A History of Rock and Dance Music

From the Guitar to the Laptop

From Chicago to Shanghai

Volume 2 (1990-2008)

*

Piero Scaruffi

*

2009

*

"If I were not a physicist, I would be a musician" (**Albert Einstein***)*

*"Most rock journalism is people who can't write, interviewing people who can't talk,
for people who can't read"* (**Frank Zappa**)

Scaruffi, Piero

A History of Rock and Dance Music

All Rights Reserved © 2009 by Piero Scaruffi

Volume 2: ISBN 978-0-9765531-6-8

Rock, Heavy metal, Psychedelia, Progressive, Ambient, Electronic, Singer-songwriter, Disco, Rap, Hip-hop, Funk, Techno, House, New Wave, Punk, Industrial, Hardcore, Pop, Noise, New Age, World-music, Grunge, Emo, Grind, Doom, Drum'n'bass, Trip-hop, Glitch

For information: www.scaruffi.com

Printed and published in the USA

Photo credits: Piero Scaruffi

Contents

VOLUME 1

The Indie Revolution

The Early 1990s: After the Cold War

In november 1989 an ecstatic crowd of young people climbed on the Berlin Wall and began dismantling it. That event marked the end of the Cold War that had spawned 50 years of worldwide proxy wars and a nuclear arms race. Coincidentally, four months earlier the very same city, Berlin, had held the first "Love Parade", a festival of electronic dance music attended by one million people. Two years later the Soviet Union would collapse altogether. In 1992 the treaty of Maastricht created the European Union, that spent the next two decades expanding and absorbing former satellites of the Soviet Union. As a consequence, the whole world (with the exceptions of a few small countries) converted to capitalism (even Russia and China), and most of the world also converted to democracy (with the notable exceptions of the Islamic world and China). The USA system had won the Cold War, the USA was the only superpower left, and all the other countries were struggling to emulate its winning system. The number of wars around the world decreased rapidly, as dictators were forced to retire. The USA, though, intervened militarily in Panama (1989), Iraq (1991), Somalia (1992), Haiti (1994), and got involved in the civil war of Yugoslavia until eventually it had to bomb Serbia (1999). These were wars fought on non-ideological grounds, in which the USA behaved like the police officer of the world.

The USA had reasons to celebrate. There were, however, disturbing signs of social disease. Street gangs terrorized entire neighborhood of the large cities. Racial riots erupted in 1992 in Los Angeles and other cities, leaving 48 people dead. Some of the problems of the previous decades had fathered worse problems. In 1989 Bush declared a "war" against hallucinogenic drugs (that was really a war against the cartels of Colombian and other "drug lords"). By the end of 1999 the World Health Organization estimated that 16 million people in the world had died of AIDS (more than half the victims being under the age of 25).

If the early 1980s had been the age of street gangs, during the rest of the decade the concepts and ideals of the street gang were progressively transferred to the digital world. Computer "hackers" realized that the Internet (the old "ArpaNET", renamed "Internet" in 1985 and extended to a much broader audience) made it possible to violate institutions such as banks, government agencies and even nuclear labs. The press started publicizing the digital exploits of the "Legion of Doom" (formed in Texas in 1984) and the "Masters of Deception" (formed by Elias Ladopoulos, aka "Acid Phreak", in 1989 in the Queens), who were brought to court in 1992. One of the legendary early hackers, Kevin Lee Poulsen, was finally apprehended in 1991. The term "cyberpunk" had been coined in 1980 by Bruce Bethke in a tale that basically predicted the advent of digital terrorism, and then William Gibson's "Neuromancer" (1984) publicized the notion of human beings that can connect into computer networks.

The "cyber" world was also becoming a substitute for the decline of the sense of community. For example, in 1985 the "Whole Earth Review", founded by Howard Rheingold in 1973 in Sausalito, established the "Whole Earth Lectronic Link" (or "WELL"). These were "sites" where people with similar interests could exchange ideas. The "usenet" on the Internet was divided in interest groups. And perhaps the first cyberspace for ordinary people was a game, "Dungeons & Dragons", introduced in 1980 by British student Roy Trubshaw, the first case of "MUD" ("multi-user dungeon").

Games were in fact evolving rapidly, from the first "Pong" invented in 1975 for the Atari by Nolan Bushnell and Alan Alcorn to Toshihiro Nishikado' "Space Invaders" (1978), the first blockbuster videogame, to Toru Iwatani' "Pac-Man" (1980) to Rick Dyer's and Don Bluth's "Dragon's Lair" (1983), an interactive animated film and the first game on laserdisc, to the Atari Lynx (1986), the first portable game system, to the boom of 1989-90, when the Sega Mega Drive and the Super Nintendo Entertainment System became mass phenomena.

Over the decades, rock music has always been the soundtrack of alternative youth lifestyles. The lifestyle of the generation of the 1990s was basically a transitional one, torn between the anger and frustration of the 1980s and the cyberworld to come.

Perhaps the most dramatic change in lifestyle affected the girls. They were the daughters of the women who had fought for emancipation and equality in the 1960s. They were the children of the sexual revolution. Women were becoming less and less dependent on men, and less oriented towards a family-based future. The "riot-grrrrls" movement that came out of Seattle was only the tip of the iceberg of a widespread grass-roots phenomenon of young women asserting their identity, their problems and their values; and beginning to create a history of their own, after centuries of male-dominated history. It is not a coincidence that the 1990s witnessed a boom of female musicians.

Musically, the 1990s saw the rock genres of the 1980s grow apart rather than fuse. Each of those genres (lo-fi pop, industrial, gothic, roots-rock, noise-rock, indie-pop, techno, ambient, etc) multiplied and evolved in a fashion largely independent of the others.

The 1990s marked, in many ways, the revenge of the "province". While the "new wave" and punk-rock (and rap and disco) had been centered around the big metropolitan areas in the North and in the West, the 1980s had slowly opened up to the rest of the country. By the time Bill Clinton became president (1992), the South, for example, had regained its grip on down-to-earth popular music, slowly establishing a supremacy over the whole gamut: alt-rock, pop, and, of course, roots-rock. The 1990s were also the age of Seattle, another relatively "provincial" center.

An involuntary catalyst for the commercial success of the various subgenres was the magazine Billboard, that finally changed the way it ranked singles and albums by tallying actual sales at retail stores instead of using the industry-manipulated word of mouth. Suddenly, rock outsold pop, and "minority" genres such as hip-hop and country entered the charts. This, in turn, led the industry to invest more in these genres.

There were perhaps fewer new genres created in the early 1990s than in any of the previous ages. Even grunge was, fundamentally, just a revival of hard rock. On the other hand, old genres diverged much more than in any previous decade, de facto splitting rock music into a loose federation of subgenres.

Female Rock

Psychedelic feminism, 1989-92

The early 1990s marked a dramatic change in the gender balance. Not only did many female singer-songwriters emerge, but their artistic achievements generally ranked higher than those of the men. The emergence of the female auteur was partly a consequence of the riot-grrrls movement and partly a sign of a changing social and psychological landscape.

The ladies had their own styles (plural). First of all, at the turn of the decade, an eccentric figure of lo-fi psychedelic storytellers emerged out of New York's underground lofts.

Multi-instrumentalist Azalia Snail (12) devoted her career to enigmatic and arcane reconstructions of the hippie era. **Snailbait** (1990) featured a parade of folk-psychedelic vocal impersonations as well as erratic guitar playing with no rhythm section, and peaked with a 23-minute collage of singing, distorted tapes, found noises and assorted turbulence, *So Much More To Go*. **Burnt Sienna** (1992) indulged in psychedelic effects, amid distorted vocals and dissonant music, leading to the chaotic **Fumarole Rising** (1994), the culmination of her program of disintegration of the pop song.

The Swans' vocalist Jarboe (11) resumed that band's apocalyptic folk on **Thirteen Masks** (1992), a set of majestic odes, oneiric visions, psychodramas, fairy tales, religious psalms and ethnic nightmares that ran the gamut from purely acoustic to subtly electronic. While not as magical and emotional, the vocal tour de force of **Sacrificial Cake** (1995) upped the ante: each song "was" a different voice, and the album as a whole sounded like a grotesque conventicle of personas.

Already early in her career, Lida Husik (22) couldn't decide whether she wanted to be a popster or a sound painter. **Bozo** (1991), produced by Kramer, was a collection of ethereal and dreamy lullabies for voice, guitar, organ and beats. Each song was programmed to sink slowly into the listener's subconscious, like a magic potion. **Your Bag** (1992), on the other hand, was devoted to experimental compositions based on collage techniques. Both albums were drenched in hallucinogens. As she emerged from the haze of drugs, Husik turned to the political stance of **The Return Of Red Emma** (1993), which sounded like a theater piece set to a vast catalog of possible musics. Leaving behind the hallucinated nightmares of her acid-induced early years, Husik regressed to the childish folk tunes of **Joyride** (1995) and **Fly Stereophonic** (1997), which were also her most touching works (particularly the former), while, at the same time, venturing into electronica with the astral lounge music of **Green Blue Fire** (1996), a collaboration with ambient specialist Beaumont Hannant, and with the trance-collages of **Mad Flavor** (1999), which were, first and foremost, aural experiences.

Post-feminism, 1989-95

At the same time, the ladies (particularly in New York and Los Angeles) continued the stark and intellectual self-searching saga inaugurated by Joni Mitchell.

Composer, pianist and vocalist <u>Robin Holcomb</u> (11), a staple of New York's jazz avantgarde (Wayne Horvitz's wife and main composer for his New York Composers' Orchestra), debuted with the mostly instrumental improvisations of **Larks They Crazy** (1989), accompanied by the supergroup of Horvitz, Doug Wieselman, Marty Ehrlich, David Hofstra and Bob Previte. A similar ensemble wove the delicate tapestry of **Robin Holcomb** (1990) for her simple, sweet melodies, sung in a register which evoked Nico's glacial and melancholy lament. With these brainy nursery rhymes she achieved a unique fusion of classical, jazz and folk music. Further removed from her jazz roots, **Rockabye** (1992) was a collection of sophisticated songs delivered by an aristocratic chanteuse.

One of the most moving voices of the decade was a humble violinist from Indiana: <u>Lisa Germano</u> (122). Her albums were comparable to the harrowing ending of a thriller. Rather than songs, the carefully assembled elements of **On The Way Down From The Moon Palace** (1991) were humble concertos that straddled the line between country, classical and new-age music. Her mournful melodies were reminiscent of Pachelbel's *Canon* and Albinoni's *Adagio* while the instrumental setting was a lesson in psychology. **Happiness** (1993) "universalized" her grief, but also climbed one tier down into her personal hell. Past, present and future merged in her feeble and confused stream of consciousness. **Geek The Girl** (1994) was both a self-portrait and an allegorical concept. It was both an epic diary of insecurity and a Dantesque journey into the psyche of a girl. It was her most atmospheric work, but also her most personal. In telling the story of her story, and making it the story of all (women's) stories, she performed the miracle of a kind of simplicity bordering on madness. The majestic dejection of the episodes worked like the exhausting grief of a lengthy funeral. In the process, Germano reenacted Nico's most lugubrious nightmares as well as Leonard Cohen's saddest fables. Her songs had become pure existential shivers. **Excerpts From A Love Circus** (1996) saw the light at the end of the tunnel, although the scene was still unfocused. Leaving behind the claustrophobic excesses of the previous albums, Germano entered a less creepy landscape. Rather than soliloquies, these songs sounded like dialogues between her touching voice and her ghostly violin. But the romantic interlude ended with the maniacal intensity of **Slide** (1998), back to the inner wasteland that ever more eccentric arrangements likened to Alice's Wonderland.

Los Angeles-based vocalist and pianist <u>Tori Amos</u> (3) fused Kate Bush's operatic falsetto, Joni Mitchell's piano-based confessional odes and Cat Stevens' romantic piano figures on **Little Earthquakes** (1991). Its ballads were simple but profound, personal but universal, melodic but discordant, thus achieving a synthesis of emotional states, not only of musical styles. The violence of hyper-realism seemed to prevail over the fairy-tale magic of introversion on **Under The Pink** (1994), a work derailed by syncopated rhythms, dissonant lashes, gospel organs, hysterical fits, orchestral flourishes and moody vocals. Leveraging the experiments of that album, the harpsichord-obsessed **Boys For Pele** (1996) sounded like a work of uncontrolled musical genius: it indulged in timbric juxtaposition, but mostly for its own sake. Backed by a rock'n'roll band and enhanced by electronic arrangements, Amos eventually chose a simpler career, starting with the much more accessible (and trivial) **From The Choirgirl Hotel** (1998).

The powerful and disorienting vocals of South Carolina's <u>Danielle Howle</u> increased the appeal of her deep thoughts on her second album, **About To Burst** (1996).

Los Angeles' street singer <u>Sheryl Crow</u> was the best seller of the bunch thanks to the hummable shuffles of **Tuesday Night Music Club** (1994).

However, the most influential female singer-songwriter of the 1990s was not Anglosaxon: Sugarcubes' singer <u>Bjork</u> (2) Gudmundsdottir came from Iceland, of all places. **Debut** (1993) employed massive doses of electronic keyboards and synthetic rhythms (conducted by producer Nellee Hooper of Soul II Soul) to sculpt dance-pop tunes that combined the savage, vital spirit of rhythm'n'blues with the psychic devastation of the post-industrial age. Along the way, Bjork garnered debris of gospel, jazz, house, hip hop, Broadway show-tunes, etc. Her eccentric vocal style, which was the musical equivalent of cinematic acting, dominated **Post** (1995), an album that focused more openly on the groove and that the producers (Hooper, 808 State's Graham Massey, Howie B and Tricky) turned into a hodgepodge of fashionable sounds. Her traumas sounded more sincere on **Homogenic** (1997), which was also her most cohesive album, while her crooning on **Vespertine** (2001) merely admitted her fundamental travesty of kitsch, easy listening and orchestral pop of the past. In a sense, her definitive statement was **Medulla** (2004), which she recorded with no instruments: just her voice and studio wizardry.

British avantgarde oboe player <u>Kate St John</u> (1) concocted an elegant fusion of chamber music and free-jazz on **Indescribable Night** (1995).

The pop-soul divas continued to rule the best-sellers' charts, notably <u>Mariah Carey</u>, one of the most successful artists of all times.

Confessional songwriters, 1992-94

The veterans were influential in shaping the musical landscape for women by reinventing the confessional vein of Suzanne Vega.

Juliana Hatfield (12), the Blake Babies' bassist and vocalist, continued to offer a moderate view of youth's troubles. **Hey Babe** (1992) was a masterpiece of whim and contrarian morals, penned by girlish voice, modest melodies, and graceful guitar rock. The self-pitying and self-loathing themes that recurred throughout the album painted a charming and anthemic biography of a teenager growing up. That existential implosion began to show a muscular side on **Become What You Are** (1993), whose sound ranged from folk-rock to hard-rock, and Hatfield definitely lost her (musical) virginity with **Only Everything** (1995), which submerged her artful whining with loud and furious riffs.

Kristin Hersh (2) carried out a solo parallel career to her band Throwing Muses with the acoustic collections **Hips And Makers** (1994), a tender and shy self-tribute via a stream of consciousness that reached the depths of her soul, and **Strange Angels** (1998), two albums of a music that was as cold as ice, as ascetic as a nun's rosary. **Sky Motel** (1999), on the other hand, sounded like a Throwing Muses reunion, and broke the spell.

Poi Dog Pondering's violinist Susan Voelz enveloped the mournful ballads of her second album **Summer Crashing** (1995) in a solemn haze.

Grrrrrls, 1990-94

Several female musicians bridged the gap between the "riot-grrrls" movement and the scene of modern singer-songwriters. Propelled by the success of their decade-old anti-folk movement, these musicians took on a wilder, angrier, more sarcastic tone.

Lois Maffeo, one of the leaders of Olympia's "riot grrrrls" movement, best summarized her age on the acoustic **Butterfly Kiss** (1992), featuring Bratmobile's drummer Molly Neuman and the Young Marble Giants' bassist Stuart Moxham.

Buffalo's fiercely independent folksinger Ani DiFranco (3) reached maturity with her fifth album, **Out Of Range** (1994). Her songs vibrated with raw energy and emotion, bit with sarcasm and wit, and pondered with angst and depression. DiFranco's art was both personal and social: while she hunted her post-menstrual demons, she also delved into poignant commentary. Her staccato acoustic guitar was no less original, a highly emotional fusion of Delta-blues and Appalachian folk picking. Parables and rants acquired new life with the less spartan format of **Not A Pretty Girl** (1995) and especially the "noisy" **Dilate** (1996) and the jazzy **To the Teeth** (1999), that also emphasized her ductile classy vocals, while **Little Plastic Castle** (1998), that presented a kinder, gentler folksinger who was less at war with society and more at ease with her own life, was even sprightly and goofy.

The music of mad Englishwoman <u>Polly Jean Harvey</u> (1) was born at the crossroad between punk rage and a nervous breakdown. Dominated by her vulgar, hysterical voice, reminiscent of Patti Smith and Sinead O'Connor, the country-blues bacchanals of **Dry** (1992) and especially **Rid Of Me** (1993) tore apart very personal and often scabrous dirges. Harvey's soul struggled between pleasure and pain, affection and libido, frustration and desire, and ultimately exposed a psyche that was metaphorically nymphomaniac. **To Bring You My Love** (1995) and **Is This Desire** (1998) evolved her style towards labyrinthine production jobs that increased the doses of electronics and downplayed the role of Harvey's voice, as she ended up sounding more like a spectator than a protagonist.

Chicago's <u>Liz Phair</u> (11) came to prominence with a highly intellectual post-modernist and post-feminist exercise, **Exile In Guyville** (1993), theoretically a diary of brutal confessions (and superficially a hyper-realistic orgy of lust) but in practice a vast fresco of the women of her generation, musically modeled after the Rolling Stones' masterpiece but also quoting everybody from Bob Dylan to Juliana Hatfield. Less cynical and more romantic, **Whip-Smart** (1994) and especially **Whitechocolatespaceegg** (1998) focused on her eclectic musical skills. Phair now engaged in a more oblique approach to her sexual and moral appetites, to reconciling sex and love, an approach which revealed her as an impressive innovator of the folk-rock idiom.

<u>DQE</u> (1), the project of Atlanta-based singer-songwriter and guitarist Grace Braun, erupted highly personal, visceral, unpleasant confessions via a frantic vocabulary of shrieks, yelps, roars, whispers and wails on **But Me I Fell Down** (1994).

The rebellious stance of these performers influenced Til' Tuesday's <u>Aimee Mann</u>, who resurrected a changed woman on her second solo, **I'm With Stupid** (1995).

A turning point was represented by the success of a Canadian teenager and former disco diva, now transplanted in Los Angeles and acquainted with the punk ethos, <u>Alanis Morissette</u> (10). Her carefree vocal style and romantic exuberance, enhanced by producer Glen Ballard's edgy rock and hip-hop arrangements (which enlisted the likes of the Red Hot Chili Peppers' Dave Navarro and Flea), transformed the songs of **Jagged Little Pill** (1995) into generational and gender anthems.

The avantgarde

There were also extreme forms of experimentation on the female voice, that took advantage of the experiments of Meredith Monk, Joan LaBarbara and Diamanda Galas (not coincidentally all women).

<u>Anna Homler</u> (1) invented her own language, both a vocal language and an instrumental language, to simulate international timeless folk

music. **Do Ya Sa' Di Do** (1992) and **Piewacket** (2001), by the project Puppetina, a collaboration with multi-instrumentalist Stephanie Payne, were in some way the vocal equivalent of the Penguin Cafe Orchestra.

A synthesis of sorts was offered by Pamela "Z" (1) Brooks in projects such as **Echolocation** (1988) and the ones composed between 1986 and 1997 and collected on **A Delay Is Better** (2005): the operatic vocal acrobatics were reminiscent of Meredith Monk while the setting within the context of live electronic music followed Diamanda Galas' example, although extended to sampling and found percussion. Rather than focusing on a dramatic persona (as Galas does), her large-scale multimedia pieces *Parts of Speech* (1995) and *Gaijin* explore universal ambience and the collective subconscious.

Post-rock

Louisville's post-rock 1989-92

The single most important regional school at the turn of the decade may well have been the one that came from one of the most unlikely of musical scenes and the one that sold the least records: Kentucky's "post-rock". Louisville's musicians introduced a convoluted, angular, cerebral style, that had little in common with rock'n'roll's hedonistic foundations. Basically, theirs was progressive-rock for an age that did not appreciate emphatic emotions anymore. The origins of this school go back to Squirrel Bait. From their ashes a number of bands were born: guitarist Brian McMahan formed Slint and For Carnation; guitarist David Grubbs formed Bastro, Bitch Magnet, and Gastr Del Sol; vocalist Peter Searcy formed Big Wheel.

Slint (101), who also featured drummer Britt Walford, bassist Ethan Buckler and guitarist David Pajo, represented a major shift in musical purpose: they were more intimidating than exciting. The mostly-instrumental music of **Tweez** (1989) kept the tension and the neurosis of hardcore but lost the passion and the narrative logic. It was "pointless" music. It was a stylistic black hole which sucked the history of rock music, in which the history of rock music virtually ended. It wasn't exactly acid-rock, although it indulged in a similar free-form approach, it wasn't progressive-rock although it exhibited the same brainy stance, it wasn't heavy-metal, although it relied on forceful guitar work, it wasn't free-jazz or avantgarde classical music, although it shared with them a penchant for innovative structures. **Spiderland** (1991) was even more abstract. Its harmonic zigzags through irregular tempos, fractured melodies and discordant counterpoint were as disorienting as notes scribbled in an unknown language. Vapid moribund passages were inundated by sudden tidal waves of sound, or, better, given the glacial tone of the band's jamming, arctic quiet was shaken by icebergs cracking in the ocean. The whole album flew in an inorganic manner, but still retained an odd sense of unity. It sounded like the stream of consciousness of a mathematician's brain as it was solving a difficult theorem.

In the meantime, the explosive metal-punk mix of Bitch Magnet (11) highlighted the innovative styles of guitarist David Grubbs, debuted in earnest on Bastro's **Diablo Guapo** (1989), and vocalist Sooyoung Park. **Umber** (1989) was a magnificent essay on how destructive and constructive processes could coexist in art, of how the irrational (fear, angst, anger) and the rational (determination, calculation, cold execution) could coexist within the same narrative. Alien riffs, psychotic melodies and truculent rhythms carried over to **Ben Hur** (1990), that reduced the role of vocals to mere decoration.

Gastr Del Sol (12), an evolution of Bastro's last line-up, i.e. the trio of David Grubbs on guitar, Bundy Ken Brown on bass and John McEntire on drums, gave new meaning to the word "subtlety" with **The Serpentine Similar** (1993), which inherited from Slint the grammatical mistakes but replaced the hardcore energy of Slint with an anemic nonchalant flimsiness. Despite the mood swings, the music bordered on free-form "slo-core" and John Fahey's transcendental suites. Jim O'Rourke joined the ranks for the chamber lied *Eight Corners* (1994) and the chamber concerto of *The Harp Factory On Lake Street* (1995), both monopolized by his ambient dissonances and derailed by anarchic jamming. Gastr Del Sol became basically a duo of Grubbs and O'Rourke for the alienated scores of **Upgrade And Afterlife** (1996) and **Camoufleur** (1998), that virtually reinvented the format of the "ballad" for the post-rock generation (dissonant chamber music loosely anchored to an off-key melody). Gastr Del Sol's research program was basically continued by the solo albums of David Grubbs (11), beginning with the solo sonatas of **Banana Cabbage, Potato Lettuce, Onion Orange** (1997). **The Thicket** (1998), recorded by a supergroup featuring John McEntire on drums, Josh Abrams on bass, Joe Bishop on trumpet, and Tony Conrad on violin, was an exercise in angst-filled settings for a new style of story-telling, of mixing timbric exploration and folk melody. Its compositions betrayed and fused Grubbs' influences: Red Crayola, Pere Ubu, John Fahey and John Cage. After the avant-jazz jams of **Apertura** (1999) and **Avocado Orange** (2000), Grubbs returned to the idea of his masterpiece with **The Spectrum Between** (2000), although in a simpler and lighter tone.

King Kong parodied B52's and Talking Heads on amusing collections such as **Funny Farm** (1993).

Another Louisville band, Rodan (10), set a standard for music that was neither atmospheric nor abstract, but a bit of both, with the lengthy conceptual compositions/improvisations of **Rusty** (1994). The interplay among Jason Noble's and Jeff Mueller's guitars, Tara Jean O'Neil's bass and Kevin Coultas' drums (plus Christian Frederickson's viola and Eve Miller's cello) contained elements of rock, jazz and classical music, but the "songs" didn't quite fall into either category. Mueller went on to form June Of 44, and Noble went on to form Rachel's, thus starting a new genealogy of Kentucky's post-rock.

Chicago's post-rock 1989-94

Post-rock was codified in Chicago with a German accent (as in "Can, Faust and Neu") by Tortoise and their countless descendants and affiliates.

Jim O'Rourke (4), Illusion Of Safety's guitarist, introduced into rock music an abstract concept of music that drew from the likes of John

Cage, Karlheinz Stockhausen, Anthony Braxton and Derek Bailey. The improvisations for "prepared" guitar of **Remove the Need** (1989), the ambient/industrial noise of **The Ground Below Above Our Heads** (1991), the electronically-manipulated chamber music of **Tamper** (1991), the musique concrete of the monumental **Disengage** (1992) and of **Scend** (1992), the chaotic free-noise of **Terminal Pharmacy** (1995) revealed one of the most eclectic, visionary and radical minds of the decade. His first venture into a more accessible style was Brise-Glace, a collaboration with other Chicago luminaries (Dazzling Killmen's bassist Darin Gray and Cheer Accident's drummer Thymme Jones), which yielded the ambient blend of jazz, rock and dub of **When In Vanitas** (1994) and then mutated into a new project, **Yona-Kit** (1995). O'Rourke's experimental fury subsided with the tributes to Tony Conrad's droning music of **Happy Days** (1997) and to John Fahey's "primitive guitar music" of **Bad Timing** (1997). And then, suddenly, he reinvented himself in the tradition of orchestral pop and easy listening with **Eureka** (1999).

Tortoise (21) basically reinvented progressive-rock for the new millenium when they anchored their musical drifting to dub and jazz pillars. The geometry of their sound started with the very foundations of the line-up, which was basically the union of two formidable rhythm sections, Poster Children's drummer John Herndon and Eleventh Dream Day's bassist Doug McCombs plus Gastr Del Sol's rhythm section (drummer John McEntire and bassist Bundy Ken Brown), augmented with Tar Babies' percussionist Dan Bitney. They were not only inspired by the historical rhythm sections of funk and dub, but they set out to obscure that legacy with a more far-reaching approach. On **Tortoise** (1994) each musician covered a lot of ground and alternated at different instruments, but basically this was a band founded on rhythm. With Slint's guitarist Dave Pajo replacing Brown on bass, **Millions Now Living Will Never Die** (1996) streamlined the mind-boggling polyphony of their jams and achieved a sort of post-classical harmony, a new kind of balance and interaction between melodies and rhythms. *Djed*, in particular, could swing between sources as distant as Neu and Steve Reich while retaining a fundamental unity, flow and sense of purpose. The jazz component and academic overtones began to prevail. The sextet (McEntire, Herndon, Bitney, McCombs, Pajo and black guitarist Jeff Parker) that recorded **TNT** (1998) had in mind the Modern Jazz Quartet and Miles Davis' historical quintet, not King Crimson or Slint, but the result was nonetheless a magisterial application of *Djed*'s aesthetics.

Rex (1), the new project by Codeine's and June Of 44's drummer Doug Scharin with singer/guitarist Curtis Harvey, Red Red Meat's bassist Phil Spirito and cellist Kirsten McCord, penned the lengthy, downbeat, convoluted jams coalescing in cloudy ballads of **Rex** (1995). The "intricate" became "majestic" on **C** (1996), Rex's most accomplished work. Him (1) were born as Rex's dub side-project with the dreamy extended pieces of **Egg** (1995) and **Interpretive Belief System** (1997), but then switched to jazz-rock for **Sworn Eyes** (1999), with Rob Mazurek's cornet playing the ghost of Miles Davis, and to ethno-funk music for **Our Point Of Departure** (2000).

The Denison-Kimball Trio (2), or DK3, formed by Jesus Lizard's guitarist Duane Denison and Laughing Hyenas/Mule/Firewater's drummer James Kimball, played nocturnal jazz with a profusion of atonal and abrasive tones on **Walls In The City** (1994), sounding like Lounge Lizards on drugs, and achieved a sophisticated synthesis of jazz, blues, rock and avantgarde on **Soul Machine** (1995), following the addition of jazz saxophonist Ken Vandermark, and **Neutrons** (1997).

New York's post-rock 1993-94

Hybrid vibrations, that mixed a post-punk ethos with the austere stance of progressive-rock and the spirit of dub and jazz, emanated also from New York.

Soul Coughing (12) concocted an effervescent blend of funk, hip-hop, jazz and rock propelled by Sebastian Steinberg's bass and Yuval Gabay's drums, and obfuscated by sampling-engineer Mark Degli Antoni's murky soundscapes on **Ruby Vroom** (1994). A further disorienting contrast was the setting of Mike Doughty's scat-like free-form poetry against a backdrop of cartoonish novelties a` la Frank Zappa, glued together by an ominous urban pulse. Following the eclectic and witty intellectual circus of **Irresistible Bliss** (1996), the varied and sophisticated **El Oso** (1998) was another stylistic tour de force but with an almost theatrical attitude, that continuously reinvented itself.

In Rhode Island, Six Finger Satellite (11) played industrial rock'n'roll that was both demented and visceral. The chaos and the noise of **The Pigeon Is The Most Popular Bird** (1993) were hardly in line with the aesthetics of post-rock. Skewed, jolting rhythms and off-kilter or plainly out-of-tune melodies were injected with lethal gas by John McLean's and Peter Phillips' abrasive guitars, and ripped apart by the emphatic, possessed vocals of Jeremiah Ryan, who engineered the best synthesis of Freud, Sartre and Bukowski on record, while instrumental interludes referenced everybody from John Cage to Throbbing Gristle to Chrome to the Velvet Underground. **Severe Exposure** (1995) was even more brutal and frantic, but still managed to cohere into a vision of post-nuclear wastelands.

Ui (1), a trio of two basses (Sasha Frere-Jones and Wilbo Wright) and drums (Clem Waldmann), offered perhaps the most adventurous fusion of dub, jazz and rock on **Sidelong** (1995) with compositions that harked back to the Contortions and Material and further back to Can.

West Coast post-rock, 1993

The West Coast was less affected by the post-rock movement, although many of San Francisco's eccentric bands (from the Residents to the Thinking Fellers) could be said to have predated it. Seattle's Engine Kid, the band of guitarist Greg Anderson, concocted an ugly hybrid of industrial music, progressive rock and jazz-core on **Bear Catching Fish** (1993) and **Angel Wings** (1995). It was only the beginning of Anderson's influential career. Seattle's Pigeonhed (1), a collaboration between Satchel's vocalist Shawn Smith and Pell Mell's keyboardist Steve Fisk, yielded the industrial/electronic dub-soul crossover of **Pigeonhed** (1993). Again, it was only the beginning of Fisk's influential career.

The absurdist rock of Residents and Thinking Fellers was still practiced in the Bay Area by Fibulator's **Drank From The Asphalt** (1993), and in Oregon by the New Bad Things (1), for example on **Freewheel** (1992).

Miss Murgatroid (2), the brainchild of San Francisco-based accordionist Alicia Rose, blended psychedelia, raga and minimalism on **Methyl Ethyl Key Tones** (1993) and especially **Myoclyonic Melodies** (1996), a glorious fest of eerie drones, Hendrix-ian glissandos, bombardment-like walls of noise, radio signals, gothic Bach-ian toccatas, noir atmospheres and surreal concertos for dissonant accordion and all sorts of instrumental noises.

Analog ambience 1993-94

Labradford (12), the Virginia-based duo of keyboardist Carter Brown and guitarist Mark Nelson, were influential for at least two reasons: they rediscovered the appeal of analog keyboards; and they coined an ambient/chamber form of rock music that shunned percussion and relied on drones. The mostly instrumental albums **Prazision** (1993) and **A Stable Reference** (1995), which added a bass to the equation, subverted the song format by conceiving each "song" as a slow-motion nebula of loops, drones and guitar events (hypnotic strumming, psychedelic reverbs), while barely whispered melodies glided in different directions. This "textural" form of jamming (jamming that enhanced the timbres and the contrasts, like an impressionistic watercolor) was basically a non-psychedelic (i.e., stark and austere) form of shoegazing. Labradford opted for a machine-driven sound with **Labradford** (1996), which began to add samplers and drum-machines to their arsenal of instruments, and to employ found sounds and dissonances. However, the overall ambience became warmer because the vocals had evolved into a real "voice", not just background hissing. Thanks to technology, the "emptiness" of previous albums had been "filled", but the "containee" was no less frightening than the container: a barren and spectral landscape, enveloped in a ghostly calm, that emerged out of a nightmarish fog. After the formulaic **Mi Media Naranja** (1998) and **E Luxo So** (1999), that indulged in the "panoramic" element of their music, Labradford returned to the aseptic mood of Brian Eno's original ambient program, albeit one in which details matter, with the four lengthy tracks of **Fixed::Context** (2001), each piece overflowing with "dark matter", with invisible sounds that were nonetheless the substance, whereas the whole was merely a vehicle, a backdrop, a context.

Fundamentally, Seattle's Jessamine (1) reprised the electronic rock format of the Silver Apples and the United States Of America, and upgraded it to My Bloody Valentine's shoegazing. **Jessamine** (1994) introduced the droning music of keyboardist Andy Brown and guitarist Rex Ritter, but **The Long Arm Of Coincidence** (1996) added a number of subtleties to the model that set it apart from other droning ensembles: a predisposition to Can-like structures, a twisted rhythmic emphasis, jazzy synth ectoplasms and occasional echoes of Soft Machine's prog-rock. Andy Brown continued the experiment in Fontanelle (1), a collaboration with guitarist Rex Ritter, whose **Fontanelle** (2000) offered instrumental jams that were evocative, trance-oriented recapitulations of Soft Machine, John Cage and Miles Davis.

Instrumental post-rock 1993-94

Post-rock's focus on instrumental interplay indirectly fostered a resurgence of instrumental rock. Oddly creative combos had been around independently of post-rock. For example, born in Boston from the ashes of Human Sexual Response, the Concussion Ensemble (1) offered a mixture of minimalistic repetition, free improvisation and hard-rock on **Stampede** (1993).

Instrumental post-rock found its prophets and visionaries in Pennsylvania's Don Caballero (12), the first band, with Virginia's Breadwinner (who never recorded an album), to consciously and thoroughly explore the innovations of Bitch Magnet and Slint. One could find countless references inside **For Respect** (1993), from Neil Young's neurotic progressions to MC5's monster riffs, from Arto Lindsay's atonal screeches to Chrome's manic distortions, from King Crimson's progressive-rock to Black Flag's progressive-hardcore. The barbaric duels of guitarists Mike Banfield and Ian Williams, and the colossal "blunders" of the rhythm section (Damon "Che" Fitzgerald on drums and Pat Morris on bass) created a deviant, menacing wall of noise. Technically, **2** (1995) was even better, as it introduced a quartet of sophisticated, skilled players, and not just an enigmatic whole. Four lengthy tracks summarized 40 years of intellectual rock music, from Soft Machine to Metallica, and unloaded a cornucopia of odd time signatures and intense/elaborate textures. **What Burns Never Returns** (1998) was an alchemic work that retained little of the original verve.

Don Caballero's guitarist Ian Williams pursued his experiments in Storm & Stress (2), featuring bassist Eric Topolsky and drummer Kevin Shea. **Storm & Stress** (1997) and **Under Thunder And Fluorescent Light** (2000) were ambitious attempts at playing music while intentionally forgetting the song that they were playing. The technique resonated with theories borrowed from John Cage, Ornette Coleman and Einsturzende Neubaten. A chronic lack of a gravitational center permeated all of their jams. At times, harmony was so loose that it appeared to be random.

Chicago's Trenchmouth (1), led by vocalist Damon Locks and guitarist Chris DeZutter, mixed heavy-metal solos, and elements of ska, funk, reggae and jazz on the philosophical concept albums **Inside The Future** (1993) and **Vs The Light of The Sun** (1994), to the point that their final **The Broadcasting System** (1996) was virtually a tribute to the dub civilization.

Australian trio Dirty Three (23), comprising Warren Ellis on violin, Mick Turner on guitar and Jim White on drums, chiseled lenthy evocative jams that aimed for a folk-jazz-raga-rock fusion, a sort of culmination of four decades of crossover. **Sad And Dangerous** (1994) and **Dirty Three** (1995) evoked John Fahey, Albert Ayler, the Third Ear Band and the Turtle Island String Quartet, but, ultimately, were quite unique thanks to Ellis' violin, that could imitate John Cale's viola and Jimi Hendrix's guitar as well as an Indian sitar or a jazz trumpet. More importantly, the narrative masterpieces of **Horse Stories** (1996) delivered emotions without exploiting the conventions of emotion in music. The trio's music transcended stylistic boundaries and technical vocabularies, but somehow managed to be intuitive and user-friendly. Abandoning the punkish undulations of the early works, the austere chamber music of **Ocean Songs** (1998) upped the ante. It was delicate, lyrical and pictorial, without the harsh edges of the early works. The emotional content was much higher because the album was a tribute to nature and also a somber meditation on the human condition, the violin rising to universal voice of the century's existential angst. The six extended compositions of **Whatever You Love You Are** (2000) hastened the convergence with classical music, as the jazz and folk influences faded away.

Montage, 1990-94

The Vampire Rodents (121), a project of Toronto guitarist/vocalist Anton Rathausen (real name Daniel Vahnke) and keyboardist Victor Wulf, were possibly the greatest composers of collage-music of the decade. **War Music** (1990) merely set the existential tone of their opus by juxtaposing recitals of horror stories against industrial music performed by Neanderthal men on stone instruments. **Premonition** (1992), featuring Andrea Akastia on violin and cello, transposed that program to another dimension, making music out of a frantic collage of sources. On one hand, the combo created a music in which sound effects, not instruments, became the element of composition. On the other hand, they retained the feeling of jazz and avantgarde chamber music. Their savage art of montage reached a demented peak with **Lullaby Land** (1993). Rhythm permeated this work at least on two levels: a disco/funk/house beat that propelled the track; and the pace at which snippets were glued together to form "songs". At both levels the verve was palpable. The songs were gags, and each gag was an assembly of cells. It was entertaining, and it was terrifying. The whole recalled the grotesque and unpredictable merry-go-rounds of Frank Zappa's early works and the Residents' early suites. Vampire Rodents' "lullaby land" was set in a Freudian nightmare and that nightmare played at double speed in a very chaotic theater. **Clockseed** (1995) added more acoustic instruments and more drum-machines, and offered a more linear, rational and focused take on the same idea. It was another symphony of chaos and multitude, that, indirectly, harked back to composers of urban cacophony such as Charles Ives and Edgar Varese (and composers of cartoon soundtracks such as Carl Stalling). It was still a cannibal and schizophrenic art, that continuously devoured itself and that continuously changed personality. **Gravity's Rim** (1996), instead, returned to the format of the pop song, thus closing an ideal loop. Layers of samples merely provided the "arrangement" for the melodies carried by the vocals. Vampire Rodents' art shared with Dadaism and Futurism the aesthetic principle that avantgarde and clownish novelty should be one and the same.

Bugskull (12), the brainchild of Oregon's guitarist and vocalist (and former folksinger) Sean Byrne, coined a style of arrangement that was the post-rock equivalent of Brian Wilson's orchestral productions: a catalog of musical mistakes instead of an abundance of instrumental counterpoint. The "songs" of **Phantasies And Senseitions** (1994) were jams of found sounds, electronic sounds, distortions, out-of-tune passages, abstract noise, and, last but not least, senseless lullabies. **Snakland** (1996) focused on the core (the tune) rather than on the shell (the cacophony), but the program remained one of wrapping tunes into layers and layers of cacophony. **Distracted Snowflake Volume One** (1997) marked the formal triumph of his techniques of lo-fi avantgarde. Each piece was carefully sculpted with a myriad of sounds, resulting in "songs" that were both overwhelming and exhilarating.

British post-rock, 1992-94

At the same time that the post-rock aesthetic was spreading in the USA, England boasted a significantly different school of intellectual rock.

Napalm Death's drummer <u>Mick Harris</u> recreated the original line-up of that band (namely, guitarist Justin Broadrick and vocalist Nick Bullen) for his new project, <u>Scorn</u> (11) but the music they played on **Vae Solis** (1992), was from another planet: Harris operated sampling machines and sequencers, and sculpted arrangements that incorporated industrial music and dub in a brutal and lugubrious framework, reminiscent of Public Image Ltd and Killing Joke. The bleak, hallucinated, horror soundscapes of this album enabled the stately psychodramas of **Colossus** (1994). The territory was still scoured by heavy beats and ghastly distortions, but there were real souls wandering in the miasmatic mist. It was a music of agonizing, paranoid rhythmic patterns, and rhythm rapidly became the focus of Scorn: **Evanescence** (1994) incorporated the syncopated beat of hip-hop, and Scorn retreated to a spectral ambient format with the instrumental **Gyral** (1995), once Bullen had left Harris alone at the helm. As the music of Scorn became more trivial, the music of its alter-ego, <u>Lull</u>, became more complex. The electronic poems of **Dreamt About Dreaming** (1992) evolved into the ambient monoliths of **Cold Summer** (1995) and **Continue** (1996), influenced by two crucial collaborations: the four lengthy **Murder Ballads** (1994), sung by Martyn Bates, at the border between gothic and ambient music; and the two ambient suites of **Somnific Flux** (1995), a joint venture with Bill Laswell. The sheer scope of Harris' work was stunning. Free-jazz, ambient music and grindcore found an improbable meeting point in <u>Painkiller</u>, the trio formed by Harris with Bill Laswell and John Zorn, best represented by **Buried Secrets** (1993).

<u>Disco Inferno</u> (1), after becoming the creature of producer Charlie McIntosh and vocalist/guitarist Ian Crause, delivered one of the most challenging albums of the era, **DI Go Pop** (1994).

<u>Pram</u> (12) twisted the old craft of progressive-rock to the point that it became a container for all sorts of odd structures. Rosie Cuckston's childish vocals inhabited a wonderland painted by the surreal colors of Max Simpson's samples and keyboards, plus the occasional trumpet or saxophone, and was constantly challenged by the grotesque charge of a power-trio ignited by Matthew Eaton's guitar. Elements of jazz, dub and electronica permeated **The Stars Are So Big The Earth Is So Small** (1993), thus it was not surprising that **Helium** (1994) sounded like Daevid Allen's Gong playing trip-hop. Its creative chaos had few rivals in those years. Despite the number and density of sonic events, the loose structures of **Sargasso Sea** (1995) sounded like pure abstractions, mirages, phantasms, and eventually led (on a more earthly plane) to the exquisite muzak of **North Pole Radio Station** (1998) and **Museum Of Imaginary Animals** (2000).

Moonshake (2), the creature of singer-songwriters Dave Callahan and Margaret Fiedler, reduced the song format to a plasma of rhythmic and melodic fragments on the atmospheric experiments of **Eva Luna** (1992). A bold synthesis of psychedelia, trip-hop and jazz, their sound basically upgraded Public Image Ltd's sound to the age of sampling. As **The Sound Your Eyes Can Follow** (1994) provided sturdier scaffolding for the melodies, the mood settled halfway between Pere Ubu-like hysteria and Contortions-like neurosis. The more robust **Dirty & Divine** (1996), without Fiedler, further polished the edges and displayed similarities with Talking Heads' rhythmic juggernauts and hypnotic fanfares.

Laika (11), the new project of Moonshake's co-founder Margaret Fiedler, continued the exploration of Moonshake's stylistic crevices while focusing on electronic keyboards, sampling machines, flute and polyrhythms. **Silver Apples Of The Moon** (1994) delivered circular jazz-funk bacchanals reminiscent of Rip Rig & Panic and ethno-ambient frescoes reminiscent of Jon Hassell. **Sounds Of The Satellites** (1997) refined the production technique and achieved a super-fusion that stretched from Miles Davis' jazz-rock to Morton Subotnick's musique concrete.

Scottish guitarist Richard Youngs specialized in "lo-fi" improvisations inspired by Terry Riley's minimalism and John Fahey's instrumental folk music, notably the three lengthy spectral improvisations of **Advent** (1988) and the three lengthy "ballads" of **Sapphie** (1998). Significant detours included **Summer Wanderer** (2005), a moving a-cappella album, and **Multi-Tracked Shakuhachi** (2006). Since the late 1980s he had also been collaborating with avantgarde composer Simon Wickham-Smith, creating lengthy free-form noise collages/jams such as **Ceaucescu** (1992), *The Proof Of The Point*, off **Kretinmuzak** (1994), *Diabetes* for more than 20 instruments, off **Asthma And Diabetes** (1994), *More Urban Music for the Middle Of Nowhere*, off **Enedkeg** (1996) and *Angels From CT* with sampler, rhythm machine and synthesizer, off **Veil** (1997).

Italian post-rock 1990-94

Post-rock was particularly fertile in Italy, a country that since the 1970s had been on the leading edge of progressive music. In general, the sonic model was a mixture of Big Black, Sonic Youth and Fugazi, while the themes coined a sort of neo-existentialism, very much concerned with the psychodramas of ordinary kids. It all sounded like a brain scan at the edge of a nervous breakdown.

Afterhours' stylistic tour de force of **Hai Paura del Buio?** (1997) achieved an eclectic fusion of hardcore, grunge, folk and pop.

Uzeda (1) cemented a dark noise-rock style that was both brutal and lyrical, physical and psychological, while fusing atonal guitar, jazzy rhythm section and hardcore vocals on their third album **Different Section of Wires** (1998).

Starfuckers (1) merged rock and electronic sounds on the ambitious aesthetic manifesto of **Sinistri** (1994) and especially on **Infrantumi** (1997), a blend of free-jazz, cubism, dissonant avantgarde, musique concrete and Faust-like structures.

Massimo Volume's subtle second album, **Lungo I Bordi** (1995), was an oneiric and noirish journey into a Fugazi-esque hell.

Marlene Kuntz's existential noise-rock on **Il Vile** (1996) sounded like a synthesis of European and USA moods.

Three Second Kiss devoted **For Pain Relief** (1996) to free-form noise-rock.

The post-rock renaissance of the 1990s somehow emancipated the rest of the nation, fostering innovation in many different genres. Both Epsilon Indi's ambient exotic monolith **A Distant Return** (1992) and Timoria's melodic concept **Viaggio Senza Vento** (1993), their fourth album, heralded a boom in new genres. Elio E Le Storie Tese, a six-member unit, became Italy's most relevant disciples of Frank Zappa with **Elio Samaga Hukapan Kariyana Turu** (1989).

A sign that Italian prog-rock was about to stage a major come-back was Eris Pluvia's baroque **Rings Of Earthly Light** (1991), particularly its five-movement title-track. Deus Ex Machina indulged in a vehement, torrential fusion of classical, jazz and rock, that slowly became more cerebral as they progressed from the rock opera **Gladium Caeli** (1991) to the jazzy fantasias of **Cinque** (2002). Finisterre's **Finisterre** (1994) saluted the revival of Italy's prog-rock school with an unusual balance of classical piano and rock guitar. Bluvertigo delivered the progressive cauldron of **Metallo non metallo** (1997).

Technogod fostered an industrial-rap-rock fusion with **Hemo Glow Ball** (1992), while Assalti Frontali, the leading hip-hop posse of Italy, unleashed the confrontational manifestos **Terra di Nessuno** (1992) and the hardcore-tinged **Conflitto** (1996).

Almamegretta coined a new form of world-music on **Sanacore** (1995), an ambitious encyclopedic revision of traditional codes that bridged the ancient folk tradition of Napoli (Naples), electronic dance music, dub production techniques and Middle-Eastern scales.

Ordo Equitum Solis (a duo of guitar and vocals) crafted sets of solemn, melancholy folk ballads redolent of medieval music such as **Solstitii Temporis Sensus** (1990).

Germany 1994

Germany didn't have a post-rock school with a unified style until the second half of the decade, but it always had musicians who tried wildly unusual avenues.

Mouse On Mars (3), the Duesseldorf-based duo of Andi Toma and Jan Werner, applied the post-rock aesthetics to post-techno dance-music. The pseudo-psychedelic trance of **Vulvaland** (1994) was unusual mainly because of its tragic, gloomy mood, but **Iaora Tahiti** (1995) layered elements of dub, jungle, hip-hop inside a shell of warped ambient/cosmic cliches, thus creating a new kind of futurism, one that was not Kraftwerk's paranoia of machines but a very bodily (and current) neurosis. **Autoditacker** (1997) consolidated that style in a baroque synthesis of light polyrhythms and bizarre electronics, while **Instrumentals** (1998) was perhaps the most austere enunciation of their deconstruction technique. The "thickness" of sound effects on **Idiology** (2001) gave rise to an hallucinated symphony of instrumental colors, while assembling a catalog of impossible beats.

The instrumental quartet Bohren & der Club of Gore (2) penned the modest ambience for piano and guitar of **Gore Motel** (1994). That idea transcended its original scope on the double-disc **Midnight Radio** (1995), whose pieces were rendered hypnotic, subdued, slow, stark and evocative by super-heavy bass notes and catatonic drumming; and finally morphed into the minimal ambient noir jazz of **Sunset Mission** (2000) and **Black Earth** (2002), with a saxophone replacing the guitar.

Noisier than Rock

New York's legacy 1990-94

The 1980s had witnessed a more or less subliminal process of deconstruction of rock music: angular melodies, irregular rhythms, strident counterpoint. The instruments and the line-up were consistent with the stereotype of rock'n'roll but the result was almost antithetical: brainy, un-hummable, depressing and mostly instrumental. During the 1990s this form of intellectual rock was recognized as a major vehicle for the message of a musician, the same way that a memorable melody had been the main vehicle for most musicians of the 1960s.

The influence of Sonic Youth was perhaps the most visible. Mostly unknown during the 1980s, Sonic Youth came slowly to represent "the" quintessential alternative band. An even more "alternative" act, Pussy Galore, was a close second. No surprise, then, that a few of the new leaders emerged from those two bands. Bewitched (1) were formed by Pussy Galore's drummer Bob Bert, and recorded a boldly experimental work, **Brain Eraser** (1990).

Jon Spencer's wife Cristina Martinez led Boss Hog (1), that re-invented party-music first on **Cold Hands** (1990), featuring Honeymoon Killers' bassist Jerry Teel and Unsane drummer Charlie Ondras, and then on **White Out** (2000), both clever revisitations of rock stereotypes.

Like Pussy Galore, the Jon Spencer Blues Explosion (3) was a bass-less trio playing careless, amateurish, skeletal and grotesque blues. The difference is that Spencer had dispensed with the "punk-rock" factor. A stylist of bad taste, Spencer carried out a postmodernist deconstruction of the blues, first on the cacophonous and viscerally crude **Jon Spencer Blues Explosion** (1992), which was virtually an insult to the great bluesmen of the past, then with the childish **Extra Width** (1993), and finally with the streamlined **Orange** (1994), which was in many ways his most accomplished (albeit not innovative) collection. These works contained psychotic rave-ups, demented jamming and scary vocals, which represented a "hip" kind of background music for the distorted values of the post-punk generation. The sophisticated sloppiness of **Now I Got Worry** (1996) and **Acme** (1998), the first Spencer album that featured a bass, further diluted the original outrage and presented a more civilized (i.e. less beastly) con-man.

Spongehead (2), a guitar-sax-drums trio, crafted a loose fusion of blues, funk and jazz that resembled Pere Ubu's abstract pop-art on the tentative **Potted Meat Spread** (1989) and on the more mature **Legitimate Beef** (1990). Dave Henderson's tenor sax and Doug Henderson's atonal guitar worked wonders on **Curb Your Dogma** (1993), an emotional as well as technical miracle that ran the gamut from expressionist psychodramas to rowdy pow-wows. **Infinite Baffle** (1996) even applied the group's recipe to roots-rock with boogie overtones a` la ZZ Top.

New York, which had been the birthplace of noise-rock, had the most varied and crowded scene of noise-rock bands: the Dustdevils, fronted by the unpleasant vocals of Jaqi Dulany; Babe The Blue Ox, with the odd dynamics of **Babe The Blue Ox** (1993); St Johnny (1), whose **High As A Kite** (1993) was derivative of Sonic Youth; Bunny Brains, who delivered the creative chaos of **Bunny Magick** (1994); Versus (1), whose **Secret Swingers** (1996) fused Television's transcendental acid-rock and Sonic Youth's atonal pop; Lotion (1), with the mildly psychedelic **Nobody's Cool** (1996); Sleepyhead, disciples of Sonic Youth who moved on to psychedelic folk.

Overall, noise-rock was a metropolitan, intellectual affair, relatively removed from the populist issues of the heartland of the USA.

The legacy of apocalyptic hardcore 1989-92

Chicago's noise-rock was heavily influenced by the subculture of hardcore, and by Big Black's apocalyptic noise. Jesus Lizard (13) summarized the style better than anyone else. The historical line-up of Scratch Acid vocalist David Yow, Scratch Acid bassist David Sims, Phantom 309's drummer Mac McNeilly, and guitarist Duane Denison, was the vanguard of a new kind of hardcore punk-rock that had absorbed funk, noise and industrial music. The EP **Pure** (1989) and the full-length **Head** (1990) were dramas of macabre hyper-realism, immersed into urban neurosis as viewed from Yow's sick mind. **Goat** (1991), their most accomplished work, found a magical balance between Yow's psychotic mumbling and screaming (and perverted visions), Denison's elegant vocabulary of grinding, scathing, sobbing and lashing sounds, and a repertory of ever-mutating epileptic rhythms. The quartet penned lugubrious, visceral, vulgar, truculent and abrasive nightmares. A less disordered and less pathological affair, **Liar** (1992) was still highly energetic, sometimes chaotic, and always galvanizing. The instrumental technique refined on **Down** (1994) stood as an impressive contribution to redefining the very essence of rock music. But their music was, first and foremost, a music of fear, the fear of a young urban population whose life was reduced to a series of agonizing spasms. The central character of their stories, a sort of mythological psychopath, was the collective subconscious of that population. If punk-rock had been the sound of a battlefield, the sound of Jesus Lizard was the sound of the wounded who rattled in the cold of the night.

Nebraska's 13 Nightmares bridged the ferocious Detroit school of MC5 and the Minneapolis school of the Replacements on **Shitride** (1989).

In Minnesota <u>Flour</u> (1), the project of former Rifle Sport's bassist Peter Conway, recorded albums such as **Luv 713** (1990) that wed Big Black's violence with dance beats and heavy-metal riffs.

A Southern version of extreme hardcore was heralded by <u>Phantom 309</u> (1), based in Mississippi but led by Indiana's guitarist and vocalist John Forbes, a band that applied the hardcore propulsion to a blues and rockabilly foundation on **A Sinister Alphabet** (1989).

Among the most oppressive followers of Jesus Lizard's convoluted power-rock were Missouri's <u>Dazzling Killmen</u> (2), no less brutal but a little jazzier. The cross-fire between vocalist Nick Sakes and guitarist Tim Garrigan, and the rhythm section's jarring movement, molded the infernal atmospheres of **Dig Out The Switch** (1992). The band relished horror psychodramas of ferocious intensity, an art that culminated on **Face Of Collapse** (1994).

Jesus Lizard's main disciples in Chicago were perhaps <u>Shorty</u>, led by guitarist Mark Shippy and vocalist Al Johnson, with the eerie violence of **Thumb Days** (1993).

<u>Unsane</u> (11), formed in New York by Jon's brother Chris Spencer and drummer Charlie Ondras, concocted a dissonant and violent form of rock'n'roll that borrowed the sheer impetus of hardcore but emptied it of any emotion and melody. The catastrophic riffs, hammering rhythms and uncontrolled vocals of **Unsane** (1991) performed glacial and relentless surgery on the body of a zombie. Cascades of atrocious sounds destabilized its songs and generated a form of hysterical tribalism. Compared with Sonic Youth, the music was spasmodically tragic, not calmly intellectual. Vincent Signorelli replaced Ondras (who had died prematurely) on **Total Destruction** (1994), another work drenched in superhuman angst, another bleak, claustrophobic and painful vision of subhuman life. Even compared to the extreme sound of Big Black, Unsane's music was a further step down the stairway to hell, and the damned weren't even crying anymore.

San Diego's <u>Three Mile Pilot</u> (2), a guitar-less trio of vocals, bass and drums led by singer Pall Jenkins (Paolo Zappoli), revived Jesus Lizard's post-hardcore dejection on **Na Vucca Do Lupu** (1992), a brutal and passionate work, and **Chief Assassin to The Sinister** (1994), a tortured, stark and obscure testament.

Kansas City's <u>Season To Risk</u> played similar heavy, tortured music on albums such as **In A Perfect World** (1995).

Los Angeles' <u>Distorted Pony</u> (1) delivered the gloomy, heavy and terrifying wall of noise of **Punishment Room** (1992), while <u>Slug</u> wed Big Black to an assortment of turntables and hip-hop rhythms, not to mention the monster assault of two basses, on **Swingers** (1993).

San Francisco-based <u>Oxbow</u> (3), fronted by nightmarish vocalist Eugene Robinson, concocted an insane free-form collage of atonal instruments, vocal rants, noise, angst-ridden punk energy and sheer nonsense on **Fuckfest** (1991) and especially **King of the Jews** (1992) and **Serenade in Red** (1996). After a long hiatus, **An Evil Heat** (2002) even included a 32-minute coda of musique concrete for distorted guitar and moribund groove, *Glimmer Shine*.

In New York, both Drunk Tank (1) with the bleak **Drunk Tank** (1991), and Cell, with **Slo Blo** (1992), further explored the edges of this style.

These bands increasingly mixed noise-rock, grunge and industrial music.

Midwestern introversion, 1993-94

Several Midwestern bands took advantage of the harmonic revolution of noise-rock to craft personal, introverted and disturbing styles.

Indiana's Antenna, formed by former Lemonheads' and Blake Babies' guitarist John Strohm, evolved into Velo-Deluxe (1), whose **Superelastic** (1994) better represented the leader's fusion of roots-rock, power-pop, the Velvet Underground and My Bloody Valentine.

Ohio's Brainiac (2) concocted a surreal hybrid of new wave and industrial music. Abandoning the punk-rock verve of their Devo-inspired debut album **Smack Bunny Baby** (1993), the short demented songs of **Bonsai Superstar** (1994), featuring new guitarist John Schmersal, revealed a lighter, gentler version of Pere Ubu, the Pixies and Sonic Youth. Chaotic and retro, that album capitalized on those masters' innovations but, thanks to Tim Taylor's naive synthesizer and to a childish aesthetic, discarded the apocalyptic overtones. **Hissing Prigs In Static Couture** (1996) was a better organized madhouse, despite the relentless, frantic chaos.

East Coast dissonance, 1992-95

Later into the decade, a new generation of bands came around playing non-linear, dissonant song-oriented music, and North Carolina (namely, Chapel Hill) was its epicenter. Polvo (12), which were in many ways the leaders of this school, resurrected Television's guitar counterpoint, which straddled the line between neurosis and ecstasy, between western existentialism and eastern transcendentalism, but pushed it to the brink of cacophony and chaos. The effect was to give "atonal" a "subliminal" meaning. The intricate and repulsive guitar collisions of Ash Bowie and Dave Brylawski propelled **Cor-Crane Secret** (1992) inwardly, while shifting and incoherent tempos lent the journey a Freudian intensity, and twisted melodies plunged the "stories" into the realm of Alice In Wonderland. A more erudite effort, **Today's Active Lifestyles** (1993) was, de facto, a series of dissonant micro-concertos, which in turn evoked a gallery of abstract miniatures, not unlike Captain Beefheart's masterpieces. **Exploded Drawing** (1996), possibly their masterpiece, perfected their manual of harmony. While the surface still sounded like a spastic version of Henry Cow, the nonchalant and detached way with which the players secretly toyed with elements of raga, blues and folk amounted to a jungle of improper signs, to a semiotic disaster of the same magnitude as Arto Lindsay's and Mayo Thompson's most heretical endeavors. The more careful arrangements of **Shapes** (1997) revealed that the scaffolding of their sonic kaleidoscope bore psychedelic stigmata. Shunning the over-extended progressive/acid format, Polvo advanced the concept of noise in the format of the pop song more than anyone else since Sonic Youth.

Boston boasted an equally original scene. Live Skull's vocalist Thalia Zedek and guitarist Chris Brokaw (ex-Codeine) formed Come (1) to indulge in noisy Royal Trux-ian blues jamming and neurotic Neil Young-ian ballads. **Don't Ask Don't Tell** (1994) was a collection of nightmarish streams of consciousness.

The Supreme Dicks (11) were among the most intriguing practitioners of the aesthetic that equates "creative" and "primitive". The theatrical bacchanals of **The Unexamined Life** (1993) managed to combine ideas from the Holy Modal Rounders, Kurt Weill and Lou Reed. That kind of drunk, dissonant folk music evolved towards the avantgarde and psychedelia on **The Emotional Plague** (1996), a vastly more ambitious work that resorted to sparse, dilated and warped structures.

In Pennsylvania, Latimer's **LP Title** (1995) was typical of Sonic Youth's nation-wide influence.

Two of the most original bands were from Washington (and not coincidentally related to Unrest). Tsunami (1), the band of ebullient singer Jenny Toomey, played frantic and muddled roots-rock on **Deep End** (1993). Pitchblende (1), the band of guitarists Justin Chearno and Treiops Treyfid, molded a vehement and jagged attack on **Kill Atom Smasher** (1993).

Broc's Cabin (1991), by Florida's Rein Sanction, was bleak and ominous like a cross between voodoo and noise-rock.

Atlanta's Pineal Ventana offered a bold mixture of improvisation, tribal drumming, saxophone drones and edgy screaming on **Living Soil** (1995).

International noise-rock, 1992-94

England was awash in Brit-pop, but still managed to deliver some of the most creative bands of the era.

Gallon Drunk (11) was one of the most aggressive and intimidating outfits of its time. **You The Night And The Music** (1992) served rock'n'roll and rhythm'n'blues played by a pack of rabid wolves, skewed tribal dances derailed by awkwardly distorted guitar and organ and by demonic changes of tempo and mood. The album revived the lascivious and sinister musical universe of Birthday Party, the Cramps and the Scientists, but in a more catastrophic setting, and amid mutant echoes of Creedence Clearwater Revival and Bo Diddley. The slightly jazzier and more rational **From The Heart Of Town** (1993), featuring reed player Terry Edwards, turned that wild flight of the imagination into a style.

Therapy? (1) unleashed another brutal work, **Nurse** (1992), a trip in a Freudian maze. The style of Jacob's Mouse (1) was even looser. Their **No Fish Shop Parking** (1992) was a cauldron of noise-rock styles. The Faith Healers (1), featuring guitarist Tom Cullinan, imitated Pixies and Sonic Youth on **Lido** (1992). Prolapse (1) specialized in angular and abrasive noise-rock, which on the early albums, such as **Backsaturday** (1995), sounded like vitriolic indictments of pop music. Boyracer behaved like childish hellraisers on **More Songs About Frustration And Self-Hate** (1994), that contains brief songs played with full-throttle clumsiness and clownish nerdiness. Rosa Mota unleashed the triple guitar assault of **Wishful Sinking** (1995).

The "Halifax school" in Canada was briefly a phenomenon. Representative albums were **Love Tara** (1993), by Eric's Trip (1), which included Rick White and Julie Doiron, and Jale's **Dreamcake** (1994). The group to emerge from this crowd was Sloan, that from the noise-pop hybrid of **Smeared** (1993), a synthesis of the musical zeitgeist of the time, via the Sixties tribute of **One Chord To Another** (1996) to the pop behemoth **Never Hear The End Of It** (2006) cultivated a fixation for the most naive form of melody.

Germany's 18th Dye explored noir atmospheres via noise-rock on their second album **Tribute To A Bus** (1995).

Progressive Sounds

East Coast 1988-94

At the beginning of the 1990s, Phish, more than anyone else, established alternative rock on mainstream radio. Phish were more than just a surrogate of the Grateful Dead for the 1990s. They legitimized a return to the aesthetics of progressive-rock, particularly on the East Coast.

In the age of hardcore punk-rock, the aesthetics of Phish (22), a quintet based in Vermont, bordered on the suicidal. Nonetheless, the band became one of the most significant phenomena of the decade. Phish focused on the live concert, a concept that had been anathema during the 1980s, and rediscovered the guitar solo, the ornate keyboard arrangements, prog-rock tempo shifts, group improvisation and the whole vocabulary of intellectual hippie music, as proven with the lengthy tracks on the cassette **Junta** (1988). The encyclopedic tour de force of **Lawn Boy** (1990) focused on mostly-instrumental melodic fantasies that quoted from an endless list of genres. Guitarist Trey Anastasio inherited Frank Zappa's clownish compositional style, which blended rock, jazz and classical music in pseudo-orchestral fashion, while his cohorts inherited Grateful Dead's dizzy jamming style, and keyboardist Page McConnell added a strong and elegant jazz accent. Their art of stylistic montage peaked with **A Picture Of Nectar** (1992). Its kaleidoscopic suites balanced the melodic center of mass and the centrifugal forces of the instrumental parts, while surfing through an impressive catalog of styles, juxtaposing kitsch sources (exotica, lounge, easy-listening, doo-wop) and chamber duets or jazz solos. The smoother and slicker sound of **Hoist** (1994) closed the epic phase and opened the commercial one in the lighter vein of the Band, the Doobie Brothers, Little Feat and the Allman Brothers. Phish, the first creative group to be completely indifferent to the punk aesthetics, had just changed the world.

Blues Traveler (1) were a simpler, domestic, rootsy version of Phish. **Blues Traveler** (1990) offered a judicious mixture of ballads and jams, and the band would eventually match and surpass Phish's commercial success.

Motherhead Bug (10) was a bizarre orchestra (accordion, trumpet, saxophone, percussion, trombone, violin and piano), led by multi-instrumentalist David Ouimet, that performed soundtracks for imaginary films. **Zambodia** (1993) was influenced by the music-hall, the circus, cartoons, marching bands, nursery rhymes and Sullivan's operettas. It was the equivalent of the Penguin Cafe' Orchestra for the new generation. Their offshoot Sulfur (1), formed by Ouimet and vocalist and keyboardist Michele Amar, carried out a similar work of stylistic collage, but the mood of **Delirium Tremens** (1998) was tragic rather than comic, and the atmosphere evoked Beckett's absurd theater.

The <u>Spin Doctors</u> became stars with the jovial and catchy ditties of **Pocket Full Of Kryptonite** (1991), that recycled stereotypes of funk, soul, blues, reggae, and rock music.

One of the leading groups of instrumental neo-prog came out of Boston: <u>Cul De Sac</u> (12). The lengthy tracks on **Ecim** (1992) bridged German rock of the 1970s, John Fahey's transcendental folk, Terry Riley's minimalism and Pink Floyd's psychedelic ragas. Their most innovative work, **China Gate** (1996), increased the doses of jazz and world-music, thus achieving both a convoluted and a hypnotic state of mind. The narrative largely revolved around the counterpoint between Robin Amos' atonal synthesizer and Glenn Jones' post-surf guitar. On **Crashes To Light** (1999) that contrast, enhanced with sophisticated arrangements, became a slick texture that enhanced the melodic center of mass, and even lent the music a spiritual overtone, halfway between trance and fairy tale.

Florida's <u>Home</u> (1) stood out from the crowd, thanks to a broad stylistic range (from cinematic prog-rock instrumentals to spastic pop songs) and to a focus on mundane events of the youth of the USA (like a more serious Frank Zappa). Works such as **IX** (1995), containing the operetta *Concepcion*, **X** (1996), arranged by the Devil's Isle Orchestra (horns, strings and choir), **Netherregions** (1998), their most deranged excursion, **XIV** (2000), a set of richly-arranged madrigals of abstract, psychedelic music, and **Sixteen** (2006), a concept on sex, called the bluff on rock music, both lyrically and musically.

British progressive music 1989-92

The <u>Ozric Tentacles</u> (13), "the" progressive band of the 1990s (although it began releasing cassettes in the mid 1980s), took Gong's legacy (fusing jazz-rock, hard-rock and acid-rock into an energetic, shining and variegated sound) and copied Mike Oldfield's invention (collating melodic and stylistic events into elegant fantasies) to produce a synthesis that sounded both ambitious and natural. Unrelenting rhythms, gurgling synthesizers, stratospheric guitars and exotic atmospheres permeated **Pungent Effulgent** (1989), and the effect was both vibrant and hypnotic. The "band" was an open ensemble, anchored to the pillars of guitarist Ed Wynne, keyboardist Joie Hinton, drummer Merv Pepler, flutist John Egan and percussionist Paul Hankin. The quantity of ideas and experiments, each realized with slick magisterial precision, was overwhelming on **Erpland** (1990), an instrumental tour de force recorded by a ten-unit ensemble (including two electronic keyboards, a sampler, four percussionists, flute, bass and guitar) and displaying an almost baroque elegance. The Ozric Tentacles had mastered, at the same time, the melodic ingenuity of classical music, the fluidity of jazz-rock and the drive of hard-rock. The sound was so cohesive and shimmering as to evoke Colosseum's jams. **Strangeitude** (1991) blended as many sources but also added dance beats to its galloping symphonic poems and colorful festivals of sounds. Far from being improvised, its intricate collages were clockwork mechanisms. **Jurassic Shift** (1993) continued to move towards the taste of the time via increasing nods to ambient, cosmic, new-age and ethnic music.

British saxophonist Kevin Martin launched a number of projects that explored the unlikely marriage of jazz, industrial, dub and punk-rock. The three lengthy jams of **Possession** (1992) and especially the chaotic nightmares of **The Anatomy Of Addiction** (1994), both credited to God (1), were relatively old-fashioned excursions in mood reconnaissance and neurotic stream of consciousness; but Techno Animal (11), a collaboration with Godflesh's guitarist Justin Broadrick, unleashed the destructive force of **Ghosts** (1990), a meeting of Foetus, Karlheinz Stockhausen and Anthony Braxton and one of the most powerful works of its time; a vision that was matched by the brutal and visceral sound of **Under The Skin** (1993), credited to Ice (1). Techno Animal's **Re-Entry** (1995), instead, delved into the claustrophobic darkness of ambient dub, summoning the likes of Jon Hassell, Bill Laswell and Brian Eno. **Tapping The Conversation** (1997), a collaboration between Kevin Martin and Dave Cochrane credited to The Bug (2), crafted an obsessive sense of fear through a psychophysical torture of extreme hip-hop and dub deconstruction. The massive, grinding, claustrophobic digital arrangements of the Bug's **London Zoo** (2008) would be perceived by the crowd of 2008 as an extreme form of dubstep (a genre that he had basically invented with the first Bug album).

Roger Eno attempted a music at the border between classical, jazz and prog-rock with the ensemble Channel Light Vessel (featuring Kate St John, Bill Nelson, Laraaji and Mayumi Tachibana) on **Automatic** (1994) and **Excellent Spirits** (1996).

Solo 1990-94

More spices were added to the progressive-rock scene by New York-based instrumental virtuosos. Marc Ribot (1), who had played with the Lounge Lizards, John Zorn, Tom Waits, and the Jazz Passengers, demonstrated his fluid style, capable of bridging cacophony and melody in a smooth and swinging manner, on **Rootless Cosmopolitan** (1990), featuring jazz masters Don Byron on clarinet and Anthony Coleman on keyboards, and one of the few albums to evoke Peter Green's **End Of The Game**. Ribot followed that achievement with the minimalist noir jazz of **Requiem For What's His Name** (1992) and the relentless sonic (and frequently dissonant) assault of **Shrek** (1994).

Nicky Skopelitis (2), who had played with Anton Fier, Bill Laswell and Sonny Sharrock, concocted a subtle form of ethnic funk-rock, orchestrated for small multi-national ensembles, on **Next To Nothing** (1989) and **Ekstasis** (1993), the latter featuring bassist Jah Wobble and Can's drummer Jaki Liebezeit.

Blind Idiot God's guitarist Andy Hawkins (1) penned the four abstract extended improvisations of **Azonic Halo** (1994) at the border between free jazz, heavy metal and droning music.

Buckethead (1), Brian Carroll's extravagant project, specialized in a goofy fusion of heavy-metal, funk and psychedelic music, which he administered on Frank Zappa-esque concept albums devoted to cyberpunk themes, such as **Bucketheadland** (1992) and **Dreamatorium** (1994), credited to Death Cube K. His best album, **Day Of The Robot** (1996), marked a more serious exploration of ambient and dance music. Despite a hiatus as Guns N' Roses' guitarist, Buckethead continued to reshape his futuristic funk-metal fusion on albums such as **Monsters And Robots** (1999), **Cuckoo Clocks Of Hell** (2004), **Island Of Lost Minds** (2004) and **Kaleidoscalp** (2006).

A unique case, Loren Mazzacane Connors (2) devoted his career to a solo instrumental music that transcended stylistic boundaries, particularly when it crafted abstract country/blues/gospel/folk meditations on **Come Night** (1991) and **Evangeline** (1998). A spectral, purer, zen-like quality, amid a John Fahey fixation, characterized the more ambitious multi-part suites of **The Little Match Girl** (2001) and **Sails** (2006).

Just like in the previous decade, a number of Frank Zappa alumni launched solo careers based on unique (and uniquely iconoclastic) styles. Ant-Bee (11), Billy James' project, was responsible for one of the most crazed albums of the decade, **Pure Electric Honey** (1990), that wed Brian Wilson's flair for eccentric arrangements with Frank Zappa's passion for deviant dynamics, and mixed up the result with techniques borrowed from musique concrete and psychedelic freak-outs. **Lunar Muzik** (1997), that collected veterans of the Mothers Of Invention (Bunk Gardner, Don Preston and Jimmy Carl Black), Gong (including Daevid Allen himself), Alice Cooper and Hawkwind (Harvey Bainbridge), was another madhouse party.

The compositions of Mike Keneally (1), whether the sprawling ones on **Hat** (1994) or the microscopic ones on **Boil That Dust Speck** (1995), whether the poppy ditties of **Sluggo!** (1997), his best album, or the all-instrumental tracks of **Nonkertompf** (1999), sounded like sprightly fragments of rock operas.

Gary Lucas (1) was instead a veteran of Captain Beefheart's band. The swirling, cyclical structures of **Skeleton At The Feast** (1991) overflowed with otherworldly guitar inventions.

Run On's guitarist <u>Alan Licht</u> concentrated on anarchic and dadaist noise with the lengthy improvisations of **Sink The Aging Process** (1994), **Rabbi Sky** (1999) and **Plays Well** (2001).

King Crimson's bassist <u>Tony Levin</u> fused world-music and chamber jazz on **World Diary** (1995).

Former Frank Zappa's and Missing Persons' drummer <u>Terry Bozzio</u> (1) lived several lives in parallel, performing solo drum improvisations, such as the ones on **Drawing the Circle** (1998), as well as composing surreal symphonic music worthy of his master, notably the two **Chamberworks** (1998) for drums and orchestra.

Thinking Plague's guitarist <u>Bob Drake</u> (1) recorded highly original instrumental albums of avantgarde roots-music: **What Day Is It** (1993), a post-modernist deconstruction of country cliches; **Little Black Train** (1996), a reckless venture into progressive bluegrass; **Medallion Animal Carpet** (1999), a wild ride down the dark but fascinating alleys of a very perverted musical mind, one that evoked the lunacy of the Residents and of the Holy Modal Rounders; and **The Skull Mailbox** (2001), which focused on pop melody, but Drake had enough imagination, and enough perversion, to turn each melody into a musical nonsense.

West Coast 1990-91

Mixing demented novelty tunes and goofy instrumental workouts, San Francisco's <u>Primus</u> (13) seemed to emulate Frank Zappa's versatile and iconoclastic irreverence. **Frizzle Fry** (1990) was typical of their capricious art: like an amusement park, it was a combination of rollercoaster rides, comedy shows, relaxing strolls and childish games. The changes in speed, mood and fashion were as abrupt as virtuoso, thanks to the inventions of bassist Les Claypool (one of the all-time greats), to the quirkiness of former Possessed guitarist Larry Lalonde, and to the monumental support of drummer Tim Alexander. King Crimson-ian instrumental convolution was offset by funny lyrics and a self-demystifying attitude. The intellectual puzzles became popular songs on **Sailing The Seas Of Cheese** (1991) and **Pork Soda** (1993), when the fusion of heavy-metal, funk, jazz and music-hall reached an almost mechanical efficiency. The trio's sonic exploration in **Tales From The Punchbowl** (1995) was more adventurous, but also highlighted the limits of the pop format.

Faith No More-associates <u>Mr Bungle</u> (1) were inspired by Frank Zappa and George Clinton on their debut, **Mr Bungle** (1991).

Seattle-based multi-instrumentalist <u>Amy Denio</u> (2) led and collaborated with a number of bizarre jazz-rock projects in the vein of the Canterbury school, notably the <u>Tone Dogs</u> (1), whose **Ankety Low Day** (1990) was a quirky flight of the imagination, and <u>Degenerate Art Ensemble</u>, that straddled the line between jazz, classical and rock.

Tongues (1993) set forth her ambitious program of deconstruction of world folk music, that can evoke Pere Ubu's abstract sonatas for accordion and synthesizer as well as Dario Fo's onomatopoeic theater. This led to a string of albums, culminating in **The Danubians** (2000), that were dominated by Denio's bizarre phonetic wordplay and by her spirited accordion playing. With these works she proved to be a devil of a composer, of an arranger, of a performer, and of a conductor.

The same scene spawned Portland's Caveman Shoestore (1), a guitar-less trio formed by vocalist and keyboardist Elaine DiFalco and by veteran jazz players Fred Chalenor (bass) and Henry Franzoni (drums). Their **Master Cylinder** (1992) ran the gamut from pop melody to Soft Machine-esque jazz-rock to dadaistic cacophony to Art Bears-esque lieder.

The Thessalonians (1), based in San Francisco and featuring percussionist Larry Thrasher, guitarist David James and keyboardists Kim Cascone, Don Falcone and Paul Neyrinck, performed live improvisations for electronic and acoustic instruments, documented on **Soulcraft** (1993), that were the ultimate cybernetic-psychedelic ragas. Falcone's own Melting Euphoria were disciples of Ozric Tentacles' cosmic-progressive rock.

Zazen (formed by four veterans) added Eastern overtones to the style of Yes and Genesis on **Mystery School** (1991).

Virginia 1992-94

During the 1990s, progressive-rock staged a come-back (although it had never truly disappeared), and mainly in the USA. Throughout the decade, Virginia and the Washington area were the epicenter, with bands such as Echolyn (1), whose **Suffocating The Bloom** (1992) contained the 11-movement suite *A Suite For The Everyman*, and Boud Deun, whose best album was probably **Astronomy Made Easy** (1997). They were typical of the genre, derivative of the Canterbury school and of King Crimson.

The most creative group was perhaps Bill Kellum's Rake (11). After the two lengthy improvisations of **Rake Is My Co-Pilot** (1994) that evoked a demented form of free-jazz rather than conventional prog-rock, Rake indulged in **The Art Ensemble Of Rake** (1995), four lengthy suites that ran the gamut from minimalistic repetition to distorted guitar workouts to blues bacchanals to bubbling Moogs to ghostly ambience. **Intelligence Agent** (1996) betrayed the band's stylistic debts towards Pink Floyd, Jimi Hendrix, Mahavishnu Orchestra and Can.

On the other hand, the most successful Virginia act was the racially integrated Dave Matthews Band, whose collections, such as **Under The Table And Dreaming** (1994), offered a sophisticated blend of jazz-rock, world music, folk and rhythm'n'blues.

Noise-punk-jazz 1992-94

God Is My Co-pilot (1) inherited Half Japanese's miniaturized dementia. **I Am Not This Body** (1992) packed 34 brief, childish and dissonant pieces that parodied all sorts of genres. Their chaotic approach bordered on free-jazz cacophony, and on party music for a madhouse.

In San Francisco, the Molecules, formed by former Rat At Rat R guitarist Ron Anderson, had already done something similar on **Steel Toe** (1991). Ditto for Love Child in New York and their **Witchcraft** (1992).

God Is My Co-pilot's idea was pursued, among others, by Spiny Anteaters in Canada, especially on their third goofy, amateurish **Last Supper** (1998), and by Blowhole in Seattle, on **Gathering** (1995), that also featured Amy Denio.

Chicago's Flying Luttenbachers (12), the quintet of drummer Weasel Walter (the only stable member), saxophonists Chad Organ and Ken Vandermark, trombonist/bassist Jeb Bishop, guitarist Dylan Posa, explored the punk-funk-jazz-rock fusion pioneered by the Pop Group and the Contortions, as well as the epileptic noise-jazz of John Zorn, on **Constructive Deconstruction** (1994) and **Destroy All Music** (1995). A new line-up recorded the even more spastic and chaotic **Revenge** (1996), the six-movement suite **Gods Of Chaos** (1998) and the free-jazz chamber music for cello, trumpet, clarinet, violin and percussion of **The Truth Is A Fucking Lie** (1999), while Walter alone penned the delirious *Rise Of The Iridescent Behemoth*, off **Systems Emerge From Complete Disorder** (2003).

Boston's Debris were a punk-jazz outfit featuring horn players next to a power-rock trio and improvising chaotic jams in the vein of Frank Zappa and Henry Cow on **Terre Haute** (1993).

International progressive music 1992-96

In France, Philharmonie experimented with the unusual format of a guitar trio, particularly on **Les Elephantes Carillonneurs** (1993). The creative and unorthodox aesthetics of the Canterbury school was revived by Xaal, a French instrumental progressive trio whose most ambitious work was **Second Ere** (1995).

The Belgian instrumental combo Die Anarchistische Abendunterhaltung (DAAU), formed by four classically-trained musicians (violin, cello, clarinet and accordion), played a hybrid of baroque chamber music, Frank Zappa-inspired jazz and Slavic folk music on the acoustic and drum-less **Die Anarchistische Abendunterhaltung** (1995).

In Canada, <u>Slow Loris</u>' **The Ten Commandments And Two Territories** (1996) straddled the border between free-jazz and acid-rock.

Sweden continued to enjoy a fertile progressive scene. For example, <u>In The Labyrinth</u>, i.e. Peter Lindahl, blended neoclassical and ethnic music on **The Garden Of Mysteries** (1994).

Norway's <u>Motorpsycho</u> (1) offered perhaps the most eclectic take on the cliches of psychedelic hard-rock on monumental albums such as **Demon Box** (1993) and **Timothy's Monster** (1994). They displayed musical ambitions that went beyond the power guitar riff, and often ended in quasi-symphonic magniloquence. The four colossal suites of **Little Lucid Moments** (2008) stood as virtually a recapitulation of jam-oriented rock music from the 1960s to the 1990s.

Australian duo <u>Pablo's Eye</u> wed Brian Eno, David Sylvian and Miles Davis with the jazzy ethnic ambient music. **You Love Chinese Food** (1995).

In Japan, <u>Happy Family</u> betrayed the influence of King Crimson, Frank Zappa, Magma and Univers Zero on their second album, **Toscco** (1997).

Italian-Swiss guitarist <u>Luigi Archetti</u> (2) debuted with the brief demential/dissonant guitar vignettes of **Das Ohr** (1993) in the vein of Fred Frith, while the cubistic and dissonant post-psychedelic music of **Adrenalin** (1994) originated at the intersection of abstract electronic music, convoluted prog-rock, tribal folk music, loose free-jazz and demented chamber music. **Cubic Yellow** (1999), credited to the <u>Hulu Project</u>, added sampling, electronics and drum machines to his eclectic and surreal guitar soundscapes. The electronic watercolors of **Transient Places** (2004) bordered on ambient, droning and microtonal music, an idea that peaked with the atonal "concrete" symphony of **Februar** (2005).

After 1991, when the Berlin wall fell, Eastern Europe developed a very creative brand of rock music, often indebted towards the local folk traditions and often looking to the avantgarde. <u>Uz Jsme Doma</u>, in the Czech Republic, were perhaps the most adventurous with their progressive-rock performed with punk-rock fury, that freely mixed cabaret, folk, noise, ethnic, classical and dance music on albums such as **In the Middle of Words** (1990).

Psychedelic Songwriting

East Coast 1988-94

Psychedelic music was the single greatest invention of the 1960s and remained the dominant genre in the 1990s. The 1960s coined a number of psychedelic styles, and they were still the basic psychedelic styles of the 1990s: the psychedelic pop of the Doors, the psychedelic freak-out of the Red Crayola, the psychedelic trance of the Velvet Underground, and the acid jam of the Grateful Dead. Among the innovations introduced during the 1980s, dream-pop and shoegazing were still popular in the 1990s. Far from merely plagiarizing the classics, the most significant bands of the decade contributed to re-define the art of the sonic trip.

Boston's Galaxie 500 (12), comprised of guitarist Dean Wareham, bassist Naomi Yang and drummer Damon Krukowski, went against the trend when they created an anti-theatrical style devoted to urban alienation. **Today** (1988) was a moonlit tide of languid litanies and whispered singalongs. It was expressionism turned upside down: angst and terror, but in the form of a bloodless stupor, not a loud scream. The trio played back the third Velvet Underground album, Pink Floyd's *Set The Controls For The Heart Of The Sun* and Television's *Torn Curtain*, but filtered of any residual vitality. **On Fire** (1989), their most personal work, was an existential anesthetic. There were echoes of the (acid-rock) past but they were ethereal, sleepy and ghostly: they had been reduced to an inner language of the subconscious. The setting was a wasteland roamed by zombies devoid of any passion, resigned to their emotional impotence and moral isolation, capable only of articulating the emptiness of their lives in a vocabulary of negative words. These were confessions of people who did not even know anymore how to grieve for their own sorrow. These dirges were the exact opposite of the anthemic call to arms of rock'n'roll. An excessive trance dazzled the acid jams of **This Is Our Music** (1990), the most ambitious but also terminal leg of their "trip". Parting ways with Wareham, the former rhythm section of Galaxie 500, Yang and Krukowski assumed the moniker Damon & Naomi (1) and recorded **More Sad Hits** (1992), whose gentle breeze was the ideal appendix to Galaxie 500's mission.

Mercury Rev (111), originating from upstate New York and featuring John Donahue on guitar and Dave Fridmann on bass, achieved a synthesis of historical proportions. **Yerself Is Steam** (1991) was a psychedelic extravaganza that spanned three decades and three continents. Emotionally, it ran the gamut from Red Crayola's anarchic freak-outs to contemplative/meditative ecstasies in the vein of new-age music. Technically, it blended and alternated pop melody, ambient droning, mind-boggling distortion, oneiric folk, martial tempos, pastoral passages, infernal noise and lyrical lullabies. Far from being merely a nostalgic tribute to an age, Mercury Rev's operation started with the hippie vision of nirvana on the other side of a swirling and chaotic music, but tempered the optimism of that program with an awareness of the human condition, and poisoned it with fits of neurosis and decadent atmospheres. The fantasies of **Boces** (1993) were even more variegated and imaginative, veritable collages of sonic events. The dense and busy arrangements, that owed more and more to Fridmann's command of keyboards and orchestration, did not interfere with what was fundamentally a much gentler mood, a distant relative of Kevin Ayers' fairy-tales. The progress towards a joyful and serene sound continued on **See You On The Other Side** (1995), which frequently embraced poppy melodies and facile rhythms, whereas **Deserter's Songs** (1998) marked the zenith of their phantasmagoric orchestrations.

Luna (1), formed by Galaxie 500's guitarist and vocalist Dean Wareham, Feelies' drummer Stanley Demeski and Chills' bassist Justin Harwood, specialized in shy, tender, whispered/conversational pop tunes, best on **Bewitched** (1994).

In Minnesota, Polara (1), the project of 27 Various' guitarist Ed Ackerson, bridged late Sonic Youth, Jesus & Mary Chain's feedback-pop and the "Madchester" sound on **Polara** (1995).

In Indiana, Arson Garden (1) sounded like the Jefferson Airplane performing renaissance psalms on **Under Towers** (1990).

Flaming Lips' lunatic pop influenced New Jersey's Tadpoles (1), whose **He Fell Into The Sky** (1994) matched the demented grandeur of the masters; while Kramer's school of psychedelic pop continued to yield cauldrons of melodic oddities, for example Uncle Wiggly's **There Was An Elk** (1993).

Minneapolis' Shift, the brainchild of keyboardists Marc Ostermeier and Eric Ostermeier, harked back to a lyrical version of shoegaze and dream-pop with the EP **A Folding Sieve** (1995). Eric Ostermeier's Motion Picture (2) achieved zen-like grandeur with the fragile folk-rock embedded in quasi-classical grace and quasi classical arrangements of **Every Last Romance** (1998), and employed a chamber quartet of cello, violin, French horn and English horn on **A Paper Gift** (2001).

In Pennsylvania, Original Sins' bizarre leader John Terlesky created one of the most irrational corpus of music ever recorded under the moniker Brother J.T. (2). Albums such as **Vibrolux** (1994) and **Music For The Other Head** (1996) conceived composition as an utter mess. Mostly, his "songs" were a hysterical rambling over cacophonous imitations of rock'n'roll. The longer tracks sounded like hippie music of the Sixties sucked, chewed and defecated by a psychedelic black-hole. It was a (hazy, incoherent, deranged) mental state, not an art.

West Coast 1988-95

Towards the end of the decade in the USA, psychedelic rock mutated into a whole new genre, less involved with studio trickery and/or guitar mayhem, more focused on songwriting while still preoccupied with textures and soundscapes.

Medicine (1), formed in Los Angeles by Brad Laner, ex-Savage Republic's drummer but now on guitars and keyboards, delivered **Shot Forth Self Living** (1992), a therapeutic shock that owed both to My Bloody Valentine and to Sonic Youth. Trance and noise were also the pillars of follow-up **The Buried Life** (1993).

Seattle's Sky Cries Mary (11), which had adopted an eclectic fusion of jazz, funk, world-music and acid-rock on the EP **Exit At The Axis** (1992), converted to hippie/new-age spirituality with **A Return To The Inner Experience** (1993), which blended Klaus Schulze's cosmic music, David Byrne's African polyrhythms and Nico's catatonic ballads, thereby coining an anti-rhetorical form of psychedelia, one that was more an ambience than an ideology. Their masterpiece, **This Timeless Turning** (1994), focused on the intersection between early Pink Floyd and dance music, but hip-hop beats, Hendrix-ian riffs, industrial tornados and ancestral rites percolated through the loose, flaccid lattice.

Quasi, formed in Oregon by Donner Party's guitarist and Heatmiser's bassist Sam Coomes, specialized in applying old-fashioned, and frequently out-of-tune, keyboards to catchy pop tunes, for example on **Early Recordings** (1995).

The dominant styles of the 1980s and 1990s were still being revised, but the well was clearly drying up.

USA shoegazing 1992-94

The influence of My Bloody Valentine and of the whole "shoegazing" movement became pervasive in the USA from 1992 on. Notable among the early albums of the genre were Fudge's **The Ferocious Rhythm Of Precise Laziness** (1992) in Virginia, and Drop Nineteens's **Delaware** (1992) in Boston.

Pennsylvania's Lilys (1) evolved from the quiet transcendental bliss of **In The Presence Of Nothing** (1992) to the dilated, majestic amorphous melodies of **Eccsame The Photon Band** (1995).

Boston's Swirlies (1) added mellotron, Moog and found noises to the guitar tremolos of **Blonder Tongue Audio Baton** (1993).

Chicago's Catherine (1) bridged shoegazing and grunge on **Sorry** (1994).

Windy & Carl (12), the project of Detroit's guitarist Carl Hultgren, added Windy Weber's ethereal vocals to the equation. **Portal** (1994) indulged in the angelic hypnosis of the shoegazers, but the drifting nebulae of **Drawing Of Sound** (1996) created friendly soundscapes for vocals to roam, despite the monumental spires of guitar distortion and the absence of rhythm. By demoting the guitars to the background and promoting the electronic keyboards to the forefront, the three lengthy tracks of **Antarctica** (1997) veered towards German "kosmische musik" of the 1970s. The organic and fibrillating **Depths** (1998) developed that idea into a full-fledged marriage of heaven (the cosmic drones) and hell (the menacing density of the sound).

Beyond space-rock 1992-94

By fusing the extreme styles of psychedelia that favored the extended, free-form jam (acid-rock, space-rock and raga-rock) over the oddly-arranged tune, a number of groups sculpted epic sonic endeavors.

Lengthy and mostly improvised space jams took up ambitious albums such as: Fuzzhead's **Mind Soup** (1993) from Ohio; Lorelei's **Everyone Must Touch The Stove** (1996) from Virginia: Temple Of Bon Matin (1)'s **Bullet Into Mesmer's Brain** (1997) from Pennsylvania; etc.

Crawlspace (2), the creature of Indiana-via-L.A. singer Eddie Flowers, produced works such as **Sphereality** (1992) and **The Exquisite Fucking Beauty** (1995), both anarchic and erudite, that went even further into the formulation of psychedelic free-jazz.

Mooseheart Faith, formed by the Angry Samoans' bassist Todd Homer (now on autoharp) and (black) guitarist Larry Robinson, squeezed the entire psychedelic vocabulary (from space-rock rave-ups to dilated ballads, from catchy ditties to abstract electronic passages) into **Magic Square of the Sun** (1991).

A group of Los Angeles musicians straddled the line between industrial music and acid-rock, and produced intriguing works such as Pressurehed's **Sudden Vertigo** (1994), featuring vocalist Tommy Grenas and keyboardist Len Del Rio. Del Rio also played on the Anubian Lights' **The Eternal Sky** (1995), while Grenas played on Farflung's **25,000 Feet Per Second** (1995).

Chicago's Sabalon Glitz (1), led by keyboardist Chris Holmes and vocalist Carla Bruce, offered a more electronic version of Hawkwind's space-rock on **Ufonic** (1994).

Detroit's Gravitar (12) were the noisiest of the bunch, and one of the noisiest groups of all times. **Chinga Su Corazon** (1993) and **Gravitar** (1995), totally improvised, were maelstroms of cacophony. Truculent rock'n'roll progressions built thick walls of noise. Each piece (especially on the second album) was a symphony of spectral dissonances harking back to Throbbing Gristle's macabre "industrial" rituals. Gravitar had endowed Lou Reed's **Metal Machine Music** with a rhythm. **Now The Road Of Knives** (1997), featuring a new guitarist, brought a bit of structure into their abominable chaos, revealing Chrome and Jimi Hendrix as the band's role models.

Texas 1990-95

By far the most active scene was in Texas. Texan psychedelia had been the craziest since the 1960s, and it claimed again that supremacy in the 1990s, led, of course, by the achievements of the Butthole Surfers. Except that, during the 1990s, this school diverged from punk-rock and moved towards a more experimental form of music, hardly "rock" at all. Spearheading the renaissance were severely irrational Butthole-ian bands.

There were three distinct schools of psychedelic rock in Texas: one based in Austin (Ed Hall, ST 37), one in Houston and one in Dallas.

If possible, <u>Ed Hall</u> (14) even increased the psychedelic-madness quotient of the Butthole Surfers, beginning with the repellent bacchanals and hallucinations of **Albert** (1988). At the least, they grotesquely increased volume and speed on their classic **Love Poke Here** (1990), a gargantuan, shameless blunder that evoked Captain Beefheart's blues, voodoo exorcisms, drunk cowboys' hoedowns, Jimi Hendrix, breakneck hardcore and redneck boogie. **Gloryhole** (1991) was the punk equivalent of Beckett's absurd theater. The slightly more serious (at times even melodramatic) **Motherscratcher** (1993) and the slightly better structured (at times even linear) **La-La-Land** (1995) were also their densest stews of heretical sonic events.

The <u>Cherubs</u> (1), a spin-off of Ed Hall, added sampling, dissonance and hard-rock riffs to Ed Hall's already explosive mix, particularly on their second album **Heroin Man** (1994).

<u>ST 37</u> (1), instead, followed in the footsteps of lysergic cosmic couriers a` la Hawkwind on albums such as **Glare** (1995).

Among the elders of Dallas' psychedelic tribe were <u>Bag</u>, documented on **Midnight Juice** (1991), and <u>Lithium Xmas</u>, represented by **Helldorado** (1994). But the glory days of Dallas' psychedelia came a bit later with the Vas Deferens Organization and its offsprings.

The Houston school was centered around one group: <u>Mike Gunn</u> (1) displayed a morbid fascination with Black Sabbath and Jimi Hendrix on **Hemp For Victory** (1991) and capitalized on it for the slow-motion ragas of their most original work, **Almaron** (1993). Mike Gunn's bassist Scott Grimm became <u>Dunlavy</u>, devoted to instrumental space-rock.

Mike Gunn's guitarist Tom Carter started <u>Charalambides</u> (3), who experimented with deranged ballads, bizarre samples, guitar freak-outs and tape manipulation on the 100-minute cassette **Our Bed Is Green** (1992) and especially the double record **Market Square** (1995). The monolithic psychological explorations of **Joy Shapes** (2004), recorded by a trio of guitarists, even ventured into avantgarde music and free-jazz. Pared down to the duo of Christina and Tom Carter, Charalambides eventually achieved the naked melodic quintessence of **A Vintage**

Burden (2006), that almost sounded like the negation of their original "acid" program.

Linus Pauling Quartet (1), who originated from the same proto-group as Mike Gunn, filled **Immortal Classics Chinese Music** (1995) with languid, whacky ballads a` la Flaming Lips but the extended jams *Improvise Now* (1996) and *The Great Singularity* off their best album, **Killing You With Rock** (1998), aligned them with the boldest sonic surgeons of their era.

San Francisco's noise psychedelia, 1991-92

Mason Jones was a San Francisco-based guru of noisy, post-psychedelic, post-ambient, post-cosmic and post-industrial music. His manifestos were the first two collections of experiments released under the moniker Trance (1), **Automatism** (1991) and particularly **Audiography** (1993), whose compositions range from symphonic movement to ethnic watercolor. The formidable wall of noise of **Delicate Membrane** (1996) began the saga of Jones' Subarachnoid Space (12), featuring Melynda Jackson on guitar. The pieces were fully improvised, the sound was majestic, and the mood ranged from suspenseful trance to sheer horror. **Ether Or** (1997) showed that the distance between their therapeutic mayhems and free jazz was negligible. The idea was further refined on **Almost Invisible** (1997), a massive hodgepodge of astral chaos, frantic ragas, oceanic psalms and abstract soundpainting that represented an ideal soundtrack for the marriage of heaven and hell. Jones had virtually resurrected early Pink Floyd and provided their biography with an alternative ending: a terrible mutation of *A Saucerful Of Secrets* rather than **Dark Side Of The Moon**. **Endless Renovation** (1998), their first studio recording and a more sophisticated variant on that idea (that quoted casually from Frank Zappa, Terry Riley or Colosseum) and **The Sleeping Sickness** (1999), a collaboration with the Walking Timebombs (the Pain Teens' Scott Ayers), simply increased the stylistic confusion around Jones' and Jackson's wild guitar distortions.

Mandible Chatter unleashed Helios Creed-ian guitar fury on the black mass **Serenade For Anton** (1992), before turning to sound manipulation on **Hair Hair Lock & Lore** (1994).

The golden age of British psychedelia, 1989-94

The golden age of British psychedelia was not the 1960s: it was the 1990s. Never had England witnessed such a deluge of psychedelic bands. The scene of raves created an inexhaustible demand for drug-induced, drug-related and drug-facilitating music.

The poppy version of psychedelia (the one that wrapped facile melodies in eccentric arrangements) went hand in hand with the booming phenomenon of Brit-pop: the Telescopes's **Taste** (1989), a more robust version of shoegazing; the Inspiral Carpets, who focused on the nostalgic Farfisa-driven sound on **The Beast Inside** (1991); Verve's **A Storm In Heaven** (1993), which predated their world-wide hit *Bitter Sweet Symphony* (1997); Sundial's **Reflecter** (1992), a bridge between California's Paisley Underground and British shoegazers; the Auteurs's **New Wave** (1993), a nostalgic tribute to the hippie era; Whipping Boy's **Heartworm** (1995), in Ireland, a work drenched in neoclassical melancholy. What was truly remarkable about these bands is how derivative and predictable they could sound.

A more sophisticated form of psychedelic pop song was devised by Curve (1), whose **Doppelganger** (1992) aimed for a lush, catchy and dance-oriented form of dream-pop; the Cranberries (1), an Irish band whose **No Need To Argue** (1994) was an album of desolate lullabies propelled by the operatic, guttural and melismatic vocals of Dolores O'Riordan; Rollerskate Skinny (1), also from Ireland, who were among the few bands to match the soulful madness of Mercury Rev on **Shoulder Voices** (1993). In Belgium, dEUS crafted the eclectic and baroque **Worst Case Scenario** (1994).

The hippie spirit, and their favorite style, raga-rock, was resurrected by Gorky's Zygotic Mynci, particularly with the eccentric **Tatay** (1994), which Euros Rowlands's keyboards and John Lawrence's guitar turned into, alternatively, a poppier Incredible String Band, a less caustic Bonzo Band, or a more bizarre Brian Wilson. The latter's orchestrations would provide the inspiration for the more conventional **Barafundle** (1997) and **Gorky 5** (1998).

Far less successful commercially, although far more creative, in Britain was the noisy and free-form version of psychedelia that wed Hawkwind's space-rock and early Pink Floyd's interstellar ragas.

Porcupine Tree (2), the project of guitarist Steven Wilson, went through three stages. **On The Sunday Of Life** (1992) was a compendium of Pink Floyd-ian sounds, from Syd Barrett's oblique ballads to **Ummagumma**'s symphonic pieces. Then Japan's keyboardist Richard Barbieri helped fine-tune the languid, fluid and transcendental mini-concertos of **The Sky Moves Sideways** (1994). And, finally, a cohesive combo crafted **Signify** (1996) and **Stupid Dream** (1999) in a fashion reminiscent of early King Crimson's majestic ambience, an idea that eventually led to the slick production of **In Absentia** (2002).

Terminal Cheesecake (2) played space-rock the way avantgarde composer Karlheinz Stockhausen would have played it. Echoes of Chrome, Pop Group and Throbbing Gristle turned **Johnny Town Mouse** (1989) and **Angels In Pigtails** (1991) into nightmarish experiences.

Skullflower, a loose group of musicians affiliated with guitarist Matthew Bower, performed heavy, droning psychedelic music on **Obsidian Shaking Codex** (1993) and **Argon** (1995), a symphony in four movements. Another Matthew Bower project was Sunroof, devoted to a psychotic version of cosmic music on the double-disc **Delicate Autobahns Under Construction** (2000). After a hiatus of seven years, Bower resurrected Skullflower to erect the impressive walls of noise of **Exquisite Fucking Boredom** (2003), containing the four-part super-doom suite *Celestial Highway*, **Orange Canyon Mind** (2004) and **Tribulation** (2006), slowly drifting towards the idea of music as one long modulated massive distortion.

Latter-period shoegazers abounded. Ride (1) adjusted the cliche` to the era of raves on **Nowhere** (1990). So did Ride's best imitators, Blind Mr Jones, on the mostly instrumental **Stereo Musicale** (1992). Swervedriver (1) turned guitar distortions into an art of quasi-zen vespers, best on **Mezcal Head** (1993), while bridging the gap between the shoegazing acid-rock of My Bloody Valentine and the hard-edged garage-rock of the Stooges. The Times' mastermind Ed Ball formed the Teenage Filmstars to play eccentric shoegaze music overloaded with studio effects on **Star** (1992).

Both Loop and Spacemen 3 spawned a new generation of bands:

Spacemen 3's guitarist Jason Pierce formed Spiritualized (3) as the natural sequel to his old band, with the same rhythm section, Mark Refoy on guitar and newcomer Kate Radley on keyboards. **Lazer Guided Melodies** (1992) was notable for the wildly schizophrenic dynamics that flung most songs between acoustic and quasi-symphonic passages. Pierce's abuse of drones and tremolos to create hypnotic lullabies and wavering ragas reached an almost baroque peak on **Pure Phase** (1995), recorded by the trio of Pierce, Radley and bassist Sean Cook. By then, Pierce had developed a process of scientific layering of sounds that was, basically, an exaggeration of Phil Spector's and Brian Wilson's production styles of yore. The lush trance-pop of **Ladies And Gentlemen We Are Floating In Space** (1997) was almost the antithesis of his old "shoegazing" style. Overflowing with quotations from multiple genres, traditions and styles (and a penchant for gospel music), it exuded grace and majesty, even when it indulged in instrumental orgies. Pierce's cynical reappropriation of other people's music induced a Babylonian merry-go-round that outdid everybody at their own game while not playing their games at all. Abandoned by both Cook and Radley, Pierce recorded **Let It Come Down** (2001) with help from dozens of external musicians, but the result was a concept album on the subject of "getting high" that did not break any new ground. In general, the point with Spiritualized was whether theirs was art or technology.

Other spin-offs were Darkside, formed by Spacemen 3's bassist Pete "Bassman" Bain, Alpha Stone, formed by the same Bain, Hair And Skin Trading Co , formed by Loop's rhythm section, Slipstream, formed by Mark Refoy, the veteran Spacemen 3 and Spiritualized member, and

Lupine Howl, formed by Spiritualized bassist Sean Cook. They marked the meeting point of shoegazing and ambient music.

Dream-pop was no less popular than shoegazing. The influence of the Cocteau Twins was felt on works as different as Kitchens Of Distinction's **Love Is Hell** (1989) and Miranda Sex Garden's **Suspiria** (1992), a disco-oriented reconstruction of medieval music, Lush's **Spooky** (1992), scoured by the abrasive guitars and sugary vocals of Emma Anderson and Miki Berenyi, Earwig's **Under My Skin I Am Laughing** (1992), and the Cranes' **Loved** (1994).

A few acts matched, if not surpassed, the masters of dream-pop, while exploring different nuances of the genre.

The Pale Saints (1), who had debuted in the ethereal and oneiric style of **The Comforts Of Madness** (1990), introduced hard-rock into dream-pop on **In Ribbons** (1992).

The trance administered by Slowdive (11) relied on the vocal harmonies of Neil Halstead and Rachel Goswell, and on triple-guitar arrangements. The hypnotic, velvety whispers, and the smooth, bright sound of **Just For A Day** (1991) reached for a psychological and even mystical level, that a game of echoes and reverbs merely enhanced. **Souvlaki** (1993) reinterpreted shoegazing as an abstraction of two formats: Strauss' symphonic poem and Brian Eno's ambient music.

Levitation (1), led by former House Of Love guitarist Terry Bickers, were reminiscent of Echo & The Bunnymen's baroque hypnosis on **Coterie** (1991).

Catherine Wheel (1) debuted with a formidable synthesis of Neil Young's neurotic folk and Brian Wilson's eccentric pop, **Ferment** (1992), whose hammering mandalas wove colossal braids of distortions around naive refrains.

Graham Sutton's Bark Psychosis (10) upped the ante of dream-pop with the extended singles *All Different Things* (1990) and *Scum* (1993), which were abstract mini-concertos built around ineffable melodies. The method was refined with the slow, lengthy sonic puzzles of **Hex** (1994), which fused dissonances, electronics, swirling ragas, jazz drumming, ghostly drones, lounge music, soft funk polyrhythms and so forth, into an organic whole.

Whether the pop, shoegazing or dream-pop variation, England was awash in psychedelic rock as never before.

Hyper-psychedelia in the Pacific, 1992-94

Perhaps the most intriguing take on psychedelia came from New Zealand. One of the most significant musicians of the 1990s, Roy Montgomery (23) created a successful hybrid of all these styles with his ensembles Dadamah (10), Dissolve (1), and Hash Jar Tempo (the collaboration with Bardo Pond). Dadamah's **This Is Not A Dream**

(1992), featuring bassist Kim Pieters, keyboardist Janine Stagg and Scorched Earth Policy's drummer Peter Stapleton, was a magic recreation of the Velvet Underground's psychedelic trance, updated to the new-wave zeitgeist of the Modern Lovers, sprinkled with effervescent oddities in the surreal vein of Pere Ubu. Dissolve's **That That Is** (1995) was merely an ectoplasm for two guitars, but their **Third Album For The Sun** (1997), by adding keyboards, percussions and cello to the guitar jamming, attained a spiritual solemnity.

In the meantime, Montgomery's solo albums walked an even more arduous path: the impressionistic vignettes of **Scenes From The South Island** (1995) harked back to the transcendental spirit of John Fahey, to the divine introspection of Peter Green, and to the dreamy psalms of David Crosby; while an obscure, symbol-drenched metaphysics and an obsessive preoccupation with the afterlife led Montgomery through the stages of the imaginary Calvary of **Temple IV** (1996). His song-oriented career peaked with **And Now The Rain Sounds Like Life Is Falling Down Through It** (1998), which contrasted introspective melody and metaphysical setting, resulting in a set of rarified, hermetic prayers, each wrapped into a different universe of haunting sound effects. But his philosophy was better expressed with the free-form soundpainting of **True** (1999). **The Allegory of Hearing** (2000) overflowed with innovative guitar techniques and included the 17-minute tour de force of *Resolution Island Suite*, which recapitulated Montgomery's theory of transcendental harmony the same way that the *Art of the Fugue* summarized Bach's and *Rainbow In Curved Air* summarized Terry Riley's. The sonic mandala of *For A Small Blue Orb*, off **Silver Wheel Of Prayer** (2001) continued his exploration of the individual's relationship with the eternal.

Dean Roberts (1) pursued similar experiments, first with Thela's two albums of lengthy artsy/noisy jams, **Thela** (1995) and **Argentina** (1996), then with his solo project White Winged Moth, that devoted albums such as **I Can See Inside Your House** (1996) to instrumental vignettes located halfway between John Fahey and Derek Bailey, and finally with the spiritual, ambient, psychedelic and ethnic collections under his own name, such as **Moth Park** (1998) and **All Cracked Medias** (1999), his masterpiece.

The saga of the bands built around Scorched Earth Policy's drummer Peter Stapleton was one of the most intriguing and influential of New Zealand. He joined forces again with guitarist Brian Cook for the second album by the Terminals (1), the spaced-out **Touch** (1992), derailed by tribal drumming and dissonant organ. At the same time, Stapleton recorded the Dadamah album with Roy Montgomery. Flies Inside The Sun (1) were born from the ashes of Dadamah (Stapleton, Pieters, Cook and guitarist/keyboardist Danny Butt), but **An Audience Of Others** (1995) and especially **Flies Inside The Sun** (1996) and **Le Mal**

D'Archive (2001), the first one without Pieters, dramatically increased the degree of improvisation and cacophony: dissonant and disjointed music halfway between free-jazz improvisation a` la Art Ensemble of Chicago, psychedelic freak-outs a` la Red Krayola and atonal chamber music. In fact, Stapleton, Pieters and Butt recorded the even more abstract **Sediment** (1996), this time credited to Rain, with the guitars replaced by synthesizers; and then the trio of Stapleton on drums, Pieters on bass and Dead C's Bruce Russell on guitar formed a (free-noise) "supergroup" that recorded the six instrumental improvisations of **Last Glass** (1994). Finally, Stapleton and Pieters launched the project Sleep (NZ) with **Enfolded in Luxury** (1999).

New Zealand's Alastair Galbraith (1) recorded albums, particularly between **Talisman** (1994) and **Cry** (2000), that were not so much collections of songs as experiments on sound.

RST was the solo project of New Zealand's guitarist Andrew Moon who, inspired by Skullflower and Sunn O))), experimented with overdubbing and manipulating his electric guitar into hostile soundscapes of heavy drones on **Event Horizon** (1995) and especially in the three hyper-diluted colossal suites of the triple-disc **Other Machines** (2007).

Post-noise in Japan, 1990-92

The most extreme kind of psychedelia (free-form jams that hark back to Grateful Dead, Red Crayola, early Pink Floyd and Hawkwind) was practiced mainly in Japan. The most imitated band was High Rise, but the man who, over a 30-year career, propelled Japanese acid-rock to the top of the world was Keiji Haino, whose numerous projects were rediscovered during the 1990s.

The all-female band Angel In Heavy Syrup (1), fronted by guitarists Mine Nakao and Fusao Toda, toyed with Pink Floyd's neurotic trips, Gong's lysergic kaleidoscopes and Amon Duul's tribal propulsion on **III** (1995).

Shizuka, led by a female vocalist and featuring Fushitsusha's second guitarist Maki Miura and Fushitsusha's drummer Jun Kosugi, were Japan's answer to My Bloody Valentine's shoegazing-rock for melodic distorted guitar on **Heavenly Persona** (1994).

Maso Yamazaki's Masonna represented the link with the previous generation of noise-makers on albums devoted to lengthy free-form jams such as **Shinsen Na Clitoris** (1990) and **Noisextra** (1995).

Similar to Fushitsusha were guitarist Kaneko Jutok's Kousokuya (1), whose **Kousokuya** (1991) indulged even more in free-jazz improvisation.

Ghost (12), led by guitarist and vocalist Masaki Batoh, fused Japanese folk music and ambient music on **Ghost** (1990). The surreal orchestration and "ghostly" effects of **Lama Rabi Rabi** (1996), increased the gothic quotient, while the four-part title-track of **Hypnotic Underworld** (2004) was the crowning formal achievement of a group of visionary jazz-rock musicians, equally adept at pop songwriting and bizarre avantgarde. **In Stormy Nights** (2007) featured the 28-minute collage of *Hemicyclic Anthelion*, constructed in studio by Batoh assembling snippets of live performances.

Michio Kurihara's White Heaven (1) continued the tradition of High Rise with **Out** (1991), inspired by the same demigods (Blue Cheer, Iron Butterfly and Jimi Hendrix).

L (Japanese singer-songwriter Hiroyuki Usui) released a pioneering work of acid folk and blues, **Holy Letters** (1992), replete with Tibetan monks.

The most original interpretation of space-rock of the 1970s was perhaps advanced by Japan's gothic punks Death Comes Along in the two suites of **Heavy Psychedelic Schizoid God** (1994).

Garage Music for the Generation X

Blues-punk, 1990-93

Jon Spencer was not the only one to adapt the blues to punk-rock. New takes on the blues and rhythm'n'blues were experimented by bands throughout the nation, from New York's <u>Railroad Jerk</u> (1), with the subnormal psycho-blues of **Railroad Jerk** (1990), to Ohio's <u>Prisonshake</u>, with **A Girl Named Yes** (1990), from Los Angeles' <u>Clawhammer</u> (1), led by former Pontiac Brothers' guitarist Jon Wahl, that fostered the unlikely wedding of Captain Beefheart and Devo on **Clawhammer** (1990), to Kansas' <u>Mercy Rule</u> (1), formed by 13 Nightmares' guitarist John Taylor and thundering vocalist Heidi Ore, with **God Protects Fools** (1993). Their sloppy, primitive, barbaric sound resonated with the suicidal psyche of the Generation X.

Ohio's <u>Gits</u> (1), featuring the witchy vocals of Mia Zapata, crossed punk-rock and blues-rock, halfway between X and Sex Pistols, with the addition of an angry feminine touch, on **Frenching The Bully** (1992).

Michigan's <u>Mule</u> (1), formed by guitarist Preston Long and Laughing Hyenas' formidable rhythm section (Jim Kimball and Kevin "Munro" Strickland), played blues-rock for hell's saloons. **Mule** (1993) offered harsh, truculent and discordant music that borrowed from Z.Z.Top, Captain Beefheart, Lynyrd Skynyrd, Jimi Hendrix and Creedence Clearwater Revival but savagely deformed the original sources.

Chicago's <u>Red Red Meat</u> (12) started from similar premises but evolved towards a more intellectual exploration of music. **Red Red Meat** (1992) and **Jimmy Wine Majestic** (1993) unleashed the dirty, feverish and unstable vibrations of all the blues irregulars of the past (the Rolling Stones, Captain Beefheart, Pussy Galore, etc), but the atmospheric **Bunny Gets Paid** (1995) veered towards desolate free-form "pieces" that felt like scarred remnants of pop songs. This, in turn, led to the abstract framework of **There's A Star Above The Manger Tonight** (1997), replete with synthesizer and other sophisticated arrangements, which was, de facto, a postmodernist exercise in stylistic deconstruction, bordering on trip-hop and ambient music while retaining the cacophony of Captain Beefheart and Pussy Galore. Red Red Meat guitarist (and original founder) Tim Rutili, drummer Ben Massarella and bassist Tim Hurley set out to further investigate this unfocused sea of sounds as <u>Califone</u> (2). The brooding acid-blues sound of their early EPs, **Califone** (1998) and **Califone** (2000), and of their full-length albums **Roomsound** (2001) and **Quicksand Cradlesnakes** (2003) absorbed jazz, post-rock, samples and loops into the canon of blues depression and gospel ecstasy. **Heron King Blues** (2004) further disintegrated the format of the roots-rock song, with the mostly instrumental jam *Heron King Blues* performing a bold balancing act between organic free-form abstraction and geometric pulsing pattern, a worthy addition to the program of Captain Beefheart's **Mirror Man**. The dusty interplay of voice, guitars, banjos, hurdy gurdies, drums and electronics concocted an understated post-everything mayhem.

In Australia, <u>Bloodloss</u> (1), which were basically Lubricated Goat with Mudhoney's vocalist Mark Arm replacing Stu Spasm, assembled some of the ugliest blues albums of all times: the sinister **In A Gadda Da Change** (1993) and especially **Live My Way** (1995), disfigured by saxophones, trumpets and keyboards, and influenced by Captain Beefheart and the Rolling Stones.

Garage-rock, 1992-94

San Francisco's <u>Mummies</u> (1) were perhaps the ideological leaders of the garage revival, even if they lasted only one album, the orgiastic and lo-fi **Never Been Caught** (1992).

Notable albums from the Pacific Northwest included **Wrecker** (1992) by the <u>Mono Men</u> and **Outta Sight** (1993) by <u>Sinister Six</u> (1). Seattle's <u>Makers</u> (1) unwound a manic frenzy of fuzz, treble and feedback at full throttle on **Howl** (1994), and enhanced the show with nihilistic overtones on **Makers** (1996).

Ohio boasted two of the best rock'n'roll groups. Heirs to MC5's bacchanals, but also a bridge to contemporary genres such as grunge, thrash-metal and hardcore, <u>God And Texas</u> (2) drenched the songs of **History Volume One** (1992) and **Criminal Element** (1993) with feverish distortions and catastrophic drumming. The <u>New Bomb Turks</u> (2) were even more barbaric and breathtaking, particularly on **Destroy Oh Boy** (1993), but anchored the songs of mature albums such as **At Rope's End** (1998) to linear progressions and anthemic melodies.

MC5's agit-prop was also relived in Washington's <u>Love 666</u> ferocious anthems, notably on the EP **Love 666** (1994) and the mini-album **American Revolution** (1995).

The <u>Dynamite Masters Blues Quartet</u>, fronted by Shinji Masuko, played raw, abrasive and loud rock'n'roll on **DMBQ** (1995) and **EXP** (1996), like a marriage of the Boredoms, Blue Cheer and the Stooges.

Crampsiana, 1993-95

The spring of garage-rock was not dry yet. The Cramps' punkabilly, in particular, was a massive influence on USA garage-rock, from Tennessee, where the <u>Oblivians</u> recorded the mini-album **Never Enough** (1994) and especially **Popular Favorites** (1996), to Kentucky, where <u>Bodeco</u> recorded **Bone Hair And Hide** (1992). <u>Reverend Horton Heat</u> (Texan rocker Jim Heath) continued the tradition of mad rockabilly on albums such as the demonic **The Full Custom Sounds** (1993).

Seattle's <u>Gas Huffer</u> (2) played epileptic rock'n'roll with the psychotic impetus of the Heartbreakers and the Cramps but also with the childish silliness of the Ramones. **Janitors Of Tomorrow** (1991) and **Integrity Technology And Service** (1992) were collections of time-warp aberrations.

The Honeymoon Killers' leader Jerry Teel went on to join the <u>Chrome Cranks</u> (1), with whom he produced at least one aberration worthy of the Honeymoon Killers, **Chrome Cranks** (1994).

In North Carolina, <u>Southern Culture On The Skids</u> (2) delivered a stew of old-fashioned styles (surf, rockabilly, country, garage-rock and rhythm'n'blues) with a punk attitude, reaching back to Rolling Stones, Creedence Clearwater Revival and Cramps. They were at their best when they let the bad vibrations flow, such as on **For Lovers Only** (1993), a madhouse of a roots-rock album, and the even more eclectic and exuberant **Ditch Diggin'** (1994).

In Minnesota, the veterans of the <u>Lee Harvey Oswald Band</u> (1) concocted the infernal party of **A Taste Of Prison** (1994), which also indulged in the most perverted side of life.

Instrumental revival, 1993-94

Instrumental music staged a massive revival during the 1990s, searching for a balance of sorts between nostalgic revival and post-rock ambitions.

Raised on sci-fi serials and horror movies, Alabama's <u>Man Or Astroman</u> (2) invented a cyberpunk version of Shadowy Men On A Shadowy Planet's postmodernist surf that recalled Devo's satirical/mythological philosophy but dispensed with the silly lyrics. From the naive and exuberant **Is It Man Or Astro-man?** (1993) to the more adventurous **Experiment Zero** (1996), they defined a science of epic guitar twangs, epileptic surf hoedowns, suspenseful vibratos and menacing reverbs.

Seattle's <u>Pell Mell</u>, the group of Pigeonhed's keyboardist Steve Fisk, carried out a similar program on collections such as **Interstate** (1994), whereas groups such as the <u>Phantom Surfers</u> in San Francisco were paying tribute to Los Angeles's surf music and to the Northwest's garage-rock on albums such as **The Exciting Sounds Of Model Road Racing** (1994).

The <u>Mermen</u> (3), from San Francisco, altered surf music via Neil Young's blues-psychedelic neurosis and Jimi Hendrix's devastating spasms on **Food For Other Fish** (1994), and achieved a miraculous balance between revival and experimentation with the three creative jams of **A Glorious Lethal Euphoria** (1995). Their compositions, led by guitarist Jim Thomas, alternated between slow and tortured dirges that flowed towards controlled cacophony, somber and colloquial meditations, majestic and symphonic twang-drenched odes, John Fahey-ian East/West fusion, jazz-rock and raga. **The Amazing California Health And Happiness Road Show** (2000) contained their tour de force, *Burn*.

Lo-fi Pop

Oceania, 1991-94

Lo-fi pop, the great invention of New Zealand's independent musicians, became one of the main phenomena, world-wide, of the 1990s.

The scene in New Zealand was largely dominated by members of the old bands, and little was added to the canon by the new generations. Graeme Jefferies' Cakekitchen (1) concocted the adult blend of austere melodies, bitter philosophy and elegant arrangements of **World Of Sand** (1992), eventually achieving the intrepid and rarefied atmosphere of **The Devil And The Deep Blue Sea** (1996). Bailter Space (1), led by guitarist Alister Parker, gave their best with the hypnotic and atmospheric noise-rock of **Vortura** (1994), that capitalized on the innovations of My Bloody Valentine and Galaxie 500.

The Underground Lovers (1) updated the psychedelic canon with **Leaves Me Blind** (1993), drenched in exotic and mystical sounds. King Loser were unique in producing a huge noise a` la Blue Cheer on **Sonic Super Free Hi-Fi** (1994) and **You Cannot Kill What Does Not Live** (1996). More conventional hard-rock was played by the 3Ds.

In Australia, former Cannanes guitarist Randall Lee's Nice (Australia) and Ashtray Boy were typical of how the dynasties of the 1980s survived the 1990s. **All Souls Alive** (1994), by the Blackeyed Susans (1), formed by vocalist Rob Snarski and bassist Phil Kakulas, owed the charm of its folk/country chamber elegies to Triffids' guitarist David McComb, Dirty Three's violinist Warren Ellis and drummer Jim White. The Moles' **Untune The Sky** (1991), featuring Richard Davies, was perhaps the most charming oddity, worthy of New Zealand's classic pop.

USA, 1990-94

The legacy of lo-fi pop was felt much stronger in and around the colleges. Olympia, near Seattle, ruled by Beat Happening, boasted the most fertile scene: Al Larsen's Some Velvet Sidewalk with their second album **Whirlpool** (1995); Rebecca Gates' Spinanes, with the shy and soulful **Manos** (1993); the Kicking Giants with **Halo** (1993); Sam Jayne's Lync, pioneers of "emo" with **These Are Not Fall Colors** (1994).

One pioneer of the style was actually a veteran. Sebadoh (1) was born as the home project of Dinosaur Jr's bassist Lou Barlow, who enjoyed sketching very brief songs (sort of nursery rhymes) in a variety of minimal settings. The early material was collected on **The Freed Man** (1989), but a group sound did not emerge until Jason Loewenstein on guitar and Eric Gaffney on drums helped him record **III** (1991), a much more focused document of youth's alienation. As the role of Barlow's partners increased (and pushed Sebadoh's sound towards the pop mainstream), Barlow regressed to his claustrophobic roots with his alter egos Sentridoh and Folk Implosion.

Some acts embodied the concept that humility was the secret to artistic success. For example, the naive pop of Florida's <u>Vulgar Boatmen</u> (1) on **You And Your Sister** (1989) was devoted to simple stories of everyday life.

However, the most influential lo-fi band of the 1990s was California's <u>Pavement</u> (2). **Slanted And Enchanted** (1992) was more attitude than art (and certainly more epigonic than original), but the chaotic, erratic and unassuming delivery was precisely the point, especially when combined with Stephen Malkmus' bizarre philosophy. **Crooked Rain Crooked Rain** (1993) was even catchy and marginally innocuous.

Malkmus helped David Berman's <u>Silver Jews</u> (1) in Virginia coin a "lo-fi" version of the Velvet Underground's boogie-trance, like a cross between Luna and Pavement, on **Starlite Walker** (1994).

Rock music was flooded by a new generation of independent bands armed with the most spartan of musical skills and influenced by loony independents of the past such as Syd Barrett, Jonathan Richman, Robyn Hitchcock and Daniel Johnston. Among the most interesting were: Los Angeles' <u>Refrigerator</u>, who penned **How You Continue Dreaming** (1995), an adult and romantic concept dedicated to their suburban community; New York's <u>Fly Ashtray</u>, best represented by the nonsensical ditties of **Tone Sensations Of The Wonder-Men** (1993); Matt Suggs' <u>Butterglory</u> in Kansas, with the hummable psychodramas of **Crumble** (1994);

Unfortunately, Pavement's idea was frequently misunderstood as meaning that a mediocre musician could produce an unlimited amount of music while at the same time disregarding any musical obligation. Independent musicians became more and more prolific, and often less and less interesting.

Primitivism, 1992-95

The more creative strand, the one that descended from Half Japanese and the Residents, was kept alive by groups that shunned linearity.

San Diego's <u>Trumans Water</u> (2) were the stereotypical "antimusical" act. **Of Thick Tum** (1992) sounded like a group of musicians who had no desire to play anything, and therefore each song was a bit of a torture. Their music was the opposite of "entertainment", as **Spasm Smash XXXOXOX Ox and Ass** (1993) proved: a carousel of spastic gestures. It was rock'n'roll filtered by the no wave and Royal Trux's **Twin Infinitives**.

Trumans Water's bassist Glen "Galaxy" Galloway dedicated his project, <u>Soul Junk</u>, to Christian themes, starting with **1950** (1993) and peaking with **1952** (1995).

Maryland's <u>Velocity Girl</u> (2) synthesized the new sounds of their time: Sonic Youth's noise-rock, Uncle Tupelo's alt-country and Pavement's lo-fi dynamics. The dissonant pop of **Copacetic** (1993) was a study in contrast: effervescent tempos, wildly off-key guitars, Sarah Shannon's seductive pop-soul register, naive melodies; **Simpatico** (1994) merely capitalized on the primitive style of strumming/jamming that they had invented to produce a postmodernist dissection of pop, soul and even jazz cliches.

Between Individualism and Populism

Bleak folk, 1990-94

In a sense, the 1990s "were" the decade of the singer songwriter, as more and more artists decided to go "solo" rather than look for a band. Both the technology (that allowed individuals to arrange their own compositions) and the loose networking of the post-punk generation (that favored more fluid partnerships) helped increase the number of musicians who recorded simply under their own name.

In general, singer-songwriters of the 1990s tended to be more subdued and humbler than in the 1980s and in the 1970s. Their masters were Joni Mitchell and Leonard Cohen, not Bob Dylan or Bruce Springsteen. One of the most influential styles of the 1990s was the moody and depressed one pioneered by Chris Isaak, Smog and American Music Club in San Francisco. It spread like a disease and almost became a stand-alone genre. Bleak dirges were strummed everywhere.

Georgia's <u>Vic Chesnutt</u> (2), confined to a wheelchair, shared with Smog the honor of having pioneered the style. **West Of Rome** (1992) and **Drunk** (1994) took southern gothic to a very personal and highly emotional level. Later his art became not only more pensive but also more austere via longer compositions and a penchant for sound that sometimes obscured the singing: **Silver Lake** (2003), with a full-fledged roots-rock band; **Ghetto Bells** (2005), with VanDyke Parks on accordion and Bill Frisell on guitar; **North Star Deserter** (2007), with a small orchestra of post-rock soundsculptors.

The Screaming Trees' <u>Mark Lanegan</u> (12) sculpted the agony of **Winding Sheet** (1990), a journey through the eternal damnation of a soul that was both lyrical, existential and lugubrious. Even more rarified and metaphysical, **Whiskey For The Holy Ghost** (1993) ventured deeper inside in a tender and doleful register, halfway between Leonard Cohen and Nick Cave, while the atmosphere was reminiscent of David Crosby's first solo album, and occasionally claustrophobic like in Tim Buckley's psychedelic nightmares. Lanegan's dilated mind seemed to be imploding on the fragile **Scraps At Midnight** (1998).

In Los Angeles, <u>Mountain Goats</u> (3), John Darnielle's project, was a bizarre experiment for voice, acoustic guitar and cheap organ whose major career was devoted to concept albums such as **Zopilote Machine** (1994), **Sweden** (1995), and **Tallahassee** (2003), mostly about disintegrating relationships, which were as lyrically ambitious as musically humble.

In Oregon, Heatmiser's singer and songwriter <u>Elliott Smith</u> (1) employed spare, acoustic arrangements and anemically whispered lyrics on **Roman Candle** (1994) to pen tuneful vignettes of daily life that merged Nick Drake's melancholia and Simon & Garfunkel's romanticism. Smith kept delving deeper into the human psyche with **Elliott Smith** (1995), that focused on heroin addiction, and **Either Or** (1997), but then resorted to Brian Wilson-ian arrangements of violins, reeds and keyboards for **Xo** (1998).

In New York, Jeff Buckley (1) was condemned to re-live his father Tim's turbulent and brief life, but **Grace** (1994) boasted a denser sound, more reminiscent of Van Morrison's soul-jazz ballads.

Toronto's Ron Sexsmith (1) crystallized the idea in the naive/tender style of Tim Hardin and Paul Simon on **Ron Sexsmith** (1995), while wedding it to Jackson Browne's arduous meditations.

Dinosaur Jr's bassist Mike Johnson (2), who had also collaborated on Mark Lanegan's masterpieces, became the most credible candidate to the title of "Leonard Cohen of the 1990s" with the funereal ballads of **Where Am I** (1994), **Year Of Mondays** (1996), which marked the zenith of his angst, and **What Would You Do** (2002), which marked an emotional nadir.

His main competition for that title was Nebraska's Simon Joyner (4), a philosopher equipped with Leonard Cohen's deep baritone and doleful vision, but also with a much grander musical ambition. After formative works entirely played by Joyner in a spartan folk style, such as **Room Temperature** (1993), he turned to atmospheric textures with **Heaven's Gate** (1995), arranged with a small chamber ensemble, and achieved his maturity with the long oneiric elegies of **Songs for the New Year** (1997). The trilogy recorded with Mike Krassner, beginning with **Yesterday Tomorrow and In Between** (1998) and continuing with the lengthy ballads of **The Lousy Dance** (1999) and **Hotel Lives** (2001), progressively increased the complexity of his compositions, capitalizing on an impressive cast of distinguished jazz, folk and rock musicians (Ken Vandermark on clarinet, Fred Lonberg-Holm on cello, Jeb Bishop on trombone, Ernst Long on flugelhorn, Will Hendricks on vibes), that augmented a rock trio (Ryan Hembrey on bass, Glenn Kotche on percussions, Michael Krassner on guitar). It was a wedding of chamber and pop settings that transported the slow, hypnotic music to a metaphysical dimension, while retaining a deeply-moving, humane dimension.

Suicidal dirges and stark odes to loneliness were the soundtrack of the 1990s. Notable albums in the style included: Matt Keating's **Scaryarea** (1994), from New York; Dave Schramm's **Folk Und Die Folgen** (1994), from New York; Karl Hendricks' **Misery And Women** (1994), from Pennsylvania.

Neo-pop, 1989-94

However there was a powerful countercurrent. The century-old tradition of the pop songwriter, that had peaked in the period between the

"Brill Building" and "Motown", was restored to its original glory by a new generation of shameless tunesmiths.

The scene was dominated by Boston's Stephen Merritt (14). His multi-faceted career began under the moniker Magnetic Fields as a humble amateur of pop music who vented his fear and nostalgia via formally impeccable melodies and arrangements. The formative **Distant Plastic Trees** (1991) and **The Wayward Bus** (1992), sung by Susan Anway, and his first masterpiece, **Holiday** (1993), which was also the first album sung by Merritt himself, coined a form of "introverted kitsch" that quoted the Sixties without sounding derivative and that employed electronic rhythm and instruments in a discreet manner. Despite being light like feathers, Merritt's ditties sounded like tributes to Brian Eno's early albums and to the classics of synth-pop. The concept album **The Charm Of The Highway Strip** (1994), his second masterpiece, perfected the idea. Leaving behind his synth-pop roots, Merritt wed the idyllic register of a Donovan, neoclassical orchestrations and the persona of a bashful lunatic. The algebraic precision of his musical artifacts was only apparently a continuation of Brian Wilson's and Van Dyke Parks' program: Merritt shunned their symphonic opulence and favored the small, intimate format of the chamber ensemble. **Get Lost** (1995) was, first and foremost, an exercise in laying out chamber instruments; but it was also his bleakest statement, and thus redeemed the indulgence with deeply felt emotions. At the same time, Merritt's mission was very much a thorough reexamination of the pop tradition, from Burt Bacharach to Phil Spector, from Tin Pan Alley to doo-wop: his ultimate sin of vanity, the colossal **69 Love Songs** (1999), was a catalog of variations on cliches of pop music. Merritt had managed a synthesis of historical proportions but he carried it out with the humble attitude of an everyman who hardly knew anything about history. In the meantime, he had also released albums as the 6ths and the Future Bible Heroes. The 6ths albums, **Wasps' Nests** (1996) and **Hyacinths and Thistles** (2000), were collection of sugary ditties performed by impressive casts of guest vocalists. The importance of arrangement and production had eventually taken over the importance of lyrics and melodies, and thus wrecked the whole idea of innocent, sincere, heartbreaking music. Most tunes on later albums such as **I** (2004), credited to the Magnetic Fields, **The Tragic Treasury** (2006), credited to the Gothic Archies, and **Distortion** (2008), credited again to the Magnetic Fields, did not serve any purpose other than Merritt's post-modernist strategies, but a few songs revealed that he still had a soul, the soul that in the 1990s had conquered the indie-pop and pre-emocore generation.

In Britain, David Gray was a sophisticated bard in the tradition of Van Morrison who scoured a broad emotional and musical territory, from the passionate confessions of **A Century Ends** (1993) to the vibrant power-ballads of **Sell Sell Sell** (1996), from the fragile pop vignettes of **White**

Ladder (2000) to the bleak introspection of **A New Day At Midnight** (2002).

Disguised as <u>Divine Comedy</u>, Irish songwriter Neil Hannon rediscovered orchestral pop for the nostalgic operetta **Promenade** (1994) and then anchored **Casanova** (1996) to old-fashioned arias.

Several veterans of the alt-rock movement recorded albums in this "neo-pop" style.

Husker Du's <u>Bob Mould</u> (4) was unique in excelling both at dejected, personal statements and at catchy popular music. The cathartic self-flagellation of the mostly-acoustic **Workbook** (1989) led to the brutal and bitter introspection of the wildly electric **Black Sheets Of Rain** (1990), which evoked Neil Young's storming and martial nightmares. Both albums were trips into his fragile psyche, mythomaniac orgies that collapsed into the punk contradiction of a nirvana of eternal damnation. **Copper Blue** (1992), instead, credited to his new band Sugar, offered guitar-driven power-pop which was only slightly neurotic and alienated, and the solo **Bob Mould** (1996), on which he played every instrument, crowned his quest for a sound that was both the sound of his music and the sound of his psyche, and turned out to be his most melodic effort.

Violent Femmes' drummer <u>Victor DeLorenzo</u> (1) found an unlikely balance of country-rock, expressionist cabaret and noir soundtracks on **Peter Corey Sent Me** (1990).

<u>Frank Black</u> (1), the new alias of former Pixies' vocalist Charles "Black Francis" Thompson, now relocated to Los Angeles, indulged in his trademark "scream of consciousness" on his solo albums **Frank Black** (1993) and **Teenager Of The Year** (1994), still characterized by erratic structures and reckless melodies.

Scottish transplant <u>Chris Connelly</u> (1), who had played in Chicago's industrial combos Ministry and Pigface, reinvented himself as a pensive pop crooner on albums such as **Shipwreck** (1994) and **The Ultimate Seaside Companion** (1998), the latter credited to the Bells.

In Australia both the leaders of the Go-Betweens recorded solo albums, and at least <u>Grant McLennan</u>'s **Horsebreaker Star** (1995) lived up to their reputation.

Neo-folk: the men, 1990-94

Los Angeles happened to be the next stop in the evolution of the genre. <u>Beck</u> (2) Hansen turned eccentricity into stardom and changed the way singer-songwriters sounded and were perceived by the mainstream. With the carefree eclecticism of **Mellow Gold** (1994) Beck invented folk music for the age of hip-hop and proved that stylistic confusion can appeal to the masses. A more organic approach to the fusion of folk, blues, rap, garage-rock and pop enhanced the overall sound of **Odelay** (1996). The fact that his lyrics were free-form associations, and only vaguely hinting to social reality, was somehow consistent with his superficial approach to musical integration (an operation that other musicians had carried out at a deeper level). **Mutations** (1998), reminiscent of Radiohead's subtle orchestrations, and **Midnite Vultures** (1999), a sort of tribute to soul music, rapidly removed the sheen from one of the decade's most over-rated artists.

Beck may have learned his tricks from an obscure and insane folksinger, Paleface, whose **Paleface** (1991) was a bizarre product of the anti-folk movement.

Far more original was the artistic mess concocted by former Red Hot Chili Peppers' guitarist John Frusciante (1) on **Niandra Lades And Usually Just A T-Shirt** (1994), a neurotic and hysterical version of Daniel Johnston halfway between agonizing blues and demented singalongs.

Neo-populists, 1989-93

The populists (a` la Bruce Springsteen, Tom Petty, John Mellencamp, etc) were mainly veterans of the punk generation.

A witty populist, sadly overlooked, delighted Canada: Blue Rodeo's keyboardist Bob Wiseman (1) penned the hilarious philosophizing of **In Her Dream** (1989) in an eclectic range of styles, and the desolate heartbreak of **Theme and Variations** (2006).

The greatest of this (not so wild) bunch was perhaps Freedy Johnston (3), a New York transplant who introduced himself as Neil Young gone cow-punk on the effervescent, edgy and eclectic **Trouble Tree** (1990), but then was rapidly converted to a smoother and streamlined sound. The bleak stories of betrayal, failure and guilt on **Can You Fly** (1992) and **This Perfect World** (1994), featuring guitarist Marc Ribot, cellist Jane Scarpantoni and drummer Butch Vig, relied on impeccable melodies, as if Simon & Garfunkel were playing funeral music. By the time **Never Home** (1997) came out, Johnston had transformed into a more superficial pop auteur.

The solo work of former Dream Syndicate's vocalist Steve Wynn (1) favored melancholy and introverted confessions at the intersection of Lou Reed, Bob Dylan and Neil Young. **Kerosene** (1990) was too obviously derivative, but **Melting In The Dark** (1996) let loose his passion for Sixties garage-rock, which overflowed on the propulsive, noisy and emphatic **My Midnight** (1999). Wynn's quest for a balance of youthful punk-rock and adult roots-rock, of a music capable of roaring, sweating and bleeding, culminated with **Here Come The Miracles** (2001), a survey of his emotional territory, a varied set of solemn, mournful, upbeat, tender, romantic, rough, demonic and harsh ballads and rave-ups.

Firehose's and Minutemen's bassist <u>Mike Watt</u> (1) entrusted the vignettes of **Ball-Hog Or Tugboat** (1994) to an extraordinary cast of vocalists.

The Replacements' <u>Paul Westerberg</u> remained a bard of ordinary anguish, but only **Suicaine Gratifaction** (1999) went close to fully realizing his vision.

Neo-blues, 1991-94

White blues singer-songwriters were obscured by the stars of lo-fi pop and neo-pop. Canada's <u>Sue Foley</u>, a Bonnie Raitt-soundalike, came to prominence with **Young Girl Blues** (1992) but matured as a songwriter with **Walk In The Sun** (1996). Texas' <u>Chris Whitley</u> used his spectacular guitar technique to vent teenage angst on **Living With The Law** (1991) the way punk's anti-heroes did. Los Angeles' <u>Ben Harper</u> (1), an eclectic African-American folksinger, debuted with **Welcome To The Cruel World** (1994), a monumental exercise in stylistic excursion.

The Second Coming of Industrial Music

Chicago's Industrial Music, 1989-92

Towards the end of the 1980s, Chicago became the epicenter of the new industrial genre (Ministry's, not Throbbing Gristle's), thanks to a plethora of bands. The most infernal atmosphere and beats were packed on **Disco Rigido** (1989), the debut album by Die Warzau (1).

Chicago also benefited by the work of former Killing Joke's drummer Martin Atkins, whose supergroup Pigface (1) interpreted industrial music as a producer's product, not unlike the producer of hip-hop: rhythm and noise form the foundation for a slew of guest vocalists such as Chris Connelly, Trent Reznor (Nine Inch Nails), Nivek Ogre (Skinny Puppy), Mary Byker (Gaye Bykers On Acid) and En Esch (KMFDM) to deliver shocking lyrics on albums such as **Fook** (1992).

From this fertile soil Trent Reznor's Nine Inch Nails (12) were born, and the fate of industrial music changed dramatically. Reznor created a persona that was a cross of Dostoevsky's "demons", Goethe's Werther, Nietzsche's "ueber-mensch", and De Sade's perverts. Technically, Reznor took elements from Throbbing Gristle, Pere Ubu, Foetus and Ministry and filtered them through the new computer technology. Reznor thus changed the very meaning of "rock band": the band was him, singer and arranger. Brutal music, nihilistic lyrics and claustrophobic atmospheres turned **Pretty Hate Machine** (1989) into the manifesto/diary of an entire generation. Few albums better summarize the spirit of the 1990s than **The Downward Spiral** (1994). Each song is both a battlefield for the highest possible density of truculent sound effects and a largely-autobiographical ode-psychodrama. The thundering polyrhythms, the chaotic and cacophonous orgies, the grotesque "danse macabres", the chamber blues pieces, the harsh counterpoints and the mournful melodies were carefully assembled to deliver the sense of a man without a past or a present or a future, a man who was a pure abstraction in search of meaning, pure form in search of content. Reznor's industrial music was never a well-defined genre: it was merely a label for heavily-arranged post-guitar rock music when sound-sculpting becomes mood-sculpting. Reznor retreated towards a simpler format, albeit using the same tools (psychotic screaming, killer synths, metallic percussions and brutal distortions), on the double album **Fragile** (1999). Reznor showed that he was not interested in angst for the sake of angst, and cared more for meditation on his own angst; that he was not indulging in insanity but merely puzzled by it.

Followers of Nine Inch Nails in Chicago included Filter, i.e. Richard Patrick and Brian Liesegang, who were most effective on **Short Bus** (1994) and Stabbing Westward, with **Ungod** (1994).

Electric Hellfire Club, on the other hand, indulged in the gothic-dance version of the genre with **Burn Baby Burn** (1993).

But even in Chicago the fad was dying out. A few years later the cyberpunks were already old-fashioned, and "industrial music" was mutating into something far less consumable. Illusion Of Safety, the project of Dan Burke and Jim O'Rourke, specialized in macabre anguish on albums such as **Cancer** (1992).

Post-industrial music, 1989-92

New York's Cop Shoot Cop (12) carried out a devastating attack against the conventions of popular music with **Consumer Revolt** (1990). Their songs were terrifying kammerspielen of the post-industrial age: noisy, percussive and unstable bacchanals. Ominous bass lines wove fear against a wall of guitar distortions and lugubrious organ drones. Melodies were torn apart by sudden bursts of noir-tinged big-band swing a` la Foetus, by demented collages of sound effects, by piercing guitars and obsessed drumming. Proving that their fury was not only an incontrollable urge, **White Noise** (1991) was an encyclopedic work, whose songs quoted the most disparate traditions without belonging to any of them. The band learned to play on **Ask Questions Later** (1993), and thus revealed their "blues" soul, despite drowning it into a catastrophic landscape of fractured rhythms, grotesque noise and desolate vocals.

Texas' Angkor Wat (11), led by guitarists Adam Grossman and Danny Lohner, coined the futuristic grindcore of **When Obscenity Becomes The Norm** (1989) that was both epic, hysterical and apocalyptic, while **Corpus Christi** (1990) was a more psychological work of morbid atmospheres.

Steel Pole Bath Tub (2) in San Francisco adopted an abrasive and psychological sound/stance that basically fused psychedelic trance, anthemic punk-rock and heavy-metal bloodshed on **Butterfly Love** (1989) and the EP **Lurch** (1990). An even darker mood envelops their most mature album, **Tulip** (1990), the definitive document of their depressed hyper-realism.

Their tape-oriented side-project Milk Cult (2) made ample use of samples, loops, rhythm boxes, filtered vocals and electronic sounds, but, unlike SPBT, the results are humorous, not tragic. Dada and Salvador Dali would be proud of the sketches on **Burn Or Bury** (1994) and **Project M-13** (2000), that deconstruct and satirize genres while offering a different take on reality. Humor and avantgarde coexist and complement each other.

Boston's Think Tree's **Like The Idea** (1992) mixed folk, cacophony, free jazz, dance beats, orchestral sounds and electronic techniques.

The most original group was <u>Girls Vs Boys</u> (11), formed in Washington by Soulside's guitarist Scott McCloud, drummer Alexis Fleisig and bassist Johnny Temple, plus Edsel's keyboardist Eli Janney (Silas Greene). Their hardcore roots were erased by Janney's bleak, noir and jazzy soundscapes on **Tropic Of Scorpio** (1992), a work that explored the morbid, expressionist backdrop of industrial music rather than its brutal undertones. Janney doubled on bass for the more cohesive **Venus Luxure No.1 Baby** (1993), which alternated between calm, atmospheric meditations and devastating bursts of power, the former radiating infernal spleen and the latter charging with atonal guitar and dissonant keyboards on top of spasmodic rhythms (hammering bass lines and catastrophic drumming). Nick Drake' mortal anemia met Big Black's harsh, abrasive psychodramas. **Cruise Yourself** (1994) and **House Of GVSB** (1996) focused on the ugliness of that sound, leveraging denser kaleidoscopes of sound effects. McCloud later pursued his sonic research with a new project, <u>New Wet Kojak</u> (2), whose **New Wet Kojak** (1995) and **Nasty International** (1997) were dark, textural studies that mixed electronics and jazz to create eerie atmospheres reminiscent of Robert Wyatt and Morphine.

Aggro and beyond, 1990-94

Born as one of the sub-genres of the new wave, industrial music had explored a wide and wild spectrum of styles, from dance music to white noise.

Throughout the 1990s, the brutal style of Nine Inch Nails (NIN) was pervasive in the USA. Industrial music became a mass phenomenon with NIN's visceral punk ethos applied to mechanical rhythms and arrangements. At the same time, the influence of KMFDM's "aggro" style was less obvious but no less ubiquitous, with most bands trying different variations on the idea of fusing heavy-metal guitars and machines. Finally, Ministry's epileptic style was the equivalent of a cultural totem.

Texas' <u>Skrew</u> (2), formed by Angkor Wat's frontman Adam Grossman, propelled the hysterical frenzy of **Burning In Water Drowning In Flame** (1992) with keyboards, samplers and drum-machines, while the Ministry-like synthesis of torrential dance beats and sinister grunge riffs achieved a claustrophobic sense of grandeur on **Dusted** (1994), an album that sounded like a diary of madness via the many voices of the leader (rap, gospel, opera, etc).

New York's <u>Sister Machine Gun</u> (1), the project of keyboardist Chris Randall, offered a more melodic version of KMFDM on **Torture Technique** (1994).

San Francisco's Grotus showed new ways of fusing industrial music and rock music by utilizing a battery of synthesizers, samples, turntables and real drums on **Slow Motion Apocalypse** (1993).

New York's Chemlab, with **Burn Out At The Hydrogen Bar** (1993), Los Angeles' Ethyl Meatplow , with **Happy Days Sweetheart** (1993), San Francisco's Hate Dept, with **Meat Your Maker** (1994), Los Angeles' Drown, with **Hold On To The Hollow** (1994), were among the pioneers of a genre that was rapidly replacing hardcore as the vehicle of choice for venting existential angst.

San Francisco's Xorcist (Peter Stone) was the most successful of the gothic dance acts, best heard on **Damned Souls** (1992).

Texas' Mentallo & The Fixer (2) fused synth-pop, EBM and dissonant electronics for the infernal visions of **Revelations 23** (1993) and **Where Angels Fear To Tread** (1994), a case of unstable retro-chic.

Britain's Cubanate (1) blended anthemic guitar riffs, devilish electronic pulses and sub-human screams like noone else on **Cyberia** (1994).

In Europe, aggro progressed thanks to works such as **Excluded** (1990) by Denmark's Klute (Claus Larsen of Leaether Strip), and **Transmission Pervous** (1995) by Germany's Steril.

EBM or "electro" (Cabaret Voltaire, Front Line Assembly, Skinny Puppy, Front 242) became more abrasive, brutal and visceral with **Brainstorming** (1992) by Germany's Yelworc (Domink van Reich), **Solitary Confinement** (1992) by Denmark's Leaether Strip (Claus Larsen), **Stored Images** (1995) by Belgium's Suicide Commando (i.e., Johan Van Roy), **Bunkertor 7** (1995) by Germany's :Wumpscut: (Rudy Ratzinger).

Industrial nightmares, 1990-96

Several "industrial" musicians were turning to the original concept of Throbbing Gristle: pure noise.

Namanax, the project of Philadelphia-based multi-instrumentalist Bill Yurkiewicz, produced loud noise through the layering of multiple sources of sound on **Multi-Phase Electrodynamics** (1993).

The percussive pandemonium of San Diego's Crash Worship (1) was quite unique and hardly documented on **Triplemania II** (1995). Their live raves in warehouses were based on ritualistic non-stop drumming.

Seattle's Tchkung, too, staged tribal shows that offered vivid views of industrial decay, accompanied by political rants on **Tchkung** (1995).

Germany's Genocide Organ, the brainchild of Wilhelm Herich, used power electronics to terrifying effect on **Leichenlinie** (1989). An affiliate project also devoted to electronic industrial horror, Anenzephalia (German electronic musician Michael Rief) progressed from the naive **Fragments Of Demise** (1993) to the imposing eight-movement symphony of **Noehaem** (2003).

Britain added relatively few new names to the ranks. Perhaps the only significant addition to the canon came from Towering Inferno (1), who summarized twenty years of experiments with the terrifying multimedia opera **Kaddish** (1994).

Omit, the project of New Zealand's isolated electronic musician Clinton Williams, refined a hybrid of Throbbing Gristle's early industrial music and Klaus Schulze's cosmic music on bleak works such as **Interior Desolation** (1999), recorded in 1996.

Digital hardcore, 1992-94

Several bands had been toying with a fusion of techno and rock. For example, Los Angeles' Babyland played techno with the fury of punk-rock on **You Suck Crap** (1992).

A far stronger synthesis was achieved in Germany by Atari Teenage Riot (10), the project of Berlin's programmer and anarchist Alec Empire (Alexander Wilke) and two vocalists (Carl Crack and Hanin Elias). The "digital hardcore" (supersonic beats, heavy-metal riffs, agit-prop lyrics and videogame-ish sound effects) of **Delete Yourself** (1995) straddled the line between punk-rock and techno. On his own, Alec Empire (2), the angry young man of techno, toyed with all sorts of styles, notably: the all-electronic **Les Etoiles Des Filles Mortes** (1996), which displayed the influence of avantgarde composer Karlheinz Stockhausen and had gothic overtones; the glacial ambient noise of **Low On Ice** (1995); the cubistic, psychedelic downtempo music of **Hypermodern Jazz 2000.5** (1996); the "drill and bass" of **The Destroyer** (1996); and the nightmarish free-jazz electronica of **The Curse of the Golden Vampire** (1998), a collaboration with Techno Animal's mastermind Kevin Martin.

"Gabber" was a subgenre of hardcore electronic dance-music that evolved in the Netherlands by fusing elements of industrial, techno and punk, and therefore strictly related to digital hardcore. It was characterized by frenzied pace, overdriven bass drums, distorted synthesizers and brutal vocals; and indulged in the kind of violent themes usually associated with the punk-rock or black-metal scenes. The single that pioneered it was *We Have Arrived* (1990) by Mescalinum United (German producer Marc Trauner).

Japanese cacophony, 1993-94

Space Streakings (11) were the greatest disciples of the great tradition of Zeni Geva and Boredoms. **Hatsu-Koi** (1993) concocted an ebullient amalgam of jazz, noise, electronica, hip-hop and hardcore that sounded like a music-hall sketch performed on doomsday. And the end of the world came with **7-Toku** (1994), the soundtrack of absolute chaos, of Babel-like confusion, of decades frantically played back in the last few seconds of civilization. Its cacophonic fantasies were the last rational beings in an ecosystem of grotesque mutations.

<u>Ground Zero</u>, the brainchild of guitarist and turntablist Otomo Yoshihide, transposed Zeni Geva's noise-core to the age of sampling. **Null And Void** (1993) was typical of their improvised symphonies for noise and samples, while **Revolutionary Pekinese Opera** (1995) was virtually a post-modernist essay, a piece of music constructed out of samples of an opera and of snippets of television commercials and soundtracks.

A few bands specialized in fast-paced noise-core that mixed the speed of hardcore and the cacophony of industrial music. Representative albums of this brutal, possessed, loud and frenzied style included: **Scratch Or Stitch** (1995) by <u>Melt-Banana</u> (1), **God Is God** (1995) by <u>Ultra Bide</u> (1), and **Missile Me** (1996) by <u>Guitar Wolf</u>.

Slo-core

Slo-core, 1991-94

One of the most important innovations of the 1990s in the canon of psychedelic folk-rock was "slo-core". Variously defined depending on local flavors, it basically referred to a slow, dreamy, melancholy version of dream-pop. It was a direct descendant of Galaxie 500 and Yo La Tengo that typically manifested itself via lengthy and subdued compositions.

Slo-core was sanctified in Chicago by <u>Codeine</u> (11) with **Frigid Stars** (1991). John Engle's guitar distortion was so dilated it sounded like an organ, Chris Brokaw's drumming evoked bells tolling for a funeral, and Stephen Immerwahr's sleepwalking litanies evoked Nick Drake and Tim Buckley. That emotional "black hole" attained nirvana with **White Birch** (1994), featuring new drummer Doug Scharin, thanks to longer songs, deeper trance and slower tempos, as if they were aiming for a song with no title in which the group does not play and does not sing.

North Carolina's <u>Seam</u> (12), the project of former Bitch Magnet's vocalist Sooyoung Park, fashioned the floating timbres and shimmering textures of **Headsparks** (1991) but, more importantly, the unstable filigree of **The Problem With Me** (1993), a sedate but also forceful work that seemed to merge tender folk-pop and neurotic hardcore, and felt like the slow-motion replay of a volcano's eruption. **Are You Driving Me Crazy?** (1995) was both an even more personal show of the leader and a less abstract, almost "poppier" affair, which led to the atmospheric melodies of **The Pace Is Glacial** (1998).

San Francisco's <u>Red House Painters</u> (111), an acoustic quartet led by introverted poet Mark Kozelek, penned the depressed mantras of **Down Colorful Hill** (1992): shy guitars that played chords as if they were reciting rosaries, and moribund dirges that seemed to end before beginning but then lasted for eternity, creating quietly unnerving atmospheres that blurred the border between sorrow and ecstasy. Like with the music of Leonard Cohen, Tim Buckley and Nick Drake, the effect was both subdued and majestic, a contradiction that became the quintessence of their art. The demo-quality of those recordings contributed to the sense of philosophical melancholy, but **Red House Painters** (1993), also known as **Rollercoaster**, revealed a much lighter and brighter mood: rather than whining, Kozelek was contemplating the universe. Each song was a moment in time, an impressionistic watercolor. **Ocean Beach** (1995) brought even more life to the compositions, dispensing with the most austere elements of their slow acoustic chamber folk. Mark Kozelek's next project, <u>Sun Kil Moon</u>, interpreted Kozelek's existential spleen in the 14-minute cryptic tour de force *Duk Koo Kim*, off **Ghosts Of The Great Highway** (2003), and especially in the sprawling streams of consciousness of **April** (2008).

Minneapolis' trio <u>Low</u> (15) also resurrected the depressed and anemic mood of Nick Drake, but then wed it to LaMonte Young's droning minimalism and to the Cowboy Junkies' lounge melodies. **I Could Live In Hope** (1994) was the quintessential case of "the whole is more than the sum of its parts": the parts were trivial and scant, but the whole was a triumph of unbridled creativity. Ascetic more than mournful, it sounded like the rock equivalent of Japanese haiku and Tibetan tangka, an art of frigid ballads that drowned in a lattice of empty notes. Low's "song" was chamber music for emotions that slowly faded away, that were never truly felt. At the same time, the unbearable delay and dilation of musical structures fostered and maintained an intensity of feeling that an ordinary refrain would have released in a few seconds. The tranquil jams of **Long Division** (1995) were as musical as circles spreading in a pond, but were given a soul by the whispered thoughts of guitarist Alan Sparhawk and drummer Mimi Parker. **The Curtain Hits The Cast** (1996) turned to electronic keyboards in order to relieve the gloom and lighten up the ambience, and **Secret Name** (1999) expanded the instrumentation by adding a string section, piano and timpani. Low regressed to a more conventional format for **Things We Lost In The Fire** (2001) and attained formal perfection with **Trust** (2002), a masterpiece of subtle metamorphoses, glacial counterpoint and ghostly religious music.

<u>Brick Layer Cake</u>, the project of veteran Minneapolis drummer Todd Trainer, bridged slo-core and post-rock on **Tragedy-Tragedy** (1994).

Texas' <u>Bedhead</u> (2), led by Matt Kadane, explored a state of mind between psychedelic trance and teenage angst on **What Fun Life Was** (1994) and **Beheaded** (1996). Their ameobic pieces "grew" rather than simply existed: they were the object of a gradual, evolutionary (and potentially never-ending) process that slowly brought the emotions into focus.

Ethereal pop, 1990-93

A variant on "male" slo-core was a style of fragile folk-pop ballads for female whispers and understated arrangements, more or less inspired by the Cowboy Junkies.

The concept was pioneered by a group that originated from the psychedelic movement, <u>Mazzy Star</u> (2). Guitarist David Roback of Rain Parade and Opal replaced Kendra Smith with a more delicate vocalist, Hope Sandoval, and greatly expanded the scope of his music on **She Hangs Brightly** (1990), a melting pot of acoustic folk, Delta blues, oneiric acid-rock and laconic lounge jazz. **So Tonight That I Might See** (1993) barely increased the melodic element of their tender lullabies, which reached alternatively for the galactic, subliminal, mystical and impressionistic levels.

Somewhat related to this atmospheric and psychological school were the electronic vignettes of His Name Is Alive (3), the brainchild of Michigan's multi-instrumentalist Warren Defever who employed different female singers for each album. Rhythm was optional on **Livonia** (1990), an experimental work that indulged in tape loops and samples but mostly relied on an elegant combination of ghostly neoclassical vocals and surreal electronic effects. Guitars were given more prominence on **Mouth By Mouth** (1993), and the group sound was more earthly, bridging Laurie Anderson's musical theater and dream-pop. The sophisticated, almost ambient **Stars On E.S.P.** (1996), was reminiscent of Brian Wilson's productions but in a skewed, unorthodox way. Defever's arrangements did not shun the obvious: they recreated the obvious in another dimension.

Illinois' Moon Seven Times (1), featuring Lynn Canfield, specialized in ethereal madrigals that boasted the spiritual depth of a raga on **Moon Seven Times** (1993).

Congo Norvell, led by former Gun Club's guitarist Kid Congo Powers and vocalist Sally Norvell, gave one of the best imitations of the Cowboy Junkies with their **Lullabies** (1993).

The atmospheric ballad, 1990-94

Whether it was slo-core or simply "slow pop", whether the influence of alt-country or a by-product of psychedelia, the slow, atmospheric ballad became fashionable again in indie music.

Los Angeles' Idaho (2), i.e. singer Jeff Martin and guitarist John Berry, were both the most existential and the most psychedelic. **Year After Year** (1993) was a set of suicidal psalms imbued with documentary lyrics and recited in a pensive tone halfway between Leonard Cohen and Lou Reed. Martin's indolent pessimism reached new heights of sweetness on **This Way Out** (1994).

Acetone (1) continued the tradition of (in reverse chronological order) Dream Syndicate, Television, Neil Young and Grateful Dead with collections of transcendental pseudo-country ballads such as **Cindy** (1993).

Pennsylvania's acoustic quintet Low Road (1) wed the aesthetic of slo-core to country music on **The Devil's Pocket** (1994).

Los Angeles' Love Spirals Downwards concocted a gothic/exotic/medieval/spiritual variant of the dream-pop cliches made popular by the Cocteau Twins and Dead Can Dance, for example on **Ardor** (1994).

Seattle's progressive ballad, 1993-94

Seattle (and the Northwest in general) originated a close relative of "slo-core", a form of "textural rock" that hanged somewhere between the extremes of roots-rock and post-rock, and emphasized non-linear guitar-based soundscapes. Built To Spill (13) were the reigning champions of the genre throughout the decade. Formed in Idaho by guitarist Doug Martsch, with Caustic Resin's guitarist Brett Netson and Lync's rhythm section, **Ultimate Alternative Wavers** (1993) was mostly a guitar tour de force, but already displayed their slovenly, messy and noisy fusion of Neil Young, Grateful Dead and Sonic Youth. **There's Nothing Wrong With Love** (1994), instead, focused on structure, constraining Martsch's imagination. **Perfect From Now On** (1997) summed the two, granting the guitar several degrees of freedom while anchoring it to a spectacular group sound (the Spinanes' drummer Scott Plouf, Nelson's bass, cello, mellotron and synthesizer). These articulate and elegant compositions relied both on lengthy hypnotic jamming and on simple, manageable form. Martsch's relentless guitar ruminations created the noise-rock equivalent of John Fahey's "primitive guitar": introspection, meditation on the meaning of life, contemplation of the universe, and worship of the absolute. **Keep It Like A Secret** (1998) simply channeled that creative force in the format of the rock song. When Built To Spill finally returned to the science of abstract jamming, on **You In Reverse** (2006), its blend of pensive transcendence and manic depression sounded like the perfect soundtrack for the zeitgeist of the new century. Martsch's guitar had a unique way to penetrate the inner core of a song's melody, and transform it into a cathartic experience. Marstch's tormented solos were the antidote to an era that increasingly strived for simplicity and superficiality.

Silkworm (2) boasted the depressed noise of guitarists Joel Phelps and Andy Cohen. Cohen's introverted mood and neurotic guitar dominated **In The West** (1993) and **Libertine** (1994). Pared down to a trio after Phelps' departure, **Firewater** (1996) veered towards the distorted, metaphysical folk-rock of Dream Syndicate and Neil Young, while highlighting the creative rhythms of drummer Michael Dahlquist and bassist Tim Midgett. **Developer** (1997) was another subtle essay of musical imagery, and perhaps even more arduous.

Dance-music in the Age of House

Madchester, 1989-90

The 1980s were almost over when a movement came out of Manchester that came to symbolize the hedonistic spirit of the era: "Madchester", a fusion of psychedelia, techno and pop. It was 1988 when anthems such as KLF's *What Time Is Love* imported acid house from the USA. The decade that had begun as the age of depressed cyberpunks was ending as the age of the wildest parties ever.

Manchester's 1988 "summer of love" became a musical movement with the debut of Stone Roses (2), one of the most influential English bands of the decade. **Stone Roses** (1989) epitomized the fusion of hypnotic disco beats, catchy melodies, surreal arrangements, and Sixties-style naive enthusiasm. Mixing Byrds with Abba, and Hendrix with Petula Clark, and James Brown and the Mamas & Papas, songs such as *I Wanna Be Adored*, *She Bangs The Drums* and *Made Of Stone* bridged different languages and civilizations while setting the foundations of a new language and a new civilization. Credit went not so much to vocalist Ian Brown and guitarist John Squire, but to the rhythm section of Alan John "Reni" Wren (drums) and Gary Mounfield (bass). Squire's guitar was more predominant on **Second Coming** (1994), a work heavily infected by hard-rock and southern boogie.

Shaun Ryder's Happy Mondays (1), who had already debuted with the psychedelic funk music of **Squirrel And G-Man Twentyfour Hour Party People** (1987), co-founded the movement with **Bummed** (1989), which embodied the ecstatic trance of raves but also a proletarian approach to it. Ryder, a sarcastic, nonchalant (and heroin-addicted) "primadonna" of techno, focused on the grooves with the disco-fied **Pills'N'Thrills And Bellyaches** (1990). Years later, he upgraded Madchester to the generation of Beastie Boys and Red Hot Chili Peppers with a new band, Black Grape (1), basically a rapper fronting a horn and keyboard orchestra, and with the multifaceted dance music (funk, hip-hop, jungle, raga, house, reggae and heavy-metal) of **It's Great When You're Straight** (1995)

Tim Burgess' Charlatans (UK) (1) were emblematic of how "Madchester" soon became more of a social phenomenon than a musical one. **Some Friendly** (1990) merely offered old-fashioned organ-based psychedelic pop-soul.

The idea was infectious and spread from rave to rave throughout the Kingdom. Psychedelic dance albums of the era (often characterized by an orgiastic frenzy) include: Renegade Soundwave (1)'s **In Dub** (1990), and the Shamen's **Boss Drum** (1992); whereas Pop Will Eat Itself's **This Is The Day** (1989) and Jesus Jones' **Liquidizer** (1989) imported into the rave scene the fusion of dance beats and rock guitars already pioneered in hip-hop by the likes of Run DMC.

Throughout the decade there were countless remnants of the rave season, in the form of exuberant pop-dance singles and albums: EMF's **Schubert Dip** (1991), that boasted an infectious mixture of bubblegum, psychedelia and rap; Utah Saints's **Utah Saints** (1993), that basically replaced the idea of the "cover song" with the idea of a song made of samples of other songs; Carter The Unstoppable Sex Machine's **The Love Album** (1992), that offered cartoonish glam-rock and synth-pop embellished with punk rage and scathing satire.

Body Music, 1991-95

It took a decade for techno and house to become the dominant dance styles, but, when they did, they spread like wildfire around the globe. The masses reacted enthusiastically, as they had in the 1960s to the hippy phenomenon. Over the years, the difference between techno and house blurred, and most ravers would not know which one was which (techno was mostly instrumental and descended from Kraftwerk, whereas house was mostly vocal and descended from soul, funk and disco music).

Belgium was one of the epicenters of the fad, perhaps fueled by the school of "electronic body music" (Front 242). **Lust** (1991), by the Lords Of Acid (1), offered wildly throbbing as well as openly erotic dance-music with a female vocalist. From Belgium, the new dance-craze spread to Holland and France. Soon, all the European countries overflowed with techno acts.

France's Laurent Garnier, with **Shot In The Dark** (1995), and Japan's Ken Ishii, with **Jelly Tones** (1995), were quintessential techno musicians of the era.

Sweden's Ace Of Base specialized in Abba-like melodies sung to the techno beat, such as *All That She Wants* (1992) and *Beautiful Life* (1995).

Norway's Apoptygma Berzerk (Stephan Groth) explored gothic techno on **Soli Deo Gloria** (1994).

Other international hits of the mid-1990s included: Corona's *Rhythm Of The Night* (1993), from Italy; Real McCoy's *Runaway* (1994), from Germany; 2 Unlimited's *Get Ready For This* (1994), from Holland; veteran USA r&b vocalist Judy Cheeks' *Reach* (1996); Playahitty's *Summer Is Magic* (1996), from Italy; No Mercy's *Where Do You Go* (1996), from Miami; although the biggest sensation worldwide was a much simpler production, Los Del Mar's flamenco-infected *Macarena* (1993).

Australia's most creative techno musician was perhaps David Thrussell, who evolved from the naive techno sound of Snog's **Lies Inc** (1992) to the almost avantgarde industrial-ambient-ethnic fusion of Black Lung's **Silent Weapons For Quiet Wars** (1994) to the

sophisticated techno sculptures of **Hollow Earth** (1994), credited to
Soma (1), a duo with Pieter Bourke.

German body Music, 1991-95

Germany, where the Berlin wall had just fallen, boasted the most
varied and fertile scene. An impressive number of sub-genres were
created within just a few years.

Disc-jockey Sven Vath (1) virtually invented Frankfurt's "progressive-
house" (or, simply, "trance") with the ambient **Accident In Paradise**
(1993).

Palais Schaumburg's keyboardist Thomas Fehlmann, became a
respected Berlin-based producer, formed 3MB with Moritz von Oswald
and Detroit's titan Juan Atkins, and then joined his pupil's "micro" scene
with works such as **Visions Of Blah** (2002). Maurizio (Palais
Schaumburg's percussionist Moritz Von Oswald) coined in Berlin a dub-
inflected style of techno, a progenitor of "micro-techno", with the many
singles under different monikers: Cyrus' 18-minute *Inversion* (1994),
Quadrant's 20-minute *Dub* (1994), Maurizio's *M-4* (1994), etc. From
those foundations Basic Channel (as producers Moritz Von Oswald and
Mark Ernestus renamed themselves) created one of the most influential
scenes.

Air Liquide (10), i.e. Ingmar "Dr Walker" Koch and Cem "Jammin`
Unit" Oral, spearheaded Cologne's psychedelic techno with the ambitious
The Increased Difficulty Of Concentration (1995), at the border
between collage and stream of consciousness, an album that included the
colossal *Robot Wars Symphony*, replete with movements that harked
back to (alternatively) Klaus Schulze, Tangerine Dream and Brian Eno.

La Bouche, formed in Frankfurt by two African-American vocalists,
became the most successful act of melodic techno after they concocted
the Euro-techno hits *Sweet Dreams* (1994) and *Be My Lover* (1995);
while L@n (1), the Duesseldorf-based duo of Rupert Huber and Otto
Mueller, belonged to the avantgarde with the Neu-influenced robotic
madly-psychedelic techno of **L@n** (1996).

X Marks The Pedwalk continued the tradition of the industrial dance of
the 1980s.

Ian Pooley (Ian Pinnekamp) was one of the prime innovators of "hard"
house, as documented on the compilation **The Times** (1996).

USA body Music, 1991-95

The USA, the homeland of techno, on the other hand, was mostly
derivative of the European styles. The jovial romps of New York's Deee-
Lite and Los Angeles' Crystal Method were old-fashioned party music
adapted to the new instruments.

Detroit's second (third?) generation was best represented by the work of <u>Jeff Mills</u>, founder of the "Underground Resistance" collective, particularly his experiments on stripped-down techno beat begun with *Waveform Transmission Vol 1* (1992) and culminating with the multi-part symphony **Time Machine** (2001). Another Detroit act, <u>Drexciya</u>, i.e. the duo of James Stinson and <u>Gerald Donald</u>, between 1991 and 1996 fused the electro sound of the 1980s with space-jazz and cosmic music. Stinson pursued that avenue until the transcendent soundscapes of **Harnessed the Storm** (2002), while Donald concocted cryptic revisions of techno stereotypes for the post-cyberpunk age on Dopplereffekt's **Linear Accelerator** (2003) and Der Zyklus' **Biometry** (2004). <u>Robert Hood</u> invented "minimal techno", originally motivated by the desire to return to the soul-inspired style of the forefathers of Detroit techno. His brutally stripped-down approach to dance music was first announced by **Internal Empire** (1994) and the single *Moveable Parts Chapter 1* (1995). <u>DJ Assault</u> (Craig Adams) publicized the "ghetto tech" style, influenced by hip-hop culture. <u>Felix Da Housecat</u> was a purveyor of old-fashioned Chicago house but his alter-ego <u>Thee Maddkatt Courtship</u> unfurled lengthy languid jams on **By Dawn's Early Light** (1994). <u>BT</u> (Los Angeles-based composer Brian Transeau) invented "epic house" (or "progressive house" or "trance") with the single *Embracing The Sunshine* (1995), and his album **IMA** (1996) pushed the boundaries towards out-of-space electronica (the 43-minute *Sasha's Voyage Of IMA*).

The exception was San Francisco, perhaps the only place where a truly national style emerged. **President's Breakfrast** (1990) by <u>President's Breakfast</u>, a San-Francisco based ensemble led by drummer and sampler technician Click Dark played an insane fusion of dub, funk, hip-hop and jazz. Starting with the EP **Magick Sounds of the Underground** (1992), <u>Hardkiss</u>, a trio of disc jockeys and producers, began bridging the hippie and the rave eras by specializing in eccentric psychedelic electronica via lush, hallucinatory and orgasmic jams of acid, cosmic, techno-dub.

Daum Bentley became part of that San Francisco movement, that also included Single Cell Orchestra, Young American Primitive, High Lonesome Sound System, etc. His own project, <u>Freaky Chakra</u> (1), adapted Chicago house, European body music and British techno to acid-rock. *Trancendental Funk Bump/ Halucifuge* (1993) and *Peace Fixation* (1994) upped the ante for the entire movement thanks mainly to their cornucopia of electronic effects. The trippy tracks of **Lowdown Motivator** (1995) spiraled out of control, soaring over a jungle of manically pulsing synths and sequencers.

Ambient House, 1989-94

An unusual form of dance-music became popular in England during the 1990s: "ambient house". The idea (originally from 808 State) was to offer music to "chill out", but soon the soundtracks for "chill-out rooms" created a genre of its own, at the border between techno and minimalism. It caused a major stylistic revolution.

An influential pioneer of ambient house was <u>William Orbit</u> (1), who proved to be an innovative electronic arranger (and world-class producer) with the electronic instrumentals of **Strange Cargo** (1988) and especially **Strange Cargo 3** (1993). At the same time he jumped on the bandwagon of acid-house with **Set The Controls For The Heart Of The Bass** (1990), credited to Bassomatic.

<u>808 State</u> (2), formed by the trio of producers Martin Price, Graham Massey and Gerald Simpson, but mostly dominated by Massey, were masters of the new electronic instruments and thus the ideal successors to Kraftwerk. Their techniques (which borrowed from Terry Riley's minimalism, Brian Eno's ambient music and Jon Hassell's "fourth-world" music) revolutionized house, techno and industrial music with tracks such as *Pacific State* (1989). The (mostly instrumental) electronic ballets of **808:90** (1989), one of the most elegant house albums of all times, and **Ex:el** (1991), were fluent in jazz-rock and world-music, bordering on progressive-rock.

The manifesto of "ambient house" was **Chill Out** (1990), by the wacky duo of Bill Drummond and Jimmy Cauty, <u>KLF</u> (1), who mixed field recordings, celestial organ drones, languid guitar tones, musical samples, and electronic sounds.

The idea was given artistic depth by pioneers such as <u>Irresistible Force</u> (2), the project of disc-jockey Mixmaster Morris (Morris Gould). **Flying High** (1992) was inspired by avantgarde composers such as Harry Partch and Karlheinz Stockhausen, and was reminiscent of Brian Eno, Steve Reich and Tangerine Dream, while revealing affinities with Terence McKenna's hallucinogenic metaphysics. **Global Chillage** (1994) showcased both the psychedelic factor and the (almost baroque) producer's skills, thus wedding the postmodernist aesthetics of assemblage and acid-rock (after all, his suites were merely a new take on the old form of the free-form jam).

<u>Orb</u> (11), formed by disc-jockey Alex Paterson (who had worked for Paul Oakenfold's "chill-out rooms") with assistance from former KLF's mastermind Jimmy Cauty, codified the revolution that was underway. The music of the EP **A Huge Ever Growing Pulsating Brain That Rules From The Centre Of The Ultraworld** (1989), a cosmic mantra for water and synthesizer, and of the album **Adventures Beyond The Ultraworld** (1991) sounded like new-age music. The lengthy tracks of **U.F. Orb** (1992) were born at the crossroad between Brian Eno's impressionistic landscapes, the postmodernist ideology of stylistic recycling, the new technologies of sampling and the techno beat. They did not have an emotional impact, and they did not unravel in a narrative way: they slowly morphed. *Blue Room* (a 40 minute-long single)

featured guitarist Steve Hillage and bassist Jah Wobble, and was Paterson's tour de force of montage and mixing. Paterson had transformed the disc-jockey into a classical composer and transferred collage art to electronic dance music. Rather than fully endorsing the "ambient" style that he had contributed to create, Orb continued to experiment with new forms of dance music: **Orbus Terrarum** (1995) and **Orblivion** (1997) rely on a subtle art of choreography to deliver an experience that is both unsettling and hypnotic.

Ultramarine (2), i.e. Paul Hammond and Ian Cooper, laid an unlikely bridge between Canterbury's prog-rock of the 1970s and ambient house. Their ethereal, pastoral vision began to form on **Every Man And Woman Is A Star** (1992), which was virtually a collection of chamber pieces for flutes, trumpets, pianos, string section, samples and electronic machines, and blossomed on **United Kingdoms** (1993), which added stronger dub and jazz ambience and Robert Wyatt's divine vocals.

Cabaret Voltaire's Richard Kirk (2) experimented with ambient techno, first as Sandoz on psychedelic albums such as **Digital Lifeforms** (1993), then as Electronic Eye and the jazz, funk and dub fusion of **Closed Circuit** (1994), and finally as himself on the monumental **Number Of Magic** (1993), a labyrinth of ideas.

Ambient house transformed into avantgarde music with Scanner (1), born Robin Rimbaud. His works achieved intense melodrama through either hypnotic layering of found sounds or subliminal repetition of soundbites and beats. His early recordings, such as **Mass Observation** (1994), focused on austere sound-collages of telephone conversations. Exposing the existential nudity of the wireless society, Rimbaud contented himself with providing a passive documentary of the city's aural cacophony. His most challenging soundscapes were on **Spore** (1995) and the **Lauwarm Instrumentals** (1999), a bold excursion from new-age meditational pieces to symphonic apotheoses.

Psychick Warriors Ov Gaia (1), the project of Dutch electronic musician Reinier Brekelmans, introduced exotic ambient house with **Ov Biospheres And Sacred Grooves** (1992).

Norway's multi-instrumentalist Geir Jenssen (ex-Bel Canto), who had pioneered ambient house with Bleep's **North Pole By Submarine** (1990), produced one of the most lyrical albums of ambient house, **Microgravity** (1991), credited to his new project, Biosphere (1). And that project evolved towards a rhythm-less "arctic sound", set in an icy wasteland of sonic bliss, notably with **Substrata** (1997).

By 1992 the masters had all debuted and were spawning countless imitations. Global Communication (1), i.e. Mark "Link" Pritchard and Aphex Twin co-founder Tom Middleton, penned the cosmic, minimalist and melancholy soundpaintings and subtle, bionic mutations of **76:14** (1994).

Jonah Sharp's <u>Spacetime Continuum</u> (1), who had collaborated with psychedelic philosopher Terence McKenna, electronic soundpainter Tetsu Inoue and ambient dub master Bill Laswell, joined the ambient fray with the polished production, the chromatic arrangements, the organic flow and the psychodramatic tension of **Sea Biscuit** (1994).

George Fleming-Saunders, disguised under the moniker <u>Solar Quest</u> (1), blended minimalist repetition and ambient stasis on **Orgship** (1994).

Toby Marks, better known as <u>Banco De Gaia</u> (1), was quick to jump on the bandwagon with the alternatively ambient and dance postcards of **Maya** (1994) and **Last Train To Lhasa** (1995).

Paul Frankland's <u>Woob</u> (1) delivered the exotic and impressionistic **1194** (1994), ambient house's musical equivalent of Gauguin's and Rousseau's paintings.

German musicians active in the ambient and atmospheric variant of techno/industrial music, with slower tempos and sophisticated arrangements included: <u>Project Pitchfork</u>, with the romantic and exoteric **Entities** (1992); <u>Bionaut</u> (Joerg Burger), with the tender, delicate minimalism of **Ethik** (1993); <u>Haujobb</u> (1)'s charming lounge-techno on **Solutions For A Small Planet** (1996).

<u>Drome</u>, i.e. German Keyboardist and vibraphonist Bernd "Burnt" Friedman, was one of the first to incorporate hip-hop breaks into chill-out grooves with his album **Final Corporate Colonization Of The Unconscious** (1993).

IDM, 1991-94

Numerous outfits experimented with the format of techno and house music, and with the sampling technology (the real protagonist of this generation's dance-music). The Intelligent Dance Music (IDM) mailing list was set up on the Internet in August 1993 to discuss the works of these artists, and the name stuck.

<u>Orbital</u> (12), i.e. Paul and Phil Hartnoll, crowned the season of raves. Their **Green Album** (1991) and **Brown Album** (1993) did to techno what Art Of Noise had done to hip-hop: they transformed it into a sophisticated art of complex compositions by intellectual "auteurs". The latter, in particular, was a parade of stylish gestures and poses, from sci-fi dissonances to dilated drones, from angelic voices to dadaistic collages, from staccato repetition a` la Michael Nyman to machine-like industrial cadences. **Snivilisation** (1994) and especially **In Sides** (1996) turned to narrative logic and emotional content, using the dance beats as mere background.

<u>Eat Static</u> (2), a side project of Ozric Tentacles' drummer Merv Pepler and keyboardist Joie Hinton, used techno beats to reach the same orbit as Gong's effervescent space-hippie prog-rock. The craft of **Implant** (1995) was both insane and imaginative, and was channelled into smoother

structures on **Epsylon** (1995), eventually leading to the sophisticated and elegant art of transglobal samples and stylistic cross-breeding of **Science Of The Gods** (1997).

London's disc-jockey Andy Weatherall was one of the men who revolutionized the scene with the <u>Sabres Of Paradise</u> (1), a project that evolved from the inventive techno music of **Sabresonic** (1993) to the loose, fractured and ghostly downtempo music of **Haunted Dancehall** (1994), a style that spilled over onto the evocative soundscapes of his next project, <u>Two Lone Swordsmen</u>'s **The Fifth Mission** (1995), that blended dub, breakbeats and noise.

<u>Future Sound of London</u> (1), i.e. electronic musicians Garry Cobain and Brian Dougans, incorporated natural sounds (often as a rhythmic element), Klaus Schulze's cosmic music and exotic voices into **Lifeforms** (1994). The harmonic puzzle of **Dead Cities** (1996) returned to frantic rhythms, and used the feverish stylistic changes as yet another rhythmic element.

<u>Black Dog Productions</u> experimented with jazz, minimalism, cosmic and ethnic music on **Spanners** (1994). <u>Plaid</u> (1), an emanation of Black Dog Productions, revolutionized with new rhythmic patterns on **Mbuki Mvuki** (1991), predating jungle.

The general impetus towards "intelligent" dance-music yielded the grotesque phenomenon of electronic musician <u>Richard James</u> (1). The three EPs credited to AFX, starting with **Analogue Bubblebath** (1991, 1992 and 1993) contained harsh, abrasive dance-music, sometimes sounding like a disco version of Morton Subotnick's electronic poems (and they remained his most valuable musical statements). In the meantime, the catchy singles credited to Aphex Twin, *Quoth* (1993) and *On* (1993), were fusing techno and pop, aiming for the charts, and Polygon Window's **Surfing On Sinewaves** (1992) was traditional, throbbing techno music, aiming for dancefloor appeal. To further confuse his persona, Aphex Twin's **Selected Ambient Works 1985-92** (1992) and **Selected Ambient Works Volume II** (1994) were experiments in ambient house and abstract electronic/concrete composition. They were childish and antiquated (and perhaps a joke on music critics), but they increased James' reputation, making him the first star of ambient house. **I Care Because You Do** (1995), his most cohesive work, cleaned up his act, offering atmospheric dance-music with occasional hints to his old virulent style.

Ontario-based disc-jockey Richie Hawtin, better known as <u>Plastikman</u> (2), refined techniques developed over the years from Kraftwerk to Cabaret Voltaire to achieve the minimal and psychedelic aesthetics of **Musik** (1994) and **Consumed** (1998).

<u>Perfume Tree</u>, a trio of Vancouver disc-jockeys, induced trance on **The Sun's Running Out** (1994) through a blend of dream-pop, hip-hop, dub and electronica.

In the USA, the most famous techno artist of the 1990s was Richard Melville Hall, aka Moby (1). His early anthems, *Go* (1991) and *Drop A Beat* (1992), were soon superseded by the ambient/new age/neoclassical/minimalist ambitions of **Ambient** (1993) and **Everything Is Wrong** (1993), a passion confirmed by Voodoo Child's **The End Of Everything** (1997), a collection of electronic vignettes a` la Brian Eno, and possibly his best work. Vapourspace (1), i.e. disc-jockey Mark Gage, produced the 35-minute single *Gravitational Arch of 10* (1993) and the **Themes From Vapourspace** (1994), that are reminiscent of avantgarde electronic music and reference Kraftwerk, Philip Glass and Klaus Schulze. But, again, the USA was only the periphery: Britain was the center for IDM.

Italian disc-jockey Robert Miles established a new trend in melodic dance music, shifting the emphasis from the beat and the drugs back to simple emotions with *Children* (1995).

Transglobal dance, 1991-94

Another powerful innovation to come out of England was the "transglobal dance" craze. By fusing world-music, electronic arrangements and dance beats, these ensembles coined the ultimate synthesis of the 1990s.

The idea was pioneered by the multiracial group Transglobal Underground (2), featuring Natacha Atlas' exotic melisma, Nick "Count Dubulah" Page's creative sampling, Alex Kasiek's surreal keyboards and Hamid Mantu's forest of percussions, on **Dream Of 100 Nations** (1993) and **International Times** (1994), that fused dance, ambient and ethnic styles. It was not a sterile exercise of Arabic-African-Indian fusion, but a stab at reinventing rhythm itself: their "world beat" was solidly rooted in ethnic traditions from around the world, but was no longer any of them. As they replaced samples with real instruments, they also achieved a warmer (and more authentically "ethnic") sound on **Psychic Karaoke** (1996).

Another multiracial ensemble, Loop Guru (2), overdubbed tape loops, field recordings, vocal samples, and exotic instruments in a way that emanated stronger ambient and jazz flavors. **Duniya** (1995), which included their tour de force, *The Third Chamber*, sounded like a blend of Orbital, Jon Hassell, Brian Eno and Weather Report, and the mellotron-heavy **Amrita** (1995) made the experiment more accessible.

Future Primitive (1994) was the manifesto of former Tangerine Dream member Paul Haslinger (12). Swinging from extreme violence to extreme calm, Haslinger unleashed demonic orgies of percussions, techno-funky tempos, heavy-metal riffs, chamber music interludes, industrial beats, screams, electronic distortions and pounding polyrhythms. That futuristic collage technique intensified on **World**

Without Rules (1996), which also boasts a stronger ethnic flavor and the sheer violence of a heavy-metal band, while remaining anchored to the format of dance-music. **Score** (1999) completed the trilogy in a more technical vein.

Michael Paradinas, better known as <u>Mu-ziq</u> (1), unleashed the polyrhythmic bacchanals of his third album **In Pine Effect** (1995), that worked more like a therapeutic shock than dance grooves, an idea refined on his most complex work, **Lunatic Harness** (1997), that ran the gamut from symphonic music to jazz, from lounge music to drum'n'bass.

The multiracial quartet <u>Cornershop</u> (1), led by Tjinder Singh, fused Indian, hip-hop and techno music on **Woman's Gotta Have It** (1995) and on the more commercial **When I Was Born For The 7th Time** (1997).

In the USA, the closest thing to "transglobal dance" was probably <u>Tulku</u>, the project conceived by Native American keyboardist Jim Wilson: **Transcendence** (1995) and **Season Of Souls** (1998), were experiments in ethnic trance music that drew inspiration from various indigenous styles of the world.

Big Beat, 1992-94

The last dance "cross-over" of the decade was to be the one between techno and rock music (or "big beat"). This happened almost by accident, as a number of British producers and djs reacted to the intellectual wing of dance-music by focusing on more accessible dance-music that relied on shameless, old-fashioned catchy breakbeats and silly, novelty-like samples. Because it did not depend so much on studio trickery, it could be performed live, thus meeting the demand of the rock audience. Because it could be performed live, it reasserted the importance of the "front-man", the distinctive trait of rock music.

The idea was pioneered in England by Liam Howlett's <u>Prodigy</u> (1) with the hyperkinetic numbers of **Experience** (1992), the versatile and cosmopolitan **Music For The Jilted Generation** (1995) and the super-synthesis of **The Fat Of The Land** (1997), which ran the gamut from ambient to heavy-metal (albeit in a very superficial manner). The Prodigy became the first superstars of the rave culture. Howlett was the brain behind the act, but Keith Flint (the singer) attracted the tabloids. It was techno for the rock market.

An even more obvious premonition was contained in the music of <u>Underworld</u> (2), the trio of disc-jockey Darren Emerson, vocalist/guitarist Karl Hyde and keyboardist Rick Smith. Rock guitars, electronic dance beats and spoken-word parts found a magic intersection in the lengthy tracks of **Dubnobasswithmyheadman** (1994), each a chameleon continuously changing in texture, melody and tempo without ever losing its identity. The album, a tour de force of dance production techniques, referenced the insistent sequencers of Giorgio Moroder's disco-music but was mainly a container of sound effects, polyrhythms and haunting melodic fragments. **Second Toughest In The Infants** (1996) reprised the combination of existential mood and fantasia-like melodic collage.

Musically speaking, the frenzy increased with the Chemical Brothers (2), i.e. "Madchester" veterans Tom Rowlands and Ed Simons, whose **Exit Planet Dust** (1995) and **Dig Your Own Hole** (1997) recycled overdoses of funk, heavy-metal and hip-hop, confusing the languages of Public Enemy, Kraftwerk and the Stooges.

The prophecy of "big beat" was fully realized later into the decade by Norman Cook, better known as Fatboy Slim (2). The "songs" on **Better Living Through Chemistry** (1996) and **You've Come a Long Way Baby** (1998) were wacky collages of styles set to dance beats and fragmented into jerky segments, a praxis that, despite the high-school prank mood, was reminiscent of the deconstruction/reconstruction techniques of postmodernist art.

The only rivals of the British big-beat masters were France's Daft Punk, whose **Homework** (1996) featured a retro fixation for Giorgio Moroder's disco-music while exploiting various styles of production (hip hop, ambient, funk, industrial and house).

Trip-hop, 1989-94

One of England's great inventions at the turn of the millennium was "trip-hop", the style that bridged downtempo breakbeats, psychedelic dub trance and soft-jazz atmosphere. Pioneered in the 1980s by dance collectives such as A R Kane and Coldcut, by sophisticated singers such as Sade and Neneh Cherry, and by pop bands such as Cowboy Junkies and Blue Nile, trip-hop was born in earnest in Bristol, England, the home base of the collectives that turned the world of dance music upside down. Soul II Soul, the project of disc-jockey Jazzie B (Beresford Romeo) and arranger Nellee Hooper, launched the genre in march 1989 with *Keep On Movin'*, a whispered, sensual scat over shadowy bass lines, softly hypnotic beats and orchestral counterpoint. Bristol created a clear demarcation between techno/house/jungle and atmospheric, ethereal dance music. Massive Attack (1), an emanation of the sound system Wild Bunch (disc-jockey Grantley "Daddy G" Marshall, rapper Robert "3-D" Del Naja and rhythm engineer Andrew "Mushroom" Vowles), formalized that dividing line on their influential **Blue Lines** (1991), featuring vocalist Shara Nelson, which established the sonic standard of trip-hop: a blend of soul vocals, dub bass lines, languid strings, ambient electronica, intricate drum patterns, and eerie atmosphere. The idea was not terribly original (it was basically a revamping of easy-listening, new-age music, orchestral soul and cocktail-lounge music for the affluent white disco crowds), but the choreography was clearly more important than the music, as **Mezzanine** (1998) proved in an even more seductive manner.

Portishead (10), formed by producer Geoff Barrow, vocalist Beth Gibbons, sound engineer Dave McDonald and guitarist Adrian Utley, were the ultimate creation of Bristol's fertile scene. The spectral and funereal lieder of **Dummy** (1994) set desolate laments to a casual backdrop of electronic music and let them float over a disorienting flow of syncopated beats. They had blurred the line between the pop ballad and the abstract chamber piece.

Tricky (1), a former member of the Wild Bunch, hired Martina Topley-Bird to imitate Portishead on **Maxinquaye** (1995), adding more neurotic dynamics. The album credited to **Nearly God** (1996) featured guest vocalists such as Bjork, Neneh Cherry and Alison Moyet interpreting or backing up Tricky's "songs". Fullfilling his progression towards a more personal and sincere form of music, the bleak **Pre-Millenium Tension** (1996) set his depressed toasting against nightmarish soundscapes.

Luke Vibert devoted his project Wagon Christ (1) to the ambient side of the trip-hop equation with **Phat Lab Nightmare** (1994) and especially with the celestial trance of **Throbbing Pouch** (1995), exuding abandon and fatalism. Massive sampling of orchestral sounds gave **Tally Ho!** (1998) an almost symphonic grandeur.

Minimal techno, 1989-94

The career of Manchester-based disc-jockeys Sean Booth and Rob Brown, better known as Autechre (22), actually comprised two careers. The first one was about dance music whose beat had been deformed and suppressed, melted into a watery substance and emptied of its narrative content, but was still relatively warm and organic. The smooth and detached tones of **Incunabula** (1993), perhaps the most austere and implacable album in the history of dance music, coined a new form of ultra-minimal techno that was expanded on the more colorful **Amber** (1995), insinuating those minimal/artificial sounds in the most obscure orbits of the subconscious, and on the more claustrophobic **Tri Repetae** (1996), that resorted to metallic sounds and subsonic frequencies. These works were inspired by Steve Reich's minimalism, Kraftwerk's robotic trance, and Brian Eno's ambient music, but their emotional content (if any) was radically different. **Chiastic Slide** (1997) was the dividing line, the discontinuity that caused a phase shift. The menacing texture of digital beats, repetitive noises and dejected melodies mutated into alien beings with a life of their own. Autechre's second career, best represented by **LP5** (1998) and **Confield** (2001), was about dissonance, icy ambience, irregular rhythm and non-linear development. Both careers were characterized by austere, meticulous and intricate sound design.

Autechre's tracks often seemed to be labyrinthine mirages: the closer one went, the more lost one felt.

Foxcore

The riot-grrrrls of Seattle, 1991-94

Hardcore punk-rock had been mostly a male phenomenon. Girls were excluded from hardcore the same way they were excluded in society from many other male-only rituals, whether street gangs or USA football. The "riot grrrls" movement of the 1990s changed the sociopolitical landscape of punk-rock by introducing the "girl factor" into the equation of frustration/ depression/ desperation/ anger.

The riot-grrrls movement originated largely in and around Seattle (Olympia, to be precise), and indeed it was Seattle that boasted the most fertile scene for female-only bands. The movement's manifesto was the article "Women, sex and rock and roll", published by "Puncture" in 1989. The first radio program to address the angry young girls was "Your Dream Girl", conducted by Lois Maffeo on Olympia's KAOS. One of the earliest riot-grrrls was Molly Neuman, who joined Allison Wolfe to create the fanzine "Girl Germs", one of the main alternative media for college girls. In the summer of 1991 they celebrated themselves at the Olympia campus, shouting their slogan "Revolution Girl Style Now!" The mood had been changing throughout the 1980s: the magazine "Sassy" had been founded already in 1987 as an alternative, not afraid to tackle brutal themes, to the conventional magazines for teenage girls.

Artistically, these young girls harked back to New York's female folksingers of the 1980s (who began singing about the female condition in hyper-realistic terms, not only from a sociopolitical point of view but also from an intimate-diary point of view), to California's all-female punk bands (Runaways, Pandoras, Frightwig and L7, not to mention Sugar Baby Doll, formed in San Francisco in 1986 by future foxcore stars Kat Bjelland, Courtney Love and Jennifer Finch), and to a few creative all-female British bands (Raincoats, X-Ray Spex and the Slits). To some extent, female intellectual rockers such as Patti Smith, Chrissie Hynde, Exene Cervenka, Lydia Lunch and Kim Gordon were all influential in defining the riot-grrrl ethos. Seattle/Olympia was one of the areas with the most sophisticated "do it yourself" infrastructure: it was not difficult for these girls to began releasing their own cassettes and CDs (e.g., via the label founded by Beat Happening's Calvin Johnson). In nearby Vancouver, anarchic poetess Jean Smith had formed Mecca Normal in the mid-1980s to create polemic works such as **Calico Kills The Cat** (1988), which became an inspiration for the riot-grrrls of Seattle.

This was a musical movement founded on the lyrics, not on the music, so their sound varied wildly. But, mostly, the vocals were quite unattractive (they tended to imitate a scream, rather than enhance a melody) and the playing was quite amateurish. The female voice had been treated as an instrument (a sound) in the male-dominated musical culture: it now became a vehicle for a message. The rest of the music was largely redundant and/or optional.

They were rebels, but only to an extent. Their message was not revolutionary: their message was intimate. They dealt with the real problems of teenage girls, from rape to loneliness. Their fanzines were not agit-prop pamphlets, they were blackboards to write on about their intimate experiences. The fundamental fact of the riot grrrls was that their heroine was not terrible: she was terrified.

Musically, the riot-grrrl phenomenon began in february 1991, when Kathleen Hanna and Tobi Vail formed Bikini Kill at Olympia's Evergreen College, and released the cassette **Revolution Girl Style Now** (1991), followed by the even more furious mini-abum **Pussy Whipped** (1993). Hannah would later clean up her act, and, dressed like a housewife from the Sixties, release a solo album credited to **Julie Ruin** (1998), offering her post-feminist meditations in a surprisingly radio-friendly format (a fusion of electronica, dub, and hip-hop). Even more accessible was **Le Tigre** (1999), the album recorded with video director Sadie Benning and music critic Johanna Fateman.

Even less musical was **Pottymouth** (1993), the debut album of Molly Neuman's Bratmobile. Other original riot-grrrls were Calamity Jane, who released **Martha Jane Cannary** (1992) four years after the first singles; Dickless, whose **Saddle Tramp** (1990) revealed the roaring vocals of Kelly Canary that would detonate the Teen Angels' **Daddy** (1996); Donna Dresch's Team Dresch, who hailed lesbianism on **Personal Best** (1994). They mostly played ragged rock'n'roll overflowing with angst and propelled by screeching guitars and primitive drumming.

Courtney Love's Hole (1) was one of the bands that launched the new female aesthetics nation-wide, thanks to Love's slutty attitude (an extension of the kind of depraved punk provocation already inaugurated by the likes of Lydia Lunch and Madonna) and to her marriage with Nirvana's Kurt Cobain. **Pretty On The Inside** (1991) was indeed a powerful statement of psychological devastation, its desperate ballads delivered in spasmodic fits.

Unrelated to the political movement, but sharing its visceral and raw approach to rock'n'roll, Seven Year Bitch (1) delivered **Viva Zapata** (1994), and Sleater-Kinney (1), i.e. songwriters Corin Tucker and Carrie Kinney, delivered **Call The Doctor** (1995), two albums that easily matched the emphasis of the early riot-grrrls while focusing on the music.

California's foxcore, 1991-94

The contagion soon spread to California, that had nurtured rock girl-groups since the 1960s.

San Francisco, whose Frightwig had pioneered the idea, boasted the Mudwimin, formed by Frightwig's guitarist Mia Levin and Tragic Mulatto's drummer Bambi Nonymous, with **Skiz** (1992); Stone Fox, lesbians who played melodic hard-rock on **Burnt** (1994); 4 Non Blondes, whose **Bigger Better Faster More** (1992) was highlighted by the Janis Joplin-style roar of openly-lesbian Linda Perry; Tribe 8, a radical lesbian band that played loud and fast "homocore" on **Fist City** (1995); and more moderate groups such as Tiger Trap, the project of Sacramento-based Rose Melberg, who played romantic punk-pop on **Tiger Trap** (1993), and Ovarian Trolley, with the even less aggressive **Crocodile Tears** (1993).

The spectrum was broad, but was eventually unified and sold to the masses by the Donnas, a novelty act (four teenage girls from Palo Alto all named Donna who played tight punk-rock with a strong Ramones fixation) equipped with producer Darin Raffaelli's catchy, energetic, anthemic tunes on **The Donnas** (1996), released when they graduated from high school, and **American Teenage Rock 'N' Roll Machine** (1998).

Los Angeles (where L7 had ruled) was home to some of the most successful and influential bands. The mostly female Creamers (1) recorded one of the most powerful albums in the frantic style of the New York Dolls (whirling rock'n'roll and catchy hooks), **Love Honor And Obey** (1989). The Red Aunts (1) evolved into a sort of cross between the Sex Pistols and the Rolling Stones on **#1 Chicken** (1995). That Dog, featuring violinist Petra Haden and bassist Rachel Haden (daughters of jazz great Charlie Haden), honed the intellectual **Totally Crushed Out** (1995). The Muffs (1) were a vehicle for former Pandoras bassist Kim Shattuck, who seemed to re-live the careers of wild female rockers of the past on **Blonder And Blonder** (1995).

Midwestern foxes, 1990-94

The Midwest (where Scrawl were already a legend) was no less prolific of girl-only bands. Minnesota's Zuzu's Petals were perhaps the best heirs to the Scrawl with **When No One's Looking** (1992). On the other hand, Veruca Salt, led by the songwriting duo of Nina Gordon and Louise Post, offered little more than power-pop on **American Thighs** (1994).

The most impressive musicians of the entire scene were Minneapolis' Babes In Toyland (11), led by vocalist and guitarist Kat Bjelland. **Spanking Machine** (1990) was already an eruption of cathartic violence, but **Fontanelle** (1992) stood as a set of psychological traumas, a witchy pandemonium of voodoo/pow-wow rhythms, hysterical screams and massive distortions, from which Bjelland vomited harrowing lyrics, mad with rage, disenchantment, hopelessness and frustration. The trio managed to express the schizophrenic coexistence of the innocent, apprehensive and defenseless child with the experienced and corrupt slut, junkie and juvenile delinquent. The Babes In Toyland invented an art of extreme emotions: more than singing or playing theirs was "acting", and it was "acting" one's own life.

Sugarsmack (10) were the vehicle for the Fetchin Bones' vocalist Hope Nicholls, one of the most extraordinary voices of her generation. **Top Loader** (1993), assembled with help from Pigface's Martin Atkins, came through as a catalog of terrifying neuroses, mixing industrial music, rap, heavy-metal, blues and acid-rock, and conveyed in her visceral, guttural and demonic style that fused Patti Smith's hysteria and Lydia Lunch's depravation.

Eastern foxes, 1990-94

The phenomenon was hardly visible on the East Coast. New York's Free Kitten were mostly a supergroup of female intellectuals (mainly Pussy Galore's Julia Cafritz and Sonic Youth's Kim Gordon). Luscious Jackson, featuring keyboardist Vivian Trimble, were white female rappers lost in disorienting soundscapes of jazz, funk and lounge music, best on the mini-album **In Search Of Manny** (1992). The Murmurs were a duo of female folksingers, capable of running the gamut from angelic folk to distorted hard-rock on **Pristine Smut** (1997), their third and best album. Cake Like were the closest thing to a riot-grrrrl group in New York, particularly on **Delicious** (1994).

Washington's Slant 6 were punk-poppers, catchy and amusing on **Soda Pop = Rip Off** (1994).

Picasso Trigger in North Carolina, featuring acrobatic vocalist Kathy Poindexter, were perhaps the best riot-grrrrls of the South, as proved by the bacchanals of **Fire In The Hole** (1994).

Brit and non-Brit pop

Brit-pop 1990-94

As was often the case in rock music, the most publicized phenomenon was also the least artistically interesting. "Brit-pop" became a derogatory term, one associated with ephemeral and dubious acts that speculated on facile melodies and trivial arrangements. If the British Invasion of the 1960s had at least revitalized the USA scene, the "Brit-pop" invasion of the 1990s... was hardly an invasion at all. The Brit-pop bands were all terribly similar and, mostly, tedious. In the end, only a few of them managed to have one or two world-wide hits, and most of them added very little to the history of rock music (other than yet another proof of the aberrations of its industry).

In 1990 Brit-pop had not materialized yet as a "fad", but the seeds were already being planted by bands such as Lightning Seeds, with their retro' classic **Cloudcuckooland** (1990), and La's, with **La's** (1990), specializing in sculpting memorable and unassuming melodies. Teenage Fanclub produced one of the best imitations of Big Star with **Bandwagonesque** (1991).

Heavenly (2) inherited the Primitives' passion for melodious simplicity. Fronted by former Talulah Gosh's singer Amelia Fletcher, they resurrected the age of Petula Clark, the girl-groups and bubblegum music on **Heavenly Vs Satan** (1991). Their romantic and naive approach to the pop tune evolved with **Le Jardin De Heavenly** (1992) and **Decline And Fall** (1994) into a new form of revisionist art, one that transformed Britain's perennial Sixties revival into an international language.

Pulp, fronted by Jarvis Cocker's out-of-fashion dandy style, were the quintessence of glam, retro` and kitsch on albums such as the erotic concept **His 'N' Hers** (1994) and singles such as *My Legendary Girlfriend* (1991), *Babies* (1992) and *Common People* (1995).

Scotland's Eugenius, the new project by former Vaselines' guitarist/singer Eugene Kelly, with **Oomalama** (1992), and Ireland's Frank And Walters, with **Trains Boats And Planes** (1992), also predated the 1994 explosion.

The massive Brit-pop phenomenon began in earnest with the bands destined to rule the world (according to the British press of the time): the Boo Radleys (1), who went "retro" with **Giant Steps** (1993), Blur, who attained stardom with **Parklife** (1994), and Oasis, the band (or the "bluff") that best personified the fad, from the exuberant **Definitely Maybe** (1994) to the multi-million seller **Morning Glory** (1995).

The most stunning feature of these bands was their absolute lack of imagination. They continued a British tradition, dating from at least the

Beatles, of pop musicians who had nothing to say but said it in a sophisticated manner.

Then it became a race to produce ever more predictable music. Each "next big thing" hailed by the British press was merely a copy of a copy of a copy of something that was not particularly exciting even the first time around.

If nothing else, Suede (1), featuring guitarist Bernard Butler and vocalist Brett Anderson, offered an original take on glam-pop on **Suede** (1993).

Former Microdisney's guitarist Sean O'Hagan proved his stature as a Brian Wilson-style arranger on the second and third albums by the High Llamas (1), **Gideon Gaye** (1995) and especially on the elaborate and monumental **Hawaii** (1996).

Supergrass sounded like the heirs to the Buzzcocks' punk-pop, at least on **I Should Coco** (1995).

One "next big thing" led to another "next big thing", and soon England was embroiled in a revival of the "mod" culture of the 1960s (read: the Who and, more recently, the Jam). Pioneered by Ocean Color Scene's **Moseley Shoals** (1996), the neo-mod school peaked with the Wildhearts, the most energetic and blasphemous of the pack, notably their album **Earth Vs The Wildhearts** (1993).

Inspired by the new wave of the 1970s, bands such as Elastica, fronted by Justine Frischmann and harking back to Blondie's and the Cars' disco-punk sound of the 1970s on **Elastica** (1995), and Sleeper, also relying on a female voice (Louise Wener) on **Smart** (1995), offered a less trivial kind of commercial rock.

Retro futurism, 1991

Brit-pop was just the tip of the iceberg. British rock was being swept by a tidal wave of melodic innovation. One facet of it consisted in the transposition of synth-pop and new-wave forms into the body of kitsch music. The theme of bridging nostalgia and futurism harked back to the decadent rockers of the 1970s (and, above all, Brian Eno). The new generation disposed with the decadent poses, and retained only the aesthetic.

Stereolab (12) were not the first and were not the only ones, but somehow they came to represent a nostalgic take on Sixties pop music that employed electronic rhythms and arrangements. Built around the collation of keyboardist Tim Gane (ex-McCarthy) and French vocalist Laetitia Sadier, i.e. the juxtaposition of hypnotic, acid instrumental scores and surreal, naive vocals, as refined by their early EPs **Super 45** (1991) and **Super-Electric** (1991), Stereolab walked a fine line between avantgarde and pop. As they continued to fine-tune the idea on **Peng** (1992), echoing the trance of the Velvet Underground, Neu and Suicide, while increasing the doses of electronic sounds, Sadier's voice became a sound and an instrument, contributing more than catchy refrains to the allure of the mini-album **Space Age Bachelor Pad Music** (1993), the aesthetic manifesto of their chamber kitsch. Stereolab probably reached their zenith with the singles of *John Cage Bubblegum* (1993) and *Jenny Ondioline* (1993), that inspired the stylistic tour de force of **Transient Random Noise Bursts With Announcements** (1993). Stereolab had coined a new musical language, as austere as classical music and as light as easy-listening. New keyboardist Katharine Gifford contributed to the elegant and smooth sound of **Mars Audiac Quintet** (1994), their most accomplished fusion of nostalgia and futurism, although not as innovative as the previous album. **Emperor Tomato Ketchup** (1996) was even more impersonal, pure sound for the sake of sound, pure abstraction of kitsch music. Stereolab injected Soft Machine's progressive-rock, Terry Riley's minimalism, Neu's robotik rhythm and Pink Floyd's atmospheric psychedelia into the fragile melodic skeleton of British pop music.

"Retro futurism" was pioneered also by <u>Saint Etienne</u> (2). Bob Stanley and Pete Wiggs bridged Depeche Mode's synth-pop, the Sixties pop revival, sensual disco-like vocals (Sarah Cracknell) and almost neo-classical arrangements on the sophisticated production exploits of **Foxbase Alpha** (1991) and **So Tough** (1993). They were unique in crafting a celestial, effervescent and ghostly fusion of jazz, funk, lounge and house music. **Tiger Bay** (1994) achieved pure nirvana, pure ambience and pure style. At their best, it felt as if a Broadway star of the 1950s was backed by Giorgio Moroder on electronic keyboards and by an orchestra conducted by Ennio Morricone.

<u>State Of Grace</u> (1) matched Saint Etienne's achievements on **Jamboreebop** (1996).

<u>Space</u> devised a form of kitsch that basically bridged Brit-pop and "Madchester" on **Spiders** (1996).

But it was in Japan that the genre found the most fertile terrain. <u>Pizzicato Five</u> (1), who had turned supermarket muzak into a sub-genre of synth-pop with **Couples** (1987), became one of the leading retro bands when they enrolled eccentric vocalist Maki Nomiya, the ideal alter ego of electronic keyboardist Yasuharu Konishi. The single *Lover's Rock* (1990), possibly their masterpiece, and the album **This Year's Girl** (1991) celebrated their passion for icons of the Sixties (James Bond soundtracks, hare-krishna chanting, novelty numbers, silly dance crazes), whereas later collections such as **Bossa Nova** (1993) and **Happy End Of The World** (1997) experimented with a format closer to orchestral disco-music.

Art-pop, 1993

Despite all the trivial music cooked up by the assembly chains of Brit-pop, some British bands experimented with different ideas of what a song is supposed to be.

The Tindersticks (1) deployed elegant quasi-orchestral arrangements, that relied mostly on the delicate polyphony of guitar, keyboards and violin, on **Tindersticks** (1993). Its songs were the ideal soundtrack for brothels packed with philosophers. Stuart Staples' voice (a Chris Isaak soundalike) was lost in the labyrinth of his own visions, haunted by the giant shadows of Tom Waits, Nick Cave and Leonard Cohen. But the subtlety of that work drained away as the band (a "big" band) opted for orchestral pop and lounge music on **Tinderstick** (1995) and **Curtains** (1997).

Radiohead (2), the most hyped and probably the most over-rated band of the decade, upped the ante for studio trickery. They had begun as third-rate disciples of the Smiths, and albums such as **Pablo Honey** (1993) and **The Bends** (1995) were cauldrons of Brit-pop cliches. Then **OK Computer** (1997) happened and the word "chic" took on a new meaning. The album was a masterpiece of faux avantgarde (of pretending to be avantgarde while playing mellow pop music). It was, more properly, a new link in the chain of production artifices that changed the way pop music "sounds": the Beatles' **Sgt Pepper**, Pink Floyd's **Dark Side Of The Moon**, Fleetwood Mac's **Tusk** and Michael Jackson's **Thriller**. Despite the massive doses of grandiloquence a` la U2 and of facile pathos a` la David Bowie, the album's mannerism led to the same excesses that detracted from late Pink Floyd's albums (lush textures, languid melodies, drowsy chanting). Since the production aspects of music were beginning to prevail over the music itself, it was just about natural to make them "the" music. The sound of **Kid A** (2000) had decomposed and absorbed countless new perfumes, like a carcass in the woods. All sounds were processed and mixed, including the vocals. Radiohead moved as close to electronica as possible without actually endorsing it. Radiohead became masters of the artificial, masters of minimizing the emotional content of very complex structures. **Amnesiac** (2001) replaced "music" with a barrage of semi-mechanical loops, warped instruments and digital noises, while bending Thom Yorke's baritone to a subhuman register and stranding it in the midst of hostile arrangements, making it sound more and more like an alienated psychopath. Their limit was that they were more form than content, more "hype" than message and more nothing than everything. However, Radiohead were emblematic of a new trend in rock music that conceived each song as an isolated and saturated microcosmos of studio effects; each song as an ecosystem of interacting sounds in motion.

Alt-pop

Pop renaissance in the USA

During the first half of the 1990s, pop music vastly outnumbered underground/experimental music. It was the revenge of melody, after a quarter of a century of progressive sounds. A cycle that began with the demise of the Beatles and the rise of alternative/progressive rock, and that continued with the German and Canterbury schools of the 1970s, and then punk-rock and the new wave, and peaked with the alt-rock and college-pop of the 1980s, came to an abrupt, grinding halt in the 1990s.

The more fashionable and rewarding route was, however, the one that coasted the baroque pop of latter-day Beach Boys, Van Dyke Parks, Big Star and XTC, the one that coupled catchy refrains and lush arrangements. The single most important school may have been San Francisco's, which had originated in the 1980s with the Sneetches. Jellyfish (2), featuring guitarist Jason Falkner, wrote perhaps the most impeccable melodies of the time. **Bellybutton** (1990), a milestone of naive, bubblegum melodic music inspired by Merseybeat and later Beach Boys, was both cartoonish and shimmering, while the arrangements on **Spilt Milk** (1993) were almost baroque.

Other devoted followers were Imperial Teen, led by former Faith No More's keyboardist Roddy Bottum, the Mommyheads, MK Ultra, Overwhelming Colorfast, Smash Mouth, Orange Peels, masters of the retro` on **Square** (1997), Beulah, with **Handsome Western States** (1997), etc.

In Seattle, the melodic tradition of the Green Pajamas and the Young Fresh Fellows was continued by Juan Atkins' project, 764-Hero, with **Get Here And Stay** (1999), and by Super Deluxe with **Famous** (1995).

Elsewhere, similar sounds were produced by Velvet Crush in Rhode Island; Material Issue in Chicago, with **International Pop Overthrow** (1991); Rembrandts in Los Angeles; etc.

The Eggs (1), in Virginia, were among the most creative, particularly on their second album, **Exploder** (1993), that featured exotic instruments, synthesizer, trombone, and oboe.

New York-based Fountains Of Wayne, on the other hand, became the USA's prime Brit-poppers through **Fountains Of Wayne** (1996) and **Utopia Parkway** (1999).

Quite unique was the style of the Ben Folds Five in North Carolina, because keyboardist and vocalist Folds was an unusual disciple of Todd Rundgren and Elton John, best heard on the ballads of **Ben Folds Five** (1995).

In Oklahoma, Tyson Meade's Chainsaw Kittens (1) launched a revival of glam-pop with **Violent Religion** (1990), a concentrate of Aerosmith, New York Dolls, T. Rex, Cheap Trick, Patti Smith, Stooges, Velvet

Underground, etc. Glam-pop's comeback continued with <u>Sponge</u> in New York, and <u>Running With Scissors</u> in Seattle.

In Texas, the hyper-pop muzak of Tim DeLaughter's <u>Tripping Daisy</u> evolved from the sugary **Bill** (1992) to the grandiose and baroque **Jesus Hits Like The Atom Bomb** (1998).

Canada's most successful pop bands were the <u>Barenaked Ladies</u>, revealed by **Gordon** (1992), and the <u>Crash Test Dummies</u>, with **God Shuffled His Feet** (1993).

Non-pop 1990-95

The Pixies invented the most creative form of pop of the 1980s, one that conveyed the fractured tics of hardcore punk-rock and the enigmatic dynamics of the new wave into a melodic format that was not straightforward at all but sounded like it. The greatest disciples of the Pixies' late quirky-pop sound were the <u>Breeders</u> (2), a supergroup featuring the Pixies' bassist Kim Deal (now on guitar) and the Throwing Muses' guitarist Tanya Donelly. **Pod** (1990) explored a broad range of tones, from the ecstatic nursery-rhyme of a naive little girl to the harsh, syncopated riff of a hard-rock band. The band continued to blur daydreaming and nightmare on **Last Splash** (1993), having replaced Donelly with Kim's twin sister Kelley, an even more powerful post-feminist statement that employs an even wider repertory of "voices" (girl-groups, jangling folk-rock, country, even grunge). Donelly went on to create <u>Belly</u> (1) and craft the charming and subtly primitive **Star** (1993), while the twins remained more faithful to the eccentric rhetoric of the Pixies, Kim with the Amps and **Pacer** (1995), and Kelly with the <u>Kelly Deal 6000</u> and **Go To The Sugar Altar** (1996).

Boston was also the home base of one of the greatest bands of the decade, <u>Morphine</u> (112), a guitar-less trio whose style borrowed heavily from blues and jazz but shared with the Pixies the same casual, detached approach to melody. Three masterpieces established them among the masters of the "noir" atmosphere. **Good** (1992) highlighted their ability to turn ballads and rockers into metaphysical dialogues between bass and saxophone. The languid crooning of former Treat Her Right's bassist Mark Sandman, who chiseled one of the most evocative voices of the era, added another layer of meaning, a Tom Waits-like mourner and Nick Cave-like preacher floating inside the stark, unreal, heavy fog of the music. The trio contrived melodies that offered a quiet vivisection of post-industrial anxiety. Sandman refined the way he rode (like a surfer) the gloomy and occasionally even lugubrious lines of Dana Colley's saxophone on **Cure For Pain** (1993), a less claustrophobic and more accessible work, featuring drummer Billy Conway (also ex-Treat Her Right). **Yes** (1995) followed the route that seemed less congenial to the trio, by emphasizing rhythm over melody. Less depressed and distressed, it almost sounded like a return to rock'n'roll and rhythm'n'blues of the 1950s. Their representation of reality provided an anti-spectacular synthesis of transcendental and mundane elements, additionally soaked into premonitions of a merciless destiny. After the mediocre **Like Swimming** (1997), Morphine's last album, **The Night** (2000), released after Sandman died of a heart attack on-stage in 1999, turned out to be both their most introspective and their most orchestrated work (piano, cello, horns, organ and choir).

Georgia was still a favorable turf for alternative pop. Magnapop (1), the band of vocalist Linda Hopper and guitarist Ruthie Morris, played in a style halfway between folk-rock and hard-rock on **Magnapop** (1992). Toenut delivered unsettling tunes on **Information** (1995).

Los Angeles' Madder Rose (2) was an oddly schizophrenic band that relied on the contrast/friction (rather than the amalgam/fusion) of Billy Cote's abrasive guitar and Mary Lorson's sweet vocals. **Bring It Down** (1993) and **Panic On** (1994) were poetic, idyllic works whose mood fluctuated between autumnal singalongs and tormented rockers. They converted to trip-hop with **Tragic Magic** (1997) and reinvented themselves with the surreal stylistic melange of **Hello June Fool** (1999).

Also in Los Angeles, Further (1) toyed with Dinosaur Jr-style noise-pop on **Sometimes Chimes** (1994).

North Carolina, which had become one of the main centers for alternative rock, was also one of the venues in which musicians truly tried to speak new melodic languages.

The brand of power-pop concocted by the Archers Of Loaf (2) on **Icky Mettle** (1993) and **Vee Vee** (1995) mixed the eccentric dynamics of the Pixies and the anthemic tone of the Replacements, and added a generous dose of Television's guitar noise. Archers Of Loaf's guitarist/vocalist Eric Bachmann (1), disguised as **Barry Black** (1995), revealed his real self (and ambitions) with a program of all-instrumental chamber music that was both demented and virtuosic. His next project, Crooked Fingers (1), capitalized on that experiment for a chaotic and eclectic repertory of carefully-arranged, dark, pensive ballads, particularly on their second album **Bring On The Snakes** (2001).

Other notable albums of the North Carolina school were Small 23's **True Zero Hook** (1993) and Spatula's second album **Medium Planers and Matchers** (1995).

Franklin Bruno's Nothing Painted Blue (1) in Los Angeles experimented with an introverted and intellectual form of power-pop on their second album **Power Trips Down Lovers Lane** (1993).

Vancouver's Superconductor, led by Carl Newman, toyed with a bizarre six-guitar line-up on the loud and tuneful **Hit Songs For Girls** (1993) and the rock opera **Bastardsong** (1996).

Holland was perhaps the most fertile place for college-pop, outside the USA. The Dutch contingent was led by Daryll-Ann (1), who pursued an implosion of country-rock and folk-rock stereotypes on their lyrical third album **Weeps** (1996), and <u>Bettie Serveert</u> (1), who served cold clever melodies on **Palomine** (1992).

Lounge-pop 1990-94

A brief fad in the USA was "lounge-pop", that was rediscovered in Rhode Island by <u>Combustible Edison</u>: the soundtrack to their "Combustible Edison Heliotropic Oriental Mambo and Foxtrot Orchestra", partly collected on **I Swinger** (1994), was its manifesto, while their third disc, **The Impossible World** (1998), wed it to the other big fad of the time, trip-hop.

In Canada, <u>Zumpano</u>, the new project of singer/guitarist Carl Newman, fully acknowledged that zeitgeist on their second album, **Goin' Through Changes** (1996), adopting lounge music and easy-listening within the alt-rock framework.

In Sweden the <u>Cardigans</u> wrapped Nina Persson's soft, sensual and dreamy phrasing around sophisticated and lush lounge-pop arrangements, notably on their second album **Life** (1995).

Two Georgia bands flirted with easy-listening: <u>Jody Grind</u>, whose vibrant jazzy vocalist Kelly Hogan propelled **One Man's Trash Is Another Man's Treasure** (1990), and the <u>Opal Foxx Quartet</u>, with the elaborate **The Love That Won't Shut Up** (1993).

Seattle's <u>Satchel</u> (1), featuring Pigeonhed's vocalist Shawn Smith, crafted elegant pop-soul-jazz ballads, inspired by both Steely Dan and Prince, on **EDC** (1994).

Grunge

The golden age of Seattle

Grunge was one of the big phenomena of the 1990s, although it was largely confined to the United States. Grunge was essentially a revival of 1970s' hard-rock. However, it was also identified with the musical renaissance of Seattle, that suddenly became one of the world's centers for rock music, and "grunge" came to include just about any band that played in that city.

The road had been opened in the late 1980s by Pearl Jam, Soundgarden, Melvins and Mudhoney, with four distinctive styles that involved "hard" vibrations. Those were the four cardinal points of Seattle's grunge. Nirvana had turned grunge into a slot machine.

Alice In Chains (1) perfected a form of gloomy pop-metal and of power-ballad with **Facelift** (1990) and especially the stark melodrama of **Dirt** (1992), the intimate portrait of a drug addict. Layne Staley's psychotic vocals and Jerry Cantrell's sharp riffs transformed their confessions into bloodsheds.

Followers of their bittersweet hard-rock included My Sister's Machine, with **Diva** (1992), Truly, with **Fast Stories** (1995), and the most successful band of the second generation, the Foo Fighters, formed by Nirvana's drummer David Grohl, Germs' guitarist Pat Smear and Sunny Day Real Estate's rhythm section, with the even poppier **Foo Fighters** (1995), which was truly a Grohl solo album.

A multitude of derivative bands appeared after Nirvana's 1991 success: Love Battery, with the EP **Between The Eyes** (1990); Green Apple Quickstep, with **Wonderful Virus** (1993); Sweet Water, with their second album **Superfriends** (1994); Candlebox; etc.

Nearby Oregon had Sprinkler and Pond, but mainly Everclear.

Few bands truly experimented with the format. Hammerbox (1) were possibly the most imaginative: their fusion of punk, country, blues, funk and metal elements on **Numb** (1993) was unrivaled.

GodHeadSilo (2), the duo of bassist Mike Kunka and drummer Dan Haugh, played nightmares not sounds. The gargantuan pieces of **Scientific Supercake** (1994) were catalogs of terrifying sounds borrowed from Chrome, Unsane and Melvins. **Skyward In Triumph** (1996) did not sound human at all, submerged by an irrational noise of galactic riffs, demonic screams and crushing cadences.

An even more claustrophobic atmosphere was penned by Hammerhead (1) with the ugly, post-hardcore sludge of **Ethereal Killer** (1993).

Atomic 61 (1) wed the Melvins' apocalyptic sensibility to Jimi Hendrix's blues-rock on **Tinnitus In Extremis** (1993).

Portland's Everclear (1), the project of Art Alexakis, a sincere populist, bard of the misfits, expressed teenage angst via a mythological review of provincial life on **Sparkle And Fade** (1995) and especially **So Much For The Afterglow** (1997), the latter embellished with layers of keyboards, horns, strings and choirs. His mission peaked (morally, if not artistically) with the solemn and touching concept album **Songs From An American Movie** (2000), whose lush arrangements were almost symphonic.

Grunge in California

Southern California, long the main center for heavy-metal, jumped on the bandwagon with Scott Weiland's Stone Temple Pilots (1), who virtually cloned Pearl Jam and Soundgarden, especially on their second album **Purple** (1994), and Blind Melon, two of the most successful grunge bands of the 1990s, but also two of the most derivative. More original were perhaps Failure on **Magnified** (1994).

Tool (3) was the most innovative band to emerge from grunge's second generation. **Undertow** (1993) announced their sinister, threatening and (in a subtle way) explosive blend of Led Zeppelin, grunge, heavy-metal and progressive-rock. The lengthy and brainy suites of **Aenima** (1996) displayed a shimmering elegance that was almost a contradiction in terms, but that was precisely the point: Tool's art was one of subtle contrasts and subdued antinomies, one in which existential rage and titanic will competed all the time. It was also a diary of primal angst, and the lyrical level truly paralleled the instrumental level. **Lateralus** (2001) expanded on that two-level approach, with tracks that, musically, were multi-part concertos or mini-operas, and, lyrically, were Freudian sessions that elicited all possible interior demons. In parallel, Tool's vocalist Maynard James Keenan was adapting grunge to the claustrophobic and neurotic atmospheres of industrial music and post-rock on **Mer De Noms** (2000), the debut album by his supergroup A Perfect Circle.

An even more original assimilation of progressive-rock's language was carried out by a San Diego band that relocated to England, God Machine (1), on **Scenes From The Second Storey** (1993).

Grunge in New York

Helmet (1), formed by Band Of Susans' guitarist Page Hamilton, were the undisputed leaders of New York's grunge. **Strap It On** (1990) defined their sound: stormy, dense and dark; a dull, continuous, torrential noise that created a manic tension.

Quicksand, formed by Gorilla Biscuits' guitarist Walter Schreifels, fused hardcore and grunge in a more straightforward manner on **Manic Compression** (1995).

Surgery (1) were to Helmet what the Rolling Stones were to the Kinks. The supercharged blues-rock frenzy of **Nationwide** (1990) and the savage and incendiary sound of EP **Trim 9th Ward Highrollers** (1993) had no class and no artistic pretenses: they simply displayed animal instincts.

Barkmarket (11) coined a form of "progressive grunge", an explosive mixture of Jesus Lizard and Sonic Youth that relied on David Sardy's uncontrolled histrionics (reminiscent of Mick Jagger at his worst) and guitar bacchanals a` la Surgery to craft the chaotic, incendiary atmospheres of **Vegas Throat** (1991). And **Gimmick** (1993) added sound effects and samples to an already frantic cacophony.

Austria's H.P. Zinker (relocated to New York) offered a jazzy version of grunge on **Beyond It All** (1990).

Scarce (1), formed in Rhode Island by guitarist/vocalist Chick Graning on the ashes of Anastasia Screamed, penned the memorable **Deadsexy** (1995), one of the most melodic and melodramatic grunge albums of the era.

Grunge in Chicago

Chicago had actually co-pioneered the genre with Urge Overkill, particularly on their second album, **Americruiser** (1990), a compromise between their experimental debut and the melodic style that would make them famous. Bands such as Hum and Soil kept it alive.

Out of Chicago also came the only hard-rocking band that could compete with the popularity of Seattle's grunge: the Smashing Pumpkins (2). **Gish** (1991) crossed the boundaries of grunge, progressive-rock and acid-rock, unifying the power of riffs and the subtlety of dynamics. **Siamese Dream** (1993) gave the idea psychological depth and dramatic emphasis: languid melodies were delivered in a neurotic register by Billy Corgan while James Iha's guitar screeched a wall of noise. They were more "recitations" than songs, and the band's achievement was to strike a balance between elegance and savagery. The monumental **Mellon Collie And The Infinite Sadness** (1995) sounded like a series of uncontrolled urges to experiment with all sorts of formats (symphonic, acoustic, bubblegum, glam, easy-listening and avantgarde). The common denominator of these schizophrenic fits was the atmosphere, a disorienting blend of fairy tale and Freudian confession.

Soon in the Midwest a few crossover experiments tried to expand the horizons of the genre. Detroit's Big Chief fused grunge with funk, blues, hip-hop and soul on **Face** (1991); and Minneapolis' Walt Mink added jazz and psychedelia on **Miss Happiness** (1992).

In the south, grunge merged with the local tradition of "southern boogie" and with the countless flavors of blues, soul and gospel: Alabama's Verbena, with **Souls For Sale** (1997); Georgia's Collective

Soul, with **Hints Allegations And Things Left Unsaid** (1994);
Texas' Toadies, with **Rubberneck** (1994); etc.

British grunge

England's contingent was not as numerous and not as significant. Bush
were the most successful thanks to **Sixteen Stone** (1994); and Fudge
Tunnel were the most devastating with **Hate Songs In E Minor** (1991).
On the other hand, the Manic Street Preachers merely watered down
Guns N'Roses' street rock on **Generation Terrorists** (1992).

The Golden Age of Hip-hop Music

Generally speaking, the rule for hip-hop music of the 1990s was that behind every successful rap act there was a producer. Rap music was born as a "do it yourself" art in which the "message" was more important than the music. During the 1990s, interest in the lyrics declined rapidly, while interest in the soundscape that those lyrics roamed increased exponentially. The rapping itself became less clownish, less stereotyped, less macho, and much more psychological and subtle. In fact, rappers often crossed over into singing. Hip-hop music became sophisticated, and wed jazz, soul and pop. Instrumental hip-hop became a genre of its own, and one of the most experimental outside of classical music.

East-Coast rap

The most significant event of the early 1990s was probably the advent of Wu-Tang Clan (1), a loose affiliation of rappers, including Gary "Genius/GZA" Grice, Russell "Ol' Dirty Bastard" Jones, Clifford "Method Man" Smith and Dennis "Ghostface Killah" Coles, "conducted" (if the rap equivalent of a classical conductor exists) by Robert "RZA" Diggs, the musical genius behind **Enter the Wu-Tang** (1993), a diligent tribute to old-school rap. It was RZA's three-dimensional sound experience and his cerebral gutter beats (and occasional philosophical/mystical tone-poems) that gave meaning to the voices of those rappers, although the sumptuous arrangements of **Wu-Tang Forever** (1997) threatened to take away precisely that meaning. This "clan" (not "gang") spun off a number of successful solo careers. Ol' Dirty Bastard's **Return to the 36 Chambers** (1995), Method Man's **Tical** (1994), Raekwon's **Only Built 4 Cuban Linx** (1995) and GZA/Genius' **Liquid Swords** (1995), the most dramatic and cinematic of the bunch, were produced by RZA. However, when the Wu-Tang Clan began a rapid artistic decline, it was Ghostface Killah who emerged as the voice of his generation with the brutal, death-obsessed cinematic storytelling of **Supreme Clientele** (2000) and **Fishscale** (2006).

The Wu-Tang clan were one of the few East Coast acts that stood up to the past standards of the city's hip-hop. A number of New Jersey acts, in particular, cast a doubt on the future of hip-hop: the duo P.M. Dawn, with **Of the Heart of the Soul of the Cross** (1991), Naughty By Nature, with **Naughty By Nature** (1991), Kris Kross (the pre-puberal duo of Chris "Daddy Mack" Smith and Chris "Mack Daddy" Kelly), produced by teenager Jermaine Dupri, with the disco energy of **Totally Krossed Out** (1992), and the trio of the Lords of the Underground, with **Here Come the Lords** (1993), produced by Marley Marl. Washington multi-instrumentalist Basehead (Michael Ivey), with **Plays With Toys** (1992), was also crossing over into pop and soul territory. Trevor "Busta Rhymes" Smith's **The Coming** (1996) was as bizarre as it was accessible (basically an extension of the absurdist style of Public Enemy's William "Flavor Flav" Drayton). The nonsensical dialectic of Das Efx (Andre "Dre" Weston and Willie "Skoob" Hines) on **Dead Serious** (1992) was only functional in creating novelty acts.

Main Source's **Breaking Atoms** (1991), Poor Righteous Teachers' second album **Pure Poverty** (1991), permeated by Islamic philosophy, **Mecca and the Soul Brother** (1992) by producer Pete Rock (Phillips) & rapper C.L. Smooth (Corey Penn), Reggie "Redman" Noble's **Whut? Thee Album** (1992), **Enta Da Stage** (1993) by short-lived trio Black Moon, and New Kingdom's tribal-psychedelic **Heavy Load** (1993) were among the few albums that dared to experiment. East Coast hip-hop was losing to the West Coast. If nothing else, Kendrick "Jeru the Damaja" Davis's **The Sun Rises in the East** (1994) briefly brought back party-rap's original sound.

New York's duo Organized Konfusion (Larry "Prince Poetry" Bakersfield and Troy "Pharoahe Monch" Jamerson) refined the dramatic/poetic skills of rap music, from the ghetto vignettes of **Organized Konfusion** (1991) to the psychologial hip-hopera **The Equinox** (1997)

Philadelphia's The Goats (1), led by Oatie Kato (Maxx Stoyanoff-Williams), orchestrated the "hip-hopera" **Tricks of the Shade** (1992), a concept album built around the evils of the USA way of life, with both samples and a live band, deep grooves and a canvas of jazz, funk and rock.

"Prince Paul" Huston (1), the producer of De La Soul's **3 Feet High and Rising** and the equally psychedelic **My Field Trip To Planet 9** (1993) by Justin Warfield, penned Gravediggaz's gothic **6 Feet Deep** (1994) with Wu-Tang Clan's Robert "RZA" Diggs, and the solo albums **Psychoanalysis: What Is It?** (1997) and especially the concept album **A Prince Among Thieves** (1999).

Philadelphia-born Roots' collaborator Ursula Rucker was a black spoken-word artist who coined a new form of art with her single *Supernatural* (1994), a dance hit created by a-capella vocals. After being a mere novelty on other people's songs, she emancipated her voice and her stories of black women on **Supa Sista** (2001).

Alien to the street culture of much hip-hop, New York's J-Live (Justice Allah) was one of the MCs who turned rhymed storytelling into a veritable art, both on **The Best Part** (1996), released five years after being recorded, and **All Of The Above** (2002).

Gangsta-rap

On the West Coast, "gangsta-rap" was the dominant theme. Schoolly D had invented it in 1984, but, starting with Ice-T in 1986, it was in Los Angeles that the form found its natural milieu. In 1992, when racial riots erupted (following the police beating of a black gangster), Los Angeles was said to have 66 gangs of teenagers, mostly black, with daily shootings among them. They reached a temporary truce in april. It is not a coincidence that gangsta-rap became a national phenomenon in the following twelve months. Gangsta-rap was not so much about gangster lives as about a metaphorical, solemn, doom-laden recreation of the noir/thriller atmosphere of the urban drug culture. It was more than a mere depiction of their lives, just like psychedelic music had been more than a mere reproduction of the hallucinogenic experience. Gangsta rap was about the mythology and the metaphysics of the gang life, with sexual and criminal overtones. As Greg Kot wrote, "The gangster rappers depict a world in which gangbangers and crack-heads fester in a cesspool of misogyny, homophobia and racism". Invariably dismissing women as teasers or sluts, these rappers indirectly revealed the sordid and desperate conditions of the women of the ghettos. Their justification was that they were not promoting that kind of violence, but merely documenting it: gangsta-rap was a documentary of daily life in the ghetto. Furthermore, the arrogance of these self-appointed super-heroes was often accompanied by a fatalistic mood: gangsta-rap was not about immortality, albeit about survival. N.W.A. (1), or "Niggaz With Attitude", formalized "gangsta-rap" on **Straight Outta Compton** (1988), and two of its former members, O'Shea "Ice Cube" Jackson with **AmeriKKKa's Most Wanted** (1990), a total immersion in a nightmarish atmosphere, and Andre "Dr Dre" Young (1) with **The Chronic** (1992), featuring rapper Calvin "Snoop Doggy Dogg" Broadus, and later with **2001** (2000), gave it its masterpieces. The latter, heavily influenced by George Clinton's psychedelic funk, also coined a subgenre called "G Funk".

Houston's Geto Boys, featuring young rapper Brad "Scarface" Jordan, were one of the first crews from the South to become known nation-wide, thanks to the the terrifying gangsta-rap of their second album **Geto Boys** (1990). Robert-Earl "DJ Screw" Davis, who died at 30 of an overdose, became a Houston legend by slowing down ("screwing") rap hits into psychedelic, dilated melodies.

Gangsta-rap became mainstream via albums such as **Doggystyle** (1993) by Los Angeles native Calvin Broadus, better known as Snoop Doggy Dogg (1), produced by Dr Dre, and **Me Against The World** (1995), the third album from Oakland's 2Pac (aka Tupac Shakur, born Lesane Parish Crooks, shot to death in 1996), produced by Sam Bostic, which was followed by **All Eyez on Me** (1996), the first double album of hip-hop music.

As gangsta-rap generated sales, rappers found it almost obligatory to spin the usual litany of hard-boiled tales of drugs, sex and murder.

One of the main sources of creativity for the Los Angeles scene was the the Freestyle Fellowship crew, responsible for the elaborate collages of **To Whom It May Concern** (1991) and especially **Inner City Griots** (1993). The second album, **A Book Of Human Language** (1998), by Aceyalone, a founding member of the "Freestyle Fellowship" crew, was lavishly arranged by Matthew "Mumbles" Fowler, and retained a literate approach that contrasted with the old "gansta" style. **Magnificent** (2006) featured beats by Jon "RJD2" Krohn.

Los Angeles was also the birthplace of Latino hip-hop, which debuted with **Escape From Havana** (1990) by Cuban-born Mellow Man Ace (Sergio Reyes) and **Hispanic Causing Panic** (1991) by Kid Frost (Arturo Molina). Kid Frost's *La Raza* (1990) and Mellow Man Ace's *Mentirosa* (1990) became the reference standards for all subsequent Latin rappers. The artistic peak of West-Coast rap was probably reached by a semi-Latino group, Cypress Hill (1), the project of producer Lawrence "Muggs" Muggerud and rapper Louis "B Real" Freeze, with their hyper-depressed trilogy of **Cypress Hill** (1992), **Black Sunday** (1993) and **Temples of Boom** (1995). The large Latino collective Ozomatli offered ebullient salsa-funk-rap on **Ozomatli** (1998), featuring wizard turntablist Cut Chemist (Lucas MacFadden).

Oakland was the headquarters of most black rappers from the San Francisco Bay Area. The main acts were the crew Digital Underground (1), the brainchild of Greg "Shock G" Jacobs and the main hip-hop purveyors of George Clinton's eccentric "funkadelia", notably on **Sex Packets** (1990); and rapper Del tha Funkee Homosapien (Teren Delvon Jones), also inspired by the P-funk aesthetics on **I Wish My Brother George Was Here** (1991). The Mystic Journeymen, formed by rappers Pushin' Suckas' Consciousness (PSC) and Vision The Brotha From Anotha Planet (BFAP), were important not so much for their **4001: The Stolen Legacy** (1995), but as founders of the Oakland collective "Living Legends".

San Francisco produced some of the most virulent agit-prop rap of all times: the Beatnigs, with **Beatnigs** (1988), Consolidated (1), with **The Myth Of Rock** (1990), and the Disposable Heroes Of Hiphoprisy (1), with **Hypocrisy Is The Greatest Luxury** (1992).

Gangsta-rap reached the East Coast with Onix's **Bacdafucup** (1992), Nasir "Nas" Jones' powerful **Illmatic** (1994), the Notorious B.I.G. (Christopher "Biggie Smalls" Wallace)'s **Ready to Die** (1994), produced by Sean "Puffy" Combs and others (Wallace was shot to death in 1997), and Mobb Deep's second album **The Infamous** (1995), featuring Albert "Prodigy" Johnson.

Fat Joe (Joseph Cartagena), the first major Latino rapper from the Bronx, also embraced the gansta-rap aesthetic, notably on his second album **Jealous One's Envy** (1995). Fat Joe was the most notorious member of New York's rap collective D.I.T.C. (Diggin' In The Crates), formed by Joe "DJ Diamond D" Kirkland and first tested on Diamond D's **Stunts, Blunts & Hip Hop** (1992). The other notable member, Lamont "Big L" Coleman (shot to death in 1999), released perhaps the best of their albums, **Lifestylez Ov Da Poor & Dangerous** (1995), produced by Anthony "Buckwild" Best.

Progressive-rap

Progressive-rap of the kind pioneered by Public Enemy thrived with works such as Arrested Development (1)'s **3 Years 5 Months and 2 Days In The Life** (1998), the product of Atlanta-based rapper Todd "Speech" Thomas and disc-jockey Timothy "Headliner" Barnwell; Movement Ex's **Movement Ex** (1990), a concentrate of stereotyped conspiracy theories from Los Angeles; Oscar "Paris" Jackson's second album **Sleeping With the Enemy** (1992), from the Bay Area; Public Enemy associate "Sister Souljah" (Lisa Williamson)'s **360 Degrees of Power** (1992); Brand Nubian's **One For All** (1990); X-Clan's **To the East Blackwards** (1990) from New York, KMD's **Mr Hood** (1991), featuring rapper Daniel "Zen Love" Dumile (later known as MF Doom), and **Return Of The Boom Bap** (1993) by former Boogie Down Productions mastermind KRS-One (Lawrence Krisna Parker). These groups harked back to the radical, militant, Afro-nationalist ideology of the Black Panthers and the Nation of Islam. They basically represented the "positive" alternative to gangsta-rap: instead of advocating rape and murder, they confronted issues of both local and global politics. Even feminism found its hip-hop voice: Yolanda "Yo-Yo" Whittaker, who debuted with **Make Way for the Motherlode** (1991) and founded the "Intelligent Black Woman's Coalition" to promote self-esteem among women.

This subgenre reached a fanatical peak with **Steal This Album** (1998) by Oakland's duo The Coup, that reads like Mao's "Red Book" or a Noam Chomsky pamphlet.

Jazz-hop

This was also the decade of "jazz-hop" fusion. Jazz-hop fusion had distinguished predecessors. Some consider Miles Davis' **On The Corner** (1972) the precursor of hip-hop. For sure, in the 1990s the Last Poets, a Harlem-based trio of former jail convicts who had converted to Islam (led by Jalal Mansur Nuriddin), were using "spiel" (as rap was called in those days) over a jazz background: their political sermons inspired by Malcom X relied on the arrangements of jazz producer Alan Douglas on

The Last Poets (1970), which became a hit, and developed into "jazzoetry" on **Chastisement** (1972).

Within the rap nation, jazz-hop was pioneered by: Grandmaster Flash's remixes of jazz master Roy Ayers; scratcher Derek "D.ST" Howells's collaboration with jazz pianist Herbie Hancock, *Rockit* (1983); the Jungle Brothers' **Straight Out the Jungle** (1988), possibly the first example of full-fledged jazz-hop fusion; **And Now The Legacy Begins** (1991), the eclectic multi-stylistic manifesto of Toronto-based duo Dream Warriors (with the prophetic *My Definition of a Boombastic Jazz Style*); A Tribe Called Quest's **The Low End Theory** (1991), which featured guest musician Ron Carter; Carlton Douglas "Chuck D" Ridenhour's big-band tribute to Charlie Mingus (1992). Jazz returned the favor with post-bop saxophonist Greg Osby's **3D Lifestyles** (1993), with Miles Davis' very last recording, **Doo-Bop** (1992), and with the "acid-jazz" scene of San Francisco (such as Broun Fellinis and Alphabet Soup).

Besides being one of the first groups to follow in the footsteps of Public Enemy's militant hip-hop, Gang Starr (1), rapper Keith "Guru" Elam and producer Christopher "DJ Premier" Martin, pioneered the mature exploitation of jazz on **Step In The Arena** (1990) and **Daily Operation** (1992), and then ventured beyond jazz-hop on **Moment of Truth** (1998). Martin's extensive use of jazz sampling and percussion loops revolutionized the way "raps" ought to be orchestrated.

Jazz-hop became the sensation of 1993 with Guru (1)'s own **Jazzmatazz Volume 1** (1993), US3's **Hand on the Torch** (1993), for which British producer Geoff Wilkinson mined the Blue Note catalog, the Digable Planets' **Reachin'** (1993), from Boston, Pharcyde's dadaistic, carnivalesque **Bizarre Ride II the Pharcyde** (1993), from Los Angeles, and **Plantation Lullabies** (1993) by Washington's Me'Shell Ndege' Ocello (Mary Johnson). The trend was amplified in the following years by albums such as **One Step Ahead of the Spider** (1994), the third album by Dallas' white rapper Mark Griffin, better known as MC900 Ft Jesus (1), the Fun Lovin' Criminals' **Come Find Yourself** (1996).

Philadelphia's Roots (1) approached jazz not via samples but through live instrumentation, led by the rhythm section of drummer Ahmir-Khalib "?uestlove" Thompson and bassist Leon "Hub" Hubbard and by keyboardist Scott Storch, on **Do You Want More** (1994), the album that introduced spoken-word artist Ursula Rucker. A quantum jump in arrangements (notably James "Kamal" Gray's electronic keyboards) made **Phrenology** (2002) a case in point for the marriage of technology, composition and performance, transforming hip-hop music into avantgarde architecture; and its successors **Game Theory** (2006) and **Rising Down** (2008) refined their invention (catchy, agitprop, beat-based and cross-stylistic music) by wedding those lush production values with dark and high-energy vibrations.

The horizon further expanded with Chicago's <u>Common Sense</u> (Lonnie Rashied Lynn), who evolved from the mellow jazz-hop of **Resurrection** (1994) to **Electric Circus** (2003), an experiment reminiscent of psychedelic and progressive-rock, and with New York's Dante "<u>Mos Def</u>" Smith (1), who reacted to gangsta-rap by bring back the serious-minded philosophy of the "Native Tongues" posse while at the same time accomodating rock, soul and funk on the phantasmagoric **Black on Both Sides** (1999).

Basically, hip-hop music had fragmented along three seismic faults of rebellion: one could vent negro anger as a gangsta, as an Afronationalist militant or... by playing jazz music.

Hip-hop domination

By the mid 1990s, hip-hop had dramatically evolved from an art of "messages" that were spoken in a conversational tone over an elementary rhythmic base to an art of cadenced speech in an emphatic and melodramatic tone over an intricate rhythmic collage. Regardless of the "message" that was now being broadcasted, the sense of black self-affirmation had moved to the forefront. The main continuity with the original form of Grandmaster Flash was in the "urban" setting of the music: except for free-jazz, no other form of black music had been so viscerally tied to the urban environment.

During the 1990s, hip-hop spread outside of its traditional bases (New York and Los Angeles), reaching the far corners of the globe.

Acid-rap, a morbid style related to Gravediggaz's horrocore, was coined by Detroit's rapper and producer <u>Esham</u> (Rashaam Smith), both on his solo album **Boomin' Words From Hell** (1990), recorded when he was 15, and on the harsh and disturbing **Life After Death** (1992), credited to his group <u>NATAS</u> ("Satan" spelled backwards).

Southernplayalisticadillacmuzik (1994) by Atlanta's <u>Outkast</u> (1), the duo of Andre "Dre" Benjamin and Antwan "Big Boi" Patton, was representative of the rise of southern hip-hop, with its emphasis on soul melodies and pop arrangements. Outkast turned hip-hop into a new form of space funkadelia on their sumptuous kaleidoscopes of aural ecstasy, **Aquemini** (1998) and **Stankonia** (2000) Another product of the Atlanta school was <u>Goodie Mob</u>'s **Soul Food** (1995), fronted by vocalist Thomas "Cee-Lo Green" Callaway and credited with starting the "Dirty South" movement; while Master P assembled the No Limit posse in New Orleans.

The limitations of Southern gangsta rap were well represented in Texas by <u>UGK</u> (Underground Kingz), the rapping duo of Bun B (Bernard Freeman) and Pimp C (Chad Butler), who debuted with **The Southern Way** (1992). The "hard" sound of that album rapidly disappeared in favor of a smooth radio-friendly sound, leading to the bestsellers **Ridin'**

Dirty (1996) and **Underground Kingz** (2007). While Pimp C died in 2007 from a drug overdose, the effervescent Bun B launched a successful solo career with the eclectic and star-studded **Trill** (2005) and **II Trill** (2008).

In Britain, Fundamental, the brainchild of Aki "Propa-Gandhi" Nawaz, attempted an original and brutal fusion of hip-hop, industrial music and world-music on **Seize The Time** (1994), propelling his agit-prop raps with a style reminiscent of Tackhead, Consolidated and Public Enemy. And Asian Dub Foundation, a London-based sound system of ethnic Indian musicians halfway between Tackhead and Clash, concocted the militant ethnic-punk-folk-dance music of **Rafi's Revenge** (1998).

Irish communist rappers Marxman sounded like the British version of Public Enemy on **33 Revolutions Per Minute** (1992), but without the musical talent.

The most influential idea was perhaps the one pioneered by the Ragga Twins (Trevor and David Destouche) on **Reggae Owes Me Money** (1991): the fusion of reggae and hip-hop breakbeats (that would lead to a whole new genre, "jungle").

MC Solaar (Senegal-born Claude M'Barali) catapulted French hip-hop to the forefront of the international scene with the brilliant **Qui Seme le Vent Recolte le Tempo** (1991) and **Prose Combat** (1994).

Assalti Frontali, the leading hip-hop posse of Italy, unleashed the confrontational manifestos **Terra di Nessuno** (1992) and the hardcore-tinged **Conflitto** (1996).

Instrumental hip-hop

Crucial for the development of an atmospheric pseudo-dance genre was instrumental hip-hop.

Instrumental hip-hop was largely legitimized by a Los Angeles native resident in London, DJ Shadow (1), born Josh Davis. A legendary turntablist, Davis used prominent bass lines and scratches to detonate his extended singles *Entropy* (1993) and *In/Flux* (1993), and basically bridged classical music and hip-hop on elaborate, multi-part compositions such as *What Does Your Soul Look Like* (1995). **Endtroducing** (1996) was possibly the first respectable album of all-instrumental hip-hop, entirely composed on the sampler but nonetheless lushly orchestrated.

The dub-tinged soundscapes of New York's Skiz "Spectre" Fernando (2) were best deployed on the imposing gothic, post-apocalyptic trilogy of **The Illness** (1995), **The Second Coming** (1997) and **The End** (1999), each of them the hip-hop equivalent of a William Blake poem.

Japanese dj DJ Krush added a jazzy tinge to the idea on **Strictly Turntablised** (1994) and **Ki-Oku** (1998), featuring trumpeter Toshinori Kondo.

With DJ Shadow, Spectre and DJ Krush operating in three different regions, the genre of instrumental, sample-based hip-hop became an international koine.

Urban soul

"Urban" was the nickname grafted to the smooth and sophisticated rhythm'n'blues ballad of the late 1980s, best personified by Janet Jackson (Michael's sister) and Whitney Houston. Jackson debuted with **Control** (1986), crafted by producers Jimmy Jam (James Harris) and Terry Lewis that offered urban soul music tinged with hip-hop beats to propel her sensual whisper. Houston exploded with *Saving All My Love For You* (1985), *How Will I Know* (1985), *Greatest Love Of All* (1985), *I Wanna Dance With Somebody* (1987), *Didn't We Almost Have It All* (1987) and *One Moment In Time* (1988).

Urban soul came to dominate pop music as well, thanks to the Los Angeles-based stars of Shalamar's singer Jody Watley, Brandy Norwood and Macy Gray (born Natalie McIntyre), revealed by the moribund growl of *I Try* (1999), a rousing ballad composed with keyboardist Jeremy Ruzumna, bassist David Wilder and guitarist Jinsoo Lim.

The fact that black female artists such as Whitney Houston and Janet Jackson came to dominate the charts and set new sale records was, if nothing else, proof that black artists and female artists had made tremendous progress in being accepted by a world that used to worship only male white idols such as the Beatles and Elvis Presley.

Urban soul became a much more rhythmic affair in 1988, after Jimmy Jam and Terry Lewis produced Janet Jackson's **Control** (1986), Antonio "L.A." Reid and Kenneth "Babyface" Edmonds produced the Pebbles' **Pebbles** (1987) and after Teddy Riley produced Keith Sweat's **Make It Last Forever** (1987). Finally, Teddy Riley's own group Guy and Bobby Brown's second album, **Don't Be Cruel** (1988), also produced by L.A. Reid and Babyface, fused urban soul with hip-hop to create "new jack swing". Bobby Brown had beeen a member of teenage-group New Edition, whose biggest hit, *Cool It Now* (1984), was probably the first to use rapping in a pop-soul context. Jimmy Jam and Terry Lewis topped everybody else with Janet Jackson's second album, **Rhythm Nation 1814** (1989). Later, the style was perfected by producer Sean "Puffy" Combs on Mary J. Blige's **What's the 411?** (1992), and by producers/writers Tim "Timbaland" Mosley and Melissa "Missy" Elliott on the second album by teen-idol Aaliyah (Haughton), **One In A Million** (1996).

The most successful of the new jack swing artists were Philadelphia's Boyz II Men, who established their "hip-wop" style (new jack swing plus four-part harmonies a` la doo-wop) with **Cooleyhighharmony** (1991), produced by Michael Bivins of the New Edition, and churned out colossal hits such as the Babyface-penned *End of the Road* (1992), that broke a record held by Elvis Presley since 1956, *I'll Make Love to You* (1994), another Babyface creation (which even beat the previous record), *On Bended Knee* (1994), produced by Jimmy Jam & Terry Lewis (a hit which beat their own record), and *One Sweet Day* (1995), a duet with Mariah Carey (which, again, broke their own previous record). The era of new jack swing ended with Usher (Raymond)'s **My Way** (1997), produced by Jermaine Dupri, Babyface and Sean "Puffy" Combs, and by multi-instrumentalist Robert "R" Kelly, whose double album **R** (1998) marked a revival of classic soul music. Kelly later premiered his campy, cartoonish television soap hip-hopera **Trapped In The Closet** (2005-07) that looked like a parody of the whole scene.

The spiritual message and the Caribbean-pop-rap fusion of London-born Des'ree Weekes came to focus on **I Ain't Movin'** (1994).

Assembled in 1988 by Los Angeles writers/producers Denzil Foster and Thomas McElroy (both former Club Nouveau), the female quartet En Vogue rejuvinated the concept of the "girl group" for the video age with their second album **Funky Divas** (1992). However, the new vanguard of female rhythm'n'blues groups was represented by TLC, the brainchild of producer Dallas Austin, that debuted with **Oooooooohhh** (1992). They, in turn, inspired Houston's Destiny's Child (featuring the rising star of Beyonce Knowles), who came to dominate the charts at the turn of the century.

The Minneapolis sextet Mint Condition was the most competent combo of mainstream rhythm'n'blues throughout the 1990s, from *Breakin' My Heart* (1991) to *What Kind of Man Would I Be* (1996).

A revival of soul music, updated to the technology of the hip-hop era, was heralded by D'Angelo's **Brown Sugar** (1995), and by Maxwell's **Urban Hang Suite** (1996), a sumptuous Marvin Gaye-style romantic concept album.

In fact, the soul revival had been predated by, yet again, the influential production duo of L.A. Reid and Babyface, for example on Toni Braxton's two massive bestsellers, **Toni Braxton** (1993) and **Secrets** (1996), the latter containing one of the most famous ballads of all times (*Un-break My Heart*, composed by Diane Warren).

Roots-rock in the Age of Alt-country

Alt Country

A revolution in roots-rock began in the late 1980s in Chicago with Souled American and Uncle Tupelo, and in the 1990s became a new genre altogether. It was Nashville's country music transposed into the small bedrooms of the disaffected youth in the small towns of the heartland. Those bands had rediscovered country and folk music for the hardcore generation: their descendants dumped hardcore for the most spartan and traditional of sounds.

Led by singer-songwriters Jay Farrar and Jeff Tweedy, Uncle Tupelo (1) pretty much invented a new genre when they released **No Depression** (1990), a collection of country ballads played with the fury of hardcore. Abandoning the punk edge and focusing on the depressed stories, the acoustic tour de force of **March 16-20 1992** (1992) invented more than a genre: it created a movement for sincere, populist and political music. **Anodyne** (1993) hinted at the mainstream appeal of this idea. After they parted ways, the two leaders would form two of the most influential bands of the 1990s: Son Volt and Wilco.

Kentucky's Will Oldham (1), who also recorded under the monikers Palace Brothers, Palace Songs, Palace Music, Palace and Bonnie Prince Billy, virtually jumpstarted the "alt-country" movement with **There Is No One What Will Take Care Of You** (1993), an album that displayed the qualities of independent alternative rock while playing old-fashioned country music. Oldham's acoustic folk was not terribly emotional: **Days In The Wake** (1994) was perhaps his most personal statement.

The acoustic revival spread to Kentucky, where Freakwater had already been active. A collaboration between Eleventh Dream Day's drummer Janet Bean and Catherine Ann Irwin, two singer/songwriters who seemed little concerned with the alternative/avantgarde rock of their time, Freakwater began in the vein of primitive folk music but evolved with **Old Paint** (1995) to deliver a bleak vision of humankind in a stark, neutral style.

Alt-country, or (from Uncle Tupelo's classic album) "no-depression folk", ruled the second half of the decade, and influenced even bands that had little to do with the acoustic revival.

New York's Ida delivered the old-fashioned, melancholy folk ballads of **Tales Of Brave Ida** (1994).

Chicago's Handsome Family (1) composed the solemn parables of **Milk And Scissors** (1996), infused with a cruel sense of urban alienation, and reached their "literary" peak with the dark, obsessive vignettes of **In the Air** (1999).

Los Angeles' Grant Lee Buffalo (1), led by Shiva Burlesque's guitarist Grant Lee Phillips, penned **Fuzzy** (1993), whose style was power-pop that sounded like folk music, an odd hybrid of American Music Club, Woody Guthrie and Big Star.

Tennessee's <u>Lambchop</u> (11) coined a form of "chamber folk". The pieces on **I Hope You're Sitting Down** (1994) were artful disguises of a gentle and downbeat minstrel (guitarist/frontman Kurt Wagner) in a maze of keyboards, horns and strings. The music was more often funereal than exuberant, and the atmosphere was the equivalent of "film noir" in a Nashville setting. **How I Quit Smoking** (1996) was a more private affair, but still wrapped in arrangements that were pastoral, neoclassical, nostalgic and dreamy. If sometimes Lambchop's albums sacrificed substance for elegance and occasionally veered into a bland hybrid of country and soul balladry, ever more formidable ensembles helped to craft works such as the rock opera **Nixon** (2000) that were poetic but formulaic, austere but diluted, gentle but superficial, transcendental but mundane: this intermediate state became the metaphysical location of Wagner's art, the ecosystem where the crystalline ambient elegies of **Damaged** (2006) and **OH** (2008) thrived. As Wagner's skills as an arranger matured, the most effective instrument on his crowded songs became his rough voice, simply because it was the ultimate antithetic sound to the gentle symphony that lay underneath.

Quite unique was the baroque, new-age sound of Louisiana's <u>Subdudes</u>, for example on **Annunciation** (1994).

Country-rock

Modern country-rock was best represented by Detroit's <u>Volebeats</u> (1), whose eclectic and schizophrenic style, that incorporated surf music, world music, Ennio Morricone and many other influences, was best immortalized on their fourth album **Solitude** (2000).

Ohio's <u>Ass Ponys</u> (1) concocted one of the most original variants on country-rock on **Mr Superlove** (1990), that was rustic in principle but afflicted by urban neurosis in practice.

Boston's <u>Blood Oranges</u> fused bluegrass and grunge on **The Crying Tree** (1994).

Among the works that renovated the country style with the impetus and eccentricity of alternative rock were: **Bottle Rockets** (1993), by Missouri's <u>Bottle Rockets</u>; **Toreador Of Love** (1993), by Oregon's <u>Hazel</u>, featuring guitarist Peter Krebs; **Play Cell** (1994), by San Francisco's <u>Tilt</u>; **For The Sake Of Argument** (1995), the second album by Kentucky's <u>Stranglmartin</u>; **The Medicine Is All Gone** (1998), the third album by Idaho's <u>Caustic Resin</u>; **Too Far To Care** (1997), the third album by Texas' <u>Old 97's</u>.

At the same time, cow-punks mutated into something even weirder. Chicago's <u>New Duncan Imperials</u> applied Bonzo Dog Band's aesthetics to the country and blues tradition on **Hanky Panky Party Voo** (1990);

Pennsylvania's Strapping Fieldhands applied the Holy Modal Rounders aesthetics (atonal guitars and grotesque vocals) to Appalachian folk music on **Discus** (1994).

The Grifters (11), the project of Tennessee songwriters Scott Taylor and David Shouse, were the terrorists of alt-country: **So Happy Together** (1992) was to roots-music what Sonic Youth's noise-rock had been to classic rock, a barbaric psycho-industrial bacchanal that rarely coalesced, a merry-go-round of drunk vocals, atonal guitars and erratic rhythms. Just a bit less grotesque and abrasive, **One Sock Missing** (1993) still evoked the specters of Captain Beefheart, Red Crayola and Pussy Galore. A better structured and bluesier approach surfaced on **Crappin' You Negative** (1994) and the EP **Eureka** (1995) achieved a synthesis of sorts, offering "tunes" that were both catchy and demonic. Not surprisingly, **Ain't My Lookout** (1996) and **Full Blown Possession** (1997) ended up sounding like the Rolling Stones.

Southern blues-rock staged a powerful comeback with Georgia's Black Crowes (1), whose tasty imitation of the Rolling Stones and the Faces (but more soul-rock than blues-rock) on **Shake Your Money Maker** (1990) was briefly a sensation.

Folk-rock

Several San Francisco-based groups significantly updated the folk-rock canon: X-Tal, with **Reason Is 6/7 Of Treason** (1990), Harm Farm, with **Spawn** (1990), Bedlam Rovers, best on **Wallow** (1993), Tarnation, with **Gentle Creatures** (1995). Best of this batch were Swell (1), who derailed the archaic structures of blues and country music with extravagant dynamics and arrangements. **Swell** (1991) and especially **Well?** (1993) were festivals of the irregular, coupled with existential lyrics.

But the most successful were the Counting Crows, whose style on **August And Everything After** (1993) was a humbler take on classic roots-rock (Van Morrison-ian vocals, Byrds-ian guitar jangle and gospel organ a` la Band).

Cracker (1), led by former Camper Van Beethoven's vocalist David Lowery, unleashed the virulent roots-rock of **Kerosene Hat** (1993).

Sacramento's Cake toyed with country, blues, tex-mex, funk, reggae and salsa stereotypes dressing them up on **Motorcade Generosity** (1994) with quirky arrangements and an eclectic sense of humour that evoked Camper Van Beethoven and Primus.

A South Carolina band, Hootie & The Blowfish, which debuted with the charming **Cracked Rear View** (1994), was responsible with the Counting Crows for the continuing popularity of folk-rock. They were also the first rock band fronted by a black vocalist (Darius Rucker) to attain mainstream success.

Louisiana's <u>Better Than Ezra</u> (1), led by Kevin Griffin, attained a higher standard of philosophical depth with their second album **Deluxe** (1995).

Pan-ethnic music

World-music got more and more sophisticated, but fewer and fewer artists offered original ideas. Notable among creative works that used ethnic styles were **Rapid** (1997), by Hungary's <u>Kampec Dolores</u>, **Mlah** (1990), by the French acoustic mini-orchestra <u>Les Negresses Vertes</u>, **Allegria** (1990), by French combo the <u>Gypsy Kings</u>, **Phyidar** (1992), by Belgium's <u>Raksha Mancham</u>, **Monostress 225L** (1992), by French steel band <u>Les Tambours Du Bronx</u>, and **The Rhythm Of The Ritual** (1994), by Belgium's <u>Hybryds</u>.

Perhaps the most creative world-music ensemble in the world was the Polish ensemble <u>Atman</u> (2), whose **Personal Forest** (1993) and **Tradition** (1999) were collages of surreal blends of Eastern and Western music, in the vein of the Third Ear Band and the Incredible String Band. Atman's multi-instrumentalist Marek Styczynski and vocalist Anna Nacher started a new project, Projekt Karpaty Magiczne, or <u>Magic Carpathians Project</u>, devoted to an ambient, cosmic, jazz version of Atman's pan-ethnic music on **Ethnocore II** (2001).

One of the effects of globalization was that traditional ethnic music was being rapidly abandoned by the new generations for modern USA-style pop ballads or melodic rock music. The biggest stars in both China and India were singers of original material modeled after USA's pop melodies (and often set to electronic rhythms). Latin America, Sub-Saharan Africa and the Middle East were perhaps the areas that best incorporated the traditional instruments and rhythms. However, globalization was creating a more and more uniform musical landscape across the globe. For example, Chinese superstar Han Hong, a Tibetan female singer who debuted on album in 1983, sang pop ballads over western rhythms. Even traditional songs and "classical" music were often performed with string orchestra and drums. Basically, ethnic music as such was rapidly disappearing and being replaced by music rooted in western ideas of melody, harmony and rhythm.

The Age of Emocore

Emocore, 1989-94

While magazines kept publicizing the "death of punk-rock", hardcore became a pervasive movement that did not leave any town (or country) untouched. As if galvanized by its own death, the movement took on a life of its own and became a genre within the genre. In the 1990s that genre, in turn, spawned a number of sub-genres.

First and foremost, there was "emocore", the style invented in the late 1980s by Rites Of Spring and the Washington contingent. Their "emotional" hardcore alternated quiet and furious musical parts, admitted moody arrangements, indulged in time changes and mid-tempo rhythms, leveraged emotional singing that could whisper as well as shout within the same song, and was not limited to the short/fast format of hardcore. In other words, it was almost the negation of hardcore.

While the genre was, by definition, rather loose, bands that fell into the category during the 1990s included: San Francisco's Jawbreaker, with **Unfun** (1990); Oregon's Heatmiser, the group of songwriter Elliott Smith and bassist Sam Coomes (formerly of Donner Party), with **Dead Air** (1993); Los Angeles' Weezer, the most successful of the batch, with **Weezer** (1994).

Seattle's Sunny Day Real Estate (2), the vehicle for songwriter Jeremy Enigk (the prototypical anguished voice of emocore), legitimized artistically the genre with the lengthy and elaborate compositions of **Diary** (1994) and **How It Feels To Be Something On** (1998).

Seaweed (1) moved from the popcore of **Weak** (1992) to the grunge, metal and punk hybrid of **Four** (1993) to the power-ballads of **Spanaway** (1995), showing a maturity that was unusual within the hardcore scene; and then vocalist Aaron Stauffer, a worthy heir to the melodic/populist tradition of Bob Mould (Husker Du) and Paul Westerberg (Replacements), formed Gardener (1) with Screaming Trees' bassist Van Conner, which released the natural evolution of Seaweed's sound: the romantic **New Dawning Time** (1999).

New Jersey's Wrens invented a form of "emo-pop" with **Secaucus** (1996) and perfected it to a manic degree on **Meadowlands** (2003).

Emocore represented the terminal point of the trajectory of punk-rock that started in 1976. Back then punk-rock was nihilistic: it boasted that it had no meaning, that it had no interest in society, that it had no emotion. However, shortly thereafter, punks began to show political awareness. Punk-rock acquired a meaning (whether left-wing or right-wing), displayed not indifference for society but a deep-seated anger, and basically transferred the power of the music to the public level. Not only did emocore have a meaning, but that meaning was now highly private, retreating from the social sphere to the individual sphere. Not only did emocore display emotions, but it was highly emotional. Despite the similarity in tone, emocore represented almost the exact opposite of what punk-rock aimed to be in 1976.

Washington's progressive hardcore

Washington was still the home of a highly-creative hardcore scene, the epitome of "progressive hardcore".

Nation Of Ulysses (10) concocted the explosive, theatrical agit-prop sound of **Plays Pretty For Baby** (1992), an album that was the Clinton-age equivalent of MC5 and Public Enemy. The band's cacophony was tamed by hysterical vocalist Ian Svenonius in an epic way. Guitarist Tim Green moved to San Francisco and formed the Fucking Champs, while Svenonius reformed the band with a slightly different line-up and a new name, Make-Up (2): **Destination Love** (1996), a conceptual exercise of community-based music, and the more organic **In Mass Mind** (1998) experimented with a deranged gospel-funk-rock sound borrowed from Gang Of Four, Pop Group and Contortions.

Shudder To Think (1) became the King Crimson of hardcore with **Get Your Goat** (1992) and **Pony Express Record** (1994), featuring new guitarist Nathan Larson, that were full of sophisticated and eccentric nuances.

Jawbox (1), led by former Government Issue's bassist Jay Robbins, created an opus that was both melodic and eclectic, charged with pathos as well as neurosis, on **Grippe** (1991) and **Novelty** (1992), only to increase the doses of electricity on **For Your Own Special Sweetheart** (1994).

Edsel (1) not only applied the noise-rock lessons of Sonic Youth, Dinosaur Jr and My Bloody Valentine on **Everlasting Belt Co** (1993) but continued to evolve it until they reached the level of polish, adulteration and elasticity of **Techniques Of Speed Hypnosis** (1995)

Lungfish (2) were the vehicle for Daniel Higgs' sociopolitical philosophizing. His favorite medium was the tension-filled and almost messianic simplicity of **Pass And Stow** (1994), and eventually he and his cohorts fell under the spell of Indian ragas and Buddhist trance on **Indivisible** (1997) and **Artificial Horizon** (1998).

Circus Lupus (1) experimented with post-hardcore ideas that were as adventurous and irregular as Minutemen's and Saccharine Trust's on **Super Genius** (1992), displaying a technical prowess that was virtually unmatched. Circus Lupus' vocalist Chris Thomson and guitarist Chris Hamley started Monorchid (1) to pursue a sound that was even more jarring and feverish, as documented on **Let Them Eat** (1997).

No other scene in the world mustered so many talents as Washington's.

Ska-core

The fusion of ska and punk-rock, pioneered in Britain in the late 1970s, became extremely popular everywhere in the USA during the 1990s.

The San Francisco Bay Area was one of the epicenters of the ska-punk revolution. Operation Ivy were part of Berkeley's legendary "Gilman Street" scene, but their album **Energy** (1989) stretched beyond punk-rock, encompassing ska and surf. From their ashes, two groups were born. Their guitarist, Tim "Lint" Armstrong, formed Rancid (1), and proceeded to sell the idea to the masses. **Rancid** (1993) and especially **Let's Go** (1994) disguised the rebellious spirit of hardcore under the appearance of exuberant wit, irresistible rhythms and catchy refrains. It was Clash's recipe for a new generation. The less threatening potion of **And Out Come The Wolves** (1995) found an even bigger audience. The other group, Dance Hall Crashers (1), boasted two female singers and favored joyful fanfares played with a naive verve more akin to girl-groups of the Sixties than hardcore of the Nineties, particularly on **Lockjaw** (1995).

Commercial success came with Boston's Mighty Mighty Bosstones, who penned amusing collections such as **Question The Answers** (1994), and Florida's Less Than Jake, who delivered the explosive **Pezcore** (1994).

Los Angeles became the capital of ska-core thanks to: Bradley Nowell's Sublime (1), who coined one of the most anthemic styles on **40 Oz To Freedom** (1992); No Doubt, fronted by a female vocalist (Gwen Stefani), who broke through with **Tragic Kingdom** (1995); Voodoo Glow Skulls, with generic packages such as **Band Geek Mafia** (1998).

Best in England were probably Citizen Fish, born from the ashes of the Subhumans, and best in the rest of Europe were probably Sweden's Millencolin.

Punk-pop

Hardcore climbed the charts (twenty years after it was invented by the Ramones) with "popcore", the new variation on Buzzcock's punk-pop. It was, again, San Francisco that bridged the gap between the charts and the punks.

By capitalizing on the style pioneered in the mid 1980s by Mr T Experience, Green Day (1) became one of the money-making machines of the decade, thanks to the infectious hooks and riffs of **Dookie** (1994) and to the generic pop of *Time Of Your Life* (1997) and *Minority* (2000).

The Seattle scene, which had been primed by the Fastbacks, yielded several of the best pop-core bands.

Rusty Willoughby's Pure Joy belonged to the generation of the Fastbacks, but emerged only with **Carnivore** (1990). Willoughby and the Fastbacks's drummer Nate Johnson formed Flop (1), who revisited the deceptive simplicity of Cheap Trick and the Buzzcocks on impeccable packages such as **Flop & The Fall Of The Mopsqueezer** (1992) and especially **Whenever You're Ready** (1993).

Although its bands (Descendents, Bad Religion and the likes) had inspired Green Day, in the 1990s Los Angeles was, de facto, a colony of San Francisco, recycling whatever was successful up north. Pennywise (1) led the charge with **Pennywise** (1991), and a sound that, while respectful of the masters of "beach punk", was also more pensive and atmospheric, eventually achieving the depth of **Unknown Road** (1993). Many of the Los Angeles bands of this generation surfaced after Green Day's breakthrough, but had been roaming the city's clubs for years. Most successful of them all were Offspring, that competed with Green Day's mass appeal on **Smash** (1994).

The Humpers sounded more sincere than the average of these clones of Screeching Weasel, because their **Positively Sick On 4th Street** (1992) harked back to the original style of the Ramones and the New York Dolls.

Chicago, the city where Screeching Weasel had preached the gospel of punk-pop, boasted perhaps the greatest of punk-poppers, Pegboy (11). Formed by Naked Raygun's guitarist John Haggerty and other hardcore veterans, they crafted a sound that was frantic and barbaric, but that, at the same time, carried hummable tunes. Every single beat of **Strong Reaction** (1991) was "wrong" in a unique way that made it just about "perfect", delivering a dynamite emotional punch straight to the core of Haggerty's stories. Abandoning the excesses of that stormy and visceral style, Pegboy penned **Earwig** (1994), hell's version of Green Day.

Rick Valentin's Poster Children started out with the brainy noise-rock of **Tool Of Man** (1992), featuring drummer John Herndon, but converted to a more accessible style on **Junior Citizen** (1995).

Another bastion of punk-pop was located in North Carolina: Mac McCaughan's Superchunk (1) resurrected the original spirit of punk-rock, but without the negative overtones (the Ramones rather than the Sex Pistols). The exuberant mood of their second album, **No Pocky For Kitty** (1991), was almost the anti-thesis of hardcore. Mac McCaughan's alter-ego, Portastatic, originally formed to vent the more introspective side of his art, eventually merged with Superchunk's punk-pop, and possibly obscured it, on **The Summer of the Shark** (2003) and **Bright Ideas** (2005).

New Hampshire's Queers (1) delivered a barrage of catchy, pummeling refrains on **Love Songs For The Retarded** (1993), coupled with outrageously decadent sex/drugs lyrics, and eventually turned their career into a tribute to the Ramones.

England's punk-pop elite basically comprised five bands: Leatherface, whose **Mush** (1991) was perhaps the greatest album of this generation, Senseless Things, Ned's Atomic Dustbin , Mega City Four and Seers.

While they probably did not deserve the notoriety granted to them by the British press, their sound at least stood up to the avalanche of Brit-pop.

The sound of Green Day was exported to Canada by <u>Cub</u>, with **Betti-Cola** (1993), and to Australia by <u>The Living End</u>, who found mainstream success with **The Living End** (1998).

California garage-punk

An eclectic punk-rock style was pioneered in San Diego by <u>Pitchfork</u>, the band of guitarist John Reis and vocalist Rick Farr, who recorded **Eucalyptus** (1990) and went on to form <u>Drive Like Jehu </u>(11), one of the most innovative punk bands in the world. They first turned angst into a shimmering cascade of emotions on **Drive Like Jehu** (1991), and then proceeded to compose the soundtrack of a nervous breakdown on **Yank Crime** (1994), one of the most catastrophic and excoriating albums of the time, whose vocabulary was so complex and effective that guitar-based punk songs began to sound like hyper-dramatic mini-symphonies.

<u>Rocket From The Crypt</u> (11), the new band formed by Drive Like Jehu's guitarist John "Speedo" Reis, embodied the quintessence of both 1960s' garage-punk and 1990s' hardcore. **Paint As A Fragrance** (1991), a parade of lethal, abrasive, turbo-charged acts of fury, was only the appetizer for **Circa Now** (1993), an anthemic synthesis of wild rock'n'roll that evoked the Fleshtones as well as the Heartbreakers. Their art of riffs was so recklessly retro that albums such as **Scream Dracula Scream** (1995) and **RFTC** (1998) sounded like collections of covers.

Albums such as <u>aMiniature</u>'s **Plexiwatt** (1992) and <u>Fluf</u>'s **Mangravy** (1993) laid the foundations for the scene that eventually yielded the commercial success that Tom Delonge's <u>Blink 182</u> attained with their fifth album **Enema Of The State** (1999).

In San Francisco, <u>Zen Guerrilla</u> (2) blended punk's demented speed with black music (blues, soul and rhythm'n'blues) on the roaring **Positronic Raygun** (1998), the fervent **Trance States In Tongues** (1999) and the visceral **Shadows On The Sun** (2001), albums that capitalized on many earlier EPs.

Jazzcore

"Jazzcore" thrived in the background, but the idea (that had been pioneered by the likes of the Minutemen, Universal Congress, Saccharine Trust and others) fueled the creative work of numerous bands. The Los Angeles school was continued by <u>Bazooka</u> (1), saxophonist Tony Atherton's hardcore adaptation of the ideas of Frank Zappa, Albert Ayler and Thelonious Monk, particularly on **Perfectly Square** (1993), and by <u>Trash Can School</u>, whose **Sick Jokes And Wet**

Dreams (1992) harked back to the visceral blues-punk sound of Pop Group and Birthday Party.

Utah's Iceburn (2) fused the languages of progressive-rock, jazz, metal and hardcore on **Firon** (1992) and on the monumental **Hephaestus** (1993). The latter's brainy jams opened a number of stylistic avenues that would take the band a decade to fully explore. **Poetry Of Fire** (1995) introduced elements of classical music and atonal avantgarde, not to mention Indian ragas, while veering towards the loose structures of free-jazz, a metamorphosis that continued on Iceburn Collective's **Meditavolutions** (1996), featuring the suite *Sphinx*, one of their most terrible and accomplished works, and was completed with the three lengthy group improvisations of **Polar Bear Suite** (1997).

San Diego's Creedle unleashed **Silent Weapons For Quiet Wars** (1994), inspired by John Zorn's hyper-kinetic nonsense jazz.

Old school

More or less straightfoward hardcore punk-rock was still pervasive, from New York's crowded scene to Los Angeles' super-crowded scene. Best in New York (and most faithful to the Ramones and the Sex Pistols) were D Generation, with **D Generation** (1994). New York also boasted a vigorous "straight-edge" movement, best represented by Shelter, the new band of Youth Of Today's singer Ray Cappo.

Seattle boasted two of the best revival bands. Supersuckers (1) indulged in Ramones-ian verve on **The Smoke Of Hell** (1992), and Zeke (1) unwound a breathless parade of lightning-speed bullets on their second album **Flat Tracker** (1996).

Ohio's Gaunt, with rapid-fire collections such as **Kryptonite** (1996), were also among the best disciples of the Ramones and the Clash.

The heirs to Siege's grinding hardcore were Rhode Island's Drop Dead, who, just like their mentors, recorded very little, mostly on **Drop Dead** (1993).

England was awash in the sweet sound of Brit-pop and could hardly nurture a hardcore scene. However, Silverfish (1) propelled (and, at the same time, sabotaged) angry young girl Lesley Rankine's roars and wails with an anthemic and seismic mixture of unrefined adrenaline and concentrate vitriol on **Fat Axl** (1991) and **Organ Fan** (1992).

Norway's glam-punks Turbonegro (1) eventually recorded one of the most impressive hardcore works of the decade, their fourth album **Apocalypse Dudes** (1998), that sounded like a hardcore version of Alice Cooper and Kiss.

The atonal ferocity of Sweden's Brainbombs was devoted to the most lascivious, sadistic and murderous instincts, like a seriously (not comically) deranged version of the Cramps. The sound of **Burning Hell**

(1992) and **Genius and Brutality Taste and Power** (1994) was a sloppy exaggeration of the Stooges with cameos from a jazz trumpet.

Post-hardcore

The influence of avantgarde hardcore bands such as Fugazi, Henry Rollins and Jesus Lizard led to a "post-hardcore" style that was convoluted, jittery, sinister and ugly.

Seattle's Unwound (14), the vehicle for Justin Trosper's epileptic sermons, learned the lessons of Sonic Youth, Fugazi and Jesus Lizard and applied them to the brutal, harrowing vision of **Fake Train** (1993), broadening the lexicon of hardcore with techniques that borrowed from the blues as well as from the avantgarde, while maximizing the emotional impact. It was music that transpired angst and alienation, music of harsh tones, agonizing tempos and demonic vocals. Unwound's essay in intolerable tension continued with **New Plastic Ideas** (1994) and **The Future Of What** (1995), that channelled Trosper's hellish angst into a Morse code of ghastly shrieks and gut-wrenching riffs. While flirting with jazz and avantgarde manners, **Repetition** (1996) and **Challenge For A Civilized Society** (1998) clarified the subtle mission of the band: a sound that was as loud as the sense of confusion and insecurity of their generation.

Phatom 309's vocalist/guitarist John Forbes recorded the raw and vulgar **Sahara Of The Bozart** (1992) with Dirt and then the frenzied and dark **Put The Creep On** (1994) with Mount Shasta.

Texas bred a school of musicians who blended elements of different local schools of the 1980s: hardcore (e.g., Poison 13), psychedelic (e.g., Butthole Surfers) and industrial (e.g., Pain Teens). Crust (1) crafted **Crust** (1991) and especially **Crusty Love** (1994), a chaotic, claustrophobic and cacophonous post-industrial symphony. Drain (1), the side-project of Butthole Surfers' drummer King Coffey, mixed Red Crayola, John Cage and nursery-school mayhem on **Pick Up Heaven** (1992). The music of **Pistol Swing** (1993) by Johnboy (1) sounded like a chain reaction inside a nuclear reactor, a repulsive magma of manic impulses and subhuman hallucinations.

Several bands from Illinois and Minnesota straddled the line between hardcore and grunge, notably Janitor Joe, on **Big Metal Birds** (1993), and Tar, on **Jackson** (1991).

The "crossover" style of the early 1980s, pioneered by hardcore bands that incorporated heavy-metal elements (Agnostic Front, Bad Brains, Corrosion of Conformity) was revitalized in New York by two bands that, de facto, invented "metalcore": Judge, the new band of Youth of Today's Mike Ferraro and John Porcell, with **Bringin' It Down** (1989), and Killing Time with **Brightside** (1989).

From Grindcore to Stoner-rock

A metal nation

If the 1980s had been the golden age of heavy metal, the age when heavy metal was accepted by the masses and climbed the charts, the 1990s saw the fragmentation of the genre into rather different styles, that simply expanded on ideas of the 1980s.

As usual, pop-metal, the genre that appealed to the masses, was, artistically speaking, the least significant variant of heavy metal. It spawned stars such as Los Angeles' Warrant, with **Cherry Pie** (1990); Boston's Extreme, who specialized in "metal-operas" a` la Queen such as **Pornograffiti** (1990); and Pennsylvania's Live, with **Throwing Copper** (1994); etc.

Los Angeles had to live with remnants of its "street-scene" (Guns N' Roses, Jane's Addiction), although they sounded a lot less sincere and a lot less powerful than the original masters: Ugly Kid Joe, Life Sex And Death, Dishwalla, Ednaswap, etc.

Glam-metal staged a comeback of sorts in Florida with Marilyn Manson (1), the product of Brian Warner's deranged mind. Propelled by the brutal sounds of keyboardist Madonna Wayne-Gacy and guitarist Daisy Berkowitz, Warner's theatrical exhibition of degenerate, depraved animal instinct wed Alice Cooper's scum-rock and Nine Inch Nails' industrial-hardcore on **Portrait Of An American Family** (1994). By borrowing the energy of speed-metal, **Antichrist Superstar** (1996) sold the gimmick to the masses.

The connection between hardcore and heavy-metal ("metalcore") had been kept alive by New York's Biohazard, especially on **Urban Discipline** (1993), and Boston's Converge, best on later albums such as the explosive **Jane Doe** (2000) and **You Fail Me** (2004). Converge also exhibited the influence of post-rock and therefore pioneered "mathcore". So did New Jersey's Rorschach on **Protestant** (1993).

Prog-metal

Progressive-metal was more capable of producing new ideas. Notable USA albums of the 1990s in the style of Queensryche and the likes included: **Last Decade Dead Century** (1990), by Michigan's Warrior Soul; **Wonderdrug** (1994), by New York's Naked Sun; etc.

Dream Theater (11), formed at Boston's prestigious Berklee College of Music, established a new standard for progressive metal. Their second album, **Images And Words** (1992), constructed lengthy melodic fantasias that relied on symphonic magniloquence (Kevin Moore on keyboards), fluid instrumental passages (John Petrucci on guitar), haphazard rhythms (Mike Portnoy on drums) and romantic emphasis

(James Labrie on vocals). At the same time breathless and catchy, rock and neoclassical, impulsive and brainy, this style became even more elaborate on **Awake** (1994), although it lost some of its bite, which got further diluted in the seven-movement suite *A Change Of Seasons* (1995). At the same time colossal pieces such as *Octavarium* (2005) became compendia of the prog-rock vocabulary.

Texan band <u>Absu</u>, fronted by drummer Proscriptor (Russ Givens) and featuring a synthesizer, coined an erudite and epic black-metal style devoted to esoteric and exotic themes with their second album **Sun of Tiphareth** (1995).

Likewise in Europe there were a few significant prog-metal contributions such as the symphonic metal of **Land Of Broken Hearts** (1993) by Denmark's <u>Royal Hunt</u>.

Switzerland's <u>Alboth!</u> (2), a piano-bass-drums trio, invented a new genre at the border between jazz and industrial metal, between Cecil Taylor and Young Gods. The jackhammer rhythms and torrential piano clusters of **Liebefeld** (1992) and **Ali** (1996) were both visceral and sophisticated.

Death-metal

The terrifying sound of grindcore and death-metal continued to thrive in the USA thanks to New York's <u>Brutal Truth</u> (1), with **Extreme Conditions Demand Extreme Responses** (1992), Buffalo's <u>Cannibal Corpse</u>, with **Tomb of the Mutilated** (1992), and Louisiana's <u>Acid Bath</u>, with **When The Kite String Pops** (1994). However, Death's **Human** (1991) led to a "technical" renewal of the field, of which the main proponents were two bands from New York: <u>Suffocation</u> with their **Effigy of the Forgotten** (1991), and <u>Immolation</u> with **Dawn Of Possession** (1991).

Thanks to the creative work of three groups in the USA, "death-metal" was rapidly mutating into something at the same time more terrible and more musical.

<u>Type O Negative</u> (101) in New York achieved the most shocking fusion of metal, industrial and gothic languages. With vocalist Peter "Steele" Ratajczyk convincingly impersonating a psychopath who uttered nihilist, racist, sexist and fascist invectives, keyboardist Josh Silver molding grandiose sonic architectures, and guitarist Kenny Hickey highlighting the turpitude of the stories with excoriating noises, the terrifying vision of **Slow Deep And Hard** (1991) acquired a metaphysical dimension besides and beyond its hyper-realistic overtones, bridging the philosophical themes of sex and death the way a black mass would do. Moral ambiguity translated into musical ambiguity, as anthemic choruses wavered like funereal dirges, epic riffs shrieked like agonizing spasms in the struggle for survival, and homicidal fantasies

peaked with evil apotheosis. Contrasts and juxtapositions blurred the difference between hell and paradise. Each song was structured as a sequence of movements, each movement arranged in a different fashion, and the sequence leading to unrelenting suspense. They sounded like Wagnerian mini-symphonies composed in Dante's Inferno and supercharged with fear and despair. The apocalypse subsided on **Bloody Kisses** (1993), a more sincere fresco of urban violence.

Today Is The Day (23), in Tennessee, straddled the border between grindcore, noise-rock, death-metal, hardcore, progressive-rock and industrial music. The visceral nightmares of **Supernova** (1993) were full of sonic experiments and stylistic twists, but **Willpower** (1994) went beyond the "ambience" to extract sheer angst from Steve Austin's screams and the trio's assorted cacophony. Each song sounded like a natural catastrophe, each song was the soundtrack of an irrational state of mind. Scott Wexton's sampling machines (replacing the bass player) bestowed an electronic flavor to **Today is The Day** (1996). The effect was to enhance the progressive-rock part of the equation, a fact that helped sustain the stylistic collage of **Temple Of The Morning Star** (1997): no less macabre and emphatic, the music also felt surreal and cathartic. It was still the sound of a psychological torture, but one that mirrored some kind of supernatural beauty. After the brief bursts of super-charged grindcore and religious fervor packed on **In The Eyes Of God** (1999), Austin unleashed the orgy of experimentation of the satanic monolith **Sadness Will Prevail** (2002), running the gamut from eerie piano ballads to Jimi Hendrix-style cacophony to Middle-Eastern music.

Fear Factory (11), in Los Angeles, painted their harrowing mural of urban decadence with an emphasis on rhythm: thrashing, grinding beats spread like neurotransmitters inside the nervous system of the cyberpunk manifesto **Soul of a New Machine** (1992). Songs evolved rather than just erupted. The music of **Demanufacture** (1995), featuring Front Line Assembly's keyboardist Rhys Fulber, seemed to come from another world, saturated with blasphemous truths about this world. Its cascading bombshells kept morphing into cingulate beasts and emanating poisonous miasmas.

This triad pretty much subverted the conventions of the genre, and created a new kind of music, tailored for the issues and the mood of the cyberpunk generation.

A rare attempt to fuse death-metal with progressive-rock and even jazzcore was carried out simultaneously in Florida by Atheist on **Unquestionable Presence** (1991), and by Cynic on their lone album, **Focus** (1993). Gorguts' third album **Obscura** (1998), the first one by the line-up of vocalist Luc Lemay, guitarist Steeve Hurdle, bassist Steve Cloutier and drummer Patrick Robert, offered an even more explosive fusion of atonal avantgarde, free jazz and death-metal.

Pennsylvania-based trio Exit-13, featuring vocalist Bill Yurkiewicz and guitarist Steve O'Donnell, turned **Green Is Good** (1990) into a caricature of grindcore by injecting elements of doom, jazz, acid-rock and even music-hall; basically, grindcore the way Frank Zappa would have done it.

Sweden, instead, boasted an Iron Maiden-inspired melodic death-metal movement that peaked with At The Gates' **The Red In The Sky Is Ours** (1993), Dissection's **Storm of the Light's Bane** (1995) and In Flames's **The Jester Race** (1996).

On the other hand, Sweden's Entombed embobied the classic sound of death-metal, especially on their second album **Clandestine** (1991).

Czech band Forgotten Silence ranked among the most experimental death-metal bands of their age. They established their progressive death-metal style with the double-disc **Senyaan** (1998), a concept in seven (lengthy) chapters with interludes, while the esoteric/mystical Egyptian theme became more prominent. *Come With Me As Far As Behind The Horizon*, off the mini-album **Bya Bamahe Neem** (2004), and the three extended suites of **Kro Ni Ka** (2006) unfurled stylistic kaleidoscopes that transcended the genre.

Scandinavian black metal

More or less independently of death-metal, a new school of "black metal" arose out of northern Europe, particularly in Norway where Mayhem and Bathory had planted the seeds.

Darkthrone's **A Blaze In The Northern Sky** (1991) and the bass-less **Under a Funeral Moon** (1993) coined a raw, brutal and buzz-intense sound, almost like a "garage" version of their forefathers Bathory and Mayhem, while the growling noise coming out of vocalist Ted "Nocturno Culto" Skjellum's mouth enhance the sense of damnation.

Forgotten Woods' **As The Wolves Gather** (1994), and Immortal's **Battles In The North** (1994) were the other albums that launched the genre.

Enslaved (1) were emblematic: they employed medieval and epic arias inspired by the Scandinavian folk tradition in lengthy majestic songs of dark, piercing, intense agony enhanced with synthesizers and piano on **Vikingligr Veldi** (1994), transitioning towards progressive-rock on **Eld** (1997), etc.

In The Nightside Eclipse (1994) by Emperor (1) stood as a concentrate of violence (thanks to lightning-speed drumming, satanic shrieks and frantically distorted guitar), but also as a metaphysical (and symphonic) inspection of the otherworld.

Satyricon (1) experimented with a fusion of folk music and dark metal on **Dark Medieval Times** (1993), while their "metal opera" **Nemesis**

Divina (1996) stuck to the basics, erecting a dense and intricate wall of guitar distortions and epileptic beats.

Burzum (2), the project of former Mayhem's Christian "Count Grishnackh" Vikernes (who was in prison for murder), coined an original ambient version of dark metal with the four massively droning, distorted, glacial tracks of **Hvis Lyset Tar Oss** (1994). On the other hand the instrumental monolith *Rundtgaing Av Den Transcendentale Egenbetens Stotte*, off the more eclectic **Filosofem** (1996), was just a sparse, drum-less, riff-less, drone-less electronic soundscape. Besides providing the demonic vocals, Grishnackh played all the instruments, mixing romantic keyboards with extremely distorted guitars, setting the music to demented rhythms, and screaming the lyrics like a damned soul burning in hell.

Sweden's Katatonia represented the suicidal extreme of doom-metal with **Dance of December Souls** (1993), wrapped in romantic guitar solos and atmospheric keyboards.

Sweden's Marduk (fronted by guitarist Morgan Haakansson) and Norway's Gorgoroth invented a lightning-speed version of black metal on albums such as the former's **Those of the Unlight** (1993) and **Opus Nocturne** (1994) and the latter's third album **Under The Sign Of Hell** (1997).

Finland's Beherit (1) sounded like a black-metal band drawn into a psychedelic freak-out on **Drawing Down The Moon** (1993), as close to white (black?) noise as black metal had ever come, dominated by satanic vocals (Marko Laiho) that were more interested in hissing and growling like an invisible demon than in shrieking like a wild beast.

Thanks to the harrowing lives (and deaths) of its protagonists, black metal now competed with hip hop as the most anti-social form of music in the world, having displaced hardcore punk-rock from that title.

Outside of Scandinavia, the most influential practicioners of black metal were perhaps England's Cradle Of Filth, who wed the ever more malevolent guitar riffs and drum beats of the genre with a theatrical and literary gothic stance and with symphonic keyboards on the vampire-based concept **Dusk and Her Embrace** (1997); and Abigor, an Austrian trio of black metal that featured a vocalist, a guitarist and a drummer but no full-time bassist, especially on the third album **Nachthymnen/ From the Twilight Kingdom** (1995).

Russia's Forest were faithful disciples of Burzum, except that their debut cassette **Forest** (1996) also contained the 20-minute psychedelic and progressive suite *Winter Howl* (recorded in 1994).

Graveland, the brainchild of Polish multi-instrumentalist Rob "Darken" Fudali, embraced a brooding midtempo style on their fourth album **Immortal Pride** (1998), with its two lengthy epics, on **Creed of Iron** (2000), with four lengthy visions of medieval warfare, and on **Memory**

And Destiny (2002), steadily moving towards an ambient pagan folk-metal.

The 1990s also witnessed the birth of an influential school of black metal in France. Among the pioneers were the two duos that shared the split cassette album **March to the Black Holocaust** (1995): Vlad Tepes and Belketre. Most influential of all were Willy Roussel's Mutiilation, whose **Vampires of Black Imperial Blood** (1995) was the best approximation of the Scandinavian classics.

Dark ambient music in continental Europe peaked with Paysage D'Hiver (Swiss guitarist Tobias Moeckl), whose keyboard-based **Die Festung** (1999) was even reminiscent of Popol Vuh's spiritual ambience. Its alter-ego was the massive super-heavy glacial hypnotic drone of the 21-minute *Die Zeit des Torremond*, off **Schattengang** (1999). *Welt Aus Eis*, off **Paysage D'Hiver** (2000), added violin to the keyboards in a soundscape devastated by blastbeats and hysterical guitars.

Doom metal

"Doom-metal" (a slow, gothic, baroque exaggeration of Black Sabbath's deadly grooves) became more and more popular in England thanks to a number of progressively more sophisticated groups. Paradise Lost, that debuted with **Paradise Lost** (1990), were not particularly creative, but Cathedral (1), featuring vocalist Lee Dorrian (ex-Napalm Death), invented a new format with the lengthy and stately elegies of **Forest Of Equilibrium** (1991), whose relation with progressive-rock was evident in colossal suites such as *The Voyage of the Homeless Sapiens* (1994) and *The Garden* (2006). Anathema (1) gave the movement a spiritual dimension with **Serenades** (1993) and a delirious medieval dimension with the mini-album **Pentecost III** (1995). My Dying Bride (1) perfected that format with an almost baroque grandeur on their third album **The Angel & The Dark River** (1995). Solstice's second album **New Dark Age** (1998) mixed epic riffs with Celtic and medieval influences.

Doom-metal in the USA had fewer and lesser adherents. Los Angeles' Obsessed, the band of former Saint Vitus member Scott "Wino" Weinrich, stood out with the cadaveric dirges of **The Obsessed** (1990) and **Lunar Womb** (1991). North Carolina's Confessor offered a technical version of doom-metal on **Condemned** (1991). **Into The Depths Of Sorrow** (1991) by Texas' Solitude Aeturnus was the epitome of epic doom.

Super-doom

The Melvins had pioneered a different kind of "doom rock", a style that manically emphasized and extended the psychedelic grooves of

Black Sabbath. Their "super-doom" grunge was continued in Seattle by Earth (11), who were the most extreme of Seattle's "doom-rockers". The titanic instrumental tracks of the EP **Extra-Capsular Extraction** (1991) and the album **2** (1993) relied on colossal drones and heavy rhythms seen through the distorted lense of Dylan Carlson's neurosis. Earth's music sounded like the casual jamming of extraterrestrial monsters. It merged elements of LaMonte Young's avantgarde minimalism and Eastern music's transcendental ecstasy and drenched them into gothic-scifi atmospheres. They were not "songs", they were hyper-psychedelic states of mind. **Phase 3** (1995) and the more accessible **Pentastar - In The Style Of Demons** (1996) continued Carlson's virtual sampling of historical riffs of hard-rock in a more earthly setting. Compared with their evil symphonies, Lou Reed's *Metal Machine Music* was classical music.

Karp (1) packed a mad carnival of cacophonous maelstroms, spasmodic psychodramas, rowdy voodoobilly and monolithic trance on **Mustaches Wild** (1994).

Louisiana's Eyehategod (2), who debuted with the ferocious **In the Name of Suffering** (1990), opened the way to an entire "sludge-core" scene in the South dedicated to truculent, feedback-laden, deep-groove rock music. Their third album **Dopesick** (1996) was the ultimate feedback experience.

Two bands coined dreamy introspective styles that stood out amid the bombast of their peers.

Finland's Thergothon pioneered a slow-motion otherworldly version of doom for cadaveric vocals and funereal keyboards on **Stream From The Heavens** (1992).

Australia's Disembowlment crafted **Transcendence Into The Peripheral** (1993), an album of contrasts in which blasts of noise crashed into lakes of ghostly melodies.

Esoteric (1) pioneered an epic version of doom with their triple guitar attack and their passion for colossal (double-disc) albums such as **Epistemological Despondency** (1994) and **The Pernicious Enigma** (1997), devoted to minimal quasi-ambient hyper-psychedelic meditations.

Stoner rock

"Stoner-rock" was an evolution of Blue Cheer's brutal hard-psychedelic-blues sound: super-distorted, super-heavy and super-loud.

The genre was first pioneered in southern California by Kyuss (11). **Wretch** (1991), basically, expanded on Chrome's hurricanes from the perspective of hard-rock (Chrome without the new-wave frills), but **Blues For The Red Sun** (1992) was a majestic work in a completely new dimension, a collection of disturbing symphonies for bulldozers and bombers, with disorienting interludes worthy of acid-rock. The waves of feedback and the cascades of melting steel coming from Josh Homme's guitar, the vibrant eloquence of John Garcia's crooning, the seismic bass of Nick Oliveri and the tribal drums of Brant Bjork, combined to produce the effect of high-tension electroshocks, breakneck gallops and incandescent lava. **Welcome To Sky Valley** (1994), on the other hand, was almost baroque in the way it fused all those elements into a uniform and organic one, like an act of vanity from a bunch of cannibals.

Stoner-rock thrived in the San Francisco Bay Area. <u>Sleep</u> (1), the band of vocalist Al Cisneros and guitarist Matt Pike, bridged doom-metal and stoner-rock with the slow, dark, booming dirges of **Volume One** (1992). And then it fell prey to a Black Sabbath obsession on **Sleep's Holy Mountain** (1993). Everything came into focus (i.e., to a virtual standstill) with the cryptic lumbering hour-long suite of **Jerusalem** (1998), originally recorded in 1995 and reissued in its 63-minute entirety as **Dopesmoker** (2003), one of the most austere attempts at scoring the deepest torments of the human psyche, a turgid mass of convoluted guitar monologues and werewolf howls which actually sounded like one deep coma.

Sleep's guitarist Matt Pike built a career from stretching out Black Sabbath's riffs into earth-shaking hyper-lysergic trances. His next project was <u>High On Fire</u>, that debuted with **Art Of Self Defense** (2000).

In the meantime Cisneros had formed a bass-and-drums duo, <u>Om</u>, devoted to trancey stoner jams, best on the mini-album **Conference of the Birds** (2006)

The second epicenter of stoner-rock was New York, where <u>Monster Magnet</u> (1), led by guitarists David Wyndorf and John McBain (and later Ed Mundell), concocted a crazy variant of Hawkwind's space-rock on **Spine Of God** (1991). It almost sounded like a parody of (soon to be called) stoner-rock, but the sound actually became heavier on **Superjudge** (1993), although Jimi Hendrix's soul-blues blood ran through its veins. These cathartic baths in guitar distortions dissolved into the heavily arranged (mellotron, strings, sitar) **Dopes To Infinity** (1995) and the more conventional grunge sound of **Powertrip** (1998).

<u>Acrimony</u> was perhaps the best of the British stoners, having discovered a hypnotic way of wrapping catchy riffs into droning and repetitive structures, especially on their second album **Tumuli Shroomaroom** (1996).

Funk-metal

The real money machine of the 1990s was funk-metal. In the 1980s bands such as Red Hot Chili Peppers and Primus had coined a style that was a hybrid of funk and hard-rock. Earlier, Run DMC had already experimented with a fusion of rap and heavy-metal. These two simple ideas made up the scaffolding of much heavy-metal of the 1990s.

Los Angeles was funk-metal's home turf: Infectious Grooves, the side-project of Suicidal Tendencies' vocalist Mike Muir, with **The Plague That Makes Your Booty Move** (1991); Eleven, with **Eleven** (1993); etc. But, more importantly, rap-metal was headquartered in Los Angeles. Rage Against The Machine (1), the band that launched the style worldwide, realized one of the most important leitmotivs of the decade: a fundamental unity of purpose between the music of black urban rebels and the music of white urban rebels. **Rage Against The Machine** (1992), one of the most violent albums of the time, a worthy heir to MC5's homicidal fury, sustained seismic shocks after seismic shocks thanks to Tom Morello's guitar explosions (from Hendrix-ian glissandoes to Page-esque hard-rock riffs), Zack de la Rocha's visceral and frantic rapping and ultra-syncopated hail-like rhythms. The sinister and morbid atmosphere of **Evil Empire** (1996), virtually a philosophical essay on willpower, and the passionate call to arms of **The Battle of Los Angeles** (1999) reached new depths although they lost most of the bite.

Rap-metal turned into something completely different, halfway into the decade, with the advent of Korn (1). Jonathan Davis embodied the post-yuppie pessimism at the turn of the century, and made a career of focusing on the anxieties of disaffected teenagers of the middle-class. Thus the tone of **Korn** (1994) was bleak, and, while not as aggressive as other funk-metal bands, it had few rivals in terms of dramatic tension. It was only fitting that **Life Is Peachy** (1996) and **Follow The Leader** (1998) were confused and insecure albums, compensating a lack of songwriting skills with an emphasis on mood swings and claustrophobic atmospheres.

The main representatives of funk-rock in New York were Scatterbrain, the new band by Ludichrist's vocalist Tommy Christ and guitarist Glenn Cummings, whose **Here Comes Trouble** (1990) in fact predated the fad.

Gothic Rock

Nordic gothic

The gothic brand of punk-rock ("dark-punk"), that had seen the light in the heydays of the new wave, redefined gothic rock as a deeper and stronger mood than the one originally served by Black Sabbath and Alice Cooper. Gothic rock was, first and foremost, an attitude, and remained such during the 1990s. In the 1990s, that attitude was refined by a generation of musicians that could take advantage of improved studio technology and electronic instruments.

Somewhat surprisingly, the leadership moved from Britain to the United States. Britain's gothic was limited to late purveyors of apocalyptic folk such as Rose McDowall's Sorrow, for example on **Under The Yew Possessed** (1993), and Michael Cashmore's Nature And Organisation, for example on **Beauty Reaps The Blood Of Solitude** (1994).

Germany's gothic school was far more imposing. Aurora (11), formed by Project Pitchfork's members Peter Spilles and Patricia Nigiani, crafted two of the eeriest and most powerful works in the genre: **The Land Of Harm And Appletrees** (1993), typical of their bleak and majestic overtones, overflowing with memorable melodies and eclectic arrangements (symphonic, acoustic, danceable, dirge-like, and so forth). The apocalyptic lieder of **Dimension Gate** (1994) covered an even broader territory, evoking both medieval religious music and ancestral tribal music, mimicking at the same time cosmic, techno and new-age music, sounding like a meeting of Popol Vuh and Dead Can Dance in Sven Vath's studio.

Das Ich (1), i.e. vocalist Stefan Ackermann and multi-instrumentalist Bruno Kramm, composed **Staub** (1994), a symphonic work of heroic proportions.

However, it was Sweden that came to rule European gothic. Roger Karmanik, the mastermind of Brighter Death Now and the founder of the Cold Meat Industry label, was the inspiration behind Sweden's gothic scene. Deutsch Nepal's **Deflagration Of Hell** (1991) was still under the influence of industrial music (the genetic source of this scene), but soon Scandinavia coined an original language: the "sound constructivist" school, that merged elements of ambient, gothic and industrial music, and, in general, relied on atmospheric keyboards and sometimes classical instruments to create terrifying visions of the otherworld; a genre that often sounded closer in spirit to classical music than to rock music. The works of In Slaughter Natives, such as **Sacrosancts Bleed** (1992), were feasts of excesses, relying on heavy-metal guitar and stormy beat-boxes as well as Gregorian litanies, Wagnerian choirs, martial drumming, etc. Love Is Colder Than Death's **Teignmouth** (1991) bridged the ancestral and the modern, the middle ages and cybernetics, ecstasy and hedonism, via a sequence that led from monk psalms, funereal tempos and organ drones to disco beats and bombastic arrangements. Mortiis (1), the brainchild of Emperor's bassist Haavard Ellefsen, transposed Klaus Schulze's symphonic grandeur and Brian Eno's majestic ambient ecstasy into gothic music, particularly with the two lengthy suites of **The Songs Of A Long Forgotten Ghost** (1993). Ordo Equilibrio (1), the project of multi-instrumentalist Tomas Pettersson, specialized in the glacial, desolate electronica first pioneered on **Reaping The Fallen** (1995). Arcana (1) refined the neoclassical, symphonic style on **Dark Ages Of Reason** (1996). The most abstract project was Morthound (Benny Nilsen), who sculpted the electroacoustic suites of **This Crying Age** (1991).

The master of nordic landscapes was Peter Andersson, known as Raison D'Etre (2), who experimented with both the "industrial folk" style of **Prospectus I** (1993), a set of psalms for string section and percussion instruments, and the "dark ambient" style of **Within The Depths Of Silence And Phormations** (1995), his most daring collage of samples, drones, monk-like chanting and futuristic electronics; a progression that led to the six neoclassical and mystical suites of **In Sadness Silence And Solitude** (1998).

Swedish composer Henrik "Nordvargr" Bjorkk was an original founder of Maschinenzimmer.412, or MZ.412, an outfit that helped define metal-industrial music with works such as **In Nomine Dei Nostri Satanas Luciferi Excelsi** (1995). Violence remained the common denominator of his subsequent projects: Folkstorm, best represented by the brutal sound of **Information Blitzkrieg** (1999); Toroidh, that debuted with the "European Trilogy", each episode being a romantic collage of wartime soundbites, notably **Europe is Dead** (2001); and Hydra Head 9, whose devastating wall of noise **Power Display** (2002) topped anything he had done before. The bleak electronic works released under his own name, Henrik Bjorkk, such as **I End Forever** (2004), **The Dead Never Sleep** (2005) and **Vitagen** (2005), on which he mastered the techniques of musique concrete, applied the same philosophy of terror to post-industrial droning music.

Swedish duo Abruptum (Marduk's multi-instrumentalist Morgan Haakansson and vocalist-guitarist Tony Sarkka) specialized in exhausting improvised meandering trance-metal pieces such as the 51-minute **Obscuritatem Advoco Amplectere Me** (1993), that leaned towards abstract cacophony, and the hour-long **In Umbra Malitiae Ambulabo In Aeternum In Triumpho Tenebrar** (1994), that leaned towards droning gothic ambience.

American gothic

In the United States, gothic rock was anchored around the label Projekt, founded by Black Tape For A Blue Girl's mastermind Sam Rosenthal, which mainly recruited bands in Arizona and California and promoted a similar, "classical-oriented" approach to atmospheric music.

Lycia (22), the brainchild of guitarist and vocalist Michael Van Portfleet, achieved a solemn and profound synthesis of cosmic electronics, synth-pop, psychedelic-rock, and industrial music. **Ionia** (1991), featuring Dave Galas on keyboards, coined Van Portfleet's favorite setting of ghostly vocals floating in a soundscape of electronically-processed guitar tones and glacial orchestral counterpoints. A heavily-layered instrumental backbone sustained the emotional tension of the formally impeccable **A Day In The Stark Corner** (1993): on one hand, a lyrical, idyllic, dreamy undercurrent that percolated every fibre of the music; and, at the same time, a haunting and harrowing sense of despair, hinting at inescapable supernatural forces. The monumental **The Burning Circle And Then Dust** (1995), with Tara Vanflower on vocals, completed the moral Calvary of the previous works: a less catastrophic atmosphere revealed an ocean of somber melancholy, a foreign sense of beauty that underlined a process of self-discovery. This album codified Lycia's message, halfway between a philosophical treatise, a religious prophecy and the last thoughts of a dying man. By now free of the semiotic burden of his two masterpieces, Van Portfleet proceeded to sculpt the abstract ballads of **Cold** (1996), in a vein that evoked Dead Can Dance and that amounted, de facto, to a repudiation of his gothic roots.

Arizona's contingent also featured: Michael Plaster's Soul Whirling Somewhere (1), whose **Soul Whirling Somewhere** (1996) was a cosmic and neoclassical update of Dead Can Dance's sound, a fragile polyphony of ethereal madrigals bridging Constance Demby's symphonic new-age music and Harold Budd's celestial ambient music; Lovesliescrushing, whose **Xuvetyn** (1996) bordered on ambient music; Julianna Towns' Skinner Box, also influenced by Dead Can Dance on **The Imaginary Heart** (1991).

Remnants of the army that followed Christian Death in Los Angeles included Faith And The Muse and Cradle Of Thorns (1), who penned the barbaric psychodramas of **Feed Us** (1994), woven around the contrast between the death-metal growl of a male singer and the operatic contralto of his female counterpart (Ty Elam and Tamera Slayton), and propelled by a mixture of disco-music, punk-rock and industrial rhythms.

Johnny Indovina's Human Drama (1) rose above the gothic scene of Los Angeles. A mostly-acoustic work, **The World Inside** (1991), introduced not only fairy-tale atmospheres and neoclassical passages but also the archaic undercurrent that resurfaced on **Songs Of Betrayal** (1995), a philosophical meditation that achieved anthemic overtones as well as plunged into suicidal dejection. These works were so heavily arranged that each song sounded like a symphonic poem, when it was not as spare and austere as a chamber sonata.

Offshoots of that school were to be found in Chicago, such as Padraic Ogl's Thanatos.

In San Francisco, the gothic clubs of SOMA reveled in the music of Switchblade Symphony, and especially Children Of The Apocalypse (1), who recorded the exoteric **Ta 'Wil** (1997).

In Australia, Darrin Verhagen's Shinjuku Thief (2) assembled collages of industrial, ambient, jazz and dance elements on **Bloody Tourist** (1992) and achieved the magniloquent orchestral gothic of **The Witch Hammer** (1993).

Post-ambient Music

Electronic Ambience, 1989-93

New studio techniques and new electronic and digital instruments allowed rock music and avantgarde music to develop new kinds of composition and performance. Ambient and cosmic music, in particular, reached an artistic peak. Noise was employed in a less irreverent and more calculated manner. Electronic sounds became less alien and more humane. Sound effects became the center of mass, not the centrifugal force. Overall, the emphasis shifted from melody/rhythm to "sound" and "ambience". And, in a way, this was the terminal point of a movement begun at the outset of the 20th century to emancipate music from the dogmas of classical music.

French combo Lightwave (20) was still composing electronic tonal poems in the spirit of the German "cosmic couriers" of the 1970s, but they added intrepid new ideas. Serge Leroy and Christoph Harbonnier harked back to Klaus Schulze's early works on **Nachtmusik** (1990), but enhanced that cliche' with techniques borrowed from avantgarde music. **Tycho Brahe** (1993), that added Paul Haslinger (ex-Tangerine Dream) and violinist Jacques Deregnaucourt to the line-up, offered elegant, dramatic and highly dynamic chamber-electronic music of a kind that had never been heard before. Electronic music had matured into something both more conventional (like a traditional instrument) and more alien (like a supernatural harmony). **Mundus Subterraneus** (1995) reached new psychological depths, while furthering their soundpainting both at the microscopic and at the macroscopic levels. A spiderweb of metabolizing structures, an organic blend of timbres, drones and dissonances, it blurred the line between rationality and chaos, showing one as being the sense of the other. The spirit of Lightwave's music recalled the allegorical, encyclopedic minutiae of medieval treatises, an elaborate clockwork of impossible mirages and erudite quotations. Ultimately, it was a journey back to the roots of the human adventure.

In Germany, Uwe Schmidt's multi-faceted saga began with Lassigue Bendthaus and unfocused electronic soundscapes such as the ones on **Render** (1994). His ambient/atmospheric project Atom Heart was more successful, particularly with **Morphogenetics Fields** (1994). N+'s **Built** (1996), which was virtually a tribute to cosmic music, and the numerous collaborations between Bill Laswell and Pete Namlook completed his training in the field of lengthy, static electronic poems. But his activity ranged from Latin music, explored by Senor Coconut Y Su Conjunto, for example on **El Gran Baile** (1997), to the digital ambient/industrial jazz-rock of Flanger, a collaboration with percussionist Bernd Friedman, on **Templates** (1999). His partnership with Japanese visionary Tetsu Inoue was particulary relevant. The third Datacide (1) album, **Flowerhead**

(1994), toyed with a noise-based form of ambient music that sounded like organic matter slowly developing into an embryo. The duo recorded ambient works under several names, notably Masters Of Psychedelic Ambiance's **MU** (1995) and Second Nature's **Second Nature** (1995).

Tetsu Inoue, Uwe Schmidt's partner in Datacide, was even more delicate on **Ambiant Otaku** (1994).

In Belgium, Vidna Obmana (2), Dirk Serries' project, practiced electronic soundpainting on the ambient trilogy begun with **Passage In Beauty** (1991), but **Echoing Delight** (1993) shifted the emphasis towards spiritual and tribal evocations. This is the genre in which Serries gave his most original and poignant works, first **Spiritual Bonding** (1994), a collaboration with Steve Roach and Robert Rich, and then **Crossing The Trail** (1998).

In Holland, Ron Boots's **Different Stories and Twisted Tales** (1993) straddled the border between sequencer and ambient music. In Portugal Nuno Canavarro produced one of the most atmospheric works of early ambient music, **Plux Quba** (1988).

San Francisco's Kim Cascone (1) mined the border between ambient music and musique concrete both on Heavenly Music Corporation's **In A Garden Of Eden** (1993) and on PGR's **The Morning Book of Serpents** (1995).

A Produce (2), Barry Craig's project, also from California, crafted **Reflect Like A Mirror** (1993), an impeccable follow-up to Brian Eno's and Harold Budd's ambient classics, as well as the majestic albeit brainy world-music of **Land Of A Thousand Trances** (1994).

Happy The Man's keyboardist Kit Watkins (1) composed the austere **Thought Tones** (1992) and especially **Circle** (1993), a suite for electronic sounds and natural sounds.

In Canada, Delerium (3), an offshoot of Front Line Assembly, crossed over into gothic, dance and pop music with meticulously and lushly arranged albums such as **Stone Tower** (1990), **Spiritual Archives** (1991) and **Spheres** (1994). Their associates Will (1) composed the pagan mass **Pearl Of Great Price** (1991) in a similar vein.

Arizona-based Life Garden (1) sounded like the electronic version of Popol Vuh on **Caught Between The Tapestry Of Silence And Beauty** (1991).

The "organic sound sculpting" of Voice Of Eye (2), the Texas-based duo of Bonnie McNaim and Jim Wilson, was inspired, at different levels, by Steve Roach, Harold Budd, and Karlheinz Stockhausen. **Mariner Sonique** (1993), the seven **Vespers** (1994), imbued with medieval spirituality and zen transcendence, and the six movements of **Transmigration** (1996) co-founded the religious version of electronic world-music with Life Garden.

The most challenging and political form of ambient music was perhaps the one invented in New York by Terre Thaemlitz, for example on **Soil** (1995).

Liquid Mind (2), the project of Los Angeles-based composer Chuck Wild, sculpted the ecstatic **Ambience Minimus** (1994): memorable melodies slowed down, came to a standstill and decomposed in celestial chimes, echoes of angels and breathing of nebulae. The neo-classical **Unity** (2000), instead, let strings and woodwinds float, multiply and merge as if an entire repertory of "adagios" was being played in slow motion and out of sync by an orchestra of orchestras.

In a lighter mood, Richard Bone (2) was equally at ease with the surreal synth-pop of **Vox Orbita** (1995) and the ambient symphony of **Eternal Now** (1996).

Dutch duo Beequeen (Frans De Waard and Freek Kinkelaar) dabbled in droning compositions inspired by ambient, cosmic and industrial music, notably on their most austere recordings, such as **Music For The Head Ballet** (1996) and **Treatise** (2000).

Electronic Ambient World Music, 1988-94

By exploiting Steve Roach's ideas, a number of musicians scoured the territory at the border between new-age music, ambient music and world-music.

San Francisco's "modern primitivism" movement was best represented by a multi-national commune that emerged with the music of Lights In A Fat City (1), centered upon Canadian electronic composer Kenneth Newby, British-born didjeridoo player Stephen Kent and percussionist Eddy Sayer. **Somewhere** (1988) was possibly the first electronic album built around the sound of the didjeridoo, and juxtaposed hypnotic rhythms to a madly droning background. **Sound Column** (1993) was a more philosophical work, comprising four improvisations for didjeridoo and acoustic instruments recorded inside a huge pillar. That project evolved into Trance Mission (12), formed by Newby and Kent with Club Foot Orchestra's clarinetist Beth Custer and percussionist John Loose. **Trance Mission** (1993), a dense maelstrom of jazz improvisation, transcendental exotica, atmospheric electronica and tribal rhythms, took a new route to Brian Eno's ambient trance and to Jon Hassell's fourth-world music. That wedding of futuristic and ancestral elements was abandoned on **Meanwhile** (1995), for a more facile dance-exotic fusion that evoked the vision of the Third Ear Band mixed by a techno producer; while later works such as **Head Light** (1997) veered towards an alien form of free-jazz. Kent and harpist Barbara Imhoff (accompanied by a percussionist and a vocalist) explored a simpler kind of electronic folk music under the moniker Beasts Of Paradise on **Gathered On The Edge** (1995).

Kenneth Newby (10), a member of the Trance Mission collective, crafted **Ecology Of Souls** (1993), perhaps the most accomplished fusion of electronic music and exotic instruments of the era. Four lengthy suites explored a magical, surreal, mythological landscape roamed by rhythmic patterns and primordial sounds, swept by intergalactic winds and tidal waves of cosmic radiations, while melodramatic and ethereal moments alternated at creating a metaphysical suspense.

Germany's Enigma (2), the project of Romanian-born veteran disco producer and electronic composer Michael Cretu (aka Curly M.C.), elaborated a pseudo-ethnic ambient style that would be very influencial on mainstream music. **MCMXC A.D.** (1990) mixed Gregorian chanting, dance beats, new-age ecstasy and exotic fascination. **The Cross Of Changes** (1994) was a tour de force of juxtapositions and layering that roamed the world for inspiration (French chansons, African polyrhythms, Middle-eastern cantillation, Peruvian flutes, operatic choirs, etc).

France's Deep Forest (1) were successful on **Deep Forest** (1992) with a similar idea: an atmospheric potion of ethnic samples and dance beats.

Mo Boma (12), the duo of German multi-instrumentalist Carsten Tiedemann and Iceland-born jazz bassist Skuli Sverrisson, achieved a brilliant fusion of Brian Eno, Jon Hassell, Klaus Schulze, Weather Report and Pat Metheny, for the age of raves on **Jijimuge** (1992) and especially on the more electronic, primitive-futurist **Myths Of The Near Future** (1994). The first part of a trilogy recorded in South Africa in 1993, the latter set the foundations for the sophisticated ethno-jazz of **Myths Of The Near Future Part Two** (released in 1995) and the lush, symphonic "thickness" of **Myths Of The Near Future Part Three** (1996). Overall, the trilogy represented a majestic celebration of the human race.

Australia's Eden (11), the brainchild of vocalist Sean Bowley, displayed the combined influence of Dead Can Dance's exotic/medieval music and Nico's ancestral folk on the madrigals of **Gateway To The Mysteries** (1990), performed by a chamber ensemble (rich in ancient instruments) and sung in lugubrious ecclesiastical tones. The macabre and decadent ballads of **Fire And Rain** (1995) added Paul Machliss' electronic arrangements.

Veteran British guitarist Mike Cooper, who had played blues in the 1960s and jazz in the 1970s, coined "ambient electronic exotica" (reminiscent of Jon Hassell's "fourth-world music") for guitar, electronics, samples of old records, and field recordings from exotic countries on albums such as **Kiribati** (1999), **Globe Notes** (2001) and **Rayon Hula** (2004).

Transglobal trance, 1992-94

It was not avantgarde, but Britain's "transglobal dance" was a natural consequence of the merger of electronica and world-music in the age of raves.

TUU (2), mainly Martin Franklin's project, delivered arcane, sacred and ethnic trance on **One Thousand Years** (1992), evoking both Third Ear Band and Popol Vuh. **All Our Ancestors** (1995) approached chamber music and Jon Hassell's fourth-world music, while the more electronic **Mesh** (1997) was influenced by Steve Roach's sinister soundscapes.

Voices Of Kwahn offered an elegant fusion of quirky vocals and electronic/ethnic ambience on their second album **Silver Bowl Transmission** (1996).

Guitar drones

An important thread for ambient music was started in Britain when the post-shoegazing psychedelic groups began playing music anchored to guitar drones. Seefeel (2) pioneered the idea on **Quique** (1993) and **Succour** (1994). The combination of Sarah Peacock's stunned vocals, Mark Clifford's minimalist guitars, Justin Fletcher's proto-rhythms and Darren Seymour's dub bass lines dissolved the music of My Bloody Valentine and Spacemen 3 in nebulae of abstract sound.

Drone-based symphonies became the bread and butter of most shoegazing veterans.

Spacemen 3's guitarist Sonic Boom (Peter Kember) began a stubborn quest for the mystical qualities of sound. His first success was with **Soul Kiss** (1991), the second, ultra-ethereal album by Spectrum (1). Kember's second success came with Experimental Audio Research (2), or E.A.R., the experimental trio formed with God's Kevin Martin and My Bloody Valentine's Kevin Shields, who produced at least two innovative recordings: the four cosmic-ambient suites of **Mesmerised** (1994) and the three futuristic concertos of **Millennium Music** (1998).

Main (2), the new project of Loop's Robert Hampson, was an obsessive probe into the power of drones. Over the course of a number of EPs, **Hydra** (1991), **Calm** (1992), **Dry Stone Feed** (1993) and **Firmament** (1993), and the album **Motion Pool** (1994), Hampson's style evolved from a dark, cold, dynamic sound to a softer, static, almost mystical sound. The two colossal tracks of **Firmament II** (1994) and the six multi-part suites of **Hz** (1996) coined a sophisticated art of nuances that, far from being only cacophonous and monotonous, was rich in the way that a black hole is rich of invisible gravitational energy. Hampson's technique was perhaps the closest a rock musician had come to repeating Karlheinz Stockhausen's experiments of the 1960s.

Sound manipulation of acoustic sources became the focus of many artists of this generation.

Rapoon (3), the brainchild of Zoviet France's Robin Storey, gave new meaning to the fusion of Indian and western music on albums such as **Vernal Crossing** (1993) and **The Kirghiz Light** (1995), exalted orgies of samples, loops and mixing that "used" drones and rhythms rather than "playing" drones and rhythms. He then converted to the mystical/contemplative style of **Darker By Light** (1996), **Easterly 6 Or 7** (1997) and **The Fires Of The Borderlands** (1998), that basically reconciled his experiments with new-age music.

O.Rang (1), the new project of Talk Talk's rhythm section of Lee Harris (percussions) and Paul Webb (now on keyboards), manipulated the sounds of a small orchestra of friends on **Herd Of Instinct** (1994).

Flying Saucer Attack (2), i.e. the duo of multi-instrumentalists Dave Pearce and Rachel Brook, were among the groups that transformed psychedelic rock into an austere form of chamber music. The albums **Flying Saucer Attack** (1993), **Further** (1995) and **New Lands** (1997) refined a kind of shoegazing that relied increasingly on melody, yielding delicate elegies set against a disturbing background of cosmic music, free-jazz, Throbbing Gristle's industrial noise, LaMonte Young's droning music or contemplative new-age music.

German guitar trio Maeror Tri (1) co-pioneered doomsday's music for guitar-drones, although their white-noise hurricanes, particularly on the monumental **Myein** (1995), recorded in 1992 and 1993, were reminiscent of both Glenn Branca's symphonies and Throbbing Gristle's industrial nightmares.

Ambient avantgarde, 1989-94

At the turn of the century, ambient composers abounded all over the world.

Veteran British music critic David Toop (2) aimed for Brian Eno's ambient ecstasy via a mix of natural sounds, electronic sounds and acoustic instruments on **Buried Dreams** (1994), a collaboration with Max Eastley, basically reinventing musique concrete for the ambient generation. **Screen Ceremonies** (1995) was the austere manifesto of this fusion of ethnic and concrete music. Toop used real buildings as well as imaginary buildings as sources of inspiration, conceiving them as sentient organisms, notably for the 26-minute eco-suite *Smell of Human Life*, off **Museum Of Fruit** (1999).

Belgian composer Benjamin Lew (1) crafted **Le Parfum Du Raki** (1993) for an ensemble of electronic, ethnic and acoustic instruments.

Alio Die (2), the project of Italian composer Stefano Musso, assembled electronic pieces such as **Sit Tibi Terra Levis** (1991) that continued Harold Budd's program of angelic music. In **Suspended Feathers** (1995) tiny instances of natural sounds appear in calm soft soundscapes and create disorienting shifting perspectives, the sonic equivalent of a camera that slowly moves around the landscape. The drone symphony **Password for Entheogenic Experience** (1997) evolves in time instead of space, as the initial pastoral setting gets stretched and dilated into a dreamy mournful adagio and then modulated into the geometry of a baroque fugue and then channeled into the austere macabre grandeur of a requiem.

British audio-visual technician Andrew Lagowski launched both the dark ambient project of <u>Legion</u>, that released **False Dawn** (1992) for found sounds and white noise, and especially **Leviathan** (1996), a six-movement symphony of exoteric electronica, and the project <u>SETI</u>, at the border between techno, ambient and dub.

German electronic musician <u>Pete Namlook</u> (Peter Kuhlmann), one of the most prolific musicians of all times (not a compliment), focused on the untapped potential of analog synthesizers, often developing or extending the instruments in his own laboratory. Most of his 200+ recordings were collaborations with influential artists of his time, and many were repeated collaborations (i.e., with sequels): **Silence** (1992) with Dr Atmo, **The Dark Side Of The Moog** (1994) with Klaus Schulze, **Psychonavigation** (1994) with Bill Laswell, **Jet Chamber** (1995) with Atom Heart, etc. Namlook's own music, the series that started with **Air** (1993), endorsed one or a combination of the following: German "kosmische musik", Brian Eno's "discreet" music, free-jazz and/or Eastern classical music.

After familiarizing himself with the soft, slowly-decaying gong drones of **Teimo** (1992), German composer <u>Thomas Koner</u> (1) penned the drone-based ambient music of **Permafrost** (1993). These pieces laid the foundations for hour-long compositions such as *Daikan* (2001), the zenith of his icy ambience, and *Une Topographie Sonore* (2003), that obsessively explores a magical and ethereal soundscape of natural sounds and eerie drones.

Australian composer <u>Paul Schutze</u> (15) was inspired by Brian Eno's ambient music, Miles Davis' jazz-rock and Pierre Henry's musique concrete for the one-hour collage of **Deus Ex Machina** (1989) and for the claustrophobic *Topology Of A Phantom City*, off **New Maps Of Hell** (1992), perhaps the best formulation of his "chaotic minimalism", a psychological puzzle of dissonance, trance, jazz, psychedelia, tribal frenzy, raga and ambient melodrama. The same urban neurosis tore **The Rapture Of Metals** (1993) apart, and disfigured **Apart** (1995), an imposing summary of his techniques, particularly the cryptic and sinister suite *Sleep*. **Nine Songs From The Garden Of Welcome Lies** (1997) employed organs instead of synthesizers to improvise soundscapes halfway between Monet's abstract impressionism and Tibetan mantras.

Indiana-based ambient guitarist <u>Jeff Pearce</u> employed layers and layers of electronically-processed guitar melodies to compose **The Hidden Rift** (1996).

New York-based pianist <u>Ruben Garcia</u> (1) opted for a more emotional version of Harold Budd's ambient piano minimalism in *Eleven Moons*, off **Room Full of Easels** (1996).

Alaska resident <u>John Luther Adams</u> composed static music in the minimalist tradition but scored for chamber orchestras. Thus his colossal *In The White Silence* (1998), *The Light That Fills the World* (2000) and *The Immeasurable Space of Tones* (2001) for violin, vibraphone, piano, keyboard and contrabass.

Concrete Avantgarde

(The following is an excerpt from my book on avantgarde music).

The avantgarde of ordinary sound

Innovative concepts in the arts of field recording and of collage were introduced during the 1990s.

Gen Ken Montgomery assembled the environmental noise symphony *Father Demo Swears* (1989), a terror-inducing wall of noise for amplified violin, voice, street noise and (massive) feedback.

David Dunn (1) used computers to assemble "environmental sound works", works that manipulate field recordings, such as *Chaos And The Emergent Mind of the Pond* (1992), off **Angels And Insects** (1992).

Under the moniker Crawling with Tarts the San Francisco-based duo of composer Michael Gendreau and Suzanne Dycus concocted **Operas** (1993), or, better, "surface noise operas" (operas composed out of field recordings and studio manipulations) via "transcription discs", a program refined on **Grand Surface Noise Opera Nrs 3 (Indian Ocean Ship) and 4 (Drum Totem)** (1994), the former scored for four turntables and the latter scored for turntables and percussion. Michael Gendreau's **55 Pas de la Ligne au nø3** (2002) was devoted to the excruciating sound of a rotating disk on a modified turntable. *Grand Surface Noise Opera Nr 7 - The Decadent Opera - Rococo* (1995) first assembled voices (taken from various sources) and then injected all sorts of musical snippets into the process, each grotesquely deformed, as in a collaboration between Frank Zappa and Karlheinz Stockhausen.

By electronically and digitally processing the sounds of objects and places, Steve Roden created "possible landscapes", such as **Humming Endlessly in the Hush** (1996), credited to In Be Tween Noise, that require "deep listening" to appreciate the subtlety of slight variations in the mostly silent wasteland; while **Four Possible Landscapes** (1999) bordered on the glitch aesthetic of Bernhard Guenter.

Deathprod, the solo project of Motorpsycho's keyboardist Helge Sten, pushed the abstract electronic soundsculpting of **Treetop Drive 1-3/ Towboat** (1994) into the age of digital audio manipulation with **Morals and Dogma** (2004). Using low-tech home-made recording devices, and emphasizing the very limitations of those devices (the hiss of an old tape recorder, or the distortion of a defective sampler, or the deteriorating sound of a digital-to-analog transfer), and then mixing them with traditional instruments, Deathprod de facto ventured into digital chamber music.

Fueled by Dadaistic eccentricity, the Argentinean trio Reynols (drummer Miguel Tomasin and guitarists Roberto Conlazo and Anla

Courtis) released all sorts of sarcastic musique-concrete symphonies, from **Gordura Vegetal Hidrogenada** (1995) to **10.000 Chickens Symphony** (1999) for chicken sounds ("the only record in the world where all the participants were killed and eaten afterwards") to **Blank Tapes** (Trente Oiseaux, 2000) for amplified blank tapes. In parallel, Anla Courtis continued to use the tape as his main instrument in a series of extremely chaotic works, especially the 16-minute expressionist nightmare of *Encjas de Viento* (1996).

Ellen Band bridged musique concrete and deep-listening music with collages such as *Radiatore* (1998) in which apparently harmless (and lifeless) sounds collected in the streets are scrutinized, repeated, amplified, deformed, enhanced until they become very much alive. The mundane becomes extraordinary: "no sound is ordinary".

The electronic processing of microscopic bodily noises by Daniel Menche yielded the monstrous intensity of **Screaming Caress** (1997).

The compositions of John Hudak employ minimalist and subsonic repetition of electronically-processed found sounds, as in **Pond** (1998), that uses underwater insects as its main source.

Heir to the glorious French traditions of musique concrete and sound collage, French sound-sculptor Christian Renou, aka Brume, specialized in the dense, rapid-fire sonic montage that culminated with the concrete symphony **Fragments and Articulations** (2002).

Spanish composer Francisco Lopez, one of most prolific composers in history (not a compliment), focused on collages of field recordings and sound-manipulation of natural phenomena. The resulting music was often static subsonic ambient music (frequently bordering on utter silence) rather than traditional (noisy) concrete music. Typical of his method was the trilogy of **La Selva** (1998), a collage of sounds from the tropical forest, **Buildings** (2001) and **Wind** (2007), a repertory of wind sounds from Patagonia,

German composer Marc Behrens used a computer and feedback-based devices to organize the collage of field recordings of **Elapsed Time** (2001).

Sacramento-based digital composer Joe Colley specialized in generating sounds from negative feedback loops, achieving an austere and mature balance of tones with the droning **Everybody Gets What They Deserve** (1999) and the almost serene **Stop Listening** (2000), released under his moniker Crawl Unit, a phase that culminated with the 19-minute **Static For Empty Life** (2001) and the two pieces of **Sound Until The World Ends** (2001). His art of ad-hoc feedback-driven installations was refined on **Desperate Attempts At Beauty** (2003) and especially the "industrial" symphony **Psychic Stress Soundtracks** (2005), five lengthy collapse of noises from mechanical devices, and acquired expressionist overtones on **Waste Of Songs** (2006).

The early recordings of British composer Janek Schaefer (2) focused on two elements: studio manipulation of field recordings, and his self-built twin and triple armed varispeed turntables. The resulting collage is unusually dense and dynamic, culminating with the concrete symphony *Cold Storage* (2004), **Songs For Europe** (2004), a collaboration with Philip Jeck that builds ambient soundscapes from old Greek and Turkish records as well as radio broadcasts, the dance soundtrack **Migration** (2006), concocted out of manipulated field recordings, and **In The Last Hour** (2006), a piece in four movements that leveraged the combination of live instrumentation and turntable-derived textures to create an electronic poem that was both lugubrious and romantic.

The hyper-realistic field recordings of Japanese composer Toshiya Tsunoda consist in capturing the sound of inert matter. Each object has a "sound": it is just a matter of finding a way to render that sound so that it can be appreciated by the human ear. The music of **Pieces Of Air** (2001), literally recordings of air vibrations, is thus one of minimal subsonic vibrations.

Seth Nehil sculpted the quiet blurred pieces of **Tracing the Skins of Clouds** (1998) for found objects and instruments.

More traditional collages of field recordings survived in the work of three French soundsculptors. Syllyk (a collaboration between Eric LaCasa and Sylvie Laroche) dedicated their ambitious collages of manipulated field recordings to mythological themes: the 27-minute *Le Sacrifice*, off **O Comme Icare** (1992), the 19-minute *Terre Ciel Soleil Feu*, off **Frontieres** (1992), and especially the 66-minute piece of **Ascendre A L'Ombre Du Vent** (1996). Eric LaCasa's four lengthy compositions collected on **L'Empreinte de L'Ivresse** (1999) represented an ambitious fresco of human life. Jean-Luc Guionnet, also a free-improvising jazz saxophonist, and Eric Cordier, also a body art performer, created the two installations of **Synapses** (1999) in which a sound produced on an instrument was propagated to other instruments. a way that plucking one string causes a chain reaction of sounds. Guionnet was investigating the synthetic masses of musique concrete in a serene context bordering on new-age music, as displayed in the three works for electronics and natural sounds composed between 1989 and 1996 and collected on **Axene** (2000). Cordier reconstructed audio sources to compose the sound sculptures of **Houlque** (1996), whereas **Digitalis Purpurea** (Ground Fault, 2003) collects four audio installations for multiple loudspeakers, one of his specialties. Jean-Luc Guionnet, Eric LaCasa and Eric Cordier constituted the musique-concrete ensemble Afflux that focused on electronic improvisation with environmental sounds as they occur in an open landscape, a method first documented on **Azier St. Martin-Sur-Mer Dieppe** (2002).

The 1990s, as the sampler became ubiquitous in popular music, witnessed a generation of sound sculptors who toyed with samples of the musical repertory, field recordings and acoustic instruments.

Bob Ostertag, one of the earliest free-jazz improvisors at the electronic keyboards, embraced the sampler and realized the string quartet *All The Rage* (1992), that employed popular music and sounds of a riot (as well as string instruments) as sources.

David Shea, who had already established his reputation as one of the first turntablists (mainly in John Zorn's ensembles), further legitimized the sampler as an instrument with his works, both the ones for ensemble, such as *Shock Corridor* (1992) for samples and instruments (Anthony Coleman on piano and organ, Shelley Hirsch on voice and electronics, Ikue Mori on drum-machine, Zeena Parkins on electric harp, Jim Staley on trombone and didjeridoo, Jim Pugliese on percussion), a kaleidoscopic merry-go-round of stylistic detours, and those for solo sampler, such as *Alpha* (1995), a real-time collage of record snippets, *Satyricon* (1997), a sophisticated survey of the collective unconscious, *Sita's Walk Of Fire* (2001), a demented study in frenzy and contrast.

The avantgarde of computer sound

While the pioneers of computer music (basically from the 1950s to the 1980s) were mostly fascinated by a tool that challenged the pillars of western music (i.e., the relationship between performer and composer, and even the very notions of composer and performer), the wide diffusion of software for composing music on relatively cheap and portable computers (or "laptops") made it possible for a new generation of musicians to simply use the compositional algorithms and the synthesized sounds of a laptop in broader contexts. Fundamentally, computers had contributed to the breakdown of the traditional concept and role of harmony. The new generation exploited that very breakdown to create a kind of music directly referencing "sound". Basically, computers helped musicians focus more on the "sound" that they wanted to produce and less on the process to obtain it.

The eclectic Japanese musician Ikue Mori went through several stages before arriving at computer music: first as a drummer for the experimental rock band Mars, then as a free-jazz improviser, then as the electronic composer of the five long meditations for drum machines and samplers of **Garden** (1996), and finally as the laptop soundpainter of **Labyrinth** (2000) and **Myrninerest** (2005). Thus she was ideally suited to bridge the aesthetics of dissonance, improvisation and machine music.

Achim Wollscheid used household objects as percussion instruments "played" according to a computer algorithm for **Moves** (1997).

Germany's <u>Lutz Glandien</u> composed the wildly dissonant music of **The 5th Elephant** (2002) assisted by a computer in selecting and assembling "samples" from recordings of acoustic instruments.

<u>Furt</u>, the duo of British electronic musicians Richard Barrett and Paul Obermayer, assembled the tetralogy "Out Of Time", notably **Angel** (1995) and *Ultimatum* (2000), off **Defekt** (2002), of free-form studio collage.

The Cyber Age

The Late 1990s: Globalization

The new world order yielded an era of global growth on a scale that had never been witnessed in the world. Asia, in particular, staged one of the most spectacular economic booms in history, with China leading the way (China had been one of the most isolated communist countries until the early 1980s). Many in the West fell to the illusion of perennial prosperity. Many in the developing world sensed the end to poverty and starvation.

Bill Clinton, elected in 1992, the youngest president of the USA since John Kennedy and the first "baby boomer" to become president, well represented the new era, that basically amounted to one long huge party. The economic expansion during his eight years was the longest in the history of the USA.

The demographics had also changed significantly: in 2000 the population of the USA was 280 million, and most of the growth took place in the South and the West. The most populated state was now California with over 30 million people, and Los Angeles (which a century earlier was a town of 100,000 souls) had become the second largest metropolis in the country.

The USA was rocked by one of the most influential inventions of all time, the Internet. Throughout the decade, more and more innovative software changed the way people lived their lives. In 1991 the World-Wide Web invented by Tim Berners-Lee in Geneva debuted on the Internet. From that moment on, an endless stream of new companies progressively demolished the "American way of life": Marc Andreessen's Netscape in 1994 to browse the World-Wide Web; Jerry Yang's Yahoo in 1994 to search the Web; Craig Newmark's Craigslist in 1995 to serve the community; Amazon.com in 1997 to sell books over the Internet; Al Lieb's and Selina Tobaccowala's Evite in 1997; Larry Page's and Sergey Brin's Google in 1998; Pierre Omidyar's Ebay in 1998; Shawn Fanning's Napster in 1999 (a system to share music files); Jimmy Wales' Wikipedia in 2001, a collaborative encyclopedia edited by the whole Internet community. A new economy appeared in the USA, the "net" economy, whose drivers were the "dot.com" companies. By 1999, the US had 250 billionaires, and thousands of new millionaires were created every year by an ebullient stock market. By 2000 e-mail had become pervasive, replacing traditional ("snail") mail and even telephones as the main medium of long-distance communication.

Novels and films speculated on the ideas of "cyberspace" (the space of data, that could be interpreted as a universe of its own) and "virtual reality" (a computer simulation of real life in cyberspace).

Even in the middle of the boom the USA society remained one of the most violent in the world, particularly for young people. In 1999 a new worrisome phenomenon took hold of the USA: 13 students and teachers died during a high-school shooting at Columbine, Colorado.

Internationally, the security of the USA was no longer threatened by major powers but by a small group of terrorists: Al Qaeda, led by an Islamic fanatic from Saudi Arabia, Osama bin Laden, from his base in Afghanistan. In 1993 they tried to blow up New York's World Trade Center, and in 1998 they bombed two USA embassies in Africa, killing scores of people.

The economic boom ended soon, and with a bang. In April 2000 the stock market for high-technology companies crashed, wiping out trillions of dollars of wealth. The mood turned to gloom when, at the end of the decade, George W Bush of the Republican Party became president on a technicality, beginning one of the most divisive presidencies of all times.

Thus the world, and in particular the USA, went through one of the most breathtaking decades in memory. The 1990s were roughly the equivalent of the roaring 1920s: a senseless party before a big crisis.

Generation X

However, the new generation, dubbed "Generation X" (people born between the mid 1960s and 1981), was living largely in the shadow of the generation of their parents, the "baby boomers", the most analyzed generation in history. The contrast was not encouraging for the kids. The Baby Boomers grew up in the 1950s, in a world of unlimited economic opportunities, while the Generation X grew up in the 1980s, in a world of economic recession, AIDS, drugs, climate change and street gangs. The Baby Boomers grew up in a world of stable families, while the Generation X grew up in a world of pervasive family breakdown. Their parents were turning to spirituality and environmentalism, having been "reborn" in the 1980s after having "changed" the world in the 1960s. When the generation Xers became adults, the world was dominated by Baby Boomers: a baby boomer (Microsoft's founder Bill Gates) had become the world's richest man, and a baby boomer had become the world's most powerful man (USA president Bill Clinton).

There was also a stark contrast between Generation X and their baby-boomer parents in the way body and mind were perceived. Their parents had fostered aerobics and the culture of gyms, but mainly as devices to enhance inner, psychological health, not just bodily health. Generation X seemed only interested in the bodily part, so much so that this was a generation in which the traditional relationship between smoking cigarettes and doing drugs was reversed: kids were more likely to do drugs (that hurts your mind) than smoke cigarettes (that hurts your body). They were more likely to engage in random sexual activities (that may terminate their emotional life) but always using "protection" (to avoid contracting AIDS, that would terminate their physical life). The "gym culture" was by now pervasive: it was important to look good (as opposed to boast one's mental skills), to be artificially athletic (as opposed to being knowledgeable), to perform courageous acts for the sake of proving one's fitness (as opposed to accomplishing something for the sake of an ideal).

When it comes to the rest of the world, an important shift took place in the mindset of this generation. The influx of immigrants from non-Christian parts of the world (India, Middle East, Far East) abolished the Christian monopoly on moral values, creating a higher degree of cultural relativism. Generation X was less prejudiced against non-European cultures.

Fast forward

Musically, the ebullient atmosphere of the age and the introduction of digital sound-making devices finally led to the birth of truly new genres: post-rock, trip-hop, drum'n'bass, glitch music, etc. If the early 1990s had been devoted to revisiting the past, the late 1990s laid the foundations for a completely different future. What these new genres had in common was a sense of alienation and disorientation. While the huge party was punctuated by the thumping rhythms and catchy melodies of house and pop music, the new genres hinted at a latent existential malaise. They expressed the growing gap between the (jubilant) collective psyche and the (subdued) individual psyche. The arts embraced a form of neo-expressionism under the pretense of post-modernism.

Popular music at the turn of the millennium was also characterized by the confluence of two revolutionary trends. The first was world music. The 1990s had been the decade of world music, when Western musicians pillaged the rhythms, melodies and timbres of other ethnic cultures. In reality, Western musicians had only scratched the surface of the vast repertoire of sounds created over the centuries by the rest of the world. The exploration and integration had just begun. The second trend was electronic/digital music. New instruments had always determined musical revolutions, because, tautologically, they allowed for new forms of music. The electronic/digital "instrument" was bound to have an even bigger impact because the new forms of music that it enabled were virtually infinite. It also released the musician from the burden of finding a "band" and a "producer" before being able to deliver her music to the audience.

The commodization of atmosphere

Two trends were the two sides of the same coin. One was widespread among the pop crowd, that veered towards more and more sophisticated arrangements, longer songs, complex stories. The other one was typical of the avantgarde crowd, that veered towards ever more abstract soundscapes, whether of colossal post-psychedelic drones or of futuristic electronic cacophony, with a direction that was clearly towards an ever greater reliance on computers. The age of chamber pop and of digital soundscapes was basically the same age. Both deemphasized the central power of the melody and decentralized sound so that peripheric elements (whether acoustic timbres or artificial sounds) became more and more relevant. The aesthetic principle was the same of so much "atmospheric" music of the past, except that now it didn't require an orchestra and a sophisticated producer. In the new century, crafting atmospheres had become as commonplace as writing software.

The loser was the punk generation. That momentum had clearly drained away. What was left of the punk aesthetic was the sloppiness not the fury. Both singer-songwriters, one-man bands, regular bands and avantgarde combos often displayed a preference for a casual, careless attitude in delivering music (even though sometimes it had been painstakingly composed). That was punk's true legacy: another nail in the coffin of the Western musical tradition of aiming for the perfect combination of sounds.

The Age of Mediocrity

The boom of independent music at the turn of the millennium had changed the dynamics of the music industry. At about the same time, the CD (cheap to manufacture) replaced the vinyl album (expensive to manufacture). Shortly thereafter, the Internet allowed musicians to directly distribute their music, thus bypassing the selection of the old-fashioned "record label".

Unfortunately, the combined effects of these phenomena resulted in a boom of mediocrity. Among independent/avantgarde musicians, it became commonplace to release just about anything they recorded or just thought of recording. Needless to say, only a few minutes of the hours of recording that they released were truly indispensable.

Among mainstream musicians, it became commonplace to release an album that contained only one or two songs worthy of being released. The rest was filler, but was filler that increased the price of the release, i.e. the profits of the label and of the artist.

Both sides shamelessly took advantage of technology that allowed to print and distribute albums very easily. The cost of printing compact discs kept going down, and the Internet allowed to bypass the traditional, cumbersome marketing and distribution processes. The net result was a flood of poor-quality recordings.

The music press soon revealed itself to be part of the problem, not of the solution. Instead of helping screen and select the few outstanding recordings, countless magazines, fanzines and webzines promoted just about every recording as a masterpiece, no matter how trivial, derivative and amateurish it was. Basically, anyone could make a CD and count on at least ten critics writing a good review of it; which was enough to sell enough copies to break even. The free marketing provided by the music press increased the motivation of musicians to release as much as possible. It was one of the few infallible business plans of the age. The music press was in turn rewarded with free promo CDs: Darwinian competition forced critics to compete for access to promos (no reviews, no advertisers). Thus the musician (not the music critic) held the reins of power and could "blackmail" the music critic into writing positive reviews.

The whole scene was the ultimate in capitalism and consumerism. The idealism of the hippie age and of the punk age had been buried for good.

Mediocre artists were soon releasing their eighth or eleventh album, and with worldwide distribution. But then the very meaning of music-making had changed. More and more artists came to view music-making as simply an endless refinement for one simple idea. De facto, their music was wallpaper. Their first album introduced a mood, a tone, a style, and usually did so without having enough experience, skills or simply help from the producer. The following albums refined that very same trademark sound. The songs were mostly faceless. Each album was simply a repeat of the previous one with slightly different melodies, lyrics and arrangements. The listener could purchase any of their albums and find the same product, except that more recent "releases" of that product were likely to be more refined. The motivation to innovate became inversely proportional to the low cost of making albums.

The Disappearing Album

On the other hand, it was unfair to compare the quality of the "albums" released during the vinyl era (when making and distributing an album was an expensive process) with the quality of the "albums" released during the CD era (when making and distributing an album had become a cheap process). No wonder that the average quality of albums in the 1960s was so much higher than in the late 1990s: in the 1960s record labels could not afford to release an artist's album until it contained the best music that the artist could produce. The "album" of the 1990s, instead, was merely a snapshot of the artist at the time the artist made that album.

Ultimately, the "album" was rapidly becoming an obsolete concept.

The 1990s saw the apex and the downfall of the music industry. In 1979 Sony and Philips had invented the compact disc (CD), a digital storage for music, and the same year Sony had launched the "Walkman" portable stereo. In 1981 MTV debuted on cable tv. During the 1980s these innovations spread and redesigned the way music was marketed and sold. As the new paradigm took hold, the music industry seemed to enjoy its best time ever. In 1996 Mariah Carey's *One Sweet Day* topped the U.S. charts for an unprecedented 16 weeks, breaking all the Presley and Beatles records. In 1997 Elton John's *Candle in the Wind* became the best-selling song of all times, overtaking Bing Crosby's *White Christmas*. In 1999 'N Sync set the new record of sales in the first week of a new release (2.4 million copies)

In 1999 the world's music market was worth 38 billion dollars. The music world was ruled by five "majors" (Universal, Warner, Sony, EMI, BMG) that controlled 95% of all albums sold in the world, and 84% of the 755 million albums sold in the USA. The USA accounted for 37% of world sales, Japan for 16.7%, Britain for 7.6%, Germany for 7.4%, France for 5.2%, Canada for 2.3%, Australia for 1.7%, Brazil for 1.6%, Holland for 1.5%, Italy for 1.4%. Basically, the compact disc had helped the music industry to multiply its revenues.

Drum'n'Bass

Jungle

Dance music of the 1990s largely rejected the simple, jovial, hedonistic approach to body movement that had ruled since James Brown invented funk music in the 1960s. Disco, techno and house had simply imported new technologies (both for rhythm and arrangements) into the paradigm of funk. The 1990s continued that process, but further removing the "joy" of dancing from the beats, and, in fact, replacing it with fits of acute neurosis. One of the most important ideas to come out of Britain was "jungle" or "drum'n'bass", a syncopated, polyrhythmic and frantic variant of house, a fusion of hip-hop and techno that relied on extremely fast drum-machines, epileptic breakbeats and huge bass lines.

Precursors of jungle included, in the USA, *Bug In The Bassbin* (1989), the rhythmic workout of Carl Craig's Innerzone Orchestra, and, in Britain, Perfecto's *Baz De Conga* (1989). The experiments of Plaid and Meat Beat Manifesto also laid the foundations of jungle.

Jungle saw the light in 1992 in London with tracks such as Leakage Trip's *Psychotronic*, Nebula II's *Flatliners* and Johnny Jungle's *Johnny*, followed by Andy C's *Valley Of The Shadows* (1993) and Ed Rush's *Bloodclot Attack* (1993), while Omni Trio's *Renegade Snares* (1993) and especially LTJ Bukem's *Music* (1993) invented "ambient jungle" (a calmer, introverted version of that hyperkinetic dance music). The name originated from the London club that first promoted the new style, the "Jungle". Jungle (the style) spread like wildfire through other club venues, such as "Roast", "Roller Express", "Telepathy", "Desire", "A Way Of Life", "Jungle Rush", "Jungle Fever", "Thunder And Joy", "Thrust", etc. In 1994, the style began to be called "drum'n'bass", and in 1995 Goldie turned it into a mass phenomenon. The London club "Rage", thanks to disc-jockeys Fabio and Grooverider, became the epicenter of drum'n'bass.

Few genres of popular music underwent so many changes and reached such ambitious heights as jungle did. Within a few years, jungle musicians were already composing abstract and ambient pieces, integrating breakbeats with pop vocals, adopting jazz improvisation.

The golden age of drum'n'bass

4 Hero (2), the duo of Dego MacFarlane and Mark Mac, coined a sort of "armchair jungle", a groundbreaking marriage of fusion-jazz and ambient music that even employed lush strings and free-form electronics with the sci-fi concept album **Parallel Universe** (1994) and with the ambitious **Two Pages** (1998).

The first star of jungle, Goldie (1), born Conrad Price, made his name with the extended singles *Terminator* (1993) and *Timeless* (1994), which were mini-symphonies of hardcore techno, and the groundbreaking **Timeless** (1995), that used breakbeats to construct atmospheric music. Thanks to his skills at sound manipulation, he turned songwriting into sound painting. And the hour-long composition *Saturnzreturn* (1998) removed any boundaries from his studio explorations.

Another milestone for "ambient jungle" was the tour de force of **Waveform** (1996), by T Power (Marc Royal).

Roni Size (1), the leader of Bristol-based dj collective Reprazent and one of the first "auteurs" of drum'n'bass, blended jungle's breakbeats with live instruments and singing on the monumental double disc **New Forms** (1997), and reconciled dance music's suite format with the traditional song format of pop/soul music.

Other musicians who merged drum'n'bass with jazz were Photek, born Rupert Parkes, with **Modus Operandi** (1997), and James Hardway (real name David Harrow), with **Deeper Wider Smoother Shit** (1996).

Major additions to the drum'n'bass canon came from varius directions. Fila Brazillia, the duo of Steve Cobby and Dave McSherry, were perhaps the most adventurous in cross-fertilizing different genres, particularly on their later albums, such as **Power Clown** (1998) and **A Touch Of Cloth** (1999). Adam Fenton's **Colours** (1997) was also an album of diverse stylistic experiments. Boymerang (1), the new project of former Bark Psychosis frontman Graham Sutton, sculpted **Balance Of The Force** (Regal, 1997), a conceptual work of art that straddled the boundaries between pop, jazz and avantgarde. The imaginary soundtrack **Exorcise The Demons** (1999) qualified Source Direct, i.e. veterans Jim Baker and Phil Aslett, as jungle's equivalent of Barry Adamson.

In the meantime, new styles continued to emerge from London clubs, such as "techstep" (a fast, brutal fusion of techno and jungle probably invented by DJ Trace in 1994), "speedgarage" (mainly a production technique, developed by Armand Van Helden in 1996, of huge breakbeats and bass lines, which he himself defined as "a cross between house and drum'n'bass"), "two-step garage" (interplay of frantic breakbeats and velvety soul vocals, emerging in 1997) and "drill'n'bass" (very fast drum'n'bass). Garage music (only vaguely related to Larry Levan's "garage" of the 1980s, and closer to the style perfected by disc-jockey Tony Humphries of New Jersey's "Zanzibar" club) was refined by groups such as the Dreem Teem and Tuff Jam, and began to climb the British charts with Shanks & Bigfoot's *Sweet Like Chocolate* (1999) and Dj Luck & Mc Neat's *A Little Bit of Luck* (2000).

Germany's Panacea (1), i.e. Mathis Mootz, borrowed elements from death-metal and industrial music for the "drill'n'bass" sound of **Low Profile Darkness** (1997).

Animals on Wheels, the brainchild of British electronic musician Andrew Coleman, employed a kaleidoscopic assembly of jazz samples, frantic breaks and downtempo electronica on **Designs And Mistakes** (1997) for his brand of drill'n'bass.

Japan's Bisk, born Naohiro Fujikawa, introduced a very ornate, baroque, manically-crafted style on albums such as **Strange Or Funny-haha** (1997).

Propellerheads, i.e. Alex Gifford and David Arnold, led "big beat", the subgenre of drum'n'bass that assimilated tribal African beats, with **Decksandrumsandrockandroll** (1998).

Avantgarde jungle

Thanks to ever more intricate beats and to free structures borrowed from jazz, jungle music rapidly became the foundation for a new kind of avantgarde music, "conceptual jungle", pursued by the most austere of the genre's visionaries.

Spring Heel Jack (23), the project of John Coxon and Ashley Wales, subverted the rules of ambient jungle with the symphonic extravaganzas **There Are Strings** (1995) and especially **68 Million Shades** (1996). The experiments with jazz and minimalism of **Busy Curious Thirsty** (1997) blossomed on **Treader** (1999), a wild excursion into 20th century classical music. Most of its tracks sounded like symphonic poems: lush, thematic orchestral narratives built out of samples, loops and echoes. The jazz elements became predominant with **Disappeared** (2000), a work that alternated calculated geometry and Wagnerian intensity. Storming, Foetus-like spasms crushed a steady flow of sonic debris, while elsewhere melodic fragments morphed into alien structures. **Masses** (2001) completed their conversion to avantgarde jazz with a chamber concerto performed by the sensational ensemble of Matthew Shipp (piano), Evan Parker and Tim Berne (saxophones), Roy Campbell (trumpet), Daniel Carter (flute and saxophones), Ed Coxon (violins), Mat Maneri (viola) and William Parker (bass). And **Amassed** (2002), featuring Han Bennink (drums), Ed Coxon (violin), John Edwards (bass), Evan Parker (saxophone), Paul Rutherford (trombone), Matthew Shipp (piano), Kenny Wheeler (trumpet), and the "shoegazing" guitar of Spiritualized's Jason Pierce, was one of the most exhilarating stylistic orgies of modern jazz, straddling not one stylistic border but pretty much all possible borders.

Tom Jenkinson, better known as Squarepusher (2), coined a cubistic version of drum'n'bass on **Hard Normal Daddy** (1997): a wild assembly of manic breakbeats, spirited electronica and disjointed samples concocted a whirling cacophony a` la Morton Subotnick. Visceral intensity and impeccable fluidity coexisted and enhanced each other. Each piece on **Go Plastic** (2001) was, de facto, a treatise on a new form of Dadaistic, disjointed, beat-based music in which the drum-machine became the equivalent of a jazz instrument for a creative solo improvisation while approaching the abstract intensity of chamber electronic music (basically, musique concrete imbued with punk frenzy).

Brazilian-born Amon Tobin (12) well impersonated the classical composer in the hip-hop age. Instead of composing symphonies for orchestras, Tobin glued together sonic snippets using electronic and digital equipment. **Adventures in Foam** (1996), released under the moniker Cujo, and especially his aesthetic manifesto and masterpiece, **Bricolage** (1997), unified classical, jazz, rock and dance music in a genre and style that was universal. Tobin warped the distinctive timbres of instruments to produce new kinds of instruments, and then wove them into an organic flow of sound. Tobin kept refining his art of producing amazingly sophisticated and seamless puzzles on **Permutation** (1998), **Supermodified** (2000) and, best of his second phase, **Out From Out Where** (2002). Once he had exhausted the possibilities of instruments and samples, Tobin turned to found sounds and field recordings as the sources for **The Foley Room** (2007), without basically changing style. In effect, Tobin carried out several philosophical debates at once (e.g., on the irrelevance of the message, on the irrelevance of time), while entertaining his audience with catchy numbers of an extra-terrestrial music hall. Tobin was debating on the meaning of music itself, on the nature of composition, on the viability of communication, on the ultimate constituents of sound. His neglect of form was a new kind of form, a form that had reduced form to the annihilation of form. The dualism of content versus form was resolved by the post-modernists as a non-issue: Tobin redefined it as a process, a process of form-abatement by which content is created, as if content and form were the same substance, and more of one meant less of the other one.

Matt Elliott's Third Eye Foundation (1) evolved from the atmospheric blend of guitar textures and jungle breakbeats of **Semtex** (1995) to the sample-based disorienting puzzles of **Ghost** (1997) and especially **You Guys Kill Me** (1998).

Twisted Science (1), the project of disc-jockey Jon Tye, was to techno what Sonic Youth were to rock'n'roll: a scaffolding of hard-core techno was brutalized by layers of abrasive electronica, distorted hip-hop beats, jungle polyrhythms and industrial cacophony on **Blown** (1997).

Witchman (1), born John Roome, contaminated drum'n'bass with gothic, techno, industrial, dub and ambient music on **Explorimenting Beats** (1997).

Faultline (1), the brainchild of clarinet player and studio wizard David Kosten, fused chamber music, industrial techno and free-form noise on the melancholy multi-part sonatas of **Closer Colder** (1999).

Klute (Tom Withers) indulged in intricate and psychotic arrangements on **Casual Bodies** (1998).

Andrea Parker (1), a classically trained cellist, a disc-jockey and an electronic composer with a penchant for analog synthesizers, mixed string orchestrations, hip-hop beats and heavy bass to create the highly seductive music of **Kiss My Arp** (1999).

Neotropic (2), the project of female electronic dance musician Riz Maslen, offered a dreamy, deconstructed version of trip-hop and drum'n'bass on **15 Levels Of Magnification** (1996), although the tracks floated weightlessly (and beat-lessly) in the fragile, haunting electronic soundscapes of **La Prochaine Fois** (2001).

Icarus (2), the London-based duo of Ollie Bown and Sam Britton, dislocated beats and melodies on **Fijaka** (1998) while adopting a digital and minimalist aesthetic that would lead to pieces such as *Three False Starts*, off **I Tweet the Birdy Electric** (2004), at the border between ambient, jazz, concrete and glitch music.

Venetian Snares (2), the moniker of Canadian electronic musician Aaron Funk, established his trademark "breakcore" style of complex, brutal, distorted, skittering, whirling drum programming (with a manic passion for the 7/4 time signature and often only consisting of "clicks and cuts") on **Printf("shiver in eternal darkness/n")** (2000) and especially on **Doll Doll Doll** (2001). Innovative tracks of the period include the ten-minute *Twisting Ligneous*, off **2370894** (2002), the 15-minute *A Giant Alien Force More Violent & Sick Than Anything You Can Imagine* (2002), the nine-minute *Marty's Tardis*, off **The Chocolate Wheelchair Album** (2003), the digital pastiches of glitchy videogame-like drill'n'bass of **Find Candace** (2003), and the ferocious bombardments of the mini-album **Winnipeg is a Frozen Shithole** (2005); while *Badminton* (2003) and *Moonglow* (2004) toyed with jazz. Funk transformed from punk terrorist to nostalgic dreamer and existential philosopher with the "Hungarian" album **Rossz Csillag Allat Szuletett** (2005), that introduced strings, horns and piano. His split personality then yielded works such as **Meathole** (2005) in the old brutal style and works such as **My Downfall** (2007) in the orchestral style.

Noize Creator (1), the project of Dresden's disc-jockey Stefan Senf, emerged with harsh, visceral cut-up breakbeat decostructions that sounded like Nine Inch Nails playing drum'n'bass, and **Deferred Media** (2002), a barrage of syncopated beats set against wildly disjointed soundscapes.

New York's progressive jungle

Jungle came to the US in the second half of the decade, thanks to British expatriates such as DJ Dara Gilfoyle, sculptor of the cerebral, sinister, post-industrial soundscapes of **Rinsimus Maximus** (1997). New York became the main USA center for jungle. We (1), featuring Gregor "DJ Olive" Asch, demolished the cliches of dub, trip-hop, drum'n'bass and jazz on **As Is** (1997). Datach'i (2), Joseph Fraioli's brainchild, spun the chaotic high-speed digital novelties of **10110101** (1999) and the hyper-kinetic pandemonium of **We Are Always Well Thank You** (2000). Dylan Group (2), i.e. percussionist Adam Pierce and dj Dylan Cristy, retooled drum'n'bass for the post-rock generation with the jazzy, vibraphone-driven **It's All About** (1997) and the more relaxed **More Adventures In Lying Down** (1999), even expanding into progressive-rock with **Ur-Klang Search** (2000). Dylan Group's multi-instrumentalist Adam Pierce also had his own project, Mice Parade (1), that was even more adventurous on **The Meaning Of Boodley Baye** (1998) and on the the symphonic **Ramda** (1999), a dazzling take on dub, jazz and techno.

The musicians of the New York school created such bold experiments that the term "progressive jungle" was more appropriate.

At the same time, New York was home to the "Illbient" movement (as christened by DJ Olive).

Paul Miller, better known as DJ Spooky (5), the star of the Illbient movement, opted for a chaotic flow of rhythmic and non-rhythmic electronic sounds that harked back to Italian futurism and to electronic-music pioneers such as Morton Subotnick and Karlheinz Stockhausen. **Songs Of A Dead Dreamer** (1996) explored the least visited interstices of genres such as ambient, dub, electronica, trip hop, drum'n'bass. The tracks on **Riddim Warfare** (1998) were not so much dance grooves as catalogs of sound effects that turned drum'n'bass into an electronic symphony. His most ambitious work, **Viral Sonata** (1998), credited to Paul D. Miller, was an amorphous aural architecture that evoked a post-apocalyptic wasteland roamed by ghosts. **File Under Futurism** (1999) was chamber electronic music. **Optometry** (2002), performed by the quartet of pianist Matthew Shipp, bassist William Parker, saxophonist Joe McPhee and drummer Guillermo Brown, was one of the works that blurred the line between live and sampled jazz music.

The Illbient disease contaminated even avantgarde composer Bob Neill, a former member of La Monte Young's ensemble, who collaborated with DJ Spooky and We's DJ Olive on **Triptycal** (1996).

DJ Olive himself demolished and redirected the entire movement with **Buoy** (2004) and **Sleep** (2006), that contained only one colossal track each, and each a titanic endeavor of abstract soundsculpting, musique concrete, glitch art and ambient droning.

Mocean Worker (1), the project of New York-based vocalist and bassist Adam Dorn, followed in the footsteps of the jazz and drum'n'bass fusion of Spring Heel Jack, duly updated to the age of digital soundsculpting, on **Home Movies From the Brain Forest** (1998).

In Los Angeles, Medicine's guitarist/keyboardist Brad Laner used the moniker Electric Company to carry out a study in deconstruction of drum'n'bass as Kraftwerk would have done it, on **Studio City** (1997).

San Francisco-based disc-jockey Jhno (John Eichenseer) offered a bold fusion of ethnic, ambient, jazz and techno music on **Understand** (1995), while **Kwno** (1998) mixed drum'n'bass and computer-generated improvisation and **Membrane** (2000) focused on inventing a new vocabulary of irregular rhythms and eerie soundscapes.

Demolition Squad (1), the Los Angeles-based duo of jazz saxophonist Jim Goetsch and Japanese keyboardist Kim Koschka, integrated drum'n'bass, dub, trip-hop, world-music, orchestral and electronic effects to craft **Hit It** (2000).

Under the moniker Hrvatski, Boston's electronic and digital composer Keith Fullerton-Whitman (2) began composing drum'n'bass soundscapes that were actually audio collages of breakbeats, as documented on **Oiseaux 1996-1998** (1999). He began a more austere career of soundsculptor under his own name, first with the mini-album **21:30** (2001), an abstract piece for guitar and laptop computer that borrows the "phasing" technique of minimalist composer Steve Reich, and then with the album **Playthroughs** (2002), also dominated by electronically-manipulated guitar tones. The mini-album **Antithesis** (2004) and the full-length **Multiples** (2005) were split between droning trance, ambient nebulae, minimalist undulations and guitar psychedelia. All these strands came together on his masterpiece **Lisbon** (2006), a 41-minute live improvisation that also ventured into field recordings and Alvin Lucier-inspired feedback-driven music.

Trip-hop

The golden era of trip-hop 1995-99

Bristol's greatest invention, trip-hop, became one of the most abused languages of dance music.

After the success of Portishead came the deluge: Funki Porcini (James Braddell), with the pastoral **Hed Phone Sex** (1995); Rockers Hi-Fi, the Birmingham-based sound system of Richard "DJ Dick" Whittingham and Glyn Bush, with **Rockers To Rockers** (1995); Andrew Barlow's Lamb (1), with the psychodramas of **Lamb** (1996); Morcheeba, fronted by sensual chanteuse Skye Edwards, with **Who Can You Trust** (1996); Red Snapper (1), who sculpted the complex, arcane and recombinant **Prince Blimey** (1996); the Sneaker Pimps, the project of keyboardist Liam Howe and guitarist Chris Corner, fronted by singer Kelli Dayton, whose **Becoming X** (1997) was trip-hop for the generation that never heard the new wave; all the way to gothic, decadent chanteuse Alison Goldfrapp and her elegant, sexy and slow **Felt Mountain** (2000).

London-based producer Howie Bernstein, better known as Howie B (2), who had engineered the atmospheres of Soul II Soul's records, followed a different route on his solo albums: the instrumental tone poems of **Music For Babies** (1996), the stylistic studies **Turn The Dark Off** (1997), ranging from vibraphone-based lounge shuffles to big-band dancehall exuberance, and the elegant ballet of noises and instrumental sounds of **Snatch** (1999), works that elevated him to the jazz counterpart of Brian Eno and the hip-hop counterpart of Robert Fripp. Skylab (1), a collaboration between avantgarde composer Mat Ducasse and Howie B, crafted a wild collage of manipulated sounds, **#1** (1995), an essay in the absolute dissolution of identity that sounded like John Cage reborn as a disc-jockey.

In other countries musicians influenced by trip-hop produced an atmospheric form of sound collage that ventured beyond the original premises of trip-hop.

An atmospheric sound similar to trip-hop hovering in an ether halfway between dub, hip-hop and ambient music, was often produced via a technique of cut-up that was the equivalent of cinema's montage. For example: Grassy Knoll (1), the project of San Francisco-based disc-jockey, filmmaker, photographer and composer Bob Green, on **Grassy Knoll** (1995); or Russian-born Andre Gurov, better known as DJ Vadim, who focused on collage of micro-samples with **The Theory Of Verticality** (1996).

DJ Cam (French dj Laurent Daumail) sculpted the subliminal jams of **Substances** (1996), that frequently employed samples of obscure jazz records, and the doleful, impressionistic sonatas of **Loa Project Vol. 2** (2000).

Towa Tei, a Korean-Japanese former member of Deee-Lite in New York, assembled jazz, world-music and all sorts of retro styles on **Future Listening** (1995).

A number of "atmospheric" groups were also more or less related to trip-hop. Iceland's Gus Gus (1) coined an anemic, sleepy, out-of-focus kind of pop-soul-jazz ballad on **Polydistortion** (1995), that sounded like the equivalent of be-bop in the age of trip-hop: a dejected soundtrack for the neuroses of the urban crowd. Sweden's Whale incorporated sensual crooning and heavy-metal guitars into the trip-hop sound of **We Care** (1995). Tosca, i.e. Austrian producers and disc-jockeys Richard Dorfmeister and Peter Kruder, achieved the majestic mannerism of **Opera** (1997) and especially **Suzuki** (2000), which was replicated by the Sofa Surfers, an Austrian quartet led by Wolfgang "I-Wolf" Schloegl, on **Cargo** (1999).

Chris "P'taah" Brann (1), a white dj from Atlanta (Georgia), who had already contaminated house music with jazz and Latin elements, caused a sensation with the twisted fusion of futuristic jazz-rock, funk, downtempo and acid-jazz on **Compressed Light** (2000). He even adopted the austere, quasi-classical composure of the ECM sound for **Staring At The Sun** (2003).

Towards the end of the decade all these innovations circled back to influence British trip-hop.

Iranian-born London-based dj Leila Arab abstracted the stereotypes of trip-hop to create the surreal electronic folk of **Like Weather** (1998), each song being painstakingly sculpted and then caressed by a guest vocalists (mostly Luca Santucci). After an eight-year hiatus, Leila applied the same ideology to the otherworldly digital ambience of **Blood, Looms, And Blooms** (2008).

The Cinematic Orchestra (1), led by bandleader John Swinscoe, devoted **Motion** (1999) to a tribute to film soundtracks of the 1950s. It was one of the works that marked a turning point in avantgarde, when "reconstructing" started prevailing over "deconstructing" (that had been the dominant buzzword throughout the era of postmodernism).

The Groove Armada, i.e. London-based disc-jockeys, Tom Findlay and Andy Cato, "reconstructed" the romantically retro **Vertigo** (1999).

Western dub

Dub had a life of its own in the western world. Notable works included: **Sounds from the Thievery Hi-Fi** (1996) by Thievery Corporation (1), the project of Washington-based disc jockeys, Eric Hilton and Rob Garza; the series that culminated with **Dub Voyage** (2000) by Twilight Circus Dub Sound System, i.e. Holland-based multi-instrumentalist Ryan Moore; **Rome** (1996) by Rome, a Chicago instrumental trio of bass, drums and sampling keyboards sculpting dissonant electronic dub; **Dancehall Malfunction** (1997) by <u>Sub Dub</u> (the quartet of bassist John Ward, programmer Raz Mesinai, vocalist Ursula Ward and saxophonist Grant Stewart), which spearheaded a fusion of hip-hop, ambient house, world-music and dub; **CD 1** (1998) by <u>Pole</u>, i.e. Berlin-based sound engineer Stefan Betke, who became the master of a starkly minimalist form of dub-based dance music. Influenced by Bill Laswell's and Jah Wobble's experiments of the 1980s, not to mention Adrian Sherwood, the Pop Group and Tackhead, they reinvented the genre as a stark and austere form of art.

British dance hybrids, 1996-2000

Inevitably, in a world that lived on continuous change, the days of traditional techno and house were numbered. In 1996, for example, legendary British disc-jockey Paul Oakenfold launched "Goa Trance" at the "Full Moon Party", yet another dance craze ("Goa Trance" was literally Sven Vath's "trance" via the hippie tribes of Goa, in India), one that actually took hold in Germany and produced such production masterpieces as Paul Van Dyk's *For An Angel* (1998) and Andre Tanneberger's *9pm Till I Come* (1999). It was, however, the last of the major dance crazes.

<u>Spaceheads</u> (1), i.e. the duo of trumpeter Andy Diagram and percussionist Richard Harrison, alumni of Pop Group-style avant-jazz-funk-rock outfits such as the Honkies during the "Madchester" era, wed the collage techniques of the avantgarde, jazz improvisation and the angular rhythms of the post-techno dancefloor (a mixture of hip-hop, drum'n'bass and acid-jazz) on **Spaceheads** (1995), enhancing the textures of their "prepared" instruments with loops and overdubs.

<u>Leftfield</u>, i.e. the duo of Neil Barnes and Paul Daley, created techno for non-dancers (slower, softer, lighter) with **Leftism** (1995).

British producer, disc-jockey and tablas virtuoso <u>Talvin Singh</u> was an erudite purveyor of "transglobal dance" transplanting ethnic styles (and their traditional instruments) to a field of electronic beats and techno production techniques on **OK** (1998).

<u>Death In Vegas</u> (1), the brainchild of multi-instrumentalist Richard Fearless, contributed the ambient-dub-techno-rock stew of **Dead Elvis** (1998).

Inspired by "garage house", the style born in the late 1980s out of New York gay clubs that basically set sexy rhythm'n'blues crooning to a techno beat, <u>Basement Jaxx</u>, i.e. British disc-jockeys Felix Burton and Simon Ratcliffe, composed real songs out of exuberant, catchy, frantic post-techno music with reggae and Latin overtones on **Remedy** (1999).

<u>Faithless</u> (1), the project of producers and disc-jockeys Rollo Armstrong and Ayalah "Sister Bliss" Bentovim, penned the elaborate, acrobatic, chameleon-like arrangements of **Reverence** (1996).

The Lo-Fidelity Allstars opted for a "street" approach to dance music, rooted in urban alienation and decadence, with albums such as **How To Operate With A Blown Mind** (1998), while the music sampled (literally and metaphorically) half a century of dance styles, from soul to funk, from dub to house, from hip hop to trip-hop.

Luke Slater (1) crafted **Freek Funk** (1997), an eclectic potpourri of hip-hop, propulsive funk and ambient textures.

Christian Vogel was a significant composer of "dissonant" techno, particularly challenging on **Specific Momentific** (1996) and the programmatic **All Music Has Come To An End** (1998). Super Collider was a collaboration with producer and vocalist Jamie Lidell that fused soul crooning and ambient techno on **Head On** (1999). On his own Jamie Lidell concocted the deranged dissonant funk music of **Muddlin Gear** (2000) and injected different brands of old-fashioned soul music into the body of techno music on **Multiply** (2005).

South-African born and British-based dj Mira Calix (Chantal Passamonte) conceived a dance style that was an unlikely fusion of folk tunes, orchestral arrangements, oneiric ambience, twitching beats and field recordings, peaking with **Eyes Set Against the Sun** (2006).

In Ireland, David Holmes composed works, such as his third album, **Bow Down To The Exit Sign** (2000), that mixed audio verite` segments and an eclectic range of black musical styles (soul, acid-jazz, funk and hip-hop).

Cassius, a pair of veteran French producers of dance music, blended house music, dub, pop and hip-hop on **Cassius** (1999).

Post-dance music, 1999-2001

By the end of the decade the cross-pollination of dance styles had reached a level that either produced abstract stylistic collages or stifled the very nature of dance-music.

As One (1), i.e. British techno dj/producer Kirk Degiorgio, pursued a techno infused with elements of jazz and soul in the tradition of Squarepusher, notably on **Planetary Folklore** (1997) and on the luxuriant **21st Century Soul** (2001).

In Japan, Susumu Yokota (1) wove the intricate grooves of **Cat Mouse And Me** (1996) in a continuum of sonic bliss before turning to ambient house with **Magic Thread** (1998), a stylistic journey that would lead to an art akin to Brian Eno's impressionistic soundpainting on **Sakura** (2000) and **Grinning Cat** (2001).

Seattle's Entropic Advance (1), the project of Seattle-based avantgarde musicians Wesley Davis and Casey Jones, best summarized on the double-disc **Red Yellow Noise** (2002), concocted a collage of warped melodies, digital arrangements, multi-layered rhythms, ambient electronica, found sounds, free jazz, hip-hop, ethnic and industrial music.

The theatrical fusion of disco-music, punk-rock and dissonant electronica packaged by Detroit's <u>Adult</u> on their early EPs, starting with **Dispassionate Furniture** (1998), peaked with *Hand to Phone* (2001), one of the earliest electro-clash classics. **Anxiety Always** (2003), however, was a visceral and brutal work that betrayed their punk personas.

The German dancing avantgarde, 1997-2001

Germany, in particular, was still a leader in the fusion of avantgarde and dance music.

Robert Hood, a Detroit producer, was widely credited for "inventing" minimal techno. However, similar ideas had been pursued in Berlin since 1993 by Basic Channel (producers Moritz Von Oswald and Mark Ernestus), who were more influenced by dub music than funk/soul music. Monolake and Porter Ricks were the first major protagonists of minimal techno.

<u>Monolake</u>, the Berlin-based duo of Robert Henke and Gerhard Behles, bridged minimal dub-techno music and abstract digital soundsculpting, as documented on the compilation of singles **Hong Kong** (1997).

<u>Porter Ricks</u>, a duo with Andi Mellweg, was Thomas Koner's brainy and ghostly techno project, first documented on **Biokinetics** (1996).

Most purveyors of this subliminal languid psychedelic brand of "deep" techno, that basically de-emphasized the rhythm, were assembled around Chain Reaction, a Berlin-based record label owned by the Basic Channel duo: <u>Scion</u> (German techno producers Rene Lowe and Peter Kuschnereit) who had pioneered the sound with *Emerge* (1995), <u>Vainqueur</u> (Rene Lowe) whose anthemic *Lyot* (1992) had already been a hit and whose first album was **Elevations** (1997), <u>Substance</u> (Peter Kuschnereit) whose first album was **Session Elements** (1998), <u>Fluxion</u> (Konstantinos Soublis) whose first album was **Vibrant Forms** (1999), and <u>Hallucinator</u> (Anna Piva, Trevor Mathison and Edward George) whose first album was **Landlocked** (1999).

<u>Gas</u>, one of the many projects of <u>Wolfgang Voigt</u> (the godfather of Cologne's dance scene), inaugurated "minimal ambient techno" with **Zauberberg** (1997) and especially **Konigforst** (1998), on which he achieved a haunting fusion of the three elements. The dancefloor beat coexisted with abstract drones obtained by manipulating samples of classical music, tiny digital noises and a sense of cosmic dub. Another pioneer of Cologne's ambient techno was <u>Markus Guentner</u>, whose **In Moll** (2001) almost hid the beats behind the feathery, breathy drafts of electronics.

German house producer Rajko "<u>Isolee</u>" Mueller spearheaded "microhouse" (a fusion of glitch aesthetic, minimal techno and house music) with **Rest** (2000).

Rechenzentrum, the project of digital composer Marc Weiser and visual artist Lillevaen, engineered **Rechenzentrum** (2000), a subtle venture into the realms of minimal techno and hip-hop.

Komet, the project of German digital composer Frank Bretschneider, specialized in skeletal highly-processed glitch-techno music for microscopic events, notably on **Rausch** (2000) and **Curve** (2001).

Austrian drummer and electronic composer Bernhard Fleischmann (1) packaged a disorienting combination of glitch music and synth-pop on **Pop Loops for Breakfast** (1999). The two lengthy suites of **Tmp** (2001) and especially the double-disc **Welcome Tourist** (2003) pioneered the marriage of post-rock and dance music.

Post-post-rock

The Louisville alumni 1995-97

The Squirrel Bait and Rodan genealogies continued to dominate Kentucky's and Chicago's post-rock scene during the 1990s.

Half of Rodan, i.e. Tara Jane O'Neil (now on vocals and guitar) and Kevin Coultas, formed Sonora Pine with keyboardist and guitarist Sean Meadows, violinist Samara Lubelski and pianist Rachel Grimes. Their debut album, **Sonora Pine** (1996), basically applied Rodan's aesthetics to the format of the folk lullaby.

Another member of Rodan, guitarist Jeff Mueller, formed June Of 44 (11), a sort of supergroup comprising Sonora Pine's guitarist Sean Meadows, Codeine's drummer and keyboardist Doug Scharin, and bassist and trumpet player Fred Erskine. **Engine Takes To The Water** (1995) signaled the evolution of "slo-core" towards a coldly neurotic form, which achieved a hypnotic and catatonic tone, besides a classic austerity, on the mini-album **Tropics And Meridians** (1996). Sustained by abrasive and inconclusive guitar doodling, mutant rhythm and off-key counterpoint of violin and trumpet, **Four Great Points** (1998) metabolized dub, raga, jazz, pop in a theater of calculated gestures.

Post-rock was clearly more "instrumental" than "vocal", and Rachel's (2), formed by Rodan's fourth member, guitarist Jason Noble, merely formalized this fact with an all-instrumental format and a chamber ensemble built around Rachel Grimes' piano and Christian Frederickson's viola. **Handwriting** (1995) augmented the rock trio with strings and keyboards, but, rather than aiming for an orchestral sound, it downplayed the multitude of "voices" in favor of an artful exploration of timbres, while the narrative languished somewhere between the Club Foot Orchestra's dark soundtracks (minus the expressionistic overtones) and the Penguin Cafè Orchestra's minimalist dances (minus the nostalgic and exotic factors). By the time of **The Sea And The Bells** (1996), this somber hybrid had evolved into hermetic and severe avantgarde music.

For Carnation (1), the new project of Slint's guitarist Brian McMahan, followed Gastr Del Sol's route to subtle dynamics and wasteland-evoking soundscapes on two EPs, **Fight Songs** (1995) and the superb **Marshmallows** (1996). They refined the art of low-key, sparse but nonetheless complex compositions to the point that **For Carnation** (2000) betrayed virtually no emotions, just illusions of emotions.

Slint's guitarist Dave Pajo (11) contributed to dispel the notion that instrumental music had to be atmospheric with **Aerial M** (1997), which delivered languid sub-ambient slo-core in which elements of lounge jazz, Ennio Morricone's soundtracks and Rachel's semi-classical scores were carefully defused. His minimalist and transcendental technique, equally inspired by Pat Metheny (jazz), Robert Fripp (rock) and John Fahey (folk), reached an existential zenith on Papa M's **Live From A Shark Cage** (1999), a phantasmagoria of cubist de-composition, the instrumental equivalent of Tim Buckley's music.

Rodan's guitarists Jeff Mueller and Jason Noble reunited when they formed Shipping News (1) with drummer Kyle Crabtree, and recorded the oblique, undulating jams of **Save Everything** (1997). They refined their approach with the slow-forming filigrees of **Very Soon And In Pleasant Company** (2000), impersonating not so much brainy improvisers as consummate storytellers spinning enigmatic tales, full of twists and surprises. Rodan's wreckage of classical harmony left behind flotsam of dub-like ecstasy and hard-rock fits.

The Chicago alumni, 1995-98

The Tortoise genealogy constituted the epicenter for Chicago's post-rock of the 1990s.

Shrimp Boat (1), featuring vocalist Sam Prekop, coined a jazz-soul-country fusion that sounded like a cross between Camper Van Beethoven and the Minutemen, particularly on their second album, **Duende** (1992). Prekop's next band Sea And Cake (1) almost wed post-rock and easy-listening. The drunk, sleepy delivery of the vocalist was matched on **Sea And Cake** (1994) by a gentle, low-key, Steely Dan-ian soundscape of jazz and soul phrases laid down by guitarist Archer Prewitt and Tortoise's multi-instrumentalist John McEntire. The idea led to the sumptuous keyboard arrangements of **Nassau** (1995) and eventually the electronica of **The Fawn** (1997).

Jazz was a major factor in alienating the Chicago school from the traditional foundations of rock music. More and more units looked to jazz for inspiration: Isotope 217, the project of Tortoise's black guitarist Jeff Parker; Euphone, the brainchild of drummer Ryan Rapsys, whose **The Calendar of Unlucky Days** (1999) was devoted to improvised, instrumental jams mixing electronics, acoustic instruments and syncopated beats; Bill Ding, veterans of the jazz scene who performed chamber music for electronics, vibraphone, cello, trumpet and violin on **Trust In God But Tie Up Your Camel** (1997); Brokeback, a collaboration between Tortoise's bassist Douglas McCombs and Chicago Underground Quartet's bassist Noel Kupersmith, which delivered the quiet, ethereal, sparse watercolors of **Field Recordings From The Cook Country Water Table** (1999) and **Morse Code In The Modern Age** (2001).

Duotron (1) played abstract pieces in a psychotic form that ran the gamut from progressive-rock to noise to absurdist vaudeville to no wave and free-jazz, particularly on **We Modern We Now** (1995).

The instrumental group Town And Country (1) articulated an aesthetics of baroque trance that wed Harold Budd's hypnotic bliss and

Bill Evans' romantic jazz. The lengthy pieces of **Town And Country** (1998) and **It All Has To Do With It** (2000), straddling the line between jazz improvisation and classical composition, led to the mature post-fusion synthesis of **C'mon** (2002), performed by Jim Dorling on harmonium and bass clarinet, Ben Vida on guitar and cornet, Liz Payne on guitar, Josh Abrams on bass and celeste.

The Scissor Girls (1), led by keyboardist Azita Youssefi and drummer Heather Melowicz, devoted **We People Space With Phantoms** (1996) to a schizoid (and largely improvised) form of punk, funk and electronic music.

Zeek Sheck (the brainchild of Roseanna Perkins Meyers) composed a Residents-like pentalogy on an imaginary race starting with **I Love You** (1998), a chaotic assemblage of violin, flute, clarinet, harmonica, tuba, guitar, bass and electronics, including Cheer Accident's keyboardist Thymme Jones and cellist Fred Lonberg-Holm.

Frontier ran the gamut from shoegazing to King Crimson to Can to Tortoise on **Heather** (1997).

Dianogah, a trio of two basses and drums, betrayed the influence of Slint on the mostly-instrumental **As Seen From Above** (1997).

Boxhead Ensemble (4) was an impromptu project of the Chicago rock avantgarde that involved members of Tortoise, Jim O'Rourke and Ken Vandermark, assembled by composer Michael Krassner to score the soundtrack for a film, **Dutch Harbor** (1997), a set of austere, erudite, low-key and gloomy improvisations, of high-caliber noir and chamber jazz. Another stellar cast (Krassner, bassist Ryan Hembrey, violinist Jessica Billey, drummer Glenn Kotche, Souled American's guitarist Scott Tuma, cellist Fred Lonberg-Holm) improvised the smoky, sleepy chamber music of **Two Brothers** (2001), the seven transcendent **Quartets** (2003) and the eight zen-like **Nocturnes** (2006). The Lofty Pillars (10) recycled a few members of the Boxhead Ensemble to perform compositions by Krassner and keyboardist Will Hendricks. Like the Penguin Cafè Orchestra, **Amsterdam** (2001) was caught in a time warp, plotting a fusion of old-fashioned genres (Leonard Cohen-ian dirges, Dylan-ian odes, gospel and country hymns a` la Band) and modern aesthetic values, while delivering clockwork performances worthy of classical music.

Chicago's L'Altra (1) introduced a sublimely elegant fusion of pop, jazz and classical music with their EP **L'Altra** (1999). The effect of **Music Of A Sinking Occasion** (2000), ten madrigals for a small chamber ensemble played with a lazy renaissance grace, was to transpose atmospheric and intellectual pop music to another temporal dimension, in the vein pioneered in the 1970s by the Penguin Cafè Orchestra. **In The Afternoon** (2002), featuring cellist Fred Lonberg-Holm, crystallized their method: lush and oneiric soundscapes accompanying dual vocal harmonies.

The towering figure of this generation was cellist <u>Fred Lonberg-Holm</u>, who played in and led a number of orchestras and ensembles, notably <u>Pillow</u>, a quartet with the Flying Luttenbachers' reed player Michael Colligan, and two members of Town And Country, bassist Liz Payne and guitarist Ben Vida, best documented on their second album **Field On Water** (2000), and **Terminal 4** (2001), that offered rock music for a pseudo-jazz quartet of cello, guitar (Ben Vida), bass (Josh Abrams) and trombone (Jeb Bishop), the <u>Terminal 4</u>.

Chicago's trio (saxophone, bass and drums) <u>Bablicon</u> (1), featuring Neutral Milk Hotel's drummer Jeremy Barnes, was influenced by Soft Machine's progressive-rock, Slint's post-rock and Frank Zappa's irreverent musique concrete. The noisy, spastic, psychedelic jazz-rock of **In A Different City** (1999) and of the mini-album **Orange Tappered Moon** (2000) led to **A Flat Inside A Fog, The Cat That Was A Dog** (2000), a gloriously incoherent statement of piano-based ambient cacophony.

The golden age of post-rock, 1995-1997

The most obvious link between post-rock of the 1990s and progressive-rock and German avant-rock of the 1970s was a band from Maryland, <u>Trans Am</u> (1), a trio led by guitarist/keyboardist Philip Manley. The keyboards-driven instrumental rock of **The Surveillance** (1998) was unique in that it exhuded the rhythmic exuberance of dance music. The group moved towards a less distinctive but more accessible prog-pop sound that culminated with **Red Line** (2000), under a broad range of influences, from Devo's futuristic rock'n'roll to Frank Zappa's noise-jazz bacchanals.

<u>Jackie-O Motherfucker</u> (2), the project of New York-based multi-instrumentalist Tom Greenwood, relied heavily on free-jazz improvisation for **Alchemy** (1995), **Cross Pollinate** (1996) and especially **Flat Fixed** (1998), featuring female guitarist Honey Owens, although his most intriguing works were probably the ones that moved away from those roots. **Fig 5** (1999) piled up elements of acid-rock, folk, blues, noise-rock and soul; and the jazz elements all but disappeared on the double-disc **Magick Fire Music** (2000), an epic journey from noise collage to ambient melancholia.

The recordings of the <u>No-Neck Blues Band</u> (3), a loose New York-based collective of improvisers, were mainly devoted to long chaotic instrumental jams that drew inspiration from the Art Ensemble Of Chicago, Captain Beefheart, Amon Duul II and Pink Floyd. **Letters From The Earth** (1996), recorded on a roof in 1996 and including the 38-minute jam *Isopropyl Ocean*, and **Sticks And Stones May Break My Bones But Names Will Never Hurt Me** (2001) ran the gamut from an anthropological recapitulation of primal shamanic music to free-jazz improvisation. At their best, the jams were minimalist fanfares of sorts, combining a number of repetitive patterns into a tribal acid trip of loose guitar/mandolin threnodies, polymorph multi-instrumental beats, loose aggregates of free-jazz horns and languid trance-like droning instruments. **Qvaris** (2005) dressed that dadaistic vice into a more austere format, bordering on electroacoustic chamber music and musique concrete.

Boston's Karate were emblematic of post-rock's ambition to concoct loose and jazzy song structures, notably on **In Place of Real Insight** (1997).

In San Francisco, the iconoclastic tradition of the Residents and Thinking Fellers Union Local 282 was continued by albums such as: Double U's **Absurd Fjord** (1996), Ubzub (1)'s **Alien Manna For Sleeping Monkeys** (1996). Deerhoof (1) was an avant-pop concept that balanced cacophony and melody, abstraction and organization, and evolved from the blissful Captain Beefheart-esque anarchy of **The Man The King The Girl** (1997) to the prog-garage ingenuity of **Reveille** (2002).

Instrumental post-rock 1995-99

Instrumental rock music became more and more ambitious in the second half of the decade.

Chicago's 5ive Style (2), formed by guitarist Billy Dolan, Tortoise's drummer John Herndon, bassist LeRoy Bach and Lonesome Organist's keyboardist Jeremy Jacobsen, concocted first the angular funk and rhythm'n'blues of **5ive Style** (1995), which sounded like the Meters playing for Schoenberg, and then the nostalgic Caribbean nonsense of **Miniature Portraits** (1999), replete with demonic picking and kitschy vibraphone.

Salaryman (1), the all-instrumental subsidiary of the Poster Children, toyed with a kaleidoscope of genre deconstructions on **Salaryman** (1997).

San Francisco's A Minor Forest indulged in the lengthy instrumental improvisations of **Flemish Altruism** (1996).

North Carolina's Tractor Hips glued together remnants of Soft Machine's jazz-rock, Can/Faust's kraut-rock and John Zorn's avant-jazz on **Tractor Hips** (1996).

The Fucking Champs (1), hailing from San Francisco, leveraged the double-guitar attack of Josh Smith and Tim Green (ex-Nation Of Ulysses) on **III** (1997), released under the moniker C4AM95, one of the few works to bridge heavy-metal and post-rock since the pioneering work of Bitch Magnet.

Paul Newman were Don Caballero's disciples in Texas with albums such as **Frames Per Second** (1997).

Minnesota's prog-rockers <u>Gorge Trio</u> (1) applied Don Caballero's art of counterpoint to **Dead Chicken Fear No Knife** (1998) and **For Loss Of** (1999).

Dazzling Killmen's bassist Darin Gray and Cheer Accident's drummer Thymme Jones who had been the rhythm section for O'Rourke's projects Brise-Glace and Yona-Kit, formed <u>You Fantastic</u> with guitarist Tim Garrigan, whose **Homesickness** (1999) contained brief experiments at the border between hardcore and free-jazz.

San Diego's <u>Tristeza</u> (1) seemed to wed new-age music and instrumental post-rock with the slow, gentle pieces of **Spine And Sensory** (1999).

<u>Out of Worship</u> was a collaboration between San Francisco-based guitarist/bassist Joe Goldring and Codeine/Rex/Him's drummer Doug Scharin, whose **Sterilized** (1999) achieved a sophisticated and colorful fusion of jazz, raga, psychedelia and dub (thanks to Ill Media's turntables, Tony Maimone's bass, Julie Liu's violin and Adheesh Sathaye's tablas).

<u>Turing Machine</u>'s **A New Machine For Living** (2000), the new project by Pitchblende's Justin Chearno, wed four generations of jamming (1960s' acid-rock, 1970s' kraut-rock, 1980s' noise-rock and 1990s' post-rock).

Industrial nightmares 1998-2000

<u>Laddio Bolocko</u> (1), featuring Drew StIvany on guitar, Ben Armstrong on bass, Marcus DeGrazia on saxophone and ex-Dazzling Killmen's drummer Blake Fleming, mixed the neurotic introspection of post-rock and the psychotic attack of hardcore on **Strange Warmings** (1997), whose jams also referenced free-jazz and acid-rock. As structures exploded and imploded, the listener was taken on a rollercoaster of stylistic mirages. The soundscape got blurred on the EPs **In Real Time** (1998) and **As If By Remote** (1999), that abandoned the frenzy of the debut album to concentrate on textural explorations. After the group split, bassist Ben Armstrong and guitarist Drew St.Ivany formed <u>Psychic Paramount</u> with a drummer and de facto continued the same mission of Laddio Bolocko on **Gamelan Into The Mink Supernatural** (2005).

<u>Phylr</u> (1), the new project of Cop Shoot Cop's keyboardist Jim Coleman, indulged in Foetus-like gothic and industrial overtones on **Contra La Puerta** (1998).

Minnesota's space-rockers <u>Salamander</u> (1) indulged in abstract soundpainting on **Red Ampersand** (1998) and turned the title-track of **Red Mantra** (1999) into an avantgarde concerto.

San Francisco's <u>Burmese</u> were a guitar-less trio or quartet (two basses and one or two drums) who, inspired by Whitehouse's horror free-form noise, by the more abstract forms of grindcore and occasionally by

Earth's subsonic drones, crafted the dense, chaotic, frenzied and heavy 21 brief songs of **Monkeys Tear Man To Shreds, Man Never Forgives Ape, Man Destroys Environment** (2000).

San Diego-based Tarantula Hawk delivered post-industrial doom and psychedelic delirium on two self-titled albums, **Tarantula Hawk** (2000) and **Tarantula Hawk** (2002).

Ebbing and flowing 1995-2000

As instrumental post-rock lost its hardcore component and shunned the trance-oriented approach of ambient music, it developed into a new form of music, both dynamic and atmospheric.

Rake's guitarist/keyboardist Bill Kellum and Pitchblende's guitarist Justin Chearno formed a keyboards-guitar-drums trio, Doldrums (12), that concocted an atmospheric blend of Main's ambient shoegazing, Tangerine Dream's cosmic music, Grateful Dead's *Dark Star* and Pink Floyd's *A Saucerful Of Secrets*. **Secret Life Of Machines** (1995) and **Acupuncture** (1997) contained multi-part suites that, under the apparent staticity, mutated continuously, each an amorphous plasma of sounds that went from exuberant to ecstatic, from chanting to droning, from tribal drumming to abstract doodling. **Feng Shui** (1998) was a more artificial work, the product of studio editing, but that technique was refined on **Desk Trickery** (1999), a multitude of carefully-crafted sonic events seeping through the shapeless jelly.

Scenic (2), the new project by Savage Republic's founding member Bruce Licher (now living in Arizona), interpreted desert music in an almost cosmic setting. If **Incident At Cima** (1995) was still impressionistic and sketchy, **Acquatica** (1996) and **The Acid Gospel Experience** (2002) were ambitious frescoes of the musician's environment and, indirectly, of the musician's psyche.

Seattle's Hovercraft (2), the project of keyboardist/guitarist/samplist Ryan Campbell, created the musical equivalent of action painting performed by an epileptic acrobat on phantasmagoric albums such as **Akathisia** (1997) and **Experiment Below** (1998). Their atonal mini-symphonies recalled alternatively Sonic Youth, Red Crayola and King Crimson, but also wove a supernatural suspense and inspired apocalyptic fear.

Their cousins Magnog (1) incorporated the aesthetics of post-rock into the plot-less synth-tinged instrumental tracks of **Magnog** (1996), that offered a tuneless and mantra-oriented form of space-rock.

San Francisco's Tarentel (2) sculpted **From Bone To Satellite** (1999), a magnificent plateau of desolate, dilated, arpeggiated, minor-key, synth and guitar-driven scores a` la Godspeed You Black Emperor. A more humane feeling surfaced from the stark, carefree solemnity of **The Order of Things** (2001). The four-volume series of **Ghetto Beats On**

The Surface Of The Sun (2006) zeroed on skeletal rhythms piercing through a jelly of glitchy ambience. Their "ghetto" was a psycho-musical ghetto, a mythological "place" of the mind that manifested itself in a plethora of disorienting soundscapes.

Montage, 1996-99

In New York, M'lumbo (1) bridged dissonant avantgarde, free-jazz and dance music with the free-form collages of **Spinning Tourists in a City of Ghosts** (1999), that applied the collage technique to the most diverse sources.

Boston's Land Of The Loops (1), the project of Boston keyboardist Alan Sutherland, produced the cartoonish collages of samples, dance beats and ethereal vocals of **Bundle Of Joy** (1996).

Bran Van 3000 (1), the project of Montreal-based multi-instrumentalist Jamie DiSalvio, assembled **Glee** (1998), a surreal, dissonant, hyper-realistic collage of hip-hop, conversations, scratches, jazz improvisation, choirs, loops, orchestral instruments, that magically retained the traditional song format.

In Holland, Solex (12), the project of Dutch used-record specialist Elizabeth Esselink, updated the soul-jazz diva to the age of samplers and drum machines. The songs on **Pick Up** (1999) and especially **Low Kick And Hard Bop** (2001) were fragments of music glued together and propelled by disjointed beats. The difference between her compositions and the audio cut-up of the avantgarde was that her compositions were actually "songs", and even "melodic" ones. Her silky voice blended naturally with the frigid textures of her collages. Few composers could turn a cold, artificial art of puzzle recomposition into a warm, personal art of personality decomposition, as she proved on another painstaking, almost surgical, cut-and-paste tour de force, **Laughing Stock Of Indie Rock** (2004).

The Australian ensemble Avalanches (1) coined a new form of sample-based dance music with their early singles and perfected it with the clockwork collages of **Since I Left You** (2000).

German post-rock 1994-98

Post-rock owed a huge debt to German rock of the 1970s. Thus, it was not surprising that Germany rapidly became one of the centers for post-rock.

Ronald Lippock's To Rococo Rot (1) basically unified the aesthetics of trip-hop and post-rock on **Veiculo** (1997), achieving on **The Amateur View** (1999) a gentle, subliminal blend of hypnosis and vitality. Lippock's side-project Tarwater (1) infused the robotic rhythms and alien noises of **11/6 12/10** (1996) with romantic melodrama.

Laub (1), the duo of vocalist Antye Greie-Fuchs and keyboardist Juergen "Jotka" Kuehn, explored alien soundscapes on **Kopflastig** (1997) and especially **Unter anderen Bedingungen als Liebe** (1999).

Markus Archer's Notwist (1), featuring Martin "Console" Gretschmann on samples, were fluent in the idioms of hardcore, noise-rock and post-rock, which they applied simultaneously to the pastiches of **12** (1997). By the time that they crafted the carefully orchestrated and absurdist ballads of **Neon Golden** (2001), instead, they were pioneering the digital folk-rock of the new decade. Their cousins Village of Savoonga (1) straddled the line between expressionist drama, psychedelic doom and stream of consciousness on **Philipp Schatz** (1996) and on the mini-album **Score** (1998). And their other cousins Tied & Tickled Trio (1) revived cool jazz for the digital generation on **Tied & Tickled Trio** (1998) and **EA1 EA2** (1999), while horns-driven **Observing Systems** (2003) and the keyboards-driven **Aelita** (2007) balanced the elegant flow of a jazz improvisation and the cold geometry of a classical composition.

Workshop were the main heirs to the "krautrock" tradition during the late 1990s, especially on **Meiguiweisheng Xiang** (2000).

The "songs" built by Notwist's sampling engineer Console (born Martin Gretschmann) on albums such as **Pan Or Ama** (1997) and **Rocket In The Pocket** (1999). were tributes to studio technique, concentrates of electronic and computer trickery, complex hodgepodges of synthesizer melodies, spastic beats, samples, dissonances, reverbs, computerized voices.

Kreidler (1), featuring keyboardists Andreas Reihse and Detlef "DJ Sport" Weinrich, toyed with jazz, disco and glitch music on **Weekend** (1996) and with austere post-rock chamber music on the mini-album **Eve Future** (2002).

Lali Puna, the project of Munich-based vocalist and multi-instrumentalist Valerie Trebeljahr, crafted minimal and alienated form of synth-pop on **Tricoder** (1999).

Austrian electroacoustic trio Radian (1) vivisected glitch electronica, post-rock and digital processing with surgical precision on the instrumental tour de force **TG11** (2000).

These German projects made up a formidable generation of experimental musicians, worthy of their predecessors Can, Neu and Faust.

British post-rock, 1995-99

Piano Magic, the project of guitarist Glen Johnson, offered the fragile electronic tapestry of **Popular Mechanics** (1997), performed on cheap keyboards and reminiscent of Young Marble Giants and Brian Eno.

Scotland's Mogwai (1) anchored the blissful, impressionistic ambience of **Young Team** (1997) to atmospheric guitar sounds, ranging from celestial drones to hellish walls of distortions. Removing the impetus of that work, **Come On Die Young** (1999) revisited the desolate soundscapes of "slo-core", music that wandered, drifted, diluted itself into myriad variations of its own theme. The slowly-unfolding ballads of **The Rock Action** (2001) and the carefully orchestrated, organic, rational sonatas of **Happy Songs For Happy People** (2003) were practical applications of that theory.

Other notable albums of the second half of the decade included: **Precious Falling** (1997) by Quickspace, the new project of Faith Healers' guitarist Tom Cullinan; the trilogy of concept albums begun with **Caledonian Gothic** (1997) by Fiend, the brainchild of Mogwai's drummer Brendon O'Hare; **Slow Motion World** (1998) by Snowpony, the supergroup of Stereolab's keyboardist Katharine Gifford, My Bloody Valentine's bassist Deborah Googe and Rollerskate Skinny's drummer Max Corradi; **Hammock Style** (1998) by Ganger; **Little Scratches** (1998) by Rob Ellis' Spleen; **Fried For Blue Material** (1998) by Davey Henderson's Nectarine #9, inspired by the Pop Group and Captain Beefheart; and **Volume One** (2000) by Richard Warren's Echoboy.

Fridge was the post-rock project of English multi-instrumentalist Kieran Hebden that reached maturity with the evocative melodies of **Eph** (1999) and **Happiness** (2001). His alter-ego Four Tet (2) better revealed the composer's ambitions, starting with the encyclopedic 36-minute rhythmic vortex of the single *Thirtysix Twentyfive* (1998) and the electronic ethnic-jazz fusion of **Dialogue** (1999). **Pause** (2000) and **Rounds** (2003) repeatedly crossed over into "jazztronica" and digital beat-based folk music. Four Tet's "digital folk" became an abstract exercise in layering contrasting patterns over unassuming melodies and disappearing rhythms.

Appliance conceived **Manual** (1999) and especially **Imperial Metric** (2001) at the confluence of post-rock and shoegazing, a notion that would become more and more popular in the coming decade.

Post-rock primitivism 1995-97

Chicago's U.S. Maple (2), formed by Shorty's guitarist Mark Shippy and vocalist Al Johnson, were among the "primitivists" of post-rock. The post-modernist blues of **Long Hair In Three Stages** (1995) used a confused vocabulary of spastic jamming, acid singing and crooked geometry, inspired by Red Crayola and Captain Beefheart. US Maple's surgical strike on tradition achieved an immaculate purity on **Talker** (1999) and **Acre Thrills** (2001). Both impeccable in their execution of the science of musical flaws and faults, they represented a genuine confession of love for what the band hated.

Seattle's Old Time Relijun (2) were possibly the greatest disciples of Captain Beefheart in the 1990s, devoted to organizing musical structures out of sheer chaos. The psychotic jazz-rock of **Songbook Vol 1** (1997) evoked a meeting of the Contortions and Albert Ayler, but the more experimental **Uterus And Fire** (1999), with Phil Elverum of the Microphones on drums, was reminiscent of Jon Spencer's deformed blues except that the focus was on DeDionyso's vocal histrionics, while atonal guitars and childish drums created a divine mayhem. The leader's saxophone solos and a demented rhythm section graced **Witchcraft Rebellion** (2001).

Chicago's Joan Of Arc (2), featuring multi-instrumentalist and singer Tim Kinsella and keyboardist Jeremy Boyle, inhabited a niche of sub-folk music with the likes of Nick Drake and Smog, but they focused on the disturbing process of a neurotic soul in the making. **A Portable Model** (1997) shunned the edgier, harshest overtones of post-rock and reached out to Will Oldham's anti-folk. That format was perfected with the rambling and sparse ballads of **How Memory Works** (1998), a cybernaut's journey through the extreme periphery of German avant-rock and electronic music. After a calm and subdued **Live in Chicago** (1999), Kinsella's ensemble crafted a frail music of scant and tentative emotions with the unstable and unfocused structures of **The Gap** (2000).

Colossamite (1) was the Gorge Trio augmented with the unholy growl of Dazzling Killmen's vocalist Nick Sakes. **All Lingo's Clamor** (1997) and **Economy Of Motion** (1998) unleashed brief but terrifying firestorms of dissonant guitars, chaotic drumming and beastly screams.

Oregon's Rollerball (1), that featured Mae Starr (vocals, keyboards, accordion), Amanda Wiles (sax) and Shane DeLeon (trumpet), indulged in Pop Group-inspired, spastic, psychedelic, progressive and free rock that peaked with **Trail Of The Butter Yeti** (2001).

Post-post-rock 1996-99

Lowercase (1), San Francisco's guitar-drums duo of Imaad Wasif and Brian Girgus, staged unstable, suicidal psychodramas via the slow, lengthy dirges of **All Destructive Urges** (1996) and especially **Kill The Lights** (1997), which basically reenacted over and over again a descent into a personal hell.

Chris Leo conducted the textural experiments of Van Pelt's **Sultans Of Sentiment** (Gern Blandsten, 1997) and Lapse's **Heaven Ain't Happenin'** (2000).

I Am Spoonbender, the trio of Pansy Division's drummer Dustin Donaldson, Cub's guitarist Robynn Iwata and keyboardist Brian Jackson, mined the border between Brian Eno's retro-pop and Can's austere avant-rock on **Sender/ Receiver** (1998).

Indiana's Tombstone Valentine (1), fronted by vocalist Richelle Toombs, renewed the art of space-rock with **Hidden World** (1998), an album which blended the surreal element of Pink Floyd's **Piper At The**

Gates Of Dawn, the percussive element of 1970s' German avant-rock, and the exotic element of the Third Ear Band.

New York's Oneida (1) carved an odd niche for themselves with the convoluted psychedelic and post-rock freak-outs of **A Place Called El Shaddai's** (1998), a mixture of Blue Cheer, Sonic Youth, and Can that blossomed on the sophisticated and harrowing **Each One Teach One** (2002).

Fantomas, a supergroup formed by Faith No More's vocalist Mike Patton, Melvin's bassist Buzz Osbourne on guitar, Mr Bungle's bassist Trevor Dunn and Slayer's drummer Dave Lombardo, debuted with an explosive blend of heavy metal and abstract sound-painting on **Fantomas** (1999). Their third album **Delerium Cordia** (2004) was instead a 74-minute chamber concerto for rock band, vocalist and electronics that sculpted an ambience inspired by progressive-rock, glitch electronica, post-rock and dark metal.

The core of the New York-based Animal Collective (3) was guitarist Avey Tare (real name David Portner) and drummer Panda Bear (real name Noah Lennox). The extraterrestrial android vaudeville of **Spirit They're Gone Spirit They've Vanished** (2000), credited to the duo, evoked Flaming Lips and Mercury Rev in their most anarchic moments, establishing an aesthetic of tenderly dissonant post-psychedelic electronica that was (deliberately) chaotic and unfocused. After the more abstract **Danse Manatee** (2001), credited to "Avey Tare, Panda Bear and Geologist", **Here Comes The Indian** (2003), the first album credited to the Animal Collective, was even more erratic and amoebic. The Animal Collective now resided firmly on the soundsculpting side of the musical universe. Rhythms and melodies had been subjected to a process of purification and distillation resulting in a complete loss of identity. The Animal Collective tempered its quirkiness on **Sung Tongs** (2004), although regained some of its wild edge on **Strawberry Jam** (2007). Meanwhile, Panda Bear (1) performed a spectacular deconstruction of pop and folk music on his solo album **Person Pitch** (2007) with multi-part vocal harmonies, cheesy bubblegum melodies and trance-inducing tribal rhythms, weaving singalongs that rode layers of humble arrangements according to an ancestral logic of tribal repetition and jovial self-parody.

Georgia's San Augustin (David Daniell and Andrew Burnes on guitar, Bryan Fielden on drums) specialized in introspective slow-motion low-volume free improvisation, documented on the live **Amokhali** (2000).

The Music Tapes (1), the brainchild of Neutral Milk Hotel's multi-instrumentalist Julian Koster, conceived **First Imaginary Symphony For Nomad** (1999) as a gigantic, mad collage in the vein of the Fugs' *Virgin Forest* with notable parts for singing saw and bowed banjo. Another cartoonish survey of a whole musical century, **Music Tapes for**

Clouds & Tornadoes (2008), turned sound quality into a co-protagonist by recording all the songs on vintage equipment of yore.

Noise-rock's epitaph 1995-97

In the mid-1990s noise-rock picked up steam again. The new generation was led by creative outfits that reinvented rock music by embedding twisted melodies into atonal structures and, sometimes, irregular rhythms. Frequently, their songs were aural puzzles soaked in the history of rock music. Occasionally, their method straddled the line between trance and dissonance. Significant albums in this genre to come out of New York included: Poem Rocket's **Felix Culpa** (1996), Lynnfield Pioneers' **Emerge** (1997) , **Fantastic Spikes Through Balloon** (1996) by Skeleton Key (1), **In An Expression Of The Inexpressible** (1998) by Blonde Redhead (1).

Firewater (2) was a noise super-group formed by Cop Shoot Cop's vocalist Tod Ashley, Jesus Lizard's guitarist Duane Denison, Motherhead Bug's pianist/trombonist Dave Ouimet, Soul Coughing's percussionist Yuval Gabay and Laughing Hyenas' drummer Jim Kimball. Ashley's tormented soul dominates **Get Off The Cross** (1997) and **The Ponzi Scheme** (1998), wandering in the paleo-gothic purgatory inhabited by the likes of Tom Waits and Nick Cave.

In Britain, 50 Tons Of Black Terror's **Gutter Erotica** (1997) was an album of brutal, convoluted, harsh music in the tradition of Jesus Lizard.

Mood music, 1998-99

Calexico (12), which was Giant Sand's rhythm section of bassist Joey Burns and drummer John Convertino, coined one of the most distinctive and traditional styles of the era. The languid, introspective and touching mood of **The Black Light** (1998) relied on humble but eccentric orchestration and an hallucinated, oneiric take on mariachi music and Ennio Morricone's soundtracks. Austere but friendly, they sounded like the equivalent of the Penguin Cafè Orchestra for the Arizona desert. With **Hot Rail** (2000), Calexico opted for a more intimate form of expression, for a stylish, somber, bleak ballad that is often drenched in psychedelic reverbs and accented by jazz instruments. **Feast of Wire** (2003) was, instead, an album of film-noir gloom.

Black Heart Procession (11), a collaboration between Three Mile Pilot's singer Pall Jenkins and keyboardist Tobias Nathaniel, switched to melancholy, funereal music, sparsely arranged with analog keyboards, guitars, xylophone and trumpet. The skeletal lullabies of **1** (1997) led to the dark and creepy **2** (1999), which basically coined a new form of existential ballad, one that leveraged and transcended the abused stereotypes of Nick Drake, Leonard Cohen and Nick Cave. **3** (2000) wrapped the naked agony of that album into sophisticated arrangements, that, enhanced with Matt Resovich's violin, led to the post-psychedelic trance-y ballads of **The Spell** (2006).

Maquiladora (3), a trio from San Diego (vocalist Phil Beaumont, drummer Eric Nielsen, guitarist Bruce McKenzie), filled **Lost Works of Eunice Phelps** (1998) with lunatic ballads baked by the hot sun of the desert that ran the gamut from the drugged folly of the Holy Modal Rounders to the calm poetry of Leonard Cohen, from Syd Barrett's mad folk to the eerie stupor of Cowboy Junkies. **White Sands** (2000) refined the idea by adding several keyboards and string instruments to their arsenal, a move that somehow highlighted the similarities with Calexico's hallucinated country-rock. Far from being only an intellectual exercise, Maquiladora packed an impressive amount of poetry in the brief vignettes of **Ritual Of The Hearts** (2002).

Colorado's Czars (1) progressed from the low-key bittersweet laments of **Before... But Longer** (2000) to the atmospheric **The Ugly People Vs The Beautiful People** (2003), enhanced with the stately voice of John Grant.

Georgia's Japancakes achieved an almost transcendental fusion of post-rock, alt-country and atmospheric instrumental rock on their third album **Waking Hours** (2004).

Italy 1996-2001

At the turn of the century, Italy's post-rock scene had become one of the most vibrant in the world.

Ossatura indulged in a mixture of abstract electronic soundscaping, free-jazz improvisation, concrete collage and progressive-rock on **Dentro** (1998).

The Dining Rooms (Stefano Ghittoni and Cesare Malfatti) ventured into trip-hop with a cinematic twist on **Subterranean Modern Volume Uno** (1999).

Yuppie Flu's **Days Before The Day** (2003) offered charming folk vignettes arranged with analog electronic keyboards.

Maisie (Alberto Scotti and Cinzia La Fauci) penned the dissonant and cartoonish divertissement **The Incredible Strange Choir Of Paracuwaii** (1999) under the aegis of Captain Beefheart and Dada.

Quintorigo's postmodern chamber workout **Rospo** (1999) was Italy's best attempt at classic-jazz-rock fusion since the heydays of progressive-rock.

Minimal duo My Cat Is An Alien (1) delivered a post-rock version of Tim Buckley's sublime dejection on the totally improvised three-part jam **Landscapes Of An Electric City** (1999). The (improvised) music on the triple-CD **The Cosmological Eye Trilogy** (2005) attained an even higher form of nirvana: astral and subliminal soundscapes sculpted with an arsenal of sound-producing objects at the transcendental border where acid-rock meets post-rock and free-jazz.

A Short Apnea (former Afterhours' guitarist Xabier Iriondo, guitarist Paolo Cantu and vocalist Fabio Magistrali) blurred the borders between post-rock, free-jazz and electronic avantgarde in the three jams of their second album, **Illu Ogod Ellat Rhagedia** (2000).

Bron Y Aur played a devastating kind of improvised post-rock on **Bron Y Aur** (Beware, 2000).

Giardini di Miro` (1) assembled an intriguing combination of hypnotic instrumental textures, deconstructed melodies, dilated psychedelic improvisation, and melodramatic soft-loud glacial/vibrant dynamics on **Rise and Fall of Academic Drifting** (2001).

Notable was also Yo Yo Mundi's instrumental post-rock puzzle **Sciopero** (2001).

Zu (1) revived the school of jazzcore from the perspective of the post-rock generation with the brutal, free-form instrumental music of **Igneo** (2002).

Jennifer Gentle (1), perhaps the premier psychedelic band of Italy, penned the surreal folk-pop of **Funny Creatures Lane** (2002) for rock quartet, strings, accordion and sitar.

To The Ansaphone's **To The Ansaphone** (Heartfelt, 2003) harked back to the angst-filled no wave of the late 1970s (Pop Group, Contortions, DNA).

Larsen were among the most creative groups to try and bridge the aesthetics of post-rock and glitch electronica with the austere, brooding, hypnotic atmospheres of **Rever** (2002) and **Play** (2005).

Canada 1998-2000

The most important school of instrumental post-rock to emerge at the end of the decade actually came from Canada.

Godspeed You Black Emperor (3), a large ensemble from Montreal, revolutionized (mostly) instrumental rock with the three slow-building compositions of **f#a# Infinity** (1998): they were not melodic fantasies (too little melodic emphasis), they were not jams (too calculated), and they were not symphonies (too low-key and sparse), but they were something in between. Emotions were hard to find inside the shapeless jelly, dark textures and sudden mood swings. The four extended tracks of **Lift Your Skinny Fists Like Antennas To Heaven** (2000) were more lively, but no less enigmatic, alternating baroque adagios for chamber strings, majestic psychedelic crescendos, martial frenzy, noise collages and, for the first time, tender melodies. **Yanqui UXO** (2002) was a collection of glacial, colorless holograms with no dramatic content, massive black holes that emitted dense, buzzing radiations.

Three members of Godspeed You Black Emperor (guitarist Efrim Menuck, violinist Sophie Trudeau and bassist Thierry Amar) contributed to the two lengthy multi-part suites of **He Has Left Us Alone But Shafts Of Light Sometimes Grace The Corners Of Our Rooms** (2000), credited to <u>A Silver Mt Zion</u> (1), that presented a more humane face of Godspeed's music, bending the techniques of the baroque adagios and allegros to fit the spleen (if not the aesthetic) of post-rock. Two Godspeed members (drummer Aidan Girt and violinist Sophie Trudeau) also contributed to <u>Set Fire To Flames</u>' **Sings Reign Rebuilder** (2001), a much more noise-experimental work.

<u>Fly Pan Am</u> (1), the project of Montreal's guitarist Roger Tellier, followed the example of Godspeed You Black Emperor for the lengthy and stately instrumental suites of **Fly Pan Am** (1999).

The <u>Shalabi Effect</u> (2), organized in Montreal by Sam Shalabi, employed vintage electronics, ethnic percussions, manipulated instruments and found sounds to produce the propulsive and trancey scores of **Shalabi Effect** (2000). The same orchestra of ethnic, western and electronic instruments performed **The Trial Of St Orange** (2002), wedding Third Ear Band, Amon Duul II and Taj Mahal Travellers; while Sam Shalabi's solo **On Hashish** (2001) was a more pretentious experiment with field recordings, free improvisation, droning and glitches.

Toronto's instrumental combo <u>Do Make Say Think</u> imbued **Do Make Say Think** (1998) and **Goodbye Enemy Airship the Landlord Is Dead** (2000). with irregular flows of electronic, electric and acoustic sounds, yielding a fragile hybrid of free jazz, psychedelic dub, Canterbury-style spleen and progressive-rock. The sprawling **Winter Hymn Country Hymn Secret Hymn** (2006), structured as a set of three-movement suites, achieved a quiet grandeur.

Scandinavian alienation 1999-2000

Towards the end of the decade the marriage of the old post-rock aesthetic and the new digital aesthetic led to intriguing contrasts in the northern lands.

Norwegian duo <u>Alog</u> (1) composed **Red Shift Swing** (1999), a set of chamber lieder for acoustic ensemble, homemade instruments, found sounds and electronics.

Iceland's <u>Mum</u> (2) offered a delicate mixture of glitch electronica, chamber instruments and atmospheric vocals on **Yesterday Was Dramatic Today Is Ok** (2000) and **Finally We Are No One** (2002) applied the idea to a vast spectrum of music. The first album was a brainy disquisition. The second one was the object of that disquisition.

Finland's prolific <u>Circle</u> (1), a mostly instrumental combo fronted by bassist, vocalist and keyboardist Jussi Lehtisalo, adopted a stance that wed progressive-rock, metal riffs, repetitive patterns a` la Steve Reich's minimalist music, "motorik" rhythms a` la Neu, and mystical trance on **Andexelt** (1999) and **Guillotine** (2003), while **Miljard** (2006) removed the "metal" element altogether indulging in quasi new-age atmospheres. Suites such as *Puutiikeri*, off **Tulikoira** (2005), and *Steel Torment Warrior*, off **Tyrant** (2006), were more atmospheric than violent.

Norway's Salvatore, played instrumental hypnotic droning propulsive abstract rock a` la Circle on **Jugend - A New Hedonism** (2000).

Progressive music 1995-99

The Babel of music that did not abide by the linear conventions of pop music proliferated more than ever.

New York boasted talented and innovative combos that descended from the prog-rock bands of the 1980s. The veterans who ran Run On (11), drummer Rick Brown and bassist Sue Garner of Fish & Roses, plus guitarist Alan Licht of Love Child, and violin player Katie Gentile, showed how prog-rock could yield engaging songs and not only difficult constructs. **Start Packing** (1996) was a festival of instrumental lunacy, brainy hypnosis, eccentric arrangements, and lightweight cacophony that mostly stuck to the format of the pop song. The oneiric folk-rock of **No Way** (1997), inconspicuously raised on acid-rock and Indian music, homaged the classics (Bob Dylan, Lou Reed, Neil Young) while steering away from classic rock. Nothing in these albums was obvious. Every note was where it was because "that" was not where it should have been, if one were a traditional composer. Brown and Garner's vision of music was a place where we should (obviously) all have been but have never even dreamed of being. **Still** (1999), credited to Garner and Brown, was, de facto, a late addition to the Run On canon.

One of the most eccentric musicians of his time, Dave Soldier (the violinist of the renowned Soldier String Quartet), organized the **Thai Elephant Orchestra** (2001), an ensemble of elephants playing large custom-made instruments and performing their own improvisations and some compositions by Soldier and others. He also organized the **Tangerine Awkestra** (2000), a vocal ensemble of schoolchildren performing free improvisation.

New York's Escapade (1) performed all-instrumental music straddling the line between kraut-rock, hyper-psychedelia and progressive-rock. The three lengthy acid jams of **Searching For The Elusive Rainbow** (1996) and the two epic-length excursions of **Inner Translucence** (1997) led to **Citrus Cloud Cover** (1998), containing the 30-minute *The Sunlight*, a tour de force within the tour de force, and the best formulation of their conflagration of free-jazz and avantgarde electronic music.

New York's <u>Rasputina</u> (1) were a trio of female cellists who played minor-key waltzes, sounding like the Penguin Cafè Orchestra fronted by Nico on **Thanks For The Ether** (1996).

New York's quartet <u>Gutbucket</u> (bassist Eric Rockwin, saxophonist Ken Thompson, guitarist Ty Citerman, drummer Paul Chuffo) played music of a frenzied and caustic wit straddling the border between punk-rock and progressive-rock on **Insomniacs Dream** (Knitting Factory, 2001),

An erudite form of instrumental progressive-rock was coined in Boston by <u>Cerberus Shoal</u> (3). The neoclassical suites of **And Farewell To Hightide** (1997) and **Elements Of Structure/ Permanence** (1997), particularly *Permanence*, sounded like Grateful Dead's *Dark Star* performed by a chamber ensemble. Deeper jazz and world-music undercurrents destabilized the two tours de force of **Homb** (1999), while the pieces on the transitional **Crash My Moon Yacht** (2000) sounded like collages. **Mr Boy Dog** (2002), both irreverently amusing and wildly creative in the tradition of Frank Zappa, offered sonic charades that mixed Albert Ayler, Nino Rota, Sonic Youth and Pink Floyd while deconstructing world-music, funk and free-jazz. The dense orchestration and inventive dynamics capitalized on three decades of progressive-rock.

<u>Bright</u>'s **Bright** (1996) in Boston bridged Cul De Sac and shoegazing.

The <u>Amoebic Ensemble</u> was a small chamber ensemble led by accordionist Alec Redfearn in Rhode Island that straddled the border between progressive-rock and cartoon music on **Limbic Rage** (1995). <u>The Eyesores</u> were a large chamber ensemble formed by Redfearn that evolved from the cabaret-influenced style of **May You Dine on Weeds Made Bitter by the Piss of Drunkards** (1999) to a more abstract, avantgarde, progressive style, peaking with the 23-minute fantasia *Gutterhelmet Ascending*, off **The Smother Party** (2006).

Rhode Island's <u>Space Needle</u> (2), featuring keyboardist Jud Ehrbar, were responsible for the titanic nonsense of **Voyager** (1996), a deliberately amateurish work pushing the boundaries of progressive, psychedelic and cosmic music with mystical overtones. The no less cryptic hodgepodge of **The Moray Eels Eat The Space Needle** (1997) indulged in instrumental prog-rock jamming, ambient ballads and shoegazing ecstasy.

<u>Bent Leg Fatima</u> (1) from Philadelphia played a more ethereal version of Soft Machine's progressive-rock on **Bent Leg Fatima** (2000). When they reformed under the new name <u>Need New Body</u>, their **UFO** (2003) opted for a fragmented and demented format.

Florida's <u>Big Swifty</u> (1) crafted the austere compositions of **Akroasis** (1997) around drones a` la LaMonte Young, minimalist repetition a` la Terry Riley and microtonal techniques.

Also in Florida, <u>Meringue</u> mixed the verve and imagination of Frank Zappa, Captain Beefheart and Gong on the monumental **Music From The Mint Green Nest** (1996); while <u>Obliterati</u>'s **Havy Baubaus**

Inflience (1998) sounded like a meeting of the Art Bears and the Contortions.

Washington's El Guapo (1) added manic doses of electronics to its stew of Soft Machine, Contortions, Pop Group and the Fall on their third album **Super System** (2002).

Michigan's Larval, an open ensemble formed by Bill Brovold (a veteran of Rhys Chatam's groups), played progressive-rock tainted with avantgarde techniques on **Larval** (1997), that featured a rock band, and on **Larval 2** (1998), a free-form freak-out that expanded the rock band to classical and jazz instruments.

Aloha (1), from Cleveland (Ohio), merged progressive rock, free jazz, minimalism and post-rock in the intricate pieces of **That's Your Fire** (2000).

Ohio's Witch Hazel (1), the project of multi-instrumentalist Kevin Coral, indulged in a poppy and baroque form of progressive-rock on **Landlocked** (1995).

Inspired by Japanese noise-core, Chicago's TV Pow, a trio of electronic musicians (including Brent Gutzeit), compiled albums of atonal and chaotic electronic music such as **Away Team** (1998) and **Television Power Electric** (1999).

The Progressive West-Coast

In San Francisco, the Tin Hat Trio (1) evoked the Penguin Cafè Orchestra and the Lounge Lizards on **Memory Is An Elephant** (1999) with a mixture of tango, jazz, folk, avantgarde and world-music. **Helium** (2000) was its cerebral counterpart, a kaleidoscope of quasi-dissonant jamming, pseudo-Balkan frenzy and atonal lounge melodies.

Spaceship Eyes, the new project by Melting Euphoria's keyboardist Don Falcone, pushed progressive-rock towards a sort of acid electronic ethnic ambient music on **Kamarupa** (1997).

San Francisco's Species Being (1) penned the 11-movement suite **Yonilicious** (1998), an adventurous sonic odyssey through the musical genres.

Idiot Flesh were a Dada-inspired rock cabaret act and a colorful commune of dancers and noise-makers in San Francisco. Their shows, performed in outrageous costumes, would mix puppets, psychedelic lights, pyrotechnics, visuals and theatre. Their albums, from **Tales of Instant Knowledge and Sure Death** (1990), featuring guitarist Gene Jun, bassist Dan Rathbun, drummer Chuck Squier, keyboardist Daniel Roth and multi-instrumentalist Nils Frykdahl, to **Fancy** (1997), continued the tradition of eccentrics such as the Residents and Thinking Fellers Union Local 282.

Estradasphere, a Bay Area-based quintet (with saxophone and violin) that participated in the community of Mr Bungle and Secret Chiefs 3, concocted a frenzied Frank Zappa-esque carnival of styles (ambient, jazz, metal, country and classical music) on **It's Understood** (2000), notably the 20-minute *Hunger Strike*.

The Climax Golden Twins, the Seattle-based duo of Rob Millis and Jeffery Taylor, crafted surreal lo-fi collages of field recordings, electronic noise and sampled voices organized as madcap free-form pseudo-psychedelic jams on albums such as **Imperial Household Orchestra** (1996), **Locations** (1998) and **Session 9** (2001).

A progressive world, 1996-99

Symphonic rock was pursued in England by Guapo (1). After toying with samplers and electronics on **Hirohito** (1998), they fell under the influence of the Ruins and crafted **Great Sage** (2001), including the 16-minute epic *El Topo*. A more comprehensive summation of their art was the five-part suite **Five Suns** (2004).

In France, Volapuk (1) continued the neoclassical school of Art Zoyd and Univers Zero with albums such as **Slang** (1997). Tear Of A Doll, featuring guitarist Francois L'Homer, fused progressive-rock, punk-rock, jazz, exotica and noise on **Tear Of A Doll** (1996). Later Francois L'Homer relocated to Burma and started Naing Naing, a project devoted to "music without instruments", as demonstrated on **Toothbrush Fever** (2004) for natural sounds, computer and studio mixer.

The slow, thick and majestic compositions of Ulan Bator (2), a French ensemble led by guitarist Amaury Cambuzat, linked post-rock with French progressive-rock, especially on **Vegetale** (1997) and **Ego Echo** (2000).

Canterbury's melodic jazz-rock survived in the music of the Forgas Band Phenomena, founded by veteran French composer and drummer Patrick Forgas. They debuted with the two lengthy suites of **Roue Libre** (1997) for a sextet with saxophone, vibraphone and keyboards. The 34-minute *Coup De Theatre* appeared on **Soleil 12** (2005) and a "short" excerpt of *Double-Sens* appeared on **L'Axe du Fou** (2008).

Aavikko, the project of Finnish drummer Tomi Leppanen, penned the frenzied electronic instrumentals of **Derek** (1997), full of syncopated beats, old-fashioned analog keyboards, lounge jazz atmospheres, garage-surf rave-ups, and catchy melodies. The way the whole was sequenced and layered evoked alien noir soundtracks.

Norwegian horns-based combo Jaga Jazzist (1), a collective of multi-instrumentalists founded by Lars Horntveth and including Jorgen Munkby, straddled the border between the Canterbury (melodic jazz-rock) sound of Soft Machine and the Chicago (brainy post-rock) sound of Tortoise on **A Livingroom Hush** (2001). The electronic and "orchestral" **The Stix** (2003) veered towards atmospheric jazztronica for the masses.

Norwegian improvisers <u>Supersilent</u> (3), featuring Motorpsycho's keyboardist Helge "Deathprod" Sten, set a terrifying standard of violent and cacophonous jazz-rock on their triple-CD **1-3** (1998), an orgy of dissonant instruments, electronic noise and tribal drums, somewhere between free jazz and Japanese noise-core. All the extremes were painstakingly explored on the wildly improvised **5** (2001), while **6** (2003), instead, achieved an otherworldly balance of moods and sounds in six compositions (not only improvisations) of subtle counterpoint.

<u>Koenjihyakkei</u>, the Magma-inspired side-project of Ruins' mastermind Tatsuya Yoshida that debuted with **Hundred Sights of Koenji** (1994), eventually achieved a baroque complexity on **Angherr Shisspa** (2005).

Vajra's dummer <u>Toshiaki Ishizuka</u> constructed ambient music for an "orchestra" of tonal percussion instruments on **In The Night** (1999) and **Drum Drama** (2006).

Ambience

prootgarde world music, 1995-1999

The technology of sampling and the broad availability of ethnic instruments turned world-music into a sort of commodity. Generally speaking, the studio became the real center of the new "high-tech" world-music.

Georgia's Macha (1) penned the mostly improvised **Macha** (1998) and the quasi-symphonic **See It Another Way** (1999); while New York's Badawi, Raz Mesinai's project, fused traditional Middle-Eastern instruments, simple reggae figures and syncopated drumming at a deeper level on **Jerusalem Under Fire** (1997).

Tuatara (1), a supergroup made of REM's Peter Buck, Screaming Trees' drummer Barrett Martin, Luna's bassist Justin Harwood and jazz saxophonist Skerik (Nalgas Sin Carne), indulged in studio magic on the all-instrumental **Breaking The Ethers** (1997).

Michigan's Fibreforms (1) performed instrumental world-music a` la Penguin Cafe Orchestra on **Treedrums** (1996), but based on the haunting sound of the African bounkam. They changed their name to Kiln (1) and repeated the exploit with **Holo** (1998).

Hochenkeit, led by guitarist Jeff Fuccillo of Portland's Irving Klaw Trio, concocted the psychedelic/electronic world-music cauldron **I Love You** (1999), inspired by German avant-rock of the 1970s.

Britain's Bob Holroyd integrated Deuter's eastern spirituality, Jon Hassell's fourth-world atmosphere and Deep Forest's sampling on **Fluidity And Structure** (1995).

The lush electronic arrangements and soothing melodies of **Mythos** (1998) by Canada's Mythos were the obvious bridge with new-age music.

Dead Can Dance's multi-instrumentalist Brendan Perry (1) returned with **Eye Of The Hunter** (1999), an intensely personal statement arranged for (synthesized) orchestra and a plethora of acoustic instruments, but more reminiscent of Nick Cave and Leonard Cohen than of his old band.

In Japan, Onna-Kodomo offered a languid and spiritual fusion of western classical music and eastern classical music on **Syuuka** (1997), in a vein similar to Popol Vuh's **Hosianna Mantra**.

Terra Ambient (1), the project of electronic musician Jeff Kowal, employed percussion, didjeridoo, guitar and ethnic instruments for the "fourth-world music" of **The Gate** (2004).

Ambient guitar noise 1995-2000

In the USA, ambient guitar noise was generally more subdued than it had been in Britain at the beginning.

Pennsylvania's <u>Azusa Plane</u> (1), the project of guitarist Jason DiEmilio, formalized a mystical psycho-acoustic art of guitar drones and overtones on **Tycho Magnetic Anomaly And the Full Consciousness of Hidden Harmony** (1997) leading to the chamber ambient dissonant music of **America Is Dreaming Of Universal String Theory** (1998).

The genre of instrumental drone-oriented psychedelic music was perfected by Oregon's <u>Yume Bitsu</u> (11). The lengthy, trancey, ethereal suites with a dramatic edge of **Giant Surface Music Falling to Earth Like Jewels From The Sky** (1998) were reminiscent of both German cosmic music and British shoegazers. On **Yume Bitsu** (1999), the quintessential album of extended psychedelic jams, guitarists Adam Forkner and Franz Prichard painted (or, better, drilled) soundscapes of incredible brightness, enhanced by the surreal palette of Alex Bundy's keyboards. Texture and mood were the two fundamental axes of Yume Bitsu's art. Their technique was mainly "pointillistic": a thick layer of colored dots (percussions, guitar tones, repeated chords) that created the illusion of shapes and stories.

<u>Surface of Eceon</u> (1), formed in New York by former Yume Bitsu's guitarist Adam Forkner, penned **The King Beneath the Mountain** (2001), an album of epic-length triple-guitar textures, adrift in a solemnly calm sea of languid notes that recalled both Popol Vuh and Pink Floyd, but refracted through the lenses of Dali's surrealism. Forkner's stylistic journey eventually rediscovered the land of Terry Riley's **Rainbow In Curved Air** and Brian Eno's **Discreet Music** with <u>White Rainbow</u>'s **Prism Of Eternal Now** (2007).

<u>Pan American</u> (2), the side-project of Labradford's guitarist Mark Nelson, used the extended (and mostly instrumental) compositions of **Pan American** (1998) and especially **360 Business 360 Bypass** (2000) to craft ambient music for the post-house age. Mixing wavering beats, organic pulses, digital noise, processed instruments and voices, Nelson built minimalist soundscapes and populated them with slow-motion events. The process of music-making was hardly recognizable anymore, especially when all that was left was a weak, unfocused signal. Whenever instruments or voices resurrected harmony, Nelson killed it again, at a deeper level. Wadded rhythms drifted through the music rather than supported it. **The River Made No Sound** (2002) whispered languid tones into liquid, murky textures. **Quiet City** (2004) was music of environments that are, first and foremost, in the mind. The events within those environments are modest and tidy, but generate intense poetry, as in the sonata of *Christo in Pilsen*. Mark Nelson's still nature, which prefers pale colors and smooth surfaces, reveals itself in a discreet, almost fearful manner. The subtleties and innuendos of Nelson's compositions gave ambient music a new meaning.

San Francisco's <u>Bethany Curve</u> bridged pop song and ambient guitar on **Gold** (1998). Michigan's <u>Tomorrowland</u> seemed to play old-fashioned "kosmische musik" on **Stereoscopic Soundwaves** (1997) even though all sounds were produced by manipulating acoustic instruments.

Ambient avantgarde, 1995-2001

Ambient music was another example of an avantgarde genre that, by the end of the decade, had become a commodity. A handful of composers took it as an inspiration to create new forms of "light" electronic music.

<u>Cevin Key</u> (1) of Skinny Puppy composed a magniloquent symphony for "subconscious electronic orchestra", **Music For Cats** (1998).

A former member of Chicago's Illusion of Safety, <u>James Johnson</u> recreated Harold Budd's ethereal ecstasy with the computer-generated music of **Surrender** (1999).

<u>Stars Of The Lid</u> (2), the Austin-based duo of Adam Wiltzie and Brian McBride, manipulated found sounds, acoustic instruments and electronics to produce the ambient concertos of **Ballasted Orchestra** (1997); and an even more austere exploration of melody and movement was carried out on **The Tired Sounds Of Stars Of The Lid** (2001).

Los Angeles-based tuba improviser <u>Tom Heasley</u> manipulated the sound of the tuba in order to produce the ambient music of **Where the Earth Meets the Sky** (2001) and **On the Sensations of Tone** (2002).

New York-based clarinetist and saxophonist <u>William Basinski</u> (3) specialized in gentle compositions for loops and drones, whether derived from snippets of radio broadcasts, such as on **The River** (2002), or composed with electronic keyboards, such as on **Watermusic** (2001), or obtained by letting tapes slowly deteriorate, such as on **The Disintegration Loops** (2003), or created out of variations on simple melodic patterns, such as on **The Garden of Brokenness** (2006) and **Variations For Piano And Tape** (2006).

<u>Eliane Radigue</u> (1) proved to be La Monte Young's greatest disciple on **Trilogie De La Mort** (1998).

Pendulum (1999) by <u>Kevin Keller</u> (1), featuring David Darling on cello and Jeff Pearce on guitar, achieved a magical balance of lyrical and cerebral elements by juxtaposing cosmic drones of guitar and cello against slow piano notes.

Other notable ambient recordings included <u>Robert Scott Thompson</u>'s **Music for A Summer Evening** (1997), and <u>Akira Rabelais</u>'s **Spellewauerynsherde** (2004).

The **Metachoral Visions** (1997) by <u>Larry Kucharz</u> (1) signaled an original (and somewhat neurotic) take on the repetitive music of minimalist Steve Reich, with a preference for timbres that approach the busy signal of the telephone.

Rick Cox's 25-minute piece of the EP **Fade** (2005) was typical of
the ever more popular strategy of creating ambient music via tone
exploration: the instruments improvised around each other's sustained
dreamy tones, patiently weaving a labyrinthine celestial atmosphere.

Ashera (1), Australian electronic sound-sculptor Anthony Wright, was
a faithful disciple of the paradisiac ambient music of Harold Budd on
Colour Glow (2000).

British ambience, 1995-2001

An important contribution to ambient music of the mid-1990s came
from the British collective Ora (1), that included Colin Potter, Darren
Tate and Andrew Chalk. Their droning music was quite humble, peaking
with the eight vivid rural landscapes of **Amalgam** (2000).

Andrew Chalk (1), who had debuted in 1985 with the industrial noise
of his project Feral Confine and had collaborated on David Jackman's
project Organum, emerged solo with the crystalline, shimmering ambient
music of **East of the Sun** (1997), and soon became a specialist in ringing
overtones. **Over the Edges** (1999) contains three untiled works of 1997
obtained by exciting only two strings of an acoustic guitar with an e-bow
(an experiment along the lines of old ideas by Alvin Lucier and Ellen
Fullman). The 74-minute droning symphony of **Shadows From The
Album Skies** (2004) was devoted to extended droning-guitar monoliths
whose overtones harked back to the experiments of Phill Niblock and
Eliane Radigue. **The River That Flows Into The Sands** (2005) and **The
River That Flows Into The Sands II** (2006) explored oneiric and
ghostly guitar soundscapes. Among his most evocative works of deep-
listening music were **Sumac** (1999), a 71-minute collaboration with
Jonathan Coleclough, **Fall In The Wake Of A Flawless Landscape**
(2004), and the 51-minute solo-piano suite **Blue Eyes Of The March**
(2006). Mirror was a prolific collaboration between Christoph Heemann
of HNAS and Andrew Chalk, whose manifesto, **Eye Of The Storm**
(1999), created a thick blend of natural sounds, ringing percussion,
fluttering electronics and Heeman's sustained bowing drones.

Colin Potter had started releasing cassettes in 1979, but his first solo
CD was **And Then** (2000).

Monos was the new project of Darren Tate that focused on the droning
manipulation of field recordings, a project that often involved Colin
Potter (de facto, a continuation of Ora without Chalk). Despite the
abrasive sound of early pieces such as the 32-minute **Promotion** (2000),
Monos was more often concerned with the thick, rich drones of pieces
such as **360 Degrees** (2001) and **Sunny Day In Saginomiya** (2001), that
explicitly referenced natural sounds. However, **Nightfall Sunshine**
(2002), that delved into the "concrete" sound of vintage analogue
electronics, and the 47-minute **Collage** (2003) were more ambitious in

that Potter's studio work all but totally eclipsed the original sources, a process that peaked with the four extended pieces of the double-disc **Generators** (2005).

Paul Bradley became part of the same scene via his collaborations with Colin Potter and Darren Tate. His major solo works of droning computer-manipulated field recordings were disc-length pieces such as: the 54-minute **Liquid Sunset** (2005), the 40-minute **Sketches From Dust** (2006) for guitar and piano drones, the 41-minute **Memorias Extranjeras** (2006), the 57-minute **Pastandpresentcollide** (2006), the 40-minute **Sketches From Dust** (2006).

British sound sculptor John Coleclough (1) operated at the border between droning ("deep listening") music and abstract electronic music on sophisticated poems such as **Cake** (1998). His **Period** (2001) ranked as one of the most soothing and monolithic compositions in the repertory of droning music.

Nick "Farfield" Webb coined a form of ambient music for tape collage of electronic sounds, found sounds and instruments on **The Edges of Everything** (1999).

Hwyl Nofio (1), the brainchild of veteran British guitarist Steve Parry, prepared droning and drifting collages of treated keyboards and guitars (including Danish guitarist Fredrik Soegaard and Hungarian guitarist Sandor Szabo) for **The Singers And Harp Players Are Dumb** (1999) and **Hymnal** (2002), while the more radical **Anatomy Of Distort** (2005) epitomized his nonlinear fusion of free jazz, Indian raga, ambient music, musique concrete and minimalist repetition.

The disease had already spread to continental Europe.

Arovane, the project of Berlin multi-instrumentalist Uwe Zahn, wed ambient music, Debussy's impressionism and new-age relaxation on **Tides** (2000).

Russian classical pianist Anton Batagov penned ambient music inspired by Buddhism on the triple-cd **The Wheel Of The Law**, originally recorded in 1999, containing three compositions/improvisations for organ, glockenspiel, xylophone, piano and percussion: *Circle Of Time, Voidness cycle, Liberation Through Listening In The Between*.

Noise

On the more radical front of noise and sound manipulation, countless musicians worldwide composed symphonies of "textures" (as opposed to "instruments"), sometimes with abrasive overtones and sometimes with an ambient/new-age feeling: Gareth Mitchell's Philosopher's Stone in England, with **Preparation** (1997); Klangkrieg in Germany, with **Das Fieber der Menschlichen Stimme** (1999); RhBand in Los Angeles, with **Third Order Parasitism** (1997); and Ether in Utah, with **Hush** (1997).

Campbell Kneale's <u>Birchville Cat Motel</u> (1) in New Zealand inaugurated his career with a tour de force of sound manipulation, **Siberian Earth Curve** (1998). This laid the groundwork for the later symphonic frescoes of **We Count These Prayers** (2001), **Beautiful Speck Triumph** (2004) and **Birds Call Home Their Dead** (2007), that alternated between droning, layered nightmares and cascading, distorted, pulsating space-rock jams and whirlwinds of visceral musique concrete.

<u>Randy Greif</u> (1) indulged in hypnotic, percussive, tribal pieces like **Bacteria and Gravity** (1987) and especially **Verdi's Requiem** (1997), reminiscent of Morton Subotnick's chaotic scores, but also coined a novel technique of postmodernist deconstruction and recomposition of texts with **Alice In Wonderland** (1992) and **War Of The World** (2001).

<u>Thomas Dimuzio</u>'s **Sonicism** (1997), created by distorting an arsenal of instruments, samples and field recordings, was perhaps the best example of dark ambient industrial music.

<u>Oophoi</u> (prolific Italian composer Gianluigi Gasparetti) created "dark ambient" music for analog synthesizer, notably the 49-minute three-movement suite *Space Forest*, off **Three Lights at the End of the World** (1996), the live double-disc album **The Spirals of Time** (1998), and the 67-minute piece of **Behind The Wall Of Sleep** (1998), that set the standard for the monoliths of his subsequent releases.

Further developments

<u>Hood</u> (1) began as followers of Flying Saucer Attack with **Cabled Linear Traction** (1994), but, via the dilated melancholic folk-rock of **Rustic Houses Forlorn Valleys** (1998), they mutated into a different band. Their most original achievement, **Cold House** (2001), juxtaposed gentle melodies, acoustic instruments, layers of cutting-edge electronica, digital clicks and fractured beats.

Canadian composer and inventor <u>Jean-Francois Laporte</u>, pursued his own original version of "deep-listening" music with the symphony of loud abrasive drones *Dans Le Ventre Du Dragon* (1997), performed by an air compressor equipped with car horns and trumpet bells inside a reverb-inducing ship; with the spectacular 20-minute "dronescape" of the EP **Mantra** (2000); and with *Tribal* (2002) for an orchestra of invented instruments.

In Iceland, <u>Sigur Ros</u> (2) specialized in lengthy suites that leveraged celestial vocals and orchestral drones on **Agaetis Byrjun** (1999). The dilated fabric of **( )** (2002) evoked the image of frail organisms crawling on spectral landscapes, particularly *Death*, thirteen minutes of cataleptic suspense and understated raga.

Neil Campbell's <u>Vibracathedral Orchestra</u> (2) in Britain drew inspiration from droning-minimalist composers such as LaMonte Young and Pauline Oliveros. Working with a variety of acoustic instruments, as well as electronics, they turned the chaotic **Lino Hi** (2000), **Versatile Arab Chord Chart** (2000) and **Dabbling With Gravity** (2002) into mystical experiences, specializing in a dense and blurred mixture of guitar mayhem and ambient bliss.

English duo <u>Jazzfinger</u> (Ben Jones and Hasan Gaylani) merged the schools of noise, drone and glitch music on **The Little Girl On The Plane Who Turned Her Dolls Head Around To Look At Me** (1998).

Finnish jazz drummer <u>Terje Isungset</u> employed instruments made of ice (including gamelan-sounding percussion and moaning simulations of horns) as well as eerie wordless vocals for his "all-ice trilogy": the ghostly turbulent **Iceman Is** (2001), the more soothing and tribal **Igloo** (2006), and the more shamanic **Two Moons** (2007).

<u>Troum</u>, the brainchild of Maeror Tri's Stefan Knappe, created pagan/shamanic droning ambient music on a trilogy dedicated to the aboriginal "dreamtime", **Tjukurppa - Harmonies** (2000), **Tjukurppa - Drones** (2001) and **Tjukurppa - Rhythms And Pulsations** (2003), while the three-movement **Sigqan** (2003), the "circular" suites of **Autopoiesis** (2004) and the 51-minute piece of **Shutun** (2007) in collaboration with All Sides (Nina Kernicke) were studies on the organization of sound that transposed into music the combination of biological metabolism, Freudian stream of consciousness, and sci-fi cinematic visions.

Africa

North Africa

Morocco's gnawa music is a kind of folk music that originated among the Gnawas, descendants of black slaves. It retains central-African characteristics such as propulsive syncopated beats and pentatonic melodies, and employs instruments such as the sintir lute and the karkabas castanets, besides the human voice. The music usually accompanies ceremonies of healing based on creating an atmosphere of trance. The cult (which is probably related to the voodoo of Haiti and the macumba of Brazil) is centered in the city of Essaouira. A distinguished gnawa musician is Maleem Mahmoud Ghania, who collaborated with jazz giant Pharoah Sanders on **Trance of Seven Colors** (1994).

Hassan Hakmoun (1) plays the sintir lute and concocts fusion tracks of trancey gnawa, lilting rock and USA dance music on albums such as **Trance** (1993).

Maleem Abdelah Ghania, a virtuoso of the Moroccan guimbri guitar, released the trancey **Invocation** (2000).

Egyptian percussionist Hossam Ramzy (1) drew from the rituals of Arabian Bedouin tribes and from the belly-dance rhythms of the Middle East for **Source of Fire** (1995).

With **Sudaniyat** (1997) Sudanese singer-songwriter Rasha (1) concocted a mishmash of jazz, pop, reggae and USA dance music that achieved pan-ethnic pathos in the tracks arranged with an orchestra of violins, accordion, saxophones, oud and percussion.

Black Africa

Mali remained the leading scene of Africa in the 1990s.

Malian guitarist Djelimady (or Jalimadi) Tounkara of the Super Rail Band developed a style that evokes the sound of the kora harp, the balafon xylophone and the ngoni lute.

Habib Koite' (1), who had played guitar in the band Bamada (*Cigarette A Bana*) since 1990, fused griot philosophy, the trancey folk music of the desert (he plays the guitar like a ngoni lute) and the blues jamming of the forest on **Muso Ko** (1995).

Issa Bagayogo updated the traditions of Mali to the age of electronic dance music (house, techno, hip-hop, dub) on **Sya** (1998) and **Timbuktu** (2002).

Mali's female singer-songwriter Oumou Sangare (1) single-handedly revolutionized African music with **Ko Sira** (1993), devoted to feminist issues from the perspective of a young African woman, sung in a majestic register, and accompanied by danceable music for violin, lute and percussion.

Mali's <u>Lobi Traore'</u> (1) bridged distant ages on **Bambara Blues** (1991) and **Bamako** (1994) by harking back to the original feeling of the blues while adopting the burning guitar riffs of hard-rock and underpinning them with frantic cerimonial percussion.

Mali's <u>Rokia Traore'</u> (1) expressed her anguish in a gentle tone on **Wanita** (2000) over hypnotic rhythmic patterns based on the kora harp, the ngoni lute and the balafon xylophone, but rather neutral in terms of ethnic origin.

Originally from Mali but formed in an Algerian refugee camp, <u>Tinariwen,</u> a desert-blues band of Tuareg nomads with electric guitars, were the main musicians to emerge from the first "Festival au Desert" that was held in january 2001 at Tin Essako in the Sahara of northeastern Mali. **The Radio Tisdas Sessions** (2002), **Amassakoul/ Traveller** (2004) and **Aman Iman/ Water is Life** (2007) documented the music they had been playing since the mid 1980s.

Jean-Marie Ahanda's <u>Les Tetes Brulees</u> took Cameroon's music into the punk age, with a provocative attitude and a demented and energetic sound. **Hot Heads** (1991) offered ancient bikutsi rhythms of the rain forest replacing the balafon xylophone with the electric guitars of rock music.

Senegalese vocalist <u>Baaba Maal</u> (1) mixed traditional African instruments with the western aesthetics on **Baayo** (1991).

Ghana's percussionist <u>Kwaku Kwaakye Obeng</u> (1) delivered the imposing, intricate and hypnotic polyrhythmic maelstroms of **Awakening** (1998).

Raised in Europe, fluent in the musical traditions of the Middle East and of African-Americans, Congolose vocalist Marie Daulne founded <u>Zap Mama</u> (1), an all-female a-cappella group, to sing tunes inspired by the music of the world, such as on **Adventures in Afropea I** (1993).

Madagascar's <u>Tarika</u> (1) is led by female vocalist Hanitra Rasoanaivo who is on a musicological as well as sociopolitical mission to rediscover the roots of her land on albums such as the bleak (but nevertheless rhythmically upbeat) concept **Son Egal** (1997).

Glitch Music and Digital Minimalism

Glitch Music, 1994-2000

In the second half of the 1990s, a new style was born in Europe that employed digital events (such as the "glitches" of defective compact discs) to produce disconcerting ambient music and even "dance" music. Glitch music originated from Germany (Oval) and Britain (Autechre).

Markus Popp's Oval (1) had the idea of applying the avantgarde technique of musique concrete to the static, droning, ethereal fluxes of ambient music. **Systemisch** (1994) "composed" tracks by using the "glitches" of defective compact discs as an instrument (an adaptation to the digital age of the ideas of Czech artist Milan Knizak), thereby inventing a whole new musical genre ("glitch music"). The "mechanical" effect of compositions such as the 25-minute *Do While* (1996), off **94 Diskont** (1996), was akin to the aesthetics of Futurism. Oval's Popp and Mouse On Mars' Jan Werner pursued a similar strategy of accident-prone electronic music under the moniker Microstoria on works such as **Init Ding** (1995).

Another precursor was Pita (2), the project of Austrian electronic musician Peter Rehberg, who contributed to formalize the "glitch" aesthetics with **Seven Tons For Free** (1996), a concerto for pulse signals, and **Get Out** (1999), which was the cacophonous equivalent of a romantic symphony. KTL (2), his collaboration with Sunn O)))'s Stephen O'Malley (playing "strings, FX and amps"), coined a new art of textural nuances that sounded like the equivalent of the "cosmic music" of the 1970s updated to the digital age. **KTL** (2006) juxtaposed two antithetical methods: the 24-minute computer-based *Estranged* fused the glitch aesthetic and the doom-droning aesthetic into an eerily futuristic soundscape of shadows and echoes, while the 40-minute guitar-based suite *Forest Floor* consisted in a stoic attempt at modulating a melody out of chaos and dissonance. **KTL 2** (2007), an even gloomier and louder cosmic/psychological journey into some obscure place of the mind, wove a massive sound sculpture out of layers and layers of wavering drones.

Finland's digital composer Mika Vainio imported the wildest forms of electronic music (Pierre Henry's musique concrete, Morton Subotnick's dadaistic electronica, Suicide, Kraftwerk, Throbbing Gristle, Einsturzende Neubauten) into the format of ambient dance music. Brian Eno's **Before And After Science** was the main influence on the surreal vignettes of **Metri** (1994) and **Olento** (1996), credited to Vainio's solo project 0 (or, better, the symbol used in computer science for the digit zero). Pan Sonic (3), mostly a duo of Vainio with Ilpo Vaisanen, specialized in samples-driven minimal techno. Their albums **Vakio** (1995), **Kulma** (1997) and especially the poetic **A** (1999) evoked futuristic wastelands roamed by faint signs of life (digital beeps, echoes, scrapes, warped beats, clicks, clangs, radio frequencies) amid a lot of silence. The "arctic" beat became their trademark. The four-disc set of **Kesto** (2004) was both a compendium of state-of-the-art techniques (the vehicle) and a Dante-esque journey from organic and violent structures to chaotic stasis (the message). In a sense, this album was also a compendium of the civilization of 2004, a representation of the contemporary zeitgeist, of the state of humanity. It was not an album for people to listen to, but a message to be decoded by future generations. The albums credited to Mika Vainio in person, such as **Onko** (1998) and **Ydin** (1999), revealed the avantgarde composer of cacophonous concertos. There was beauty in the monotonous minimalism of Vainio's art, just like in haiku and epigrams. Angel (1), a collaboration between Ilpo Vaisanen of Pan Sonic, Dirk Dresselhaus of Schneider TM and cellist Hildur Gudnadottir, yielded the romantic ambient droning glitchy industrial music of the 70-minute piece **In Transmediale** (2006).

Alva Noto (born Carsten Nicolai in Germany) was one of the composers who switched to the computer. His audio installations, documented by albums such as **Prototypes** (2000), employed techniques as diverse as minimalistic repetition, abstract soundpainting, musical pointillism and industrial noise, but, ultimately, subscribed to a notion from Physics, that the vacuum is alive and that reality hides in the interstices of the spacetime grid.

Vladislav Delay (11), born Sasu Ripatti in Finland, employed slow-motion, glacial, watery, organic pulsations, often with an undercurrent of Terry Riley's minimalist repetition, to craft the digital landscapes of **Ele** (1999). **Multila** (2000) specialized in distant tremors of breezes that pick up glitches along the way. **Anima** (2001), his 61-minute masterpiece, was a prime example of digital soundscaping that draws inspiration from both musique concrete and industrial music. Melodic fragments and disjointed noises coexisted and blended into each other in a sort of "call and response" format. Delay's alter-ego Uusitalo performed four lengthy techno suites on **Vapaa Muurari Live** (2000) that sounded like techno's version of Terry Riley's minimalism, while Luomo was Ripatti's creative disco/house project, documented on **Vocalcity** (2000). Delay pursued its ambient dub/glitch aesthetic with surgical precision on **The Four Quarters** (2005) and **Whistleblower** (2007), works of meticulous production and cryptic coldness, while Uusitalo's **Karhunainen** (2007) did to techno what Luomo had done to house.

France's Tone Rec (1) harked back to French musique concrete of the 1950s. Digitized noise, hypnotic loops, raw statics, dub-like bass lines, and post-techno beats populated **Pholcus** (1998).

Ryoji Ikeda (1) wed LaMonte Young's living drones and Pan Sonic's glitch electronica on his trilogy of +/- (1997), **0 Degrees Celsius** (1998) and **Matrix** (2000).

Nobukazu Takemura concocted jams of minimal glitch techno such as *Pendulum* , on **Funfair** (1999), credited to his alter-ego Child's View, *On A Balloon*, on **Scope** (1999), and *Souvenir In Chicago*, on **Sign** (2000), with members of Tortoise.

Neina (Japanese keyboardist Hosomi Sakana) proved to be a subtle follower of Oval with **Subconsciousness** (2000).

Nerve Net Noise, the Japanese duo of Tsuyoshi "Tagomago" Nakamura and Hiroshi Kumakiri, specialized in minimalist, glitch and noise music produced with homemade analogue synthesizers on the provocative **160/240** (1998) and on the concept album about the lifestyle of teenage girls **Various Amusements** (2001).

Russian-born Swedish-based laptop player Ivan "Coh" Pavlov (2) turned to ambient glitch soundsculpting with the intimidating **Enter Tinnitus** (1999) and especially with the four **Seasons** (2003) for processed instruments and noise. The bleak three-movement suite of **Netmork** (2002) and the 24-minute EP **Patherns** (2006) refined his art of cryptic audio signs and gave it an existential meaning. His technique peaked with **Strings** (2007), which completed the mission by emphasizing the espressionistic overtones.

Norwegian electronic duo Jazzkammer (John Hegre and Lasse Marhaug) established themselves as the Scandinavian version of Merzbow with the insane digital mayhem of **Hot Action Sexy Karaoke** (2000) but then veered towards glitchy ambient music with the 32-minute piece of **Pulse** (2002) and even doom ambient music a` la Sunn O))) with the 35-minute piece of **Panic** (2006).

The San Francisco school

Matmos (2), the San Francisco-based electronic duo of Drew Daniel and Martin Schmidt, pioneered the use of "organic" samples (noises, not instruments) to compose dance music. More importantly, **Matmos** (1997) bridged three levels of the electronic avantgarde: the chaotic and atonal bleeps and squeaks of the electronic poems of the 1960s, the dilated and warped structures and rhythmic patterns of the German avant-rockers of the 1970s, and Pierre Henry's "musique concrete" of the 1950s. **A Chance To Cut Is A Chance To Cure** (2001), based on sounds taken from hospitals, was even playful and effervescent. In the meantime, the duo had experimented with traditional instruments on **The West** (1999), a work that basically "remixed" the history of the United States and let a "human" quality transpire through the dense jelly of the digital "arrangements".

Kid 606 (1), Venezuela-born San Francisco-based digital composer Miguel Trost-Depedro, topped Matmos' madness on **Down With The Scene** (2000), an edgy collage of white noise, sampled voices and frantic breaks. The schizo-chaotic **The Action Packed Mentallist Brings you**

the Fucking Jams (2002) for terminal post-ecstasy nervous breakdowns abused the notion of creating dance-music out of samples, of employing cut-up art to achieve dance nirvana.

Joshua Kit Clayton (1), also from San Francisco, added dub-like echo effects and robotic rhythms a` la Neu to the usual blend of stormy electronics, found sounds and digital glitches on **Nek Sanalet** (1999) and especially **Lateral Forces - Surface Fault** (2001).

San Francisco-based dj Sutekh crafted **Fell** (2002), a laptop-based excursion into free-form glitch/techno music.

Electric Birds, the project of Bay Area-based computer composer Mike Martinez, sculpted the lyrical glitch-ambient laptop music of **Gradations** (2002).

Glitch-pop, 1997-2000

The dance music of British dj Matthew Herbert (1) replaced drum-machines and synthesizers with beats and melodies manufactured out of random noises of everyday life, an idea pioneered on **Around The House** (1998), that employed the sounds of household objects, and transferred to the song format with the electronic jazz ballads of **Bodily Functions** (2001) and **Scale** (2006). Herbert refrained from simply sampling instruments. Each melody and rhythm was meticulously constructed in the studio. Herbert shared with Matmos the honor of having pioneered the use of "organic" samples (noises, not instruments) to compose dance music. The sound of everyday life became not only the source but also the meaning of his art.

Boards Of Canada (1), i.e. the duo of Scottish electronic musicians Michael Sanderson and Marcus Eoin, were among Autechre's most original followers, capable of secreting the sound of **Geogaddi** (2002), straddling the border between ambient, new age, glitch and hip-hop music.

The ambient glitch-pop presented on **Soup** (1998) by Bola (the project of English electronic musician Darrel Fitton) was similar in scope to Boards Of Canada's: wrapped in spectral breakbeats and lush electronic ambience.

Max Tundra (1), the solo project of British electronic musician Ben Jacobs, represented the singer-songwriter as it evolved into a computer technician. Each instrumental piece on **Some Best Friend You Turned Out To Be** (2000) and each vocal song on **Mastered By Guy At The Exchange** (2002) was a smooth albeit energetic and chaotic digital collage that mined soul, funk and/or synth-pop of past ages and transposed them into contemporary cacophony, manufactured by painstakingly assembling electronic sounds and samples of live instruments (all played by Jacobs himself). Computers enabled him to dispel the notion that chaos means dissonance.

Of all the musicians who worked on "jazztronica" perhaps the most successful hailed from Germany. Kammerflimmer Kollektief (3), a German collective led by Thomas Weber, not only fused jazz, rock and electronica but also emphasized the visceral aspect of each on **Maander** (1999). Then **Hysteria** (2001), **Cicadidae** (2003) and **Absencen** (2005) coined a sound that was the equivalent of ECM's jazz-rock for the era of glitch music an elegant balance of post-rock, droning ambient, glitch techno, sampling and improvised music.

Digital minimalism, 1995-2000

Bernhard Guenter (13) represented the link with the classical avantgarde. The guru of digital, dissonant minimalism, he sculpted sub-atomic soundtracks that picked up the sounds from the crevices between one quantum event and the next one. His **Un Peu De Neige Salie** (1993) and **Details Agrandis** (1994) were works of musique concrete that manipulated noises of ordinary life to the point that they became unrecognizable, and then turned them into cold, dark, monolithic structures of silence, terrible depths from which there emerge unidentified and barely-audible bursts of "implied sound". **Time Dreaming Itself** (2000) and **Then Silence** (2001) opened a new phase of sonic exploration, "active" rather than "passive", and frequently reminiscent of Morton Feldman. **Redshift - Abschied** (2002) bridged this hyper-minimal music and chamber music.

German musician Thomas Brinkmann (1) transposed the minimal aesthetic of glitch music into the subliminal ideology of dub music on **Klick** (2001), the natural link between sound sculpting and dance-floor beats. **Klick Revolution** (2006) continued the program of **Klick** with another set of subliminal, anemic, dilapidated techno music assembled out of defective vinyl records.

By expanding the principle of the remix, German composer Ekkehard Ehlers conceived music composition as a samples-driven art reminiscent of Burroughs' cut-up technique. Autopoieses' **La Vie A Noir** (1999), a duo with Sebastian Meissner, employed jazzy film-noir soundtracks and his **Betrieb** (2000) used classical music to build expressionistic sonic architectures.

German laptop musician Sebastian Meissner used a similar principle to craft the abstract glitch music of Random Industries' **Selected Random Works** (2000) and the ambient music of Random Inc's **Jerusalem Tales Outside the Framework of Orthodoxy** (2001), based on vintage recordings made by Jewish and Palestinian musicians. That program terminated with the "pop ambient" of his works as Klimek, such as **Milk & Honey** (2004), basically beat-less minimal techno "extracted" from acoustic sources.

Inspired by the desire to communicate with the otherworld via the microsounds hidden in silence, Swedish composer Carl Michael von Hausswolff achieved a noble fusion of glitch, ambient and cosmic music on **Stroem** (2001).

The microscopic exploration of the space between sounds and silence conducted by Washington-based disc-jockey Richard Chartier (1), particularly on his fourth solo album **Series** (2000), highlighted the relationship between digital minimalism, "silence music" a` la Bernhard Guenter and "deep listening" a` la Oliveros. "Micro-textured" albums such as **Of Surfaces** (2002), **Tracing** (2006) and **Incidence** (2006) simultaneously austere and angelic, were fundamentally studies in what one does not hear when listening to music.

New York-based composer Taylor Deupree redefined digital minimalism as a form of sporadic musique concrete, like a panorama that is periodically disturbed by brief catastrophic events, on **Occur** (2001).

Australian guitarist Oren Ambarchi explored minimal events, silence and static sound on **Suspension** (2001) by manipulating the sounds of his guitar via a number of electronic and digital devices. Overdubbing live instruments and manipulating them with a mixing board, Ambarchi achieved the fragile melancholia of **Grapes From The Estate** (2004) and **Pendulum's Embrace** (2007).

Australian electronic composer Pimmon (Paul Gough) specialized in sound manipulation and sample collaging that yielded the wastelands of ghostly, minimal glitch-pop documented on **Waves And Particles** (1999) and **Kinetica** (2000).

Australian digital musician Philip Samartzis set the very background noise that sound engineers try to remove from a recording (tape hiss, vinyl crackles, electrical buzzes, radio interference and so on) against a vast stark backdrop of unnerving silence on compositions such as the 39-minute piece of **Windmills Bordered By Nothingness** (1999), the 18-minute *Microphonics*, off the compilation **Grain** (2003), and the six untitled movements of **Soft And Loud** (2004).

Japanese techno veteran So Takahashi crafted the ambient glitch electronica with spare beats and found sounds of **Nubus** (2000).

Exuberance

The top economist in the world, Alan Greenspan, famously described the behavior of the stock market as "irrational exuberance". In many ways that expression could be used to label the behavior of the youth of the era. They were growing up inside an (economic) bubble, but they didn't know. They partied like no generation ever had, without knowing that they were as vulnerable as the previous ones. There was a general belief that things could only get better. The difference between mainstream music and alternative music had become the difference between optimism and pessimism.

The last gasps of Brit-pop, 1996-97

The leaders of the second generation of Brit-pop were the Super Furry Animals, whose distinctive feature was the lush, elaborate arrangements. **Fuzzy Logic** (1996), a witty version of Suede's glam-pop, laid the foundations for the more ambitious Brian Wilson-ian constructs of **Rings Around The World** (2001) and especially **Phantom Power** (2003).

The ultimate product of Brit-pop was the Spice Girls, as hyped and inept as any of the Mersey-beat groups of 30 years earlier, despite selling more than 20 million copies of the awful albums **Spice** (1996) and **Spiceworld** (1997).

Reacting to Brit-pop, 1996-99

Trembling Blue Stars, the project of former Field Mice's frontman Bob Wratten, continued Field Mice's "bedroom-pop" on a more personal basis, notably on their third album **Broken By Whispers** (1999), a parade of elaborate and sumptuous ballads dwelling halfway between Lycia's gothic depression and the Cure's somber existentialism.

Scotland's Usurei Yatsura were unusual in that they embraced Pavement's lo-fi approach on **We Are** (1996).

The Delgados (1) started out from the same premises on **Domestiques** (1997), but then turned to sumptuous orchestral pop, a style that peaked on **The Great Eastern** (2000).

The mellow, whining and evocative pop of the Smiths staged a comeback towards the end of the decade. It was best represented by the Doves (1) with the slow, mellow ballads of **Lost Souls** (2000) and the impeccable orchestrations of **Last Broadcast** (2002).

Radiohead inspired the "post-pop" generation of 1997-98, notably Six By Seven, whose **The Things We Make** (1998) was basically a neurotic version of the "Madchester" sound of the Stone Roses; and Coldplay, whose **Parachutes** (2000) was mainly a display of dynamic and emotional ranges.

The stylistic evolution of <u>Broadcast</u> (1) from the singles compiled on **Work And Non Work** (1997), that juxtaposed cheesy electronica, childish vocals and noir atmospheres, to the cubistic remixes of pop stereotypes on **Haha Sound** (2003) fostered the decline of Stereolab's space-age pop.

These bands laid the foundations for the success of <u>Add N To X</u> (12), a British trio on analog keyboards whose retro-futurism was inspired by Tangerine Dream, Suicide, Cabaret Voltaire, Kraftwerk and Devo. **On the Wires of Our Nerves** (1998) evoked a dark, claustrophobic, teutonic fantasy of mechanical monsters gone mad. It wasn't electronica the way Led Zeppelin's music was not blues. They discovered a rougher and deeper dimension of electronica, just like Led Zeppelin had discovered a rougher and deeper dimension of blues. They discovered "hard electronica" just like Led Zeppelin discovered "hard rock". **Avant Hard** (1999), instead, put aside the uncompromising sonic onslaught for a more mature symphony of tones and textures; whereas the poppy, danceable, electronic rock'n'roll of **Loud Like Nature** (2002), drowned in an orgy of digital cacophony, heralded a new form of post-industrial decadent futuristic punk cabaret.

<u>Bent</u>'s **Programmed To Love** (2000) in England was the best post-modernist essay that Air never wrote.

The sound of <u>Clinic</u> (1), notably the singles later compiled on **Three Piece** (2001) and the mini-album **Internal Wrangler** (2000), bridged the Sixties-revival of the 1990s with the new wave of the late 1970s.

<u>Muse</u>, fronted by operatic vocalist and shoegazing guitarist Matthew Bellamy, hit the jackpot with the grandiose sound of **Origin of Symmetry** (2001).

Japanese Kitsch 1996-99

Surprisingly, it was in Japan that bands excelled at this parodistic and futuristic approach to kitsch and muzak. Pizzicato Five had shown the way.

<u>Cibo Matto</u> (1), the duo of Miho Hatori and Yuka Honda, specialized in musical satire inspired by junk food and implemented via a casual assembly of jazz, hip-hop, funk and dissonances. **Viva La Woman** (1996) performed a clownish postmodernist massacre of stereotypes.

<u>Fantastic Plastic Machine</u> (1), the creature of producer Tomoyuki Tanaka, debuted with **Fantastic Plastic Machine** (1998), a collection of ultra-hip, glamourous cross-cultural tunes composed via a montage of cliches of western pop music.

<u>Buffalo Daughter</u> (1) wed both a retro and a progressive ideology. **Captain Vapour Athletes** (1996) and especially **New Rock** (1998)

delivered ebullient, quirky synth-rock for electronic keyboards, turntables and samplers.

Multi-instrumentalist Cornelius (1), born Keigo Oyamada, composed "pop tunes" by overdubbing "found" samples and stereotypical music, achieving on **Fantasma** (1997) and, partially, on **Point** (2002) a kind of eclectic postmodernist nonsense. The most creative aspect of his compositions was how elements of "musique concrete" (found noises that were sampled, looped and refined) got to be integrated with the rhythmic and melodic infrastructure of the songs without sacrificing their aural appeal.

Ooioo (1), the side-project of Boredoms's drummer Yoshimi "P-We" Yokota and a few of her female friends that began as an exercise in hyper-deconstruction of kitsch, juxtaposed all sorts of musical debris in the suites of **Feather Float** (1999) and **Taiga** (2006), vaguely reminiscent of the aesthetic ambitions of progressive and psychedelic music but insanely playful.

USA Kitsch, 1995-99

While not as successful as Air, April March (Elinore Blake) in Los Angeles pursued similar routes to disorienting pop muzak with the eclectic and campy **And Los Cincos** (1998) and **Chrominance Decoder** (1999).

By bridging the Pixies' eccentric pop with new wave's eccentric dance music, Wisconsin's Garbage (1), a trio of veteran producers (including Butch Vig on drums) fronted by sexy and trashy vocalist Shirley Manson, obtained the success that had eluded the Pixies with their **Garbage** (1995).

North Carolina's Squirrel Nut Zippers reached further back in time, to the ballroom blues-jazz combos of the 1940s and the calypso of the 1950s, on their second album **Hot** (1996).

Joey Burns and John Convertino of Calexico highlighted the melancholy country and blues meditations of **The Shadow Of Your Smile** (1995), by the Friends Of Dean Martinez (1), a work centered on the atmospheric picking of Naked Prey's guitarist Bill Elm.

The Aluminum Group performed the unlikely wedding of Burt Bacharach's easy-listening and Tortoise's post-rock on **Plano** (1998).

The Scud Mountain Boys' vocalist Joe Pernice in Boston turned to pop orchestration with the Pernice Brothers on **Overcome By Happiness** (1998).

Texas' Spoon, the vehicle for Britt Daniel, evolved from the neurotic, Pavement-influenced **Telephono** (1996) to the linear punk-pop of **Girls Can Tell** (2001) to the minimalist power-pop of **Gimme Fiction** (2005) and **Ga Ga Ga Ga Ga** (2007), almost the opposite of Phil Spector's "wall of sound".

Nebraska's the <u>Faint</u> refined their synth-driven nostalgic exercise in retro-futurism until they became stars of the electroclash generation with **Danse Macabre** (2001),

The prolific San Diego-based singer-songwriter and guitarist <u>Rob Crow</u> launched a slew of parallel projects, starting with the progressive hardcore of <u>Heavy Vegetable</u>, documented on **The Amazing Undersea Adventures Of Aqua Kitty And Friends** (1994). He built a bizarre sound around vintage keyboards as <u>Optiganally Yours</u> on **Spotlight On Optiganally Yours** (1997) and **Presents Exclusively Talentmaker** (2000). An acoustic quartet named <u>Thingy</u> penned the avant-melancholia of **To The Innocent** (1999). Then he found a compromise of sort in <u>Pinback</u>'s somnolent lullabies at the border between post-rock, new wave, psychedelic-rock and folk-rock, first on **This Is Pinback** (1999) and especially the EP **Offcell** (2003). Pinback kept twisting the formula of power-pop until they achieved a slightly angular format of lo-fi song on **Summer In Abaddon** (2004) and **Autumn of the Seraphs** (2007).

Elephant 6, 1996-98

The breakthrough in this quest for the perfect melody came from the south, from Georgia and Louisiana, where a group of bands (the "Elephant 6" collective) started the single most influential school of the decade in pop music. Robert Schneider, founder of the movement and founder of the <u>Apples In Stereo</u> (1), was the Phil Spector of this generation: the songs on **Tone Soul Evolution** (1997) were miracles of pop metabolism, incorporating one century of melodic tricks.

Will Hart's <u>Olivia Tremor Control</u> (2) struck an elegant balance between retro-Sixties sound and state-of-the-art production techniques on **Dusk at Cubist Castle** (1996) and **Black Foliage** (1999), which were, first and foremost, tours de force of eccentric and oneiric pop arrangements. Each song was a mini-collage of oddities and spaced-out harmonies, and the albums in their entirety could be viewed as one giant, frantic collage, a work of pop-art a` la Andy Warhol.

<u>Neutral Milk Hotel</u> (1), Jeff Mangum's creature, codified that style on **In the Aeroplane Over The Sea** (1998), one of the most perfect pop albums of all times, thanks to drummer Jeremy Barnes and multi-instrumentalist Julian Koster.

<u>Elf Power</u>'s **A Dream In Sound** (1999), their best album, was fundamentally bubblegum music: cheesy pop for brainless people. Nonetheless, it was the elegance and the decorum that still made it unique even within that garbage can.

The works by <u>Of Montreal</u>, or Kevin Barnes, such as **The Gay Parade** (1999), were whimsical collections of carefully-crafted pop tunes assembled and sequenced in a way to compose a flamboyant psychedelic vaudeville. Having moved towards baroque and lively digital and electronic arrangements with **The Sunlandic Twins** (2005), his ninth album **Hissing Fauna Are You The Destroyer?** (2007) even set existential depression to the beats of dance music.

These bands dramatically raised the qualitative standard of pop songs, a fact clearly visible in popsters of the next generation: Ladybug Transistor (1), the project of New York-based vocalist Gary Olson, particularly with the sumptuous arrangements of **Beverley Atonale** (1997) and **The Albemarle Sound** (1999), featuring guitarist Jeff Baron and keyboardist Sasha Bell; Art DiFuria's Photon Band (1), from Pennsylvania, with the sophisticated and encyclopedic **All Young In The Soul** (1998); Flake in New Mexico, with **Flake Music** (1997); Marcy Playground in Minnesota, with **Marcy Playground** (1998); and Superdrag in Kentucky, with **Regretfully Yours** (1996).

Teen-pop 1995-99

But the real million-sellers in the USA were the "teen pop" sensations of the south: Florida's Backstreet Boys, whose **Backstreet Boys** (1995) sold some 13 million copies in five years, Oklahoma's Hanson, Louisiana's Britney Spears, whose **Baby One More Time** (1999) sold ten million copies in just one year, New York's Christina Aguilera, whose **Christina Aguilera** (1999) boasted more robust vocals and an explicit sexual image, Florida's N'Sync, whose second album **No Strings Attached** (2000) sold more than one million copies on the first day it was released and spawned the career of Justin Timberlake, whose solo debut **Justified** (2002) sold even more.

Natalie Imbruglia became one of Australia's all-time best-sellers with **Left of the Middle** (1997).

International Kitsch, 1997-99

Outside Britain and Japan, there were other significant centers of "futuristic kitsch".

French duo Air (1), Nicolas Godin and Jean-Benoit Dunckel, indulged in the nostalgic sound of vintage analog keyboards on **Moon Safari** (1998), a work marked by a zany campiness that exuded Pink Floyd's psychedelic majesty, jazz's subdued ambience, random quotations from the history of soul, funk and disco music, and more than a passing mention of Burt Bacharach's and Ennio Morricone's scores.

Stereo Total, the project of Berlin-based vocalist and electronic wizard Brezel Goering, concocted a goofy, anarchic, exuberant, multi-ethnic (and multi-linguistic) fusion of new wave, punk-rock, disco music and synth-pop, bridging girl-groups, funk, Giorgio Moroder and the Ramones, which turned **Monokini** (1997) into the sonic equivalent of a Marx Brothers movie.

Beanfield (1998) proved that the heart of Munich-based Michael Reinboth, better known as Beanfield, was in jazz fusion, but his subconscious was still entangled in the genres of his childhood.

Le Hammond Inferno, the project of Berlin-based producers and disc-jockeys Marcus Liesenfeld and Holger Beier, mimicked Pizzicato Five on **Easy Listening Superstar** (1999).

Starting with **Intervision** (1997), Finnish-born singer and multi-instrumentalist Jimi Tenor played kitsch music (and sang in a sexy falsetto) to a techno beat with an approach that was the musical equivalent of Andy Warhol's pop art but that mocked everybody from soul to glam.

A satirical, kitschy synth-pop style was coined in Sweden by Aqua (1) on the exuberant **Aquarium** (1997).

The Concretes were the heirs of the Cardigans in the realm of the atmospheric Nordic pop ballads. **The Concretes** (2003), when they had become an eight-piece ensemble, transposed that style to the fragile and ebullient sound of the 1960s, wrapping them in lush orchestrations that, in scope, went beyond chamber pop and towards a "maximalist" form of pop music.

North-American kitsch 2000

A spectacular revival of the pop tune took place at the turn of the century throughout the USA and Canada.

Fronted by vocalist and keyboardist Jenny Lewis and vocalist and guitarist Blake Sennet, Los Angeles-based Rilo Kiley played mellow country-pop muzak on their second album **The Execution of All Things** (2002).

San Francisco's Aislers Set evoked the age of Phil Spector and the girl groups on **The Last Match** (2000).

Mates Of State, the San Francisco-based duo of drummer Jason Hammel and keyboardist Kori Gardner, penned romantic ballads for boy/girl harmonies and vintage keyboards on **My Solo Project** (2000).

Minnesota's Lifter Puller, featuring vocalist Craig Finn and guitarist Tad Kubler, used the synthesizer to ornate the ambitious quasi-concept **Fiestas & Fiascos** (2000).

New York-based British-born androgynous vibrato baritone Antony Hegarty debuted with the noir, expressionistic ambience and the sophisticated arrangements of **Antony & The Johnsons** (2000), reminiscent of Roxy Music; while **I Am a Bird Now** (2005) was surprisingly a warm, intimate and humane portrait of his obsessions.

Trivial punk-pop still existed, best represented by the third album **Dressy Bessy** (2003) of Colorado's Dressy Bessy, but was becoming less and less relevant.

Zumpano's vocalist Carl Newman formed the New Pornographers, a supergroup of sorts with Neko Case and Destroyer's Dan Bejar. **Mass Romantic** (2000) and **Electric Version** (2003) were manuals of gleeful melodies, retro arrangements, multi-part harmonies, bouncy guitars and peppy rhythms.

Dan Bejar's Destroyer, based in Vancouver, packaged quirky parades of impeccable pop tunes filled with the pathos of glam-rock on albums such as **This Night** (2002), achieving an almost delirious, baroque zenith with the lush, electronic **Your Blues** (2004) and the lean **Destroyer's Rubies** (2006).

Transcendence

Textural pop, 1995-99

The legacy of slo-core was still being felt at the end of the decade on countless recordings devoted to fragile, slow ballads. For example, Fuck in San Francisco, notably their second album **Baby Loves A Funny Bunny** (1996), and Kingsbury Manx in North Carolina, with the gentle, bucolic odes of **Kingsbury Manx** (1999).

Texas' American Analog Set (1) advanced the oneiric sound pioneered by Galaxie 500, especially on their second album, **From Our Living Room To Yours** (1997). The extended single *Late One Sunday* (1997) wove together two hypnotic patterns, respectively a country guitar twang and a dub bass line, against a backdrop of intense drumming and floating voices.

New York's trio Calla (1) sculpted shadowy melodies that slowly crept out of their fragile envelopes on the stark and stately **Calla** (1999), a softly-hallucinated music reminiscent of Ry Cooder's soundtracks and Calexico's desert ambience.

Seattle's Red Stars Theory (2) turned Built To Spill's brainy trance upside down, emphasizing the trance, on their mostly-instrumental albums **But Sleep Came Slowly** (1997) and especially **Life In A Bubble Can Be Beautiful** (1999), which fused psychedelic, chamber and country music. Their songs were amoeba-like pseudo-jamming lattices that freely elaborated on a theme relying more on atmosphere and feeling than on structure or dynamics.

Built To Spill's second best pupils were Death Cab For Cutie (1), whose painstakingly detailed stories of alienation and defeat on **Something About Airplanes** (1999) employed the "textural" technique of the masters.

Boston's Helium (1), led by Mary Timony, bordered on feedback-pop on **Dirt Of Luck** (1995).

In England, Drugstore's **Drugstore** (1995) was a work of subtle seduction a` la Cowboy Junkies and Mazzy Star.

Mojave 3 (1), the new project by Slowdive's vocalists Neil Halstead and Rachel Goswell, were modern bards that harked back to the golden age of country-rock and folk-rock (Bob Dylan's **Blonde On Blonde**, early Donovan, Leonard Cohen) but added a metaphysical dimension. **Ask Me Tomorrow** (1996) and especially **Excuses For Travellers** (2000) were devoted to folk and country ballads that a lacerating pain had emptied of all energy and filled with a zen-like acceptance of the mystery of life.

Movietone (1), the project of Flying Saucer Attack's vocalist Rachel Brook and Third Eye Foundation's guitarist Matt Elliot played melancholy twilight ballads a` la Mazzy Star on **Day And Night** (1997).

Seattle's <u>Microphones</u> (1), the brainchild of Phil Elvrum (also the drummer for Old Time Relijun), found a different way to baroque psychedelic-pop. The sophisticated orchestration of his third album **The Glow Pt 2** (2001), dedicated to fire, following two concepts dedicated to air and water, namely **Don't Wake Me Up** (1999) and **It Was Hot We Stayed in the Water** (2000), laid the foundations for the five lengthy suites of **Mount Eerie** (2003), audio fantasies that absorbed and metabolized apparently disconnected sounds to produce perfectly rational organisms.

Space-rock, 1995-99

The wilder and looser strain of guitar-driven psychedelic music staged an impressive comeback.

Oregon's <u>King Black Acid And The Womb Star Orchestra</u> (1) crafted some of the most eclectic, encyclopedic and exhilarating space jams on **Womb Star Sessions** (1995).

Oregon's power-trio <u>Davis Redford Triad</u>, fronted by Faust's guitarist Steven-Wray Lobdell, were the main purveyors of the heavy psychedelic freak-out with the Fushitsusha-grade tornadoes of guitar distortion of **The Mystical Path Of The Number Eighty Six** (1997), as well as venturing into mellower dilated Eastern-tinged psychedelia with **Ewige Blumenkraft** (1998).

<u>Pelt</u> (2), in Virginia, further experimented on the format with **Brown Cyclopedia** (1995), a studio-savvy cross between Royal Trux's **Twin Infinitives**, Sonic Youth's **Daydream Nation**, the Velvet Underground's **White Light White Heat** and Pink Floyd's **Ummagumma**. The free-form instrumentals of **Burning Filament Rockets** (1996) and **Max Meadows** (1997), that merged mind-bending psychedelic distortions and mind-opening world instrumentation, the three epic tracks of **Techeod** (1998), that obviously homaged minimalism and free-jazz, and the colossal title track from **Empty Bell Ringing In The Sky** (1999), led to the tour de force of **Ayahuasca** (2001), whose "ragas" defined a post-psychedelic and post-ambient music bridging John Fahey, Grateful Dead, Ravi Shankar and LaMonte Young. That set the standard for Pelt's massive cacophonous drone-based post-industrial hyper-psychedelic ragas, such as *Pearls From the River*, off **Pearls From The River** (2003), *II*, off **Pelt** (2005), *Bestio Tergum Degero*, off **Skullfuck** (2006), and *Cast Out To Deep Waters*, off **Dauphin Elegies** (2008).

Connecticut's <u>Primordial Undermind</u> (2) evolved from the garage-rock of **Yet More Wonders Of The Invisible World** (1995) and the space ballads of **You And Me And The Continuum** (1998) to the Hawkwind-style jams of **Universe I've Got** (1999) and the free-form space-rock of **Beings Of Game P-U** (2001), two albums which rank among the most "cosmic" and transcendental of the time.

Towering over every other space-rock band of the era, Philadelphia-based Bardo Pond (12) turned the acid-rock jam into a major art. **Bufo Alvarius** (1995) coined a new form of music built around supersonic drones. The average piece was a rainstorm of guitar distortions, strident turbulences and catastrophic drumming, halfway between MC5's heavy blues and Spacemen 3's shoegazing. It was the soundtrack of a cosmic trauma that still haunts the firmament. While no less brutal, **Amanita** (1996) revealed a spiritual element that harked back to both Popol Vuh's **Hosianna Mantra** and Pink Floyd's *A Saucerful of Secrets*; but nothing could be less religious than the apocalyptic chaos of **Lapsed** (1997). These albums were as musical as Einstein's relativity.

The members of Bardo Pond (guitarists John and Michael Gibbons, drummer Joe Culver, bassist Clint Takeda) also shone on two magnificent collaborations with guitarist Roy Montgomery, both credited to Hash Jar Tempo (110), **Well Oiled** (1997) and **Under Glass** (1999). The former, a seven-movement instrumental jam, is a cosmic hymn of monumental proportions, the psychedelic equivalent of a symphonic mass. Guitars compete for and concur to a universal "om", first running against each other, battling for the highest form of enlightenment, and then joining together in unison. The music emerges from spacetime warps, propelled by seismic rhythms, only to delve into deeper and deeper abysses, hypnotized by an unspeakable force. The second album was even more experimental, less dependent on guitars, and explicitly inspired by classical music. It alternated between glacial, imposing structures and chaotic noise collages, reconciling Wagner and Amon Duul, Verdi and Hawkwind, Bach and Red Crayola.

Beyond shoegazing, 1995-2000

My Bloody Valentine's droning psychedelic lullabies turned out to be one of the most influential inventions of the late 1980s. A decade later, they inspired an entire generation of younger musicians.

New York's Saturnine 60 (1) sculpted languid ballads that soared with epically distorted apotheoses on **Wreck At Pillar Point** (1995).

New Jersey's Lenola expanded the genre both forward, in terms of structure, and backwards, in term of melody, on **The Last Ten Feet Of The Suicide Mile** (1996). So did Georgia's Seely on **Julie Only** (1996).

New York's Bowery Electric (1), after the embryonic **Bowery Electric** (1995), a collection of lengthy guitar drones, enhanced their trance with dub reverbs, sampler, loops and drum-machines on **Beat** (1996).

Kansas' Shallow enhanced shoegazing with quasi-orchestral arrangements of flute, dulcimer, piano, organ and cello, besides loops and samples, on their second album **High Flyin' Kid Stuff** (1997).

New Jersey's Flowchart wed My Bloody Valentine's droning symphonies and Enya's magical fairy tales on **Cumulus Mood Twang** (1998).

Florida's Windsor For The Derby (1) sculpted the dreamy, wadded bliss of **Calm Hades Float** (1996) with guitar, Farfisa and drums.

Seattle's Kinski were heirs to the tradition of Bardo Pond's ambient space-rock. The jams of **Spacelaunch for Frenchie** (1999) and **Be Gentle With the Warm Turtle** (2001) valued repetition and texture but also unleashed brutal maelstroms of distortions, a compromise between British shoegazing and Japanese noise.

In Britain, Richard Walker's Amp (2) continued Flying Saucer Attack's mission with the chaotic ambience of **Sirenes** (1996) and the ethereal space ballads for female vocals (Karine Charff) and guitar maelstroms of **Stenorette** (1998), while at the same time indulging in the more abstract improvisations of **Astral Moon Beam Projections** (1997) and **Perception** (1997).

Droning psychedelia, 1995-2000

The next (transcendent) step in the evolution of acid-rock and shoegazing music consisted in shifting the focus of the music from the melody to what had been the background noise.

The area around Detroit (that had a tradition stretching from the Stooges to Gravitar) boasted one of the most fertile scenes. Fuxa harked back to both German avant-rock of the 1970s and Spacemen 3's shoegazing nightmares on **Very Well Organized** (1996). The wild, improvised, cacophonous jams of Asha Vida's **Nature's Clumsy Hand** (1998) stretched as far as free-jazz and musique concrete. Medusa Cyclone (1), the new project by Viv Akauldren's keyboardist Keir McDonald, ran the gamut from synth-pop to cosmic music on their debut album, **Medusa Cyclone** (1996).

The hypnotic, transcendental form of acid-rock was also popular in Texas. Furry Things (1) crafted the feedback-driven trance of **The Big Saturday Illusion** (1995) at the intersection of prog-rock, ambient music and acid jams. Its "songs" were grotesque deconstructions of rock'n'roll that twitched under clouds of swirling drones. 7% Solution (1) gave more melodic and dynamic depth to the drone-driven ambient psychedelia of the shoegazers on **All About Satellites And Spaceships** (1996).

The Dallas scene was particularly vibrant. The Vas Deferens Organization (12), or VDO, founded by New Orleans-natives Matt Castille and Eric Lumbleau, highlighted the link between psychedelic culture and the century-old cultures of dadaism and futurism. They specialized in a form of narrative nonsense for electronics and percussions that relied on a vast sonic puzzle. The three mad suites of **Transcontinental Conspiracy** (1996), featuring Medicine's guitarist

Brad Laner, fluctuated between the most childish compositions of Frank Zappa and the most daring pieces of the classical avantgarde. **Saturation** (1996) combined the Mahavishnu Orchestra's wild jazz-rock with Terry Riley's keyboards-driven minimalism, musique concrete with raga. Abandoning the reckless frenzy of those early works, the five compositions on **Zyzzybaloubah** (1997) flew with more aplomb, displaying a brainy, pretentious attitude where merry pranksters used to play.

The VDO tribe spawned countless projects. Matt Castille recorded a lengthy suite of psychedelic excesses on **Muz** (1998). Eric Lumbleau formed Sound (USA) (1) and recorded the audio montage of **Drunk On Confusion** (1999), worthy of Frank Zappa's most amusing and iconoclastic moments. Mazinga Phaser (1) assembled the unfocused collages of **Cruising In The Neon Glories** (1996) by juxtaposing chamber music, elegiac bebop, gothic dub, space soul, ethereal bossanova and discordant drum'n'bass. Scott Sutton vented his Jimi Hendrix fixation on **Late Nite Songs** (1996), as J. Bone Cro, and his Syd Barrett fixation on **Owners Manual** (1997), as Jaloppy. Further emancipating themselves from the stereotype, Ohm (1), a keyboards-bass-clarinet trio, composed ethnic and electronic music on **O2** (1997).

The droning school found a fertile soil also in San Francisco, where Helios Creed and Subarachnoid Space had long advocated guitar mayhems.

Guitarists Steven Smith and Glenn Donaldson focused on free-form instrumental psychedelia with Mirza's mini-album **Ursa Minor** (1996). In addition, Steven Smith released several solo works of eerie instrumental pieces created via a process of gradual composition, from **Gehenna Belvedere** (1996) to **Tableland** (2000) to **Lineaments** (2002). Those dense and meticulous blends of ancient, modern, acoustic, electric, western and ethnic instruments reenacted Smith's private ghosts, the primordial spleen that was the undercurrent of his avantgarde projects (the abstract and cacophonous Thuja, the pan-ethnic Hala Strana). Donaldson is also half of the Skygreen Leopards who released collections of lazy and hazy psych-folk ditties such as **She Rode On A Pink Gazelle & Other Dreams** (2001), **One Thousand Bird Ceremony** (2004) and **Life & Love In Sparrow's Meadow** (2005).

The Double Leopards (1) orchestrated thick cosmic drones for a quartet featuring three guitarists (Chris Gray, Marcia Bassett, Mike Bernstein) and a keyboardist (Maya Miller) on the double-disc **Halve Maen** (2003), containing the 21-minute *A Hemisphere in Your Hair*. Full of suspense and drama, their sound bridged LaMonte Young, early Throbbing Gristle and Zen meditation. They achieved expressionistic intensity with the three lengthy noisescapes of **A Hole Is True** (2005) and with **Out Of One, Through One, And To One** (2005), a colossal improvisation with Samara Lubelski.

Dead Voices On Air (1), formed in Vancouver by former Zoviet France's collaborator Mark Spybey, sculpted droning ambient-industrial nightmares on **New Words Machine** (1995).

Ashtray Navigations, the brainchild of super-prolific English multi-instrumentalist Phil Todd, specialized in sloppy droning free-form acid-rock for guitar and synthesizer, for example on **Four Raga Moods** (1997) and **Tristes Tropiques** (2000), a style that peaked with the six jams of **The Love that Whirrs** (2005), featuring drummer Alex Neilson and guitarist Ben Reynolds.

Scotland's Beta Band devoted their first two EPs, **Champion Versions** (1997) and **The Patty Patty Sound** (1998), to intense sound sculpting and disco-oriented shoegazing.

Treated guitar drones and noises reached a new dimension with the work of Austrian-born Christian Fennesz (3), both in his harsh cacophonies, such as **Hotel Paral.Lel** (1997) and the nightmarish **Plus Forty Seven Degrees 56'37" Minus Sixteen Degrees 51'08"** (1999), and in his melodic glitch-pop mirages, such as **Endless Summer** (2001) and **Venice** (2004). The interaction between guitar and computer reached a psychological peak with **Black Sea** (2008) that sounded like the cold and gloomy meditation of a painter turned philosopher.

Australian guitarist Chris Smith piled up layers of guitar drones and drenched them in crackling background noise to sculpt the stately architectures of his second album **Replacement** (2000), reminiscent of both Roy Montgomery and Flying Saucer Attack.

Noise-folk, 1996-2000

Six Organs of Admittance (2), the project of acoustic guitarist Ben Chasny, coined a psychedelic form of Sandy Bull's and John Fahey's western ragas with east-west meditations such as *Sum of All Heaven*, off **Six Organs of Admittance** (1998), and *VIII*, off **For Octavio Paz** (2003).

Largely improvised noise-folk-rock music with strong psychedelic overtones was offered in England by Volcano The Bear (1) on **Five Hundred Boy Piano** (2001), notably the three-movement suite *The Tallest People In The World*, **The Idea Of Wood** (2005) and especially the double-CD **Classic Erasmus Fusion** (2006), that ran the gamut from naive lullabies to convoluted fantasias.

Japanese acidcore, 1996-2000

In Japan, Mainliner (11), formed by High Rise's bassist Asahito Nanjo with Acid Mothers Temple's guitarist Makoto Kawabata, unleashed two of the most brutal works of the era, **Mellow Out** (1996) and **Sonic** (1997), nuclear tornados of cacophonous Feedtime-like chaos and

Chrome-like martian beats. The former's wall of noise signaled the advent of a new kind of "rock" music, one that relied on unrelenting impetus (just like hardcore) while retaining the mind-expanding qualities of acid-rock.

The most prolific of this prolific Japanese school of space-rockers was, by far, Makoto Kawabata, the (demented) brain and the (logorrheic) guitar behind <u>Acid Mothers Temple & The Melting Paraiso U.F.O.</u> (4). Synthesizer-heavy progressive jams in the vein of freaks such as Magma and Gong filled their early albums, **Acid Mothers Temple & The Melting Paraiso Ufo** (1997) and **Pataphysical Freak Out Mu** (1999), but subsequent collections, such as **La Novia** (2000), became more chaotic and orgiastic. The mini-album **41st Century Splendid Man** (2002), featuring Tatsuya Yoshida of the Ruins, adopted instead a celestial trance bordering on ambient and cosmic music, and **Univers Zen Ou De Zero A Zero** (2002) found perhaps the middle path between the two extremes. This natural evolution towards a synthesis of styles led to **Nam Myo Ho Ren Ge Kyo** (2007) and *Electric Psilocybin Flashback*, off **Crystal Rainbow Pyramid Under The Stars** (2007), colossal jams built around the ancient Buddhist mantra of the title. Ethereal soprano Cotton Casino was to Kawabata in AMT what Gilli Smyth was to Daevid Allen in Gong.

<u>Musica Transonic</u> (1), a supergroup with Acid Mother Temple's guitarist Makoto Kawabata and Ruin's drummer Tatsuya Yoshida, specialized in a less barbaric fury and even jazzy stylings on albums such as **Introducing** (1995), **A Pilgrim's Repose** (1996) and **Orthodox Jazz** (1997).

<u>Christine 23 Onna</u> (the duo of Masonna's Maso Yamazaki and Fusao Toda of Angel In Heavy Syrup) specialized in wild, distorted, chaotic retro-analog electronic sounds on **Shiny Crystal Planet** (2000) and **Acid Eater** (2002).

Violence

Garages, 1995-2000

The revival of garage-rock continued unabated throughout the decade with decadent acts such as Georgia's <u>Nashville Pussy</u>, whose **Let Them Eat Pussy** (1998) harked back to Cramps' porno-billy.

Ohio's <u>Thomas Jefferson Slave Apartments</u> (1), led by Great Plains vocalist Ron House and guitarist Bob Petric, delivered a concentrate of Cramps, Stooges and Ramones on **Bait And Switch** (1995) and especially **Straight To Video** (1997).

Both the hippies' philosophy and sound reincarnated in a bizarre San Francisco project, Anton Newcombe's <u>Brian Jonestown Massacre</u> (2). Despite the clumsy recording quality and the amateurish stance, **Methodrone** (1995) and **Their Satanic Majesties' Second Request** (1996) were monumental encyclopedias of psychedelic music, from the Jefferson Airplane to Hawkwind, from the Rolling Stones to the Velvet Underground. Subsequent albums alternated between superbly derivative, such as **Take It From The Man** (1996) and **Give It Back** (1997), majestically musical, such as **Thank God For Mental Illness** (1996), arranged with a wealth of instruments, and dreamy/melancholy, such as **Strung Out In Heaven** (1998). Newcombe mostly followed in the footsteps of deranged street folksingers like David Peel, but his naive folly could also explode in noise collages.

Inspired by the depravity of the Stooges and the New York Dolls, Seattle's <u>Murder City Devils</u> (1) added the screams of vocalist Spencer Moody and the gothic overtones of an organ to the mayhem of **Empty Bottles Broken Hearts** (1998).

A more personal and intimate take on garage-rock was offered by Seattle's <u>Love As Laughter</u>, fronted by Lync's Sam Jayne, whose fusion of Royal Trux's artsy retro-rock, irregular post-rock structures and Jim Morrison-ian histrionics peaked on third album **Sea To Shining Sea** (2001).

The punk approach to the blues and to soul music was refined by Washington's <u>Delta 72</u> (1), whose **The R&B Of Membership** (1996) and particularly **Soul Of A New Machine** (1997) were derailed by Sarah Stolfa's organ and Gregg Foreman's primordial howl. Their conceptual revisitation of black music eventually led to imitate the Rolling Stones circa **Exile On Main Street** on the more professional **000** (2000).

New Jersey's <u>Danielson Famile</u> (2) reinvented Christian music in the form of gospel hymns with an off-kilter instrumental backing and frantic harmonies worthy of the Holy Modal Rounders and David Peel on **A Prayer For Every Hour** (1995), a program of 24 songs, one for each hour of the day, the manic **Tell Another Joke At The Ol' Choppin'**

Block (1997), and **Tri-Danielson!!!** (1999), a quirky philosophical concept.

Louisiana's one-man band Quintron devised the demented and largely improvised percussive experiment **Internet Feedback 001-011** (1996). The mini-album **Satan Is Dead** (1998), replete with nostalgic overtones and dance beats, added a new dimension to the genius of this musical clown.

Texas' Sixteen Deluxe (1) practiced the psychedelic pop tune on **Backfeed Magnetbabe** (1995).

Texas' Sincola unleashed the post-feminist rants of **What The Nothinghead Said** (1995).

Oregon's most hyped band of the 1990s, the Dandy Warhols (1) managed to fuse Brit-pop and the Velvet Underground on **Dandys Rule OK** (1995), but then sold out to generic power-pop with **Come Down** (1997) and **Thirteen Tales From Urban Bohemia** (2000).

The Deadly Snakes, a sextet from Toronto with guitar, keyboards and horns, played rowdy epileptic soul-tinged garage-rock reminiscent of Fleshtones, J Geils Band and New York Dolls on **Love Undone** (1999).

In Britain, Kula Shaker penned the derivative but exuberant **K** (1996).

Comet Gain resurrected the neo-mod sound of the Wildhearts with a more hysterical attitude, especially on **Tigertow Pictures** (1999).

The Heads concocted **Relaxing With** (1996), a demented soup of Stooges, MC5 and Blue Cheer.

Scotland's Long Fin Killie updated Pentangle's folk-rock to the age of trip-hop and post-rock on **Houdini** (1995).

During the 1990s, the single most impressive concentration of garage-rock bands was perhaps in Scandinavia. Hanoi Rocks had led the way, and, one decade later, a number of Scandinavian bands followed their lead.

MC5, Motorhead and New York Dolls were the role models for Sweden's Hellacopters (1), who delivered the impressive punch of **Supershitty To The Max** (1996) and **Payin' The Dues** (1997), and for Norway's Gluecifer, who stormed through a program of acrobatic rock'n'roll numbers on the mini-album **Dick Disguised As Pussy** (1996).

The Hives (1) opted for anthemic overtones on the mini-album **Barely Legal** (1997) and especially the album **Veni Vidi Vicious** (2000).

Santa Cruz-based Comets On Fire (3), featuring vocalist/guitarist Ethan Miller and keyboardist Noel Harmonson, played acid-rock with a punk vengeance on **Comets on Fire** (2000), one of the most intense albums of distorted and anthemic rock'n'roll since MC5. Loud, fast, apocalyptic waves of guitar distortions and gigantic rhythm shake **Field Recordings From the Sun** (2002). Adding Ben Chasny of the Six Organs of Admittance, **Blue Cathedral** (2004) lent intellectual depth to the most primal, barbaric emotional bursts. Their most effective weapon was the sheer density and frenzy of their playing.

Hugh Golden's Lowdown, that shared Noel Harmonson with the Comets On Fire, transitioned from **Revolver II** (1999), a sarcastic, cacophonous and anarchic collection of jams, to **Y Is A Crooked Letter** (2003), a rather different beast that harked back to the intense maelstroms of Japan's noise-core bands.

Instrumental nostalgia, 1996-98

While not as original as their counterparts of the early 1990s, an impressive number of groups still offered witty and creative takes on instrumental rock. Notable albums of the period included: **The Utterly Fantastic and Totally Unbelievable Sound** (1995) by the Los Straitjackets in Tennessee; **At Home With Satan's Pilgrims** (1995) by the Satan's Pilgrims in Oregon; **Savage Island** (1996) by the Bomboras in Los Angeles; **Battle Of The Loons** (1998) by Shark Quest (1), in North Carolina, that contaminated surf music with flavors of country and folk; New York's Mooney Suzuki, who played old-fashioned high-adrenalin garage-rock on **People Get Ready** (2000).

In Canada, Mark Brodie And The Beaver Patrol resurrected the vibrato melodies of the Ventures and Dick Dale on **The Shores Of Hell** (1996), thus following in the footsteps of Shadowy Men On A Shadowy Planet.

Post-punk, 1995-2000

The languages of punk-rockers continued to multiply, although few bands were able to stand up as generational icons.

There were those who still played the original style. The Streetwalkin' Cheetahs rediscovered catchy punk-rock for Los Angeles' "street" generation on **Overdrive** (1997). Minnesota's Dillinger Four matched their verve on the sociological trilogy that began with **Midwestern Songs Of The Americas** (1998). New York's Chavez became contenders for the title of greatest Mission Of Burma disciples with the huge riffs of **Gone Glimmering** (1995).

Towards the end of the decade punk-pop had become as mainstream as pop muzak thanks to groups such as Florida's New Found Glory, who had started out with the "old school" sound of **Nothing Gold Can Stay** (1999) but later achieved stardom with a much watered-down version of punk-pop, and Scotland's Idlewild, with **Hope Is Important** (1999). England's Skunk Anansie, a multi-racial group fronted by bold black lesbian feminist Deborah Anne "Skin" Dyer, unleashed a politicized blend of funk, blues, hardcore, reggae, hip-hop and metal on albums such as **Stoosh** (1996).

Other bands, particularly in the Midwest, came up with original styles indebted to Fugazi and Jesus Lizard. Minneapolis' Calvin Krime played ferocious "old school" hardcore on **You're Feeling So Attractive**

(1998). New Jersey's <u>Rye Coalition</u> fused emocore and hard-rock, Fugazi and AC/DC, starting with **Hee Saw Dhuh Kaet** (1997). A similar maturation was displayed by Florida's <u>Hot Water Music</u> on **Fuel for the Hate Game** (1996). Ohio's <u>Terrifying Experience</u>, the project of Guided By Voices' guitarist Mitch Mitchell, experimented with progressive hardcore on **Supreme Radial** (1999). So did Los Angeles' <u>Stanford Prison Experiment</u>, that tried to bridge that style and funk-metal on **The Gato Hunch** (1995).

Jazzcore, 1996-2000

Avantgarde hardcore bands tried to revitalize the genre mostly by incorporating jazzy idioms. New York's <u>Stratotanker</u> offered atonal punk-jazz on **Baby Test The Sky** (1996) that evoked the unlikely wedding of Captain Beefheart and Miles Davis. <u>Dysrhythmia</u> (1), a Philadelphia-based instrumental trio, were heirs to the tradition of instrumental jazz-tinged punk-rock of Universal Congress and Saccharine Trust on **Contradiction** (2000) and **No Interference** (2001). Oregon's <u>Irving Klaw Trio</u> wed the spastic dementia of Red Crayola and Captain Beefheart with the avant-jazz architecture of Frank Zappa and Can on **Utek Pahtoo Mogoi** (1997). The Minutemen were still an important reference point for the dissonant, angular hardcore of combos such as Maryland's <u>Candy Machine</u>, for example on **A Modest Proposal** (1994), and Virginia's <u>Kepone</u>, mostly on **Ugly Dance** (1994). Sweden's <u>Refused</u> (1), featuring vocalist Dennis Lyxzen, gave their spiritual and artistic testament with their third album **The Shape of Punk to Come** (1998), whose title paraphrased Ornette Coleman's jazz masterpiece. Their militant jazzcore bridged the generation of the 1980s and the generation of post-rock.

The golden age of emocore, 1995-2000

Meanwhile, the deluge of emocore continued in the second half of the 1990s, indirectly making it less and less relevant.

Wisconsin's <u>Promise Ring</u> epitomized the conventions of that generation, shifting from the litanies of **30 Degrees Everywhere** (1996), fueled by Davey VonBohlen's passionate screaming and crooning, towards the rousing singalongs, reminiscent of the Replacements' populist rock'n'roll, of **Nothing Feels Good** (1997). The natural outcome of that evolution was the blue-collar rock of <u>Maritime</u>, fronted by VonBohlen and featuring two virtuosi such as Dismemberment Plan's bassist Eric Axelson and Promise Ring's drummer Dan Didier, especially on their second album **We The Vehicles** (2006).

There was hardly a month without a new significant addition to the "emo" canon: Illinois' <u>Braid</u>, with **The Age Of Octeen** (1996); Texas'

And You Will Know Us By The Trail Of Dead with **And You Will Know Us By The Trail Of Dead** (1997); Texas' At The Drive In, featuring guitarist Omar Rodriguez and singer Cedric Bixler, with the highly technical and emotional **In Casino Out** (1998); Kansas City's Get Up Kids, with **Four Minute Mile** (1998), which were among the most popular; Chicago's Alkaline Trio, with the razor-sharp anthems of **Goddamnit** (1998); Arizona's Jimmy Eat World, with **Clarity** (1999), the most popular at the turn of the decade; Kentucky's Elliott, with **False Cathedrals** (2000); Kansas' Appleseed Cast, with **Mare Vitalis** (2000), Buffalo's Snapcase, with **Designs for Automotion** (2000); Dashboard Confessional, the project of Florida-based singer and guitarist Chris Carrabba, with **Swiss Army Romance** (2000); Florida's Underoath, with the electronic arrangements and intricate melodies of their fifth album **Define The Great Line** (2006); New Jersey's Thursday with their third album **War All the Time** (2003) that transposed the intimate angst of old emocore into the collective psyche; etc. Most of them emphasized melody over fury, and emotions over rebellion.

Towards the end of the decade a number of bands tried to introduce new elements.

One of the best, Wisconsin's Rainer Maria (1), relied on the male/female vocal harmonies of Kyle Fischer and Caithlin DeMarrais, and on complex dynamics for the psychological studies of **Past Worn Searching** (1997).

The early works of Cursive (2), the project of Nebraska's guitarist and vocalist Tim Kasher, displayed the leader's erudite and tortured persona, as well as his ambition to craft a post-emocore punk ballad. Kasher reached a remarkable musical and lyrical maturity on the concept album **Domestica** (2000), that introduced Lullaby For The Working Class' guitarist Ted Stevens. **The Ugly Organ** (2003), adding cellist Gretta Cohn to the line-up with Kasher increasingly toying with keyboards, mixed emocore melodrama and the angular punch of noise-rock in uniquely eccentric formats. If fear was the overarching theme of that album, then anger was the leitmotiv of **Happy Hollow** (2006), a scathing indictment of organized religion. Kasher's side-project Good Life complemented Cursive with the stark and melancholy ballads of third album **Album of the Year** (2004).

New York's Saetia invented a popular variant of emocore: "screamo". Its main attribute was the high-pitched screaming, but also the extremely furious guitar playing, as demonstrated on **Saetia** (1999).

Milestones in the emergence of screamo were the jarring and psychotic EP **Chaos is Me** (2000) by Boston's Orchid and **Document #5** (2000) by the Virginia-based septet Pg. 99.

New York's Glassjaw played emocore that sounded like the original nuclear hardcore of Black Flag on **Everything You Ever Wanted To Know About Silence** (2000).

In Texas, Will Johnson fronted <u>Centro-matic</u>, that bridged psychedelic-pop, cow-punk and emocore on **All the Falsest Hearts Can Try** (2000). A more mature version of the band, renamed <u>South San Gabriel</u>, delivered the allegorical concept album **The Carlton Chronicles** (2005).

Get Up Kids' keyboardist James Dewees formed <u>Reggie and the Full Effect</u>, that introduced a sense of humor in emocore, besides wedding catchy hooks and quasi-metal fury, notably on their second album **Promotional Copy** (2000).

Kansas' <u>Anniversary</u> flirted with both the revival of the new wave (thanks to the videogame-inspired keyboards of Adrianne Verhoeven) and with the poppy emocore that was fashionable at the turn of the century (thanks to frontmen Joshua Berwanger and Justin Roelofs) on **Designing a Nervous Breakdown** (2000).

New York's <u>Brand New</u> greatly expanded the stylistic range of the genre (from hard-rock to roots-rock to power-pop) on **Deja Entendu** (2003) and **The Devil and God Are Raging Inside Me** (2006).

Progressive hardcore, 1998-2000

In Washington, Ted Leo's <u>Chisel</u>, on **Set You Free** (1997), and especially <u>Dismemberment Plan</u> (1), on **Emergency and I** (1999), a sci-fi concept album enhanced with all sorts of studio witchcraft, fused progressive hardcore with new wave and power-pop.

<u>Les Savy Fav</u> from Rhode Island mixed angular rhythms, twisted melodies, psychotic vocals, dissonant guitar and spastic drumming on **3/5** (1997).

Los Angeles-area's <u>Thrice</u> evolved from the "screamo" style of the EP **First Impressions** (1999) to **The Illusion of Safety** (2002), an eclectic work that indulged in both grandiose pop and heavy-metal fury.

The hardcore of San Diego's <u>No Knife</u> incorporated elements of post-rock on **Hit Man Dreams** (1997). In the same city <u>Locust</u> coined a feverish and convulsive brand of electronic and noisy hardcore on **The Locust** (1998) and especially **Plague Soundscapes** (2003).

New York's <u>Mindless Self Indulgence</u> (1) played a mixture of hardcore, industrial music and hip-hop, heavily syncopated, derailed by scratching or electronics or videogames, and sung in a psychotic falsetto, notably on **Frankenstein Girls Will Seem Strangely Sexy** (1999), a 30-song self-parodistic hardcore monolith with overtones of operetta.

Seattle's <u>Juno</u> (1) specialized in open-ended structures with a wide range of dynamics on **This is the Way It Goes And Goes And Goes** (1999) and **A Future Lived in Past Tense** (2001).

Chicago's <u>90 Day Men</u>, featuring keyboardist Andy Lansangan and bassist Robert Lowe, bridged hardcore, progressive-rock and new wave on **(It (Is) It) Critical Band** (2000).

Seattle's Blood Brothers (2) virtually invented a new kind of hardcore with their blend of progressive and melodic stances on **This Adultery is Ripe** (2000). The chaotic punk-rock songs of **March on Electric Children** (2001), via cabaret piano, sampling and tape manipulation, led to the reckless stylistic chameleons and visceral nonchalance of **Burn Piano Island Burn** (2003). The vocal interplay of Johnny Whitney and Jordan Blilie was a first, pitting the high-pitched outburst of one against the melodic pathos of the other. The massive stylistic detours of **Crimes** (2004) and **Young Machetes** (2006) relied on instrumental virtuosi such as guitarist Cody Votolato and drummer Mark Gajadhar. Johnny Whitney and Mark Gajadhar also released an album under the moniker Neon Blonde, **Chandeliers in the Savannah** (2005), that wed the Blood Brothers' aesthetics to the ballad format and to dance beats.

Arab On Radar (2), from Rhode Island, played a concentrate of wildly dissonant punk-rock. **Rough Day At The Orifice** (1999) is a demented collage of feverish and feral sounds, vaguely approaching the state of music, somewhere along the twisted line that straddles Red Crayola, Pop Group, Mars and Pere Ubu. **Soak The Saddle** (2000) is the music of very angry (and very spastic) youth: psychotic melodies, manic pace, abrasive guitars, hardcore fury and extreme noise.

Industrial violence, 1995-2000

Nine Inch Nails and KMFDM imitators surfaced on both coasts as well as inland: Seattle's SMP, with **Stalemate** (1995), New York's Bile, with **Teknowhore** (1996), Missouri's Gravity Kills, with **Gravity Kills** (1996), Colorado's Society Burning, with **Tactiq** (1997), Oregon's Hellbent (Bryan Black), with **Helium** (1998).

Chicago's Acumen (1) unleashed the industrial-metal fury of **Territory = Universe** (1996) and then mutated into DJ? Acucrack (1) to experiment with a brutal, all-electronic, version of techno and drum'n'bass, best on **Mutants Of Sound** (1998).

Los Angeles' Static-X offered speed-metal for dance clubs on **Wisconsin Death Trip** (1999).

EC8OR, i.e. French keyboardist Patric Catani and German vocalist Gina D'Orio, carried out a similar campaign with **All Of Us Can Be Rich** (1997), a harrowing, excruciating, non-stop sonic assault made of bulldozer/jackhammer beats, mind-bending distortions and death-metal riffs.

Pennsylvania's God Lives Underwater (1) wed industrial music to Depeche Mode's synth-pop on the all-electronic **Life In The So-Called Space Age** (1998).

EBM was still thriving in San Francisco, where Battery relied on vocalist Maria Azevedo, best captured on **Distance** (1997), to deliver a formidable punch, and where Scar Tissue (1) crafted one of the most innovative and complex works, **TMOTD** (1997).

The third album by New York's Infidel? Castro (1), the double-disc **Bioentropic Damage Fractal** (2005), was a massive chaotic collage that ran the gamut from noise to grindcore to digital hardcore to drones to musique concrete.

New York artist Alan Dollgener, disguised under the moniker Reverb Sleep (1), only released the electronic collages of a nightmarish, ghastly intensity of **Fish Dream** (1995) before dying of AIDS.

Inheriting Throbbing Gristle's aesthetic of industrial chaos, and the brutal, visceral, dissolute abrasiveness of post-psychedelic improvisers such as Gravitar, Wolf Eyes (1), started in Michigan by vocalist and electronic musician Nate Young, crafted frantic, distorted, violent trancey electronic soundscapes on their first album as a trio, **Dread** (2001). Their futuristic vision was expressed by works such as **Dog Jaw** (2005), the mini-album **Human Animal** (2006) and the 40-minute piece **Black Wing Over The Sand** (2007) that were drenched in galactic drones, electric turbulence, vocal samples, manipulated found sounds and instrumental doodling; a form of pure abstract horror soundsculpting.

English noise-meisters Aufgehoben No Process were largely an invention of drummer Stephen Robinson, who edited in studio the savage improvisations of his quartet (guitar, electronics, two drummers) to produce the percussive and distorted mayhem of **The Violence Of Appropriation** (1999). The two "collaborations" with guitarist Gary Smith, **Magnetic Mountain** (2001) and **Anno Fauve** (2004), approached the madness of Japanese noisecore. The 27-minute *Jederfursich*, off **Khora** (2008), marked the insanely solemn zenith of Robinson's post-processing art.

British born New York-based super-prolific noise artist Dominick "Prurient" Fernow (who released more than 20 works in 2007 alone) blasted vomit-like shouts, ear-piercing eruptions of feedback and grotesque rhythms in the hour-long **Collaboration** (2000), the two colossal pieces of **Fossil** (2004), the 30-minute **The Baron's Chamber** (2005) and the four suites of **Pleasure Ground** (2006). His reputation was established by visceral live performances.

Breakcore, 1998-2000

The descendants of Atari Teenage Riot's digital hardcore could avail themselves of more advanced sampling and mixing equipment. While they may not have matched the urgency and fury of the masters, they easily outdid the master's chaotic dynamics.

The EPs, such as **Welcome To The Warren** (1997), mostly compiled on **Ambush** (2003), released by London's Toby "DJ Scud" Reynolds were emblematic of the raw electronic mayhem that underpinned breakcore.

The second album, **All Things Are Connected** (2000), by Schizoid, the project of Canada's producer Jason Smith, was the epitome of heavy violent metallic breakcore born from the ashes of drill'n'bass: distorted pounding beats, metallic guitars and evil vocals wrapped in dense grim electronic ambience.

Chicago's James Plotkin (1) used processed guitar sounds to compose subliminal works such as **A Peripheral Blur** (1998), but then ventured into the most ferocious kind of industrial music and digital hardcore on **Atomsmasher** (2001), a concentrate of drilling electronics, chaotic collages, hyper-fibrillating drums, psychotic howls and barbaric noises.

Confusion

Post-depression roots-rock 1995-1999

Dance clubs of the late 1990s reflected the general euphoria of the new generation of white-collar engineers, all of them aspiring millionaires. The rock bands rooted in the white and black traditions of the land, instead, reflected the down-to-earth attitude of the working class. Precisely because it was an age of rapid change, that was making old lifestyles obsolete and creating totally new ones, in which people were learning to shop on-line and talk on cellular phones and telecommute, it was also an age of personal confusion, of identity crisis, of insecurity.

Uncle Tupelo bred two offshoots. Jay Farrar's Son Volt were mostly a vehicle for their leader's philosophizing: **Trace** (1995) was a concept album that analyzed the collective subconscious of the people of the Mississippi river. Jeff Tweedy's Wilco (3) expanded Uncle Tupelo's vocabulary towards the Byrds' folk-rock, Neil Young's mournful ballads, the Rolling Stones' drunk rhythm'n'blues, the Band's domestic gospel-rock, Bob Dylan's **Blonde On Blonde** and Big Star's baroque pop on their second album, **Being There** (1996). Jay Bennett's keyboards helped pen arrangements that left their roots way behind. **Summer Teeth** (1999), the natural evolution of that idea, was thus a studio product that relied heavily on electronic sounds, and **Yankee Hotel Foxtrot** (2002), their most experimental album, was a majestic nonsense of eccentric arrangements, skewed melodies and lyrical meditations that bridged the Beach Boys' **Pet Sounds** and Radiohead's **OK Computer** while also delivering a very poignant meaning.

In New York, Shannon Wright's Crowsdell contaminated Pavement's style with roots-rock on **Dreamette** (1995), while Eef Barzelay's Clem Snide embodied the minimalist aesthetic of alt-country, notably on their second album **Your Favorite Music** (2000).

North Carolina's Whiskeytown (1), a punkier Uncle Tupelo (or a countryfied Replacements) who relied on the combined talents of vocalist Ryan Adams, violinist Caitlin Cary and guitarist Mike Daly, penned perhaps the best of the batch, **Strangers Almanac** (1997).

Seattle's Citizens' Utilities (1), on the other hand, crafted a baroque form of country-rock, relying on three-part vocal harmonies as much as on tension-filled dynamics and eccentric instrumental touches, with **Lost And Foundered** (1996), **No More Medicine** (1997), their most poignant work, and **Sunbreak** (1999).

Boston's Scud Mountain Boys, fronted by Joe Pernice, were almost slo-core on **Massachusetts** (1996).

Boston's Willard Grant Conspiracy (1) played elegant, evocative and melancholy country music on the introspective monolith **3am Sunday @ Fortune Otto's** (1996) that evolved into the solemn and depressed ballads of **Mojave** (1999), which often sounded like Chris Isaak interpreting Neil Young's *Harvest* or Bob Dylan's *Knocking On Heaven's Door*.

Boston's Wheat (1) penned the graceful, melancholy folk-rock of **Medeiros** (1997) and **Hope And Adams** (1999).

Punk-rock and bluegrass were fused by Bad Livers in Ohio, for example on the intimidating **Hogs On The Highway** (1997); and by Split Lip Rayfield in Kansas, for example on the grotesque **In The Mud** (1999). Ohio's Moviola struck a balance between country-pop and heavily-distorted acid-rock on **The Year You Were Born** (1996).

Boston's Dropkick Murphys were the Pogues of the 1990s, detonating traditional Irish songs and even appropriating the sound of bagpipes on **Do Or Die** (1997).

Ohio's Appalachian Death Ride (1), an open ensemble of eight to ten musicians, sounded like the USA version of the Mekons on the punkish **Appalachian Death Ride** (1996) and especially the visceral, anthemic **Hobo's Codebook** (2003).

Washington's Quix*o*tic, a trio with Slant 6's guitarist Christina Billotte, vocalist Mira Billotte and bassist Mike Barr, achieved an odd hybrid of Nico's ghostly singing and Sleater-Kinney's rabid roots-rock on their second album **Mortal Mirror** (2002).

Doo Rag, a duo from Arizona, played blues-punk with demented ferocity and sardonic humor on **What We Do** (1996). Their vocalist-guitarist Bob Log continued his unorthodox career with collections of "devoluted" (a` la Devo), spastic, sloppy, out-of-tune country blues, saloon boogie and garage rock set to a frantic drum-machine beat, notably on **Trike** (1999).

Populism 1994-99

A vibrant sector of roots-rock favored the route opened by Tom Petty: folk-rock and power-pop with populist overtones. Bands that played in this style included: Ohio's Throneberry, with **Sangria** (1994); Texas' Fastball, with their second album **All The Pain Money Can Buy** (1998); San Diego's Supernova, with **Ages 3 And Up** (1995); Los Angeles' Possum Dixon, with **Star Maps** (1996). New York's late bloomers Nada Surf started out in 1996 with a trite brand of populism but the gently melodic gems exuding anger and frustration of **Let Go** (2003) coined a new standard for the genre.

Colorado's Sixteen Horsepower (1) attacked the sonic icons of America's rural traditions (whether Louisiana's zydeco or Kentucky's bluegrass) from the vintage point of California's "acid" folk-rock on **Sackcloth & Ashes** (1996); and the painstakingly orchestrated elegies of **Low Estate** (1997) shifted the focus towards David Eugene Edwards' noble empathy.

Third Eye Blind looked for a middle path between hard-rock and folk-rock on **Third Eye Blind** (1997).

Seattle's Modest Mouse (2) was the vehicle for Isaac Brock's honest, heart-felt vignettes on **This Is A Long Drive For Someone With Nothing To Think About** (1996), a sprawling chronicle of everyday life in the 1990s. His portraits of drifters, losers and disillusioned fools became much sharper and more musically assured on **The Lonesome Crowded West** (1998), and his most experimental work was **Sharpen Your Teeth** (2002), released by his side-project Ugly Casanova (1), featuring Black Heart Procession's Pall Jenkins and Califone's Tim Rutili.

Georgia's Drive-by Truckers (1) seemed to belong to another era with their good-humored blend of roots-rock, ranging from cow-punk to southern boogie. The double-disc **Southern Rock Opera** (2001) was an explicit tribute to the three-guitar sound of Lynyrd Skynyrd. **The Dirty South** (2004) was another concept devoted to myths of the south.

Philadelphia's Marah composed a saga of life in their hometown via the com/passionate vignettes of **Let's Cut The Crap And Hook Up Later On Tonight** (1998), a diverse and exuberant rock'n'roll album.

My Morning Jacket from Louisville (Kentucky) specialized in simple country-rock melodies highlighted by luscious arrangements and haunting vocals on **The Tennessee Fire** (1999). Alt-country, southern-rock and power-pop met on **At Dawn** (2000), a monolith that packed enough refrains and riffs for an entire bar-band dynasty. Their method turned into a luscious sonic exploration of ordinary states of mind on **Z** (2005).

Rocky Votolato's Waxwing played roots-rock with punkish overtones on **For Madmen Only** (1999) in a style reminiscent of the Replacements, although **One For The Ride** (2000) steered towards U2's arena rock.

Los Angeles' Earlimart, the brainchild of singer-songwriter Aaron Espinoza, ranked among the best disciples of the Pixies on **Kingdom of Champions** (2000) before turning to the baroque folk-rock of **Everyone Down Here** (2003), with string arrangements by Fred Lonberg-Holm.

If "post-rock" was the key to understanding the 1990s, "pre-rock" (of the kind pioneered by Royal Trux) was the key to understanding the early 2000s. Michigan's White Stripes (1), the guitar and drums duo of Jack White and Meg White came up with the idea on their second album **De Stijl** (2000) of offering a wealth of sonic extracts of blues music without actually playing blues music. **White Blood Cells** (2001) refined that idea into a catchy synthesis of roots-rock and hard-rock, performed with the kind of "detached enthusiasm" that pervaded the revisionists of the time.

Chamber folk 1996-2000

In the mid 1990s, following the example of Lambchop, a new evolution of roots-rock led to a form of "chamber folk", a folk/country style that employed an expanded instrumentation and loitered at the border between noise-rock and post-rock.

Nebraska's Lullaby For The Working Class (11), led by vocalist/guitarist Ted Stevens and multi-instrumentalist Mike Mogis, used an arsenal of acoustic instruments to pen fragile, post-modernist folk songs that expanded on Palace Brothers' melancholy alt-country concept. The sounds of the instruments were scattered like ambient sounds on **Blanket Warm** (1996), turning each song into an impressionistic painting. The sound of **I Never Even Asked For Light** (1997) was sleepy and abstract, often hypnotic, as it lulled elusive melodies in a sea of warm tones; and **Song** (1999) further reduced the pace, plunging in a serene slumber. The effect fell halfway between Van Morrison's **Astral Weeks** and Hindemith's kammermusik.

Los Angeles' Geraldine Fibbers (2), fronted by former Ethyl Meatplow's vocalist Carla Bozulich, bridged the gap with urban culture in the desolate, hyper-realistic stories of **Lost Somewhere Between The Earth And My Home** (1995). The subversive power-pop of **Butch** (1997), featuring jazz guitarist Nels Cline, embedded rootsy melodies into alien structures.

Chicago's Pinetop Seven (1), Darren Richard's project, specialized in majestic and post-apocalyptic ballads arranged in a sophisticated style encompassing a wide range of settings, especially on their third album **Bringing Home The Last Great Strike** (2000).

Ohio's Mysteries Of Life, featuring Antenna's rhythm section of Jacob Smith and Freda Boner, offered another imitation of Van Morrison's neoclassical folk-soul with **Keep A Secret** (1996).

Multi Kontra Culti Vs Irony (2002), the second album by New York-based multinational quintet Gogol Bordello (Ukrainian vocalist Eugene Hutz, Russian fiddler Sergey Rjabtzev, a Russian accordionist, an Israeli guitarist and an Israeli saxophonist) was a moral and musical tribute to a nation of immigrants at the sound of a blazing Slavic and gypsy punk-pop.

Colorado's DevotchKa, equipped with violin, accordion, sousaphone and trumpet, concocted a rare hybrid of alt-country, gypsy music and Ennio Morricone-like ambience on **Supermelodrama** (2000), adding mariachi horns on **How It Ends** (2004) to create a sort of Latin-gypsy-rock.

Dengue Fever, fronted by Cambodian vocalist Chhom Nimol and featuring saxophone and keyboards, perfected a nostalgic fusion of world-music and psychedelic-rock of the Sixties on their second album **Escape From Dragon House** (2005).

British folk-rock

Folk-rock in England was revitalized by Fire & Ice's baroque **Runa** (1996), a set of languid and emphatic ballads imbued with the spirit of northern fairy-tales and embellished with keyboards and horns.

Scott 4 experimented with hip-hop tinged folk-rock on **Recorded In State LP** (1998).

An original variant of roots-rock was experimented by Gomez on **Bring It On** (1998), an album that relied on studio-production technique more than on traditional songwriting.

Scotland boasted much more original purveyors of folk-rock. Belle And Sebastian (2), one of the leading bands of the second half of the decade, rediscovered Donovan's gently whispering vocals, and his naive blend of melodic and poetic elements. **Tigermilk** (1996) focused on the intense pathos of low-key tunes, an apparent oxymoron that Stuart Murdoch's recitation and necolassical arrangements with piano, flute, harpsichord and cello (Isobel Campbell) turned into a new form of art. His fragile, modest style acquired a shimmering look and feel on **If You're Feeling Sinister** (1997). Many more instruments contributed to the magic of **The Boy With The Arab Strap** (1998) and **Fold Your Hands Child** (2000), but the lush arrangements rarely interfered with Murdoch's heart-wrenching lullabies.

Appendix Out, the project of singer-songwriter Ali Roberts, focused on elegant and cadaveric music for dramatic meditations on the spartan **The Rye Bears A Poison** (1997) and on the more seductive **Daylight Saving** (1999), a marvel of discreet chamber arrangements.

Arab Strap, the project of vocalist Aidan Moffat and multi-instrumentalist Malcolm Middleton, indulged in the moody and disorienting atmospheres of **Philophobia** (1998).

In the 2000s Gary Lightbody's brainchild Snow Patrol, from Scotland via Northern Ireland, would take the fragile folk-rock of Belle And Sebastian, turn it into the bombastic experience of **Final Straw** (2004) and propel it to the top of the charts.

Psych-folk 1996-99

At the turn of the century several groups and singers launched a revival of the psychedelic folk music of the hippies.

Amps For Christ, a prolific albeit erratic Los Angeles-based group led by instrument builder Henry Barnes, practiced "cosmic-folk" music characterized by the distorted electronic sounds produced by Barnes' home-made instruments. Albums such as the double-LP **The Plains Of Alluvial** (1995), the 34-song **Beggars Garden** (1997) and the 39-song double-disc **Electrosphere** (1999) were cauldrons of very short-term ideas that rarely managed to coalesce.

The New York-based Tower Recordings collective (including Tim Barnes and Pat Gubler) harked back to English pagan folk on albums such as **Furniture Music For Evening Shuttles** (1998). P.G. Six was the more or less solo project of Pat Gubler, who pursued a kind of progressive folk music akin to both Incredible String Band's psychedelic folk and John Fahey's raga-folk, although enhanced with both electronic and natural sounds, on **Parlor Tricks and Porch Favorites** (2001).

Fursaxa (1), the project of prolific Philadelphia-based singer-songwriter Tara Burke, indulged in psychedelic folk music on albums such as **Mandrake** (2000), her archetypical set of hymns for keyboards, dulcimer, guitar and voice, **Madrigals in Duos** (2004) and especially **Amulet** (2005), containing four extended pieces. By the time that **Lepidoptera** (2005) and **Kobold Moon** (2008) came out, her style had reached an otherworldly quality.

Los Angeles' Beachwood Sparks (1) adopted the chirping guitars of the Byrds and the rustic melodies of the Grateful Dead, i.e. the sound of the late hippie era, and grafted them onto the emerging style of chamber folk. **Beachwood Sparks** (2000) and especially **Once We Were Trees** (2001) were slightly disorienting journeys through the ages.

Solo acoustic guitar, 1996-1998

Sun City Girls' boss Sir Richard Bishop (1) launched his solo career with **Salvador Kali** (1998), a set of seriously virtuoso instrumentals that spanned ethnic, jazz and classical music. The solo guitar improvisation workouts on **Improvika** (2005) and especially **While My Guitar Violently Bleeds** (2007) took inspiration from John Fahey and Sandy Bull for their blends of raga, flamenco, jazz and folk guitar styles.

German guitarist Steffen Basho-Junghans (2) was the main European heir to the school of the "primitive guitar" (John Fahey, Robbie Basho). His early albums for solo acoustic guitar, the naive and pastoral **In Search of the Eagle's Voice** (1995) and the two volumes of raga-influenced **Fleur de Lis** (1996), indulged in hypnotic sound painting of a less metaphysical nature than Fahey's and of a less spiritual nature than Basho's, but **Song of the Earth** (2000) was a gentle and intense philosophical meditation. The more experimental **Inside** (2001) and especially **Waters in Azure** (2002) were studies in texture and ambience. He achieved a gentle synthesis of sorts with the two tours de force of **Rivers and Bridges** (2003) and with *Late Summer Morning*, off **Late Summer Morning** (2006).

Colorado's Janet Feder applied a whirlwind of Western and Eastern techniques to her second album **Speak Puppet** (2001).

They were the vanguard of another case of revival affecting a style that had been very underground in its heyday.

Depression

Desperate songwriters, 1996-99

The dejected tone of so many young songwriters seemed out of context in the late 1990s, when the economy was booming, wars were receding and the world was one huge party. They seemed to reflect a lack of confidence in society, in politics and, ultimately, in life itself.

First there was the musician who could claim the title of founder of this school in the old days of the new wave. Mike Gira (2) basically continued the atmospheric work of latter-period Swans. His tortured soul engaged in a form of lugubrious and apocalyptic folk, which constituted, at the same time, a form of cathartic and purgatorial ritual. After his solo album **Drainland** (1995), which was still, de facto, a Swans album, assisted by Jarboe and Bill Rieflin, Gira split the late Swans sound in two: Body Lovers impersonated the ambient/atmospheric element, while Angels Of Light focused on the orchestral pop element. On the one hand, Gira crafted the sinister and baroque layered instrumental music of Body Lovers' **Number One Of Three** (1998) and the subliminal musique concrete of **Body Haters** (1998). On the other hand, Angels Of Light's ethereal and supernatural folk music of **How I Loved You** (2001), a concept on sex, and **Everything Is Good Here Please Come Home** (2003), which explored simultaneously the personal, historical and political planes, renewed the similarities with Nico's stately, pagan, ancestral lied. Basically, the Body Lovers were the culmination of the Swans' experiments with magniloquent production (the "male" component of their sound), while Angels Of Light was the continuation of Jarboe's "female" component of the group's sound.

Ohio's Jason Molina, better known as Songs:Ohia (1), evolved from the cliche' of the melancholy cry of a tortured soul towards a sinister form of depression. The suicidal dirges and stately odes of **Songs:Ohia** (1997) transformed into the philosophical psalms of **The Lioness** (2000) and the metaphysical requiem of **Ghost Tropic** (2000), which in turn led to the seven lengthy meditations of **Didn't It Rain** (2002).

Los Angeles' Duncan Sheik (1) wrapped the chronic mood of desperation and heartbreak of **Duncan Sheik** (1996) into an "ambient folk-rock" style that merged lush string arrangements and the acoustic style of the troubadours.

In Seattle the stark albums of Damien Jurado (1), such as **Waters Ave S** (1997) and **Ghost Of David** (2000), were imbued with Tom Waits-grade spleen, Chris Isaak-infected apathy, Smog-tinged fatalism, and, mostly, music of moral emptiness.

Johnny Dowd in upstate New York penned the gloomy "murder ballads" of **Wrong Side of Memphis** (1998).

New York-based guitarist and electronic keyboardist <u>Greg Weeks</u>
debuted a hushed, subdued, minor-key and melancholy bedroom style,
somewhat reminiscent of Nick Drake, on **Fire In The Arms Of The Sun**
(1999).

<u>Dakota Suite</u>, the project of English singer-songwriter Chris Hooson,
best represented by **Signal Hill** (2000), was an intimate, pessimistic
philosopher in the vein of Nick Drake but gifted with a flair for mixing
soul, folk and jazz in the vein of Van Marrison.

Irish singer-songwriter <u>Adrian Crowley</u> (1) penned the quiet nightmare
of **A Strange Kind** (1999).

Baroque songwriters, 1996-2000

The existential spleen knew no musical boundaries. The trend towards
more and more eccentric and eclectic arrangements continued in the
second half of the 1990s but was rarely matched by an optimistic mood.
In fact, the "baroque" songwriters might have better reflected the
zeitgeist of the "dotcom" era, an economic boom that fundamentally
failed to create happiness.

A Brian Wilson fixation permeated the work of Australian expatriate
<u>Richard Davies</u> (3), who attained a magical balance of Syd Barrett,
David Bowie and Donovan on his collaboration with Eric Matthews,
Cardinal (1995), credited to <u>Cardinal</u>, a classic of chamber pop, and
then crafted the austere **There's Never Been A Crowd Like This** (1996)
and the surreal **Telegraph** (1998), whose vocal harmonies are
reminiscent of Crosby Stills & Nash.

His partner in Cardinal, Boston's <u>Eric Matthews</u>, indulged in VanDyke
Parks-style orchestrations on his own **It's Heavy In Here** (1995).

Michigan's humble <u>Brendan Benson</u> penned baroque songs in the
tradition of Todd Rundgren on **One Mississippi** (1996) and **Lapalco**
(2002).

Jellyfish's <u>Jason Falkner</u> played all the instruments on his shimmering
Author Unknown (1996).

The <u>Eels</u> (12), the project of Los Angeles-based songwriter Mark
Oliver Everett, worked out a storytelling style that was both humble and
sophisticated on **Beautiful Freak** (1996), locating his tone and
arrangements somewhere between Beck and the Flaming Lips. **Electro-
Shock Blues** (1998), a bleak concept album and a moving requiem for
friends who died, upped the ante by adopting Tom Waits' skewed
orchestral arrangements and topping Neil Young's manic depression. By
exploiting the disorienting sonic events generated by keyboards,
samplers and turntables, and by integrating jazz and neoclassical motifs,
Everett coined a solemn, disturbing, jarring form of folk music. By the
time of the autobiographical concept **Blinking Lights And Other**

Revelations (2005), Everett had refined his ability to modulate a monotonous discourse into graceful, colorful, mesmerizing calligraphy.

Virginia's Mark Linkous, best known under the moniker Sparklehorse (2), created studio miracles such as **Vivadixiesubmarinetransmissionplot** (1995) and **It's A Wonderful Life** (2001), which coupled oddly original music with melancholy overtones, something that harked back to the Pearls Before Swine.

Soon, eccentric arrangements became as important as the words and the refrains. Ambitious arrangements reached a paradoxical peak at the end of the decade: Sunny Day Real Estate's Jeremy Enigk, with **Return Of The Frog Queen** (1996); Washington's Sea Saw, with **Magnetophone** (1996); New York's Dean "Illyah Kuryahkin" Wilson, with **Thirtycabminute** (1999); Chicago's Fruit Bats, i.e. Eric Johnson, with the lazy, laid-back campfire ballads of **Echolocation** (2000).

Ohio's Joseph Arthur (1) wed electronica and folksinging on the eclectic **Big City Secrets** (1997), although he made his point more poignantly with the simpler and catchier songs of **Come To Where I'm From** (2000).

Boston's Jack Drag (1), John Dragonetti's project, penned **Unisex Headwave** (1997), an eclectic work that ran the gamut from blues to pop to psychedelia to hip-hop.

In Canada, Rufus Wainwright (1), the son of Loudon Wainwright III and Kate McGarrigle, went beyond Brian Wilson with **Rufus Wainwright** (1998), an erudite, melodramatic extravaganza that mixed Italian opera, Sullivan's operettas, French cabaret, Broadway show-tunes, and early Brian Eno. Wainwright progressed from vaudeville to opera with **Poses** (2001).

Visual Audio Sensory Theatre (1998), or VAST, the project of San Francisco-based multi-instrumentalist Jon Crosby, epitomized unrelenting melodrama and symphonic arrangements.

Nebraska's Bright Eyes (1), the brainchild of Conor Oberst, signaled the maturity of this movement with the multiple refracting moods and sounds of **Fevers And Mirrors** (2000). Oberst's other band Desaparecidos concocted an incendiary fusion of garage-rock and emo-core with strong sociopolitical overtones on **Real Music Speak Spanish** (2002).

By borrowing ideas from Debussy, Stravinsky and Hindemith rather than Van Dyke Parks or Brian Wilson, San Francisco's Her Space Holiday, the brainchild of Marc Bianchi, coined a form of grand, symphonic pop on albums such as **Manic Expressive** (2001).

San Francisco's For Stars rediscovered soft rock of the 1970s on **Windows for Stars** (1999).

Jason Lytle's Grandaddy (1), from Modesto (California), served quirky pop a` la Sparklehorse on **Under The Western Freeway** (1997), which became almost futuristic on the socio/sci-fi concept album **The Sophtware Slump** (2000).

Stone Temple Pilot's vocalist <u>Scott Weiland</u> (1) became the eccentric bard of **12 Bar Blues** (1998), another example of stylistic fusion and futuristic folk.

Watch It Happen (1999) and especially **A Tall-Tale Storyline** (2001), by <u>Mazarin</u>, the project of Philadelphia's singer-songwriter Quentin Stoltzfus (Azusa Plane's drummer), were miracles of lush, eccentric studio production that still maintained the aural quality of a lo-fi bedroom production.

After two collections of lo-fi vignettes and an electronic experiment, Michigan's <u>Sufjan Stevens</u> (1) reinvented himself as a sophisticated arranger with the meticulously crafted concept album **Michigan** (2003) and especially **Illinois** (2005), a 22-song cycle entirely scored and arranged by Stevens himself.

Boston's singer-songwriter <u>Ben Kweller</u> bridged Jonathan Richman's jovial lo-fi pop and Elton John's elegant grand pop on **Sha Sha** (2002).

Australia's <u>Ben Lee</u> adopted a high-tech instrumentation of computers, keyboards, samplers and drum-machines on **Breathing Tornados** (1998).

The surreal songs of Swedish singer-songwriter <u>Nicolai Dunger</u> (2) were influenced by the holy triad of Robert Wyatt, Tim Buckley and Van Morrison, especially on **Eventide** (1997), boasting neoclassical arrangements. After the trilogy of **Blind Blemished Blues** (2000), **A Dress Book** (2001) and **Sweat Her Kiss** (2002), Dunger perfected his fusion of soul, jazz and rock with the lavish arrangements of strings, horns, piano and percussion on **Soul Rush** (2001). Under the moniker <u>A Taste Of Ra</u>, Dunger delivered the six-movement suite **Morning Of My Life** (2007), the ultimate realization of Van Morrison's blues-jazz-folk fusion for small chamber ensemble.

<u>Badly Drawn Boy</u> (i.e. Damon Gough) was introduced as the British version of Beck by a series of amateurish, lo-fi, poignant bedroom-style EPs, later compiled on **How Did I Get Here** (1999). However, his sprawling 18-song album **The Hour of The Bewilderbeast** (2000) was instead a lushly arranged work that owed more to Radiohead than to his generation's singer-songwriters.

Dementia, 1998-2000

The recordings of <u>Danny Cohen</u>, a veteran Los Angeles-based freak (of Frank Zappa's generation) began to surface only at the turn of the century thanks to **Museum Of Dannys** (1999) and **Dannyland** (2004). His songs were basically twisted folk lullabies arranged for studio effects and delivered in a Tom Waits-ian tone.

MC Trachiotomy (2), a collaborator of the dreadful Mr Quintron, was a Louisiana "rapper" whose albums **Robot Alien or Ghost** (1999) and **W/Love from Tahiti** (2002) are madcap collages highlighted by terrible production, drunk vocals, sub-standard percussion and cryptic lyrics. The latter (73 minutes long) is the musical equivalent of a hurricane, devastating a vast stylistic territory: swamp blues, reggae balladry, lounge muzak, big-band swing, Broadway show tunes, and free-form jamming.

Chicago harbored two wacky satirists in the vein of David Peel. Bobby Conn (1) displayed the wicked, twisted, frequently obnoxious wit of street performers: **Bobby Conn** (1997) was a wild, uncensored ride in a labyrinth of genres, and the concept album **The Golden Age** (2001) sounded like a parody of his generation. Lonesome Organist (multi-instrumentalist Jeremy Jacobsen) evoked early Frank Zappa with **Collector Of Cactus Echo Bag** (1998), a post-modernist merry-go-round of quotations.

Indiana's isolated Dave Fischoff (1) virtually invented a new form of folk music, barely audible and mostly indecipherable, with **Winston Park** (1998).

Keuhkot, a one-man band from Finland (Kalevi "Kake Puhuu" Rainio), created one of the most confused, demented and visceral hodgepodges of musical and non-musical events since the time of Wild Man Fischer with his fourth album **Peruskivi Francon Betonia** (2002), which fulfilled the promise of his solo debut **Mita Otat Mukaan Muistoksi Sivistyksesta** (1996).

In Italy the sloppy, grotesque and eclectic garage-folk of Bugo (Cristian Bugatti) bridged Beck and Jon Spencer Blues Explosion on **La Prima Gratta** (1999) and especially on the double-disc tour de force **Golia & Melchiorre** (2004).

Rootsy songwriters, 1996-99

Protagonists of the country-rock renaissance included: in Seattle, Gerald Collier (1), with the agonizing **I Had To Laugh Like Hell** (1996), and Pedro The Lion, the project of David Bazan, with **It's Hard To Find A Friend** (1998); in Oregon Varnaline, the project of Space Needle's guitarist and multi-instrumentalist Anders Parker, with the hard-rocking **Varnaline** (1997); in Ohio, Tim Easton, with **Special 20** (1998); and in Georgia, Kevn Kinney, the former Drivin'N Crying' singer, with **MacDougal Blues** (1990).

New York's Jim White transcended the genre on **Wrong-Eyed Jesus** (1997), a sophisticated exercise in the southern gothic genre.

San Francisco's Richard Buckner (1) pursued Joe Ely's "outlaw" country with a voice reminiscent of Townes Van Zandt on **Bloomed**

(1995) and particularly on the concept album **Devotion And Doubt** (1997), backed by Giant Sand and Marc Ribot.

Duet For Guitars #2 (1999) by Oregon's Matt "M" Ward (1) was too introverted to be even classified as alt-country: it was just a very personal form of moaning. The songs of **End Of Amnesia** (2001), harkening back to pre-war country, blues and gospel music, brought to the surface the nostalgic and naive elements that were working their way through Ward's psyche. Even when he converted to a full-band sound on **Post-war** (2006), the way he constructed his songs was still an abridged version of the history of USA popular music.

The alt-country movement spawned singer-songwriters such as Chicago's Robbie Fulks, with **Country Love Songs** (1996); and Nashville's Josh Rouse, with **Dressed Up Like Nebraska** (1998).

Chicago-based violinist Andrew Bird (2) engineered a brilliant mixture of cabaret, dancehall music, jump blues, Appalachian folk, swing bands and orchestral easy-listening on the albums credited to the Bowl Of Fire, notably on their third album **The Swimming Hour** (2001). His art peaked with the dizzying stylistic whirlwind of **The Mysterious Production Of Eggs** (2005) and **Armchair Apocrypha** (2007). If Will Oldham was the troubadour of alt-country, Jeff Buckley was the intimate psychologist, Devendra Banhart was the gentle psychedelic bard, Rufus Wainwright was the sophisticated popsmith, Andrew Bird is all of them at the same time: a master of deeply-felt singing, a master of layered arrangements, a master of lyrical imagery, a master of celestial melodies, a master of the bizarre and of the subtle.

Waxwing's leader Rocky Votolato penned solo acoustic albums of simple albeit competent folk-rock and country-rock such as **Rocky Votolato** (1999) and **Makers** (2006) that magnified his ragged and powerful voice.

Chisel's vocalist Ted Leo toyed with the experimental lo-fi folk music of **Tej Leo (?) Rx/Pharmacists** (1999), in which simple themes were drenched into samples and electronics, but then turned into yet another populist bard a` la Bruce Springsteen or Tom Petty on his best effort, **Hearts of Oak** (2003).

Knotworking, the moniker of the Albany (New York)-based Edward Gorch, specialized in gentle, sparse, acoustic folk ballads halfway between Cat Stevens and Leonard Cohen, notably on his second album **Notes Left Out** (2002).

In Brazil, Vinicius Cantuaria, influenced by the new wave, offered a personal synthesis of "Tropicalia", mellow jazz and soul music on **Sol Na Cara** (1997) and **Tucuma** (1999).

The Italian dynasty of singer-songwriters ("cantautori") was continued at the turn of the century by Ivano Fossati, with **Discanto** (1990), and Vinicio Capossela's **Canzoni a Manovella** (2000).

The female psyche, 1996-2000

The 10,000 Maniacs' chanteuse <u>Natalie Merchant</u> (1) conceived the fragile, tender, sensual melodies set to sophisticated folk-jazz arrangements of **Tigerlily** (1995).

With the mostly-acoustic and autobiographical **Pieces Of You** (1995), San Diego-via-Alaska's <u>Jewel</u> Kilcher manufactured a pseudo-hippie persona akin to Joni Mitchell and her proud soprano.

<u>Patty Griffin</u> inherited the mantle of Lucinda Williams on **Living With Ghosts** (1996), for voice and guitar, until **Children Running Through** (2007) fulfilled the promises of her grating country-pop-gospel fusion.

<u>Cat Power</u> (3), the project of New York-transplant Chan Marshall, debuted with the somber and spartan **Myra Lee** (1996) and the desolate, suffocating **What Would The Community Think** (1996). The latter formulated an art that took the shy pessimism of auteurs such as Nick Drake and Laura Nyro to a new dimension of introspection. Its sketchy vignettes and self-analyses coined a subtle and almost embarrassing format, that turned the listener into a voyeur peeping through the keyhole. Marshall was, at the same time, the cameraman and the actress: she played the role of a tormented heroine while she was filming herself playing that role. Her songs were as much acting as they were singing. Marshall's cinematic genius peaked with the song cycle of **Moon Pix** (1998), enhanced with the ambient, free-form arrangements of Dirty Three's Jim White and Mick Turner. The emotional intensity packed by her half whisper in the gloomy lieder of **You Are Free** (2003) bordered on the suicidal.

Another New Yorker, <u>Fiona Apple</u> (1), conveyed the anguish of her generation (she was still a teenager) on the piano-driven **Tidal** (1996), boasting a cabaret-like blend of blues, soul and jazz, and **When The Pawn Hits The Conflicts** (1999), enhanced by Jon Brion's idiosyncratic arrangements that mixed the old-fashioned and the futuristic.

San Francisco-based <u>Hannah Marcus</u> (2) penned some of the most otherworldly atmospheres, reminiscent of Laura Nyro's ominous elegies, Nico's glacial soliloquy, Tim Buckley's folk-jazz fusion, Lisa Germano's painfully childish introspection, Jane Siberry's abstract self-reflections, as well as of Patti Smith's delirious stream of consciousness, especially on her second and fourth albums, **Faith Burns** (1998) and **Desert Farmers** (2004).

<u>Lili Haydn</u>, a vocalist and violinist who sang with Nusrat Fateh Ali Khan and performed with the Los Angeles Philarmonic Orchestra, concocted an austere blend of classical, folk, jazz, rock and pop on **Lili** (1997).

The melancholy whisper of <u>Edith Frost</u> (11) breathed real life into the hypnotic lullabies of **Calling Over Time** (1997), arranged by Chicago luminaries such as Eleventh Dream Day's Rick Rizzo, Gastr Del Sol's

David Grubbs and Jim O'Rourke. Its natural evolution was the chamber pop of **Telescopic** (1998): Frost bled angelic melodies in a shy and introverted voice, which were captured in a web of timbres (cello, violin, flute, accordion, trombone, organ) and perturbed by psychedelic guitar effects. She did to folk music what the first Velvet Underground album did to rock music: carve a bleakly subliminal, darkly metaphysical, cruelly hellish space beneath an apparently innocent surface.

The works of Ohio-based singer-songwriter Jessica Bailiff (2) were, de facto, collaborations with Low's guitarist Alan Sparhawk. **Even In Silence** (1998) set her dilated, ethereal vocals and her intimate bedroom confessions, against the backdrop of an unfocused, loose instrumental noise. She was the first to fuse folk, ambient, psychedelia and slo-core. The litanies and lullabies of **Jessica Bailiff** (2002), oddly devoid of structure, had a supernatural quality.

Heather Duby (10) owed half the artistic success of **Post To Wire** (1999) to the oneiric orchestrations of Pell Mell's Steve Fisk, soundscapes that metabolized all sorts of styles while the singer borrowed from Nico, Enya and Bjork her emotional charge.

Crowsdell's vocalist Shannon Wright (1), an accomplished pianist, penned the austere chamber folk elegies of **Flight Safety** (1999), the nightmarish, emphatic, almost expressionistic music of **Maps Of Tacit** (2000) and, best of all, the theatrical, neoclassical meditations of **Dyed In The Wool** (2001).

Boston's Ill Ease, the project of New Radiant Storm King's drummer Elizabeth Sharp, pursued Beck's beat-based lo-fi folk-rock on **Circle Line Tours** (1999).

Seattle's Laura Veirs specialized in simple but profound collections of rural folk tales, notably on her fourth and fifth albums, **Carbon Glacie** (2004) and **Year of Meteors** (2005).

Mirah Yom Tov Zeitlyn, a singer-songwriter from Olympia, explored an intriguing hybrid of Liz Phair's sexy postures, Juliana Hatfield's introverted confessions and Lisa Germano's girlish anxiety on her second album **Advisory Committee** (2002).

Los Angeles native Mia Doi Todd found a balance between philosophical concerns and progressive dynamics on her second album **Come Out Of Your Mine** (1999) that laid the foundations for the lengthy and cryptic meditations of **Zeroone** (2001). Todd embraced electronics and jazz for **Gea** (2008), highlighted by the eleven-minute suite *River of Life/The Yes Song*.

Los Angeles' Meredith Brooks bridged the aesthetic of street singers and riot grrrls with the post-feminist anthems of **Blurring The Edges** (1997).

Los Angeles-born but New York-based troubadour Nina Nastasia whispered tunes soaked in subdued, interior aching (not unlike Nico) and wrapped them in understated arrangements for a country/folk ensemble (with both strings and winds) on **Dogs** (1999) and **The Blackened Air** (2002).

Neko Case (1), a part-time member of the New Pornographers, emerged out of the alt-country legion crooning and serenading in a broad range of vocal styles to pen the mood pieces of **Blacklisted** (2002).

Ohio's transgendered keyboardist, accordionist and harpist Baby Dee used her androgynous voice to craft the warm and fragile piano-based lullabies and ballads of **Little Window** (2000) and **Love's Small Song** (2002) that hinted at the artsy cabaret of Kurt Weill and Tom Waits.

Shivaree (1), the brainchild of Los Angeles-based vocalist Ambrosia Parsley, hired arrangers Duke McVinnie and Danny McGough to populate the ballads of **I Oughtta Give You A Shot In The Head** (2000) with a little zoo of quirky noises, keyboard drones and irregular beats.

In Britain, Sally Doherty's **Sally Doherty** (1996) focused on multi-layered vocals (inspired by Cocteau Twins' dream-pop and Enya's wordless lullabies) set to a lush acoustic music reminiscent of Michael Nyman's minimalistic repetition, ancient musical forms and ethnic folk.

Beth Orton (1) bridged folk music, trip-hop and Bjork's orchestral pop on **Trailer Park** (1997) and especially **Central Reservation** (1999), spicing her pensive ballads with electronic arragements, while **Comfort of Strangers** (2006) chartered a psychological territory halfway between Joni Mitchell's austere meditations and Cat Power's naive confessions.

Not only did British commanding singer Holly Golightly devote herself to retro midtempo garage-rock starting with **Good Things** (1995), but she did it better than any man, basically transposing the male-dominated sound of the early 1960s to a female-fronted perspective.

Transglobal Underground's vocalist Natacha Atlas (1) speculated on that band's seductive world-fusion on **Diaspora** (1995), **Halim** (1997) and especially **Gedida** (1999).

Icelandic singer-songwriter Emiliana Torrini dabbled in trip-hop with Bjork-inspired electronic arrangements on **Love In The Time Of Science** (1999).

At the turn of the millennium, France raised a new generation of songwriters, inspired by the post-rock styles of the late 1990s. Soundtrack composer Yann Tiersen coined a new kind of disjointed folk music with the surreal arrangements that envelop the shy tunes of **La Valse Des Monstres** (1995) and **Le Phare** (1998). Israeli-born singer-songwriter Keren Ann Zeidel fused folk, jazz and hip-hop on **La Biographie de Luka Philipsen** (2000).

A young singer from Colombia, Shakira Mebarak, became one of the best-sold Latin artists of all times first with **Donde Estan los Ladrones?** (1998) and then with **Laundry Service** (2001), both characterized by a sprightly fusion of Latin, Arab and rock music, as well as by her guttural singing. her stylistic melange progressed from the relatively earthly *Whenever Wherever* (2001) to *La Tortura* (2005) to the sophisticated rhythmic collage of *Hips Don't Lie* (2006).

Doom

Grunge and metalcore, 1996-99

The third generation of grunge was best represented by the mediocre Pearl Jam imitation of Florida's Creed on **My Own Prison** (1997) and **Human Clay** (1999). Grunge had been born in Australia (before it was reinvented in the USA) but the Pearl Jam-form of grunge came to Australia quite late. It never amounted to more than Silverchair's **Frogstomp** (1995) or Magic Dirt's **Friends In Danger** (1997).

An impressive work of gothic rock came from Switzerland: **The Pleasures Received In Pain** (1999), by Der Blutharsch.

Germany's Blind Guardian were the only significant addition to pomp-metal of the era, with **Nightfall In Middle Earth** (1999) winking at both Queen and Iron Maiden.

Hatebreed, from Connecticut, established "metalcore" as a major genre with **Satisfaction Is the Death of Desire** (1997) and **The Rise of Brutality** (2003). Towards the end of the decade, variants on the same theme were worked out by Missouri's Coalesce (1), who vomited the formidable metal-punk maelstrom of **Give Them Rope** (1997), by Massachusetts' Cave In with **Beyond Hypotermia** (1998), and by Los Angeles' Death By Stereo with their third album **Into The Valley of Death** (2003). Metalcore emphasized the breakdown: the section of a hardcore song with a slower drum beat and single-note guitar chugging that usually invites to dance. Defying the dogmas of the genre, Shai Hulud's **Hearts Once Nourished With Hope And Compassion** (1997), from Florida, managed to sound both catchy and inventive.

Florida's Poison The Well ventured beyond metalcore on their second album **Tear From The Red** (2002), exhibiting songwriting skills worthy of emo-pop and brutality worthy of death-metal.

Washington's Darkest Hour cemented the fusion of death-metal and hardcore with the vitriolic political concept **The Mark Of The Judas** (2000) and later accomplished the conversion of the genre to the mainstream with **Undoing Ruin** (2005).

New York state's Every Time I Die simultaneously joined the ranks of screamo and metalcore with the mini-album **Burial Plot Bidding War** (2000) and **Last Night In Town** (2001).

The chaotic hardcore of Japanese quintet Envy evolved into a hybrid of extreme screamo and post-rock on **A Dead Sinking Story** (2003) and **Insomniac Doze** (2006).

Stoned, 1995-2000

The revival of psychedelic hard-rock of the 1970s picked up steam after the success of Kyuss, Monster Magnet and the grunge scene.

Ed Mundell's <u>Atomic Bitchwax</u> (1) offered a more experimental version of Monster Magnet's stoner-rock on **Atomic Bitchwax** (1999). Boston's <u>Nightstick</u> (1) even added elements of free-jazz and avantgarde noise to the "Black Sabbath meets Blue Cheer" formula of stoner-rock on **Ultimatum** (1998). Southern California remained throughout the decade one of stoner-rock's main centers, as proven by works such as <u>Fu Manchu</u>'s **In Search Of** (1996), <u>Unida</u>'s **Coping With The Urban Coyote** (1999), the new project of Kyuss' vocalist John Garcia, and <u>Nebula</u>'s **Charged** (2001). Kyuss' influence on the new generations of stoner-rockers was not only obvious but even direct. <u>Queens Of The Stone Age</u> (1), the new band formed by Kyuss' guitarist Josh Homme and bassist Nick Oliveri, offered a consumable version of Kyuss (shorter songs, emphasis on the melody, streamlined dynamics) on **Queens Of The Stone Age** (1998). After the stylistic experiments of **Rated R** (2000), they achieved a sort of hard-rock classicism on **Songs For The Deaf** (2002), featuring Foo Fighters's drummer Dave Grohl and Screaming Trees' vocalist Mark Lanegan, the ideal balance of Cream and Nirvana.

<u>Los Natas</u> founded an important school of stoner-rock in Argentina with albums such as their third **Corsario Negro** (2002) and the three lengthy progressive-rock suites of **Toba-Trance** (2003).

Other notable stoners were Canada's <u>Sons Of Otis</u>, featuring guitarist Ken Baluke, especially on **Spacejumbofudge** (1996), Italy's <u>Ufomammut</u>, with **Godlike Snake** (2000), Wisconsin's <u>Bongzilla</u>, with their second album **Gateway** (2002), and Japan's <u>Church Of Misery</u>, with **Master Of Brutality** (2001).

Scandinavian horror, 1995-2000

Sweden's <u>Watain</u> were emblematic of the continuity of black metal in Scandinavia, particularly on their second album **Casus Luciferi** (2003).

Scandinavia remained at the forefront of progressive metal.

<u>Edge of Sanity</u> (1), the brainchild of Swedish vocalist and multi-instrumentalist Dan Swano, pioneered the marriage of death-metal and progressive-rock on the melodramatic third album **The Spectral Sorrows** (1993) and the diverse **Purgatory Afterglow** (1994). The dystopian 40-minute suite of **Crimson** (1996) alternated blastbeats and midtempo, death growls and clean vocals, crushing and melodic passages.

Sweden's <u>Meshuggah</u> (2) better categorized their generation's experimental metal as a subgenre of post-rock with the angular and intricate compositions of **Destroy Erase Improve** (1995) and especially **Chaosphere** (1998), indulging in off-kilter time signatures and polyrhythmic assaults. The EP *I* (2004) was a seamless 21-minute orgy of post-metal ideas, with lots of loops, guitar drones, polyrhythmic progressions and abstract interludes, without surrendering the frenzy of death-metal.

Sweden's Opeth (2) the brainchild of vocalist, guitarist and composer Mikael Akerfeldt, penned majestic gothic fantasias that alternated between acoustic melodic passages and anthemic quasi-grindcore attacks, notably *Forest of October* from **Orchid** (1995), the monumental *Black Rose Immortal* from **Morningrise** (1996), *Blackwater Park* from **Blackwater Park** (2001), and *Deliverance* from **Deliverance** (2002).

Also innovative in Sweden was Pain Of Salvation's **One Hour By The Concrete Lake** (1999).

The super-technical style of Norway's Solefald (1) turned their third album **Pills Against the Ageless Ills** (2001) into a brainy exercise of fusion-metal.

For a country that had a population of less than five million people, Norway produced an amazing number of innovative metal bands. Norway's supergroup Ved Buens Ende pioneered the fusion between post-rock and heavy-metal on **Written In Waters** (1995). Beyond Dawn (1) invented trombone-based black metal, an unlikely juxtaposition that tinged their second album **Revelry** (1998) with ambient noir atmospheres. Ulver (1) created an "electronic black metal" with the colossal **Themes From William Blake's The Marriage Of Heaven & Hell** (1998) and **Blood Inside** (2005), that introduced elements of techno, industrial, ambient and trip-hop music as well as sampled snippets of jazz, blues, classical music, continuously recasting black metal into wildly different frameworks. Norwegian multi-instrumentalist Vidar "Ildjarn" Vaaer pioneered "lo-fi black metal" inspired by garage-rock on collections of very brief and brutal "songs" such as **Ildjarn** (1996) and **Forest Poetry** (1996). At the same time, he pursued ambient suites for electronic keyboards on **Landscapes** (1996) and **Hardangervidda** (2002). Norway's one-man band Furze (1) followed up the frenzied and cartoonish mini-album **Trident Autocrat** (2000) with the unorthodox doom-metal of **Necromanzee Cogent** (2003), containing the 23-minute post-psychedelic orgy of *Sathanas' Megalomania*.

New standards for the genre were also set in Norway by Arcturus' **La Masquerade Infernale** (1998), In The Woods' **Omnio** (1997), Borknagar's **The Archaic Course** (1998) and Carpathian Forest's **Black Shining Leather** (1998).

A new trend in black metal was orchestral/electronic arrangements: Norway's Dimmu Borgir, with **Stormblast** (1996), East Germany's Rammstein, with **Sehnsucht** (1997), Japan's Sigh, with **Hail Horror Hail** (1997), Finland's And Oceans, with **The Dynamic Gallery Of Thoughts** (1998). Tiamat, Therion, and Amorphis pursued a neoclassical version of death metal, which preferred the sound of keyboards. Norway's Theatre of Tragedy even adopted operatic vocals. Haggard indulged in symphonic arrangements.

Finland's Children of Bodom tempered their full-frontal assault with insanely fast neoclassical keyboards on **Something Wild** (1997).

European black metal, 1995-2000

France suddenly became the stage for some of the most creative bands of black metal.

Blut Aus Nord played keyboards-tinged black metal on **Ultima Thulee** (1995), but began to introduce elements of industrial music into their fourth album **The Work Which Transforms God** (2003). After the ambient detour of **Thematic Emanation Of Archetypal Multiplicity** (2005), they abandoned black metal altogether for a new gothic genre straddling the border between post-rock and doom-metal with atonal guitars and grotesque keyboards, yielding the tortured **Mort** (2006).

Antaeus toiled at the border between black metal and grindcore with their fast, intricate **Cut Your Flesh And Worship Satan** (2000).

French multi-instrumentalist Stefan Kozak was the man behind two one-man bands. He coined his frenzied hybrid of classically-influenced keyboards and wall of fuzz and distortion a` la Burzum with Mystic Forest starting with **Green Hell** (1999). The sound on Eikenskaden's **The Black Laments Symphonie** (2001) and **The Last Danse** (2002) was even more grandiose, bordering on self-parody, and actually quite hummable and stately.

S.V.E.S.T. unleashed the black-metal equivalent of a chaotic psychedelic freak-out on their lo-fi cassettes **Scarification of Soul** (1998) and **Death to Macrocosm** (1999), later collected on **Coagula** (2005), before achieving pure hell with the three lengthy pieces of **Urfaust** (2003).

Deathspell Omega adopted a new format on their third album **Si Monvmentvm Reqvires Circvmspice** (2004) and on the mini-album **Kenose** (2005): midtempo songs that were hypnotic and brainy at the same time, and full of idiosyncratic stylistic detours.

German outfit Katharsis were to black metal what Captain Beefheart was to blues music: chaotic, demonic and hysterical. **666** (2000) was their manifesto, while the third album **VVorld VVithout End** (2006) showed quasi-progressive ambitions.

Germany's Nagelfar, featuring drummer Alexander von Meilenwald, experimented with progressive and epic forms of black metal that mixed Scandinavian frenzied gothic with both acoustic and symphonic (electronic) passages on **Srontgorrth** (1999).

Germany's Nargaroth competed with the Scandinavian masters of black metal via the satanic mass **Herbstleyd** (1998) and the four colossal suites of **Geliebte Des Regens** (2003). Germany's Necrofrost followed suit with their second album **Bloodstorms Voktes Over Hytrunghas**

Dunkle Necrotroner (2001), a natural disaster of struggling growls, riffs and beats.

Romania's Negura Bunget mixed black metal, dark ambience and folk melodies in the four suites of **'N Crugu Bradului** (2002).

Russia's Old Wainds epitomized the cold style of their generation of black metal on **Zdes Nikogda Ne Skhodyat Snega/ Where The Snows Are Never Gone** (1997) and **Religion of Spiritual Violence** (2001). Born from their ashes, Nav adopted a more majestic and melodic sound on **Halls Of Death** (2004).

On a totally different note, Benighted Leams, the brainchild of English guitarist Alex Kurtagic, played cartoonish black metal on **Caliginous Romantic Myth** (1996); and Austrialian one-man band Vorak delivered the spastic, childish **Triumph Of The Will** (1996).

Melechesh, the brainchild of the Israeli Arab vocalist-guitarist Melechesh Ashmedi, melded Middle-Eastern music with death-metal on the Assyrian concept **As Jerusalem Burns Al'Intisar** (1996).

Colombian guitar-drums duo Inquisition introduced a trancey quasi-chanting vocal style on **Into The Infernal Regions Of The Ancient Cult** (1998).

West-Coast black metal, 1996-2000

San Francisco's Weakling, featuring keyboards and two guitarists (Fucking Champ's guitarist Josh Smith and John Gossard) concocted a twisted tribute to Scandinavian black metal: the five trancey monoliths of **Dead As Dreams** (2000).

John Cobbett was the anchor for a few "retro" groups based in San Francisco. The Lord Weird Slough Feg, fronted by metal baritone Mike Scalzi, harked back to the "heroic" style of Judas Priest and Iron Maiden on the mini-album **The Lord Weird Slough Feg** (1996) and the Celtic concept **Twilight Of The Idols** (1999), perfecting it into their own moderate, melodic format on **Down Among The Deadmen** (2000). The Hammers of Misfortune harked back to keyboards-based prog-metal with the rock opera **The Bastard** (2001), featuring dueling male-female vocals. Ludicra, a quintet fronted by two women (Christy Cather and Laurie Sue), displayed the influence of post-rock and space-rock on their **Hollow Psalms** (2002).

Leviathan (1) was the original "one-man band" (Jeff Whitehead) of San Francisco's black metal that later inspired many more individuals. Inspired in turn by the sound of Burzum, Leviathan released 13 cassettes since 1998, partially compiled on the double-disc **Verrater** (2001). The official debut, **The Tenth Sub Level of Suicide** (2003), bridged the gap between the classic, "heroic" style of black metal and the progressive, dischordant, unstable style of the 2000s.

The revival of black metal in the USA was also signaled by Chicago's Judas Iscariot, in particular with their second album **Thy Dying Light** (1996).

International doom, 1995-99

The greatest heirs to the throne of British doom-metal were Electric Wizard (2). Led by singer/guitarist Justin Osborn, they inflated the heaviness of doom-metal to the point that music did not flow anymore: it just boomed; a long, dull, oppressive sound. **Electric Wizard** (1995) blended the holy triad of stoner-rock (Black Sabbath, Blue Cheer and Hawkwind) in a new form that was an implosion of each of them, but its twin album **Come My Fanatics** (1997) was even more powerful (even heavier, duller, darker and more sluggish), a tidal wave of gloomy sounds. The colossal-oriented approach led to **Dopethrone** (2000), whose extended tracks towered over an even more apocalyptic wasteland.

England's Orange Goblin straddled the border between stoner-rock and doom-metal on **Frequencies From Planet Ten** (1997).

Following in the footsteps of Thergothon, Finland's bass-less trio Skepticism were the European masters of ultra doom, thanks to the massive medieval-sounding church-organ that depressed **Stormcrowfleet** (1995) and the EP **Ethere** (1997).

Georgia's Harvey Milk (1) drained the loud, slow, brutal and mean-spirited creatures of **My Love Is Higher** (1996) of any emotions, carving a niche between Type O Negative, Swans and Melvins.

Seattle's Burning Witch, featuring guitarist Stephen O'Malley, conceived doom metal as background music for the vocalist's histrionic psychodrama on **Crippled Lucifer** (1998).

Florida's Cavity, who were at their best on third album **Supercollider** (1999), were more hummable than the average doom band despite the massive riffs and drumming explosions.

After shutting down Obsessed, Scott "Wino" Weinrich formed Spirit Caravan, whose **Jug Fulla Sun** (1999) sounded like a compendium of his obsession with doom.

The lengthy pieces of Michigan's Paik (1) mixed My Bloody Valentine' shoegazing vertigoes, Sonic Youth's minimalist repetitions, and Earth's super-heavy distortions, peaking with their fourth album **Satin Black** (2004) after **Corridors** (2001) and **The Orson Fader** (2002) had transitioned from the soft to the hard edges of stoner-rock.

Earth's main followers were Seattle's Sunn O))) (3), the new project of Engine Kid's guitarist Greg Anderson and Khanate's bassist Stephen O'Malley, particularly on the four monumental concertos for bass and guitar only of **Zero Zero Void** (2000), even heavier and slower than Earth. By the time they perfected their formula with **Black One** (2005), via the super-heavy drones and sinister monoliths of cacophony of **Flight Of The Behemoth** (2002) and **White2** (2004), the whole project sounded like the doom-metal equivalent of Lou Reed's **Metal Machine Music**. Their compositions were studies on how to combine the sound of a guitar and a bass to produce infinite loops of proto-riffs, moebius strips of distorted drones. Rarely had music sounded so ugly and hostile.

Outside the USA, the main stoners and super-doomers were Japan's Boris (2), whose terrifying monoliths **Absolutego** (1996) and **Amplifier Worship** (1998) indulged in the art of transforming colossal riffs into lengthy, dark and extremely dense drones. The five-movement symphony **At Last - Feedbacker** (2004) oscillated from dark to gentle to manic to ethereal and back, emphasizing texture over atmosphere.

The Japanese quintet Corrupted (3) propelled Boris' art of huge slow-motion dirges to another (very cold and very empty) dimension. From the 42-minute piece of **Paso Inferior** (1997) to the 71-minute piece of **El Mundo Frio** (2005) they patiently escalated a hypnotic post-rock suspense a` la Godspeed You Black Emperor or Mogwai only to crush every bit of emotion under catastrophic eruptions of guitars and drums a` la Boris. The two colossal suites of the double-disc **Llenandose de Gusanos** (1999) represented two sides of the same angst: a 74-minute black hole of ambient/cosmic drones and a 50-minute tsunami of evil riffs.

Towards the end of the decade the Finnish school of ultra-doom (Thergothon, Skepticism) started proselytizing around the world. The most faithful to the gospel were perhaps New York's Rigor Sardonicus, whose glacial **Apocalypsis Damnare** (1999) relied on apocalyptic cymbals and vocals that were so guttural to the point of becoming an incomprehensible rumble.

Graven (1999), by the Danish one-man band Nortt, was perhaps the work that best evoked the sense of utter depression.

Angst, 1995-98

The intense, macabre, excruciating, self-flagellating music of Korn became the dominant factor for heavy-metal bands such as: Sacramento's Deftones (1), first with the harrowing psychodramas of **Adrenaline** (1995) and then with the sinister and titanic **White Pony** (2000); Michigan's Kid Rock (born Bob Ritchie), with **Devil Without A Cause** (1998); Florida's Limp Bizkit (1), with **Three Dollar Bill Yall** (1997), driven by Fred Durst's furnace of angst and anger and derailed by DJ Lethal's beats, scratches and samples, and with the ambitious and experimental **Significant Other** (1999); Los Angeles' Incubus, with **Science** (1997).

The Armenian-American outfit System Of A Down (2) was perhaps the most revolutionary of the Los Angeles acts, concocting with **System**

Of A Down (1998), **Toxicity** (2001) and **Mezmerize** (2005) a sonic experience that was both extremely complex and extremely violent, evoking the punk barricades of the late 1970s with visceral, vibrant political anthems while upping the ante of prog-metal with disorienting rhythmic and melodic turns.

Soulfly (1), the brainchild of former Sepultura frontman Max Cavalera, heralded an even bolder degree of stylistic fusion (dub, drum'n'bass, hip-hop) with **Soulfly** (1998) and especially **Primitive** (2000).

Frenzy, 1996-2001

Grindcore and death-metal, the most frantic of metal's subgenres, lent themselves to sonic explorations that their founders would not have imagined.

Sweden's Nasum had not the fastest but perhaps the busiest grindcore style of the late 1990s: the blistering **Inhale/Exhale** (1998) consisted of 38 micro-songs.

Maryland's Dying Fetus incorporated the breakdown into death-metal on albums such as **Killing on Adrenaline** (1998), thus pioneering "death-core".

Montreal's Cryptopsy de facto invented a new kind of death-metal with their chaotic second album **None So Vile** (1996), highlighted by Daniel Greening's tortured bark, Jon Levasseur's jagged guitar solos, Eric Langlois' abrasive jazzy bass lines and Flo Mounier's volcanic baffling blastbeats.

Iowa's Slipknot (1) played what was fundamentally death-metal, but they did so with a novel idea: **Slipknot** (1999) leveraged turntables, samples and percussions, not just guitars, to achieve maximum ferocity.

Die Apokalyptischen Reiter in Germany first coined an original form of epic and melodic (folk-ish?) death-metal, notably on **Allegro Barbaro** (1999), and then introduced non-metal instruments (harpsichord, harp, piano) to enhance the keyboards-heavy (and even catchier) **All You Need Is Love** (2000).

Germany's one-man death-metal band Necrophagist (Mohammed Suicmez) adorned the death metal of **Onset Of Putrefaction** (1999) with highly-technical guitar acrobatics.

Colorado's Cephalic Carnage perfected a labyrinthine sound on their third album **Lucid Interval** (2002) that blended metalcore, stoner-rock, jazzcore and death-metal.

At the turn of the century, the scene of death-metal was further destabilized by the arrival of South Carolina's Nile (1), the new champions of highly technical and innovative death-metal. Their experiments with keyboards, percussion and ethnic instruments peaked with lengthy pieces such as *The Dream Of Ur*, off **Black Seeds Of Vengeance** (2000), and *Unas Slayer of Gods*, off their supreme **In Their**

Darkened Shrines (2002) that also included the 18-minute four-movement juggernaut *In Their Darkened Shrines*.

Pig Destroyer, a bass-less trio from Virginia that featured guitarist Scott Hull, popularized grindcore as a less extreme genre with their third album **Prowler in the Yard** (2001), despite retaining the key attributes of the genre (vomiting vocals, lightning-speed blastbeats, insane/brutal guitar noise).

Agoraphobic Nosebleed, featuring Pig Destroyer's guitarist Scott Hull and a drum-machine instead of a live drummer, embellished the grotesquely-short miniatures of **Honky Reduction** (1998) and especially **Frozen Corpse Stuffed With Dope** (2002) with lots of samples, electronic noises and digital processing of guitars and vocals. **Altered States Of America** (2003) packed 100 songs on a short EP, most of them lasting between four and ten seconds.

Poland's Decapitated performed surgical death-metal on **Winds of Creation** (2000).

In Flames' school of melodic death-metal in Sweden fathered Arch Enemy, the leaders of the new generation with **Stigmata** (1998), and especially Soilwork, with their torrential **Steelbath Suicide** (1998) and the more complex **The Chainheart Machine** (2000). Anata unleashed a catchy dual-guitar attack on **The Infernal Depths Of Hatred** (1998) and **Dreams Of Death And Dismay** (2001).

Japanese quartet Bathtub Shitter, fronted by psychotic shouter Masato Morimoto, delivered a screwball amalgam of noisecore and death-metal on **Wall Of World Is Words** (2000).

Other impressive grindcore/death recordings at the turn of the century included: **Gore Metal** (1998) by the Bay Area's Exhumed, that invented its own subgenre; **Mondo Medicale** (2002), the second album by the Bay Area's Impaled with their triple vocal attack; and Circle Of Dead Children's EP **Exotic Sense Decay** (2000).

Progress, 1999-2001

A virtually infinite number of variations on the innovations of the early 1990s came to light in the second half of the decade.

By reinterpreting Dazzling Killmen for the crowd of metal-heads, New Jersey's Dillinger Escape Plan (1), with the unstable metal-jazz compounds of **Calculating Infinity** (1999), virtually invented a subgenre, a new form of prog-rock with the "heaviness" of metalcore: "mathcore" (already pioneered by Converge and Rorschach). Seattle's Botch, especially with their second album **We Are The Romans** (1999), offered an alternative take on the same idea.

Vermont's Drowningman offered a convulsive blend of metalcore, emo and noise-rock on their second album **Rock and Roll Killing Machine** (2000).

The prog-metal concept album **Leitmotif** (1999) by San Francisco's Dredg (1) boasted intricate multi-layered sonic patterns.

The super-fusion of New York's Candiria became denser and denser, eventually reaching full maturity on their fourth album **300 Percent Density** (2001), that incorporated death-metal, hip-hop, jazz and industrial music.

Canada's Strapping Young Lad (1), the brainchild of veteran vocalist Devin Townsend, reached a new level of sonic savagery on **City** (1997) while coining an influential huge, gloomy sound with industrial overtones.

Discordance Axis (1) played grindcore influenced by Japanese noisecore on brief albums such as **Jouhou** (1998) and especially **The Inalienable Dreamless** (2000).

Boston's Isis (2) debuted with **Celestial** (2000), an album of brutal post-industrial electronic-metal sludge in the vein of Neurosis and Godflesh, but later shifted the emphasis towards atmospheric and textural elements, notably on third album **Panopticon** (2004), taking the post-rock dynamics of Godspeed You Black Emperor and Mogwai as new reference points.

The Neurosis-sanctioned confluence of grindcore and industrial music was explored by Australia's Berzerker on their second album **Dissimulate** (2002), an unstable and explosive mix of android clangor and distorted fury.

Boston's Maudlin Of The Well, fronted by vocalist, guitarist and keyboardist Toby Driver, were an eight-piece ensemble on two complementary albums that mixed highbrow chamber music with bursts of death-metal: the dense, dark and expressionistic **Leaving Your Body Map** (2001) and the humble, ethereal and spiritual **Bath** (2001).

Other post-metal albums at the turn of the century included: Spiral Architect's **A Sceptic's Universe** (1999), sleek jazz-metal from Norway; and Mudvayne's second album **The End of All Things To Come** (2002), prog-metal from Illinois.

Hip-hop Music

Hip-hop becomes mainstream, 1995-2000

Pre-Life Crisis (1995) by Nashville's rapper, multi-instrumentalist and producer Count Bass D (Dwight Farrell) was the first rap album to feature all live instruments.

New Orleans's Master P (Percy Miller) was the leading entrepreneur of unadulterated gangsta-rap. He turned it into the hip-hop equivalent of a serial show, with releases being manufactured according to Master P's script at his studios by a crew of producers. His own albums **Ice Cream Man** (1996) and **Ghetto D** (1997) were the ultimate stereotypes of the genre. In 1998, his musical empire had six albums in the Top-100 charts.

Atlanta's producer Jonathan "Lil Jon" Smith and his East Side Boyz coined a fusion of hip-hop and synth-pop called "crunk", from the title of their debut, **Get Crunk Who U Wit** (1996).

The first star of East Coast's Latino rap was Christopher "Big Punisher" Rios, a second-generation Puertorican of New York who died of a heart attack shortly after climbing the charts with **Capital Punishment** (1998).

The British still had a difficult relationship with hip-hop culture. Roots Manuva (Rodney Smith) was a true rapper, as the oneiric production of **Brand New Second Hand** (1999) owed to drum'n'bass and trip-hop, and his Jamaican roots creeped out on **Run Come Save Me** (2001), that was also unusual for its confessional content.

In 1996 two rap singles reached the #1 spot in the pop charts. But also in the same year the Bay Area's Tupac Shakur/ 2Pac and (a few months later) The Notorious B.I.G. were murdered, two events that highlighted the violence inherent in the genre and in the industry.

A brief commercial fad was the opulent, or "jiggy", style served by producer Sean "Puffy" Combs on his own **No Way Out** (1997), credited to Puff Daddy, and on **Money Power & Respect** (1998) by rap trio LOX.

Whether it was a female response to gangsta-rap or a reaction to the new teenage idols, female rappers stepped up to the crude vocabulary of the men: New York's Kimberly "Lil' Kim" Jones, with **Hard Core** (1996), Philadelphia's Eve Jihan Jeffers, with **Let There Be Eve** (1999), Chicago's Shawntae "Da Brat" Harris, the first female rapper ever to score platinum with **Funkdafied** (1994), produced by Jermaine Dupri, and Miami's "Trina" (Katrina Laverne Taylor), with **Da Baddest Bitch** (2000), were representative of this raunch, aggressive, obscene, materialist, vulgar and profane tone.

In the second half of the decade, hip-hop artists became more conscious of the essence of hip-hop: it's the process, not the structure that makes a song a hip-hop song. Its process is a process of deconstruction, and can be applied to just about anything that has ever been recorded. The new awareness in the process resulted in a new awareness of the importance of sampling. The role of the sampling device in transforming both the sampled and the recipient material became more and more obvious to a generation of post-Malcom X African-Americans who, politically speaking, had been raised to challenge and transform stereotypes. Hip-hop artists became semiotic artists, artists who employed sonic icons to create a fantastic universe grounded in the real universe. The same process led to a rediscovery of melody (even pop crooning) and then to a rediscovery of live instruments, whose warm and humane sound linked back to the rural roots of hip-hop's urban African-Americans. The metamorphosis of hip-hop was also due to its own commercial success, which, de facto, removed it from the streets and moved it to the much more sophisticated lifestyle of Beverly Hills villas and Manhattan high-rise condos.

The obvious weakness of the entire hip-hop movement was in the lyrics, which were mostly naive, stereotyped, clumsy; and, in fact, did not age well.

Sophisticated hip-hop

The "sophisticated" age of hip-hop can be made to start with the Fugees (1), a trio from New Jersey (Lauryn Hill, Prakazrel "Pras" Michel, Wyclef "Clef" Jean) whose **The Score** (1996) fused hip-hop with jazz, rhythm'n'blues and reggae. Even more sophisticated was Wyclef Jean (1)'s first solo project, **The Carnival** (1997), a virtual tour of the black world, from Cuba to New Orleans to Jamaica to Africa, boasting eccentric arrangements.

Shawn "Jay-Z" Carter (1), the most commercially successful hip-hop artist of the era, epitomized the state of the art, from the gangsta-rap landmark **Reasonable Doubt** (1996) to the eclectic double album **The Blueprint 2 - The Gift & the Curse** (2002), mainly produced by Kanye West, to the post-modern concept **American Gangster** (2007).

New York rap was also resurrected by the success of Earl "DMX" Simmons' **It's Dark and Hell Is Hot** (1997).

Los Angeles' trio Abstract Tribe Unique offered a lyrical blend of soul and jazz on **Mood Pieces** (1998).

Ditto for Philadelphia-born Bahamadia (Antonia Reed), whose **Kollage** (1996) was a smooth, laid-back exercise in recasting the soul-jazz ballad into the context of rap music.

Chicago's hip-hop duo All Natural (rapper David "Capital D" Kelly and dj Tony "Tone B Nimble" Fields), members of the "Family Tree" posse, offered passionate raps on **No Additives No Preservatives** (1998).

At the turn of the century New York unleashed the creative geniuses of the Antipop Consortium, whose **Tragic Epilogue** (2000) created a new genre ("digital hip-hop"?) by wedding rap with the new aesthetics of "glitch" music, and of Ian Bavitz, alias Aesop Rock (1), whose albums **Float** (2000) and **Bazooka Tooth** (2003) overflowed with eccentric arrangements and haunting textures. Sensational delivered nightmarish, stoned, warped, non-linear rapping over lo-fi beats on **Loaded With Power** (1997).

New York-based spoken-word artist and hip-hop producer Mike Ladd (1) was more interested in sculpting a musical background to his poetry than in beats and rhymes on **Easy Listening 4 Armageddon** (1997) and especially **Welcome to the Afterfuture** (1999).

The most significant stylistic revolution of New York rap came with Dalek (3), the project of rapper Will Brooks and producer Alap "Oktopus" Momin. The five lengthy songs of **Negro Necro Nekros** (1998) and the electronic ethnic ambient noise hodgepodges of **From Filthy Tongue of Gods and Griots** (2002) delivered a baroque psychedelic version of Public Enemy's creative chaos. Dalek thrived halfway between the neurotic and the transcendental, the same way that industrial music did in the late 1970s. **Absence** (2004) was explosive like shrapnel, dense like a lava stream and, still, elegant like a peacock's tail. But this was barely hip-hop at all. It was just layers of sounds and noises.

Instrumental hip-hop, 1995-2000

DJ Shadow's instrumental, sample-based hip-hop music was represented in Britain by Herbalizer, i.e. disc-jockeys Jake Wherry and Ollie "Teeba" Trattles, whose most daring experiment was **Very Mercenary** (1999).

San Francisco-based disc-jockey and virtuoso of the mixing board Dan "the Automator" Nakamura (1) sculpted **Dr Octagon** (1995), a collaboration with rapper Kool Keith and turntablist Richard "Q-Bert" Quitevis, Handsome Boy Modeling School's **So How's Your Girl** (1999), with Prince Paul, and the science-fiction concept album **Deltron 3030** (2000), with rapper Del Tha Funkee Homosapien and turntablist Kid Koala.

Another notable album of abstract instrumental hip-hop was **Soulmates** (2000), by Los Angeles' Elvin "Nobody" Estela.

DJ Shadow also helped create a new artistic figure: the turntablist. As more and more genres adopted the turntable as an instrument, it was inevitable that "virtuosi" began to appear. Atlanta's DJ Faust (1) was first to record an all-scratching album, **Man Or Myth** (1998). While he never realized a significant record, drum'n'bass specialist DJ Craze (Nicaraguan-born Aristh Delgado) stunned the crowds of Miami with his acrobatic routines at the end of the decade.

New York's quartet of turntablists X-Ecutioners (1), featuring turntablists Robert "Swift" Aguilar and Anthony "Roc Raida" Williams, marked a nostalgic return to the era of virtuoso scratching with the elaborate performances of **X-Pressions** (1997), while Rob Swift (1)'s solo albums **Soulful Fruit** (1997) and the jazz tour de force of **The Ablist** (1999) were creating a new place in music for the technique.

The most influential dj collective of all times, Invisibl Skratch Piklz, consisted of turntablists from the San Francisco Bay Area and the Sacramento area of Latino and Philipino descent: Richard "DJ Q-Bert" Quitevis (1), who also released the instrumental sci-fi concept album **Wave Twisters** (1998), "Mixmaster" Mike Schwartz, who also released **Anti-Theft Device** (1998) with producer Naut Humon (of Rhythm And Noise), Philippines-native Dave "D-Styles" Cuasito of the "Beat Junkies" crew, who debuted solo with **Phantazmagorea** (2002), a collection of songs composed entirely from scratching, Ritche "Yogafrog" Desuasido, "Mixmaster Mike" Schwartz, Jon "Shortkut" Cruz, Lou "DJ Disk" Quintanilla, etc. Starting with *Invasion of the Octopus People* (1996), this collective of scratch virtuosi developed a separate art of DJ-ing.

Live Human (1), a San Francisco-based trio led by turntablist Carlos "DJ Quest" Aguilar, played sophisticated jams and adopted a technique of live sampling that continuously reinvented their compositions during live performances. The improvised music of **Live Human Featuring DJ Quest** (1997), bridged the gap between hip-hop and jazz better than any fusion or crossover project.

Canadian turntablist Kid Koala (Eric San), a spiritual disciple of Coldcut's sound collages, downplayed his virtuoso show on **Carpal Tunnel Syndrome** (2000) with an irriverent anarchic cartoonish humour.

Jason "DJ Logic" Kibler (1) contributed to redefine the turntablist as a jazz improviser on **Project Logic** (1999) and especially **Anomaly** (2001). DJ Logic seamlessly integrated the noise of his turntable with the instruments of his jazz combo (flute, saxophone, organ, violin, organ, trumpet).

White rap

During the 1990s, white rap acts caught up with blacks. Initially, white musicians such as Beck didn't quite get the whole point of rapping. Thus, for example, Everlast's **Whitey Ford Sings The Blues** (1998) merely used hip-hop as a rhythmic background for his folk-style meditations. On their debut album **G. Love & Special Sauce** (1994), Philadelphia's G. Love & Special Sauce, led by guitarist and vocalist Garrett Dutton, bridged vintage talking blues and contemporary rap.

Blaxpoitation of rap began in earnest with the most celebrated white rapper of the era, Marshall Mathers, aka Eminem (2), whose **The Slim**

Shady LP (1999) and **The Marshall Mathers LP** (2000) unleashed angry rants at the society of the USA and resonated with the masses of disaffected white kids from the suburbia.

The whole model of the "singer songwriter" was revolutionized by the advent of white rappers such as Eminem: they introduced not only the syncopated rhyming but also the brutal subjects of rap music to an audience of middle-class white kids.

One of the most influential figures at the turn of the millennium was white producer El-P, aka El Producto, born Jaime Meline in New York. He founded Company Flow (1), whose **Funcrusher Plus** (1997) and especially the instrumental **Little Johnny From The Hospital** (1999) were the most bombastic, ebullient and explosive works of the time, and crafted the soundscape of Cannibal Ox (1)'s **The Cold Vein** (2001), a project risen from the ashes of Company Flow (Vast Aire and Vordul Megilah), before releasing his first solo album, the neurotic sci-fi concept **Fantastic Damage** (2002). Throughout his work, EL-P harked back to the anthemic, ebullient and explosive mix of Public Enemy.

El-P's influence was visible on Rjyan "Cex" Kidwell's fusion of hip-hop, pop and avantgarde electronics on **Being Ridden** (2003).

cLOUDDEAD (2), a trio of white hip-hop artists from the Oakland-based "Anticon" collective (producer David "Odd Nosdam" Madson and rappers Adam "Doseone" Drucker and Yoni "why?" Wolf), transcended the canon of hip-hop music on the six-movement **cLOUDDEAD** (2001) and **Ten** (2004). They offered hip-hop distorted through the lenses of a dystopian vision or through the nervous breakdown of an urban werewolf. The sound effects constituted the core, not just the periphery, of the music, at times even reminiscent of ambient music and industrial music. Doseone also fronted Subtle (1), a sextet featuring guitarist Jordan Dalrymple, keyboardist Dax Pierson, clarinetist Marty Dowers, cellist Alexander Kort and electronic percussionist Jeffrey "Jel" Logan. Despite the jazz-like line-up, **A New White** (2004) was devoted to progressive rap-rock fusion with a fixation for the catchy Sixties. Having mastered the technique of mixing hard beats and dense textures, Subtle interjected psychedelic, glitch, illbient, hip-hop, industrial, pop and even atonal chamber music into Doseone's frantic, demented, acrobatic rapping on the better choreographed **For Hero For Fool** (2006). Subtle's trilogy of concept albums, continued by the more melodic **Exiting Arm** (2008), chronicled the life of a rapper, Hour Hero Yes.

Tim "Sole" Holland, the main brain behind the "Anticon" collective, unfolded his erudite stream of consciousness with punk fervor over a fluctuating layer of samples and live instruments on **Bottle Of Humans** (2000) and **Selling Live Water** (2003).

Another white member of Oakland's "Anticon" posse, Brendon "Alias" Whitney (1) wed introspective lyrics and downtempo atmospheres on **The Other Side of the Looking Glass** (2002), and then moved towards noir jazz with the instrumental album **Muted** (2003), thus coining a (lush) fusion of forms: singer-songwriter of the 1970s, trip-hop of the 1990s and jazztronica of the 2000s.

Anticon also nursed the talent of frenzied rapper Sage Francis (1), Paul Franklin, the best lyricist of his generation, whose **Personal Journals** (2002), mostly produced by Sixtoo, and **A Healthy Distrust** (2005), mostly produced by Alias and Reanimator, became the classics of "emo hip-hop", his interference of political and personal discourses enhanced by a new generation of beatmakers and producers.

Canadian hip-hop producer and rapper Richard "Buck 65" Terfry was, at heart, an existential hobo whose laments relied on piano and guitar as much as on the traditional hip-hop arsenal. The 45-minute long piece **Language Arts** (1997) and the concept album **Vertex** (1999) displayed a unique art of stark storytelling and philosophizing, mixing folk into hip-hop.

The border between vocal and instrumental tracks was blurred in the wasteland sculpted by Canadian dj Robert Sixtoo Squire (2), a member of the "Anticon" collective, on the lengthy jams *The Canada Project*, off **Songs I Hate and Other People Moments** (2001), *Duration Project*, off **Duration** (2002), *The Mile-End Artbike*, off **Antogonist Survival Kit** (2003), *Storm Clouds & Silver Linings* and *Boxcutter Emporium*, off **Chewing On Glass & Other Miracle Cures** (2004). The guesting MCs are merely part of the murky, downtempo, post-industrial production, just like the samples, the electronics, the fractured beats and the live instrumentation.

Atlanta's white producer Prefuse 73 (1), Scott Herren, also active as post-rocker Savath & Savalas, heralded laptop-based hip-hop with **Vocal Studies + Uprock Narratives** (2001), a tour de force of fractured, warped, incoherent stream of consciousness that mixed glitch music, deconstructed vocals and jazz patterns. Two albums later, Herren gave his project a more organic and humane face by employing a vast assortment of voices on **Surrounded By Silence** (2005).

Northern State was a trio of college-educated white female rappers from New York (Julie "Hesta Prynn" Potash, Correne "Guinea Love" Spero and Robyn "DJ Sprout" Goodmark) that rediscovered the Beastie Boys sound on **Dying In Stereo** (2002).

Party Fun Action Committee, featuring Aesop Rock's producer Tony "Blockhead" Simon, penned the goofy hip-hopera **Let's Get Serious** (2003).

San Francisco's Gold Chains, aka Topher LaFata, mixed rock, reggae and techno on **Gold Chains** (2001).

Atmosphere, the project of Minneapolis-based rapper Sean "Slug" Daley and producer Anthony "Ant" Davis, coined an introspective "emo-rap" on **God Loves Ugly** (2002).

All in all, white hip-hop music was more influential on white popular music than on hip-hop proper: it grafted the production, rhythmic and rhyming techniques of black hip-hop music onto the old singer-songwriter genre (whether political, introspective or sociological). The political "discourse" of white hip-hop remained fundamentally different from the discourse of black hip-hop. The former was conditioned by the tradition of Euro-American political idealism, which, instead, was never truly part of the Afro-American discourse, which has been traditionally centered on civil rights. Ditto for analytic/existential introspection, which was never truly part of the black repertoire (the blues was a kind of atmospheric introspection, and, in any case, a community-wide introspection, an "inter-spection"). Even the most extreme cases (such as Eminem) displayed a psychoanalytic quality that was generally missing in black hip-hop. Ditto for the sociological analysis, which was more rational than antagonistic: white rappers displayed an analytic approach to refounding society as opposed to the cynicism and fatalism of black rappers. To summarize, white hip-hop and black hip-hop had different purposes and functions. Ultimately, it was a matter of human geography: the suburbs as opposed to the ghettos. White people had an "American Dream" that is still very much part of their subconscious (whether one succeeded or failed): black people's "dream" was still Martin Luther's dream, a wildly different kind of dream.

R&B auteurs

The Fugees' vocalist <u>Lauryn Hill</u> (1) delivered in a versatile, booming voice the elegant and sincere allegories of **The Miseducation Of** (1998), across a broad stylistic range.

Virginia's singer-rapper-songwriter Melissa <u>"Missy" Elliott</u> (1) and Virginia's producer Tim "Timbaland" Mosley (members of the hip-hop production crew "Da Bassment") proved to be a lethal combination: Elliott's sultry vocals, gymnastic raps and female-centric lyrics coupled with Timbaland's stuttering, digital grooves created a mood that was simultaneously sensitive, confrontational, hedonistic, stark and futuristic on **Supa Dupa Fly** (1997). The duo veered towards a format that mixed freely intimate ballads, dancefloor tracks and angry raps on **So Addictive** (2001).

Texas-born singer-songwriter <u>Erykah "Badu"</u> Wright (2) revisited soul music via digital glitches and intense hip-hop, blending live instrumentation and samples in a fluent and never discordant manner, notably on **Baduizm** (1997) and **New Amerykah Part One - 4th World War** (2008).

At the turn of the century, <u>Kelis</u> Rogers inherited the crown of Queen Latifah and Missy Elliott with her feminist-tinged fusion of hip-hop and rhythm'n'blues on **Kaleidoscope** (1999), aggressively produced by The Neptunes (Chad Hugo and Pharrell Williams).

Missouri's laid-back pop-rapper Nelly (Cornell Haynes) became the genre's biggest seller with **Country Grammar** (2000), **Nellyville** (2002) and the double album **Sweatsuit** (2004).

Songwriter and pianist Alicia "Keys" Cook dramatically increased the level of musicianship with her **Songs in A Minor** (2001).

Outkast's Andre 3000 (Benjamin) rediscovered Prince's erotic funk-soul music on **The Love Below** (2003).

This was the age of superproducers The Neptunes (Chad Hugo and Pharrell Williams) and Tim "Timbaland" Mosley, both based in Virginia Beach, both masters of the new digital technology based on the "Pro Tools" software introduced in 1991. Both owed a lot to Teddy Riley, the Harlem producer who had made Virginia Beach the Mecca of the new sound in the first place, when he opened his "Future Recording Studios" there in 1991. The Neptunes were emblematic of the cold and thin sound of the digital age (as opposed to the warm and thick sound of classic pop, soul and rock music). Both could work on just about any kind of material, as proven by their co-production of white teenage idol Justin Timberlake's **Justified** (2002).

Timbaland pioneered the technique of custom-creating the beat via digital keyboards instead of adding a break-beat to a sample. Timbaland's strategy of musical estrangement (stuttering beats in alien timbres, unstable melodies that warp the conventions of singing along) was first experimented on Aaliyah's second album **One In A Million** (1996), and even more in the single *Are You That Somebody* (1998), whose arrangement bordered on glitch music; and blossomed on Missy Elliott's **Supa Dupa Fly** (1997) and **So Addictive** (2001), albums that were canvases on which the producer laid ever more creative beat patterns. Timbaland was, in fact, the first major hip-hop producer to cross over successfully into pop, crafting two million sellers: Nelly Furtado's **Loose** (2006) and Justin Timberlake's second album **Future Sex/ Love Sounds** (2006), albums credited to mediocre singers that the producer turned into sonic extravaganzas.

Hip-hop 2000

Other significant hip-hop albums released at the turn of the century included: **Seven Eyes Seven Horns** (1999), by producer Phillip "Scaramanga" Collington, who worked on Kool Keith's Dr Octagon project; Walter "Killah Priest" Reed's spiritual tour de force **Heavy Mental** (1998), from New York; Curtis "50 Cent" Jackson's **Power of the Dollar** (2000), from New York, a catchy product for the masses, produced by "Trackmasters" (i.e. the duo of Jean-Claude "Poke" Olivier and Samuel "Tone" Barnes), from a former crack dealer destined to become a rap superstar (**Get Rich or Die Tryin'** in 2003 and **The Massacre** in 2005 set records of sales); **Supreme Clientele** (2000) and **The Pretty Toney Album** (2004), by Wu-Tang Clan's member Dennis "Ghostface Killah" Coles; the Metabolics' **M-Virus** (1999), a New York duo produced by Bimos; Christopher "Ludacris" Bridges' **Back For The First Time** (2000), from Atlanta; **Coming Forth By Day - The Book Of The Dead** (2000), by New Jersey's jazz-hop crew Scienz of Life; and **Let's Get Ready** (2000), the fifth album by New Orleans rapper Mystikal, a pupil of Master P who adopted a James Brown-ish persona.

Houston-based Geto Boys' rapper Brad "Scarface" Jordan established himself as the existentialist philosopher of rap art and reached his narrative peak with **The Fix** (2002) that sounded like the punch-line on hip-hop's entire "comedie humaine".

People Under the Stairs' second album **Question in the Form of an Answer** (2000) was a collection of jams almost entirely created from funk and jazz samples, the project of Los Angeles Mike "Double K" Turner and Chris "Thes One" Portugal, bent on reappropriating the D.I.Y. aesthetics of early party-rap.

The new auteurs included: Kansas City's Aaron "Tech N9ne" Yates, with the horrorcore rap-rock fusion of **The Calm Before The Storm** (1999), **Anghellic** (2001) and **Absolute Power** (2002); and New York's Terrence "Tes" Tessora, with the apocalyptic post-industrial soundscapes of **Take Home** (2000) and **x2** (2003).

The idea of combining hip-hop and live instruments was explored in novel settings. For example, the Dakah Hip Hop Orchestra, organized in 1999 in Los Angeles by saxophonist Geoff Gallegos with up to 60 players and MCs, blended hip-hop, jazz and classical music on the 12-song cycle of the **Unfinished Symphony** (2004).

The master of diction and free-form rapping was New Orleans' Lil Wayne (Dwayne Carter), who had debuted with **Tha Block Is Hot** (1999), produced by Mannie Fresh (Byron Thomas), but reinvented himself on the trilogy of **Tha Carter** (2004), **Tha Carter II** (2005) and **Tha Carter III** (2008).

Digital Avantgarde

(The following is an excerpt from my book on avantgarde music).

The extended ear

New digital devices allowed more sophisticated manipulation of sound in the studio. Musique concrete evolved into cut-up, collage and montage techniques that mixed field recordings, electronic/digital sounds and conventional instruments.

The idea of "the microphone as an extended ear" propounded by Loren Chasse was best expressed in the ambient minimalist works that digitally processed field recordings: albums such as **Siphon Glimmers** (1997) and **Hedge Of Nerves** (2002) basically documented sound sculptures of musique concrete and interactive electronic/digital music. Coelacanth, a collaboartion with Jim Haynes, manipulated and layered sounds of rocks, sand, leaves, electrical devices and waves to obtain a viscous tapestry of ambient music, as on **Mud Wall** (2004). Of was a project that mixed natural sounds and live instrumental improvisations by Chasse himself, for example **The Sun And Earth Together** (2008).

Thuja's discs documented the collective improvisations of guitarists Steven Smith and Glenn Donaldson (both of psychedelic-rock band Mirza), sound sculptor Loren Chasse and pianist Rob Reger. They devoted the ambient vignettes of **Suns** (2002) and the abstract frescoes of **Pine Cone Temples** (2005) to a study on the psychological properties of natural sounds. These works exorcized urban life and aimed to recapture the essence of the human condition on Planet Earth while retaining the high-tech world that humans erected on it. Ultimately, all Thuja albums were duets between the human brain and the human environment.

British composer Simon Wickham-Smith used the computer on **Extreme Bukake** (2002) to create a collage inspired by Buddhist and Catholic religious music.

Irr. App. (Ext.), the project of San Francisco-based composer Matt Waldron, applied musique concrete to the anarchic, provocative aesthetic of surrealism, perfecting the fusion of field recordings, event music and electronic soundsculpting with the two lengthy suites of **Ozeanische Gefuhle** (2004), originally recorded in 2001.

After recording a tetralogy of albums, that focused on digital processing of natural sounds, under the moniker of Hazard, Morthound's mastermind Benny "BJ" Nilsen created the arctic and alien dronescapes of **Fade To White** (2004) and **The Short Night** (2007) by manipulating natural sounds and instruments.

Icelandic avantgarde electronic trio Stilluppsteypa, featuring Heimir Bjorgulfsson, worked out a Dadaistic multi-layered style of soundsculpting that juxtaposed with the horror or high-brow trends of the era, notably on **Reduce by Reducing** (1998) and **Interferences Are Often Requested** (1999).

The Portuguese multimedia artist <u>Alfredo Costa-Monteiro</u> produced organic flows of sound by processing paper noises on **Allotropie** (2005) and by employing pickups and turntables on **Z = 78** (2006).

Texas between the extended ear and droning minimalism

Texas boasted a vibrant electroacoustic school of droning musique concrete in the tradition of Eric LaCasa. <u>Mnortham</u>, the project of <u>Michael Northam</u>, was the virtuoso of this technique, producing dense aggregates of sound from the tiniest and slightest of sources. His first demonstration, the 30-minute piece of **Many Rivers Move Along The Surface Of The Magnet** (1995), was the manifesto for the entire Texas school. Also influential were his two collaborations with John Grzinich: **The Stomach Of The Sky** (1997) and **The Absurd Evidence** (1998). Mnortham's essays on how to acoustically reconfigure the environment picked up speed with the 21-minute piece of **Breathing Towers** (2000), the three extended compositions of **Coyot** (2001), the three extended compositions of **From Within The Solar Cave** (2001), and the 54-minute "raga" of **A Great And Riverless Ocean** (2002). <u>Seth Nehil</u> composed chamber music for found objects and instruments, as documented on **Tracing the Skins of Clouds** (1998). In 1994 John Grzinich and Seth Nehil had formed the live electro-acoustic ensemble <u>Alial Straa</u>, documented on **Tunnels/Stairwell** (1997). The duo's study of timbres, texture and dynamics reaches new heights of paroxysm on **Confluence** (2002). <u>John Grzinich</u>, a builder of amplified piano-wire instruments, was perhaps the most lyrical in this sound art of weaving together digitally manipulated field recordings. His **Intimations** (2004) diluted and abstracted piano notes, then merging them with field recordings of cicadas, birds and waves; while the sources of **Insular Regions** (2005) were all collected from a small village in Estonia, therefore creating a personal transfigured diary.

Compositional rigor highlighted the fusion of acoustic chamber music, droning minimalism, glitch music, electronic soundscaping and computer-manipulated field recordings propounded by <u>Olivia Block</u> in her trilogy of **Pure Gaze** (1998), **Mobius Fuse** (2001) and **Change Ringing** (2005). All three constructed dramatic symphonies of reverbs, pulses, drones and glitches.

Turntable music

The turntablist as an instrumentalist was an artistic person that migrated from hip-hop music into avantgarde, rock and jazz music during the 1990s. The turntable allowed musicians to achieve two goals (that were frequently overlapped): 1. quote from a musical source by another musician (and therefore create collages of quotations), and 2. produce sequences of extreme noise. Christian Marclay spearheaded the new trend towards "composing", performing and improvising using phonographic records. De facto, he applied John Cage's indeterminism and, in general, Dadaism's provocative principles of aesthetic demystification to the civilization of recorded music. His specialty consisted in devising mechanisms for letting a record evolve a sound over time, typically by having people somehow degrade its sound (as in *Record Without a Cover* of 1985, a record sold with no cover and no jacket so that it keeps deteriorating after every playing, or *Footsteps* of 1990, a totally random composition resulting from hundreds of people walking on a record).

The idea was refined in Britain by Philip Jeck and in Japan by Otomo Yoshihide.

Philip Jeck (3) created the chaotic cacophony of *Vinyl Requiem* (1993) for 180 turntables. **Vinyl Coda I-III** (2000) and **Vinyl Coda IV** (2001) documented Jeck at the peak of his virtuoso art, mixing snippets of old records in a jungle of turntable noises. The 24-minute *Skew*, off **Host** (2003), was even more radical, while the three-movement *Fanfare Song Trilogy*, off **Sand** (2008), abandoned the discontinuous, glitchy format of his beginnings and turned to crystalline, slowly-revolving, quasi-ambient soundscapes.

Otomo Yoshihide (2), Ground Zero's guitarist, harked back to the most brutal musique concrete ever conceived as well as to Morton Subotnick's electronic ping-pong music for the screeching and hissing tornadoes of **Sound Factory** (1997). The three-movement concerto of **Anode** (2000) evoked John Cage's aleatory music by only providing the performers with vague instructions.

Bionic music

In the late 1990s computer processing was becoming pervasive.

The installations of Michael Schumacher (2) often started with field recordings or accidental events, that were then processed at the computer to produce long spatial tones, as documented in the **Four Stills** (2002). A complex computer algorithm generated the sparse sounds that populated the **Room Pieces** (2003).

The "live" laptop manipulations of British musician Kaffe Matthews, such as the theremin-based **Cd Eb And Flo** (2003), yielded droning compositions that are layered to the point of becoming dense mobile textures. She also organized Lappetites' **Before The Libretto** (2005), a collaboration with Elaine Radigue (France), Ryoko Kuwajima (Japan), and Antye Greie-Fuchs (Germany), basically a multinational all-female laptop quartet, ranging in age from the 70-year old Radigue to the Japanese teenager.

In 2001 Matt Rogalsky developed his "Kash" software to interact with live performers on traditional instruments. The resulting live performances are subtle and subliminal works, in which Rogalsky toys with fictitious microtonal sounds in a very sparse and desolate soundscape. Another kind of software, "Sprawl", allows Rogalsky to operate on densely layered structures, that yield floating clusters similar to the ones that fuel ambient and cosmic music.

New Zealand's digital manipulator Rosy Parlane mixed melodic drones, sample loops and field recordings on the languid and cinematic three-movement symphonies **Iris** (2004) and **Jessamine** (2006) that emanated a sense of calm and harmony made more humane by an underworld of microscopic events.

Japanese composer Koji Asano engineered the monumental **The Last Shade of Evening Falls** (2000) for computer-processed violin and contrabass, a nightmarish exercise that ran the gamut from chaotic and wildly atonal to densely droning.

Chinese composer Fan Wang's **Sound Of Meditation Within the Body** (2001) blended Western and Eastern ways of music via musique-concrete collages of subterranean currents and otherworldly noises that slowly grow into om-like cosmic drones, oscillating between the internal and the external soundscape.

Chinese laptop composer Jun Yan explored the convergence of noise-sculpting techniques that came from musique concrete and the improvised techniques that came from jazz in lengthy creative sequences of artificial sounds.

The Digital Age

The 2000s: Decade of Fear

Within a few months the relative peace and stability of the Clinton era were totally reversed. The "dot com" bubble crashed in april 2000. The election to succeed Clinton was won by George W. Bush on a technicality (his opponent had won more votes). Nonetheless Bush interpreted the result of the elections as a mandate to pass highly divisive right-wing policies. The longest economic expansion in USA history came to a sudden halt in his first months as president. Then in september 2001 terrorists affiliated with Osama Bin Laden's Al Qaeda carried out a spectacular attack against the World Trade Center and the Pentagon, killing more than 3,000 people. The USA retaliated by bombing the Taliban out of power in Afghanistan and launching a worldwide "war against terrorism". Bush coined the expression "axis of evil" for the totalitarian regimes of Iraq, Iran and North Korea, that now represented the enemies in the post-Soviet era, and in 2003 proceeded to take out the first one, Saddam Hussein.

For the rest of the decade the USA was involved in two lengthy wars of attrition, plus intense diplomatic pressures to deter North Korea and Iran. Those wars and a generally arrogant attitude towards the rest of the world gained the USA an unprecedented degree of hostility, even among the traditional allies of Western Europe (where millions attended anti-USA demonstrations). The USA's policy of "globalization" further alienated foreign masses, that widely interpreted it as a plan for world hegemony. Suddenly the world identified the USA not as the defender of freedom but as the most polluting country in the world and the most imperialistic, a barbaric regime that still administered the death penalty and that tortured prisoners of war. Anti-USA sentiment brought to power leftist regimes throughout Latin America.

Internally the USA was rocked by political scandals while the budget deficit skyrocketed, the dollar collapsed and the trade deficit mushroomed. Signs of global decline were greeted all over the world: in 2007 China overtook the USA to become the world's second largest exporter, and Toyota passed General Motors as the world's largest car manufacturer. In 2007 the stock market hit a record high, but then oil prices started increasing dramatically and a financial crisis caused banks to collapse. One year later (in october 2008) the USA stock market had lost almost half of its value. The crisis spread from one continent to the other: markets worldwide plunged into chaos, heralding the worst recession since the 1970s and stroking fears of a new depression.

During the presidential campaign of 2008 oceanic crowds gathered to listen to the first black candidate, Barack Obama, the son of an African man, a sign that the nation had not lost hope. The following january he, a man of African and Muslim descent, became the world's most powerful person in the capital of the Western and Christian world. However, he was now presiding over a worldwide economic catastrophe.

During this era of turmoil the great social transformation within the USA took place in cyberspace. Over the decades, rock music has always been the soundtrack of alternative youth lifestyles. In the case of "Generation Y", born between 1981 and 1999, it was a "digital" lifestyle. They grew up with videogames, email, instant messaging, music downloads, movie rentals, cable television, blogs. This was the first generation for whom there was no centralized source of news and entertainment (previous generations had come of age in a world still dominated by three television networks, by five major record labels, by major movie studios and theaters, etc). This was the first generation for whom the primary source of information and news was the Internet. Larry Page and Sergey Brin had founded Google in 1998, and Google became the main interface with the world for an entire generation. Social networking software such as Facebook, founded in 2004 by Mark Zuckerberg, became their primary source of socialization. In 2001 Jimmy Wales founded Wikipedia, a multilingual encyclopedia that was collaboratively edited by the world-wide web community, and soon became the most trusted source of knowledge.

Just like in the previous decades, the biggest change in lifestyle was probably for women. The Western woman was still busy rebuilding her identity and her role in society. For example, this was the first time in history that so many women were still single in their thirties. The average age for a woman to get married had progressively increased, but now it had reached a point that made it unlikely these women would ever become mothers or even wives. Single women in their thirties constituted de facto a new social class that never existed before.

Death of the Hero

Among the many social transformations of the new century one stood out: the death of the hero. The generation growing up after the advent of cable news television had a fundamentally different kind of exposure to world news. Previous generations were fed radio or television news at a specific time of the evening, and shared that event with the entire nation. The entire nation was exposed to the same range of emotions. Not surprisingly, the response to a world event was relatively uniform across the entire nation. The fact that the news was limited to a narrow time window increased its emotional impact. As McLuhan said, the media created the message. Because the news were delivered in this fashion, they facilitated the emergence of hero figures. Bob Dylan was a product of that age. In the age of 24-hour live news, instead, that uniform collective response was lost forever. People absorbed the news at different times in different ways. The Internet further diluted the emotional impact, as people could get the news when they wanted (not when the media delivered them). Inevitably, becoming a national hero became a lot more difficult. The demise of the national hero had a profound effect on all the arts.

Each decade in the history of rock music (the ultimate international koine) was marked by an international icon (a koine within the koine).

The 1950s had Elvis Presley (best selling artist for 40 years).

The 1960s had the Beatles (still the best selling band of all times).

The 1970s had Pink Floyd (still the best selling album-oriented band of all times).

The 1980s had U2 and Madonna, and already one could see the Atlantic divide getting wider, and a non-rock artist (Michael Jackson) surpassing all rock artists in generating worldwide hysteria.

The 1990s had very pale icons compared with their predecessors. No rock artist managed to get even close to the sales of non-rock artists such as Mariah Carey, Whitney Houston, Garth Brooks, Britney Spear, Boyz II Men, etc. The best selling rock albums were one-shot deals from artists such as Alanis Morissette and Hootie & the Blowfish whose popularity lasted only a few years. Radiohead were darlings of the mainstream press, but hardly recognized by the masses or identified with a social trend. Eminem opened the 2000s with a bang, but faded rapidly in the background as the decade progressed.

Yet another definition of Rock Music

Rock'n'roll may (may) have been a well-defined genre, but starting with Buddy Holly the term "rock music" became fuzzier and fuzzier. The Beach Boys played surf music, and the Beatles' music was Mersey-beat, a variant of pop music. Dylan was a folksinger. Somehow they all got lumped into "rock music". The truth is that there was no "technical" definition of rock music to start with. During the following decades there was less and less of an agreement on what constituted rock music, as its purveyors swung wildly from jazz to world-music. By the end of the century, rock music included artists who played mainly electronic and digital instruments.

The problem is that "rock music" was never a definition of the music, but a definition of the audience. Rock music was music for young white rebels. As those young rebels grew up, it lost its "young-only" quality. As times changed and people accepted the Establishment (maybe because they had fewer reasons to attack it), the "rebellious" quality was reduced to a mere search for originality. Thus rock music evolved into music for white originals. The music itself changed dramatically, but the audience that rock music had created basically continued to exist, mutatis mutandis, across generations. Thus an identity could be found in the audience, not in the stylistic attributes of the music.

The media were largely responsible for determining what that audience listened to, and therefore what rock music was. The media's defining power was already evident in the 1960s. Hendrix happened to be classified as a rock musician mainly because his records were reviewed in rock magazines and therefore sold to a rock audience. He might as well have been classified as a blues musician, or even a jazz musician: had his records been reviewed mainly by blues magazines, his audience would have been the blues audience, and therefore he would have been part of the history of blues music, not rock music.

Ultimately, the reason some musicians were considered "rock" is that rock critics and rock historians (such as me) wrote about them. The only consistent definition of rock music is, in a sense, that rock music is what i am writing about.

The only viable definition is a "use-based" definition: rock music is the set of all musicians that the rock community writes about. Thus Klaus Schulze (an electronic musician) makes rock music, but an electronic musician raised in the classical community does not make rock music, even if their styles are very similar: the difference between the two is that the rock press writes at length about Schulze.

It is not the listener who defines what is rock music, it is the reader.

The Great Divide

Surprisingly, by the end of the century the white-black divide had not been erased at all. The world of popular music was still largely divided into white and black music. White music was mostly rock and its variations (whether heavy-metal or punk-rock). Black music was definitely not rock (hardly any black musician in heavy-metal or punk-rock bands) and mostly dance-oriented. Forty years after the peak of the civil-rights movement, there were virtually no white bands fronted by a black singer anywhere in the world. The majority of black musicians were still playing in all-black bands, and the majority of white musicians were still playing in all-white bands (or, better, bands with no black musician, because the number of Latin American and Far Eastern musicians in white bands had dramatically increased). White music was still largely "mind" music, while black music was still largely "body" music, although the corporeal music of the blacks often carried a more meaningful message than the intellectual music of the whites. Even when white musicians played black music (as it has been the case since the 1950s), they tended to do it with other white musicians rather than with black musicians. Black musicians, on the other hand, rarely bothered to play white music at all.

If one does not count the Jimi Hendrix Experience and Prince and the Revolution (neither of which was truly a band, as their titles imply), rock music had to wait until 1994 for a white band fronted by a black vocalist,

Hootie & The Blowfish, to attain mainstream success. For all its widely advertised rebelliousness, unconformity and liberal lifestyles, rock music remained the most racially segregated art/industry of all.

On the other hand, this racial barrier continued to provide an invaluable creative source. After all, rock'n'roll, ironically, originated from the segregated society of the 1950s. Rock music originated from the wall that the Establishment had erected between white and black communities. Had they coexisted as equals, white teenagers may have never been so morbidly attracted to the music of black teenagers. And probably black teenagers would have been so integrated in the USA lifestyle that soul and rhythm'n'blues and hip-hop would have never happened. Ironically, it was, to some extent, the very racial nature of these genres that kept them in a permanent state of evolution/revolution.

Rock music is ultimately the next generation's noise

For the first three decades rock music evolved in a rather turbulent manner. Every ten years or so a major socio-musical revolution caused a complete realignment of its aesthetic paradigm and induced a similar change in habits and values of young western people. Those revolutions lend themselves as generational dividing lines. The first one took place in 1955, when Chuck Berry and the other black rockers introduced a paradigm of rebellion to the USA lifestyle and a paradigm of bodily music. (Something similar took place in rhythm'n'blues music at about the same time).

A second dividing line was represented by the year 1966, when musicians such as Pink Floyd and Frank Zappa introduced a much more complex view of rock music. That led to the "psychedelic" and "progressive" sounds of the late 1960s and early 1970s. This time the music was either political (not just rebellious) or spiritual (not just anti-conformist). It was therefore a music for the mind, not the body, and that was, in retrospective, its major innovation: rock music became a more conceptual and more adult form of art than it had been in the 1950s and early 1960s. (Something similar took place in soul music).

A third dramatic change in direction came at the end of the 1960s, when the emphasis shifted from content to form, from "style" to "sound". It was the age of the electronic keyboards and, for the consumer, of the "hi-fi" stereo.

The fourth obvious dividing line is the year 1976, the "new wave", when musicians such as Pere Ubu, the Residents, Suicide, the Pop Group and Throbbing Gristle reinvented rock music as a rather depressing form of music, a music inspired by the violent and nihilistic "punk" aesthetic. It was a music of anarchy instead of order, and it marked a return to the body, away from the mind. (A parallel trend could be detected in funk/disco music and in hip-hop).

The fifth dividing line was a bit less obvious, as the 1980s witnessed an unprecedented multiplication of styles and a proliferation of musicians, but 1989 can be conveniently used as the year in which independent/alternative rock music took a different shape: the Pixies, Fugazi, Royal Trux, My Bloody Valentine, Godflesh and Tortoise (as well as Public Enemy in hip-hop) were the post-modernists of rock music, providing an "intellectual" reading of old styles, with an emphasis on the "emotional" impact that eventually led to grunge and emo-core.

Next came the age of drum'n'bass and trip-hop, that was basically another return to "sound" as opposed to "style".

The seventh revolution came with the mass adoption of electronic and especially digital devices. If electronic keyboards had simply expanded the spectrum of sounds, digital devices allowed musicians to conceive new ways of organizing those sounds. Digital music enjoyed an extra degree of freedom. Something similar happened in black music with "digital" producers and with soundsculptors such as Dalek.

Each age was not so much a rejection of the previous ages as a re-interpretation of the styles of previous ages. Hence the many "revivals" that took place in each decade.

And each age had a movement of reaction to this trend (Presley and the Beatles at the beginning, glam-pop in the 1960s, synth-pop during the new wave, pop-metal during the 1990s, and the digitally-arranged pop music of the digital era).

But, mostly, each age challenged the dogmas of the previous one. So much so that very few "fans" migrated from one generation to the next one, each generation remaining convinced that only mediocre imitation or noise was being produced by the following one. The mediocre imitations were indeed such (musicians who kept playing the same old music). But the "noise" was the new exciting music that only those in the new generation were capable of identifying with. Long-term, that "noise" was what mattered.

That "noise" was the history of rock music.

In a sense, this was the main link between each ages of "rock" music: it was meant to be incomprehensible to the previous generations.

What is Rock Music? Part Two

At the turn of the century, after so many revolutions that had created so many subgenres, each one undergoing its own peculiar mutation, the term "rock music" became less and less meaningful. It was difficult to classify Pan Sonic or Vibracathedral Orchestra as rock music, but their albums were mainly reviewed by rock critics for rock publications. Even garage-rock or heavy-metal bands were becoming so experimental that they hardly related to the classics anymore. The world of the avantgarde had moved closer and closer to the world of rock music. It was not clear who was what anymore. "Rock" had become a federation of genres rather than a well-defined genre.

This schizophrenia was already there in the 1960s, when rock music encompassed everything from Dylan's folk-rock to King Crimson's progressive-rock, and every decade added new subgenres. Eventually, rock music had become a genealogical tree of genres, each one owing its existence to some predecessor going back all the way to the generation of Chuck Berry. Rock music was never a uniform, monolithic style, but simply a historical chain of events: Chuck Berry begat the Stones who begat the Velvet Underground who begat Brian Eno who begat the new wave... etc. As the genealogical tree unfolds, one gets to musicians who play a music wildly different from Chuck Berry's, but owe their existence to a socio-musical revolution that started in the 1950s with rockers such as Berry. Thus it is "rock". But not quite.

"Rock" was born as a music of synthesis (of white and black music), and continued to remain essentially a synthesis of styles, from electronica to grindcore. Fundamentally, there was a need for a new term but nobody came up with one. Jazz also had evolved over the decades, but there had always been a prevailing jazz style (swing, bebop, free-jazz, ...) that played the role of center of mass for all the other jazz subgenres. Rock was a looser term because, at any point in time, no subgenre prevailed.

Rock music was born a music of and for young people (or, at least, young people thought so, not realizing how much their choices were being manipulated by the managers of the major recording labels). Rock music used to be a music for young people mainly because young musicians were the only ones willing to experiment, and young listeners were the only ones willing to listen to their experiments. This fact remained true to an extent throughout the following decades (each generation being reluctant to accept the styles in vogue among the new generations), but not as much as it used to be in the 1960s. The adults of the turn of the century were much more willing to listen to something "weird" than their parents had been, although there remained psychological resistance to accepting a style different from the styles one had grown up with. The gap between young people and adults was mainly due to the amount of new music that they listened to. Younger people enjoyed the huge advantage of having a lot more time to listen to music than older people. That, ultimately, was the factor that still created a gap between the generations. Despite this inevitable gap (due more to time constrains than to ideological differences), "rock" music was more "adult" than it had ever been. Both the average age of the musicians and the average age of the audience had increased dramatically from the 1960s. Thus rock music could not even be simplistically associated with young people anymore.

Reshaping the music industry

In 1999 Shawn Fanning founded the Napster on-line music service that allowed anyone with a computer and a modem to share music files with others over the Internet. They could be played on the PC itself or on the portable MP3 devices (that had been introduced in 1998). Millions of Internet users did not need to pay outrageous prices for their favorite music: in fact, they didn't need to pay anything. Even after the "file sharing" phenomenon was reined in by a series of lawsuits, life was much improved for consumers: Apple introduced the on-line music service "iTunes", which legally sold 25 million songs during just the first year. For a long time record labels had ripped off the consumer by forcing the consumer to purchase CDs, regardless of how many songs of that CD a consumer wanted to hear. A completely new dynamics was created by iTunes: consumers were finally allowed to purchase just the song that they desired. The consumer was no longer a captive in the logic of the record labels. The first dogma to collapse was the dogma of the "album": the listener was free to download any song without having to purchase the entire album.

In 2001 sales for the record industry slipped 5% (their first decline in ages), a fact that was widely blamed on the on-line sharing services. The same year, Napster was found guilty of breaching copyright law and forced to suspend its service, but others took its place. In 2000 Warner remained the only USA "major", as Universal had become French, Sony was Japanese, EMI was British, and BMG was German. Clearly, the USA was less and less interested in the business of selling CDs.

The downfall of the record industry was long overdue and welcomed by just about everybody. But it was not the only anachronism still in place. As consumers became even more song-oriented, it became even more important to pinpoint a song heard on the radio. Alas, disc-jockeys continued the old habit of not announcing the title of a song and the name of the musician. Consumers remained powerless to actually know what song they just listened to. In the 2000s it remained easier to read a review of an album that one had never heard than to discover the title of a song just heard on the radio. Millions of potential sales were still hindered by the chronic stupidity of disc-jockeys worldwide, probably in cahoots with record labels that wanted consumers to buy CDs based on the marketing campaign and not on the basis of what the songs actually sounded like.

Another positive side-effect of the "music download" civilization was the demise of the unscrupulous critic. The availability of music on the Internet, and particularly of recent releases, had a healthy impact on one vital aspect of the music industry: critics. It freed thousands of critics (both professionals and amateurs) from the psychological deference towards the labels that sent them promos for review. For decades the press and the radio stations had to rely on friendly labels to send them free promos of new music. This created a master-slave relationship that never boded too well for the objectivity of the opinions expressed by the slaves (critics and radio stations). Hence the thousands of new releases routinely rated as "masterpieces" by so many critics (only to be downgraded one year later to the status of "failure"). Indirectly, the fact that in 2001 a new release could be downloaded anonymously, without fear of reprisal by the label, allowed the rock critic to become truly independent (for the first time ever). The rock critics who still depended on promos provided by the labels now had to face the competition of truly independent rock critics, who could care less whether the labels sent them promos or removed them from their mailing lists.

A little noted side effect of the digital download and of the consequent demise of the CD was the end of an illustrious craft that dated from the dawn of recording: the cover art. That art had peaked during the 1960s and 1970s, when each album cover was carefully designed by professional artists. The advent of the CD had downgraded the cover art, simply because the CD was smaller and did not allow the artists as much space. However, CDs could still come packaged in creative manners (instead of the environmentally-unfriendly plastic wrap). Once the industry shifted to the digital download, though, the cover art died. For the first time, the music was to be enjoyed with no visual complement.

Superficial Listening

The 1990s had introduced technological innovations that changed both the way music was manufactured and the way music was consumed. Unlike the "record", that required a well-funded record label to manufacture and distribute, the compact disc had become cheaper and cheaper to manufacture, and the Internet had allowed an ever larger number of musicians to bypass the traditional distribution channels. Thus musicians were, de facto, in a position to record and release compact discs ad libitum.

The market for independent recordings was soon flooded with compact discs of mediocre quality (both artistic and technical). In a sense, the very concept of what a recording is underwent a dramatic evolution: instead of being the summa of a period (the best pieces composed during that period), it became merely a sample of the period's sound. Musicians paid less and less attention to crafting impeccable songs. They contented themselves with documenting their current sound with a one-hour long recording of it. In a sense, there was a trend towards releasing the "demo" and never reaching the point of the finished product.

The consumer, faced with dozens of recordings by an independent musician, none of them expected to be a milestone, was, in turn, sampling them in the same superficial manner.

Thus the cardinal process of the 20th century (the process away from the melody and towards the sound) became also a process of moving from deep listening to superficial listening (just the opposite of what some musicians advertised).

Furthermore, a 30-year trend towards hi-fi equipment was dramatically reversed at the turn of the century with the widespread diffusion of lo-fi equipment. Whether the laptop or an MP3 player or a iPod, for millions of young people the device of choice to listen to music became a relatively low-quality device. If psychedelic music, cosmic music and even new-age music were basically the consequence of more and more sophisticated stereo equipment, the consequence of less and less sophisticated audio equipment was a lower degree of instrumental prowess (no matter how many layers of instruments were used to arrange a piece of music). The motivation to produce chromatically beautiful music was somewhat reduced.

The Civilization of the Prosumer

Marshall McLuhan had predicted already in 1972 that technology would eventually enable consumers to become producers. Alvin Toffler's "The Third Wave" (1980) introduced the term "prosumer". Surprisingly, rock and dance music were the first fields in which their prophecies became reality. Three factors contributed to a major shift in the habits of kids of the middle class. An increased purchasing power (compared with their parents' generation) reduced the limitations of traditional entertainment (drive-in cinema, pub drinking, bowling and so forth). At the same time a highly programmed lifestyle (from childhood to graduation) reduced the percentage of time devoted to real social life (the kind of social life that kids in developing countries get from spending all their spare time in the streets with the other kids of the neighborhood). Finally, a surge in the availability of low-cost media production and distribution tools (video and audio production, distribution via the web) created a new form of solitary entertainment. These three factors (economic, social and technological) translated into a shift of interest from passive fruition (such as cinema and television) to active creation (typically on a laptop). It wasn't just an upgrade from playing electric guitar or the drums: it was a step up from depending on others (the band, the venue, the record) to being self-sufficient in doing, marketing and distributing one's creation. The transition from the electromechanical world to the digital world enabled the civilization of the "prosumer", a civilization in which the line between consumer and producer is becoming increasingly blurred.

The Democratization of Culture

Rock music, as well as jazz music and all other genres of popular music, owed its existence to one of the most significant phenomena of the 20th century: the democratization of culture. Until then only the elite had a "culture" to talk about. Popular culture used to be ephemeral: itinerant shows, variety shows and the likes provided cheap and vulgar entertainment for the masses, but the masses themselves didn't take them seriously. During the 20th century an avalanche of technological innovations (phonograph, radio, cinema, television, LP, CD, walkman, iPod, DVD, MP3) made culture readily and cheaply available to the masses. A parallel process created a growing middle-class and therefore enabled more and more people to spend time and money on cultural events and artifacts. The combination of these two phenomena led to an unprecedented boom in popular culture that tranformed popular culture into a driver of sociological change. Technology was further democratized in the 1990s through the Internet revolution that literally enabled hundreds of millions of ordinary people to share and download in their houses all sorts of cultural artifacts, from music to videogames. Highbrow culture still existed but it was becoming less and less relevant because the gap in terms of audience was beginning to be colossal.

Where to, Chuck?

Chuck Berry invented the paradigm of rock music: three minute melodic songs, mainly driven by the electric guitar over a rhythm section of bass and drums, and sometimes arranged with other instruments. Fifty years later the world audience of rock music had been served more than 100,000 collections of songs, for a grand total of more than one million songs. Every time a musician of the 2000s released an album that was a collection of three-minute songs, that musician had basically answered "yes" to the question "Does the world really need ten/fifteen more of these three-minute songs, so that the grand total goes from one million to one million and ten?"

No matter how much the magazines hailed the new album by this or that "next big thing" or "alternative artist" (obviously convinced of having a unique voice, a unique message and a unique set of refrains never heard before in the history of music), there was something terribly obsolete and (ultimately) tedious about listening to yet another batch of three-minute songs. The magazines hailed them as masterpieces, one after the other, but over a decade the same magazines would remember only two or three of the songs contained in all the "masterpieces" of an artist. This huge library of more than one million songs was fundamentally a junkyard. These boatloads of new songs were moving straight from the store to the junkyard after a brief stop in the CD player of a hapless consumer. Something was fundamentally wrong about an art whose main effect was to create the biggest garbage dump of all times.

Last but not least, the lyrics of a three-minute song are neither William Shakespeare verses nor Henry James novels, despite what most songwriters and most of their reviewers may think. Listening to a new three-minute song invariably meant listening to yet another bad example of storytelling or bad example of poetry oversold by reviewers as meaningful, poignant, touching, thrilling...

This was the mother of all crises facing rock music at the beginning of the 21st century.

Destination: Earth

Whatever the answer to that existential question, and whatever the definition of the Anglosaxon music that used to be called "rock", during the 2000s it became obvious that the Anglosaxon countries had lost their monopoly of... Anglosaxon music. That music had spread throughout the world, and other regions of the planet, especially continental Europe and Japan, were producing as much quality and quantity as the USA and Britain.

DJs and Rappers

Hip-hop and the digital producer

Hip-hop dominated the charts during the first decade of the 21st century. That represented a dramatic change from 50 years earlier, when black music had been segregated to the "race" charts. The reason why rap artists appealed to such a broad audience was probably that they boasted, on average, the best producers. Music (whether popular or classical) in the second half of the 20th century had been increasingly focusing on the soundscape, on sculpting the atmosphere, rather than on the melody. Hip-hop music completed that trend by mostly disposing of the melody and setting the lyrics in a purely atmospheric context. The producer (the sound director and sculptor) was clearly more important in hip-hop music than in other genres. Competition among producers in turn led to a generation of more and more sophisticated producers. Very few rock producers could compete with hip-hop producers in terms of instrumental creativity.

It was the black producers of the 2000s who inherited the mantle of the white producers of the 1960s (Joe Meek, Phil Spector, George Martin, Brian Wilson) who had coined the concept of the studio as an instrument.

Another appeal of hip-hop music rested on the fact that the lyrics of rappers tended to be less pompous and indulgent than the lyrics of rockers. It made sense to listen to the raps in a way that did not make sense in rock music. Rockers were largely speaking to an older audience that was still interested in personal existential journeys (the same way that country singers had been speaking to an older audience when rockers were speaking to a younger audience). The younger generation (especially in the middle class) was often more attracted to the down-to-earth lyrics of black rappers.

Hip-hop music

As white hip-hop became more competitive, black hip-hop reached a creative crisis that forced the new generations to focus on sound manipulation rather than on messages. At the turn of the century, hip-hop music was borrowing from other musical genres as well as recycling its own vocabulary of breaks, samples, and themes. New technology allowed producers to wrap everything into an original art of atmosphere/ambience sculpting. The "message" was becoming less and less important. The sociopolitical landscape was also radically changed by the 2001 terrorist attacks against New York and Washington: the debate shifted from class conflict to religious conflict, which contributed to neutralize the original sociopolitical fuel of hip-hop music.

The deluge of hip-hop albums at the turn of the century continued with works such as: Ben "Ty" Chijioke's **Awkward** (2001), an original Afro-funk-jazz-rap fusion from Britain; **Quality** (2002) by New York's Talib Kweli (Greene); **Exit** (2003) by Canada's K-OS (Kheaven Brereton); **The End of the Beginning** (2003), by veteran Los Angeles rapper Murs (Nick Carter), a former member of 3 Melancholy Gypsys (or 3MG) and, after relocating to Oakland, of the Mystik Journeymen's "Living Legends" collective, produced by 9th Wonder; Dudley Perkins' **A Lil Light** (2003), another oneiric production by Madlib; **Black Mamba Serums** (2004), by former Company Flow rapper Justin "Bigg Jus" Ingleton.

Little Brother, the North Carolina-based duo of rapper Phonte Coleman and producer Patrick "9th Wonder" Douthit, joined the ranks of soul-tinged rap music with **The Listening** (2003). Phonte then hooked up with Dutch producer Matthijs "Nicolay" Rook and the duo, under the moniker Foreign Exchange, released **Connected** (2004), an even more baroque attempt at transposing the fluidity and smoothness of classic soul into hip-hop music.

Virginia-based production team The Neptunes (Chad Hugo and Pharrell Williams), already among the most successful hip-hop producers, formed N.E.R.D. (1) with rapper Sheldon "Shay" Haley. **In Search Of** (2001), remixed the following year with live instrumentation, and especially **Fly or Die** (2004) indulged in a neurotic melange of sonic stereotypes and production techniques of metal, funk, soul and pop. They also produced the albums by Clipse (1), the duo of Virginia brothers Gene "Malice" and Terrence "Pusha T" Thornton, two of the sonic jewels of the decade: **Lord Willin'** (2002) and **Hell Hath No Fury** (2006).

Northern Californian duo Blackalicious (1), i.e. rapper Tim "Gift of Gab" Parker and producer Xavier "Chief Xcel" Mosley, crafted a lyrical and nostalgic style with **Nia** (2000).

The decadence of West-Coast rap was well represented by the groups that were supposed to rejuvenate it, and that, in fact, failed to: Dilated Peoples, whose **The Platform** (2000) featured beats created by Los Angeles' producer Alan-Daniel "Alchemist" Maman, and Jurassic 5, whose enthusiastic and amusing **Quality Control** (2000) and especially **Power in Numbers** (2002) amounted de facto to a revival of old-fashioned rap (despite Cut Chemist's presence). Even Madvillain (1)'s **Madvillainy** (Stones Throw, 2004), the much publicized collaboration between New York-based rapper Daniel "MF Doom" Dumile (the former "Zen Love" of KMD) and Los Angeles-based producer Otis "Madlib" Jackson, was mostly an impressive tour de force of production techniques; the same skills that Jackson had already displayed on several of his own recordings, notably Quasimoto's **The Unseen** (2000) and Yesterdays New Quintet's **Angles Without Edges** (2001), frequently blurring the border between psychedelic, jazz and hip-hop music. MF Doom, on the other hand, lent his rapping skills also to Dangerdoom's **The Mouse And The Mask** (2005), a collaboration with Danger Mouse.

New York's producer Brian "Danger Mouse" Burton, better known for mixing together vocals and beats from Jay Z's **Black Album** and snippets from the Beatles' **White Album** to create his **Grey Album** (2004), formed Gnarls Barkley with Goodie Mob's vocalist Cee-Lo Green. The soul, pop and hip-hop hybrid of their **St Elsewhere** (2006) signaled a shift towards a reappropriation of the past.

On the lighter side, Los Angeles' rapper Regan "Busdriver" Farquhar, mixed goofy energetic scat-tinged rapping and eclectic beats on **Temporary Forever** (2002).

Chicago's Kanye West (2) produced Jay-Z, Talib Kweli and Alicia Keys and then fashioned one of the most personal concepts of the era, the soul-infected **The College Dropout** (2004). Hyper-chromatic three-dimensional arrangements turned **Late Registration** (2005) into a stately hip-hop fresco and a distillation of the genre's existential legacy.

The combination of Gershwin "BlackBird" Hutchinson, a versatile West Coast rapper and singer, and the quasi-psychedelic imagination of producer Paris Zax yielded **Bird's Eye View** (2005).

Philadelphia-based producer and MC Jneiro Jarel (born Omar Gilyard) added a new dimension to the fusion of jazz and hip-hop music with the digital collage of **Three Piece Puzzle** (2005).

Georgia's rapper Clifford "T.I." Harris was the most successful purveyor of southern rap, thanks to **Trap Muzik** 2003) and the platinum-selling **King** (2006).

Boston's white rapper Edan Portnoy fused acid-rock and hip-hop on **Beauty And The Beat** (2005), the same way Sly Stone fused acid-rock and funk music four decades earlier.

Minnesota's white quartet Kill The Vultures wed punk, jazz and hip-hop on **Kill The Vultures** (2005).

The new star of soul music was Raheem DeVaughn, who debuted with **The Love Experience** (2005) and broke through with the more traditional **Love Behind the Melody** (2008). The rhythm'n'blues diva of the decade was Beyonce Knowles, now a solo artist after dropping the best-selling female group of all time, Destiny's Child.

Why? debuted with **Oaklandazulasylum** (2003) in the vein of San Francisco's numerous freak acts that bent genres and derided stereotypes. With the romantic **Elephant Eyelash** (2005) and the tragic **Alopecia** (2008), though, two albums that mirrored each other three years apart, Why? perfected an unlikely fusion of rap, minimalism and rock while using it as the scaffolding for frontman Yoni Wolf's brutally vivid and earnest lyrics.

Prolyphic & Reanimator, i.e. the duo of Chicago's producer Reanimator and Rhode Island's rapper Prolyphic, refined their mentor

Sage Francis' introspective and multi-layered style on **The Ugly Truth** (2008).

Instrumental hip-hop, 2001-2008

Detroit's white producer Dabrye (Tadd Mullinix) created a new instrumental format out of hip-hop, funk, jazz and electronica on **One/Three** (2001).

In Los Angeles, Busdriver's white producer Alfred "Daedelus" Roberts (1) painted the disjointed murals of **Invention** (2002), setting collages of samples to hip-hop beats, mixing sci-fi electronica and orchestral kitsch; an art that he refined and culminated with the elegant retro parade of **Exquisite Corpse** (2005), where the samples of orchestral music of the 1930s came to constitute the musical equivalent of a collective stream of consciousness.

Inspired by New York's "illbient" scene, a number of djs aimed for a hip-hop that could transcend hip-hop, that is for a new (ambient, psychological, free-form) form of art founded on the marriage of poetry and sound. Ohio-born dj Boom Bip (Bryan Hollon), a self-described "anti-dj", well impersonated the sound sculptor and collage assembler of the new wave of hip-hop with the mind-boggling exercise in hip-hop counterpoint of **Seed to Sun** (2002).

RJD2, the project of white Ohio-based producer Ramble Jon Krohn, turned **Deadringer** (2002) into a tour de force of cinematic collages of samples and wicked stuttering beats, dilating and deforming Sixties soundtracks, smooth jazz, soul themes and gloomy atmospheres.

Los Angeles' producer Paris Zax tried to fuse hip-hop and acid-rock on the all-instrumental **Unpath'd Waters** (2005).

Lucas "Cut Chemist" MacFadden rediscovered the joyful childish art of audio collage on **The Audience's Listening** (2006).

James Yancey upped the ante of instrumental sample-based (and schizophrenically fragmented) hip-hop with **Donuts** (2006), credited to both his nicknames J Dilla and Jay Dee.

Los Angeles-based producer Steven Allison, better known as Flying Lotus, was emblematic of a generation that was employing laptop computers to generate sounds that were impossible before, both in terms of (noisy) arrangement and in terms of (convulsive) rhythms. **1983** (2006) also displayed a broad range of influences.

British styles of the 2000s

London's Dylan Mills, better known as Dizzee Rascal (1), a member of the "Roll Deep Crew", promoted a new genre ("grime"), an abrasive version of "garage" (itself a variant of drum'n'bass), with **Boy in Da Corner** (2003).

The other British "next big thing" of the era was Sri Lankan-born agit-prop chanteuse Maya Arulpragasam, or M.I.A. for short, whose **Arular** (2005) simply mixed hip-hop, reggae and pop, while fostering a hard-line ideology that embraced both the political and the sexual, part Jello Biafra and part Madonna. **Kala** (2007) was less immediate but more visceral, a giant cauldron of artificial, natural, social and musical sounds.

Streets, the project of Mike Skinner, a white British rapper, jumped on the bandwagon of the latest dance fads ("garage" and "two step") and turned them into tools to construct generational anthems. **Original Pirate Material** (2002) turned Streets into the English equivalent of Eminem.

Dubstep originated in London (probably in a club called "Forward>>" in 2001) as a bass-heavy instrumental dance music derived from garage, a sort of middle ground between two-step and dub. Unlike grime, that was fundamentally orientated towards the vocals, dubstep was more about the atmosphere. Digital Mystikz, Loefah and Kode9 were among the pioneers of the scene, but it was Skream with *Midnight Request Line* (2005) that established it as a major force in dance music.

The first artist to emerge from the British dubstep scene and reach a broader audience was Will "Burial" Bevan (1). **Burial** (2006) actually seemed rather an evolution of the gloomy trip-hop ambience of the 1990s shaken by post-jungle breaks; but it included metallic post-industrial polyrhythms, miasmatic electronics and "concrete" collages of noise, voices and beats. Reintroducing the vocals, its follow-up **Untrue** (2007) wed dubstep with soul music.

Other milestones of the grime/dubstep scene included: Richard "Wiley" Cowie's **Treddin' On Thin Ice** (2004), Virus Syndicate's **The Work Related Illness** (2005), Kane "Kano" Robinson's **Home Sweet Home** (2005), Maxwell "Lethal Bizzle" Ansah's **Against All Oddz** (2005), Steve Milanese's **Extend** (2006), Barry "Boxcutter" Lynn's **Oneiric** (2006), Louise-Amanda "Lady Sovereign" Harman's **Vertically Challenged** (2006), Steve "Kode9" Goodman's **Memories Of The Future** (2006), Greg "Distance" Sanders's **My Demons** (2007), Jan "Disrupt" Gleichmar's **Foundation Bit** (2007), Rob "Pinch" Ellis' **Underwater Dancehall** (2007), Beni "Benga" Uthman's **Diary Of An Afro Warrior** (2008).

There were few musicians left who were worthy of the great drum'n'bass innovators of the past. Shitmat (1), the brainchild of British producer Henry Collins, specialized in spastic drill'n'bass and digital hardcore peppered with Jamaican-style ragga shouting on **Killababylonkutz** (2004), that contained multiple remixes of the same song in completely different directions, and on **Full English Breakfest** (2004), originally released as five EPs; and then converted to madcap breakcore collages with **Hang The DJ** (2006), a wild and witty merry-go-round of samples from such diverse sources as heavy metal and orchestral pop.

Neil "Landstrumm" Sutherland's **Restaurant Of Assassins** (2007) offered an original fusion of drill'n'bass, dubstep and glitchy noise.

Clarence Park (2001) by English electronic musician Chris Clark provided a diligent summary of English electronica of the previous decade (Squarepusher, Aphex Twin and Autechre), running the gamut from ambient music to glitch music to drum'n'bass to synth-pop.

Inspired by Shitmat, DJ Scotch Egg (Japanese producer Shigeru Ishihara, based in Brighton) used a handheld video game console to shape dance-music of the gabber genre, as documented on **KFC Core** (2005).

World-hop

Cadence Weapon, the moniker chosem by Western Canada's white rapper Rollie Pemberton, utilized a broad (and still cohesive) palette of beats and virtuoso claustrophobic studio arrangements on **Breaking Kayfabe** (2005).

Shadow Huntaz, formed by Dutch producers Don and Roel Funcken and three USA rappers, delivered a delirious fusion of glitch music and hip-hop music, influenced by the iconoclastic jams of both acid-rock and free-jazz, on **Corrupt Data** (2004).

One of the most intriguing takes on the whole scene came from Australia. Terminal Sound System (Halo's bassist Skye Klein) probed the landscape of dubstep, drum'n'bass and trip-hop, sculpting glitch-ambient music over a bed of chaotic breakbeats on albums such as **Compressor** (2007) and **Constructing Towers** (2008).

In Japan the most intriguing work was perhaps **Neutrino** (2004), by Japanese duo Neutrino (Atsuhiro Murakami and Hideki Kuroda).

Bards and Dreamers

Bards of the old world order

Traditionally, the purposefulness and relevance of a singer-songwriter were defined by something unique in their lyrical acumen, vocal skills and/or guitar or piano accompaniment. In the 1990s this paradigm was tested by the trend towards larger orchestrastion and towards electronic orchestration. In the 2000s it became harder and harder to give purpose and meaning to a body of work mostly relying on the message.

Many singer-songwriters of the 2000s belonged to "Generation X" but sang and wrote for members of "Generation Y". Since "Generation Y" was inherently different from all the generations that had preceeded it, it was no surprise that the audience for these singer-songwriters declined. Since the members of "Generation X" were generally desperate to talk about themselves, it was not surprising that the number of such singer-songwriters increased. The net result was an odd disconnect between the musician and her or his target audience. The singer-songwriters of the 2000s generally sounded more "adult" because... they were. They appealed to the more mature of the kids in their teens or twenties, and they appealed to those of the older generations who still listened to music.

The apocalyptic crowd of **The Heat** (2004) reinvented D Generation's vocalist Jesse Malin as a hyper-realist bard in the vein of Lou Reed and Bob Dylan.

Sixteen Horsepower's vocalist David-Eugene Edwards, under the moniker Woven Hand, painted bleak frescoes of the contemporary world on works such as **Woven Hand** (2002) and **Mosaic** (2006), highlighted by a calm mastery of the folk tradition and a tormented brand of existential mysticism. By **Ten Stones** (2008) Edwards' booming croon had acquired the apocalyptic quality of the gospel preachers of the Far West.

Stephen Malkmus's first solo album, **Stephen Malkmus** (2001), mostly sounded like an attempt to recreate the melodic apex of Pavement's career, **Crooked Rain Crooked Rain**. His blues-rock alter-ego, a more interesting guitarist than singer or lyricist, ended up dominating **Real Emotional Trash** (2008).

The ranks of the more or less old-fashioned folksingers included: Rosie Thomas from Seattle, whose **When We Were Small** (2001) was a collection of intimate songs in the tradition of Joni Mitchell's austere contralto and somber confessions; Whiskeytown's violinist Caitlin Cary, a darling of the old Georgia establishment (Chris Stamey, Don Dixon, Mitch Easter), who delivered highly-dignified folk and country music on **While You Weren't Looking** (2002); Clem Snide's singer Eef Barzalay, who explored a broad emotional and musical spectrum while employing minimal means on **Bitter Honey** (2006); etc.

Florida-based folksinger Samuel Beam, under the moniker Iron And Wine (1), opted for pastoral quiet on the home-made and naive **The Creek Drank The Cradle** (2002). Thus **Our Endless Numbered Days** (2004) stuck to the "less is more" aesthetic and demonstrated the power of understated emotions.

Texas-born singer-songwriter and multi-instrumentalist Jolie Holland specialized in the vintage sound of country, folk, blues and jazz, notably on **Escondida** (2004), her best revisitation of the world of Billie Holiday, Woody Guthrie, Blind Lemon Jefferson and Louis Armstrong.

The Moldy Peaches, who only released **The Moldy Peaches** (2001), were an anti-folk group (or, better, "the" anti-folk group) based in New York, centered around Adam Green and Kimya Dawson, and specializing in topics (sex) and attitudes (sarcasm) that defied the stereotypes of folk music. Kimya Dawson debuted solo with **I'm Sorry That Sometimes I'm Mean** (2002), a collection of depressing teenage bedroom pop tunes that make creative use of the human voice.

Madder Rose's vocalist Mary Lorson collected a disturbing set of jazzy piano ballads and pop-soul hymns on **Tricks For Dawn** (2002), presenting her as a serious candidate to take Joni Mitchell's and Laura Nyro's place.

Joanna Newsom (11), raised at the border between California and Nevada, sang **The Milk-Eyed Mender** (2004) in the shrill and untrained voice of a little child, accompanying herself at her polyglot harp (used like a banjo, a contrabass, a dulcimer, a xylophone...). The music of **Nervous Cop** (2004), a collaboration with two drummers and Deerhoof's John Dieterich on electronics, sounds like a nightmarish evocation of the nuclear holocaust. Newsom employed arranger Van Dyke Parks to craft **Ys** (2006), whose five songs marked a turn towards Jane Siberry's introspective melodrama but with a sense of narrative melodrama that matched **Blonde On Blonde**-era Bob Dylan. Existentially speaking, these fluid structures resembled terminal confessions of a visionary whose visions had drained her soul.

Chicago's Josephine Foster manifested a different personality in each of her first albums: the ukulele-based pop songstress of **There are Eyes Above** (2000), the retro-nostalgic hippy of **All the Leaves Are Gone** (2004), and the high-brow chamber folksinger of **Hazel Eyes I Will Lead You** (2005).

The Reminder (2007) propelled Canadian songstress Leslie Feist of Broken Social Scene to the forefront of the female singer-songwriters who were trying to bridge the Joni Mitchell generation and the Bjork generation.

The stark, skeletal **For Emma Forever Ago** (2008) introduced Bon Iver, the moniker of Wisconsin's Justin Vernon, as an introverted bard in the vein of Iron & Wine but with a versatile falsetto register.

Boston's Marissa Nadler returned to ancestral gothic folk music on **Ballads of the Dying** (2004), sung in a haunting mezzo-soprano and accompanied with acoustic guitar and little else.

Nashville's Taylor Swift was the unusual country-music star (and songwriter and guitarist) who, barely 16 when she recorded the high-school concept **Taylor Swift** (2006), addressed her songs to the younger generation.

Britain seemed to be more focused on "bands" than "bards", but nonetheless managed to nurture two stars. England's teen idol Amy Winehouse, the British equivalent of Erykah Badu, became one of the best-selling female artists with **Frank** (2003), a painful exhibition of a teenager's turbulent lifestyle disguised as a collection of soul-jazz ballads. Scotland's Kate "KT" Tunstall became a world-wide star with *Suddenly I See*, originally buried inside **Eye To The Telescope** (2004), a blues-rock shuffle sung in a casual tone. In the meantime, Fovea Hex, i.e. veteran Irish folksinger Clodagh Simonds, resurrected Nico's archaic and stately atmospheres with the three EPs titled **Neither Speak Nor Remain Silent** (2005-07).

Bards of the new world order

The 1990s had introduced a new role model, the one-man studio, i.e. the musician who not only writes and sings but also arranges the music. That also changed the very definition of "technical prowess": it was not about the vocal range or the playing of a specific instrument, but about the skills in arranging the instruments and the voice in a sophisticated manner. In a sense, this generation decreed the obsolescence of the singer-songwriter as an artist of stories that could relate to the every person and elicit an emotional response. The new singer-songwriter related to the every person and elicited an emotional response by a semiotic (not literary) device, one that relied a lot more on the sounds (on the arrangements) than on the words. It used to be that singer-songwriters were either romantic or realist. They could now afford to be mere soundmakers with only a passing interest in storytelling. However, the fundamental limitation of pop music (the mother of all limitations) was still there: predictable structures, dejavu melodies, a portfolio of abused rhythms. For the older generations these songs mostly constituted trivia ("what does it sound like?"). For the younger generations they were muzak, no matter how intelligent.

New York-based Dirty Projectors (1), i.e. Dave Longstreth, abandoned the captivating idiosyncracies of **The Glad Fact** (2003) for ambitious orchestrations: a ten-piece chamber orchestra for **Slaves' Graves and**

Ballads (2004) and cello octet, women's choir, wind septet and digital cacophony for the ambitious **The Getty Address** (2005).

Slow Learner, the project of New York-based singer-songwriter and multi-instrumentalist Michael Napolitano turned songwriting into an art of studio collage and sound sculpting on **In Their Time They Are Magnificent** (2006).

Edison Woods, the project of New York-based multimedia artist Julia Frodahl, evoked a cross between Nico and Laurie Anderson with the transcendental and graceful melancholy of **Edison Woods** (2002),

Beirut (1), the project of New Mexico's multi-instrumentalist Zach Condon, offered the unlikely marriage of baroque arrangements and street music on the guitar-less **Gulag Orkestar** (2006). Relocating to France, Condon mutated into a melancholy crooner for **The Flying Club Cup** (2007). His music referenced a nostalgic ambience of ordinary lives in old environments, a universe of resigned ancestral emotions recycled via a blatant appropriation of stereotyped sounds.

And The Gospel Of Progress (2005), a concept album about a romantic relationship by Texas-based Micah Hinson, inhabited a limbo halfway between orchestral pop and acoustic folk.

The Scissor Girls' keyboardist Azita Youssefi (1) converted with **Life On The Fly** (2004) and especially **How Will You** (2009) to the austere, erudite piano-based ballad style of Joni Mitchell and Robin Holcomb, her voice having become a fluent, eloquent, melismatic instrument.

Ed Harcourt (1), a classically-trained English pianist, displayed a fairy-tale imagination on **Here Be Monsters** (2001).

The Week That Was, the project of Field Music's drummer Peter Brewis, debuted with the densely multi-layered concept **The Week That Was** (2008), bordering on progressive-rock.

Bards of the new Nordic order

Scandinavia produced a generation of eccentric singer-songwriters who fully took advantage of the transition from the old world order to the new world order.

Swedish singer-songwriter Jens Lekman (1) demonstrated a stunning flair for crafting pop confections in his first three EPs, later compiled on **Oh You're So Silent Jens** (2005), but his art of arrangement truly took off with **Night Falls Over Kortedala** (2007), a collection of ballads overflowing with strings, horns and all manners of orchestral effects.

Dungen, the project of Swedish multi-instrumentalist Gustav Ejstes, honed his skills with **Dungen** (2001), structured as three lengthy folkish medleys a` la Mike Oldfield, and then applied them to **Ta Det Lugnt** (2004), an orgy of retro production that roamed the aural landscape of the Sixties.

Norwegian singer-songwriter <u>Hanne Hukkelberg</u> arranged **Little Things** (2004) with folk instruments, found objects and Kare Vestrheim's keyboards, and sung in a soft voice somewhere in between Billie Holiday and Bjork.

Sweden also introduced three introverted chanteuses. <u>El Perro Del Mar</u>, the project of Sarah Assbring, sung, played and arranged **It's El Perro del Mar** (2005), a set of old-fashioned sad litanies delivered in the naive lovesick crooning of the yeh-yeh girls of the 1960s but applied to the gloomy atmosphere of the 2000s. The Concretes' vocalist Victoria Bergsman debuted solo under the moniker <u>Taken By Trees</u> with **Open Field** (2007), a set of lushly arranged melancholy ballads contrasting the sound usually associated with the exuberant girl-groups of the 1960s with the existential spleen of the 2000s. <u>Lykke Li</u> (Zachrisson) sang stark dance-pop tunes with minimal arrangements (by producer Bjorn Yttling) on **Youth Novels** (2008).

Finnish-born, Swedish-raised <u>Anna Jarvinen</u> debuted solo with a collection of retro songs that harked back to the country-rock and piano ballads of the 1970s, **Jag Fick Feeling** (2007).

Swedish singer-songwriter <u>Frida Hyvonen</u> harked back to Joni Mitchell's tradition of piano-based meditations on **Until Death Comes** (2005), although Jari Haapalainen's lush arrangements turned her into a pop songstress on **Silence is Wild** (2008).

Bards of the psychedelic otherworld

Syd Barrett's vision of eccentric introverted psychedelic music continued to haunt the world three decades after his disappearance.

Texas-born but San Francisco-based <u>Devendra Banhart</u> basically bridged the rural tradition of folk music, the metaphysical tradition of church music, and the urban tradition of the singer-songwriter with his artistic journey from the lo-fi fairy tales of **Oh My Oh My** (2002) to the almost gothic production and sparse but classical chamber arrangements of **Rejoicing in the Hands** (2004).

<u>Vetiver</u>, the brainchild of San Francisco-based singer-songwriter Andy Cabic, practiced neo-hippy psychedelic-tinged chamber folk music on **Vetiver** (2004).

Relocating to San Francisco, Lungfish's vocalist <u>Daniel Higgs</u> (1) vented the spirituality at which Lungfish's albums had only hinted on his second solo album, **Ancestral Songs** (2006), containing six psalms of transcendental psychedelia for guitar, banjo, jew's harp, toy piano and voice (mostly shaman-like invocations imbued with esoteric religious imagery). Higgs the alien troubadour perfected his fusion of India and Appalachia on the six instrumental pieces of **Atomic Yggdrasil Tarot** (2007) in the vein of Sandy Bull and Robbie Basho.

Mazzy Star's vocalist Hope Sandoval (1) employed My Bloody Valentine's multi-instrumentalist Colm O'Ciosoig to recreate the magic of her former band on **Bavarian Fruit Bread** (2001).

Tanakh, the project of Virginia-based singer-songwriter Jesse Poe, resurrected the evocative, spiritual and gothic sound of the later works of Mike Gira's Swans on **Villa Claustrophobia** (2002), penned with acoustic, electric and handmade instruments.

Hush Arbors, the project of Virginia-born folksinger Keith Wood, tried a psychedelic take on old-fashioned stark rustic Appalachian music, as if Jimi Hendrix had gone alt-country, on works such as **Hush Arbors** (2003) and especially the EP **Death Calligraphy** (2005).

Los Angeles-based Nick Castro, with the naive and surreal ballads of **A Spy In The House Of God** (2004), scored for an eclectic orchestra of Western and non-Western instruments, and New York-based Edward Droste, i.e. Grizzly Bear, with the atmospheric folk-rock of **Yellow House** (2006), were also representative of the psychedelic bards of the time.

Sonora Pine's violinist Samara Lubelski breathed life into the naive folk lullabies of her second solo album **Spectacular Of Passages** (2005) by embellishing them with slightly psychedelic orchestration.

The second solo album by Jackie-o Motherfucker's female guitarist Honey Owens, **Naked Acid** (2008), credited to Valet, was an intimate psychedelic nightmare in the vein of David Crosby or Bruce Palmer.

After relocating to New York, Double U's child-like vocalist Linda Hagood debuted solo with the surrealistic cabaret of **Pink Love Red Love** (2008), the ugly side of post-psychedelic music.

New Zealand's CJA (1), a side-project by Armpit's Clayton Noone, greatly expanded the stylistic palette on the double-disc **Pink Metal** (2007), a genre-defying hodgepodge of free-form, atonal, droning and folk music. **Impact Wound** (2007) sounded like the ideal conflation of three historic strands of New Zealand's rock music: Dead C's wall of noise, Roy Montgomery's guitar soundpainting and Clean's lo-fi punk-folk.

New Zealand's Lamp Of The Universe (the solo project of Datura's bassist Craig Williamson) was devoted to elaborate chanted shoegaze-ragas, peaking with **Heru** (2005), a seven-movement chamber symphony for sitar, tabla, synthesizer and guitar.

El Guincho (Spanish vocalist Pablo Diaz-Reixa) took Panda Bear's strategy of using loops and samples to pepper a clattering and hazy art of spaced-out vocals chanting melodies over tribal rhythms and transposed it to the intersection of exotica and freak-folk on **Alegranza** (2007).

Belgium's Ignatz (Bram Devens) played ghostly psychedelic blues at a meandering pace for abstract distorted vocals and erratic guitar fingerpicking on **II** (2006).

Kiss The Anus Of A Black Cat (Belgian musician Stef Heeren) rediscovered the pagan apocalyptic folk of Current 93 and latter-days Swans on **If The Sky Falls, We Shall Catch Larks** (2005), notably the 19-minute *Sighing Seething Soothing*, and **Nebulous Dreams** (2008), notably the 15-minute *Between Skylla and Charybdis*.

Bards of the digital frontier/ USA

Pioneered by bands such as P.G. Six, "folktronica" was the inevitable consequence of the adoption of digital "instruments" by rock music. After all, rock music had been conceived mainly to deliver a message, and throughout its convoluted history it had always been used for communicating across groups of young people. The digital age was no exception to the rule. Only the sound was different.

Detroit's producer Matthew Dear wed the figure of the microhouse dj and the figure of the singer-songwriter on **Leave Luck To Heaven** (2003).

Seattle's Dntel (1), the project of Jimmy Tamborello, used laptops to craft the charming folk tunes of **Life Is Full of Possibilities** (2002) and immerse them in a glitchy soundscape.

Armed with an arsenal of electronic keyboards, Vancouver-based Scott Morgan, or Loscil (2), penned the brief instrumental vignettes of **Submers** (2002). Live instruments dented the mechanistic ambience of **Plume** (2006).

Casiotone For The Painfully Alone, the project of Chicago-based singer-songwriter Owen Ashworth, delivered literate lo-fi pop performed with drum-machine and Casiotone keyboards on **Pocket Symphonies for Lonesome Subway Cars** (2001). It is the contrast between electronic/digital instruments and acoustic/electric instruments that lends the songs of **Etiquette** (2006) a unitary theme.

Michigan's Patrick Wolf (1) introduced novel elements in the "digital folk" format inaugurated by Four Tet (blending neoclassical music, folk music and industrial music) while anchoring them to a classical form of storytelling, first with the extended allegory of **Lycanthropy** (2003) and then with the introverted and elaborate riddle of **Wind in the Wires** (2005).

Los Angeles' iconoclastic tradition of Frank Zappa and Zoogz Rift was continued by singer-songwriter, writer and painter Nate Denver. The goofy acid garage-folk of **No One Is Coming To Help You** (2005) evoked the Holy Modal Rounders transplanted in the age of death-metal and of videogames.

Benoit Pioulard (Oregon-based vocalist and multi-instrumentalist Thomas Meluch) employed found sounds, treated guitars, tape manipulations and acoustic instruments to craft the simple, dreamy and hazy songs of **Precis** (2006).

M.I.A. had signaled the coming of the "iPod" generation that wanted to shuffle musical genres the way a busy worker eats fast food. Her equivalent in the USA was, for example, Santogold, the project of Philadelphia's vocalist Santi White and multi-instrumentalist John Hill, who debuted with **Santogold** (2008), a hodgepodge of pop, dub, punk-rock, hip-hop, house, reggae, grime, psychedelic-rock and ska. That neutral, multi-faceted and faceless genre of genres (creating a new stereotype of stereotypes) was the face of the future.

Bards of the digital frontier/ Fairy queens

During the 1980s avantgarde vocalists Diamanda Galas had shown how to alter the human voice and mix it with electronic music to dramatic effects. In the 2000s a number of female vocalists, taking advantage of digital devices, transposed that idea to a less melodramatic and more surrealistic format.

Oakland's Inca Ore, the project of Eva Salens, manipulated her vocals (reverb, echo and delay) to shape the two lengthy oneiric pieces of the mini-album **A Knit of My Own Fibers/ When You Are Sleeping I Tell You Secrets** (2005).

Oregon's Grouper (1), the project of Liz Harris, drew abstract fragile spaced-out lullabies on a canvas of droning slow-motion foggy ambience of keyboards and guitars to create the avantgarde slo-core of **Way Their Crept** (2005) and **Wide** (2006) in the vein of Lida Husik. Even when she returned to a more traditional song format with **Dragging A Dead Deer Up A Hill** (2008), the music maintained the otherworldly dimension of reverb-drenched, introverted, whispered dream-pop.

The Tropes, the project of German vocalist and multi-instrumentalist Susan Bauszat, wove wordless vocals, guitar, piano, xylophone, auto harp, flute, synthesizers, strings and drum-machines into the gentle, drifting dream-pop of **Tropes** (2008).

Geraldine Fibbers' vocalist Carla Bozulich (1) gave with **Evangelista** (2006) another terrifying vision of hell that harked back to Diamanda Galas: not songs but screams, whispers and moans that wander through the inner maze of the psyche, through a soundscape of noises, samples, drones, loops and distortions.

Argentinean singer-songwriter Juana Molina (1), coined an introverted form of bedroom folktronica for voice, guitar, keyboards and percussion. Electronic effects permeated **Segundo** (2003) and **Tres Cosas** (2004) to the point that they became the protagonists of the stories, and the ethereal ambience became the ultimate meaning of those stories. Molina sounded something like a calmer Diamanda Galas, a colder Bjork and a happier Lisa Germano. **Un Dia** (2008) was at the same time more intimate, more abstract and more hypnotic, with the voice increasingly turning into an instrument and the rhythm increasingly turning into a voice.

Bards of the digital frontier/ Bay Area

San Francisco, one hour away from Silicon Valley, benefited from the futuristic environment, but also from a tradition of irreverent cabaret-like avantgarde that went back to at least the Residents.

San Francisco's Blectum From Blechdom (1), the female San Francisco-based electronic duo of Bevin "Blevin Blectum" Kelley and Kristin "Kevin Blechdom" Erickson, experimented with their own brand of digital pop on the EP **Snauses and Mallards** (2000), a madcap collage of psychedelic ideas replete with toy and cheap keyboards, and the album **The Messy Jesse Fiesta** (2000), that indulged in fragmented grooves and laptop-based harmony. After the split Blevin Blectum specialized in chaotic tapestries of beats, loops, samples and sound effects on **Talon Slalom** (2002) and **Look! Magic Maple** (2004); while Kevin Blechdom (2) straddled the line between progressive-rock, new wave and something that still had no name on **Bitches Without Britches** (2003), that summarized the EPs **The Inside Story** (2001), **I Love Presets** (2002) and **Your Butt** (2003), and reinvented pop muzak on **Eat My Heart Out** (2005), a psychotic compromise between avantgarde electronic-dance music and vintage pop music, mixing post-modern elegance and post-industrial neurosis in one powerful antidote to the prevailing aesthetic mood.

Safety Scissors (1), the project of San Francisco-based (Minneapolis-born) electronic musician and singer-songwriter Matthew Curry, littered the catchy tunes of **Parts Water** (2001) with all sorts of "glitchy" debris and drenched them into a sneaky dub-techno vibe. The beats got even more disjointed on **Tainted Lunch** (2005), while the music became even more old-fashioned.

Female vocalist Jade Vincent (1) formed a duo with keyboardist Keefus Ciancia that engulfed the fake ballads of **Vincent & Mr Green** (2004) in an atmosphere of decadence and dejection.

Black Dice's vocalist Eric Copeland created the "songs" of **Hermaphrodite** (2007) from free-form collages of guitars, field recordings, electronic sounds and manipulated vocals.

Bards of the digital frontier/ Planet Earth

Manitoba (2), the brainchild of Canadian producer Dan Snaith, debuted in the vein of Boards Of Canada's glitch-pop electronica with **Start Breaking My Heart** (2001), excelling even at jazztronica. Snaith coined a new form of anti-pop elegance with the nostalgic Brian Wilson-ian multi-layered retro-pop approach on **Up In Flames** (2003), arranged with all sorts of vintage equipment. Renaming the project Caribou (1), Snaith changed style again for **The Milk Of Human Kindness** (2005), opting for a brainy rhythm-dominated dream-pop atmosphere that fleshed out his classic sense of melody while drowning it in neurotic pulsations and post-psychedelic sounds. **Andorra** (2007) marked yet another mutation, transforming Caribou into a necrophilic exercise of Sixties revival.

Canadian producer Koushik Ghosh mixed retro-pop lullabies with collages of sound effects and hip-hop beats on **Out My Window** (2008).

Chad VanGaalen (1), also from Canada, composed, played and produced by himself **Infiniheart** (2004), arranging the songs with a large arsenal of classical instruments, self-made instruments and digital/electronic devices.

In Britain former Herbert's chanteuse Dani Siciliano turned to digital pop with **Likes** (2004).

The Earlies delighted with painstakingly-crafted orchestral-pop electronica a` la Manitoba on their early EPs, collected on **These Were** (2004).

Part Timer (Englishman John McCaffrey) filled **Part Timer** (2006) with pastoral lullabies for guitar, piano and flute, sung in an ethereal female contralto and drenched in a tapestry of glitchy and psychedelic sound manipulations pierced by murky beats and crackling ambience.

In Germany Antye Greie-Fuchs, Laub's vocalist, devised cubist puzzles of voice and rhythm on works such as **Westernization Completed** (2003), as if she had shuffled the chronology of a stream of consciousness.

Yvonne "Niobe" Cornelius penned songs that juxtaposed heavily-processed vocals against a surrealistic backdrop of jazz, exotic and electronic archetypes.

French singer and electronic keyboardist Emilie Simon mixed pop, jazz and electronica on **Emilie Simon** (2003). The film soundtrack **La Marche de l'Empereur** (2006) employed sounds of "cold" objects (such as ice), while **Vegetal** (2006) used sounds of plants (and introduced the electric guitar).

The medium was indeed the message in the case of French duo Cocorosie (1): the music of **The Adventures of Ghosthorse and Stillborn** (2007), so fragile and improbable, was diagnosing an ongoing mutation in the collective psyche and in the zeitgeist of the 2000s.

Norwegian duo Royksopp basically offered a less challenging version of Boards Of Canada with the futuristic easy-listening of **Melody A.M.** (2001).

Shugo Tokumaru (2) debuted with the mini-album **Night Piece** (2004), that revealed him as a sort of bedroom Mozart, gifted with the talent to both borrow pristine old-fashioned melodies from around the world and to play dozens of instruments like a one-man orchestra. The serene, pastoral and witty mood of the debut yielded to colder and more introspective, meticulously assembled and densely layered, clockwork mechanisms on **L.S.T.** (2005). He played more than 50 instruments (and arranged them on his laptop) for **Exit** (2007), a veritable catalog of Sixties kitsch.

Wordless bards

Solo guitar improvisation staged an impressive comeback in the 2000s, ironically just when John Fahey died. The "revival" had started in the late 1990s with Steffen Basho-Junghans and Sir Richard Bishop, but became a widespread phenomenon only after 2001. They mostly took John Fahey as a reference model and adapted him to the post-rock sensibility.

Pelt's guitarist Jack Rose was emblematic with **Red Horse White Mule** (2001), almost a remix of John Fahey's country-ragas, and **Raag Manifestos** (2004), that also experimented with electronics.

Souled American's guitarist Scott Tuma (1) ran the gamut from brief impressionistic vignettes to lengthy metaphysical brooding on the mostly unaccompanied **Hard Again** (2001), that sounded like an ambient remix of his band's most distressed songs. The soundscape got even more rarified on **The River 1 2 3 4** (2003) for guitar, harmonica, organ and harmonium (all played by Tuma himself), somewhere between Ennio Morricone's soundtracks, Far Eastern transcendence, blues dirges and folk lullabies.

Charalambides' female soul Christina Carter (1) added a fragile, intimate, introspective element to what was becoming ambient guitar music on **Electrice** (2006), a concept of sorts (all four lengthy pieces are in the same key and use the same guitar tuning).

Low's guitarist Alan Sparhawk instead leaned towards the psychedelic world on **Solo Guitar** (2006), full of drones, dissonances and reverbs.

Pakistani-born Minnesota's resident Ilyas Ahmed leaned towards the raga-psychedelic end of the spectrum with the improvisations of **Towards The Night** (2006) and the many recordings on which the acoustic guitar was not the only protagonist but the center of mass for a blurred soundscape of wordless vocals, piano, eerie drones and sparse percussion.

The humblest of the batch was perhaps Montreal-based Harris Newman (1), whose **Non-Sequiturs** (2003) felt like a fresco of evocative, bittersweet, country life, while **Accidents with Nature and Each Other** (2005) took off towards a more ambitious and unpredictable form of improvisation.

Matt Baldwin's **Paths Of Ignition** (2008) represented the spirit of the Bay Area, as far from Appalachia as possible.

English guitarist James Blackshaw (2) was perhaps the one who came the closest to Fahey's original intent with the colossal fingerpicking-intense raga-folk improvisations for twelve-string acoustic guitar of **Celeste** (2004) and **Sunshrine** (2005). Blackshaw's personal touch was the shimmering cascade of notes that sculpted a dense wavering tapestry. The droning ambience of **Lost Prayers & Motionless Dances** (2004) and the timid experiments of **The Cloud of Unknowing** (2007) charted new paths.

Fear Falls Burning (1), the new project by Vidna Obama's Dirk Serries, indulged in hugely-amplified drone-based abstract guitar soundpainting. The double-disc tour de force of **He Spoke in Dead Tongues** (2005) and the 39-minute piece of **I'm One Of Those Monsters Numb With Grace** (2006) bridged the avantgarde school of Jonathan Coleclough, the shoegazing music of My Bloody Valentine and the doom-metal school of Earth.

Paradise Camp 23's multi-instrumentalist Erik Amlee crafted the abstract psychedelic sitar or guitar improvisations of **Afternoon Dream** (2006).

Japanese guitarist Hisato Higuchi spun the slow-motion, introspective and languid solo meditations of **Dialogue** (2006), exuding zen humility, the very negation of Japanese noisecore.

Tunesmiths

Emo-smiths

The long, long tide of emocore did not recede in the 2000s.

Continuing the cross-pollination begun in the previous decade, New York's Coheed And Cambria, fronted by vocalist-guitarist Claudio Sanchez, carried out a historical fusion of the progressive-rock tradition and the emo-core tradition on their sci-fi tetralogy, notably **In Keeping Secrets Of Silent Earth** (2003).

Pioneers of "progressive emocore" were also Breaking Pangaea in Philadelphia, who crafted the lengthy progressive emo psychodrama *Turning* on **A Cannon To A Whisper** (2001). The same city later witnessed the ascent of Circa Survive, whose fusion of hardcore, pop, metal and prog-rock peaked with **Juturna** (2005).

Minus The Bear rejuvinated emo-core in Seattle by stretching Fugazi's original aesthetic to accommodate progressive jamming driven by guitarist Dave Knudson and keyboardist Matt Bayles, best on the EP **This Is What I Know About Being Gigantic** (2001) and partially on the album **Highly Refined Pirates** (2002).

Oregon's 31 Knots were perhaps the most versatile and erudite in fusing progressive-rock and melodic/melodramatic emocore, starting with **A Word Is Also A Picture Of A Word** (2002).

The epitome of the teenage melodrama was, however, to be found in the more modest songs of New York's Taking Back Sunday, e.g. on **Where You Want To Be** (2004), that featured half of Breaking Pangaea (notably guitarist Fred Mascherino).

Straylight Run coined a pensive, adult version of emocore, relying on the male-female vocal harmonies of John Nolan (formerly of Taking Back Sunday) and Michelle Nolan as well as on atmospheric instrumental accompaniments on **Straylight Run** (2004) and **The Needles The Space** (2007).

Michigan's sextet Chiodos grafted screamo vocals, metalcore attitude, and heavy-metal bombast onto Mars Volta's theatrical progressive-rock for **All's Well That Ends Well** (2005).

There were clearly two extremes. On one hand the charts-oriented punk-pop of band such as Nevada's Panic At The Disco, that scored big with **A Fever You Can't Sweat Out** (2005), or Jack's Mannequin, the project of Los Angeles-area singer-songwriter Andrew McMahon, with **Everything in Transit** (2005), or Toronto's Silverstein, with **When Broken Is Easily Fixed** (2003). And on the other hand the bands that still had roots in punk-rock. For example, Cursive's guitarist Stephen Pedersen launched Criteria in Nebraska with the high-class all-out punk attack **En Garde** (2003).

Among the former, New Jersey's <u>My Chemical Romance</u> reached their lyrical peak with the concept **The Black Parade** (2006) in a harder and quasi-metal variant of punk-pop. Emerging from the same busy scene, <u>Early November</u> fulfilled Arthur "Ace" Anders' songwriting and musical ambition on the triple-disc semi-autobiographical concept album **The Mother, The Mechanic and The Path** (2006).

The slabs of supercharged melodic hardcore of **Revolutions Per Minute** (2002) by Chicago's <u>Rise Against</u> harked back to popcore of the 1980s.

The idea of turning emo into fun was further refined in Chicago by popcore outfits such as <u>Fall Out Boy</u>, notably on **From Under The Cork Tree** (2005), and <u>Academy Is</u>, especially on **Almost Here** (2005).

Melody makers

The world, apparently, had not had enough of three-minute ditties. However, most bands in this genre had to resort to meticulous production in order to keep the project interesting.

<u>Decemberists</u> (2), fronted in Oregon by Colin Meloy, stood out from the crowd with their coupling of brainy lyrics and simple melodies. In particular, **Castaways and Cutouts** (2002), that included the ten-minute quasi-psychedelic meditation of *California One Youth and Beauty Brigade*, and **Picaresque** (2005), that included the tragicomic nine-minute fantasia *The Mariner's Revenge Song*, were tours de force of emotional storytelling.

<u>Wolf Parade</u> (1), the project of Montreal-based singer-songwriters Dan Boeckner and Spencer Krug, employed two keyboards and an encyclopedic palette for the eclectic pop structures of **Apologies To The Queen Mary** (2005).

The Bay Area's <u>Velvet Teen</u> (1), fronted by singer-songwriter Judah Nagler, presented ambitious and melodramatic pop constructs on their second album **Elysium** (2004), although they steered towards a more cerebral and electronic sound on **Cum Laude** (2006).

Chicago's <u>M's</u> dabbled in retro garage-pop with vintage guitar riffs, vintage vocal harmonies and vintage refrains that, on **The M's** (2004), evoked just about every catchy and rocking British band from the Kinks to T.Rex.

After incorporating singer and multi-instrumentalist Janie Porche, Chicago's <u>Bound Stems</u> delivered the eccentric power-pop of **Appreciation Night** (2006).

New York's trio <u>Oxford Collapse</u>, fronted by guitarist and vocalist Michael Pace, harked back to noise-rock and college-pop of the 1980s as well as to Pavement's lo-fi rock of the 1990s on the virulent and angular **Good Ground** (2005).

Australian octet <u>Architecture in Helsinki</u> (1) struck an unlikely balance between naive refrains and futuristic lounge jamming on **Fingers Crossed** (2004), arranged with a revolving cast of acoustic and electronic instruments.

Australia's <u>Art Of Fighting</u> (1) were among the few who aimed for psychological depth, in particular on their second album **Second Storey** (2004).

Less original but more commercially successful purveyors of pop included: New Mexico's <u>Shins</u>, formed by Flake's guitarist James Mercer, with their third album **Chutes Too Narrow** (2003); <u>Long Winters</u>, the brainchild of Seattle-based singer-songwriter and multi-instrumentalist John Roderick, with **When I Pretend To Fall** (2003); <u>Capitol Years</u>, the brainchild of Philadelphia-based singer-songwriter Shai Halperin, with **Let Them Drink** (2005); Canada's identical twins <u>Tegan and Sara</u> Quin, with **So Jealous** (2004); etc.

If nothing else, <u>Polyphonic Spree</u>, a large group formed in Texas by Tripping Daisy's vocalist that includes a small orchestra and a choir for a grand total of between 20 and 25 musicians, delivered pure grandiose sugary pop on **The Beginning Stages** (2001).

Nebraska's <u>Head Of Femur</u> employed 28 performers to decorate the baroque pop of **Ringodom or Proctor** (2003), an idea that evolved into the massive orchestral sound of **Hysterical Stars** (2005).

As usual, Sweden was at the vanguard of melodic rock. <u>Peter, Bjorn & John</u>, featuring producer Bjorn Yttling, were as derivative of the Sixties as possible on **Peter, Bjorn & John** (2002). <u>Love Is All</u>, fronted by the shrieking Josephine Olausson, shot the brief and slightly neurotic punk-pop bullets of **Nine Times the Same Song** (2005) and **A Hundred Things Keep Me Up at Night** (2008): retro party music with gutsy saxophone, driving rhythm and crunchy riffs.

Going against the gloomy zeitgeist of the 2000s, German quartet <u>Banaroo</u> delivered one of the most demented dance-pop anthems of all times, *Dubi Dam Dam* (2005).

Canada before the flood

The pop renaissance of the 1990s in Canada led to a generation of deft and versatile acts.

<u>P:ano</u>, the project of Vancouver-based songwriter Nick Krgovich and multi-instrumentalist Larissa Loyva, managed to sound intimate and profound on their second album **Den** (2004).

The <u>Dears</u>, fronted by Montreal's sentimental crooner Murray Lightburn, indulged in psychological analysis with the lengthy orchestral noir melodramas of **No Cities Left** (2004).

Belle And Sebastian's folk-pop was still an influence, as demonstrated by <u>Hidden Cameras</u>, the project of Toronto-based singer-songwriter Joel Gibb, on **The Smell of Our Own** (2003).

Montreal's <u>Besnard Lakes</u> (1) roamed several decades of pop styles to produce **Are The Dark Horse** (2007), although wrapping it in an elegiac mood.

Toronto's <u>Broken Social Scene</u> (1) employed 15 players to craft **You Forgot It in People** (2002), whose parade of styles was captivating in its anarchic and protean overreaching, with the music often morphing gently into its own negation within the same song.

<u>Azeda Booth</u> concocted a dreamy fusion of ambient, glitch and pop music on **In Flesh Tones** (2008), somewhat reminiscent of Mum.

Montreal's <u>Plants And Animals</u> subverted the conventions of baroque pop with the lush chamber **Parc Avenue** (2008) because each of the songs was a busy, moody and whimsical micro-suite of styles.

Britain after the flood

The land of Brit-pop was still being haunted by an endless series of "next big things" but their credibility had greatly decreased. The <u>Clientele</u> played classy psychedelic pop on **The Violet Hour** (2003) that was arranged with a cornucopia of delay, reverb and tape effects. <u>British Sea Power</u> were original on **The Decline Of** (2003), toying with elements of progressive-rock, but then converted to Brit-pop.

<u>Go Team</u> (2), a sextet formed by English wunderkind Ian Parton, concocted sample-heavy party music a` la Avalanches on albums that were hyper-arranged in an amateurish manner such as **Thunder Lightning Strike** (2004) and **Proof Of Youth** (2007). If the original songs used as blueprints were simple pop hits, in the hands of the Go Team they became the emotional equivalent of a national anthem.

More trivial were the <u>Arctic Monkeys</u>, whose **Whatever People Say I Am** (2006) became the fastest-selling debut album of all times in Britain; the <u>Guillemots</u>, also a "next big thing" for a few days, and perhaps the most melodramatic of all on **Through The Windowpane** (2006); and the <u>Libertines</u> with **Up the Bracket** (2003).

Two groups from Liverpool briefly stole the show. The <u>Coral</u>, a sextet fronted by James Skelly and boasting organ and horns, harked back to the effervescent technicolor Brit-pop of the mid-Sixties for **The Coral** (2002). The <u>Zutons</u>, a quintet fronted by David McCabe and featuring a saxophonist, sounded like a folkier version of the Animals, less bluesy and more attuned to the sugary choruses of Merseybeat, via the pub-rock of the late 1970s on the lively and entertaining **Who Killed The Zutons** (2004).

Even the <u>Last Shadow Puppets</u>, the duo of the Arctic Monkeys' vocalist Alex Turner and Miles Kane, sounded more original than the stars on **The Age Of The Understatement** (2008), the ultimate retro-pop album, sampling the styles of every master of the past with grand orchestral arrangements (courtesy of Final Fantasy's Owen Pallett).

I Am Kloot started an acoustic-pop revival in Manchester with **Natural History** (2001). The most original of the batch were probably Elbow with **Asleep in the Back** (2001) and **Cast of Thousands** (2004).

Camera Obscura started out as pupils of Belle And Sebastian's folk-pop but progressed to the lush chamber arrangements of **Let's Get Out Of This Country** (2006).

Towering over the rest of British chamber pop, Lorna (2) employed sophisticated arrangements of string, wind and keyboard instruments for the folkish ditties of **This Time Each Year** (2003) that mixed naive female vocals with lounge-style xylophone, pastoral flute, jazzy horns and neoclassical strings. **Static Patterns & Souvenirs** (2005) added a further layer of otherwordly electronic sounds.

The influence of My Bloody Valentine and the Cocteau Twins was still being felt by some left-field pop groups. The Fields peppered **Everything Last Winter** (2007) with shoegazing guitars, dream-pop orchestration, atmospheric synths and male-female harmonies.

Los Campesinos boasted non-stop fun with a punkish verve on **Hold On Now Youngster** (2008).

The Wild Beasts, a trio fronted by eccentric and theatrical singer-guitarist Hayden Thorpe, evoked different kinds of stage (exotic club, cocktail lounge, cabaret, discotheque, musical theater and punk saloon) with the eclectic stylistic stew of **Limbo Panto** (2008).

Populists

The gloomy mood of the USA during the wars of Afghanistan and Iraq was reflected by much of the grass-roots music of the late 1990s. The real protagonist of much of the stories was the collective subconscious of a country that was on a quest for a new identity. A sense of moral confusion permeated the sounds and the lyrics of the bands that harked back to the musical traditions of the USA. The moral center of mass had shifted, and it wasn't clear where.

The languid alt-country of Washington's Canyon on their debut **Canyon** (2001) was emblematic of the existential lack of focus.

New York's National (2) spun the allegorical tales of **The National** (2001) in a stately country-pop style. **Sad Songs For Dirty Lovers** (2003), a soap opera of ordinary misfits tinged with Lou Reed-ian expressionism and Leonard Cohen-ian existentialism, upped the ante, as did the atmospheric and solemn **Boxer** (2007).

New York's Hold Steady, formed by Lifter Puller's vocalist Craig Finn and guitarist Tad Kubler, concocted an old-fashioned, infectious mix of hard-rock, roots-rock and power-pop, drenched in semi-biogaphical themes of ordinary blue-collar life, on **Almost Killed Me** (2004), **Separation Sunday** (2005), which is basically a rock opera, and **Boys And Girls In America** (2006), which contained epic tales of frustrated suburban kids anchored to solid hooks and riffs.

Seattle was a good spot for bands that played folk-rock for the post-emo era: Band Of Horses, with the melancholy dreamy melodic mid-tempo country-rock of **Everything All The Time** (2006); Elected, formed by Rilo Kiley's singer-songwriter Blake Sennett, with the slightly-neurotic and sometimes harrowing autobiographical stories of **Me First** (2004); and the Fleet Foxes (1), fronted by singer-songwriter Robin Pecknold, with the disorienting multi-part harmonies of **Fleet Foxes** (2008).

The general trend around the country was to animate the songs with eccentric arrangements or sound effects. Florida's Holopaw employed an array of acoustic, electric and electronic instruments to arrange the tragic, intense tales of **Quit +/or Fight** (2005). Wisconsin's Decibully straddled the border between pop, psychedelia and soul on **City of Festivals** (2003). Central Falls, formed in Chicago by US Maple's drummer Adam Vida, stood out for the oneiric atmosphere of **Love And Easy Living** (2003). Texas' Midlake delivered the concept album **The Trials Of Van Occupanther** (2006) in a calmly melancholy tone.

Utah's Coastal (2) bordered on shoegazing psychedelia with the lengthy trancey songs of **Coastal** (2001) and the slow-motion chromatic mirages of **Halfway To You** (2004). Their music achieved a rare fusion of romantic and metaphysical themes.

Nobody better than New Hampshire's <u>Okkervil River</u> (2) personified the emerging "chamber roots-rock" aesthetic. **Don't Fall in Love with Everyone You See** (2002) and **Down the River of Golden Dreams** (2003) relied on the balance among evocative keyboards (Jonathan Meiburg), strong rhythms, tasty arrangements (horns, strings) and plaintive vocals (Will Sheff). The tight integration of storytelling and instrumental parts allowed the songs of **Black Sheep Boy** (2005) and **The Stage Names** (2007) to revolve around psychological analysis in a profound and erudite manner that had few precedents in the annals of roots-rock.

Okkervil River's keyboardist Jonathan Meiburg and Okkervil River's guitarist Will Sheff also formed <u>Shearwater</u> (1), this time fronted by Meiburg, that started in the spartan and dejected vein of Nick Drake with **The Dissolving Room** (2001) and matched Talk Talk's abstract chamber-pop meditations on **Winged Life** (2004). **Palo Santo** (2006) was basically Meiburg's solo album with guests. He borrowed from gentle and romantic songwriters such as Leonard Cohen via the introverted celestial melancholy of Jeff Buckley, adding pastoral and ecological overtones.

San Diego's <u>Castanets</u> (1) concocted a gloomy fusion of alt-country, slo-core and digital production on the brief but visionary **Cathedral** (2004) and on the turbulent **In The Vines** (2007).

Baltimore's <u>Wilderness</u> conceived the songs of **Wilderness** (2005) as a post-rock variant of the old dream-pop sound of the Cocteau Twins plus the neurotic, twitching vocals of James Johnson.

Oregon's <u>Blitzen Trapper</u> enchanced the Wilco-style country-pop of **Field Rexx** (2004) with all sorts of stylistic detours; and **Wild Mountain Nation** (2007) made the stylistic detours the whole point of the music.

San Francisco's <u>Dodos</u> (1), the brainchild of guitarist Meric Long (a student of West African drumming and blues finger-picking), redefined roots-rock for the age of post-rock on their second album **Visiter** (2008).

New Jersey's <u>Gaslight Anthem</u>, fronted by Brian Fallon, played populist bombastic punk-folk, frequently reminiscent of Bruce Springsteen, on their second album **The '59 Sound** (2008).

The catchy albeit whimsical folk-punk of Bay Area-based <u>Port O'Brien</u> on **All We Could Do Was Sing** (2008) connected the Violent Femmes with alt-country of the 1990s.

<u>Beat Circus</u> (1), the brainchild of Boston's composer, film-maker and multi-instrumentalist Brian Carpenter, matured with the multi-stylistic and nostalgic concept album **Dreamland** (2008), set in an amusement park at the beginning of the electric age, scored for a 22-piece ensemble, and weaving together a journey into the psyche of a nation and an era.

The <u>Rosebuds</u>, the North Carolina-based duo of guitarist Ivan Howard and keyboardist Kelly Crisp, updated folk-rock with the naive, energetic and catchy male-female harmonies of **Make Out** (2003).

Horse Feathers, the Oregon-based duo of singer-guitarist Justin Ringle and string-man Peter Broderick (who played all sorts of stringed instruments) coined a form of acoustic folk music with little or no percussion and no keyboards on **Words Are Dead** (2006) that sounded like a two-men string band, except that the music was drenched in reverb and the tunes were not inspired by Appalacchia but by urban spleen.

Indiana's quintet Murder By Death crafted the gloomy atmospheric country-rock of Dante-esque concept **In Bocca al Lupo** (2006) with piano and cello.

In the realm of country music perhaps the most impressive new voice was that of Georgia's singer-songwriter Kristen Hall, whose trio Sugarland scored big with **Twice the Speed of Life** (2004) in a poppy style influenced by the Indigo Girls.

Generally speaking, it wasn't easy to say something still relevant with roots-rock in the age of the laptop. Nor was it easy to relate to the rustic values of small-town America when the vast majority of the population now lived in big cities (only 20% still lived in rural areas). In a sense roots-rock was forced to undergo the evolution that Western movies had to undergo in the 1960s, when a moral shift left John Wayne in the dust the way no bandit or crook could have done on screen.

Intellectuals

As it is often the case with rock genres, "post-rock" had become a term encompassing more than one style, and sometimes simply differentiating the non-song format from the song format. There were three main schools: the "ebbing and flowing" style of post-rock (as in God Speed You Black Emperor and Mogwai), the brainy jazz-influenced style of post-rock (Tortoise), and the original style of post-rock, that was simply a form of non-linear instrumental music (Slint, Don Caballero). Prog-rock, by comparison, tended to be more exuberant (if not bombastic) and more about the technical skills of the musicians. Ambient, noise, glitch and world music all contributed to further confuse the tongue of post-rock.

Post-rock in Chicago

Aesthetically speaking, being "post" something was the artistic manifesto of many in the 2000s. It was basically a generalization of post-modernism: not only pushing the boundaries of existing styles, but reinventing, reinterpreting, recontextualizing them and, ultimately, dismantling them.

Chicago's school of post-rock was still alive and kicking in the 2000s, although its focus and scope was rapidly shifting towards the digital soundscape.

The Battles (1), a New York-based supergroup formed by Don Caballero's guitarist Ian Williams, jazz vocalist Tyondai Braxton, Helmet's drummer John Stanier and Lynx' keyboardist Dave Konopka, single-handedly reinvented post-rock for the 21st century with **Mirrored** (2007), appropriating dance rhythms, jazz improvisation and digital editing (via a meticulous process of collage) to craft erudite and intricate compositions that harked back to the Canterbury school of progressive-rock of the 1970s.

The Boxhead Ensemble's drummer Glenn Kotche recorded **Introducing** (2002), an experiment in free-form electroacoustic percussion-based music, and **Mobile** (2006), an unlikely blend of ethnic, glitch, jazz and minimalist music.

The Eternals, formed by Trenchmouth's bassist Wayne Montana and vocalist Damon Locks, experimented with the keyboards-heavy dub-jazz-funk fusion of **The Eternals** (2000), the lengthy disjointed suites of hip-hop, dub and electronica of the mini-album **Black Museum** (2002), the anarchic funk-punk jams of **Rawar Style** (2004), halfway between Material and the Contortions, until **Heavy International** (2007), with its way of deconstructing and reconstructing funk, dub, jazz and techno, began to sound like the post-rock equivalent of what the Talking Heads had done to the new wave in the late 1970s.

Town & Country's multi-instrumentalist Ben Vida, disguised under the moniker <u>Bird Show</u> (1), mixed Western and Eastern acoustic instruments, ethnic field recordings and found sounds on **Green Inferno** (2005).

<u>Yakuza</u>, fronted by saxophonist Bruce Lamont, concocted a colorful hybrid of industrial-metal, hardcore, jazz-rock and chamber post-rock on **Way Of The Dead** (2002), mostly taken up by the 43-minute atmospheric piece *01000011110011* a` la Miles Davies.

<u>Volcano!</u> (drummer Sam Scranton, guitarist Aaron With and keyboardist Mark Cartwright) harked back to Chicago's brainy post-rock tradition on **Beautiful Seizure** (2005) and **Paperwork** (2008), classic exercises in balancing the yin-yang of chaos and structure, dynamics and meditation, harmony and discord.

Post-industrial in New York

If Chicago was the epicenter of post-rock, New York was the epicenter of noise.

<u>Black Dice</u> (3), featuring Bjorn Copeland on guitar and Eric Copeland on vocals, attempted an unlikely and epileptic fusion of hardcore punk-rock and abstract electronica on **Black Dice** (2000) and the mini-album **Cold Hands** (2001), but then dropped the punk pretense for the sprawling jams of sound effects on **Beaches & Canyons** (2002), frequently sculpted with samples and loops and occasionally blending everything into a tribal orgy, with Aaron Warren's keyboards dominating soundscapes that borrowed from both Throbbing Gristle's industrial soundscapes and Godspeed You Black Emperor's post-industrial streams of consciousness. After the tour de force of sound manipulation that was the EP **Miles Of Smiles** (2004), **Creature Comforts** (2004) continued the process of dissolving the textural unity of Western music by altering timbres, confusing dynamics and diluting rhythms, thus creating a new kind of audio collage. The more organic approach of **Broken Ear Record** (2005) highlighted their surreal synthesis of the primitive and the futuristic, even evoking the psychotic "modern dance" of Pere Ubu.

The <u>Books</u> (2), a duo (Nick "Zammuto" Willscher and Paul DeJong), concocted a fusion of folk, electronica, vocal samples and found sounds on **Thought For Food** (2002) but using an anemic approach that rarified sounds and disconnected them to the point of non existence. It was Dada without a sense of humor. **The Lemon of Pink** (2003) was even more cryptic and disorienting. At times it sounded like the same solemn demystification of roots-music preached by the Holy Modal Rounders in the Sixties, however transposed from the hippie civilization to the high-tech civilization; the same surrealistic cabaret of the United States Of America, but transposed inside a videogame. There was something grand and noble to these grotesque dizzying montages. As deranged as it was, the Books' sound art was a metaphor for a higher plane of life the same way that psychedelic freak-outs were a metaphor for altered mental states.

Sightings specialized in hysterical industrial hardcore noise that evoked the Boredoms and Mars on early works such as **Michigan Haters** (2002). By setting their mayhem to a robotic beat, **Arrived In Gold** (2004), instead, took musique concrete to a disco.

Parts and Labor turned **Groundswell** (2003) into an epic feast of new-wave digressions, mostly highlighted by the electronic noises of Dan Friel.

Top Dollar (2001), the only album by Toby Dammit (1), the brainchild of New York-based percussionist Larry Mullins, was a unique artifact of that scene, a frenzied merry-go-round of techno, dub, funk, jazz, industrial, exotic and electronic elements.

Post-dada in San Francisco

Irreverence and anarchy still reigned in San Francisco, continuing a tradition that had started in the 1960s and had produced creative oxymorons in each and every decade.

Multi-instrumentalist Nils Frykdahl and bassist Dan Rathbun of Idiot Flesh formed Sleepytime Gorilla Museum with Tin Hat Trio's violinist Carla Kihlstedt and Species Being's drummer Frank Grau. **Grand Opening And Closing** (2001) was a visceral hodgepodge of convoluted prog-rock jamming, operatic/cabaret vocals, home-made instruments and loud industrial/grindcore guitars, with sudden incursions in chamber music.

Faun Fables, the Bay Area-based duo of folksinger and performance artist Dawn McCarthy and Sleepytime Gorilla Museum's multi-instrumentalist Nils Frykdahl, staged a quirky Brecht-ian cabaret on **Family Album** (2004).

Book of Knots, featuring Sleepytime Gorilla Museum's drummer Matthias Bossi, Tin Hat Trio's violinist Carla Kihlstedt and Pere Ubu's bassist Tony Maimone, penned the historical concept album **The Book of Knots** (2007) and especially the spasmodic and demented **Traineater** (2007).

Hella (1), the Sacramento-based duo of guitarist-keyboardist Spencer Seim and drummer Zach Hill, unleashed the spastic instrumental post-rock of **Hold Your Horse Is** (2002) and **The Devil Isn't Red** (2004) in a deliberately chaotic fashion. The EP **Bitches Ain't Shit But Good People** (2003) and the mini-album **Total Bugs Bunny On Wild Bass** (2003), with a prominent synthesizer, dangerously increased the instability of the formula. The mission was completed by the double-disc **Church Gone Wild/ Chirpin Hard** (2005), one disc for Hill's industrial noise and one disc for Seim's videogame cacophony.

Howard Hello (1), a percussion-less trio formed by Tarentel's bassist Kenseth Thibideau, Dilute's guitarist Marty Anderson and Court and Spark's vocalist Wendy Allen, roamed a vast territory of electronic and acoustic sounds with irregular time signatures and dissonant counterpoint on **Howard Hello** (2002).

Subtonix, that released only **Tarantism** (2002), were an all-girl band devoted to Contortions' spastic noise-jazz-punk-rock with synthesizer and saxophone.

Outside the Bay Area there were only islands of insanity. Philadelphia's Man Man (1), fronted by vocalist and keyboardist Ryan "Honus Honus" Kattner, harked back to the exuberant, eclectic and satirical music-hall of Frank Zappa augmented with an added tribal element and the leader's Tom Waits-ian sloppy baritone. The reckless romps of **Man in a Blue Turban with a Face** (2004) and especially **Six Demon Bag** (2006), featuring synthesizers, horns, strings, chaotic percussions and all sorts of vocal harmonies, were catalogs of musical mistakes cursed to an ever-shifting focus.

Post-soundpainting

Several acts were the musical equivalent of "pointillistic" painting: focusing on the pixels rather than on the overall picture in order to produce a different view of the form being painted. A complementary approach was to aim for ambient and cinematic music, for moody and cryptic atmospheres, for contemplative and meditative moods. In a sense, this "ambient" form of post-rock was the lay/secular equivalent of spiritual acid-rock. Where Eastern-tinged psychedelia had liberated the mind to wander through a transcendent dimension, ambient post-rock liberated the mind to wander through a lay philosophical dimension.

Jackie-O Motherfucker's female guitarist Honey Owens, Fontanelle's keyboardist Brian Foote and Fontanelle's percussionist Paul Dickow formed Nudge (1), whose **Trick Doubt** (2002) and **Elaborate Devices for Filtering Crisis** (2003) were experiments in sculpting glacial and fragile post-rock structures permanently on the verge of disintegrating. Nudge's vivisection of sound peaked with **Cached** (2005), a work whose eclectic excursions (from lounge soul to acid freak-out, from ambient electronica to dub-funk-jazz fusion) were meant to disorient while "re-orienting" the listener.

Aemae, the project of San Francisco-based engineer Brandon Nickell, employed software of his own design to animate **The Helical Word** (2005), a work that was emblematic of the advent of austere, erudite and high-brow noise; while **Maw** (2007) explored the concept of ambient music for the glitch generation, or industrial music for the age of abstract digital soundsculpting.

Souvenir's Young America, a Virginia-based trio featuring keyboardist Jonathan Lee and guitarist Ken Rayher, opted for an anti-bombastic, textural, autumnal, contemplative sound on **Souvenir's Young America** (2006) and especially **An Ocean Without Water** (Crucial Blast, 2007), characterized not by gigantic guitar but mournful harmonica, and by a sense of emptiness reminiscent of Calexico's desert rock.

At the same time, this generation had mastered the praxis of improvisation/composition that had been appropriated by post-rock after being refined over the centuries by classical music (the fantasia) and by jazz (the jam).

A case in point, Texas' Explosions In The Sky (1), fronted by guitarists Mark Smith and Munaf Rayani, pushed the wild dynamics of Godspeed You Black Emperor to new heights (sonically speaking) of epic instrumental post-rock on **Those Who Tell the Truth Shall Die** (2001) and **The Earth is Not a Cold Dead Place** (2003). The six impeccable pieces of **All Of A Sudden I Miss Everyone** (2007) could be used as instruction manuals for apprentice post-rockers.

Kopernik (1), formed in Georgia by upright bassist Tim Delaney and computer composer Brad Lewis, employed a postmodernist technique of collage and cut-up on **Kopernik** (2003) to create droning ambient neoclassical free-jazz as well as ornate neoclassical sonatas.

The Cloaks (Oregon's pianist Spencer Doran) dabbled in swirling minimalist repetition of piano patterns woven into intricate layers of sonic events, notably with the 32-minute *A Crystal Skull In Peru* for piano, electronics, zither and bells, off **A Crystal Skull In Peru** (2007) and the 35-minute *Dream Tape Number One* for piano and electronics, off **Serene** (2008).

Post-new

New York also witnessed the revival of the "new wave" of the 1970s, a movement that in those days had recaptured the intellectual and rebellious spirit of the late 1960s, and then wed it to pseudo-avantgarde techniques as well as to existential lyrics.

Interpol (1) led the movement with the dark, somber and claustrophobic **Turn on the Bright Lights** (2002).

The Strokes became a sensation in Britain with the album **Is This It** (2001), that found perhaps the ideal balance between dejavu and fashionable.

Yeah Yeah Yeahs expressed the quintessence of sexual frustration and existential desperation on the EP **Yeah Yeah Yeahs** (2001).

Zah Lehroff's Seconds (1), featuring Yeah Yeah Yeahs' drummer Brian Chase, penned **Y** (2001), and **Kratitude** (2006), whose sound was the closest thing to the "no wave" of DNA, Mars and Teenage Jesus.

Other Mathematics (2001) by the Ex Models (1) flew through 13 songs in just 24 minutes in a breathless manner not heard since the heydays of the "no wave".

The fusion of futuristic electronica, nostalgic pop and punk verve was best epitomized by TV On The Radio (2). **Desperate Youth Blood Thirsty Babes** (2004) was a stylistically ambiguous statement littered with encyclopedic musical quotations. Few musicians had traveled the vast land bordered by industrial nightmares and a-cappella harmonies in just one album, or even one career. The effect of squeezing together doo-wop, shoegazing and digital ambience was to make **Return To Cookie Mountain** (2006) an even more tormented sonic feast.

The Liars (1) progressed from the effervescent **They Threw Us All In a Trench And Stuck A Monument On Top** (2001), a festival of hostile vocals and gargantuan rhythms, to the abstract and expressionistic **Drum's Not Dead** (2006), once the group had relocated to Germany. Their senseless lullabies evoked anemic soundscapes that created a sense of alienation.

The High Places, a New York-based duo (vocalist Mary Pearson and digital musician Robert Barber), created the childish multi-layered multi-stylistic songs of **High Places** (2008) by assembling on a computer a repertory of samples, loops, found sounds and home-made instruments.

The cosmopolitan sound of the Talking Heads was becoming a major influence again in New York. Yeasayer (1) blended non-rock instruments, four-part harmonies and polyrhythmic beats on **All Hour Cymbals** (2007), achieving an opalescent pan-ethnic electronic rock reminiscent not only of the Talking Heads but also of Peter Gabriel and latter-day Fleetwood Mac. Vampire Weekend (1) meticulously crafted the quasi-orchestral and pan-ethnic stew of hooks and grooves of **Vampire Weekend** (2008), reminiscent of Paul Simon as well as the Talking Heads. The Ruby Suns, formed in New Zealand by USA-born multi-instrumentalist Ryan McPhun, pioneered a simpler way to bridge world-music and baroque pop on **Sea Lion** (2008).

Black Madonna (2007) by New York's duo Austerity Program (Thad Calabrese on bass and Justin Foley on vocals and guitar) was the best imitation yet of the visceral and jagged sound of Steve Albini's Big Black propelled by a seismic drum-machine.

New York State's sextet Ra Ra Riot, fronted by vibrato tenor Wesley Miles and featuring violin (Rebecca Zeller) and cello (Alexandra Lawn), filled **The Rhumb Line** (2008) with gloomy new-wave inspired dirges.

From New York the revival of the new wave spread to the rest of North America.

San Francisco's Vue ventured into a marriage of the Stooges (a crude double-guitar assault) and Suicide (pulsating keyboards) on **Vue** (2000).

The stylistic schizophrenia of Los Angeles' Mae Shi encompassed both spastic funk-punk and synth-driven new-wave eccentricity. The EP **To**

Hit Armor Class Zero (2003), running the gamut from catchy refrains to danceable rhythms to the 51-minute electronic pastiche of *To Hit Armor Class Zero II*, was the ideological manifesto of musicians that did not want to have an artistic manifesto.

Seattle's <u>Pretty Girls Make Graves</u> improved over the naive punk-pop a` la Fastbacks of the mini-album **Good Health** (2002) by superimposing a progressive/aggressive sound in the vein of the new wave on **Elan Vital** (2006).

The <u>Paper Chase</u>, a quartet from Texas fronted by singer/guitarist John Congleton and featuring Sean Kirkpatrick on keyboards and samplers, were artsy, nervous and neurotic like the early groups of the new wave on the album **Young Bodies Heal Quickly You Know** (2001) and the EP **Cntrl-Alt-Delete-U** (2002). Since the times of Chuck Berry, rock music tended to tailor the music to the lyrics. The Paper Chase's **How You Are One Of Us** (2006) was emblematic of a switch towards deliberately decoupling the two and even juxtaposing them, so that one's yin contrasts with the other's yang.

San Diego's <u>Xiu Xiu</u> (3), fronted by vocalist Jamie Stewart and featuring Yvonne Chen's and Lauren Andrews' cheesy keyboards and assorted instruments, debuted with the highly eccentric and creative **Knife Play** (2002), that bridged the wildly introverted and apocalyptic sounds of the new wave and the wildly extroverted sounds of the late 1990s. The quartet painted abstract mood pieces that simmered and boiled, but never lost control of the energy they radiated. Stewart invented one of the few truly innovative styles of singing of the decade, hardly singing at all. The use of silence and of "non-melodic" singing was even more prominent and effective on **A Promise** (2003), that continued their exploration of the border between music and non-music. Gothic in spirit, but too rarified to be anything at all, Xiu Xiu's music left behind any pretense of songwriting, focusing almost exclusively on the angst-ridden atmosphere centered around Stewart's schizoid persona. The arrangements had declined to the status of mere signs, as the accompaniment fell short of the most elementary musical qualities. Not only was each instrument limited to a few seconds of sound, and not only were those sounds mostly atonal, but there was virtually no counterpoint, harmony, polyphony. Xiu Xiu's songs relied more on silence than on sound. After going electronic on **Fabulous Muscles** (2004), Xiu Xiu achieved a subtler form of sound-painting with the meticulous, sophisticated arrangements of **La Foret** (2005), that also added keyboardist Caralee McElroy to the line-up.

Texas' <u>I Love You But I've Chosen Darkness</u> revisited Joy Division's dark-punk via Interpol on **Fear Is on Our Side** (2006).

Under the pretext of revisiting the new wave, Florida's <u>Black Kids</u>, led by vocalist Reggie Youngblood and keyboardist Dawn Watley, retailed the bouncy party music of **Partie Traumatic** (2008).

The Evangelicals, a foursome from post-Flaming Lips Oklahoma, played energetic, catchy and lo-fi garage-rock **So Gone** (2006) while adopting a "maximalist" aesthetic for the lush, thick, operatic and stately tunes of **The Evening Descends** (2008).

Connecticut's duo Have A Nice Life (1) concocted an unlikely hybrid of My Bloody Valentine's shoegaze-pop, Joy Division's dark punk, Godspeed's post-rock, Nine Inch Nails' industrial dirges and the Swans' proto-doom on the double-disc **Deathconsciousness** (2008).

Pennsylvania's Black Moth Super Rainbow, featuring keyboardist Tom "Tobacco" Fec, employed analog keyboards for the lo-fi electronic psychedelic pop of **Falling Through A Field** (2003), displaying the influence of the Boards Of Canada on the sprawling **Dandelion Gum** (2007).

Vancouver's Frog Eyes, featuring melodramatic vocalist Carey Mercer, sounded like a romantic version of Xiu Xiu or a cubistic version of Roxy Music on their first two albums, **The Bloody Hand** (2002) and especially **The Golden River** (2003), both characterized by declamations in the vein of Tom Waits and Nick Cave, by Kafkian atmospheres due to keyboardist Grayson Walker and guitarist Michael Rak, and by a fragmented stream of consciousness. **Tears Of The Valedictorian** (2007) reached for emotional and musical balance.

Post-pop

Britain and Canada were reeling from a decade of poppier and poppier bands. The injection of a new-wave sensibility helped move the scene onto more creative forms of pop.

Franz Ferdinand were basically a simplified Scottish equivalent of New York's dance-punk, and their **Franz Ferdinand** (2004) did much to launch the "new generation" of Britain. The other precursors, the Futureheads, wed Mersey-beat harmonies and dance-punk from a new-wave perspective, like a schizophrenic alter-ego of Franz Ferdinand, on **The Futureheads** (2004). Their cousins (via drummer Peter Brewis) Field Music mixed early XTC's skewed pop, new wave's arrangements and Beach Boys' harmonies on **Field Music** (2005). Paul Smith, Maximo Park's frontman, was the Ray Davies of the "new generation": a poignant chronicler of his times who used addictive hooks and riffs (and rhythms) to capture the attention of his audience: the frenzied dance-pop of **A Certain Trigger** (2005) was ultimately just a more streamlined version of Franz Ferdinand and the Futureheads, and perhaps also the catchiest of the three. Of that generation, the most valuable were perhaps Bloc Party with **Silent Alarm** (2005). Their main inspiration was the hummable punk-rock with disco-like drumming of early XTC. And, ultimately, these British bands simply augmented the eccentric and punkish tones of the new wave with Brit-pop melodies and danceable tempos. For example, <u>Kaiser Chiefs</u> harked back to early XTC's sprightly power-pop on **Employment** (2005). Later the <u>Foals</u>, fronted by Yannis Philippakis, tried to fuse dance-punk a` la Bloc Party and post-rock a` la Mogwai on **Antidoes** (2008).

Toronto's <u>Junior Boys</u> were more poignant on **So This Is Goodbye** (2006), opting for a twitching synth-pop sound that referenced the stereotypes (stately melodies, evocative electronics, erotic vocals) while destabilizing them at the root.

Even more original were <u>Holy Fuck</u> (1), an instrumental Toronto-based combo led by keyboardists Brian Borcherdt and Graham Walsh, who mixed techno, jazz and progressive-rock on the mini-album **Holy Fuck** (2005) and then penned percussive and surrealistic rave-ups on **LP** (2007). Few bands had ever used propulsion as their raison d'etre like Holy Fuck did.

Montreal's <u>Arcade Fire</u> (2), fronted by vocalist and guitarist Win Butler and featuring keyboardists Regine Chassagne and Richard Parry, crafted the magniloquent pop ballads of **Funeral** (2004), one of the most creative achievements of the decade, and of **Neon Bible** (2007). Overflowing with references to the classics, their songs elegantly blended elements of folk, blues, glam-rock, new wave and classical music.

The <u>Islands,</u> also from Montreal, absorbed the influence of Arcade Fire on their **Return to the Sea** (2006), but inhabited their own sonic niche, one that descended from slo-core and psychedelic pop, and that embraced Caribbean, hip-hop and country music.

Post-Europe

The nonlinear and cross-stylistic nature of post-rock had opened new horizons for bands worldwide. Britain, the land of the Boards Of Canada and Mogwai, was still leading the way.

<u>Electrelane</u> (1), an all-girl group from England formed around multi-instrumentalist Verity Susman, based the evil ditties of **Rock It To The Moon** (2001) on the contrast between the propulsive side of the band (intent on pounding hypnotically a` la Velvet Underground or Neu) and the contemplative side (busy weaving disturbing soundscapes). **The Power Out** (2004) applied that instrumental schizophrenia to Susman's erudite lieder.

<u>Aereogramme</u> (1) offered an ambitious mixture of prog-rock, death-metal, industrial music and emo-core on **A Story In White** (2001) and especially **Sleep And Release** (2003).

<u>65Daysofstatic</u> coined a sound for guitar, piano, noise and drum-machine that seamlessly blended Brit-pop, hard-rock and drum'n'bass on **The Fall Of Math** (2004).

Asbestoscape (one-man band Luke Shaw) blended post-rock, trip-hop, drum'n'bass and droning metal on **Asbestoscape** (2008). The Fuck Buttons, a duo that sounded like the English equivalent of Black Dice, combined electronic noise and melody on **Street Horrrsing** (2008). The Vessels indulged in instrumental post-rock that roamed a vast range of influences (folk, jazz, metal, dance, hardcore) on **White Fields And Open Devices** (2008).

Aki Peltonen, a Finnish accordionist, fused folk, classical, jazz and post-rock elements on **Radio Banana** (2005).

Huntsville, formed by three Norwegian veterans of creative jazz music (guitarist Ivar Grydeland, bassist Tonny Klutten and percussionist Ingar Zach), played their instruments in unorthodox manners and then manipulated their sounds to obtain the post-modern reinvention of folk, jazz, raga and drone music of **For The Middle Class** (2006).

French composer Cecile "Colleen" (2) Schott built the instrumental lullabies of **Everyone Alive Wants Answers** (2003) via a meticulous collage of sampled records in a way reminiscent of Solex. The same fragile textures drenched in nostalgia permeated **The Golden Morning Breaks** (2005), composed, performed and recorded in the traditional way with acoustic instruments played live. In fact, the role of the instruments, and in particular of medieval and renaissance instruments increased on **Les Ondes Silencieuses** (2007), de facto an album of adult classical music.

In Germany the abstract and syncretic post-rock school of Bohren & der Club of Gore yielded Gruenewald (guitarist Christian Kolf and drummer Florian Toyka), who experimented an oneiric and spectral fusion of slocore, jazz-rock and cosmic music with the three suites of **Gruenewald** (2008).

The Icelandic tradition of Sigur Ros and Mum was continued by the Apparat Organ Quartet, founded in 1999 by Iceland's composer Johann Johannsson and consisting of four organists and a drummer, that delivered the retro-futuristic pop of **Apparat Organ Quartet** (2006). Johann Johannsson (1) himself specialized in grandiose constructs for orchestra, choir and electronics such as the hour-long solemnly melodic piece **Virthulegu Forsetar** (2004), scored for eleven brass players, keyboards, percussion and electronics, and **IBM 1401 A User's Manual** (2006), an "opera" about a historical computer.

Finnish sextet Magyar Posse (armed with guitars, violins and keyboards) fused Godspeed You Black Emperor's elegant dynamics and Ennio Morricone's haunting ambience in the lush fluctuating melodic fantasies of the instrumental concept album **Kings Of Time** (2004).

Finnish trio Paavoharju penned the hazy, boreal and lunatic dance-pop wrapped in electronic effects of **Yha Hamaraa** (2005).

The stark, exuberant and propulsive organ-driven rhapsodies unleashed by Finnish quartet Shogun Kunitoki on the all-instrumental

Tasankokaiku (2006) occupied a niche in between Neu's "motorik" rhythm and Steve Reich's "minimalist" pulsation.

Ukrainian ensemble Moglass improvised droning music for guitars and electronics and bathed its filaments in a desolate atmosphere on **Uhodyaschie Vdal' Telegrafnye Stolby Stanovyatsa Vsyo Men'she i Men'she** (2003).

In the new century Italy was still a fertile territory for electronic and digital post-rock experiments, as proven by Claudio Rocchetti's **The Work Called Kitano** (2003), Uochi Toki's **Vocapatch** (2003), Technophonic Chamber Orchestra's **Nemoretum Sonata** (2004), Stefano Pilia's **The Season** (2004), Uncode Duello's **Uncode Duello** (2004), In My Room's **Saturday Saturn** (2005), Allun's **Onitsed** (2005), Punck's **Nowhere Campfire Tapes** (2005), Sinistri's **Free Pulse** (2005). Italian supergroup 3/4hadbeeneliminated (comprising avantgarde composers Stefano Pilia, Claudio Rocchetti and Valerio Tricoli) wove together slocore melodies, instrumental post-rock tapestries for guitars, drums and turntables, and drones constructed from field recordings and home-made instruments, on their second album **A Year Of The Aural Gauge Operation** (2005) and on **Theology** (2007).

Post-prog

In a sense progressive-rock had become an obselete concept in the 2000s. In the 1970s it was revolutionary to hear a rock band arrange a piece with non-rock instruments or incorporate elements of a different genre or shift tempo. By the 2000s just about every musician in the world could do so, and did so routinely. However, a few acts stood out for their original take on arrangement and/or dynamics.

Oregon's Menomena (2) reinvented the power-trio for the digital age. Brent Knopf, the putative guitarist, was not interested in bravura shows but in bionic synthesis: he composed songs with help from software that facilitated the creation of collages and loops. The artificial music of **I Am The Fun Blame Monster** (2003) seamlessly blended the aesthetics of baroque psychedelic-pop of the 1960s, melodic progressive-rock of the 1970s, jarring noise-rock of the 1980s, eccentric post-rock of the 1990s and agonizing emo-rock of the 2000s. The instrumental dance score **Under An Hour** (2005) focused on sophisticated placements of instruments to produce the equivalent of classical fantasias.

Kayo Dot (1), the new name chosen by Toby Driver for his Boston-based ensemble Maudlin Of The Well, achieved perhaps the most accomplished fusion yet of death-metal, post-rock, jazz and classical music by any band on **Choirs of the Eye** (2003). More obscure and abstract, **Dowsing Anemone with Copper Tongue** (2006), placed a stronger emphasis on vocal theatrics.

At The Drive In's guitarist Omar Rodriguez-Lopez and singer Cedric Bixler formed <u>Mars Volta</u> (10) with keyboardist Isaiah "Ikey" Owens. **De-loused In The Comatorium** (2003), featuring the Red Hot Chili Peppers' bassist "Flea", was characterized by collage-like structures and haphazard dynamics (that turned the codas into micro-concertos of sound effects). Each of the five cryptic, neurotic, elongated pieces of **Frances The Mute** (2005) was basically an album in itself, made of several sub-tracks that often collided with their neighbors instead of segueing smoothly from and into them. The typical Mars Volta composition was a cascade of incoherent fragments that generated a brutally disjointed but viscerally introspective stream of consciousness.

The <u>Ahleuchatistas</u> in North Carolina tried to update King Crimson's progressive-rock for the post-industrial age on the all-instrumental twin albums **On the Culture Industry** (2004) and **The Same and the Other** (2004).

Wisconsin's <u>Far Corner</u> (1), led by keyboardist and composer Dan Maske, evoked Colosseum with the energetic and elegant fusion of jazz, rock and classical music of **Far Corner** (2004) and especially of the suite **Endangered** (2007).

The instrumental post-rock of Texas' <u>By The End Of Tonight</u> was fueled by Josh Smith's jazz-rock guitar technique on the EP **Fireworks on Ice** (2004) and on the mini-album **A Tribute To Tigers** (2005).

Pennsylvania's duo <u>Zombi</u> indulged in instrumental electronic Goblin-influenced horror prog-rock on **Cosmos** (2004) and **Surface To Air** (2006).

<u>Combat Astronomy</u> (1), a transatlantic collaboration between Oregon-based bassist James Huggett (also programming the drum-machine) and three British jazz musicians (saxophonist Martin Archer, bassoon player Mike Beck and flutist Charlie Collins), straddled the border between industrial, heavy-metal and free-jazz on **The Dematerialized Passenger** (2005). Caveman Shoestore's vocalist Elaine DiFalco helped turn **Dreams No Longer Hesitate** (2008) into an expressionistic version of trip-hop.

The English quartet <u>Zukanican</u> (saxophone, trumpet, bass and drums) wed free-jazz, ambient music and prog-rock in a carnival-like atmosphere on **Horse Republic** (2006) like a meeting of the Art Ensemble of Chicago, Frank Zappa and Brian Eno.

German duo <u>Caacrinolas</u> (avantgarde musicians Bjoern Eichstaedt and Larry Luer of the free improvised trio Bretzel Killing Machine) were masters of instrumental horror ambience, from the black metal of the the single-track EP **A Thousand Cries Has The Night** (2001) to the 36-minute piece of **Valley of the Dead** (2003), that displayed the influences of Ennio Morricone and of King Crimson, and to the two lengthy suites of **Vargtimmen** (2007), this time influenced by doom-metal, German cosmic music and Hungarian composer Gyorgy Ligeti.

Japan's post-Ghost scene was one of the most fertile. Japanese instrumental quartet Mono (1) indulged in post-psychedelic chamber music with sentimental overtones that were unknown to the founding fathers of post-rock. The trilogy of **Under the Pipal Tree** (2001), that toyed with post-rock torment, the elegiac **One Step More And You Die** (2003), that included their artistic peak *Com*, and the pensive **Walking Cloud And Deep Red Sky** (2004) provided three perspectives on introversion in music, each complementing the others. Quest For Blood, featuring veteran jazz flutist Yukihiro Isso, invented the hyperkinetic flute-driven fusion of prog-rock, Japanese folk, free jazz and black metal of **Quest For Blood** (2008). Birushanah mixed Japanese scales and Western rock music to obtain the post-doom folk music of the two juggernauts of **Akai Yami** (2007) that sounded like a jam among Mogwai, Mike Oldfield and Khanate.

Post-noise

During the 1990s the "noisecore" scenes of Japan and New Zealand (remote descendants of the British "industrial" music of the 1970s) had legitimized extreme cacophony as a musical genre on its own. Digital instruments helped the genre evolve and branch out in many different directions.

Lightning Bolt (1) from Rhode Island (the duo of drummer Brian Chippendale and vocalist/bassist Brian Gibson) were among the few USA bands that could compete with the Japanese noise-core masters, notably on **Ride The Skies** (2001), that matched dissonant fury with killer speed. Chippendale's side-project Mindflayer offered an explosive fusion of free-jazz, house music and Neu on **Take Your Skin Off** (2003).

Death From Above 1979 (the Toronto-based duo of bassist and synth-man Jesse Keeler and vocalist and drummer Sebastien Grainger) delivered abrasive industrial-grade heavily-syncopated hardcore on the EP **Heads Up** (2002) and the album **You're a Woman I'm a Machine** (2004).

Ahousen (1), a Japanese quartet of saxophone, guitar, bass and drums, explored the obvious border between acid-rock and free jazz with far from obvious mood shifts on **Ahousen** (2007), notably the acrobatic explosions and implosions of the 28-minute *Ophelia*.

Japanese electronic musician Guilty Connector (Kohei Nakagawa) produced metallic ear-splitting noisescapes such as the incandescent and fibrillating fragments of **First Noise Attack** (2001), ranging from a five-second "song" to the 17-minute *Lethal Firetrap*, or the 15-minute pummeling and scraping *Brighter Than 10,000 Cacophonous Suns*, off **Cosmic Trigger/ 2AM Visit** (2004).

Armpit (the duo of Noone Clayton and Jon Sugar) were the heirs to New Zealand's tradition of atonal rock a` la Dead C. **Butta Daze** (2003) and the double-disc **The Praying Mantis** (2003) were the musical equivalent of galaxies of unstable antimatter.

Mammal, the project of Detroit's electronic musician Gary Beauvais, relished the extreme sensory experience of **Double Nature** (2003), a jungle of pummeling beats, horror shrieks and ear-piercing electronics.

Burning Star Core (1), the project of Ohio-based violinist Spencer Yeh, achieved a unique balance of droning ambience, musique concrete and psychedelic freak-out, a standard first set by the two lengthy meditations of **A Brighter Summer Day** (2002) and then magnified by **Three Sisters Who Share An Eye** (2006), his most extreme solo work. **Operator Dead Post Abandoned** (2007) inaugurated a quartet with Yeh on violin, Trevor Tremaine on percussion, Mike Shiflet on computer and Robert Beatty on electronics, performing a loud and transcendental fusion of free-jazz, acid-rock and digital soundsculpting over spastic percussive frenzy.

The Julie Mittens, a trio of Dutch improvisers, played heavily-distorted guitar-based acid-rock with free-jazzy drums, halfway between Fushitsusha and Supersilent, on **The Julie Mittens** (2008).

The audio compounds of Blue Sabbath Black Cheer (the Seattle duo of William Rage and Stan "Plethora" Reed), such as the 32-minute piece of **Drowning In Hate** (2006) and the two monoliths of **Boutranger Moor** (2007), emanated radioactive ear-piercing electronic noise with industrial rhythms and otherworldly vocals halfway between Merzbow and Wolf Eyes.

The Starving Weirdos, a group (mainly Brian Pyle and Merrick McKinlay) from Northern California, assembled oneiric free-form noisescapes that ran the gamut from ear-piercing walls of noise to otherworldly drones, all the time maintaining a gloomy underlying leitmotif, as if they were soundtracks to the post-nuclear world, for example on the double-disc **Eastern Light** (2006).

Hum Of The Druid, the project of Seattle's digital composer Eric Stonefelt, emulated the stream of consciousness of the industrial society with the obsessive reverb-drenched suites of **Societal** (2005) and the multi-faceted abrasive drones of **Raising The New Wing/ Braided Industry** (2008).

New Zealand's music promoter Antony Milton was determined to find a common denominator to industrial music, psychedelic music and droning music, as announced on his manifesto **Near/Far** (2001). Seen Through's **Extant** (2003) and Street's **School Of Religious Studies** (2004) simply revisited Throbbing Gristle's noise-core, but Mrtyu's double-disc **Blood Tantra** (2006) applied that cacophonous aesthetic to an ever-shifting kaleidoscope of guitar noise. A more humane phase began with the ethereal ambient music of **With Throats As Fine As**

Needles (2006), a supersession recorded outdoors with Campbell Kneale (Birchville Cat Motel), James Kirk (Sandoz Lab Technicians) and Richard Francis (Eso Steel), and with the even more delicate dronescapes of Nether Dawn's **Outer Dark** (2006). Glory Frckn Sun's **Vision Scorched** (2007), a collaboration with multi-instrumentalist Ben Spiers and jazz percussionist Simon O'Rorke, was a symphony of smoldering cosmic distortions.

The intense, frenzied, polyrhythmic improvised music for guitar, drums and electronics of Moha, the Norwegian duo of drummer Morten Olsen and guitarist Anders Hana, sounded like a cross of atonal jazz master Anthony Braxton and grindnoise master James Plotkin on **Raus Aus Stavanger** (2006).

Poochlatz, the duo of Israeli electronic musician Maor Appelbaum and vocalist Rani Zager, vomited the hypercharged industrial noisescape of **Victims of Self-Preservation** (2006). Adding drummer Matan Shmueli and changing their name to Grave in the Sky, their **Cutlery Hits China - English For The Hearing Impaired** (2007) bridged Throbbing Gristle's industrial music, the psychedelic freak-out and doom-metal.

Also in Israel was active the eight-piece ensemble Lietterschpich, whose **I Cum Blood In The Think Tank** (2007) was one of the most original takes on Throbbing Gristle's industrial music and Whitehouse's power electronics.

The British combo Emit terrorized the crowds of black metal with the claustrophobic electronic gothic industrial music of **A Sword Of Death For The Prince** (2005).

The Dutch combo Stalaggh added the delirious vocals of mental patients and a suidical murderer to the harrowing industrial noise of **Nihilistik Terrror** (2006) that could make even Diamanda Galas shiver.

The Scottish duo Wraiths ran the gamut from the demonic pounding industrial pow-wow of **Oriflamme** (2006) to the feedback-based black-noise ambient music of **Plaguebearer** (2007).

German duo Feine Trinkers Bei Pinkels Daheim (Jurgen Eberhard and Oswin Czerwinski) rattled the post-industrial scene with the droning and wavering collages of found sounds and white noise documented on **Apfelmost Und Essig** (1999) and by the 64-minute **Hungerhaken's Speckrolle** (2002). By adding Swedish guitarist Chris Sigdell the duo became NID and released **Plate Tectonics** (2007) that continued their hypno-cacophonous mission.

Post-ambient

The definition of "ambient" music changed as quickly as the definition of "rock" music. Generally speaking, it stood for quiet instrumental music with minimal dynamic development. But that was more appropriate of the destination than of the journey.

Connecticut's <u>Landing</u> abandoned the lengthy, dreamy, unstructured instrumentals of their second album **Oceanless** (2001) for the lush, almost symphonic sound of **Seasons** (2002), that absorbed acid-rock of the 1960s, Cocteau Twins' dream-pop, Windy & Carl's ambient madrigals and Bedhead's slo-core. That form peaked with the deeper psychological study of the EP **Fade In Fade Out** (2002), at the same time approaching the delicious trance of Harold Budd. Continuing the process of disintegration, **Passages Through** (2003) built guitarscapes that were even more ethereal and hypnotic.

The manifestoes of <u>Eluvium</u> (1), the project of Oregon's composer Matthew Cooper, were *Zerthis Was a Shivering Human Image*, a simple massive tsunami of guitar distortion, off **Lambent Materials** (2003), and *Taken*, a gently wavering geometric fantasia (reminiscent of Johann Pachelbel's *Variations*), off **Talk Amongst The Trees** (2005). Cooper did with the guitar what used to be done with electronic keyboards. **Copia** (2007) stood as the crowning achievement of his progression towards counterpoint, with chamber instruments replacing the shoegazing guitars.

Another project that imitated electronic cosmic music of the previous decades was <u>Dreamland</u>, based in Texas, whose **Underwater** (2001) evoked the tense atmospheres of Klaus Schulze via distorted guitars and electronic keyboards.

Chicago-based laptop folk musician <u>Greg Davis</u> (1) composed fragile structures that borrowed elements from both dance, concrete and folk music on **Arbor** (2002) and **Curling Pond Woods** (2003).

Boston's electronic composer <u>Brendan Murray</u> made blissed-out ambient music of shifting drones via a pointillistic and layered approach. His major works, the 41-minute piece of **Everybody Wants The Tide** (2006) and the 49-minute piece of **Commonwealth** (2008), sounded like philosophical meditations.

An exercise in nonlinear post-psychedelic music, the third album **Far Flung Hum** (2008) by <u>Christmas Decorations</u> (the duo of Rorschach's guitarist Nick Forte and Steve Silverstein) was a slowly revolving kaleidoscope of electroacoustic fragments, hinting that what mattered was not the composition but the way the sources were "remixed".

The British school founded in the 1990s by Colin Potter and Andrew Chalk continued to thrive and incubate talents, notably <u>Ian Holloway</u> who employed musique-concrete techniques to create the ambient drones of the 39-minute piece of **A Lonely Place** (2007) and the 37-minute piece of **Ashram Psych Tip** (2007).

British composer <u>Max Richter</u> transposed the avantgarde chamber and electronic music that he had been practicing for decades into the realm of popular music with **Memoryhouse** (2003). Electronic and digital effects were subdued on **Blue Notebooks** (2004), that was mainly a new interpretation of Erik Satie's "elevator music" for chamber instruments.

Tenhornedbeast (British soundsculptor Christopher Walton) mastered the style of apocalyptic ambient drones on **The Sacred Truth** (2007).

The ambient aural collages of Xela (English digital musician John Twells) became progressively darker and gloomier, with **The Dead Sea** (2006) virtually a tribute to Italian horror soundtracks of the 1970s, and the four-movement requiem **In Bocca Al Lupo** (2008) representing an emotional nadir.

Hauschka (German pianist Volker Bertelmann) turned the tables on the avantgarde when he applied John Cage's then-provocative techniques and the repetitive strategies of the minimalists to simple and pastoral folk-inspired melodies on **The Prepared Piano** (2005).

Dorine Muraille (1), i.e. French composer Julien Locquet, sculpted the post-ambient melodies of **Mani** (2002) by means of computer-processed acoustic instruments.

Deaf Center, the Norwegian duo of producers Erik Skodvin and Otto Totland, crafted the psycho-ambient music of **Pale Ravine** (2005) by setting in motion collages of found sounds and classical instruments.

New Zealand's soundsculptress Gydja (Abby Helasdottir) specialized in dark ambient electronic works such as the the shamanic concept **Liber Babalon** (2001) and the 79-minute piece of **Cold Seed** (2001).

New Zealand's Seht (Steven Clover) ran the gamut from the 60-minute surreal noisescape of **Goodbye America & Have A Nice Day** (2002) to the 40-minute aural collage of **Syddo Paragone** (2005) to the 34-minute minimal glitch piece of **Guyrz Nz You Are Thus Alienated** (2006) to the 36-minute majestic drone music of *One Moment*, off **Dead Bees** (2008).

Post-glitch

There was a tendency in digital soundsculpting towards extremes, but not so much towards the extremely noisy as to the extremely dynamic. Building on the legacy of electronic music, digital music did not conform with the laws of classical Western harmony, but was nonetheless meticulously crafted through a process of sound sculpting that was no less complex and laborious than scoring parts for an orchestra.

Apparat (Berlin's electronic musician Sascha Ring) transitioned from the "intelligent" techno music of **Multifunktionsebene** (2001) to the gentle and shy glitch music of **Duplex** (2003).

Washington-based multi-instrumentalist Chuck Bettis, a member of the avantgarde collective All Scars, was influenced by videogame soundtracks for the laptop-based compositions on **Community of Commotion** (2005).

White Flight (1), the new and wildly experimental project of Anniversary's guitarist Justin Roelofs, yielded the cacophonous collage of **White Flight** (2006), basically a "freak-out" in the vein of Red Crayola augmented with breakbeats, digital noise, vocal effects and non-rock instruments.

Jasper TX, the project of Swedish multi-instrumentalist Dag Rosenqvist, crafted shimmering instrumental textural slo-core drenched in lo-fi hissing, crackling, rattling ambience, starting with **I'll Be Long Gone Before My Light Reaches You** (2005), and peaking with the 21-minute *Some Things Broken Some Things Lost*, off **A Darkness** (2007), and the dark, cryptic and hypnotic six-movement symphony **Black Sheep** (2008).

Machinefabriek (1), the project of Dutch electronic musician Rutger Zuydervelt, sculpted hypnotic and grandiloquent soundscapes, despite the fuzzy background noise, notably the 18-minute *Lawine*, off **Marijn** (2006), the 19-minute *Licht*, off **Bijeen** (2007), the 22-minute *Still*, off **Slaapzucht** (2007), the 21-minute *Flotter*, off **Zwart** (2007), the 17-minute *Zink*, off **Ranonkel** (2008), and the 25-minute *Singel*, off **Dauw** (2008).

Oakland's Yellow Swans, the project of vocalist Pete Swanson and guitarist Gabriel Mindel-Saloman (both also on electronic/digital instruments), created the tapestries for electronics and drum-machines of **Bring The Neon War Home** (2004) and **Psychic Secession** (2005) by fusing free-jazz, musique concrete and drum'n'bass, and the latter even adding ghostly vocals by Inca Ore and Christina Carter of Charalambides.

Inspired by Zen and Sufi philosophy, and therefore more interested in stillness than in movement, British soundsculptor Keith Berry espoused Bernhard Gunter's and Steve Roden's aesthetic of silence for **The Ear That Was Sold To A Fish** (2005) and the double-disc **A Strange Feather** (2007).

Dialing In, the project of Seattle-based digital composer Reita Piecuch, painstakingly constructed the dense and glitchy ambient music of **Cows In Lye** (2006) from found sounds, found music and assorted keyboards.

Rhode Island-based Geoff Mullen composed droning and softly cacophonous music for guitar, banjo and electronics on **Thrtysxtrllnmnfstns** (2006). **The Air in Pieces** (2006) indulged in dense subsonic distortions whose original sources were impossible to detect. The double-LP **Armory Radio** (2007) increased the sense of confusion with constantly shifting textures and continuously evolving patterns. His music sounded like John Fahey's progressive folk being remixed by a glitch musician.

Tarab (Australian sound artist Eamon Sprod), a specialist in manipulating field recordings, transposed landscapes into dark and subliminal sound art on **Surfacedrift** (2004) and **Wind Keeps Even Dust Away** (2007).

Post-instrumental

Digital deconstruction of acoustic instruments played a role too.

Tim Hecker, an electronic musician from Montreal (Canada), was a more orthodox purveyor of ambient glitch-electronica. **Haunt Me Haunt Me Do It Again** (2001), inspired by Christian Fennesz's digital manipulation of guitar sounds, and especially **Presents Radio Amor** (2003) manipulated samples and field recordings to generate organic, romantic creatures.

Canadian electro-acoustic composer Mitchell Akiyama created the glitchy ambient music of the mini-album **If Night is a Weed and Day Grows Less** (2004) and of **Small Explosions That Are Yours To Keep** (2005) by manipulating live acoustic instruments.

Tuk, the project of Belgian digital musician Guillaume Graux, chopped and sliced instrumental parts, stitched them together, dilated them and contracted them, alternating slow-motion and rapid-fire tempos; and finally bathed the stuttering, malfunctioning clockworks of **Proud Princess Of A Brand New City** (2004) and **Shallow Water Blackout** (2007) in dilapidated ambience.

Swedish trio Tape (1) sculpted the seductive, minimal, slow-motion and drum-less soundscapes of their **Opera** (2002) by painstakingly merging synthesizer, field recordings and acoustic instruments (guitar, harmonium, melodica, harmonica, zither, piano, flute, accordion, trumpet and percussion) on a computer. The acoustic guitar was the dominant voice, as if John Fahey had been catapulted into an electroacoustic chamber concerto. The trio reached their formal zenith with **Rideau** (2005), whose pieces explored the ambient side of post-rock's nonlinear, abstract, unstructured equation; rural and pastoral instead of urban and neurotic (as most post-rock was).

Italian composer Giuseppe Ielasi morphed from the soundsculptor of **Plans** (2003), a 31-minute electroacoustic collage of drones, glitches, percussion and field recordings, to the puppeteer of **Gesine** (2005), an essay on minimal textures for electronics and manipulated guitar sounds that coined an original genre of concerto for acoustic instruments and languid musique concrete.

Maryland's Half Makeshift (sound designer Nathan Michael) was devoted to glitchy electronic post-rock based on piano and guitar manipulations. His project evolved from the massive 35-minute post-doom expressionist nightmare of the EP **Aphotic Leech** (2007) via the more relaxed **L'Anse Amort** (2007), set in an unstable but more humane noisescape, to the brooding four-movement drone-intense requiem for humankind **Omen** (2008).

The Fun Years, a New York-based duo of baritone guitar (Ben Recht) and turntable (Isaac Sparks), employed the "noises" of the turntable to "arrange" the music of the guitar and viceversa, exploring the complementary roles of the two instruments when locked together in a polyphony of samples, loops and drones, thereby unfurling the discreet schizophrenic meditations of **Life-Sized Psychoses** (2007) and **Baby It's Cold Inside** (2008).

Australian-born Iceland-based laptop composer Ben Frost choreographed the fanciful scenes for treated guitar of **Steel Wound** (2003) and then coupled industrial horror with glitchy post-rock dynamics, and psychedelic drones with minimal techno, for **Theory Of Machines** (2008).

Post-drones

Droning minimalism was evolving too, as composers were trying ever more creative ways to explore the tones and overtones and microtones of stationary waves.

Encomiast, the brainchild of Colorado's Ross Hagen, produced the dense, brooding, slowly-revolving dronescapes of **Winter's End** (2001) and **Espera** (2003) by digitally manipulating and blending acoustic instruments, voices, programmed rhythms and field recordings.

SourceCodex, the brainchild of North Carolina-based guitarist and digital composer John Patterson, created entirely on a computer the music for **Codex Hypnos** (2004), an ambient cosmic industrial droning symphony.

Hoor-Paar-Kraat, a trio of electronic/digital musicians led by the prolific California-based soundsculptor Anthony Mangicapra, secreted ambient music from collages of field recordings. The dark sheet of drones was disturbed by small dissonant events that sometimes rose to become tidal waves. The effect was particularly dramatic on **Asha Dasha** (2005) and the mini-album **The Nagaraja Movements** (2006).

Toronto's prolific Aidan Baker, who also played doom-metal under the moniker Nadja, practiced hushed droning ambient music on works such as the double-CD **Oneiromancer** (2006) and **Pendulum** (2006).

Ohio-based Taiga Remains (Alex Cobb) created raga-like noise music by manipulating and overdubbing the sound of an acoustic guitar on the three EPs titled **Ribbons Of Dust** (2006).

Light Of Shipwreck (the project of Delaware-based sound artist Ben Fleury-Steiner) borrowed the ebbing-and-flowing aesthetic of post-rock and applied it to a combination of ambient guitar noise and propulsive drum-machines, an odd mixture of drone and dance music, to create the three suites of **From The Idle Cylinders** (2007), the 21-minute piece of the EP **Through The Bilge Lies A Calm And Bloodless Sea** (2008), and the 49-minute piece of **In The Empty Wreckage Of A Dream** (2008).

An ever-mutating form of digital music was practiced by Germany's Black To Comm (1), the project of laptop musician Marc Richter, who first blended vinyl records, field recordings, voice and found percussion for **Ruckwarts Backwards** (2006), that ran the gamut from Phill Niblock's infinite drones to Gordon Mumma's massive walls of noise, with sprinkles of both chamber music and musique concrete; then manipulated the sounds of traditional instruments to create the variegated drones of **Wir Konnen Leider Nicht Etwas Mehr Zu Tun** (2007); and finally invoked a circus-like atmosphere for the collage of voices, analog keyboards and acoustic instruments of **Fractal Hair Geometry** (2008).

French duo Maninkari played droning gothic music for chamber instruments and electronics on the double-disc **Le Diable Avec Ses Chevaux** (2007) like a classical orchestra performing Sunn O)))'s music.

Swedish duo Skull Defekts assembled abstract, chaotic and cinematic electronic soundscapes such as the 55-minute piece of **Open The Gates Of Mimer** (2005), *Magnetic Skulls*, off **Magnetic Skulls & Intense Sound Stimulations** (2006), and the 43-minute piece of **The Sound Of Defekt Skulls And Intense Cranium Contact** (2007).

Australian inventor Tim Catlin pursued a dadaistic version of LaMonte Young's droning minimalism via works such as **Slow Twitch** (2003) for self-built guitar automata, and **Radio Ghosts** (2007) for prepared tabletop guitar (a` la Keith Rowe).

New Zealand's guitarist Peter Wright used field recordings and acoustic instruments to manufacture the oneiric dronescapes of **Catch A Spear As It Flies** (2002), with the 25-minute *The Bride Stripped Bare*, **Pariahs Sing Om** (2003), **Desolation Beauty Violence** (2004), **Yellow Horizon** (2005), the double-disc **At Last New Dawn** (2007), with the 34-minute *At Last New Dawn*, **Pretty Mushroom Clouds** (2008), with the 24-minute *The Devil Wears Sunroof*.

Post-cosmic

Germany had a prolific school of electronic/digital soundsculptors.

Stephan Mathieu used sample-based composition to create the atmospheric glitch-pop of **Frequency Lib** (2001), but the romantic chamber ambience of **The Sad Mac** (2005) led to the evocative **Radioland** (2008), created by manipulating short-wave radio signals. Christian Kleine animated delicate digital soundscapes gently ruffled by live instrumentation on **Real Ghosts** (2004). Jan Jelinek (2) blended jazz/funk bass lines (lifted from old records), repetitive minimalism, glitch music, trip-hop and house music on the groundbreaking **Loop Finding Jazz Records** (2001). He then used German records of cosmic music as the sources for **Kosmischer Pitch** (2005), an even more elegant application of the principle of slow variation within repetition. The beat all but disappeared on **Tierbeobachtungen** (2006), replaced by the rhythms of the loops that permeate the compositions.

As usual, Cologne was at the vanguard. For example, POL, formed by Carsten Schulz (C-Schulz), mixed field recordings, world-music and techno beats on **Transomuba** (1994). One of its members, Pluramon (Marcus Schmickler), meticulously rebuilt in studio the sound of an instrumental prog-rock band by layering live and computer-generated sounds on **Pickup Canyon** (1996).

Cloudland Canyon, the duo of Tennessee-based guitarist Kip Uhlhorn and German musician Simon Wojan, wed German "cosmic" music of the 1970s (the "motorik" rhythm of Neu and the analog keyboards of Tangerine Dream) with digital processing (a dense flow of manipulated vocals and instruments) to mold the two lengthy suites of **Silver Tongued Sisyphus** (2007).

Post-world

In a world that was rapidly becoming "globalized" the idea of "ethnic" music did not make much sense anymore, unless it referred to the "classical" or "folk" past of each region. Hence most of the contamination was now working in the opposite direction: the developing world incorporating the sounds and rhythms of Western music. For USA musicians, instead, the "ethnic" element was mostly just one of the many possible ingredients of an increasingly complex recipe, and it had lost much of its "novelty" appeal.

Quix*o*tic's stately vocalist Mira Billotte went on to play ethnic-folk-jazz-rock fusion with White Magic on their **Dat Rosa Mel Apibus** (2006).

The Arizona-based instrumental duo Smoke & Mirrors (1) mixed acid-rock, world-music, orchestral music and electronica on the Hindu concept album **Deities** (2004).

Turkish soundsculptor Erdem Helvacioglu (1) was emblematic of how the "ethnic" music scenes themselves were adapting to a global civilization: the ethereal, haunting and subliminal sound sculptures of **Altered Realities** (2006) belonged to a genre of post-folk music straddling the border between ambient, jazz, folk and concrete music.

Shanghai in China was rapidly emerging as a new powerhouse of avantgarde laptop-based music. Intelligent Shanghai Mono University (1), a quartet of four Shanghai-based digital musicians, explored abstract musique concrete, torrential white noise, disjointed electroacoustic chamber music, collages of manipulated samples, post-industrial cacophony and glitchy pseudo-dance music on **7.9** (2003). 718 (Sun Lei) assembled the subliminal collages of noise, samples and beats of **Nowise Assault** (2005). Li Jianhong (1) recorded juggernauts of solo guitar improvisations such as the 60-minute piece of **Talking Freely Before The Beginning** (2003) and the 51-minute piece of **San Sheng Shi** (2008).

Clubbers

Electroclash

The "electroclash" movement was basically a revival of the dance-punk style of the new wave. It was New York dj Lawrence "Larry Tee" who coined the term, and the first Electroclash Festival was held in that city in 2001. However, the movement had its origins on the other side of the Atlantic Ocean. One could argue that electroclash was born with *Space Invaders Are Smoking Grass* (1997), released by Belgian dj Ferenc van der Sluijs under the moniker I-f. At about the same time German house dj Helmut-Josef "DJ Hell" Geier was promoting a scene in Berlin that was basically electroclash.

Another forerunner was French dj Caroline "<u>Miss Kittin</u>" Herve', who had recorded the EP **Champagne** (1998), a collaboration with Michael "The Hacker" Amato that included the pioneering hit *1982*. The duo joined the fad that they had pioneered with **First Album** (2001).

Britain was first exposed to electroclash when Liverpool's <u>Ladytron</u> released *He Took Her To A Movie* (1999), that was basically a cover of Kraftwerk's *The Model*. Next came Liverpool's <u>Robots In Disguise</u> with the EP **Mix Up Words and Sounds** (2000).

Canadian folksinger Merrill Nisker converted to punk-rock, joined the Shit with fellow provocateur Gonzales, adopted the aesthetic of the riot-grrrrls, enhanced it with a quasi-porn show, moved from Canada to Berlin armed with a drum-machine and a sampler, invented the persona of rapper <u>Peaches</u>, and recorded an album of sex-centric electronic dance music, **The Teaches Of Peaches** (2001), that basically set Blondie to the rhythm of Salt'n'Pepa and Liz Phair to the rhythm of digital hardcore.

German-USA-Australian trio <u>Chicks On Speed</u>, a product of Munich's school of art and also a fashion-design unit, offered an amusing take on alternative hip retro dance on **99 Cents** (2003).

German dj <u>Ellen "Allien"</u> Fraatz turned dance-music upside down on **Berlinette** (2003) with her recipe of psychotic vocals, glitchy electronica and crunchy beats.

Other notable electroclash albums of Britain were: the noisy and metal-tinged **For Screening Purposes Only** (2005) by the <u>Test Icicles</u>, featuring two USA-born members (one of which, guitarist Dev Hynes, black); <u>Hot Chip</u>'s **The Warning** (2006); **Attack Decay Sustain Release** (2007) by <u>Simian Mobile Disco</u> (James Ford and James Shaw); and **You Have No Idea What You're Getting Yourself Into** (2008) by <u>Does It Offend You, Yeah?</u>.

One of the most infectious albums of the dance-punk revival came from Montreal's <u>We Are Wolves</u>: **Non-Stop Je Te Plie en Deux** (2005).

Electroclash in the USA

There were many "first" electroclash singles in the USA, notably Adult's *Hand to Phone* (2001). The definition of the genre was vague enough that any energetic disco-influenced song could be classified as "electroclash".

Chicago's duo Fischerspooner spearheaded the movement with their throbbing Giorgio Moroder-esque single *Emerge* (2000) and the album **#1** (2002), containing several more of those imitations.

Electronic dance-punk-pop in the vein of the new wave was practiced in New York by Semiautomatic, for example on **The Trebuchet** (2001), replete with vintage keyboards and home-made instruments, and in Los Angeles by Dance Disaster Movement, a Los Angeles duo, on **We Are From Nowhere** (2003).

Oregon's Glass Candy harked back to Blondie's disco-punk on the mini-album **Love Love Love** (2003).

Las Vegas' Killers, fronted by vocalist and keyboardist Brandon Flowers, harked back to synth-pop of the 1980s with the singles *Mr. Brightside* (2003) and *Somebody Told Me* (2004).

New York's duo Ratatat (multi-instrumentalist Evan Mast and guitarist Mike Stroud) rediscovered "big beat" (the fusion of electronic beats and rock guitars propounded by the Chemical Brothers and Daft Punk) on **Ratatat** (2004), the main difference being that their catchy instrumental electronic rock was filtered through the personality of the laptop.

LCD Soundsystem (2), the project of James Murphy (half of New York's production duo DFA or Death From Above with Tim Goldsworthy), was initially a futile exercise in rehashing beats, melodies and arrangements of the past like most of the electroclash output, as documented on the double-CD **LCD Soundsystem** (2005). However, its follow-up **Sound of Silver** (2007) asserted the primacy of the producer over the performers, and James Murphy proved to be one of the few artists since Brian Eno who could make the masses both dance and rock. And the 45-minute incidental suite *45:33* offered an encyclopedic survey of electronic dance music.

At the peak of the fad, Clap Your Hands Say Yeah became a sensation with **Clap Your Hands Say Yeah** (2005).

Ironically, it was the Scissor Sisters, emerging from the alternative queer scene of New York, who became the best-selling act of the whole movement with **Scissor Sisters** (2004) and **Ta-Dah** (2006). But they were pushing the electroclash movement towards a more superficial revival of glam-rock and disco-music.

Late comers included New York's duo MGMT (Andrew Vanwyngarden and Ben Goldwasser), who took inspiration from disco-music and synth-pop for **Oracular Spectacular** (2008).

Capitalizing on an old idea by Coldcut, Pennsylvania-based laptop musician Gregg Gillis, disguised under the moniker Girl Talk, offered hyperkinetic and hyperdemented "plunderphonics" for the dancefloor (in other words, infectious dance music created from snippets of old pop hits) on a series of albums starting with **Secret Diary** (2002) and peaking with **Night Ripper** (2006).

Disco revival

Acts such as LCD Soundsystem and the Scissor Sisters were part of a general revival of the Euro-disco format of the 1970s.

New York-based Osunlade had offered an original revision of disco-music with the Afro-spiritual hybrid of deep house, soul, jazz and world-music debuted on **Paradigm** (2001).

Norwegian producer Hans-Peter Lindstrom (1) rediscovered Giorgio Moroder's cosmic disco-music starting with the sleek hypnosis of *I Feel Space* (2005) and peaking with the 29-minute psychonaut *Where You Go To I Go Too*, off **Where You Go I Go Too** (2008).

French dj Pascal "Vitalic" Arbez concocted an original take on disco-music with **OK Cowboy** (2005).

French duo Justice (Xavier de Rosnay and Gaspard Auge), revealed by the singles *Never Be Alone* (2004) and *Waters of Nazareth* (2005), specialized in catchy, pounding and lushly-arranged retro-sounding house music for analog keyboards, leaning towards Daft Punk's "big beat" on **Cross** (2007).

Australia's Cut Copy (Dan Whitford) set the orchestral pop of **In Ghost Colours** (2008) to a retro-disco beat and then added the rock guitar in disorienting manners.

Hercules And Love Affair injected a childish optimism (in a genre that had been largely hijacked by the DFA-influenced neo-existentialist crowd) with the effervescent dance jams of **Hercules And Love Affair** (2008).

The Return of Funk-punk

The Talking Heads and underground acts like the Contortions and ESG, that established a credible format of funk-punk fusion in the early 1980s, exerted the biggest influence on the new generation.

Rapture (1), reborn in New York under the supervision of production duo DFA, turned dance-music into a self-flagellation process with the mini-album **Out Of The Races And Onto The Tracks** (2001) and the album **Echoes** (2003). The most successful songs achieved a disturbing sense of alienation and frustration by staging rituals that, as in the most orthodox new-wave aesthetics, were supposed to be hedonistic but turned out to be the opposite.

Out Hud (1), formed in Sacramento (California) by keyboardist Justin Vandervolgen, guitarist Tyler Pope and bassist Nic Offer, ranked among the earliest and most creative members of the funk-punk movement.

The conceptual centerpiece of the all-instrumental monster revisionist **Street Dad** (2002) was the twelve-minute *The L Train is a Swell Train and I Don't Want to Hear You Indies Complain*, a syncopated and tribal techno ballet that mixed oneiric guitar tones, industrial-grade panzer rhythms and a symphony of quirky background noises.

Their offshoot !!! (1), featuring the same core trio of Vandervolgen, Pope and Offer (and pronounced "chik chik chik"), concocted even more savage hybrids, such as the nine-minute *There's No Fucking Rules Dude*, off !!! (2002), contaminated with psychedelic, hip-hop, dissonant and ska elements, and the relentlessly mutating funk machine of *Me And Giuliani Down By the School Yard* (2003), off the eponymous EP. Their mission was to set up and trigger deranged groove-driven workouts that sounded like parodies but actually constituted the new avantgarde. A more austere and at times even gloomy tone permeated the hypnotic and orgiastic dance music of **Louden Up Now** (2004). While Out Hud delivered the thumping feverish eleven-minute techno locomotive *Dear Mr Bush There are Over 100 Words for Shit and Only 1 for Music* on **Let Us Never Speak Of It Again** (2005), !!! indulged in breakneck multi-layered collage-like dance numbers on **Myth Takes** (2007). The overall feeling of these albums was closer to a psychoanalysis of the post-industrial digital world than to a nostalgic reminiscence of the pre-digital era.

Erase Errata (1), four riot-grrrrls from San Francisco, harked back to the most savage purveyors of funk-punk (such as the Pop Group) for **Other Animals** (2001), showcasing hysterical vocals, dissonant guitar, stormy keyboards and torrential rhythms. **Nightlife** (2006) even showed that the stylistic spectrum was far from narrow.

The Numbers, a trio from San Francisco formed by vocalist and drummer Indra Dunis, guitarist Dave Broekema and keyboardist Eric Landmark, played neurotic robotic dance-punk, especially on **In My Mind All The Time** (2004).

Washington's Black Eyes (1) emulated the percussive nightmares of the Girls Vs Boys on **Black Eyes** (2003) thanks to two drummers and two bassists, but the chaotic structures, the funk undercurrents and the jazz shadowing harked back to Rip Rig & Panic.

English duo Mu (USA-born deep-house producer Maurice Foulton and Japanese-born vocalist Mutsumi Kanamori) adopted the deviant jazzy funk-punk of the Rip Rig & Panic tradition on **Afro Finger and Gel** (2003).

The Return of minimal techno

The Cologne school of ambient techno (Gas, Markus Guentner, etc) found a natural heir in Yagya, the project of Icelandic producer Aalsteinn Gumundsson, on **The Rhythm of Snow** (2002).

Polmo Polpo (Toronto-based producer Sandro Perri) fused minimal techno, droning textures and cello melodies on **The Science Of Breath** (2002).

Scottish dj Alex Smoke (Alex Menzies) practiced a nocturnal fusion of minimal techno and glitch music on **Incommunicando** (2005).

The Coldest Season (2007) by Echospace, the duo of Chicago-area producers Rod Modell and Steve "Soultek" Hitchell, performed on old-fashioned analog devices, sounded like a tribute to German minimal techno of the late 1990s.

Another milestone for minimal techno was **From Here We Go Sublime** (2007) by Field, the project of Swedish producer Axel Willner. Its blissful pieces owed more to collage, ambient and psychedelic styles than to the original minimal techno.

Rockers

Eastern rockers

Jon Spencer Blues Explosion's influence (loud and sloppy garage-blues) was still felt throughout the country, as proven by the Immortal Lee County Killers in Alabama with **The Essential Fuck-Up Blues** (2001); the Black Keys in Ohio with **The Big Come Up** (2002); and by the Kills in Florida, playing the version popularized by the White Stripes on **No Wow** (2005).

The Fiery Furnaces (4), formed by Matthew Friedberger and Eleanor Friedberger, siblings from Chicago who relocated to New York, exhibited a versatile and multi-faceted style on **Gallowsbird's Bark** (2003). Anti-crooning vocals and spiked guitar riffs as well as wildly unstable dynamics evoked the Rolling Stones at their most drunken/deranged, or Captain Beefheart's Magic Band fronted by Janis Joplin. At the same time the exuberant neglect of their arrangements was reminiscent of Pere Ubu. **Blueberry Boat** (2004) stretched out into longer and more ambitious songs, collages of genres and tours de force of arrangement (including electronic keyboards) that were meant to create a new form of musical theater. That form came to life on **Rehearsing My Choir** (2005), a work structured as a dialogue between an older woman and a younger one over a substratum of eccentric and cacophonous sounds. The concept was basically a suburban white folks' version of the concept of hip-hop music: analyzing life aloud against an atmospheric soundscape. Here the soundscape was the musical equivalent of hyper-neurosis, while mostly childish, spartan and even cartoonish. The shift towards the vocals continued on the even more bizarre **Bitter Tea** (2006), on which the arrangements (including greater doses of electronic noise and quaint keyboards) were inherently tied to the way the voice derailed the melody. The proceedings betrayed the influence of the futuristic vaudeville of the "Cabaret Voltaire" and to Brecht's technique of "estrangement". **Widow City** (2007), instead, marked a return to a linear, extroverted and fluid form of expression.

Breakneck garage-rock albums such as **Roitan** (2004) by Mississippi's Roitan kept alive the tradition of raw and visceral rock'n'roll.

Crude atonality and an amazing bad taste devastated **Let It Bloom** (2005), the third album by Georgia's Black Lips (1).

Heroine Sheiks, formed by the Cows' vocalist Shannon Selberg and the Swans' guitarist Norman Westberg, played confrontational rock music on **Rape On The Installment Plan** (2001) and **Siamese Pipe** (2002), sounding like the Swans playing wild Cows-ian romps or the Cows playing brainy noise-rock.

Detroit's glorious tradition of the Stooges and MC5 survived in the primal visceral rock'n'roll of the first two albums by Baltimore's Vincent

Black Shadow: **Vincent Black Shadow** (2006) and **More Deeper** (2008).

Georgia's duo Jucifer (vocalist and guitarist Amber Valentine and drummer Edgar Livengood) juxtaposed lumbering, distorted, pummeling, crushing doom-grunge and ethereal female vocals on **Calling All Cars On The Vegas Strip** (1999) and especially **I Name You Destroyer** (2002), sounding like the Melvins fronted by a daydreaming girl.

At least two combos from England were successful at revisiting both vintage garage-rock of the 1960s and punk-rock of the 1970s: Art Brut on **Bang Bang Rock & Roll** (2005), and Ikara Colt on **Chat And Business** (2002) and **Modern Apprentice** (2004). They were angrier, nastier and noisier than the average.

In Advance Of The Broken Arm (2007) by New York's guitarist Marnie Stern was a romp through heavy-metal, punk-rock, garage-rock and noise-rock filtered through the sensibility of the new wave of the 1970s. Not quite an intellectual singer-songwriter a` la Patti Smith (although as possessed a singer as her), Stern had to rely on an intricate abrasive guitar attack to bestow meaning on her songs.

Texas' trio White Denim favored the jerky, sloppy and punkish garage-rock pioneered by Jon Spencer but augmented it with artful moves worthy of the new wave and even post-rock on **Workout Holiday** (2008).

Western rockers

The main heirs to the glorious tradition of Northwestern garage-rock were the Hunches from Oregon, whose **Yes No Shut It** (2002) and **Hobo Sunrise** (2004) were the sonic equivalent of a carpet bombing campaign.

Thermals, also from Oregon, opted for a poppier sound on **The Body The Blood The Machine** (2006), a political concept album.

Garage-blues was dominated by Seattle's Gossip, unrivaled with the 24-minute 14-song album **That's Not What I Heard** (2001) and the EP **Arkansas Heat**.

California had the most innovative groups.

San Francisco's Coachwhips (1) took the cliche' of distorted garage-rock to the punk-rock extremes of the raucous frenzied orgy that was **Get Yer Body Next Ta Mine** (2003).

Los Angeles' duo No Age (1) coined a new hybrid of noise, punk and pop based on distortions and drones on **Nouns** (2008). No Age were the leaders of the "Smell-generation", named after the club in Los Angeles that launched them. Fellow "Smell" alumni Abe Vigoda attempted an unlikely marriage of new wave, shoegazing and Caribbean music on **Kid City** (2007) and especially **Skeleton** (2008).

In San Diego the saga of Drive Like Jehu and Rocket From The Crypt was continued by the bands formed by guitarist John Reis, notably the Sultans, although the punk-rock of **Shipwrecked** (2004) was more cerebral than visceral.

Stoners and space-rockers

Washington's stoners Dead Meadow (1) mixed hypnotic litanies and noisy jams on **Feathers** (2004).

Vancouver-based stoners Black Mountain spiced the retro-psychedelic hard-rock of **Black Mountain** (2005) and **In the Future** (2008) with vocal harmonies a` la Jefferson Airplane.

The Red Sparowes, formed by Isis' guitarist Bryant Meyer and bassist Jeff Caxide and based in Los Angeles, summed up two or three schools of the 1990s with the super-heavy post-shoegaze instrumental progressive-rock of **At The Soundless Dawn** (2005).

San Diego's instrumental power-trio Earthless, fronted by guitarist Isaiah Mitchell, devoted its first albums **Sonic Prayer** (2005) and **Rhythms From A Cosmic Sky** (2007) to progressive guitar-heavy stoner-rock suites, two per album, peaking with the five-movement *Godspeed*, off the second one.

Santa Cruz's Mammatus gave stoner-rock a philosophical dimension with the massive and kaleidoscopic suite *Dragon of the Deep*, a spiritual concept influenced by progressive and folk music, whose first two parts dominated **Mammatus** (2006) and whose third part appeared on the more varied **The Coast Explodes** (2007).

Los Angeles' stoners Ancestors debuted with the two sprawling groove-based acid jams of **Neptune With Fire** (2008).

Kentucky's power-trio Cadaver in Drag unleashed the guitar-driven mayhem over pummeling drums of **Raw Child** (2007) with industrial and doom-metal overtones.

Finland's Tivol offered a sloppy compendium of garage-rock, stoner-rock and space-rock with the kaleidoscopic jams of the mini-albums **Breathtaking Sounds** (2003), **Cyclobean Ways** (2004) and **Teema: Laskipaa** (2004).

Pharaoh Overlord, an all-instrumental side-project by Circle's guitarist Jussi Lehtisalo, achieved a hypnotic balance of stoner-rock and progressive-rock on **#3** (2005).

Argentina boasted a lively scene of stoner-rock, with Buffalo's Kyuss-inspired **Temporada de Huracanes** (2004) and Dragonauta's doom and trash orgy of **Luciferatu** (2003) leading the way.

Metal-heads

At the beginning of 2008 the "Metal Archives" website (http://www.metal-archives.com) listed 66,012 heavy-metal bands. There was no other musical genres that had fostered so many musicians. Each and every of metal's fringe subgenres was splintering in many new directions. The truly prominent bands were more interested in creating hybrids out of the fashionable attitudes of the 1990s; and metalcore was the most popular.

Metalcore, that wed heavy-metal's bombast and hardcore's rage, ruled the airwaves. Los Angeles' Avenged Sevenfold (1) bridged the gap between gothic rock, glam-punk and metalcore with **Sounding the Seventh Trumpet** (2001). Atreyu followed a similar strategy while contrasting snarling punk vocals and clear poppy vocals on **Suicide Notes and Butterfly Kisses** (2002) while investing in dual-guitar harmonies. These two bands conquered the post-emo masses with, respectively, the charming mess of **City Of Evil** (2005) and the catchy and retro **The Curse** (2004).

Boston (that had nurtured the first generation of punk-metal fusion) was a particularly fertile terrain, boasting bands such as Unearth, with **The Stings of Conscience** (2001), and All That Remains, with **Behind Silence And Solitude** (2002). Boston's Killswitch Engage (1) updated metalcore to the age of emo on **Alive or Just Breathing** (2002). And San Diego's As I Lay Dying updated speed-metal to the age of metalcore with their third album **Shadows Are Security** (2005).

Michigan's Black Dahlia Murder transcended metalcore on **Unhallowed** (2003) and **Miasma** (2005) by cross-fertilizing the acrobatic technique of death-metal and the emotional melody of black metal, a schizophrenia epitomized by the dual vocals, a black-metal shriek and a death-metal growl.

Following a decade-old intuition by Dying Fetus, bands such as San Francisco's All Shall Perish, with **Hate Malice Revenge** (2003), and Arizona's Job For A Cowboy, with the EP **Doom** (2005), popularized death-core, a style fusing elements of metalcore (e.g., breakdowns) and death-metal (blastbeats, shrieks), basically death-metal without the "death" themes in the lyrics. The legions of deathcore bands included Los Angeles' Suicide Silence, with **The Cleansing** (2007), and Tennessee's Whitechapel, with **The Somatic Defilement** (2007).

Canada's Protest The Hero coined an original and technical form of progressive metalcore on the Kafkian concept album **Kezia** (2006) and on the schizophrenic **Fortress** (2008).

Outside metalcore there were all kinds of crossbreds. Los Angeles' duo Black Cobra blended elements of stoner, doom-metal and grindcore thanks to abrasive vocals and seismic guitar (Jason Landrian) and manic drumming (Rafael Martinez) on **Bestial** (2006). Los Angeles' Otep (1) played gothic funk-metal on **Sevas Tra** (2002), a concentrate of expressionistic nightmares. Silentist (Oregon-based pianist Mark-Evan

Burden) concocted an insane hybrid of post-classical music, free-jazz and grindcore on **Silentist** (2008).

However, the old-fashioned stately 1980s sound of Judas Priest and Iron Maiden, already exhumed in the 1990s by the Lord Weird Slough Feg, staged a comeback with albums such as **Advance and Vanquish** (2004) by Vancouver's 3 Inches Of Blood, **Closing In** (2005) by Ohio's Early Man, **Brutality- Majesty- Eternity** (2006) by Chicago's Bible Of The Devil, etc.

Witchcraft, who debuted with **Witchcraft** (2004), led the contingent of Swedish bands that adopted a retro sound harking back to hard-rock of the 1970s; and not only Black Sabbath, but also Jethro Tull.

Britain witnessed a rebirth of the folkish pagan variant of black metal with Winterfylleth's **Ghost of Heritage** (2008) and Fen's **The Malediction Fields** (2009).

Technical metal-heads

Others focused on technical prowess, and that's where the most relevant contributions of the decade were to be found.

Washington-based duo Orthrelm (1), i.e. Quix*o*tic's bassist Mick Barr (now on guitar) and drummer Josh Blair (a member of avantgarde ensemble ABCs), followed the 99-track 13-minute EP **Asristir Vieldriox** (2002), of a hardly recognizable metalcore sub-style, with the 45-minute suite of **OV** (2005). Through the unlikely marriage of grindcore speed and minimalist repetition, this piece represented the relentless, dense and tense soundtrack to a tortured stream of consciousness.

Georgia's Mastodon (2), featuring former Today Is The Day's guitarist Bill Kelliher and drummer Brann Dailor (one of the most versatile drummers of heavy metal), debuted their cerebral, convoluted metal music on **Remission** (2002). Influenced by Dillinger Escape Plan and Meshuggah, they devised a unique fusion of stoner-rock, jazz-rock and southern boogie. The concept album **Leviathan** (2004), a work of relentless intensity but also slicker production, indulged in lightning-speed guitar improvisations, tempo-free drumming, and noisy, intricate counterpoint.

Pennsylvania's Commit Suicide played a hyper-technical form of "death-grind" metal on **Human Larvae Earthly Cleansing** (2002) and **Synthetics** (2004).

Georgia's Canvas Solaris espoused an acrobatic and intricate instrumental fusion of death-metal, industrial music and post-rock on **Sublimation** (2004) and **Penumbra Diffuse** (2006).

New York state's PsyOpus played brutal, frantic and intricate post-metal on **Ideas of Reference** (2004).

Anaal Nathrakh (the British duo of vocalist Dave "V.I.T.R.I.O.L." Hunt and multi-instrumentalist Mick "Irrumator" Kenney) topped the most extreme forms of black metal on **The Codex Necro** (2001): insanely loud and frantic drums, tortured keyboards, rudely-distorted riffs, studio-processed psychotic vocals, and deranged electronic ambience.

Italy's school of prog-metal continued to hatch new ideas. Ephel Duath, the brainchild of guitarist Davide Tiso, achieved one of the most brilliant fusions of jazz and metal on their second album **The Painter's Palette** (2003). Kailash resurrected Opeth's progressive black metal on **Kailash** (2007). Thee Maldoror Kollective bridged black metal and industrial music via digital noise, beats and samples on the gothic concept **New Era Viral Order** (2002).

Goths

By the end of the 1990s, black metal had become one of the most popular genres in rock music. However the stereotypical elements of black metal (buzz, distortion, growls, blastbeats) were limiting the imagination of its practitioners.

Black metal had also become one of the most personal and (ironically) introverted genres of the age, because so many of its purveyors were one-man bands who locked themselves in their bedroom with a drum-machine, a guitar and a tape recorder. In fact, the hiss of lo-fi recording equipment had become an integral part of the stereotype of black metal.

Marduk's blazing style of black metal was continued by groups such as Norway's 1349 with the raw no-frills **Liberation** (2003). Norway's Khold, instead, opted for melodic midtempo black metal on their second album **Phantom** (2002).

In the USA black metal was dominated by the West-coast scene, a scene started in the 1990s by Weakling and the Lord Weird Slough Feg in San Francisco.

Los Angeles' one-man band Xasthur (Scott Conner) adopted an agonizing midtempo, a wall of sound, synthesizers and low-fi production on the EPs **A Darkened Winter** (2001) and **Suicide in Dark Serenity** (2003). Their second album **Nocturnal Poisoning** (2002) sounded like the equivalent of dream-pop for black metal, or ambient music for heavy-metal sounds.

San Francisco's one-man band Draugar (Tim Lehi) penned the blacker atmosphere of **From Which Hatred Grows** (2003), and inspired another local one-man band, Crebain, who debuted with **Night Of Stormcrow** (2007).

The hypnotic extended jams of Seattle's Wolves In The Throne Room such as the ones on **Diadem Of 12 Stars** (2006) and **Two Hunters**

(2007), employed the same technique of blastbeats and repetitive riffs of Weakling, adding electronic drones and prog-rock touches.

Neo-goths

On the other hand, Chicago's Nachtmystium marked the movement away from black metal and towards a sound that incorporated catchy melodies and psychedelic passages, especially with their third album **Instinct Decay** (2006).

And it was in Chicago that one-man band Light Shall Prevail spearheaded Christian black metal (also called "white metal", already pioneered by Trouble in the 1980s), that was neither hateful nor nihilistic, with the lo-fi, convoluted, trippy **Defeat The Reign Of The Horned One Through The Light Of Christ** (2006) and with the mini-album **Unearthen Hymns Of Revolt** (2007), that boasted even more warped vocals and more spastic drum-machines. That school (and that very man) also yielded Agathothodion's sprawling midtempo jams of **Kan Guds Gjort** (2007), and Flaskavsae's **Philosophies** (2007), buried into dense, thick droning hurricanes. Njiqahdda (1), another project by the same musician, was hardly black metal at all: post-rock dynamics (augmented with repetitions, overdubs and loops) and psychedelic spatiotemporal warping (with riffs, vocals and beats seemingly coming from a parallel dimension) altered the drums-driven pieces, and the drum-less pieces were just dark ambient music. The split personality of the project was evident from the double-disc **Njimajikal Arts** (2007), the first disc devoted to post-doom metal amd the second disc devoted to static music, and the extra-metal ambitions were also on display with the 53-minute dark ambient piece of **Fortu Manske Orta** (2007), credited to Njiijn, and the 29-minute super-droning *Nostri Di Consivint Mek*, off **Almare Dosegaas Fyaltu** (2007).

There were signs of renewal also in the "redneck" states of the South. Texan quartet Bahimiron played devastating acid metal (like Gorgoroth's hysterical black metal via Butthole Surfers and Texan garage-rock) on their second album **Southern Nihilizm** (2008), whose title was an apt manifesto. North Carolina's one-man band Jabladav contaminated its black metal with post-rock and ambient drones on **Black As Pitch** (2007).

Oregon-based guitarist Eldrig VanSee wed soaring quasi-shoegazing guitar tapestry, neoclassical keyboards and thrash rhythms on **Everlasting War Divinity** (2007).

San Francisco-based Mamaleek achieved a tense hybrid of black-metal frenzy, industrial syncopation, shoegazing distortion and dark ambience on **Mamaleek** (2008), notably the 18-minute *Shout On Children*, and on the jazzier and denser **Fever Dream** (2008).

The Meads of Asphodel, from Britain, contaminated midtempo black metal with pop hooks, psychedelic keyboards, electronic effects and programmed beats on **Exhuming The Grave Of Yeshua** (2003).

Swiss guitar trio (no drums) Darkspace (1), featuring Tobias Moeckl of Paysage D'Hiver, were master purveyors of "ambient black metal". **I** (2003) juxtaposed the noise of manic guitars and drum-machines (the blastbeats being inconsequential for the tempo and merely contributing to the mayhem) with droning ecstasy to paint an alien soundscape. The three juggernauts of **II** (2005) alternated between a thick droning fog to sudden downpours of chaotic noise, a tactic very similar to electronic cosmic music.

At the same time that he endorsed the most suicidal overtones of masters such as Katatonia, Sweden's guitarist Kim Carlsson also attacked the very foundations of black metal by adopting a broader range of vocals, clean guitar riffs and post-rock dynamics both with his band Lifelover on **Pulver** (2006) and alone under the moniker Hypothermia, for example in the two repetitive minimal suites of **Kold** (2006).

Another purveyor of Katatonia-style suicidal black metal was the Danish musician disguised under the moniker Make A Change Kill Yourself, who unfurled the four colossal agonies of **Make A Change Kill Yourself** (2005) and the two suites of **II** (2007).

Nagelfar's drummer Alexander von Meilenwald launched the Ruins Of Beverast (1) to further explore the darkest aspects of Nagelfar's sound. While **Unlock The Shrine** (2004) already represented a peak of horror, the ambient doom-black dirges of **Rain Upon The Impure** (2006) stood as one of the most nightmarish moments in the history of the genre.

The Ruins of Beverast had basically founded a German school that soon numbered Kermania, whose black metal on **Ahnenwerk** (2007) was both grandiose and folkish.

Germany's Ekpyrosis debuted with the 30-minute piece of **Mensch Aus Gold** (2008) at the border between post-rock and black metal.

French progressive goths

Black metal was not born as a genre that easily allows musicians to come up with original variations. France was the one place where bands were capable of adding ever new ideas to the paradigm.

French duo Spektr (1), consisting of a guitarist and a drummer (but both also on programming and sampling), conceived **Et Fugit Intera Fugit Irreparabile Tempus** (2004) as a collage of industrial (frequently pushed to the limit of abstract noise), ambient (thick floating drones) and post-rock (indulging in extreme shifts of dynamics) elements from which only occasionally did blastbeats of black metal emerge. If that was a music of wild contrasts, **Near Death Experience** (2006) smoothed out the contrasts and was reduced to musique concrete with distant echoes of heavy metal. The stylistic implosion reached the nadir with the mini-album **Mescalyne** (2008) and its nightmarish hallucinations set in a desolate wasteland of sonic debris.

French duo Nuit Noire indulged in clownish, amateurish, punkish metal on **Lunar Deflagration** (2004).

Amesoeurs blended ecstatic shoegaze-rock and blasting black metal on the EP **Ruines Humaines** (2006). Alcest, on the other hand, almost completely jettisoned the metal component and basically returned to the sound of My Bloody Valentine on **Souvenirs D'un Autre Monde** (2007). Bands like these contributed to coin a "metalgaze" sub-sub-genre.

Peste Noire's originality on **La Sanie des Siecles** (2006) lay in the atmospheric touches.

Aluk Todolo, instead, assembled an unpredictable parade of industrial and post-rock events on **Descension** (2007).

The impact of post-rock's non-linear, convoluted, cryptic dynamics was felt on Glorior Belli's second album **Manifesting The Raging Beast** (2008).

French-Canadian duo Gris played Burzum-inspired black metal that was folkish, dreamy chamber music on **Neurasthenie** (2006) and **Il Etait Une Foret** (2007).

Another French-Canadian duo, Forteresse, delivered a "national" manifesto of sorts, **Metal Noir Quebecois** (2006).

Lo-fi demons

One of the most exciting additions to the canon of heavy metal came from the ranks of black metal. A number of bands played a music that was filthy, malevolent and sloppy while being raw, amateurish and stripped-down and while being heavily distorted and buzz-drenched. This had been the formula of garage-rock since the beginnings of rock'n'roll. Therefore these bands de facto offered a fusion of both the ethos and the sound of garage-rock and black metal. Songs were characterized by a snarling, pounding, atonal, lascivious appearance. They exuded a ferociously negative attitude.

Canadian duo Akitsa harked back to the guitar-heavy tradition of black metal with the manically droning riffs, hysterical shrieking and relentless pounding of **Goetie** (2001). But their successors rapidly abandoned the guitar as the main instrument.

Influenced by Ildjarn, the Australian one-man band Striborg was perhaps the most prolific purveyor of "lo-fi black metal" of the 2000s, with a sound dominated by keyboards and drums. **Mysterious Semblance** (2004), that contains the 20-minute *Mysterious Semblance Of Spectral Trees*, and **Spiritual Catharsis** (2004), that contains the 13-

minute *Spiritual Catharsis*, defined his routine of electronic ambience, drum-machine beats and fuzzed-out doom.

Australian outfit Portal (1) delivered the droning and cacophonous **Seepia** (2003), one of the most original death-metal albums since Gorguts, an evil symphony of squealing metallic guitars and spastic blasting drumming performed inside a forest of sound effects. **Outre** (2007) was less chaotic but more nightmarish, focusing their superhuman firepower and technique on building up a sheer sense of terror.

From here it was all downhill towards higher and higher degrees of mayhem.

Oregon's Velvet Cacoon (1) unleashed a claustrophonic orchestral squall of monster fuzz drones on **Genevieve** (2004), although it also included an extended horror-ambient piece (*Bete Noir*).

Canadian trio Wold (1) hid eerie melodies in the barrage of melodic repetitive keyboards, programmed beats and shoegazing guitars of **L.O.T.M.P.** (2005), approaching Japanese noisecore via ambient electronica on **Screech Owl** (2007) and, pared down to a duo, on the equally disturbing **Stratification** (2008).

Bone Awl, a San Francisco-based duo of guitar and drums, played black metal that bordered on white noise on **Meaningless Leaning Mess** (2007) and the EP **Undying Glare** (2007).

The Mausoleums from Chicago bridged the fury of black metal and the ambition of post-metal. **I Am The Mausoleum** (2007) explored an unlikely wedding of raw metal bordering on Japanese noisecore and intellectual metal bordering on post-rock.

Australian one-man band Nekrasov (1) managed to produce a furious and manic sound while experimenting with a broad spectrum of avantgarde techniques on **Into The No-Man's Sphere Of The Ancient Days** (2007), with ambient and industrial elements colliding with his black-metal roots and with abstract vocals that approach the noise of the guitar. **The Form Of Thought From Beast** (2008) matched the debut's ambitions with the progressive and psychedelic 20-minute juggernaut *The Form Of Thought From Beast*.

Lo-fi practitioners in Finland included Circle Of Ouroborus, with the sloppy and dissonant **Shores** (2006), and Vordr, with **I** (2004). Dead Reptile Shrine churned out **A Journey Through The Darkest Of Forests** (2005), a chaotic and dissonant mixture of folk and metal with a horror-industrial-psychedelic attitude.

Dutch duo Urfaust filled the black-metal nightmares of **Geist ist Teufel** (2004) with all sorts of grotesque events. **Verraterischer Nichtswurdiger Geist** (2005) was even dominated by droning ambient music.

Doomsayers

Of the genres of the 1990s, doom-metal had perhaps left the strongest mark on the new century. In the 2000s this (apparently) most narrow-minded of all narrow-minded subgenres managed to split into many new sub-subgenres.

Finland's Reverend Bizarre were the most faithful worshippers of the gospel of Black Sabbath and St Vitus with their defiantly repetitive and monotonous exposition of the most sinister doom stereotypes (cadaveric tempos, earth-shattering bass lines, crushing guitar riffs) over gargantuan-length pieces, notably the ones of **In the Rectory of the Bizarre Reverend** (2002).

Boston's drums and guitar duo 5ive played brutal, distorted doom-metal on **The Telestic Disfracture** (2001).

Khanate (3), a supergroup formed in New York by bassist James Plotkin, Sunn O)))'s guitarist Stephen O'Malley, Blind Idiot God's drummer Tim Wyskida and Old's hysterical vocalist Alan Dubin, turned the lengthy hypnotic jams of **Khanate** (2002) into a festival of massive sustained distortions, magniloquent passages and funereal litanies. A lot more suspense went into the four expressionistic psychodramas and harrowing soundscapes of **Things Viral** (2003). This art of silence, distortion and screams was refined manically by the two lengthy ceremonies of **Capture & Release** (2005). Their best monoliths achieved a psychological synthesis: the agony of a damned soul, the hallucination of a heroin addict and the extreme blank of a suicide bomber all combined together.

Aethenor was a collaboration among Sunn O)))'s Stephen O'Malley, Guapo's pianist/percussionist Daniel O'Sullivan and keyboardist Vincent DeRoguin (of Swiss metal band Shora) devoted to magniloquent doom metal, whose debut **Deep In Ocean Sunk The Lamp of Light** (2006), was a four-movement ambient-psychedelic-jazz-gothic symphony.

Florida's Torche reinvented pop-metal or grunge or both for the generation that had been raised on doom-metal. They sounded like a super-heavy version of Nirvana on **Torche** (2005) and **Meanderthal** (2008), packing catchy bubblegum melodies into bombshells of massive distorted riffs and seismic drumming.

Britain's Marzuraan tried to inject a romantic feeling (via melancholy melodies a` la slo-core) into droning doom-metal on **Solid Wood** (2006).

Britain's Atavist mixed doom-metal, stoner-rock, pop melody and free noise on **Atavist** (2006).

Post-doomsayers

The marriage of post-rock and doom-metal spawned yet another subgenre of heavy metal, largely inspired by Neurosis and Isis. Mostly instrumental and frequently incorporating keyboards, this was the mutation of prog-metal after the deluge of post-rock.

Swedish septet <u>Cult of Luna</u> played a creative form of metalcore on **Cult of Luna** (2001) that evolved into the synthesizer-tinged spleen of **Salvation** (2004) and **Somewhere Along the Highway** (2006), two albums drenched in shoegazing guitars.

Georgia's duo <u>Angelic Process</u> buried the aching lullabies of **Coma Waering** (2006) and **Weighing Souls With Sand** (2007) in a thick layer of blissful "shoegazing" guitars and slow-motion industrial rhythms.

Chicago's instrumental combo <u>Pelican</u> (1) gave spectacular essays in droning metal with the four terrifying pieces of the 30-minute EP **Pelican** (2003) and the stately counterpoint of drones and jagged, discordant passages of the album **Australasia** (2003).

The "post-doom" generation was heralded by Chicago's <u>Buried At Sea</u> with the three untitled pieces of **Migration** (2003), whose subliminal funereal style was later revisited in the 29-minute suite of the mini-album **Ghosts** (2007).

Maine's <u>Conifer</u> coupled the brainy dynamics of post-rock with the massive riffs of doom metal on **Conifer** (2004).

<u>Baroness</u>, hailing from Georgia, created one of the most eclectic fusions of elements on the EPs **First** (2004) and **Second** (2005) as well as on the album **Red Album** (2007). Each song was a kaleidoscope of infectious melodies, post-rock alienation, metalcore fury, stoner languor, cerebral drumming and electronic veneer.

Ohio's <u>Mouth Of The Architect</u> were the most obvious transposition into doom-metal of Godspeed You Black Emperor. **Time & Withering** (2004) was majestic and melodic despite the onslaught that devastated the lengthy, intricate and slow-building pieces.

<u>Minsk</u>, from Chicago, detonated **Out Of A Center Which Is Neither Dead Nor Alive** (2005), reminiscent of the heavy brooding psychedelic ambient doom of Isis with the addition of viscous, rumbling and droning electronic keyboards.

The tone of **Resurface** (2005) by Boston's <u>Tides</u> was mournful and solemn, with occasional dreamy/psychedelic detours, a balance of moods and dynamics that peaked with *In Their Arms*, from the EP **From Silence** (2006).

Maine's <u>Ocean</u> specialized in lengthy, slow and funereal pieces, such as the three on **Here Where Nothing Grows** (2005) and especially the two juggernauts of **Pantheon Of The Lesser** (2008), that followed the aesthetics of "ebb and flow" to mutate into psychological monsters.

Philadelphia's <u>Rosetta</u> (1) appropriately split the dense and intense **The Galilean Satellites** (2005) into a disc of crushing doom-metal songs and a disc of atmospheric and convoluted abstractions, and made them sound like they were two sides of the same coin. **Wake/ Lift** (2007) wed the fury of metalcore and the brain of industrial-metal to churn out brutal, frantic, sprawling and huge musical monoliths of apocalyptic doom.

Missouri's Warhammer 48K packed their hyper-kinetic extravaganza **Uber Om** (2006) with all sorts of abrupt shifts and crazy inventions.

England's quintet Hey Colossus packaged a three-pronged guitar attack into a hypnotic, funereal, loud, distorted fusion of doom-metal and Neu-like "motorik" rhythm on the mini-album **Hates You** (2004). Post-rock dynamics matched the trancey quality of their sound on **II** (2005), creating an even stranger (but no less "heavy") hybrid. Death-metal and white noise further destabilized **Project Death** (2007), whose harsher moments bordered on pummelling noisecore.

Hlidolf (1) (the project of Norwegian multi-instrumentalist Vidar Ermesjo) created a haunting all-instrumental blend of doom-metal a` la Earth, gothic electronica a` la Lustmord and cosmic music a` la Klaus Schulze with the 69-minute piece of **V01d** (2002).

Sweden's Funeral Mist managed to achieve both extremely pummeling speed and extremely dense heaviness on **Salvation** (2003).

Germany's Ocean Collective (1), conducted by Robin Staps and featuring multiple guitars and multiple vocalists, engineered one of the biggest sounds of their time on the double album that was released as two separate albums, **Fluxion** (2004), containing the "orchestral" pieces, and **Aeolian** (2005), devoted to hard-hitting songs. Keyboards and string section interfered with the bombast of riffs and growls. The schizophrenia worsened on the double-disc **Precambrian** (2007), one (short) disc being permeated by dissonant metalcore fury while the other disc indulged in ambient/progressive detours.

Dutch one-man band Gnaw Their Tongues (1) elaborated a hybrid of hellish shrieks, doom hypnosis, guitar noise, snippets of horror soundtracks, industrial drumming, electronic glitches and orchestral samples on the albums **Reeking Pained And Shuddering** (2007) and **An Epiphanic Vomiting Of Blood** (2007).

Australian duo Halo (drummer Robert Allen and bassist Skye Klein, also the brain behind Terminal Sound System) resurrected the ghosts of early Swans and Godflesh on **Guattari** (2001): sedate cyclopean drumming and industrial-grade bass lines regurgitating lava-like feedback that combined to create a disorienting sense of absence.

Australia's Whitehorse belonged to both the super-slow current and the post-rock current that had taken hold of doom-metal. Their best moments were on meandering improvisations full of ambient drones and walls of (feedback) noise, mostly recorded live until the EP **Fire To Light The Way** (2006) and the 22-minute *The Unwelcome Return*, off the double-disc **Whitehorse** (2007).

The Australian guitar-less trio Fire Witch (two basses and drums) followed a similar course with the two monoliths of **I Spit Lies** (2007).

British quartet Palehorse increased the amount of sinister vibrations in doom-metal by employing two basses and no guitar on **Gee That Ain't**

Well (2006). That also allowed the bassists to improvise in a number of different directions.

Spanish power-trio Orthodox debuted with the heavy doom monoliths a` la Earth of **Gran Poder** (2006) but introduced elements of jazz and of progressive-rock on **Amanecer en Puerta Oscura** (2007) .

English bass-and-keyboards duo Trollmann Av Ildtoppberg (1) began as a lo-fi version of Skepticism, relatively melodic and folkish, on **Forest Of Doom** (2001). Their music morphed into the abstract, glacial and distorted **Arcane Runes Adorn The Ice-Veiled Monoliths Of The Ancient Cavern Of The Stars** (2003) and the ambient, trance-like **Tolling Beyond The Tombs Of Ancient Grimnity** (2003) before exploding in the brutal, massive sound of **Dark Clouds Blacken The Sky On The Eve Of The Thousandth Sacrifice** (2004).

The monolithic ultra-doom dirges of the British band Moss were the ultimate embodiment of the idea of doom. **Cthonic Rites** (2005), containing the 44-minute *The Gate*, and **Sub Templum** (2008), containing the three-movement suite *Gate III - Devils From The Outer Dark*.

Other creative albums of doom-metal of the time included: **Something To Do With Death** (2005) by Chicago's Angel Eyes, **Samus Octology** (2005) by Boston's Irepress, **Message To Ourselves Outside The Dreaming Machine** (2006) by Germany's Woburn House, **Power Hor** (2007) by Seattle's Lesbian, **Peasant** (2008) by New Orleans' Thou, **Lights Bane** (2008) by Oregon's Trees, **Book Of The Black Earth** (2006) by Book Of The Black Earth (Seattle-based multi-instrumentalist Chet Scott), **Angel Eyes** (2008) by the Texan one-man band Brown Jenkins, **Murkrat** (2008) by Australian female duo Murkrat, **Salome** (2008) by Virginia's Salome (melodic doom-metal fronted by a woman), etc.

Cadavers

Skepticism's and Thergothon's super-slow doom-metal had its own disciples, practicing the kind of dense, heavy and glacial sound prophesized by "drone-lords" Eyehategod, Karp, Earth and Sunn O))). These bands worked in a fashion that resembled the work of the digital avantgarde: their slow and huge sounds sculpted vast and gloomy free-form doomscapes that worked both as hostile amphitheaters and as naked psyches.

Finland's Fleshpress (1) debuted with the super-slow doom-metal of **Fleshpress** (2002), that ranks among the supreme works of that sub-subgenre, but then evolved towards a more articulate sound with the extended *Asphalt* on the mini-album **Worm Dirges** (2004). The sparkling production of *All Hope Lost* on **III** (2005) harked back to art-rock, and the trance of **Pillars** (2007) was derailed by sudden accelerations and grindcore beats.

French quartet Monarch (1) wed the demonic vocals of a female singer (Emilie Bresson) with catatonic beats, basically stretching each riff to the limit of human tolerance. The three colossal agonies of the double-disc **666** (2005), the two blurred and disjointed dirges of **Speak Of The Sea** (2006), and the two excruciating ceremonies of **Die Tonight** (2007) drilled into the psyche of a black hole.

Two French outfits, Mourning Dawn and Funeralium, coupled the slow and heavy doom with shrieking black-metal vocals, respectively on **Mourning Dawn** (2007) and **Funeralium** (2007).

Dutch combo Bunkur concocted the lugubrious 65-minute piece of **Bludgeon** (2004) in the vein of slow monotonous doom-metal drenched in guitar feedback and deprived of rhythm by sparse narcotic drumming.

Catacombs, a one-man band from Arizona (Jon "Xathagorra Mlandroth" DelRussi), was able to carved out of the EP **Echoes Through The Catacombs** (2003) and the album **In The Depths Of R'Lyeh** (2006) something close to evocative and even touching art.

San Francisco's Asunder, featuring Weakling's guitarist John Gossard, added a cello to the recipe of super-slow doom-metal and stretched the idea to impossible lengths in the three heartless monoliths **A Clarion Call** (2004) and the 50-minute *Rite Of Finality*, off **Works Will Come Undone** (2006).

Los Angeles' Asva, featuring bassist Stuart Dahlquist, two guitarists (including Mr Bungle's Trey Spruance), Burning Witch's drummer, a female vocalist and an organist, concocted the dense drone-fests of **Futurist's Against the Ocean** (2005) and **What You Don't Know Is Frontier** (2008), each containing four lengthy jams.

Animus, a one-man band from Israel (Golan Weiss), made intelligent use of both repetition and droning to achieve the hypnotically suicidal atmosphere of **Poems For The Aching, Swords For The Infuriated** (2006), scarred by a massive guitar buzz and a robotic beat.

Black Boned Angel (1) was a project by Birchville Cat Motel's Campbell Kneale that devoted the hour-long pieces of **Bliss And Void Inseparable** (2006) and **The Endless Coming Into Life** (2008) to slow, heavy and deep music in the vein of doom-metal, augmented with a bit of post-rock dynamics.

Minnesota's Celestiial added a new dimension to slow and glacial metal by pouring natural sounds and the timbres of ancestral instruments (Celtic harp and Native-American flute) into **Desolate North** (2006).

Idaho-based duo Pussygutt performed droning doom fantasies for home-made instruments, chamber instruments, electronics and power-rock trio such as the four pieces of **Sea Of Sand** (2007) and the 47-minute piece of **She Hid Behind Her Veil** (2008).

Belgian multi-instrumentalist Stijn van Cauter became the super-specialist of ultra-doom, first with **Symphony I and II** (2001), under the moniker <u>Until Death Overtakes Me</u>, then with the monoliths of <u>Fall of The Grey Winged One</u>'s albums **Aeons Of Dreams** (2002), including the 42-minute title-track, and the more electronic **Death Time Emptiness** (2003), including the 37-minute *Emptiness*, and then with <u>Beyond Black Void</u>'s **Desolate** (2003), that was perhaps the best manifestation of his ambient muzak of crushing heaviness.

Other notable slow-motion recordings (the slower, the doomer) were: the EP **Stay Smoke Stay Stone** (2001) and the 40-minute EP **Dot (.)** (2004) by Japanese power-trio <u>Dot</u> (.); **Season Of Seance Science Of Silence** (2003) by New York's <u>Unearthly Trance</u>; the three juggernauts of **Catharsis** (2003) by Oregon's <u>YOB</u>; **Documents Of Grief** (2004) by Los Angeles' <u>Graves At Sea</u>; the 30-minute piece of the EP **Stormbringer** (2005) by Oregon's <u>Roanoke</u>; the single-song EPs **The Ancient Method** (2005), **The Destroyer Of All** (2006), **Cruelty** (2007) and **Absence** (2008) by <u>Monument Of Urns</u>; **Aftermath** (2006) by the new project of Sons Of Otis' guitarist Ken Baluke, named <u>Ox</u>; etc.

By the end of the decade, bands like these had stretched doom-music to its absolute droning limit, venturing into an art of soundsculpting based not on notes and chords but on timbres and tones, while replacing the role of melody with pure heaviness.

Doomgaze

Canadian duo <u>Nadja</u> (1), featuring the ambient composer Aidan Baker, churned out colossal drone-based jams for bass, guitar and drum-machine such as *Slow Loss*, off **Skin Turns to Glass** (2003), the 21-minute piece of the EP **I Have Tasted the Fire Inside Your Mouth** (2004), *Bug Golem* and *Memory Leak*, off **Truth Becomes Death** (2005), the three-movement suite **Bliss Torn from Emptiness** (2005), *Clinodactyl* and *Ossification*, off **Bodycage** (2005), the three monoliths of **Radiance Of Shadows** (2007), which were exemplary takes on doom-shoegaze fusion, and the 62-minute lungubrious piece of **Thaumogenesis** (2007), often sounding, basically, like a psychedelic version of Earth and Sunn O))).

Nadja's "doom-gaze" became more popular as the popularity of ecstatic droning rock increased. Explorers of this no man's land included: Florida's <u>Goslings</u> who conveyed thickly distorted doom-metal with gentle drifting female vocals, leaning towards the dream-pop end of the spectrum, on **Between The Dead** (2005); and <u>Hjarnidaudi</u> (Vidar Ermesjo of Hlidolf), who exposed the morbid connection between doom-metal and shoegazing rock on **Pain Noise March** (2006).

Cybergrind

Drumcorps, the project of German digital musician Aaron Spectre, applied the manipulation techniques of dance-music (such as instrumental hip-hop, techno and drill'n'bass) to grindcore and death-metal. The result was the brutal and frenzied collage of **Grist** (2006) in which blastbeats and metal riffs were two sides of the same (rhythmic) coin.

Philadelphia's Genghis Tron, a combo featuring multiple electronic keyboards and drum-machines but no bassist and no drummer, perfected a dizzying fusion of grindcore, techno music, glitch music and synth-pop on **Dead Mountain Mouth** (2006) and **Board Up The House** (2008).

North Carolina's Killwhitneydead saturated their ferocious music (more metalcore than grindcore) with hundreds of samples, basically using the sampler as a second vocalist, on **So Pretty So Plastic** (2005).

Japanese duo Noism (guitarist Yoshiro Hamazaki and beat programmer Tomoyuki Akiyama) assembled rabid dissonant disjointed industrial grindcore montages on the mini-album +/- (2008).

Breakcore, the successor of Atari Teenage Riot's digital hardcore via James Plotkin's Atomsmasher and Jason Smith's Schizoid, was still producing original works, such as **Cross Contamination** (2002) by Canada's Unitus: manically distorted guitars, pummeling drill'n'bass breakbeats, lugubrious electronic drones.

Punks

The punk-rock universe had split so many times into so many subgenres that they were hardly related anymore. They all continued to thrive, although few seemed still relevant, and none sounded even remotely revolutionary. However, from the ashes of hardcore's virulent nihilism there arose a generation of bands that channeled angst into new forms of sonic violence.

The visceral, harsh, convoluted hardcore of Jesus Lizard survived in Los Angeles' Icarus Line, at least on **Mono** (2001).

An anti-emo movement was led by the Hope Conspiracy, whose angry rants bridged metalcore and garage-rock on their second album **Endnote** (2002).

The punk-folk compromise was best represented by Florida's Against Me, an outfit that sounded like a progressive punk band a` la Clash fronted by a screaming bard in the Billy Bragg tradition (Tom Gabel) on the multi-stylistic **Searching for a Former Clarity** (2005), featuring longer songs and grander arrangements than the anthemic/desperate **Reinventing Axl Rose** (2002).

The cow-punks of the 1980s found their heirs in Tennessee's Kings of Leon, also influenced by southern boogie and hard rock, especially on **Aha Shake Heartbreak** (2005).

Among the few new ideas of the decade was the odd piano-driven hybrid of German cabaret and British punk-rock concocted by Boston's duo <u>Dresden Dolls</u> (1) on **Dresden Dolls** (2004) and **Yes Virginia** (2006).

Seattle's <u>Akimbo</u> pioneered the unlikely wedding of garage-rock, doom-metal and post-rock with the wild, insane, raw sound of **Elephantine** (2003).

The tradition of jazzcore was continued by New York's trio <u>Off Minor</u>, born from the ashes of Saetia, on albums such as **Heat Death of the Universe** (2003).

The <u>Magick Markers</u>, the New York-based trio of guitarist Elisa Ambrogio, bassist Leah Quimby and drummer Pete Nolan, performed chaotic dissonant free-jazz with punk fury, like a psychedelic version of God Is My Co-pilot, on **I Trust My Guitar** (2005) and **A Panegyric To The Things I Do Not Understand** (2006).

Seattle's <u>Gatsbys American Dream</u> pioneered a sort of progressive punk-pop in which the vocals alternated between hardcore and pop styles while the rhythm section alternated between mathcore and dance styles, notably with the two concept albums **Ribbons and Sugar** (2003) and **Volcano** (2005).

Los Angeles' <u>Horse The Band</u> (1) played demented and lo-fi keyboard-driven screamed videogame-infected metalcore impregnated with progressive-rock ambitions on **R. Borlax** (2003) and **The Mechanical Hand** (2005). Erik Engstrom's keyboards alternately lent melody, ambience or noise to the epileptic fits of the band, and well complemented the varied vocal theatrics of Nathan Winneke. **A Natural Death** (2007) even flirted with dance-music and musique concrete.

Toronto's <u>Fucked Up</u> (1) revolutionized both the ethos and the aesthetic of hardcore by transforming it into a studio-based art. The mini-album **Looking for Gold** (2004), a stream of untitled songs, introduced a hardcore's equivalent of Phil Spector's massive "wall of sound": painstakingly studio-constructed songs that stretched to twice or three times the usual duration of a punk rigmarole and relied on thick overdubs to capitalize on Damian Abraham's abrasive roar and the twin-guitar attack led by Mike Haliechuk. **Chemistry Of Common Life** (2008) brought that idea to fruition with a set of engaging songs and transfigured genre cross-pollinations.

By the middle of the decade, "screamo" hardcore had evolved into a more sophisticated style, that often was basically screamo without the screams. New York's <u>From Autumn To Ashes</u> came up with a hybrid of metalcore, screamo and pop, underpinned by the harmonies of singers Benjamin Perri (screaming vocals) and Francis Mark (clean vocals), on the melodic emo concept **Too Bad You're Beautiful** (2001). Their British counterpart were <u>Funeral For A Friend</u> with the equally catchy and "metallic" **Casually Dressed and Deep in Conversation** (2003).

Boston's the <u>Receiving End Of Sirens</u> employed multiple singers and guitarists plus drum machines on **Between The Heart And The Synapse** (2005). Virginia's <u>Far-less</u> alternated screamo turbulence and dream-pop ecstasy on **Everyone Is Out to Get Us** (2006).

Blue (2008) by Miami-based trio <u>Capsule</u> introduced a new form of hardcore that was part spazzy grindcore and part desperate screamo.

Baltimore's <u>Ponytail</u>, fronted by creative Yoko Ono-esque vocalist Molly Siegel and featuring two guitars but no bass, fashioned a catchy form of Japanese noisecore on **Ice Cream Spiritual** (2008).

Texan quintet <u>Black Angels</u> were the most convincingly derivative of the garage masters of the 1960s: **Passover** (2006) and especially **Directions To See A Ghost** (2008) evoked 13th Floor Elevators, Doors, Velvet Underground, etc.

New Jersey's sextet <u>Titus Andronicus</u>, fronted by singer-songwriter Patrick Stickles, wed the emphasis of blue-collar rock with the anger of punk-rock and the depression of emo-pop to produce the vehement and anthemic rants of **The Airing of Grievances** (2008).

The <u>Vivian Girls</u>, a female trio from New York delivered catchy and sprightly, albeit sloppy and noisy garage-rock on the mini-album **Vivian Girls** (2008) that bridged the Velvet Underground and Jesus & Mary Chain.

Danish duo <u>Raveonettes</u> harked back to the era of garage-rock and Phil Spector's girl-groups, but filtered through Jesus And Mary Chain's feedback-pop, on **Chain Gang Of Love** (2003).

Junk

The Butthole Surfers had unwillingly coined a new genre, a sort of "junk-rock" that overwhelmed the listener with an acid, trashy, delirious, distorted, gargantuan cacophony. Among the disciples of the 2000s were: Texas' <u>Rusted Shut</u> with **Rehab** (2005); San Francisco's the <u>Hospitals</u> with **I've Visited The Island Of Jocks And Jazz** (2005); San Francisco's <u>Wildildlife</u>, with **Six** (2007); and especially New York's <u>Health</u>, who unleashed the chaotic, dissonant and sinister pandemonium of **Health** (2007), orchestrating manic tribal beats, razor-sharp guitar attacks and vampire moans.

Philadelphia had a particularly virulent school, highlighted by the anguished abrasive noise-rock of the <u>Pissed Jeans</u> on **Hope For Men** (2007), a work devastated by Matt Korvette's agonizing vocals; by the demented and sloppy garage-rock of the <u>Violent Students</u> with **Violent Students** (2006); and by the claustrophobic post-hardcore of their successors <u>Clockcleaner</u> on **Babylon Rules** (2007).

Sixties garage-rock and Jesus & Mary Chain were the main inspiration for New York's <u>Psychic Ills</u> on **Dins** (2006).

Michigan's duo <u>Empire Auriga</u> debuted with the catastrophic industrial rock of **Auriga Dying** (2008).

The Japanese girl-duo <u>Afrirampo</u> (guitar and drums) played primitive, sloppy and witty garage-rock on **A'** (2004).

The <u>Drones,</u> an Australian band, debuted with **Here Come the Lies** (2002), a tour de force of distorted garage-rock, save revealing their folk and blues foundations on **Wait Long by the River and the Bodies of Your Enemies Will Float** (2005).

Trippers

Droning psychedelia

Rock music owed a lot to psychedelia. The search for a psychedelic sound had been the first and foremost motivation to cultivate progressive structures and creative arrangements. Without that motivation, rock music might have been stuck in Chuck Berry's riffs forever. Psychedelia was in a sense the "big bang" of rock music, from which the expansion began. However, after four decades it was difficult to see what that original impulse still had to offer that had not been heard already a thousand times.

The sound of droning guitars was not particularly exciting anymore, shoegazing ecstasy was becoming the equivalent of the new-age music of the 1980s, and psychedelic folksingers were beginning to sound senile.

Boston's Paradise Camp 23, the brainchild of multi-instrumentalist Erik Amlee, indulged in the 47-minute shapeless space-noise jam that takes up most of **Bar-BQ Dungeon** (2001) and then unleashed the 46-minute drone-based jam of **Solitaire** (2002), bathed in cosmic electronic noise.

Seattle's duo Growing turned psychedelic trance into an austere and pure science with its subliminal ambient dronescapes for guitars and electronics: *Epochal Reminiscence*, off **The Soul Of The Rainbow And The Harmony Of Light** (2004), that diluted a folkish melody into a cycle of ear-piercing tones; the pulsating galactic tsunami *Wide Open*, off **His Return** (2005); the dense hyper-dilated slowly-shifting *Blue Angels*, off **Color Wheel** (2006).

Minnesota-based duo Glass Organ (Justin Meyers and Tom Helgerson) dealt with acid/abrasive droning music on **Our** (2007), containing three pieces each lasting eleven minutes and eleven seconds, at the intersection among hyper-doom metal, psychedelic raga, Japanese noisecore and shoegazing music.

Acre, the project of Seattle-based digital musician Aaron Davis, used mixers, samplers and assorted sound effects to fashion the undulating and multi-layered cosmic drones of **Candyflipping** (2007) and **Monolith** (2008).

The abstract instrumentals of Expo'70 (1), the brainchild of Missouri-based guitarist Justin Wright, bridged the keyboard-based cosmic music of the 1970s and the guitar-based droning music of the 1990s on works such as **Mystical Amplification** (2007). **Animism** (2007) formalized Wright's ambient abstract progressive-rock, and **Black Ohms** (2008) de facto coined a new genre of austere guitar-based soundsculpting.

Expo '70 were emblematic of the trend towards the "ambient space jam", also represented by San Francisco-based one-man band Horseflesh (Dereck Donohue) with **Synthenesia I** (Chambara, 2008), and by New

York-based duo <u>Destructo Swarmbots</u> with the colossal *Banta*, off **Clear Light** (2007).

<u>Pocahaunted</u>, the Los Angeles-based duo of Amanda Brown and Bethany Sharayah, delved into the psychotic tribal droning freak-out of **Island Diamonds** (2008).

New York had a vast community of droning free-folk music. <u>Lichens</u> was a project by 90 Day Men's Afro-American bassist Robert Lowe devoted to droning improvisations for electronically-processed voice and guitar, bordering on Tibetan mantras and Indian ragas on **The Psychic Nature Of Being** (2005). <u>Hototogisu</u> was a collaboration between the Double Leopards' Marcia Bassett and Skullflower's Matthew Bower that released dozens of albums of free-form noise such as **Floating Japanese Oof! Gardens Of The 21st Century** (2004) and **Ghosts From The Sun** (2005). Bassett was also active in <u>GHQ</u> with Pete Nolan (from the Magik Markers): their **Cosmology Of Eye** (2006) and **Heavy Elements** (2006) were devoted to ethereal laid-back free-form spaced-out droning raga-folk music.

San Diego's duo <u>High Mountain Tempel</u> (Maquiladora's guitarist Eric Nielsen and noise-maker Keith Boyd) employed field recordings that exhibit an "African jungle" quality as well as ghostly human and animal voices buried deep into the mix to craft animate dronescapes that nurtured tiny metabolic events on **Pacific Sky Burial** (2007) and **A Screaming Comes Across The Sky** (2007), each album sounding like the brooding soundtrack to collective spiritual catharsis.

Los Angeles' hyper-prolific duo <u>Robedoor</u> epitomized the dark-drone movement, that borrowed from both droning psychedelia and doom-metal and produced countless lo-fi recordings such as **Hidden Ascension** (2006).

By the mid-2000s droning music (whether psychedelic or doom/metal in nature) had become a genre in which the musicianship did not matter much. <u>Vulture Club</u> (Kansas-based guitarist Thomas Lee) took that fact to its extreme consequences by almost letting the guitars play (or, better, "drone") by themselves on **Pure Agitator** (2006), scored for a guitar and amplifier. If the former album was merely a rotting corpse, **Live Young Die Fast And Leave An Exquisite Corpse** (2007) was actually alive, breathing and moving, the drones undergoing a metabolism of their own while the "music" played.

Britain's "black psychedelia" was born from a fusion of acid-rock and black metal. The dark distorted heavy hypnotic psychedelic jams of <u>Ice Bound Majesty</u>'s **A Tomb To Erect** (2007) blurred the boundaries among progressive folk, black metal and ambient music. The guitar-less duo <u>Skultroll</u> sculpted **Skultroll** (2007) with hyper-distorted bass and frenzied drums.

Ireland's <u>Bonecloud</u> (a duo featuring Tim Hurley) unfurled dreamy acid droning tides of sound such as the 44-minute *Snow Burial*, off the double-disc **Bonecloud** (2006), and the 40-minute piece of **Drawing Spirits In Crystals** (2007). The prolific Hurley was also active as Quetzolcoatl, delivering ethereal blissful ambient music for stringed instruments on works such as **Where Are We Going Sister** (2006).

Natural Snow Buildings, the French duo of male guitarist Mehdi Ameziane and female cellist Solange Gularte, alternated between brainy chamber post-rock freak-folk interludes, droning psychedelic trips and abstract ambient music on the double-disc **The Dance of the Moon and the Sun** (2006).

New Zealand's Bad Statistics (1) combined noise, doom, drone and repetition (and psychedelic vocals) for the two lengthy jams of **Static** (2007).

Post-shoegaze

New York's Asobi Seksu paid an unabashed tribute to the walls of distortions of My Bloody Valentine on **Asobi Seksu** (2004), and were perhaps the best of the orthodox shoegazers.

However, others went well beyond those premises.

Georgia-based Deerhunter (1), fronted by vocalist Bradford Cox, split **Cryptograms** (2007) between surreal instrumentals and psychedelic lullabies.

Georgia's Atlas Sound, the brainchild of Bradford Cox, took Deerhunter's pensive side to new heights on **Let The Blind Lead Those Who Can See But Cannot Feel** (2008).

New York's A Place to Bury Strangers sounded like a louder version of My Bloody Valentine's distorted bliss with Jesus And Mary Chain-style melodies and new-wavish keyboards on its debut **A Place to Bury Strangers** (2007).

San Francisco's Wooden Shjips, influenced by both the Doors and Spacemen 3, filled **Wooden Shjips** (2007) with barbed garage-grade riffs and hypnotic throbbing rhythm.

A similar combination of Spacemen 3 and the Doors also inspired New York's Religious Knives, fronted by organist Maya Miller and guitarist/synth-man Michael Bernstein (both members of Double Leopards). The lengthy trance pieces of **Remains** (2007), tinged with exotic and electronic overtones, laid the foundations for the chanted noise-songs for motorik rhythm and electronic drones of the mini-album **The Door** (2008).

Texan trio Indian Jewelry, featuring vocalist and keyboardist Erika Thrasher, gave an evil and drunk spin to shoegazing on **Invasive Exotics** (2006).

The relatively simple idea of feeding distorted music into heavy music and viceversa was pushed to a higher degree of paranoia by New York's trio Heavy Winged in the lengthy jams of **A Serpent's Lust** (2006),

Blacc Stork (2006), **Taking the Veil** (2006), **We Grow** (2007), making them the most relevant pupils of High Rise.

New Orleans' duo <u>Belong</u> (Turk Dietrich and Michael Jones) took shoegaze-rock to a higher (noisier) dimension with **October Language** (2006), a victim of the chaotic glitch aesthetic but still devoted to the psychedelic cause.

In the late 2000s a new fad was a kind of swaggering lo-fi shoegaze-pop, a fusion of sloppy instrumental mayhem and catchy vocal hooks that Adam Elliott called "romantic nihilism", something like the marriage of Dead C and Pavement. After Ohio's <u>Times New Viking</u>, fronted by Adam Elliott and featuring keyboardist Beth Murphy, debuted with **Dig Yourself** (2005), their example was followed by Ohio's <u>Psychedelic Horseshit</u> with **Magic Flowers Droned** (2008), and Oregon's <u>Eat Skull</u> with **Sick To Death** (2008).

French electronica duo <u>M83</u> (1) transposed shoegazing psychedelia into an age in which keyboards had replaced guitars as the pivotal sound-effect instrument. After the display of studio mastery and encyclopedic musical knowledge of **M83** (2001), they indulged in the idea of making heavy rock using keyboards instead of (or in addition to) guitars on **Dead Cities, Red Seas & Lost Ghosts** (2003), juxtaposing both ambient and cosmic passages.

France's <u>Abstrakt Keal Agram</u> achieved a balance of shoegaze, glitch and droning music on their album **Bad Thriller** (2004), with psychotic electronic keyboards and creative drum programming, that made them sound like an ominous version of M83.

French quartet <u>Cyann & Ben</u> evoked Bardo Pond's space-rock, Cocteau Twins' dream-pop, Mogwai's post-rock and Low's slo-core on **Spring** (2003).

Norway's late shoegazers <u>Serena-Maneesh</u> (1) blended My Bloody Valentine's introverted ecstasy and the Velvet Underground's pulsating neurosis on **Serena-Maneesh** (2005).

Folk freaks

Loose folk-rock jamming of the kind pioneered by the Incredible String Band in the 1960s ("freak folk") was one of the most abused praxes of the 2000s. By the mid 2000s several psychedelic-folk "collectives" were active on the East Coast.

The No-Neck Blues Band's keyboardist John Fell Ryan launched <u>Excepter</u> (1) with the digital psychedelic collage of **Ka** (2003), that matched if not surpassed the dementia of his old band. The album still tried to retain a semblance of the song format, but the EP **Vacation** (2003) let the sonic mess drift ad libitum. **Throne** (2005) was another "concrete" symphony for electronics, guitars and wordless vocals.

New York's Akron/Family (1) played soundscape-oriented instrumental background music for warbling surreal elegies and litanies of metaphysical loss on **Akron/Family** (2005). **Love Is Simple** (2007) was a more conceptual affair, of grander proportions, that reconstructed tribal and choral hippie music in a modern context.

New York-based psychedelic-folk collective Wooden Wand coined a tribal and dissonant form of urban folk music via **L'Un Marquer Contre La Moissonneuse** (2005), containing two free-form soundtracks for the afterlife of drug-addicted ghosts, **Buck Dharma** (2005), an evocative work approaching the ambience of latter-day Swans, and the percussive, demonic and distorted rituals of **The Flood** (2005).

Oregon's duo the Plants stretched out with the three lengthy "songs" of **Double Infinity** (2006) that were melodic fantasies for neoclassical instruments (flute, cello, piano) seesawing through slow-motion sloppy drones and setting the stage for devil-angel male-female harmonies (Joshua Blanchard and Molly Griffith).

Spectre Folk, that released **Spectre Folk** (2006), and Folk Spectre, that released **The Blackest Medicine** (2008), were the same project by the Magik Markers's drummer Pete Nolan. They were meant to sound like primitive folk recordings: warped folk lullabies drenched in crackle-and-hiss background noise, like a folkish version of shoegazing, or a slower version of garage-rock.

Department Of Eagles the duo of Grizzly Bear's guitarist Daniel Rossen and Fred Nicolaus, achieved a nostalgic fusion of orchestral pop and freak-folk on **In Ear Park** (2008).

Rhode Island's Black Forest Black Sea, one of many collectives that played improvised psychedelic folk music in the mid-2000s, marked the progress of this genre's artistic ambition by evolving from the fragmented **Black Forest Black Sea** (2003) to the two lengthy jams of **Black Forest Black Sea** (2007).

Another Rhode Island-based combo, Urdog, mixed organ-driven prog-rock and freak-folk, like a meeting of Nice and the Incredible String Band, on **Garden Of Bones** (2004).

The Vermont-based collective Feathers jumped on the bandwagon of psychedelic folk with **Feathers** (2005), that sounded like a summary of 40 years of the genre, from Donovan to the Incredible String Band to Marc Bolan.

Espers, a sextet including Greg Weeks on electronics that headed the Philadelphia scene, were more preoccupied with crafting melancholy, evocative, zen-like ambience than penning acid-folk ballads on **II** (2006).

Philadelphia's Fern Knight, fronted by singer-songwriter Margaret Wienk, played gothic folk-rock that bridged the Celtic and Appalachian worlds, and channeled the timbral opulence of their instrumentation into something akin to baroque chamber music, notably on their third album **Fern Knight** (2008).

The groups of the Midwest were harder to categorize. New Mexico's Brightblack Morning Light (1), fronted by guitarist/vocalist Nathan Shineywater, conjured the hazy slo-core atmospheres of **Ala.Cali.Tucky** (2004) and then ventured into a psychomusical journey, not unlike the ones attemped by avantgarde trumpeter Jon Hassell, on **Brightblack Morning Light** (2006): its warped funk, jazz and blues visions evoked places and ages without quoting any particular geography. Wisconsin's collective Davenport ("conducted" by Clay Ruby), as documented on **Free Country** (2004), performed electroacoustic country music that mixed primordial droning, free noise, anemic shamanic vocals, tribal beats, guitars, fiddles, keyboards, percussions and environmental sounds, sounding like a sedated version of the Holy Modal Rounders.

British combo Rameses III introduced a transcendent variant on this genre with the sweet dreamy ambient guitar vignettes of **Parsimonia** (2004).

Belgian ensemble Silvester Anfang improvised tribal satanic hippy music that bordered on both acid folk and gothic rock on **Satanische Vrede** (2006), containing the suite *Demonische Agricultuur II*, **Echte Vlaamse Geiten** (2007), containing *Demonische Agricultuur*, and **Kosmies Slachtafval** (2007), containing just two lengthy (and more ambient) pieces.

Erik Skodvin inaugurated the project Svarte Greiner with **Knive** (2006), an album of mournful slo-motion free-form acoustic folk dirges drifting through distant and murky acoustic soundscapes.

Australia's Brothers Of The Occult Sisterhood (the duo of siblings Michael and Kristina Donnelly) were among the most chaotic acts in the world: **Run From Your Honey Mind** (2005) and **Goodbye** (2006) demonstrated meandering atonal, tribal, cerimonial music sprinkled with electronics over a bed of found percussion.

San Francisco post-hippies

It was inevitable that San Francisco, the homeland of the hippy movement in the 1960s, would eventually get the lion's share of the phenomenon.

The Franciscan Hobbies, featuring three members of Thuja (Glenn Donaldson, Loren Chasse and Rob Reger) plus other local musicians, were emblematic of the loose Bay Area collectives that still congregated around the Jewelled Antler label (around the pioneers Thuja and the Skygreen Leopards) for which the communal spirit mattered more than the improvised amateurish psychedelic-folk music with mystical and idyllic overtones that they played on albums such as **Masks & Meanings** (2003).

One-man folk orchestra Steven Smith of Mirza, now disguised as Hala Strana, employed a huge arsenal of instruments (both classical, ethnic, home-made and found sounds) to revisit the traditional music of Eastern Europe on **Hala Strana** (2003) and the double-disc **Fielding** (2003).

The Alps (1) played languid lo-fi ambient drone psychedelic-folk on **Jewelt Galaxies** (2005) and **Spirit Shambles** (2006), but then absorbed German electronic "cosmic" music for **III** (2008), apparently heading towards a rhythm-less kind of atmospheric music while retaining the old scaffolding of spaced-out vocals, ghostly pianos and distorted guitars.

The Elemental Chrysalis, i.e. the duo of ambient composer Chet Scott and James Woodhead, employed an arsenal of instruments to craft the celestial atmosphere of **The Calocybe Collection** (2005), which was basically instrumental ambient folk music. The double-disc **The Dark Path To Spiritual Expansion** (2007) explored an oneiric, magic and nebulous underworld, basically a high-brow version of freak-folk.

The duo Barn Owl dreamed up meandering instrumental drumless space-folk for guitars, bass, banjo, harmonica, synthesizer, organ and drums on **Barn Owl** (2007).

Finnish elves

However it was Finland, of all places, that had possibly the most vibrant school of "freak folk", specializing in primitive electroacoustic production aesthetics.

Kemialliset Ystavat, a hippy collective a` la Incredible String Band, devoted their entire career to droning improvised freak-folk for casual chanting, atonal strumming and primitive drumming. Their philosophy of art was best summarized on their second album **Kellari Juniversumi** (2002).

Avarus (1), a collective of musicians derived from fellow Finnish ensembles, pursued the most avantgarde form of "free folk", bordering on both free jazz and musique concrete. The fundamental elements of their sonic whirlwinds of the mid 2000s were guitar feedback, primitive instrumental plucking, haphazard drumming, and amateurish garage rave-ups; but then the product was subjected to a variety of tortures in the studio, distorting it via tape loops, enhancing it with samples, playing it backwards or at variable speed. The result often resembled abstract noise. The most creative jams were those on **A-V-P** (2003), **II** (2006) and **Rasvaaja** (2007).

Islaja (Finnish female singer-songwriter Merja Kokkonen, a member of both Avarus and Kemialliset Ystavat) multitracked her voice over the sparse pastoral droning psychedelic sounds of **Meritie** (2004) and the more touching **Palaa Aurinkoon** (2005). **Ulual Yyy** (2007) added horns and electronics.

The hyper-prolific (and inevitably sloppy) <u>Keijo</u> Virtanen masterminded meandering jams of loose, improvised, cluttered and droning ambience for detuned instruments, spastic tribal drumming and erratic vocals. His first official disc was **After At Once** (2006), but he had already self-released a dozen albums in three years.

At least two female singer-songwriters graced this commune and represented a gentler side of Finnish free-folk: <u>Kuupuu</u> (Jonna Karanka), who delivered the dreamy **Yokehra** (2006), and <u>Lau Nau</u> (Laura Naukkarinen), who sang the otherwordly lullabies of **Kuutarha** (2005).

The super-prolific <u>Uton</u> were emblematic of these wildly redundant and self-indulgent forest hippies. Their sub-amateurish chaotic psychedelic freak-outs, often wed to glacial drones, were a new form of shapeless background music, and sometimes, like in the case of **Highway Nation** (2006), **Background For Silence** (2007), or **Ground's Dream Cosmic Love** (2008), they hardly moved at all.

Chaos

Madness without a method sometimes fared better than madness with a method. The generation after Bardo Pond reinvented space-rock and the "psychedelic freak-out" as a much wilder and looser form of non-music.

Philadelphia-based quintet <u>An Albatross</u> introduced themselves as sort of the Red Krayola for the age of grindcore with **Eat Lightning Shit Thunder** (2001) and especially with their second **We Are The Lazer Viking** (2003): frenzied keyboards-based acid-rock with shrieked vocals, except that they opted for grindcore-style bullets rather than side-long freak-outs.

New York state's <u>Burnt Hills</u> ventured into a hyper-psychedelic, primitive and tribal sound, which was inspired by both Dead C and Crash Worship, with their **To Your Head** (2006) for five guitars, bass and three drummers. The abrasive, propulsive one-hour piece of **Stoners Pot Palace** (2007) set a new standard for their recordings, that now became hour-long streams of consciousness, notably on **Tonite We Ride** (2008) for seven players.

Instrumental synth-spiced space-rock was best represented by New York's <u>Titan</u>, indulging in the three live jams of **Titan** (2006) and the 40-minute live jam of **Pilzmarmelade** (2006). The suites of their cousins <u>La Otracina</u> on **Love Love Love** (2006) and **Tonal Ellipse Of The One** (2007) were emblematic of the electronic intersection of acid-rock, prog-rock and post-rock.

New York's <u>Gang Gang Dance</u> (2), fronted by Liz Bougatsos and featuring guitarist Josh Diamond, keyboardist Brian DeGraw and drummer Tim DeWitt, debuted with the jam-oriented electronic psychedelic tribal music (a` la Animal Collective or Residents) of **Gang Gang Dance** (2004). They rediscovered the song format and crisp production for the surrealistic **God's Money** (2005) and then they also rediscovered the groove for **Saint Dymphna** (2008).

Chicago's <u>Plastic Crimewave Sound</u>, the brainchild of vocalist-guitarist Steve Krakow, harked back to Blue Cheer's stoner-rock and Hawkwind's space-rock, adding Eastern, orchestral, motorik and electronic elements on their second album **No Wonderland** (2006).

However, the most diligent revisionists of Hawkwind's abrasive hard-rocking space-rock were perhaps New York's <u>White Hills</u>, notably on **Glitter Glamour Atrocity** (2007).

Santa Cruz's wildly psychedelic <u>Residual Echoes</u> (the brainchild of guitarist Adam Payne) were the most extreme heirs of the Comets On Fire with a freak-out that bordered on Japanese noisecore and chaotic free-jazz, feeding on extreme shrieking and/or extreme distortion, as documented by **Residual Echoes** (2004).

Iowa's <u>Raccoo-Oo-Oon</u>, the brainchild of Shawn Reed, dabbled in dense tribal hysterical jazz-tinged acid-rock with electronically altered vocals, fuzzed guitars and gnomish synthesizers that seemed to sum up the 1970s of Hawkwind, Gong, Neu and Faust via the Animal Collective. **Is Night People** (2005) and **The Cave Of Spirits Forever** (2006) toyed with a prism of rock subgenres.

Australian collective <u>Grey Daturas</u> ran the gamut from extended guitar workouts to wildly acidic garage-rock on **Grey Daturas** (2002) and **Dead In The Woods** (2004).

<u>Shit And Shine</u> (13), an English collective featuring multiple drummers and guitarists, concocted a seriously damaged nuclear fusion of garage-rock and heavy-metal music on **You're Lucky To Have Friends Like Us** (2004). The 42-minute jam **Ladybird** (2005), featuring little more than the incessant pounding of the drums and massive distortions, was to psychedelic music what Lou Reed's **Metal Machine Music** was to progressive-rock: an abominable terminal point. Another colossal nightmare, the 30-minute *Practicing To Be A Doctor*, off the double-CD **Jealous of Shit and Shine** (2006), the two jams of the mini-album **Toilet Door Tits/ The Biggest Cock In Christendom** (2006), and **Cunts With Roses** (2007), documenting the first ever live improvisation by the band, as well as the apocalyptic single *Cigarette Sequence* (2008) for multiple drummers, bass players and electronic noise makers, displayed the same visceral and pointless impact.

In Japan the generation of Acid Mothers Temple and Ghost had laid the foundations for a more subdued form of psychedelic rock. <u>Suishou No Fune</u> (2), formed by female guitarist Pirako Kurenai and male guitarist Kageo, accompanied their reverb-drenched slow-motion lullabies with hypnotic mellow lightweight free-form twin-guitar noise. **Suishou No Fune** (2005), particularly the 17-minute *The Blue Bird - Betrayal and Freedom*, and the three improvised jams of **Writhing Underground Flowers** (2007) rehearsed the format that peaked with the mournful dilated ballads of the double-disc **Prayer for Chibi** (2007), a requiem of sorts. LSD-march, the brainchild of guitarist Shinsuke Michishita, debuted with the mellow anemic ballads a` la Lou Reed of **Shindara Jigoku** (2004) but the double-disc **Nikutai No Tubomi** (2007) contrasted the 40-minute harsh juggernaut *Nikutai no Tubomi* and a disc of ethereal fantasies, showing that it had transformed into an octopus of acid-rock, noisecore and post-rock.

Appendix

Chronology of Events

1860:
Eduard-Leon Scott invents the phonautograph and makes the first visual recording of sound

1867:
The first collection of "Slave Songs of the United States" is published

1876:
Thomas Watson, Edison's assistant, is the first person to listen to noise (on the first telephone test line) for pleasure

1877:
Thomas Edison invents sound recording, and a phonograph to play sound recorded on cylinders

1880:
The tango is born in Buenos Aires

1885:
Benjamin Franklin Keith and Edward Franklin Albee set up a nation-wide chain of vaudeville theaters

1887:
Emile Berliner builds the first gramophone, that plays sound recorded at 78 RPM on a flat record

1888:
Charles Ives' "Variations on America" is the first polytonal piece

1889:
Columbia is founded by Edward Easton

1892:
Popular music becomes big business and music publishers rent offices around Union Square in New York City, an area that is renamed "Tin Pan Alley" (sheet music is the primary "product" of popular music and the industry is dominated by music publishing houses)

1893:
Kerry Mills's *Rastus On Parade* is the first published cakewalk

1894:
Hawaiian guitarist Joseph Kekeku invents the slide guitar (by fretting the guitar with a comb)
The weekly Billboard magazine begins publication, offering "charts" of music sales

1895:
Ben Harney's *You've Been a Good Old Wagon* is the first ragtime piece to be published
The first jazz band, the Spasm Band, first performs in New Orleans
Gugliemo Marconi invents the radio

1897:
Edwin Votey invents the player piano

1898:
Emile Berliner sells the European rights to the gramophone to the Gramophone Company or HMV (His Master's Voice)

1899:
Scott Joplin's *Maple Leaf Rag* (1899) starts the ragtime craze

1901:
Emile Berliner founds the record label Victor Talking Machines
Melville Clark builds the first full 88-key player piano

1903:
Will-Marion Cook's musical revue **In Dahomey** exports cakewalk to Britain

1905:
Arnold Schoenberg composes atonal music

1906:
Thaddeus Cahill builds the first electronic instrument

1907:
Ferruccio Busoni publishes "Entwurf einer neuen Aesthetic der Tonkunst", predicting the use of dissonant and electric sound in musical composition
Fred Barrasso creates a chain of vaudeville theaters that evolves into the Theater Owners's Booking Association (T.O.B.A.).

1908:
Cubism is the new fad in Paris

1909:
The term "jazz" is used for the first time in the song *Uncle Josh in Society* (but it refers to ragtime)
Filippo Tommaso Marinetti publishes his "Manifesto Futurista" in Paris

1910:
John Lomax publishes "Cowboy Songs and Other Frontier Ballads"
Sergei Diaghilev produces in Paris the ballet "Scheherazade", the most successful of the "Ballets Russes"
The American Photoplayer Company introduces the "Fotoplayer Style", an instrument that can play orchestral music as well as sound effects

350,000 pianos are manufactured in the USA

1912:
William Spiller's band, the Musical Spillers, export ragtime to Britain
The incidental music to Richard Walton Tully's play **Bird of Paradise**
popularizes the ukulele and the steel guitar
The first blues is published, Hart Wand's *Dallas Blues*
Henry Cowell introduces "tone clusters" in *The Tides of Manaunaun* (1912) by
striking the keys with forearm and fist

1913:
Italian "futurist" Luigi Russolo publishes "L'Arte dei Rumori", in which he
proclaims noise to be the sound of the 20th century, and especially noise
produced by machines, such as his own "Intonarumori"

1914:
Jerome Kern invents the "musical" by integrating music, drama and ballet and
setting it into the present
The American Society for Composers (ASCAP) is founded to protect
songwriters

1915:
Tristan Tzara founds the Dada movement in Zurich

1916:
Henry Cowell composes quartets using combinations of rhythms and overtones
that are impossible to play by humans
The first record to be advertised as "samba" is Ernesto Joaquim Maria dos
Santos, better known as "Donga", *Pelo Telefone*
Alexander Scriabin's "Prometheus" features a light show
Piano makers Brunswick start a record label
Cecil Sharp publishes a collection of folk music from the Appalachian
mountains
Julian Carrillo writes "The Thirteenth Sound Theory" which heralds music for
microtones

1917:
The first jazz record is cut in New York

1918:
James Europe's Hellfighters export jazz to France

1919:
General Electric absorbs the American branch of Marconi Wireless Telegraph
and renames it Radio Corporation of America (RCA)
Will Marion Cook's syncopated orchestra plays jazz for King George V in
Britain

1920:
Mamie Smith's *Crazy Blues* is the first blues by a black singer to become a

nation-wide hit
Eric Satie composes music not to be listened to ("musique d'ameublement", furniture music)
Westinghouse Electric starts the first commercial radio station, "KDKA"

1921:
106 million records are sold in the USA, mostly published on "Tin Pan Alley", but control of the market is shifting to the record companies
Okeh introduces a "Colored Catalog" targeting the black community, the first series of "race records"
The Donaueschingen Festival of avantgarde music is founded

1922:
Trixie Smith cuts *My Man Rocks Me With One Steady Roll*
Texan fiddler Eck Robertson cuts the first record of "old-time music"
Laszlo Moholy-Nagy advocates the use of phonograph records to produce music, not only to reproduce it
James Sterling buys out the British division of Columbia

1923:
Bessie Smith cuts her first blues record
John Carson records two "hillbilly" songs and thus founds country music
Arnold Schoenberg completes his 12-tone system of composition (the first form of "serialism")

1924:
The Music Corporation of America (MCA) is founded in Chicago as a talent agency
German record company Deutsche Grammophon (DG) founds the Polydor company to distribute records abroad
Andre' Breton publishe the "Surrealist Manifesto" in Paris
Riley Puckett introduces the "yodeling" style of singing into country music

1925:
The Mills Brothers popularize the "barbershop harmonies"
Carl Sprague is the first musician to record cowboy songs (the first "singing cowboy" of country music)
the electrical recording process is commercially introduced, quickly replacing the mechanical one
78.26 RPM is chosen as a standard for phonographic records because phonographs at that speed could use a standard 3600-rpm motor and 46-tooth gear (78.26 = 3600/46).
Nashville's first radio station is founded (WSM) and begins broadcasting a program that will change name to "Grand Ole Opry"

1926:
Bing Crosby cuts his first record and invents the "crooning" style of singing thanks to a new kind of microphone
Blind Lemon Jefferson is the first bluesman to enter e major recording studio
Will Shade founds the first "jug band" in Memphis, inspired by Louisville's first

jug bands
The magazine "Phonograph Monthly Review" is founded
Vitaphone introduces 16-inch acetate-coated shellac discs playing at 33 1/3
RPM (a size and speed calculated to be the equivalent of a reel of film)
The British magazine "Melody Maker" is founded
General Electric founds the "National Broadcasting Company" (NBC)

1927:
Meade Lux Lewis cuts *Honky Tonk Train*, the most famous boogie woogie
Russian composer Leon Termen performs the first concerto with the "theremin"
Jimmie Rodgers, the first star of country music, adopts "yodeling" style of
singing, the blues style of black music, and the Hawaian slide guitar
Classical composer Kurt Weill begins a collaboration with playwright Bertold
Brecht, incorporating jazz, folk and pop elements in his soundtracks
Sales of "race records" reach $100 million

1928:
The United Independent Broadcasters (later renamed Columbia Broadcasting
System, or CBS) of 47 affiliate stations is founded
Clarence "Pinetop" Smith cuts *Pinetop's Boogie Woogie*
Maurice Martenot invents an electronic instrument, the Ondes-Martenot

1929:
Decca is founded in Britain by Edward Lewis as a classical music company
RCA buys Victor Talking Machines
The "Great Depression" destroys the record industry
Blind Lemon Jefferson dies

1930:
The first "fanzines", science fiction pulp magazines "Comet" and "Time
Traveller", are founded, to allow sci-fi fans to communicate
Leon Termen invents the first rhythm machine, the "Rhythmicon"
Warner Brothers buys Brunswick

1931:
EMI (Electrical and Musical Industries), formed by the merge of Gramophone
and the British subsidiary of Columbia, opens the largest recording studio in the
world at Abbey Road in London, while the USA division of Columbia is sold
Edgar Varese premieres a piece for percussions, *Ionisation*
George Beauchamp invents the electric guitar (the Rickenbacker)
Gene Autry's *Silver Hairde Daddy Of Mine* popularizes the "honky-tonk" style
of country music

1932:
Thomas Dorsey's *Precious Lord* invents gospel music in Chicago
Milton Brown and Bob Wills invent "western swing"

1933:

Cuban bandleader Ignacio Pineiro releases *Echale Salsita*, the song that gives the name "salsa" to Cuba's dance music
Only six million records are sold in the USA
Jimmie Rodgers dies
Sales of "race records" drop to $6 million

1934:
John Lomax and his son Alan begin recording black music of the southern states, and discover the gospel genre of "rocking and reeling"
Laurens Hammond invents the Hammond organ
The first magazine devoted to jazz music, Down Beat, is published

1935:
The radio program "Hit Parade" is launched
Woody Guthrie writes the *Dust Bowl Ballads* and becomes the first major singer-songwriter
Max Gordon founds the jazz club "Village Vanguard" in New York

1936:
Roy Acuff becomes the first star of Nashville's country music
Bluesman Robert Johnson cuts his first record
Carl Stalling begins scoring the soundtracks for Warner Brothers' cartoons
the Gibson company produces its first electric guitar, the ES-150

1937:
Records by the "big bands" are the best sellers
The mambo is born in Cuba

1938:
a Carnegie Hall concert by the piano trio of Albert Hammons, Meade Lux Lewis and Pete Johnson launches the boogie-woogie craze
CBS buys USA's Columbia

1939:
Leo Mintz founds a record store in Cleveland, the "Record Rendezvous", specializing in black music
John Cage composes *Imaginary Landascape N.1* for magnetic tape
The "Grand Ole Pry" moves to Nashville's "Ryman Auditorium" and is broadcasted by the national networks
The Panoram visual jukebox is invented (plays short films of records, the first music videos)

1940:
Disney's "Fantasia" introduces stereo sound
Pete Seeger forms the Almanac Singers to sing protest songs with communist overtones
Keynote is founded by Eric Bernay

1941:
Arkansas' radio station KFFA hires Sonny Boy Williamson to advertise groceries, the first case of mass exposure by blues singers
"La Discotheque" opens in paris, a club devoted to jazz music

1942:
Bing Crosby's *White Christmas* becomes the best-selling song of all times (and will remain so for 50 years)
Los Angeles bluesman T-Bone Walker incorporates jazz chords into the blues guitar with *I Got A Break Baby*

Capitol is founded in Hollywood, the first major music company which is not based in New York
Savoy is founded in Newark (NJ) by by Herman Lubinsky to promote black music

1943:
The first "disc jockeys" follow the American troops abroad
The USA army introduces V-Discs that play six minutes of music per side
Richard Rodgers and Oscar Hammerstein produce the musical *Oklahoma* that uses choreographer Agnes de Mille to design the ballets
King is founded in Cincinnati by Sydney Nathan to promote black music

1945:
Les Paul invents "echo delay", "multi-tracking" and many other studio techniques
Sam Hoffman plays the theremin in film soundtracks
White bluesman Johnny Otis assembles a combo for *Harlem Nocturne* that is basically a shrunk-down version of the big-bands of swing
Mercury is founded in Chicago
Jules Bihari founds Modern Records in Los Angeles, specializing in black music
Bill Monroe's *Kentucky Waltz* popularizes the "bluegrass" style

1946:
Louis Jordan launches "jump blues" with *Choo Choo Ch'Boogie*
Muddy Waters cuts the first records of Chicago's electric blues (rhythm and blues)
Carl Hogan plays a powerful guitar riff on Louis Jordan's *Ain't That Just Like a Woman*
Damstadt in Germany sets up a school for avantgarde composers
Raymond Scott founds "Manhattan Research", the world's first electronic music studio
Lew Chudd founds Imperial Records in Los Angeles, specializing in black music
The Metro-Goldwyn-Mayer (MGM) film company opens a recording business to sell their movie soundtracks
Specialty Records is founded by Art Rupe in Los Angeles to specialize in black popular music

1947:

Billboard's writer Jerry Wexler coins the term "rhythm and blues" for
Chicago's electric blues
Roy Brown writes and cuts *Good Rockin' Tonight* in Texas
Six majors control the music market: Columbia, RCA Victor, Decca, Capitol,
MGM, Mercury
The Hollywood-based tv program of Korla Pandit (John Red), pretending to be
an Indian guru and playing a Hammond organ, publicizes exotic sounds
Chess Records is founded in Chicago by two Polish-born Jews to promote
rhythm and blues
Ahmet Ertegun founds Atlantic in New York to promote black music at the
border between jazz, rhythm and blues and pop

1948:
Pete Seeger forms the Weavers, which start the "folk revival"
Detroit rhythm'n'blues saxophonist Wild Bill Moore releases *We're Gonna Rock
We're Gonna Roll*
Columbia introduces the 12-inch 33-1/3 RPM long-playing vinyl record
Pierre Schaeffer creates a laboratory for "musique concrete" in Paris and
performs a concerto for noises
Rodgers & Hammerstein's **Tale Of The South Pacific** introduces exotic sounds
to Broadway
Leo Fender introduces its electric guitar (later renamed Telecaster)
Moe Asch founds Folkways, devoted to folk music
Ed Sullivan starts a variety show on national television (later renamed "Ed
Sullivan Show")
Homer Dudley invents the Vocoder (Voice Operated recorder)
Memphis' radio station WDIA hires Nat Williams, the first black disc jockey
The magazine "Billboard" introduces charts for "folk" and "race" records

1949:
Moondog virtually invents every future genre of rock music
Fats Domino cuts *The Fat Man*, a new kind of boogie
Hank Williams' *Lovesick Blues* reaches the top of the country charts
Scatman Crothers cuts *I Want To Rock And Roll* (1949), with Wild Bill Moore
on saxophone
RCA Victor introduces the 45 RPM vinyl record
Fantasy is founded
Todd Storz of the KOWH radio station starts the "Top 40" radio program
The "Billboard" chart for "race" records becomes the chart for "rhythm and
blues" records
Aristocrat changes its name to Chess

1950:
Jac Holzman founds Elektra in New York to promote new folk and jazz
musicians
Les Baxter's **Music Out of the Moon** incorporates exotic themes in instrumental
music
the first major rhythm'n'blues festival is held in Los Angeles (the "Blues &
Rhythm Jubilee")
Dutch electronics giant Philips enters the recording business

1951:
The white Cleveland disc jockey Alan Freed decides to speculate on the success of Leo Mintz's store and starts a radio program, "Moondog Rock'n'Roll Party", that broadcasts black music to an audience of white teenagers
The first rock and roll record, Ike Turner's *Rocket 88*, is released
The first juke-box that plays 45 RPM records is introduced
Karlheinz Stockhausen joins the school of music at Darmstadt and begins composing "elektronische musik"
The French national radio sets up a studio to record electronic music in Paris and the West Deutsche Radio creates a similar studio in Cologne (the NWDR)
John Cage composes music for radio frequencies
Howling Wolf and Joe Turner popularize the "shouters"
Victor and Columbia agree to split the record market: Victor sells 33 RPM long-playing records and Columbia sells 45 RPM records
Gunter Lee Carr cuts the dance novelty *We're Gonna Rock*
The first Jamaican studio opens and begins recording "mento" music

1952:
Bill Haley forms the Comets, the first rock and roll band
Louis and Bebe Barron's soundtrack for the science-fiction film **The Bells of Atlantis** uses only electronic instruments
The Weavers, accused of being communists, are forced to dissolve
Bob Horn's "Bandstand" tv program airs from Philadeplhia every weekday afternoon
John-Clellon Holmes coins the expression "beat generation" to refer to Jack Kerouac and other young writers
The Cleveland disc jockey Alan Freed (aka Moondog) organizes the first rock and roll concert, the "Moondog Coronation Ball"
Oskar Sala invents the "Mixtur-Trautonium", an instrument capable of subharmonics
John Cage composes multi-media pieces that use a computer
John Cage's *Williams Mix* is an electronic collage of hundreds of random noises
John Cage's *Water Music* (1952) instructs the performers to also perform non-musical gestures
Gibson introduces its solid-body electric guitar, invented by Les Paul a few years earlier
Roscoe Gordon, a Memphis pianist, invents the "ska" beat with *No More Doggin'*
Sam Phillips founds Sun Records and declares "If I could find a white man who sings with the Negro feel, I'll make a million dollars"
Electronic engineers Harry Olsen and Hebert Belar create the first synthesizer at RCA's Princeton Laboratories, the Mark I
Charles Brown's *Hard Times* is the first hit by Jerry Leiber and Mike Stoller to enter the charts

1953:
Bill Haley's *Crazy Man Crazy* is the first rock and roll song to enter the Billboard charts
The Orioles' *Crying in the Chapel* is the first black hit to top the white pop

charts

Todd Matshikiza's musical *Makhaliphile* fuses classical, jazz and African music

Sam Phillips records the first Elvis Presley record in his Sun studio of Memphis using two recorders to produce an effect of "slapback" audio delay

Hank Williams dies at 30

CBS launches a sub-label, Epic

Delmark is founded by Bob Koester

The black market constitutes 5.7% of the total American market for records

Vee-Jay is founded in Indiana, owned by a black couple and specializing in black music

1954:

Boom of doo-wop

Bill Haley's version of "Rock Around The clock" is the first rock song used in a movie soundtrack

Joe Turner cuts the blues novelty *Shake Rattle And Roll*

The record companies switch from 78 RPMs to 45 RPMs

EMI (Electrical and Musical Industries) buys Capitol

The Country Music Disc Jockeys' Association (CMA) is founded in Nashville

Japanese electronic company TTK (later Sony) introduces the world's first transistor radio

The first Newport Jazz Festival is held, the first hazz festival in the world

Edgar Varese pioneers tape music with *Deserts*

Otto Luening's *Fantasy In Space* and Vladimir Ussachevsky's *A Poem In Cycles And Bells* pioneer "tape music" at Columbia University

1955:

"Rebel Without A Cause" and "Blackboard Jungle" establish a new role model for teenagers, the rebellious loner and sometimes juvenile delinquent

Frank Sinatra's **In The Wee Small Hours** (1955) is the first concept album of pop music

Millett Morgan releases a recording of the Ionosphere

Pete Seeger releases the first album of African music by a white musician, **Bantu Choral Folk Songs**

Lonnie Donegan's *Rock Island Line* launches a new genre in Britain, "skiffle"

Hungarian composer Georg Ligeti, while studying at Cologne, coins a "texture music" that has minimal movement

Chuck Berry cuts his first rock and roll records, the first ones to have the guitar as the main instrument, and invents the descending pentatonic double-stops (the essence of rock guitar)

Bo Diddley invents the "hambone" rhythm

The Chordettes and the Chantels are the first girl-groups

Ray Charles invents "soul" music with *I Got A Woman*, a secular adaptation of an old gospel

Indian sarod player Ali Akbar Khan performs at the Museum of Modern Art of

ABC-Paramount is founded in New York New York

The magazine "Village Voice" is founded by Dan Wolf, Ed Fancher and Norman Mailer

Ace Records is formed by Johnny Vincent in New Orleans, specializing in black music

Charlie Parker dies at the age of 35

1956:
Heartbreak Hotel starts Presley-mania
The rock'n'roll music of white rockers is called "rockabilly" (rock + hillbilly)
Screamin Jay Hawkins' *I Put A Spell On You* and his antics pioneers gothic rock
Wanda Jackson is the "queen of rockabilly"
The popularity of rock and roll causes the record industry to boom and allows independent labels to flourish
Ska develops in Jamaica
Martin Denny's **Exotica** invents a new genre
Norman Granz founds Verve to promote alternative jazz musicians
Elektra pioneers the "compilation" record, containing songs by different musicians

1957:
Golden age of the teen-idols
Link Wray's *Rumble* invents the "fuzz-tone" guitar sound
LaMonte Young composes music for sustained tones
Max Mathews begins composing computer music at Bell Laboratories
Lejaren Hiller writes a program for a computer to compose the *Illiac Suite*
Bruno Maderna's *Musica su Due Dimensioni* is the first electroacoustic composition
Harry Belafonte's *Banana Boat* launches "calypso"

1958:
Golden age of instrumental rock
Eddie Cochran overdubs all instruments and vocals on *Summertime Blues* and *C'mon Everybody*
The Kingstone Trio's *Tom Dooley* launches the folk revival
Lowman Pauling uses guitar distortion and feedback on the Five Royales' *The Slummer The Slum*
The film company Warner Brothers enters the recording business
Big Bill Broonzy dies at 65
RCA introduces the first stereo long-playing records
Don Kirshner opens offices at the Brill Building
David Seville's *The Witch Doctor* and the Tokens' *Tonite I Fell In Love* are the first novelty hits
Edgar Varese premieres his *Poeme Electronique* in a special pavilion designed by architect Le Corbusier, where the music reacts with the environment
John Fahey invents "American primitivism"
Bobby Freeman's *Do You Wanna Dance* begins the "dance craze"
Antonio Carlos Jobim's *Chega de Saudade* coins bossanova
The Columbia-Princeton studio is established in New York for avantgarde composers, with an RCA Mark II synthesizer
Stax is founded in Memphis to promote black music

1959:
Frank Zappa and Donald Van Vliet cut a record together
In Jamaica Theophilus Beckford cuts the first "ska" song, *Easy Snapping*

Rick Hall founds the FAME studios in Muscle Shoals, Alabama
The Drifters' *There Goes My Baby* introduces Latin rhythm into pop music
Babatunde Olatunji's **Drums of Passion** introduces the USA to African polyrhythms
The first Newport Folk Festival is held
John Cage performs "live electronic music"
LaMonte Young and others found the "Fluxus" movement
Barry Gordy founds Tamla Motown in Detroit to release party-oriented soul records
Chris Blackwell founds Island in Jamaica
Morton Subotnick, Terry Riley, Pauline Oliveros and others found the "Tape Music Center" near San Francisco
Raymond Scott invents the first sequencer, the "Wall of Sound"
600 million records are sold in the USA
Buddy Holly dies at 22 in a plane crash
Since 1955, the US market share of the four "majors" has dropped from 78% to 44%, while the market share of independent record companies increased from 22% to 56%
Since 1955, the US market has increased from 213 million dollars to 603 million, and the market share of rock and roll has increased from 15.7% to 42.7%

1960:
Twist is the biggest dance-craze in the year of the dance-crazes
Larry Parnes, Britain's most famous impresario, arranges a show for the Silver Beetles in Liverpool
The Shirelles' *Will You Love Me Tomorrow* coins a form of romantic multi-part vocal harmonies
The British producer Joe Meek uses the recording studio like an instrument for the space opera **I Hear a New World**
Eddie Cochran dies at 22
The word "reggae" is coined in Jamaica to identify a "ragged" style of dance music, with its roots in New Orleans rhythm and blues
The movie-jukebox "Scopitone" is invented in France (a refinement of the Panoram)
Russ Solomon opens the first Tower Records in Sacramento (California), the first music megastore
Philips buys Mercury
Frank Sinatra founds Reprise Records

1961:
Dick Dale uses the term "surfing" to describe his instrumental rock and roll
Bob Dylan arrives at New York's Greenwich Village
British bluesman Alexis Korner forms the Blues Incorporated, with a rotating cast that will include Charlie Watts, John Surman, John McLaughlin, Mick Jagger, Brian Jones, Keith Richard, Eric Burdon, Jack Bruce, Ginger Baker, etc
Howling Wolf cuts the **Rocking Chair** album, the masterpiece of rhythm'n'blues
July: The magazine "Mersey Beat" is founded in Liverpool
The Tokens' *The Lion Sleeps Tonight* uses operatic singing, Neapolitan choir, yodel, proto-electronics

Stax begins to produce soul records in Memphis
Kenny Gamble and Leon Huff found Philadelphia International to produce soul
records with orchestral arrangements
Robert Ashley and Gordon Mumma organize the first ONCE festival of
avantgarde music at Ann Arbor (Michigan)
LaMonte Young creates the "dream house", where the environment is part of the
music
MGM buys Verve
ABC-Paramount starts a sub-label for jazz, Impulse
The "Peppermint Lounge" opens in New York

1962:
The Beach Boys' *Surfin* (released in december 1961) launches surf-music in the
charts
The American producer Phil Spector creates a style of production named "wall
of sound"
the Tornado's futuristic instrumental *Telstar* is the first British record to top the
USA charts
Most pop hits are written and produced at the Brill Building
First show of the Rolling Stones at the Marquee (July 12)
First show of the Beatles at the Cavern (August 18)
Robert Wyatt and others form the Wilde Flowers, the beginning of the dynasty
of the Canterbury school
Seattle guitarist Jimi Hendrix begins working as a session-man
The bishop of New York forbids Catholic students from dancing the Twist
Golden age of the girl-groups
Herb Alpert founds A&M in Los Angeles
Boom of the Tamla Motown record label
MCA buys the American recording company Decca
The US market share of the four "majors" drops to 26%

1963:
"Beatlesmania" hits Britain
The Trashmen's *Surfin' Bird* and the Surfaris' *Wipe Out* extend the scope of surf
music
Davy Graham in Britain and Sandy Bull in the USA fuse folk, blues, jazz and
Indian raga
Eric Clapton joins the Yardbirds
Daevid Allen of the Wilde Flowers experiments with tape loops
A soul record, Marvin Gaye's *Can I Get A Witness*, becomes the anthem of
British mods
The Kingsmen stage the first *Louie Louie* marathon (playing the song over and
over again for one hour), and garage-rock is born
Pierre Henry's *Rock Electronique* employs electronic riff and rhythm
50% of American recordings are made in Nashville
Elmore James dies at 45
The FBI spies on folksingers such as Bob Dylan and Phil Ochs.
Warner buys Reprise

1964:

Don Van Vliet forms the Magic Band and adopts the nickname Captain Beefheart
Jesse Colin Young's **The Soul Of A City Boy** is a folk album that employs jazz musicians
James Brown coins a percussive style of soul, the predecessor of "funk"
The "British Invasion" exports to the USA the enthusiasm created by Beatlesmania in the UK
The riff of *You Really Got Me* by the Kinks virtually invents hard-rock
Millie Small's *My Boy Lollipop* is the first worldwide ska hit
Eric Clapton of the Yardbirds uses the guitar to produce feedback and fuzz
Debbie Reynolds makes a video for *If I Had A Hammer*, the first music video
Wilson Pickett creates an evil, ferocious kind of soul music with with *In The Midnight Hour*
Robert Moog begins selling his synthesizer
Charles Dodge and James Randall perform "computer music"
ESP is founded by lawyer Bernard Stollman
Karlheinz Stockhausen's *Mikrophonie I* is the first example of "live electronic music"

1965:
March: Bob Dylan's *Mr Tambourine Man* begins the season of psychedelic music
June: the Byrds' version of *Mr Tambourine Man* invents "folk-rock"
The Supremes have four number-one hits and the Four Tops have two, all of them written by Tamla's team of Brian Holland, Lamond Dozier and Eddie Holland
John Mayall's Bluesbreakers, featuring Eric Clapton, import Chicago's rhythm and blues to Britain and become the epitome of "blues-rock"
Country Joe McDonald releases the first "rag babies", agit-prop music to support Berkeley's civil-rights movement
Fred Neil's **Bleecker And McDougal** is a folksinger who merges folk, blues and psychedelic music
Dick Clark's "Where the Action Is" airs from a different location every time
Graham Bond plays the first mellotron on record
The Righteous Brothers' *You've Lost That Loving Feeling* launches "blue-eyed soul"
The Rolling Stones' *Satisfaction* is banned by radio stations across the UK and USA
The "Diggers" turn San Francisco's Haight Ashbury into a "living theater"
Bob Dylan cuts *Like A Rolling Stone* and unveils an electric band at the Newport Festival
Sonny Boy Williamson dies at 66
The Who's *My Generation* creates a new kind of rebellious rock anthem
In America garage-bands spring up everywhere
Robbie Basho's **Seal Of The Blue Lotus** fuses raga, jazz, blues and pop music
The Kinks' *See My Friends* (july) introduces Indian music into rock and roll
The Byrds' *Eight Miles High* invents raga-rock
The San Francisco band Charlatans perform for six days in front of a hippie crowd
Andy Warhol incorporates the Velvet Underground in his multimedia show

"The Exploding Plastic Inevitable"

The Warlocks (Grateful Dead) are hired to play at the "acid tests" (Ken Kesey's LSD parties), where they perform lengthy instrumental jams, loosely based on country, blues and jazz

Otis Redding's *I've Been Lovin' You Too Long* is soul music in which the instrumental backing has de facto replaced the gospel choir

Terry Riley and Steve Reich compose music based on repetition of simple patterns ("minimalism")

October: The Family Dog Production organizes the first hippie festival at San Francisco's Long Shoreman's Hall

November: Bill Graham opens the "Fillmore" as a venue for San Francisco's new bands

Alan Freed dies at 42 of a kidney disease

The "Whiskey-A-Go-Go" opens on Sunset Blvd in Hollywood

Noel Black's movie **SkaterDater** is the first skateboarding movie

1966:

Boom of the blues revival in the USA and Britain

The Jefferson Airplane and the Grateful Dead move to the Haight-Ashbury of San Francisco, the epicenter of "acid-rock" and of the "Summer of Love"

March: the Fugs' *Virgin Forest* experiments with collage, tapes and world-music

May: Bob Dylan's **Blonde On Blonde**, the first double record and the first concept album of rock music

The Velvet Underground cut their first record in two days in the spring of 1966

The 13th Floor Elevator's **The Psychedelic Sound Of** and the Jefferson Airplane's **Takes Off** are the first albums marketed as "psychedelic"

Paul Butterfield's *East-West* is a jam that fuses Afro-American and Indian improvisation

June: The elaborate arrangements of the Beach Boys' **Pet Sounds** define a new standard for pop music

July: Frank Zappa's **Freak Out**, the first double album of rock and roll

Brian Jones of the Rolling Stones plays dulcimer, flute, oboe, sitar, marimba, mellotron, etc on the band's singles

The Beach Boys' *Good Vibrations* is the first pop hit to employ electronic sounds

The Holy Modal Rounders invent "acid-folk"

Year of the jam: *Virgin Forest* by the Fugs, *Up In Her Room* by the Seeds, *Going Home* by the Rolling Stones, *Sad Eyed Lady Of The Lowlands* by Bob Dylan, etc

The Cream, the first "power-trio" debut and sell millions of copies with albums of improvised jams

Bob Dylan retires for a while from the music scene

First bubblegum hits

Jean Jacques Perrey and Gershon Kingsley create electronic pop on **In Sound From Way Out**

Pierre Schaeffer coins the term "acousmatic" in his book "Traite des Objets Musicaux"

London disc-jockey John Peel begins broadcasting American psychedelic music from his radio program "Perfumed Garden"

The UFO Club begins organizing "Spontaneous Underground" shows in London

The magazine "Crawdaddy" is founded in New York
Sire is founded in London

1967:
Love's **Da Capo** (january) features a side-long track, *Revelation*
A "Human Be-In" is held at the Golden Gate Park in San Francisco
June: Monterey festival
Ralph Gleason founds the magazine "Rolling Stone"
Velvet Underground & Nico (january) introduces droning, cacophony and
repetition (besides improvisation) to rock music, and connects rock music to the
avantgarde
Frank Zappa releases **Absolutely Free**, the first rock opera
Dyke And The Blazers cut *Funky Broadway*, the song that gives a genre its
name
The Doors (january) fuses rock and roll, blues, psychedelia, Indian raga, free-
form poetry and drama
The Jefferson Airplane's **Surrealistic Pillow** (february) is the first album of San
Francisco's acid-rock
Red Crayola's **Parable Of Arable Land** (march) turns psychedelic rock into
abstract sound-painting
The Incredible String Band's **5,000 Spirits** introduces medieval and middle-
eastern music into rock and roll
Jimi Hendrix debuts and turns the electric guitar into the equivalent of the
symphonic orchestra
The Pink Floyd debut and invent space-rock with *Interstellar Overdrive*
The second "Summer of Love" becomes a national phenomenon, attracting
young people from all states
Family Stone's bassist Larry Graham invents the "funk" bass lines
Swedish band Parson Sound fuses rock and minimalism in lengthy trance-drone
jams
The French composer Pierre Henry writes a rock mass, **Messe Pour Le Temp
Present**, that mixes symphonic, rock and electronic instruments
The Nice perform keyboard-driven arrangements of classical and jazz music
40 psychedelic bands perform at the "14 Hours Technicolour Dream" in London
Otis Redding dies at 26
Woody Guthrie dies at 55
John Coltrane dies at 40
Mort Garson's **Zodiac Cosmic Sounds** employs synthesizers
Warner Brothers purchases Atlantic
Byg is founded in France
Chrysalis is founded in London
The alternative press flourishes and a number of alternative papers unite in the
Underground Press Syndicate (UPS), including the Los Angeles Free Press, the
East Village Other, the Berkeley Barb, San Francisco's Oracle, Detroit's Fifth
Estate, Chicago's Seed, and Austin's Rag
In Jamaica, disc jockey Ruddy Redwood makes instrumental versions of reggae
hits
Neil Diamond's *Red Red Wine* is the first reggae hit by a pop musician
Caetano Veloso and Gilberto Gil found the "tropicalismo" movement in Brazil
Morton Subotnick releases a free improvisation on synthesizer, *Silver Apples of*

the Moon, the first work specifically commissioned for the recording medium

1968:
The Electric Prunes release a mass performed with rock instruments, **Mass In F Minor**
Gram Parsons invents "country-rock" with the International Submarine Band
The Creedence Clearwater Revival fuse Louisiana blues, soul and folk-rock
The Cockettes, a hippie-decadent musical theater troupe of drag queens, debuts in San Francisco, the first glam-rock experience
The Soft Machine debut, the leading group of the Canterbury school
The Silver Apples experiment with electronics in a rock and roll format
The Steppenwolf's *Born To Be Wild* contains the expression "heavy metal" that comes to identify a new genre
Blue Cheer debut, playing heavy psychedelic music (the prototype for stoner-rock)
Toots And The Maytals' *Do The Reggae* launches reggae in the USA
Joni Mitchell establishes the figure of the intellectual female singer-songwriter
The Band's **Music From Big Pink** invents "roots-rock" by fusing folk, gospel, country, and rock
The Pretty Things' **S.F. Sorrow** is the first British rock opera
Van Morrison's **Astral Weeks** invents abstract, free-form folk-rock by fusing soul, jazz, folk and psychedelia
Tim Buckley's **Happy Sad** fuses folk and free-jazz
John Fahey's **Voice Of The Turtle** fuses instrumental folk, jazz and raga
The Pentangle and the Fairport Convention debut, the leading groups of British folk-rock
The musical "Hair" opens on Broadway, the first musical that uses rock music
10,000 people attend the first Isle of Wight festival in England
Bob Krasnow founds Blue Thumb, that values the cover design as much as the music
Walter Carlos' **Switched On Bach** turns the synthesizer into a pop instrument
Syd Barrett, mentally unstable, leaves the Pink Floyd
Conrad Schnitzler, Hans-Joachim Roedelius and Klaus Schulze found the Zodiak Free Arts Lab in Berlin, the first venue for electronic music
The magazine "Creem" is founded in Detroit, with Lester Bangs, Robert Christgau, Dave Marsh

1969:
August: 300,000 people attend the Woodstock festival
Warner, Atlantic and Elektra are unified as WEA
King Crimson's **In The Court Of The Crimson King** and Frank Zappa's **Uncle Meat** herald the golden age of progressive-rock
Jazz giant Miles Davis records **Bitches Brew**, an album that combines funk/soul rhythms and electronically-amplified rock instruments
Neil Young invents a neurotic, dissonant form of guitar accompaniment
German group Can plays rock music inspired by the classical avantgarde and modern jazz
Led Zeppelin's debut launches hard-rock and defines the LP as rock's medium of choice

Crosby Stills & Nash popularize West Coast's vocal harmonies
Nico's **Marble Index** brings gothic, archaic and classical elements into rock music
Captain Beefheart cuts ""Trout Mask Replica"", possibly the greatest rock album ever
The Who release **Tommy**, the most famous rock opera
Brian Jones of the Rolling Stones dies at 27
150,000 people attend the rock festival at the Isle of Wight
The Third Ear Band invents "world-music"
Holger Czuckay's **Canaxis 5** fuses electronics and ethnic music
Beaver & Krause's **Ragnarok Electronic Funk** uses the Moog with acoustic instruments
Annette Peacock improvises live with the synthesizer
The MC5's **Kick Out The Jams** and **The Stooges** create a new Detroit sound founded on extreme violence
The world's music market is worth two billion dollars
Capricorn is founded in Alabama
Manfred Eicher forms the ECM label in Germany

1970:
King Tubby invents "dub" in Jamaica using the recording console like an instrument
Syd Barrett retires from music
12,000 people attend the alternative festival at Glastonbury, in England
ZZ Top and Allman Brothers launch "southern-rock"
Black Sabbath debut, playing heavy, dark rock music (the prototype for black metal and doom metal)
Todd Rundgren plays all instruments by himself on **Runt**, the first "do it yourself" production
German group Kluster (Cluster) plays keyboards-based instrumental music that is inspired by the industrial society
At the peak of British jazz-rock, the Soft Machine cut **Third**
Smokey Robinson's *The Tears Of A Clown* fuses vaudeville, classical music and soul music
T.Rex's *Ride A White Swan* opens the age of glam-rock
David Geffen founds Asylum Records
Richard Branson founds Virgin to promote alternative musicians
Pierre Boulez founds the IRCAM (Institut de Recherche et Coordination Acoustique) at the Centre Pompidou in Paris
Robert Moog unveils the Minimoog, the first portable synthesizer
September: Jimi Hendrix dies at 28
October: Janis Joplin dies at 27

1971:
Jim Morrison of the Doors dies at 27 (July 3)
The German band Tangerine Dream invents "kosmische musik", using synthesizers and sequencers
Johnny Thunders forms the New York Dolls, a band of tranvestites with a trash aesthetic that plays very fast and simple rock"n"roll
Alice Cooper mixes decadence, horror and hard-rock in his "shock rock"

Marvin Gaye, Isaac Hayes, Curtis Mayfield and Stevie Wonder begin
producing artsy soul records
The musical *Jesus Christ Superstar* by Andrew Lloyd Webber opens on
Broadway
Tonto's Expanding Head Band release **Zero Time**, the first pop album entirely
played at the synthesizer
The Joy Of Cooking debut, the first band led by feminists
Alice Cooper's **Love It To Death** launches horror-shock rock
German group Faust plays rock songs that are studio collages of rock music,
electronic sounds and "concrete" noise
Marvin Gaye's *Mercy Mercy Me* is the first ecological song
Duane Allman dies at 25
Gene Vincent dies at 36
A benefit concert for Bangla Desh is attended by rock stars
Sandy Pearlman of "Crawdaddy" uses the expression "heavy metal" for
Artificial Energy on **The Notorious Byrd Brothers**
Malcom McLaren opens a boutique in London that becomes a center for the
non-conformist youth
Rhys Chatam founds the avantgarde music program at the Kitchen Center in
New York
Alligator is founded in Chicago by Bruce Iglauer
"Creem" writer Dave Marsh coins the term "punk-rock" for the music of
Question Mark & The Mysterians

1972:
Popol Vuh's **In Den Gaerten Pharaos** is recorded inside a cathedral and fuses
electronic music and Eastern music (predating new-age music)
Deuter's **Aum** is released, a fusion of Eastern and Western religious music, of
acoustic instruments and natural sounds
Tangerine Dream's **Zeit** is a double album that contains four side-long suites
Annette Peacock's **I'm The One** fuses synthesizer and vocals
Neu! plays obsessively rhythmic music
Klaus Schulze's **Irrlicht** is a cosmic symphony played with electronic
instruments
Tom Verlaine and Richard Hell form the Neon Boys
Japanese group Taj-Mahal Travellers plays lengthy improvised psychedelic jams
David Bowie's **Rise And Fall of Ziggy Stardust** is the culmination of glam-
rock
By fusing Mersey-beat, folk-rock and hard-rock, the Big Star coin power-pop
Boom of singer-songwriters
The Vertigo label is founded to promote progressive-rock
Philips and Siemens merge their music companies into Polygram and buy
MGM/Verve
"Rolling Stone" writer Vince Aletti writes an article on "disco music"
Cameroon-born and Paris-based musician Manu Dibango invents "disco music"
with *Soul Makossa*

1973:
George Lucas' film **American Graffiti** launches the nostalgic revival of the
music of the 1950s and 1960s

Mother Mallard's Portable Masterpiece Company is an album of lengthy electronic suites
500,000 people attend the Watkins Glen festival (Allman Brother, Grateful Dead, Band)
"The Midnight Special" debuts on tv, led by Wolfman Jack and Helen Reddy
The film **The Harder They Come** brings reggae to the West
September: Gram Parsons dies at 26
Barry Oakley of the Allman Brothers dies
Pink Floyd's **Dark Side Of The Moon** invents a polished, keyboard-based sound for pop music, and would remain in the Billboard charts for over 600 weeks
Mike Oldfield cuts an album-long suite of instrumental music, **Tubular Bells**, all played by himself
A tv special uses the term "salsa" for Latin music
Asylum buys Elektra
Roland introduces the SH-1000, Japan's first synthesizer

1974:
The Rocky Horror Picture Show is released
Barry White plays orchestral soul for the discos
August: The Ramones debut at the CBGB's and launch punk-rock
The Residents reinvent rock music with **Meet The Residents**
The Grateful Dead, the most successful live band of all times, performs using 25 tons of loudspeakers
Robert Wyatt cuts **Rock Bottom**, possibly the greatest Canterbury album
Nick Drake dies at 26
Brian Eno's **Taking Tiger Mountain By Strategy** fuses electronics and pop, and introduces post-modernism into rock music
The magazine "Trouser Press" is founded to cover the British music scene
Kraftwerk's *Autobahn* becomes the first hit entirely played on electronic instruments and with an electronic rhythm, the blueprint for disco-music
July: Patti Smith's *Piss Factory* is the first single of New York's "new wave"
August: the "new wave" groups begin performing at New York's club CGBG's
Charly is founded in France
Technics introduces the Technics SL-1200, a turntable that becomes popular among New York DJs
Greg Shaw founds Bomp Records in San Francisco, specializing in garage-rock

1975:
Boom of funk music
Calhoun's *Dance Dance Dance* is the first 12" single
Giorgio Moroder releases the first tracks of European "disco-music" and invent the extended "disco mix"
Lou Reed releases **Metal Machine Music**, an album of pure noise
Jamaican disc-jockey Clive "Hercules" Campbell re-invents the breakbeat in New York, thereby inventing "rap music" and "hip hop"
The Queen film a bizarre, artistic video for *Bohemian Rhapsody*
Tim Buckley dies at 28
"Saturday Night Live" debuts on tv
Robert Moog introduces the Polymoog, the first commercial polyphonic

synthesizer
13-year old (Grand Wizard) Theodore Livingstone accidentally discovers the
"skratching" sound of a turntable and uses it at a party in the Bronx
Werner Uehlinger founds Hat Hut
December: John Holmstrom founds the fanzine "Punk" in New York, the first
fanzine for punk-rock and new-wave music

1976:
Pere Ubu cut **Modern Dance**, possibly the greatest new-wave album
Richard Hell cuts *Blank Generation*
David Grisman coins "newgrass", a fusion of jazz and bluegrass
Wanted: The Outlaws, featuring Waylon Jennings, Willie Nelson, Tompall
Glaser and Jessi Colter, is the first country album to be certified platinum
April: the first Ramones album is released
July: a Ramones tour organized by Malcom McLaren exports punk-rock to
Britain
September: the "100 Club Festival" turns British punk-rock into a national
phenomenon
September: the Saint's *I'm Stranded* is the first Australian punk-rock single
November: the Sex Pistols' *Anarchy In The UK* is the first British punk-rock
single
Boom of reggae music outside of Jamaica
Phil Ochs dies at 36
Howling Wolf dies at 66
William Ackerman invents new-age music and founds Windham Hill
New York disc-jockey Grandmaster Flash begins spinning on Boston Road,
where he experiments with "cutting" and "phasing"
The magazine "Musician" begins publication
The jazz magazine Cadence begins publication
Independent labels founded in 1976 include: Beserkley (Berkeley), Stiff
(London)
Barry Vercoe hosts the first International Conference for Computer Music
December: Blondie's first album bridges the gap between disco-music and punk-
rock

1977:
Punk spawns a self-publishing revolution ("do it yourself") both for music and
for magazines ("Ripped & Torn", "Sniffin' Glue", "48 Thrills")
The film "Saturday Night Fever" starts the disco fever by promoting disco-music
beyond gays and blacks
April: The Screamers are a punk band that uses two keyboards and no guitars
and performs at multimedia events on the Hollywood strip
Boom of independent labels
Suicide's **Suicide** fuses rockabilly and electronic music
Elvis Presley dies at 42
Peter Laughner of Pere Ubu dies
Three members of the Lynyrd Skynyrd are killed in a plane crash
Ronnie VanZandt dies at 28
Bukka White dies at 71
Marc Bolan of the T.Rex dies at 29

The disco "Warehouse" opens in Chicago and Frankie Knuckles becomes its resident disc-jockey
The magazine "OP" (later "Option") is founded in Olympia and becomes the reference for independent music of all genres
Roland introduces the first commercial rhythm machine
Martin Mills's record store Beggars Banquet becomes an independent label
London record store Rough Trade becomes an independent label
Affinity is founded by Joop Visser
October: The Avengers' *We Are The One* is the first single of the punk scene of San Francisco's Mabuhay Garden club

1978:
Brian Eno discovers the no-wave of DNA, Mars, Contortions, Lydia Lunch
Brian Eno invents ambient music
The Public Image Ltd bridge dub and punk
The disco "Paradise Garage" for black gays opens in New York and its founder Larry Levan becomes the first superstar disc-jockey
The California composer Monte Cazazza and the British band Throbbing Gristle coin "industrial music", that soon finds its headquarters in the English industrial town of Sheffield
July: The Germs' *Forming* is the first single of California's punk-rock
Fred Frith organizes the "Rock In Opposition" (RIO) festival that unites progressive-rock and militant politics
Keith Moon of the Who dies at 32
Sandy Denny dies at 31
"Crawdaddy" ceases publication
Mute is founded
Roland introduces the MC-4 sequencer, the first sequencer for the masses
Dave Smith (Sequential Circuits) introduces the Prophet-5, the world's first microprocessor-based musical instrument, and ushers in the age of digital synthesizers, replacing the voltage-controlled (analog) synthesizers
Independent labels founded in 1978 include: Ace of Hearts (Boston), Cherry Red (London), Rhino

1979:
The Pop Group's **Y** delivers agip-prop anthems in a style that fuses punk-rock, jazz, dub and funk
December: Clash's **London Calling** mixes punk-rock with reggae, ska, funk, blues, etc
The Talking Heads' **Fear Of Music**, produced by Brian Eno, fuses new wave and funk, and invents "techno-funk"
The B52's fuse new wave and dance music
The Specials launch a ska revival in Britain
Todd Rungren makes the first video-disc
Sony and Philips invent the compact disc (CD), a digital storage for music
Eleven fans die at a Who concert
Sid Vicious of the Sex Pistols dies at 21
Lowell George of the Little Feat dies at 34
Maybellene Carter dies at 70
The first New Music festival of avantgarde music is held in New York

Sony launches the "Walkman" portable stereo

The Australian company Fairlight Instruments introduces the first keyboard-based digital sampler, the CMI

Independent labels founded in 1979 include: Alternative Tentacles (San Francisco), SST (Los Angeles), Factory (London)

MCA purchases ABC

The world's music market is worth over 10 billion dollars and five "majors" control over 70% of it

September: Charles Mingus dies

1980:

Beggars Banquet employee Ivo Watts-Russell founds 4AD

The Cramps' **Songs The Lord Taught Us** invents "voodoobilly"

The Bad Brain's *Pay To Cum* fuses punk-rock and reggae in Washington

Ian MacKaye forms the Minor Threat in Washington

A psychedelic revival spreads from the UK to the US

The Minutemen play dissonant, funky, jazzy, punk-rock in Los Angeles

The Sugar Hill Gang cuts the first "hip hop" record in New York

Pioneering rap label Tommy Boy is founded

Glenn Branca composes music for dissonant and percussive guitars

David Geffen founds Geffen Records

John Bonham of the Led Zeppelin dies at 33

Bon Scott of the AC/DC dies at 25

John Lennon of the Beatles is murdered at 40

Ian Curtis of the Joy Division commits suicide at 23

Derby Crash dies at 22

Polygram buys the British recording company Decca

Warner acquires Sire

Independent labels founded in 1980 include: Wax Trax, On-U-Sound

1981:

Juan Atkins begins making "techno" records in Detroit (pounding and fast rhythm from a Roland sequencer MSK-100, stripped-down funk)

Venom's **Welcome To Hell** invents "black metal"

Billy Idol weds hard-rock and disco-music

New Zealand bands such as Tall Dwarfs and Clean invent "lo-fi pop"

New York rapper Afrika Bambaataa pays tribute to Kraftwerk with *Planet Rock* and thus invent "electro"

Boom of synth-pop in England

Husker Du and Replacements wed hardcore and pop in Minneapolis

Michael Jackson films a 15-minute, highly cinematic video for *Thriller*

MTV debuts on cable tv with the Buggles' "Video Killed The Radio Star"

Simon and Garfunkel reunite for a live concert in Central Park for a crowd of 500,000

Mike Bloomfield dies at 37

Alex Harvey dies at 32

Bob Marley dies at 34

Independent labels founded in 1981 include: Touch & Go, Epitaph, Dischord, Flying Nun

A four-day "CMJ Music Marathon", promoting dozens of indie acts, is held for the first time

1982:
The Sonic Youth invent "noise-rock"
The R.E.M. resurrect folk-rock and launch Georgia's neo-pop school
The club "Batcave" opens in London, cathering to the gothic (dark-punk) crowd
The Cocteau Twins invent dream-pop
The Violent Femmes weds the aesthetics of punk-rock and the format of roots-rock
A pacifist concert is held in Central Park attended by 800,000 people
Sequential Circuits introduces the "Prophet 600", the first keyboard enabled with MIDI (Musical Instrument Digital Interface), a system to connect music instruments to computers
Sony and Philips introduce the "compact disc"
Mike Gunderloy begins mailing "Factsheet Five", a fanzine of fanzine reviews
800,000 people attend a concert in New York's Central Park with Springsteen and others (for nuclear disarmement)
The magazine "Maximum Rock and Roll" is founded and becomes the reference point for punk-rock
The magazine "Puncture" is founded and becomes the reference point for alternative rock
Peter Gabriel organizes the WOMAD festival, dedicated to world music, art and dance
Rock critic Lester Bangs dies at 34

1983:
Metallica's **Kill 'Em All** invents speed-metal
Turntablist DST (DXT) plays a solo of "sktratch" on Herbie Hancock's *Rockit*
The Frightwig's **Cat Faboo Farm** is the first hardcore album by a female punk band
Madonna becomes the folk icon of the punkettes
The Suicidal Tendencies fuse hardcore and heavy-metal
The psychedelic revival leads to Los Angeles' "Paisley Underground"
Big Black's **Lungs** coins a claustrophobic form of hardcore
Run DMC fuse hip hop and heavy metal
Trouser Press magazine dies and the first "Trouser Press Guide", edited by Ira Robbins, is published
Yamaha introduces the DX-7, the first synthesizer to be sold by the hundreds of thousands
Muddy Waters dies at 68
A Sequential Circuits's "Prophet 600" and a Roland's "JX-3P" are connected together, the first time that two MIDI instruments are connected
Michael Jackson's **Thriller** spends 37 weeks at number one and becomes the best-selling album of all times
Tower Records lunches its own magaine, "Pulse"
Felix Pappalardi of Mountain is murdered
Independent labels founded in 1983 include: Creation, Projekt

1984:
The Chicago record store "Imports Etc" sells "house" records (as a contraction

of "Warehouse", the disco where DJs play electronic dance music built around drum-machines and soul vocals), first ones being Frankie Knuckles' *Your Love* and Walter Gibbons' *Set It Off*

A new British invasion (of dance-rock bands) sweeps America

The Red Hot Chili Peppers invent funk-metal

The Pogues' **Red Roses For Me** weds punk-rock and folk-rock ("rogue-folk")

Van Halen's *Jump* is the first heavy-metal song to top the Billboard charts

Schoolly D's *Gangster Boogie* coins "gangsta-rap"

Boom of new-age music

John Chowning founds the CCRMA (Center for Computer Research in Music and Acoustics) at Stanford University

Ensoniq introduces the synthesizer Mirage, that includes a built-in sampler, making it cheap to create samples-based music

Marvin Gaye dies at 45

Independent labels founded in 1984 include: Cuneiform, Homestead

1985:

A Chicago disc-jockey, DJ Pierre (later Phuture), invents "acid-house", built around the Roland TB-303 bassline machine

Youth Of Today invent "straight-edge" hardcore

Green River invent "grunge" in Seattle

Operation Ivy fuse ska and hardcore in Berkeley

Merzbow begins releasing cassettes of noise music in Japan

Rites Of Spring invent "emo-core" in Washington

Phranc's **Folksinger** starts the acoustic folk revival

The Jesus And Mary Chain's **Psychocandy** fuses noise and pop

"Live Aid", a multi-national benefit concert

The magazine "Spin" is founded in New York

German media giant Bertelsmann buys RCA and founds BMG

MCA buys Chess

the first concert by a foreign rock band is held in China (Wham)

Alternative Press is founded to cover the scene of independent rock

Digidesign releases recording and editing software for the Macintosh, that allows anyone to compose music and store it on a computer disk

Independent labels founded in 1985 include: Amphetamine Reptile, Def Jam, C/Z, Chemikal Underground, Ambiances Magnetiques

D. Boon of the Minutemen dies at 28

Joe Turner dies at 74

1986:

Bristol disc-jockeys form the Wild Bunch, whose sound mixes soul, dub and hip hop

Ministry's **Twitch** fuses industrial music and hardcore

The Melvins perform long, droning, super-heavy dirges

Mr T Experience and Green Day with their punk-pop style are protagonists of the "Gilman St scene" in Berkeley

Paul Simon's **Graceland** incorporates African music into folk and rock music

Richard Manuel of the Band dies at 43

Larry Harvey burns a wooden man at a San Francisco beach in front of a small crowd of friends, the first Burning Man event

Robbie Basho dies at 45
Independent labels founded in 1986 include: Silent
Subpop is founded in Seattle

1987:
The My Bloody Valentine invent "shoegazing" psychedelia
Zeni Geva's **How To Kill** is the first album of Japanese "noise"
Coldcut's *Say Kids What Time Is It* is the first dance hit made of samples
Napalm Death invents grindcore
Beastie Boys' **Licensed To Ill** is the first hip-hop album to reach the top of the
Billboard charts
Paul Butterfield dies at 45
Detroit disc-jockey Derrick May cuts *Nude Photo* and *Strings Of Life*, which are
broadcast on Alan Oldham's "Fast Forward" radio show and start the techno
revolution
Guns'N'Roses' **Appetite For Destruction** and Jane's Addiction's first album
vent the anger of Los Angeles' "street scene"
Enya fuses celtic music, electronic keyboards, and avantgarde vocals
Public Enemy play highly politicized hip-hop
The drug "ecstasy", banned in Britain and the USA, becomes popular at all-night
parties at the open-air dance club "Amnesia" of Ibiza (Spain) that attracts people
from all over Europe
After spending a summer in Ibiza, British disc-jockey Paul Oakenfold organizes
"Spectrum", the first ecstasy-based party in London
Philips acquires the whole of Polygram
The Roland D50 ushers in the age of digital keyboards for the masses
M/A/R/S/S' *Pump Up The Volume* is the first hit built as a collage of samples
Death's **Scream Bloody Gore** invents death-metal
Dave Datta at the University of Wisconsin creates an on-line archive of musical
information on the Internet
Independent labels founded in 1987 include: Invisible, Estrus
The first Bang On A Can festival is held in New York

1988:
The Pixies' **Surfer Rosa** signals the apex of "college-rock"
Fugazi play a tortured, existential form of hardcore in Washington
Soundgarden's **Ultramega OK** is the first hit album of Seattle's grunge sound
Roy Orbison dies
Nico dies at 49
Acid-house spreads from Ibiza to Manchester's club "Hacienda" (the "second
summer of love", "Madchester") via secretive, all-night house and techno parties
called "raves"
Sony buys CBS
"Creem" ceases publication
"The Source", a magazine for hip-hop music, is founded by two Harvard
students
Independent labels founded in 1988 include: Wiiija, Lookout
The first KLEM ("Kontakt Liefhebbers Elektronische Muziek") festival for
electronic music is held in Holland

1989:
Nine Inch Nail's **Pretty Hate Machine** is an electronic album of brutal hardcore
Slint's **Tweez** inaugurates the age of post-rock
808 State's *Pacific State* invents "ambient house"
The Ptolemaic Terrascope magazine is founded by Bevis Frond and Phil
McMullen
150 people attend a "rave" called "Love Parade" in Berlin organized by Dr
Motte as a political event
Polygram acquires Island
The Stone Roses debut, leading the Madchester scene
Independent labels founded in 1989 include: Matador, Merge, Sympathy for the
Record Industry

1990:
Paradise Lost invents "doom-metal"
Meat Beat Manifesto invents "jungle" (or "drum'n'bass"), a fusion of hip hop
and techno, that is adopted at the London club "Rage" by disc jockeys Fabio and
Grooverider
Stevie Ray Vaughn dies
The Burning Man sculpture is moved to Black Rock Desert
Warner merges with Time Life to become the world's largest media
conglomerate
Polygram acquires A&M
MCA buys Geffen
EMI buys Chrysalis
Independent labels founded in 1990 include: Trance Syndicate, Drag City, Ninja
Tune, Warp, Too Pure

1991:
Codeine's **Frigid Stars** invents "slo-core"
Molly Neuman forms the Bratmobile in Olympia, the first riot-grrrl band
Boom of Seattle's grunge (Nirvana's **Nevermind**, Pearl Jam's **Ten**)
The Primal Scream's **Screamadelica** fuses rock'n'roll and acid-house
Kyuss' **Wretch** coins "stoner" rock
Mariah Carey becomes the first artist ever to have her first five singles all make
#1 on the Billboard charts
N.W.A.'s **Efil4Zaggin** (1991) is the first rap album to debut at the top of the
charts
Revival of the melodic song in Britain ("Brit-pop")
The Prodigy's *Charly* pioneers "big beat"
Massive Attack's **Blue Lines** invents "trip-hop"
Garth Brooks' **Ropin' the Wind** is the first country album to debut at number
one in the pop charts
The "Lollapalooza" festival is born as the road show accompanying Jane's
Addiction's final tour, but soon becomes an itinerant display of alternative rock
Freddie Mercury of the Queen dies of AIDS
Johnny Thunders dies
Independent labels founded in 1991 include: Skin Graft, Kill Rock Stars, VHF,
The Pro Tools software is introduced
A Paul Simon concert in Central Park draws an audience of 750,000 people

Miles Davis dies at 65
Billboard begins tallying albums based on actual sales at retail stores (not word of mouth)

1992:
Rage Against The Machine's first album fuses funk, rap and heavy-metal
Atari Teenage Riot wed techno and hardcore ("digital hardcore")
D.J. Shadow is the first virtuoso turntablist on record
The Pavement's **Slanted And Enchanted** launches lo-fi pop in the charts
Boyz II Men set the new record for the longest running # single with "End Of The Road"
Disc-jockey Gregor Asch (DJ Olive) organizes the first Lalalandia multimedia party in Williamsburg and coins the word "illbient"
MP3 is invented as a format to store music in computers
EMI acquires Virgin Records
The first edition of Michael Erlewine's "All Music Guide" is published
Willie Dixon dies at 77
Independent labels founded in 1992 include: Cleopatra, Thrill Jockey, Nothing

1993:
Labradford's **Prazision** launches the revival of analogical keyboards
Beck's *Loser* is a folk song for the age of hip-hop
Pearl Jam's **Vs** sells one million copies the first week of release
Autechre's **Incunabula** turns dance music into an abstract art
LTJ Bukem's *Music* invents "ambient jungle"
In London techno and jungle merge and yield "techstep"
German disc-jockey Sven Vath's **Accident In Paradise** invents "progressive house" (or "trance")
The Transglobal Underground launch "transglobal dance"
Eric Miller founds the magazine "Magnet", specializing in independent rock
Polygram buys Motown
Frank Zappa dies of cancer
Kranky is founded in Chicago

1994:
Korn's first album fuses rap and grunge
Oval's **Systemisch** invents "glitch" music
Portishead's **Dummy** launches trip-hop
Simon Reynolds coins the term "post rock" for Bark Psychosis' **Hex**
Tortoise's first album leads the "post-rock" generation
The British government enacts the "Criminal Justice Bill" aimed at curbing raves
4 Hero's **Parallel Universe** introduces jazz in jungle
Sub Dub spearhead the fusion of hip hop, ambient house, middle-eastern folk and dub, the precursor to the "illbient" scene
Green Day's **Dookie** is the best-sold punk-rock album of all times
Piero Scaruffi begins work at this chronology
Kurt Cobain of Nirvana commits suicide
Independent labels founded in 1994 include: Rather Interesting
Polygram acquires 50% of Def Jam

1995:
The Rock And Roll Hall Of Fame And Museum opens in Cleveland
Legendary disc-jockey Wolfman Jack dies
Vivian Stanshall of the Bonzos dies
Sterling Morrison of the Velvet Underground dies
Jerry Garcia of the Grateful Dead dies, after performing 2,200 live concerts
The Chemical Brothers' **Exit Planet Dust** invents "big beat" that fuses techno
and rock
Seagram acquires MCA
Independent labels founded in 1995 include: Digital Hardcore

1996:
DJ Spooky's **Songs Of A Dead Dreamer** (Asphodel, 1996) launches the
"illbient" scene of New York with a chaotic and non-melodic fusion of drum &
bass, hip hop, dub
Naut Humon organizes "Recombinant", a multimedia festival for electronic
musicians, in San Francisco
Two rap singles reach the #1 spot in the pop charts
"Macarena" is the biggest dance craze since the twist (one of its mixes stays at
#1 for 14 weeks)
Jeffrey Lee Pierce of the Gun Club dies
Mariah Carey's *One Sweet Day* tops the U.S. charts for an unprecedented 16
weeks
The DVD is introduced in Japan
Disc-jockey Paul Oakenfold launches "Goa Trance" at the "Full Moon Party"
BMG buys Windham Hill
Independent labels founded in 1996 include: Alien8
Tupac Shakur and The Notorious B.I.G. are murdered

1997:
Roni Size's **New Forms** blends jungle's breakbeats with live instruments and
singing
Matmos uses "organic" samples (noises, not instruments) to compose music
Elton John's *Candle in the Wind* becomes the best-selling song of all times,
passing Bing Crosby's *White Christmas*
Armand Van Helden develops "garage" music
Laura Nyro dies
Tim Taylor of Brainiac dies
John Denver dies
Fela Anikulapo Kuti dies of AIDS
The "Terrastock" festival for psychedelic music is held in Providence (Rhode
Island)
Nusrat Fateh Ali dies
Townes VanZandt dies at 52

1998:
The first portable MP3 devices are introduced
Seagram acquires Polygram and combines MCA and Polygram into the
Universal Music Group, which thus comprises Polygram, MCA, Geffen,

Mercury, Polydor, London, Vertigo, Verve, A&M, Island, Motown, Decca, DG
Independent labels founded in 1999 include: Absolutely Kosher, Tiger Style

1999:
Moondog dies at 83
Mark Sandman of Morphine dies
Shawn Fanning founds the Napster service that allows people to share music over the Internet
Barry Hogan organizes the first "All Tomorrow's Parties" festival in England
'N Sync set the new record of sales in the first week of a new release (2.4 million copies)
"Option" ceases publication
The music world is ruled by five majors:
 1. Universal,
 2. Warner/Elektra/Sire/Atlantic,
 3. Sony/Columbia/Epic,
 4. EMI/Virgin/Capitol/Chrysalis,
 5. BMG/Jive/Private/American/Windham Hill.
The world's music market is worth 38 billion dollars. The five "majors" control 95% of the albums sold in the world, and 84% of the 755 million albums sold in the USA:
 1. Universal with 27% (26.3% in the USA),
 2. Warner with 20% (15.7%),
 3. Sony with 18% (16.2%),
 4. EMI with 16% (9.4%),
 5. BMG with 14% (16%).
The USA accounts for 37% of world sales, Japan for 16.7%, Britain for 7.6%, Germany for 7.4%, France for 5.2%, Canada for 2.3%, Australia for 1.7%, Brazil for 1.6%, Holland for 1.5%, Italy for 1.4%.
Independent labels founded in 1999 include: Family Vineyard
The Coachella Valley Music and Arts Festivals is born

2000:
Mum's **Yesterday Was Dramatic Today Is Ok** mixes glitch electronica, chamber instruments and folk-rock
Berlin's "Love Parade" becomes the largest dance event in the world, attended by almost one million people
27 people die of ecstasy in just one year in England
Curtis Mayfield dies
Tomata du Plenty dies
25,000 people attend the Burning Man festival at Black Rock Desert, which has become a city of art installations
July: San Francisco hosts "Skratchcon", a conference for turntablists
French media giant Vivendi buys Seagram. Warner is the only "major" that is still American: Universal is now French, Sony is Japanese, EMI is British, BMG is German
Independent labels founded in 2000 include: Def Jux

2001:

Larry Tee, owner of the "Luxx" club in Brooklyn, organizes the "Electroclash" festival, which establishes electroclash (a fusion of punk-rock and dance-music) as a stand-alone musical genre
Sales for the record industry slip 5% (first decline in ages)
Napster is found guilty of breaching copyright law
John Fahey dies
Sandy Bull dies
Fred Neil dies
Joey Ramone dies
Florian Fricke of Popol Vuh dies
"Puncture" ceases publication
62 albums released by the Universal group sell more than 1 million copies in 2001
The file-sharing service Kazaa is founded in Amsterdam by Niklas Zennstrom and Janus Friis

2002:
Dee Dee Ramone of the Ramones dies
Joe Strummer of the Clash dies at 50
Otis Blackwell dies at 72
The top-selling album of 2002 is a white rap album, Eminem's **Show**
The "Bonnaroo" festival is born as a jam-based marathon
EMI buys Mute
"Pulse" ceases publication
CD sales decrease 9%
Warner acquires Tommy Boy
Independent labels founded in 2002 include: Eastern Developments
The first "Projekt Revolution" tour promotes rap-rock fusion

2003:
Apple introduces the on-line music service "iTunes", which sells 25 million songs by december
Universal reduces the price of CDs by 30%
Market shares: Universal 26.3%, BMG 16.7%, Warner 16.1%, Sony 13.7%, EMI 11.2%
The top-selling album of 2003 is a black rap album, 50 Cent's **Get Rich or Die Tryin'** :
CD sales decrease 2%, from 649.5 million units in 2002 to 635.8 million units in 2003
Warren Zevon dies at 56

2004:
Ray Charles dies at 73
Robert Quine dies
British DJ John Peel dies
Johnny (Cummings) Ramone of the Ramones dies
143 millions songs are downloaded legally in the USA

2005:
Robert Moog dies

Link Wray dies at 76
CD sales decrease 7% in the USA to $602.2 million, while music downloads
more than doubled from $134 million to $332 million
352 millions songs are downloaded legally in the USA

2006:
Wilson Pickett dies at 64
Syd Barrett dies at 60
Arthur Lee dies at 61
James Brown dies at 73
Kazaa surrenders to the music industry
Global digital music sales double to about $2bn

2007:
"Live Earth" concerts are held all over the world to increase awareness of
climate change
The annual "CMJ Music Marathon" presents 1,000 indie rock bands
All four majors (Universal, EMI, Warner and Sony) start selling their music on
Amazon's digital-music store in the unprotected mp3 format

2008:
Bo Diddley dies at 79
Richard Wright dies at 65

Selected Discography

Albums of the 1960s

9.5/10
Captain Beefheart: Trout Mask Replica (1969)

9/10
Bob Dylan: Blonde On Blonde (1966)
Captain Beefheart: Safe As Milk (1967)
Doors: The Doors (1967)
Frank Zappa: Uncle Meat (1969)
Red Crayola: Parable Of Arable Land (1967)
Van Morrison: Astral Weeks (1968)
Velvet Underground & Nico (1967)
Velvet Underground: White Light White Heat (1967)

8.5/10
Jefferson Airplane: Volunteers (1969)
King Crimson: In The Court Of The Crimson King (1969)
Leonard Cohen: Songs Of Leonard Cohen (1968)
MC5: Kick Out The Jams (1969)
Pink Floyd: The Piper At The Gates Of Dawn (1967)

8/10
Band: II (1969)
Bob Dylan: Highway 61 Revisited (1965)
Colosseum: Valentyne Suite (1969)
David Peel: Have A Marijuana (1969)
Deviants: Ptooff (1967)
Doors: Strange Days (1967)
Family: Music In A Doll's House (1968)
Grateful Dead: Anthem Of The Sun (1968)
Grateful Dead: Live Dead (1969)
Holger Czukay: Canaxis 5 (1969)
Holy Modal Rounders: Indian War Whoop (1967)
Jefferson Airplane: After Bathing At Baxter's (1967)
Jimi Hendrix: Are You Experienced? (1967)
Jimi Hendrix: Electric Ladyland (1968)
Kaleidoscope: Beacon From Mars (1968)
Love: Da Capo (1967)
Neil Young: Everybody Knows This Is Nowhere (1969)
Nico: Marble Index (1968)
Pearls Before Swine: Balaklava (1968)
Pink Floyd: A Saucerful Of Secrets (1968)
Robbie Basho: Venus In Cancer (1970)
Sandy Bull: Fantasia For Guitar & Banjo (1963)

Stooges: Stooges (1969)
Tim Buckley: Happy Sad (1968)
United States Of America: United States of America (1968)
Who: Tommy (1969)
Frank Zappa: Freak Out (1966)
Frank Zappa: Absolutely Free (1967)
Frank Zappa: We're Only In It For The Money (1967)

Albums of the 1970s
9.5/10
Faust: Faust (1971)
Robert Wyatt: Rock Bottom (1974)

9/10
John Fahey: Fare Forward Voyagers (1973)
Klaus Schulze: Irrlicht (1972)
Neu: Neu! (1972)
Nico: Desert Shore (1971)
Pere Ubu: Modern Dance (1978)
Pop Group: Y (1979)
Popol Vuh: Hosianna Mantra (1973)
Residents: Not Available (1978)
Soft Machine: 3 (1970)
Suicide: Suicide (1977)
Third Ear Band: Third Ear Band (1970)
Tim Buckley: Lorca (1970)

8.5/10
Chrome: Half Machine Lip Moves (1979)
Gong: Flying Teapot - Radio Gnome Invisible (1973)
Harold Budd: Pavilion Of Dreams (1978)
Jon Hassell: Vernal Equinox (1977)
Klaus Schulze: Cyborg (1973)
Popol Vuh: In Den Gaerten Pharaos (1972)
Syd Barrett: Barrett (1970)
Tim Buckley: Starsailor (1970)
Van Morrison: Moondance (1970)

8/10
Amon Duul: Tanz Der Lemminge (1971)
Amon Duul: Yeti (1970)
Aphrodite's Child: 666 (1970)
Brian Eno: Before And After Science (1977)
Brian Eno: Music For Airports (1978)
Brian Eno: Taking Tiger Mountain By Strategy (1974)
Can: Future Days (1973)
Can: Tago Mago (1971)
Captain Beefheart: Mirror Man (1971)
Clash: Clash (1977)

Contortions: Buy Contortions (1979)
David Crosby: If I Could Only Remember My Name (1971)
Faust: IV (1973)
Frank Zappa: Burnt Weeny Sandwich (1970)
Frank Zappa: Weasels Ripped My Flesh (1970)
Germs: GI (1979)
Hampton Grease Band: Music To Eat (1971)
Henry Cow: In Praise Of Learning (1975)
Henry Cow: Unrest (1974)
Jean-Luc Ponty: King Kong (1970)
John Fahey: America (1971)
John Martyn: Inside Out (1973)
Joni Mitchell: Blue (1971)
Joni Mitchell: Hejira (1976)
Kevin Ayers: Shooting At The Moon (1970)
Kevin Coyne: Marjory Razorblade (1973)
Klaus Schulze: X (1978)
Magma: Mekanik Destruktiw Kommandoh (1973)
Michael Hoenig: Departure From The Northern Wasteland (1978)
Mike Oldfield: Tubular Bells (1973)
Mnemonists: Mnemonist Orchestra (1979)
Neil Young: Rust Never Sleeps (1979)
Neil Young: Tonight's The Night (1975)
New York Dolls: New York Dolls (1973)
Nick Drake: Pink Moon (1972)
Patti Smith: Radio Ethiopia (1976)
Penguin Cafè Orchestra: Music From The Penguin Cafè (1976)
Pere Ubu: New Picnic Time (1979)
Peter Green: The End Of The Game (1970)
Public Image Ltd: Second Edition (1979)
Ramones: Rocket To Russia (1977)
Residents: Eskimo (1979)
Residents: Meet The Residents (1974)
Rickie Lee Jones: Rickie Lee Jones (1979)
Robbie Basho: Song Of The Stallion (1971)
Robert Wyatt: End Of An Ear (1970)
Rolling Stones: Exile On Main Street (1972)
Roxy Music: Roxy Music (1972)
Stephan Micus: Implosions (1977)
Taj Mahal Travellers: July 15 1972 (1972)
Talking Heads: 77 (1977)
Tangerine Dream: Zeit (1972)
Television: Marquee Moon (1977)
This Heat: This Heat (1979)
Throbbing Gristle: Second Annual Report (1977)
Van Der Graaf Generator: Pawn Hearts (1971)
Velvet Underground: Live (1974)
Warren Zevon: Warren Zevon (1976)
Wire: 154 (1979)
Yes: Close To The Edge (1972)

Albums of the 1980s

9/10
Bruce Springsteen: The River (1980)
Butthole Surfers: Psychic Powerless (1985)
Diamanda Galas: Diamanda Galas (1984)
Foetus: Nail (1985)
Gun Club: Fire Of Love (1981)
Husker Du: Zen Arcade (1984)
Jon Hassell: Dream Theory In Malaya (1981)
Minutemen: Double Nickels On The Dime (1984)

8.5/10
American Music Club: California (1988)
Big Black: Atomizer (1986)
Dead Kennedys: Fresh Fruit For Rotting Vegetables (1980)
Constance Demby: Novus Magnificat (1986)
Dream Syndicate: The Days Of Wine And Roses (1982)
Nick Cave: From Her To Eternity (1984)
Pandora's Box: Original Sin (1989)
Peter Gabriel: Passion (1989)
Pixies: Surfer Rosa (1988)
Steve Roach: Dreamtime Return (1988)
Soft Boys: Underwater Moonlight (1980)

8/10
Ambitious Lovers: Greed (1988)
Angkor Wat: When Obscenity Becomes The Norm (1989)
Bad Brains: Rock For Light (1982)
Band Of Susans: Love Agenda (1989)
Birdsongs Of The Mesozoic: Magnetic Flip (1984)
Bitch Magnet: Umber (1989)
Black Flag: Damaged (1981)
Blind Idiot God: Blind Idiot God (1987)
Bongwater: Double Bummer (1988)
Butthole Surfers: Rembrandt Pussyhorse (1986)
Camper Van Beethoven: Camper Van Beethoven (1986)
Camper Van Beethoven: Telephone Free Landslide Victory (1985)
Cocteau Twins: Head Over Heels (1983)
Colin Newman: A-Z (1980)
Cows: Daddy Has A Tail (1989)
Cramps: Songs The Lord Taught Us (1980)
David Thomas: Monster Walks The Winter Lake (1986)
David Thomas: The Sound Of The Sand (1982)
Dead Can Dance: Spleen And Ideal (1985)
Death Of Samantha: Strungout On Jargon (1986)
Deuter: Silence Is The Answer (1981)
Diamanda Galas: The Litanies Of Satan (1982)
Dinosaur Jr: You're Living All Over Me (1987)

Djam Karet: Reflections From The Firepool (1988)
Einsturzende Neubauten: Zeichnungen das Patienten OT (1983)
Enya: Watermark (1988)
Faith No More: Introduce Yourself (1987)
Fear: Record (1982)
Feedtime: Feedtime (1986)
Feelies: Crazy Rhythms (1980)
Fetchin Bones: Cabin Flounder (1985)
Flaming Lips: Telepathic Surgery (1989)
Fleshtones: Roman Gods (1981)
Flipper: Generic (1982)
Foetus: Hole (1984)
Forrest Fang: The Wolf At The Ruins (1989)
Galaxie 500: On Fire (1989)
Godflesh: Streetcleaner (1989)
Green: White Soul (1989)
Guns N' Roses: Appetite For Destruction (1987)
Henry Rollins: Hot Animal Machine (1987)
Hugo Largo: Drum (1987)
Husker Du: New Day Rising (1985)
Jane Siberry: No Borders Here (1983)
Jon Hassell: Aka-Dabari-Java Magic Realism (1983)
Julian Cope: World Shut Your Mouth (1984)
King Snake Roost: Things That Play Themselves (1988)
Laughing Hyenas: You Can't Pray A Lie (1989)
Legal Weapon: Death Of Innocence (1982)
Lou Reed: New York (1989)
Mark Stewart: Learning To Cope With Cowardice (1983)
Mary Margaret O'Hara: Miss America (1988)
Metallica: Kill 'Em All (1983)
Metallica: Master Of Puppets (1986)
Michael Jones: After The Rain (1988)
Ministry: The Land Of Rape And Honey (1988)
Misfits: Walk Among Us (1982)
Missing Foundation: 1933 (1988)
Mission Of Burma: VS (1982)
My Bloody Valentine: Isn't Anything (1988)
Nick Cave: The Firstborn Is Dead (1985)
Pere Ubu: Art Of Walking (1980)
Peter Frohmader: Through Time And Mistery (1988)
Peter Michael Hamel: Colours Of Time (1980)
Peter Michael Hamel: Transition (1983)
Pop Group: For How Much Longer Do We Tolerate Mass Murder (1980)
Public Enemy: It Takes A Nation Of Millions To Hold Us Back (1988)
Public Image Ltd: Flowers of Romance (1981)
Rapeman: Two Nuns And A Pack Mule (1989)
Red Temple Spirits: Dancing To Restore An Eclipsed Moon (1988)
Replacements: Let It Be (1984)
Replacements: Tim (1985)
Richard Thompson: Shoot Out The Lights (1982)

Rip Rig & Panic: God (1981)
Savage Republic: Customs (1989)
Sinead O'Connor: The Lion And The Cobra (1987)
Sonic Youth: Bad Moon Rising (1985)
Sonic Youth: Daydream Nation (1988)
Stan Ridgway: The Big Heat (1986)
Stephan Micus: Ocean (1986)
Steve Roach: Structures From Silence (1984)
Swans: Children Of God (1987)
Swans: Cop (1984)
Swans: Filth (1983)
Tackhead: Friendly As A Hand Grenade (1989)
Talk Talk: Spirit Of Eden (1988)
Tiny Lights: Prayer For The Halcyon Fear (1985)
Tom Waits: Rain Dogs (1985)
Tom Waits: Swordfishtrombones (1983)
Tragic Mulatto: Locos Por El Sexo (1987)
Tuxedomoon: Half Mute (1980)
Univers Zero: Heatwave (1986)
Unrest: Tink Of Southeast (1987)
Violent Femmes: Violent Femmes (1982)
X: LA (1980)

Albums of the 1990s
9/10
Fugazi: Repeater (1990)
Lisa Germano: Geek The Girl (1994)
Hash Jar Tempo: Well Oiled (1997)
Mercury Rev: Yerself Is Steam (1991)
Morphine: Good (1992)
My Bloody Valentine: Loveless (1991)
Nick Cave: Good Son (1990)
Red House Painters: Down Colorful Hill (1992)
Royal Trux: Twin Infinitives (1990)
Slint: Spiderland (1991)
Type O Negative: Slow Deep And Hard (1991)
Vampire Rodents: Lullaby Land (1993)

8.5/10
Amon Tobin: Bricolage (1997)
Babes In Toyland: Fontanelle (1992)
Black Tape For A Blue Girl: Remnants Of A Deeper Purity (1996)
Built To Spill: Perfect From Now On (1997)
Cop Shoot Cop: Consumer Revolt (1990)
Dirty Three: Ocean Songs (1998)
Dogbowl: Cyclops Nuclear Submarine Captain (1991)
Lightwave: Mundus Subterraneus (1995)
Nine Inch Nails: The Downward Spiral (1994)
Phish: A Picture Of Nectar (1992)
Tortoise: Millions Now Living Will Never Die (1996)

Von Lmo: Cosmic Interception (1994)

8/10
Add N To X: On the Wires of Our Nerves (1998)
Air Liquide: The Increased Difficulty Of Concentration (1995)
Alanis Morissette: Jagged Little Pill (1995)
Ant-Bee: Pure Electric Honey (1990)
Atari Teenage Riot: Delete Yourself (1995)
Aurora: Dimension Gate (1994)
Autechre: Chiastic Slide (1997)
Autechre: Incunabula (1993)
Azalia Snail: Snailbait (1990)
Bardo Pond: Bufo Alvarius (1995)
Bark Psychosis: Hex (1994)
Barkmarket: Vegas Throat (1991)
Bernhard Guenter: Un Peu De Neige Salie (1993)
Black Heart Procession: 2 (1999)
Bugskull: Phantasies And Senseitions (1994)
Calexico: The Black Light (1998)
Church: Magician Among The Spirits (1996)
Codeine: Frigid Stars (1991)
Cul De Sac: China Gate (1996)
Dadamah: This Is Not A Dream (1992)
Dave Pajo: Live From A Shark Cage (1999)
David Grubbs: The Thicket (1998)
Dead C: Harsh '70s Reality (1992)
Doldrums: Acupuncture (1997)
Don Caballero: 2 (1995)
Dream Theater: Images And Words (1992)
Drive Like Jehu: Yank Crime (1994)
Earth: 2 (1993)
Ed Hall: Love Poke Here (1990)
Eden: Gateway To The Mysteries (1990)
Edith Frost: Telescopic (1998)
Eels: Electro-Shock Blues (1998)
Fear Factory: Demanufacture (1995)
Flying Luttenbachers: Gods Of Chaos (1998)
Fugazi: Red Medicine (1995)
Gallon Drunk: You The Night And The Music (1992)
Gastr Del Sol: The Serpentine Similar (1993)
Ghost: Lama Rabi Rabi (1996)
Girls Vs Boys: Venus Luxure No.1 Baby (1993)
Gravitar: Gravitar (1995)
Grifters: So Happy Together (1992)
Hash Jar Tempo: Under Glass (1999)
Heather Duby: Post To Wire (1999)
Henry Rollins: End Of Silence (1992)
Honeymoon Killers: Hung Far Low (1991)
Jane Siberry: When I Was A Boy (1993)
Jarboe: Thirteen Masks (1992)

Jesus Lizard: Goat (1991)
Juliana Hatfield: Hey Babe (1992)
June Of 44: Four Great Points (1998)
Kenneth Newby: Ecology Of Souls (1993)
Kyuss: Blues For The Red Sun (1992)
Labradford: Labradford (1996)
Laika: Sounds Of The Satellites (1997)
Lambchop: I Hope You're Sitting Down (1994)
Lida Husik: Bozo (1991)
Lida Husik: The Return Of Red Emma (1993)
Lightwave: Tycho Brahe (1993)
Lisa Germano: Excerpts From A Love Circus (1996)
Lisa Germano: On The Way Down From Moon Palace (1991)
Liz Phair: Exile In Guyville (1993)
Low: I Could Live In Hope (1994)
Lullaby For The Working Class: Blanket Warm (1996)
Lycia: A Day In The Stark Corner (1993)
Lycia: The Burning Circle And Then Dust (1995)
Magnetic Fields: The Charm Of The Highway Strip (1994)
Mainliner: Mellow Out (1996)
Mark Kramer: The Guilt Trip (1993)
Mark Lanegan: Whiskey For The Holy Ghost (1993)
Mercury Rev: Boces (1993)
Mo Boma: Myths Of The Near Future (1994)
Morphine: Yes (1995)
Motherhead Bug: Zambodia (1993)
Nation Of Ulysses: Plays Pretty For Baby (1992)
Neurosis: Through Silver In Blood (1996)
Orb: U.F. Orb (1992)
Orbital: II / Brown Album (1993)
Ozric Tentacles: Erpland (1990)
Pain Teens: Destroy Me Lover (1993)
Paul Haslinger: World Without Rules (1996)
Paul Schutze: New Maps Of Hell (1992)
Pegboy: Strong Reaction (1991)
Peter Jefferies: Substatic (1998)
Phish: Lawn Boy (1990)
Polvo: Exploded Drawing (1996)
Portishead: Dummy (1994)
Pram: Helium (1994)
Primus: Frizzle Fry (1990)
Rake: The Art Ensemble Of Rake (1995)
Red House Painters: Red House Painters / Rollercoaster (1993)
Red Red Meat: There's A Star Above The Manger Tonight (1997)
Robin Holcomb: Robin Holcomb (1990)
Rocket From The Crypt: Circa Now (1993)
Rodan: Rusty (1994)
Roy Montgomery: And Now The Rain Sounds Like Life Is Falling Down Through It (1998)
Run On: Start Packing (1996)

Scorn: Vae Solis (1992)
Seam: The Problem With Me (1993)
Sepultura: Roots (1996)
Shadowy Men On A Shadowy Planet: Dim The Lights Chill The Ham (1992)
Shellac: At Action Park (1994)
Six Finger Satellite: The Pigeon Is The Most Popular Bird (1993)
Sky Cries Mary: This Timeless Turning (1994)
Slowdive: Just For A Day (1991)
Smog: Julius Caesar (1993)
Soul Coughing: Ruby Vroom (1994)
Space Streakings: 7-Toku (1994)
Stereolab: Transient Random Noise Bursts With Announcements (1993)
Steve Roach: The Magnificent Void (1996)
Steve Roach: World's Edge (1992).
Subarachnoid Space: Almost Invisible (1997)
Sugarsmack: Top Loader (1993)
Supreme Dicks: The Emotional Plague (1996)
Swans: Soundtracks For The Blind (1996)
Techno Animal: Ghosts (1990)
Thinking Fellers Union Local 282: Mother Of All Saints (1992)
Today Is The Day: Temple Of The Morning Star (1997)
Today Is The Day: Willpower (1994)
Tortoise: TNT (1998)
Trance Mission: Trance Mission (1993)
Unrest: Imperial f.f.r.r. (1992)
Unsane: Unsane (1991)
Unwound: Fake Train (1993)
Vampire Rodents: Clockseed (1995)
Vampire Rodents: Premonition (1992)
Vas Deferens Organization: Transcontinental Conspiracy (1996)
Windy & Carl: Drawing Of Sound (1996)
Yo La Tengo: May I Sing With Me (1992)
Yume Bitsu: Yume Bitsu (1999)

Albums of the 2000s
8/10
Dirty 3: Whatever You Love You Are (2000)
Joanna Newsom: Ys (2006)
Lofty Pillars: Amsterdam (2001)
Mars Volta: Frances The Mute (2005)
Roy Montgomery: The Allegory of Hearing (2000)
Shit And Shine: Ladybird (2005)
Solex: Low Kick And Hard Bop (2001)
Spring Heel Jack: Disappeared (2000)
Spring Heel Jack: Amassed (2002)
Vladislav Delay: Anima (2001)

7.5/10
Amon Tobin: Out From Out Where (2002)
Animal Collective: Spirit They're Gone Spirit They've Vanished (2000)

Arcade Fire: Funeral (2004)
Battles: Mirrored (2007)
Black Dice: Beaches & Canyons (2002)
Blood Brothers: Burn Piano Island Burn (2003)
Books: The Lemon of Pink (2003)
Cannibal Ox: The Cold Vein (2001)
Carla Bozulich: Evangelista (2006)
Cat Power: You Are Free (2003)
Cerberus Shoal: Mr Boy Dog (2002)
Charalambides: Joy Shapes (2004)
cLOUDDEAD: cLOUDDEAD (2001)
Colleen: The Golden Morning Breaks (2005)
Comets On Fire: Field Recordings From the Sun (2002)
DJ Logic: Anomaly (2001)
Electrelane: Rock It To The Moon (2001)
Eluvium: Talk Amongst The Trees (2005)
Eminem: The Marshall Mathers LP (2000)
Entropic Advance: Red Yellow Noise (2002)
Fiery Furnaces: Gallowsbird's Bark (2003)
Ghost: Hypnotic Underworld (2004)
James Plotkin: Atomsmasher (2001)
Jessica Bailiff: Jessica Bailiff (2002)
Keith Fullerton Whitman: Lisbon (2006)
Khanate: Things Viral (2003)
Kopernik: Kopernik (2003)
LCD Soundsystem: 45:33 (2007)
Low: Trust (2002)
Lydia Lunch: Smoke In The Shadows (2004)
M83: Dead Cities, Red Seas & Lost Ghosts (2003)
Manitoba: Up In Flames (2003)
Maquiladora: Ritual Of Hearts (2002)
Menomena: I Am The Fun Blame Monster (2003)
Microphones: Mount Eerie (2003)
Nile: In Their Darkened Shrines (2002)
Orthrelm: OV (2005)
Pan Sonic: Kesto (2004)
Panda Bear: Person Pitch (2007)
Pelt: Ayahuasca (2001)
Robert Rich: Somnium (2001)
Scott Tuma: Hard Again (2001)
Shit And Shine: Jealous of Shit and Shine (2006)
Stars Of The Lid: The Tired Sounds Of (2001)
Steffen Basho-Junghans: Waters in Azure (2002)
Sufjan Stevens: Illinois (2005)
Suishou No Fune: Prayer for Chibi (2007)
Supersilent: 6 (2003)
Toby Dammit: Top Dollar (2001)
Today Is The Day: Sadness Will Prevail (2002)
Tool: Lateralus (2001)
TV On The Radio: Return To Cookie Mountain (2006)

Vibracathedral Orchestra: Dabbling With Gravity (2002)
Volebeats: Solitude (2000)
Wilco: Yankee Hotel Foxtrot (2002)
Xiu Xiu: A Promise (2003)
Xiu Xiu: La Foret (2005)

Made in the USA
Coppell, TX
10 October 2020